louise Mc

OXFORD EC LAW LIBRARY

General Editor: F. G. Jacobs
Advocate General, The Court of Justice
of the European Communities

THE EUROPEAN UNION AND ITS COURT OF JUSTICE

OXFORD EC LAW LIBRARY

The aim of this series is to publish important and original studies of the various branches of European Community Law. Each work will provide a clear, concise, and critical exposition of the law in its social, economic, and political context, at a level which will interest the advanced student, the practitioner, the academic, and government and Community officials.

Other Titles in the Library

EC Company Law
Vanessa Edwards

The General Principles of EC Law
Takis Tridimas

EC Sex Equality Law
second edition
Evelyn Ellis

European Community Law of State Aid
Andrew Evans

External Relations of the European Communities
I. MacLeod, I. D. Hendry and Stephen Hyett

Directives in European Community Law
Sacha Prechal

EC Tax Law
Paul Farmer and Richard Lyal

EC Competition Law
third edition
D. G. Goyder

The European Internal Market and International Trade
Piet Eeckhout

The Law of Money and Financial Services in the European Community
J. A. Usher

Trade and Environmental Law in the European Community
Andreas R. Ziegler

Legal Aspects of Agriculture in the European Community
J. A. Usher

The European Union
and its Court of Justice

ANTHONY ARNULL

Professor of European Law
University of Birmingham

OXFORD

UNIVERSITY PRESS

OXFORD
UNIVERSITY PRESS

Great Clarendon Street, Oxford OX2 6DP

Oxford University Press is a department of the University of Oxford.
It furthers the University's objective of excellence in research, scholarship,
and education by publishing worldwide in

Oxford New York

Athens Auckland Bangkok Bogotá Buenos Aires Calcutta
Cape Town Chennai Dar es Salaam Delhi Florence Hong Kong Istanbul
Karachi Kuala Lumpur Madrid Melbourne Mexico City Mumbai
Nairobi Paris São Paulo Singapore Taipei Tokyo Toronto Warsaw

with associated companies in Berlin Ibadan

Oxford is a registered trade mark of Oxford University Press
in the UK and in certain other countries

Published in the United States
by Oxford University Press Inc., New York

British Library Cataloguing in Publication Data

Data available

Library of Congress Cataloging in Publication Data

Arnull, Anthony.
The European Union and its Court of Justice / Anthony Arnull.
p. cm.—(Oxford EC law library)
Includes bibliographical references and index.
1. Court of Justice of the European Communities. 2. Courts of
last resort—European Union countries. 3. Law—European Union
countries. I. Title. II. Series.
KJE5461.A97 1999 341.242′2—dc21 99–38499

ISBN 0–19–825898–4
ISBN 0–19–829881–1(pbk.)

1 3 5 7 9 10 8 6 4 2

Typeset in Bembo
by Hope Services (Abingdon) Ltd.
Printed in Great Britain
on acid-free paper by
Biddles Ltd., Guildford and King's Lynn

To Anne,
Fran, and Tom

General editor's foreword

It is recognized on all sides that the Court of Justice has a key role in the life and work of the European Community. Set up to ensure that the Community would be subject to the rule of law, and having the last word on the meaning and effect of Community law, its role has proved more controversial as the Community's activities have developed, and above all since the Treaty on European Union. There has been growing debate, in particular, on whether the Court keeps within the limits of the Treaties or goes, on occasion, beyond those limits; on whether it engages in undue 'judicial activism'.

This book is a valuable contribution to the debate. Its focus is firmly on the role of the Court, and its perspective is the Court's case-law. It covers first the legal foundations—what might be described as the constitutional basis of the Community, itself essentially the product of the Court's case-law—including the fundamental issues of direct effect and primacy. Next it examines key central areas of substantive Community law: the free movement of goods and the free movement of persons and services, which are central components of the common market and where again the Court's case-law has been decisive; it examines the law of competition; and it considers the Court's approach to the principle of equal treatment for men and women. Finally it analyses the Court's general approach on two central issues: its methods of interpretation, and in particular how far they diverge from conventional methods; and its approach to precedent.

Throughout the book the author illuminates the subject by his careful and lucid analysis of the Opinions of Advocates General and the judgments of the Court, by his perceptive comments, and perhaps above all by his thoroughly balanced assessments. While he has little sympathy with the more radical critics, and shows that they are often ill-informed, he is as ready to criticise, on specific issues, as to approve. His judgment of Europe's judges will carry much weight.

The debate will continue. Some will no doubt continue to regard the Court as an agent for expanding the Community's powers. Other will see the Court as having laid the necessary foundations of the Community constitution; as making, in its everyday work, an indispensable contribution to the realization of the internal market; as upholding the rights of the individual and ensuring that national courts enforce those rights and provide effective remedies; and as creating a developed legal system in which the rights and obligations of the participants—individuals, Member States, Community institutions—are safeguarded.

The debate will continue, but with the help of this book it will be better informed, and the book, which will be of interest to students and practitioners at all levels, will be widely welcomed.

Francis G. Jacobs
September 1999

Preface

There is a risk that a book devoted entirely to just one of the European Union's various institutions will give an exaggerated impression of that institution's importance. In the case of the Court of Justice of the European Communities, that risk is a small one. The Community Treaties which form the core of the EU confer on the Court a central role in its functioning and it has used its powers in a creative and sometimes surprising way. This is perhaps enough in itself to justify a book on the Court's contribution to the development of the EU, but there are at least two further reasons why the publication of such a book seems timely and appropriate.

One is that the Court has not been spared the intense scrutiny to which the EU as a whole has been subjected since its creation at Maastricht. The Court has been attacked by critics some of whom have misgivings about the direction the process of European integration seems to be taking, some of whom are uneasy about the part played by the Court in that process. Much (though not all) of the criticism which has been directed at it has been based on a limited and unrepresentative selection of rulings and misunderstanding of the nature both of the role the Court is called upon to play under the Treaties and of the issues with which it has been confronted. The other factor is that the latest set of amendments to the Union Treaties set out in the Treaty of Amsterdam, far from marginalizing the Court, may require it to play an even more pivotal role than hitherto in the functioning of the Union. The Court's approach to its new powers and duties will inevitably be conditioned by the way it has discharged its responsibilities over the preceding forty years or so of its existence.

The purpose of this book is accordingly to examine the contribution the Court has made to shaping the legal framework within which the EU operates. As Professor Weiler points out in *The Constitution of Europe* (1999, p 189), '[t]here is more than one way towards an appreciation of the role of the Court of Justice and of the judicial process in the evolution of the Community and of European integration'. He would probably describe the approach taken in this book as 'classical'. It begins with an introductory chapter which considers the Court's place in the institutional architecture of the EU and its organization and working methods. The main sections of the book are devoted to an examination, with and without the benefit of hindsight, of the way the Court has dealt with specific problems in a range of contexts, both constitutional and substantive. The final section addresses certain general questions relating to the Court's overall approach. The discussion singles out for special attention decisions of the Court which were in some way surprising because they developed the law in directions which had not been widely anticipated. Notwithstanding the views of some critics, it will be seen that by no means all such decisions had the effect of expanding the scope of the Treaties or the Court's own powers or even of promoting the proper functioning of the common market. I have not hesitated to make clear my own views on the questions discussed in the following pages, but I have tried at all times to set out the issues at stake in a neutral way so that readers can assess for themselves the persuasiveness of the conclusions I reach.

The book is aimed at several types of reader. The specialist in EU law—whether academic or practitioner—who is familiar with the case law of the Court will, I hope, find in it some interesting observations. But I hope also that the book will be helpful to the non-specialist who is interested in the development of the EU and the part played by the Court. I have in mind particularly lawyers in the Member States who specialize in an area of domestic law which they find increasingly affected by developments in the EU, lawyers in third countries which aspire to membership of the EU, and lawyers in the EU's trading partners. Although this is a law book, I hope too that it might be useful to specialists in European studies who come from other disciplines.

The title of the book requires a brief word of explanation, since it refers to the EU while the Court is known formally as the Court of Justice of the European Communities. The Communities comprise only one of the three pillars of the EU. Although the Court originally had virtually no jurisdiction over the other two pillars, it has since the entry into force of the Treaty of Amsterdam enjoyed important powers in relation to one of the non-Community pillars. It therefore seems appropriate to speak of a Court of Justice of the Union, although the Court's main powers remain those applicable under the Community pillar.

The Treaty of Amsterdam introduced a further reform which, although designed to simplify matters, has in fact made the task of writing about the EU inordinately more complicated. I refer to the deletion of obsolete provisions and the attempt to tidy up the text of the EC Treaty and the Maastricht Treaty by renumbering those that remain. Those who come to the study of the EU after the entry into force of the Treaty of Amsterdam will of course learn the new numbering, but they will need to be reminded of the old numbering from time to time because it is used in pre-Amsterdam judgments, legislation, and literature on the subject. Those like me who had grown familiar with the old numbering will need regular reminders of what the new numbers correspond to. I have tried to satisfy both types of reader by indicating periodically both the old and the new numbering.

Several people were kind enough to read and comment on sections of the book while it was in draft. My colleague, Professor Evelyn Ellis, looked at chapters 2 and 13; Dr Christopher Kerse, Legal Adviser to the House of Lords Select Committee on the European Communities, looked at chapter 12; Professor Erika Szyszczak of the University of Nottingham looked at chapter 16. Another colleague, Jeremy McBride, gave very full answers, some of them in writing, to several questions I put to him on issues of public international law and the law of human rights. I have also benefited from discussing a number of the matters addressed in the book with the General Editor of this series, Advocate General Francis Jacobs, for whom I had the privilege of working as a Legal Secretary from 1989–92. I am grateful to them all: they made numerous valuable suggestions and saved me from several errors. They are not responsible for any that remain and do not necessarily agree with anything that I say (though I hope they will agree with some of it). A number of chapters were also read by David Green, the Birmingham Law Faculty Research Associate from September 1998 to February 1999. He too made several helpful suggestions but was in a previous incarnation a research assistant for a prominent Eurosceptic Member of the United Kingdom Parliament. If there is anything wrong with the chapters he read, I shall therefore know who is to blame. Finally, I should like to thank John Louth and his colleagues at OUP for dealing with the manuscript so promptly and efficiently notwithstanding my failure to deliver it on time.

It is not the purpose of this book to give a comprehensive account of the law in any particular area. However, I have tried to take account of developments up to the entry into force of the Treaty of Amsterdam on 1 May 1999.

A.A.
May 1999

Outline table of contents

Detailed table of contents

Table of abbreviations

AC	Appeal Cases
AG	Advocate General
AJIL	American Journal of International Law
All ER	All England Law Reports
Bull EC	Bulletin of the European Communities
CDE	Cahiers de Droit Européen
CELS	Centre for European Legal Studies, University of Cambridge
CFI	Court of First Instance of the European Communities
CLJ	Cambridge Law Journal
CMLR	Common Market Law Reports
CMLRev	Common Market Law Review
COM	Communication
Dec	Decision
Dir	Directive
EAEC	European Atomic Energy Community ('Euratom')
EBLR	European Business Law Review
EC	European Community
ECB	European Central Bank
ECHR	European Convention on Human Rights
ECJ	European Court of Justice (ie the Court of Justice of the European Communities)
ECLR	European Competition Law Review
ECR	European Court Reports
ECSC	European Coal and Steel Community
EEA	European Economic Area
EEC	European Economic Community
EFTA	European Free Trade Association
EHRR	European Human Rights Reports
EJIL	European Journal of International Law
ELJ	European Law Journal

ELRev	European Law Review
FIDE	Fédération Internationale pour le Droit Européen
GATT	General Agreement on Tariffs and Trade
Harv Int LJ	Harvard International Law Journal
ICLQ	International and Comparative Law Quarterly
IGC	Intergovernmental conference
ILJ	Industrial Law Journal
IntJCompLLIR	International Journal of Comparative Labour Law and Industrial Relations
JCMS	Journal of Common Market Studies
JSPTL	Journal of the Society of Public Teachers of Law
JSWFL	Journal of Social Welfare and Family law
LIEI	Legal Issues of European Integration
LQR	Law Quarterly Review
LS	Legal Studies
MCA	Monetary Compensatory Amount
MJ	Maastricht Journal of European and Comparative Law
MLR	Modern Law Review
OHIM	Office for Harmonization in the Internal Market (Trade Marks and Designs)
OJ	Official Journal of the European Communities
OJLS	Oxford Journal of Legal Studies
PL	Public Law
Rec	Recueil de la Jurisprudence de la Cour de justice et du Tribunal de première instance
Reg	Regulation
RTDE	Revue Trimestrielle de Droit Européen
SEA	Single European Act
TEU	Treaty on European Union
VAT	Value added tax
WLR	Weekly Law Reports
WTO	World Trade Organization
Yale LJ	Yale Law Journal
YEL	Yearbook of European Law

Table of cases

European Community (numerical)

Court of Justice

Court of First Instance

Opinions

European Court of Human Rights

Table of legislation

Regulations

Other EC Legislation

European Convention on Human Rights

Statute of the Council of Europe

Vienna Convention on the Law of Treaties

Statute of the International Court of Justice

1

Europe's Judges

The Court of Justice of the European Communities is a controversial institution. To some it has, from its base in Luxembourg, made a major contribution to the establishment of a polity which offers its Member States the peace, stability and prosperity they had previously found so hard to achieve. To others, it has consistently acted in the pursuit of an agenda of its own about the political shape of Europe, disregarding the terms of the Treaties where they have seemed to stand in the way of its own conception of what Europe requires. During the parliamentary debates on the bill[1] to give effect in the United Kingdom to the Treaty on European Union signed in Maastricht in early 1992, that view was reflected by Baroness Thatcher, who observed that 'some things at the Court are very much to our distaste'.[2] It had, she said, produced:

a great effect upon the powers that we have relinquished. It has by its decisions greatly extended the powers of the centralised institutions against the nation state. Its methods of interpreting the law are totally different from those of our courts and nothing like so exact or so good. The court draws upon the objective of European integration to inform all its rulings by which over a period of time it has therefore furthered decisions towards a unitary European state . . . It is busy reinterpreting so many things to give itself and the Community more powers at our expense. That court does not have constitutional checks and balances to temper its power. What was tolerable in a few cases is not bearable on the scale it is happening now, and it will accelerate under the massive opportunities provided by Maastricht . . .[3]

Although couched in less colourful language, similar concerns were expressed by the Conservative Government of John Major in the White Paper[4] it published on the eve of the intergovernmental conference (IGC) which led to the Treaty of Amsterdam. There the Government remarked: 'The functioning of the Court . . . could be further improved. There have been judgments in recent years that have given cause for concern, particularly where they have imposed disproportionate costs on Governments or business, even when they have made every effort to meet their EC obligations.'[5]

---

[1] The bill eventually became the European Communities (Amendment) Act 1993.
[2] HL Deb, 7 June 1993, col 560.   [3] Ibid, cols 563–4.
[4] 'A Partnership of Nations', March 1996 (Cm 3181).
[5] Ibid, para 37. In July 1996, the Government tabled a memorandum at the IGC containing proposals designed to address the concerns outlined in the White Paper. For a brief comment, see Arnull (1996) 21 ELRev 349.

In 1995, an attempt to add intellectual weight to what might be called the Eurosceptic analysis of the Court was made by the then Warden of All Souls College, Oxford, Sir Patrick Neill QC. He circulated a paper entitled 'The European Court of Justice: a Case Study in Judicial Activism'[6] in which he argued that many of the Court's decisions were 'logically flawed or skewed by doctrinal or idiosyncratic policy considerations'. Some of the detailed criticisms advanced by Sir Patrick Neill will be examined in the chapters which follow, but the gist of his argument was not new. In a path-finding book published in 1986,[7] Hjalte Rasmussen sought to show that excessive activism on the part of the Court threatened to undermine its authority and legitimacy. That view attracted powerful dissent[8] and Sir Patrick Neill's thesis encountered a similar reaction. One of the recipients of his paper was the House of Lords Select Committee on the European Communities, which was conducting an enquiry into the matters to be considered at the then forthcoming IGC. A number of witnesses took issue with the Neill line and it was comprehensively rejected by the Select Committee,[9] which observed:

A strong and independent Court of Justice is an essential part of the structure of the European Union. We agree with those witnesses who stressed the important role of the Court in the consolidation of democratic structures and upholding the rule of law in the European Community. We note the criticisms of 'judicial activism' which have been levelled against the Court but these appear to be based mainly on cases where the Court has made Community law effective against defaulting Member States at the instance of individuals seeking to enforce their rights. We accept that enforceable remedies are essential to the application of Community legal obligations, with a high degree of uniformity throughout the Member States.

Why has the Court provoked such strongly held yet diametrically opposed views? What contribution has it made to the legal framework within which the European Community, and now the European Union, conducts its affairs? These are among the questions which it is the purpose of this book to answer. To set the scene for the chapters which follow, it is first necessary to say something about the Court's place in the institutional framework of the Union and its membership and working methods.

---

[6] The paper was published in the Minutes of Evidence taken before the House of Lords Sub-Committee on the 1996 IGC (Session 1994–95, 18th Report, HL Paper 88, pp 218–45). In addition, it was released as a pamphlet by the European Policy Forum in August 1995. See also Hartley, 'The European Court, judicial objectivity and the constitution of the European Union' (1996) 112 LQR 95.

[7] *On Law and Policy in the European Court of Justice.*

[8] See Cappelletti, *The Judicial Process in Comparative Perspective* (1989), ch 9, and 'Is the European Court of Justice "running wild"?' (1987) 12 ELRev 3; Weiler, 'The Court of Justice on trial' (1987) 24 CMLRev 555; Toth (1987) 7 YEL 411. Cf Rasmussen, 'Between self-restraint and activism: a judicial policy for the European Court' (1988) 13 ELRev 28.

[9] See *1996 Inter-Governmental Conference* (Session 1994–95, 21st Report, HL Paper 105), para 256. See also Howe, 'Euro-justice: yes or no?' (1996) 21 ELRev 187; Tridimas, 'The Court of Justice and judicial activism' (1996) 21 ELRev 199; van Gerven, 'The role and structure of the European judiciary now and in the future' (1996) 21 ELRev 211.

The Origins of the Court

The Court's origins can be traced back to the Treaty establishing the European Coal and Steel Community (ECSC) signed in Paris on 18 April 1951. The ECSC Treaty established a common market for coal and steel to be regulated by four institutions: a High Authority, a Common Assembly, a Special Council of Ministers and a Court of Justice. Under Article 31 of the Treaty, the Court was given the general task of ensuring 'that in the interpretation and application of this Treaty, and of rules laid down for the implementation thereof, the law is observed'. In order to enable it to perform that function, subsequent provisions gave it particular powers. These included the power to quash certain acts of the other institutions,[10] jurisdiction to hear appeals against pecuniary sanctions and periodic penalty payments imposed under the Treaty,[11] and the power to order the Community to make good any injury caused by a wrongful act or omission on its part in the performance of its functions.[12] The Court also had 'sole jurisdiction to give preliminary rulings on the validity of acts of the High Authority and of the Council where such validity is in issue in proceedings brought before a national court or tribunal'.[13] By a stroke of unconscious symbolism, the Court was originally housed in the Villa Vauban in Luxembourg, a large mansion named after the great builder of defensive fortifications. The authors of the Treaty could not have foreseen the importance of the role the Court would play in building upon and defending the edifice they had started to construct.

The main responsibility for ensuring that the objectives of the ECSC Treaty were attained lay with the High Authority, the powers of which were defined by the Treaty with some precision. The detailed nature of much of that Treaty together with its limited scope meant that it has not on the whole given rise to the controversy which has surrounded subsequent developments. In particular, the workload of the Court in the 1950s was very light: its output until the delivery of its first judgment under the EEC Treaty in December 1961[14] fills just under five slim volumes of the European Court Reports. The cases themselves were confined largely to technical matters. As Advocate General Warner, writing extrajudicially, observed:

It was of course in those cases that the Court laid some of the foundations of Community law, but the actual topics with which they dealt are not on the whole of major interest today. An astonishing proportion of the cases brought (about half) concerned a levy on purchases of scrap which had been instituted by the High Authority in order to even out differences in the prices at which it could be obtained by steelworks situate in different parts of the Community.[15]

---

[10] Arts 33 and 38.   [11] Art 36.   [12] Art 40.   [13] Art 41.
[14] Case 7/61 *Commission v Italy* [1961] ECR 317.
[15] 'The evolution of the work of the European Court of Justice' in *Reports of a Judicial and Academic Conference, 27–28 September 1976* (Luxembourg, 1976), at p V-5. The office of Advocate General is discussed below. See also Hunnings, *The European Courts* (1996), pp 140–1.

The ECSC had, however, never been conceived as an end in itself. The Schuman declaration of 9 May 1950, which started the process leading to the signing of the ECSC Treaty, made it clear that the establishment of a European common market for coal and steel was merely the first step on the road to European integration. No sooner had the Treaty been signed than the Member States turned their attention to the next step. That step turned out to be a backwards one: a Treaty establishing a European Defence Community signed in 1952 by the Member States of the Coal and Steel Community never entered into force after the French National Assembly failed to approve it.[16] However, on 25 March 1957 the Member States made substantial further progress with the signing in Rome of the Treaty establishing the European Economic Community (EEC) and the Treaty establishing the European Atomic Energy Community (EAEC).

The purpose of the EAEC was a limited one which now seems somewhat dated: according to Article 1 of the EAEC Treaty, the task of that Community was 'to contribute to the raising of the standard of living in the Member States and to the development of relations with the other countries by creating the conditions necessary for the speedy establishment and growth of nuclear industries'. It has not given rise to a great deal of case law, but decisions of the Court relating to it may have wider implications because a number of its provisions were, at least initially, identical to the corresponding provisions of the EEC Treaty.

The task of the EEC was much more far-reaching. The preamble to the EEC Treaty recorded the determination of the Member States 'to lay the foundations of an ever closer union among the peoples of Europe'. According to Article 2 of that Treaty, the EEC had as its task,

by establishing a common market and progressively approximating the economic policies of Member States, to promote throughout the Community a harmonious development of economic activities, a continuous and balanced expansion, an increase in stability, an accelerated raising of the standard of living and closer relations between the States belonging to it.

Article 3 of the Treaty made it clear that the fulfilment of that task would entail, among other things, the elimination of obstacles to the movement of goods between Member States, the establishment of a common customs tariff and of a common commercial policy towards third countries, the abolition between Member States of obstacles to freedom of movement for persons, services, and capital, the adoption of common policies in certain fields, the avoidance of distortions to competition in the common market, and the approximation of national laws where necessary to ensure its proper functioning.

Both the EEC and the EAEC Treaties established sets of institutions, similar to that of the ECSC Treaty, to which responsibility for achieving the objectives of the two new Communities was entrusted: each was to have a European Parliament (originally called an Assembly), a Council consisting of representatives of the

---

[16] For a brief account, see Gormley (ed), *Kapteyn and VerLoren van Themaat's Introduction to the Law of the European Communities* (3rd edn, 1998), pp 9–13.

Member States, an independent Commission, and a Court of Justice. At the same time, steps were taken to contain the unnecessary proliferation of institutions. Alongside the EEC and the EAEC Treaties, the Member States also signed a Convention on Certain Institutions Common to the European Communities, creating a single Parliament and a single Court of Justice with jurisdiction under all three Treaties. Thus it was that the entry into force of the two Rome Treaties on 1 January 1958 gave birth to the Court of Justice of the European Communities in broadly the form in which we know it today.[17]

It will immediately be apparent that the project set in train by the authors of the EEC Treaty was considerably bolder and more ambitious than that contemplated by the authors of the ECSC Treaty. In the first place, the EEC Treaty was much broader in scope. Partly as a result of this, it was generally less detailed than its predecessor, a *traité cadre* or framework treaty which gave responsibility for putting flesh on the skeleton to the institutions of the Community, rather than a *traité loi* itself setting out a detailed programme for action.[18] Another distinction between the two Rome Treaties and the Treaty of Paris was that, while the latter was concluded for a period of fifty tears,[19] both the former Treaties were concluded for unlimited periods.[20] Moreover, the objective of forging 'an ever closer union among the peoples of Europe' was one which could by definition never be achieved: however closely the Member States became integrated, it would always be necessary to consider what further steps might be taken.

Since the signing of the EEC Treaty in 1957, a number of amendments affecting the Court both directly and indirectly have been made. Some of these have been purely technical, such as changes to the number of members occasioned by the accession of new Member States. Others have been more significant. The Single European Act, which was signed in 1986 and which introduced into the Treaty the notion of the internal market alongside that of the common market, inserted a new Article 168a making provision for a court of first instance to be attached to the Court. The Court of First Instance (CFI) is discussed in more detail below. A milestone in the development of the Community (as the ECSC, the EEC and the EAEC were often collectively known) came with the signing in the Dutch town of Maastricht on 7 February 1992 of the Treaty on European Union (TEU). That Treaty superimposed on the three existing Communities a new structure called the European Union with jurisdiction in two areas falling outside the scope

---

[17] The process of institutional rationalization was continued on 8 April 1965, when the Treaty establishing a Single Council and a Single Commission of the European Communities was signed in Brussels. The Council should not be confused with the European Council, which brings together the Heads of State or Government of the Member States and the President of the Commission: see Art 4 (ex D) TEU. The Court of Auditors, which audits the Community's accounts, was added to the list of institutions at Maastricht. See generally Craig and de Búrca, *EU Law* (2nd edn, 1998), chs 2 and 3; Hartley, *The Foundations of European Community Law* (4th edn, 1998), ch 1.

[18] The contrast between the two Treaties may be illustrated by comparing the rules on competition laid down by Arts 81 (ex 85) and 82 (ex 86) EC with the corresponding provisions of the ECSC Treaty, Arts 65 and 66.

[19] Art 97.   [20] See Arts 312 (ex 240) EC and 208 EAEC.

of the original Treaties, namely foreign and security policy (the subject of Title V of the TEU, sometimes called the second pillar) and justice and home affairs (the subject of Title VI, sometimes called the third pillar). Article L (now 46) of the TEU purported to exclude practically all these new provisions from the jurisdiction of the Court, perhaps an indication that the fears expressed by Baroness Thatcher in the House of Lords were not wholly idiosyncratic. The TEU also changed the title of the European Economic Community to European Community *tout court*, thereby catching up with a situation that had been apparent to observers for some time and which, as we shall see, the Court had had some part in shaping. In addition, important amendments were made to the statement of the Community's tasks contained in Article 2 of what was now the EC Treaty, which henceforward referred among other things to the establishment of an economic and monetary union.[21] The extent to which the institutions of the Community were entitled to legislate to achieve its objectives was from then on to be constrained by the famous principle of subsidiarity. By virtue of a new Article 3b (now 5) EC, in areas where jurisidiction was in principle shared between the Community and the Member States, the Community was to act 'only if and in so far as the objectives of the proposed action cannot be sufficiently achieved by the Member States and can therefore, by reason of the scale or effects of the proposed action, be better achieved by the Community'. The significance of the principle of subsidiarity, and of the TEU in general, is considered in more detail in chapter 16.

The TEU envisaged[22] the convening of a further IGC in 1996 'with a view to considering . . . to what extent the policies and forms of cooperation introduced by this Treaty may need to be revised with the aim of ensuring the effectiveness of the mechanisms and the institutions of the Community'.[23] By the time the IGC opened on 29 March 1996, the agenda extended well beyond the provisions for which the TEU expressly contemplated review.[24] In particular, the Member States hoped to reach agreement on a range of institutional reforms which were considered necessary to facilitate a substantial enlargement of the Union to bring in Cyprus and many of the countries of Central and Eastern Europe. The 1996 IGC led to the signing on 2 October 1997 of the Treaty of Amsterdam, which entered into force on 1 May 1999.[25] In the event, agreement on the main institutional reforms proved elusive, the Member States merely undertaking to convene a further IGC at least one year before membership of the Union exceeded twenty 'in order to carry out a comprehensive review of the provisions of the Treaties on the composition and functioning of the institutions'.[26] The Treaty of Amsterdam is likely, however, to have a significant impact on the Court. Not only does it con-

---

[21] See Title VII (ex VI) of the EC Treaty.   [22] See Art N(2), now repealed.
[23] Art B.
[24] See further Dashwood (ed), *Reviewing Maastricht: Issues for the 1996 IGC* (1996).
[25] For a useful overview, see Langrish, 'The Treaty of Amsterdam: selected highlights' (1998) 23 ELRev 3.
[26] Art 2, Protocol on the institutions with the prospect of enlargement of the European Union, annexed by the Treaty of Amsterdam to the TEU and the EC, ECSC and EAEC Treaties.

fer on it new powers, it also contains provisions which seem to envisage judicial solutions to problems of an essentially political nature.[27] The provisions of the Treaty of Amsterdam affecting the Court will be examined in more detail in the course of the following chapters.

The Members of the Court and its Working Methods

At this point it is convenient to consider briefly the members of the Court and its working methods. It should be noted that only some of the provisions governing these matters are contained in the Treaties themselves. Reference also needs to be made to the Statutes of the Court and to its Rules of Procedure, which were based originally on the Statute and Rules of Procedure of the International Court of Justice.[28] A Protocol on the Statute of the Court is annexed to the EC Treaty, the ECSC Treaty, and the EAEC Treaty. The Statutes form an integral part of, and have the same legal status as, the Treaties to which they are annexed.[29] Each Statute lays down rules on the members of the Court and the broad contours of its organization and procedure in more detail than would have been convenient in the body of the respective Treaties. The Statutes are implemented and supplemented by a single set of Rules of Procedure adopted by the Court with the unanimous approval of the Council.[30] The Statutes of the Court were modified in 1988 in the light of the establishment of the CFI, which has its own Rules of Procedure.[31]

The Court of Justice originally consisted of seven Judges assisted by two Advocates General. It has now grown to fifteen Judges[32] and nine Advocates General.[33] The term 'members' is often used to refer to the Judges and Advocates General collectively. The general function of a Judge does not call for further elaboration here. The task of an Advocate General, one of whom is assigned to each case before the Court, is to present an independent and impartial Opinion after the parties have concluded their submissions and before the Judges begin their

[27] See generally Albors-Llorens, 'Changes in the jurisdiction of the European Court of Justice after the Treaty of Amsterdam' (1998) 35 CMLRev 1273; Arnull, 'Taming the beast? The Treaty of Amsterdam and the Court of Justice' in Twomey and O'Keeffe (eds), *Legal Issues of the Amsterdam Treaty* (1999).

[28] See Plender, 'Procedure in the European Courts: comparisons and proposals' (1997) 267 Recueil des Cours 34–5; Schwarze, 'Origins of the European Courts' Statutes and Rules of Procedure' in Plender (ed), *European Courts Practice and Precedents* (1997), ch 1, p 4.

[29] See Plender (1997) 267 Recueil des Cours 35.

[30] The Rules of Procedure are themselves supplemented by Supplementary Rules and Instructions to the Registrar. See further Lasok, *The European Court of Justice: Practice and Procedure* (2nd edn, 1994), pp 3–8.

[31] And Instructions to the Registrar.   [32] Art 221 (ex 165) EC.

[33] Art 222 (ex 166) EC. The number of Advocates General will fall to 8 on 7 October 2000. For an explanation, see Tridimas, 'The role of the Advocate General in the development of Community law: some reflections' (1997) 34 CMLRev 1349, 1351, n 6.

deliberations.[34] The Opinion will typically set out any relevant facts and legislation and analyse the issues raised and the relevant case law of the Court. It will conclude with a recommendation to the Judges as to how the case should be decided. Thus, even where the Court of Justice sits as a court of first and last resort, its decisions are in effect judicially considered twice over.

It is hard to gauge empirically the influence of the Advocates General on the development of the case law.[35] The Statutes provide[36] that the deliberations of the Court are to remain secret, a rule which is strictly observed.[37] Moreover, the Court gives a single collective judgment signed by all the Judges who took part in the deliberations. Dissenting judgments are not permitted and for many years the Court's judgments did not refer explicitly to the views of the Advocates General. These factors tend to conceal any influence which the Opinion may have had. Simply comparing the judgment in a case with the Opinion which preceded it is inconclusive. They may reach the same result on some issues but not on others. Where the Advocate General and the Court are in agreement as to the result, their reasoning may differ, either wholly or in part. Nevertheless, most students of the Court would probably say that it is fairly unusual—although by no means unheard of—for the Court to depart from the Opinion of its Advocate General and there are reasons for believing that, whether or not an Opinion is followed, the Judges find it helpful.

Lord Slynn, who was an Advocate General from 1981 to 1988 and a Judge from 1988 to 1992, has written:[38] 'As an Advocate General, one always hoped that the function had some utility; as a judge I now know that it is very valuable in this kind of court to have a detailed first-round assessment on which the judges can work. The research, the analysis of fact and law, the direction indicated by the Advocate General—even if not followed—are of considerable help.' Confirmation that Lord Slynn's view is more than a purely personal one is provided by the modern practice of the Court, which is to refer expressly to the Opinion where it agrees with the line taken by the Advocate General.[39] Such references have become increasingly frequent. Indeed, the Court sometimes simply refers to the reasoning of the Advocate General without giving any independent reasons of its own. A striking

---

[34] See Art 222 EC, 2nd para; Dashwood, 'The Advocate General in the Court of Justice of the European Communities' (1982) 2 Legal Studies 202; Borgsmidt, 'The Advocate General at the European Court of Justice: a comparative study' (1988) 13 ELRev 106; Fennelly, 'Reflections of an Irish Advocate General' (1996) Irish Journal of European Law 5.

[35] See further Tridimas, 'The role of the Advocate General in the development of Community law: some reflections' (1997) 34 CMLRev 1349, 1362–5.

[36] EC Statute, Art 32; EAEC Statute, Art 33; ECSC Statute, Art 29.

[37] See eg Koopmans, 'Judicial decision-making' in Campbell and Voyatzi (eds), *Legal Reasoning and Judicial Interpretation of European Law* (1996), ch 5, p 94.

[38] *Introducing a European Legal Order* (1992), pp 157–8. See also the remarks of Judge Robert Lecourt, a former President of the Court, quoted in Wyatt and Dashwood, *European Community Law* (3rd edn, 1993), at p 106, n 26.

[39] The Court does not mention the Opinion where it disagrees with it.

example is *Hauptzollamt Hamburg-St Annen v Ebbe Sönnichsen*,[40] where a German court had put to the Court of Justice[41] two questions on the interpretation of Community regulations. In reply, the Court simply said: '[f]or the reasons indicated in the Advocate-General's Opinion of 31 March 1993, the reply to the question put by the national court must be that . . .'. The following year, in *SEP v Commission*,[42] the Court was called upon to hear an appeal against a decision of the CFI. The appellant had raised eight grounds of appeal. The Court dealt with the first five in a single sentence: 'For the reasons stated in paragraphs 21 to 42 of the Advocate General's Opinion, the first, second, third, fourth and fifth grounds of appeal must be rejected as unfounded.'[43]

As public documents published in due course in the reports of cases before the Court, the Opinions of the Advocates General also have value for others concerned with the Court's activities, be they practising lawyers or academics or simply members of the general public. Being the product of a single mind, the Opinions often have a clarity and directness which judgments of the Court, essentially committee documents, may lack.[44] The value of the Advocate General to users of the Court was underlined by the House of Lords Select Committee on the European Communities in its report on the establishment of the CFI. The Court itself had proposed that the CFI should not be assisted by Advocates General, but many of those who gave evidence to the Committee 'urged strenuously that Advocates-General should be appointed to the CFI'.[45] In the event, the CFI was given the right to call upon one of its members to perform the function of Advocate General where 'the legal difficulty or the factual complexity of the case so requires'.[46]

Judges and Advocates General 'rank equally in precedence according to their seniority in office'[47] and the rules relating to their appointment are the same.

[40] Case C–59/92 [1993] ECR I–2193, para 4.

[41] Under the preliminary rulings procedure established by Art 234 (ex 177) EC. See ch 2.

[42] Case C–36/92 P [1994] ECR I–1911.

[43] Para 21 of the judgment. The Court went on to dismiss the appeal in its entirety even though the Advocate General had concluded that the contested judgment should be quashed and the case referred back to the CFI.

[44] Although modern judgments are on the whole easier to follow than the extremely concise judgments often delivered by the Court in the early years of its existence. It is sometimes suggested that the clarity of the Court's judgments would be improved if dissenting judgments were permitted. Such a reform would have two significant disadvantages. It would cause delay and expose Judges to political pressure by making it possible to identify the line they had taken in particular cases. See Edward, 'How the Court of Justice works' (1995) 20 ELRev 539, 557–8; Slynn, op cit, pp 161–2.

[45] See 'A European Court of First Instance' (Session 1987–88, 5th Report), p 15; Millett, *The Court of First Instance of the European Communities* (1990), p 15.

[46] See Art 18 of the Rules of Procedure of the CFI. Only limited use has been made of this possibility: see Tridimas, 'The role of the Advocate General in the development of Community law: some reflections' (1997) 34 CMLRev 1349, 1384–5.

[47] Art 6, Rules of Procedure. On three occasions, Judges have become Advocates General (Trabucchi, Capotorti, and La Pergola) and Advocates General have become Judges (Mancini, Slynn, and Gulmann). Only Judges take part in the election of the President of the Court, who directs the judicial business and the administration of the Court and presides at hearings and deliberations of the full Court and who must himself be a Judge. In its report on the application of the TEU (see 'Proceedings of the Court of Justice and Court of First Instance of the European Communities', No 15/95 (22–6

Under the original version of the ECSC Treaty, legal qualifications were not required: 'independence and competence' sufficed. Two of the original Judges, Serrarens from The Netherlands and Rueff from France, were not legally qualified.[48] Since the signing of the 1957 Convention on Common Institutions, however, Article 223 (ex 167) EC and the equivalent provisions in the other treaties have required appointees to be 'persons whose independence is beyond doubt and who possess the qualifications required for appointment to the highest judicial offices in their respective countries or who are jurisconsults of recognized competence'. The term 'jurisconsult', at least in the English version of the Treaty,[49] is wide enough to cover lawyers in private practice and academic lawyers, even where they are not eligible for appointment to the Bench at home. In practice, the members of the Court have come from a variety of backgrounds, including the national judiciary, the civil service, the Bar, and the academic world.[50] A former President of the Court[51] has suggested[52] that a member's professional background can have at least as significant an influence on his approach to a case as his national origin.[53]

Critics in the United Kingdom sometimes object to the appointment of members without judicial experience. However, the House of Lords Select Committee on the European Communities, in its report on the 1996 IGC, said that 'a Treaty amendment which would exclude professors or administrators would narrow the range of professional experience available to the Court and would be seen as trying to impose on other Member States a particularly British view of the best background for senior judicial office'.[54] Brown and Kennedy point out that 'in all the original six Member States the holder of a University chair of law may be translated to the bench, sometimes at the highest levels'.[55] Of the British members to date, Sir Gordon Slynn (as he then was) had the greatest domestic judicial experience, yet it never seems to have been suggested that the Opinions he delivered when an Advocate General were systematically out of line with the general tenor of the Court's case law.

May 1995)), the Court suggested that Advocates General should be permitted to take part in the election of the President, but that suggestion was not taken up by the Member States.

[48] See Brown and Kennedy, *Brown and Jacobs' The Court of Justice of the European Communities* (4th edn, 1994), p 47.

[49] Lasok, op cit, p 15, n 97, points out that, in some language versions, it is possible to argue that the term 'jurisconsult' means a professional legal adviser and not simply a person learned in the law.

[50] For more information on the backgrounds of the Members of the Court, see Brown and Kennedy, op cit, pp 55–9; Lecourt, 'La Cour de Justice des Communautés européennes vue de l'intérieur' in Grewe, Rupp and Schneider (eds), *Europäische Gerichtsbarkeit und Nationale Verfassungsgerichtsbarkeit* (1981), p 261 at p 263.

[51] Judge Ole Due of Denmark, who, before his appointment to the Court, held a number of posts in the Danish Ministry of Justice.

[52] In an interview broadcast on BBC radio on 18 May 1990.

[53] The importance of the group identity engendered among the Judges of the Court by the qualifications needed for appointment and its working methods is emphasized by Chalmers, 'Judicial preferences and the Community legal order' (1997) 60 MLR 164, 168–70.

[54] Op cit, para 260.   [55] Op cit, p 46.

According to Article 223 (ex 167) EC, the members of the Court are appointed 'by common accord of the Governments of the Member States for a term of six years', which is renewable. This means that a member's appointment can in theory be blocked by any of the Member States. Unlike the European Commission,[56] there is nothing in the Treaties about the national composition of the Court.[57] In practice, however, one Judge is appointed from each Member State. There is in principle one Advocate General from the five largest Member States,[58] while the remaining posts rotate among the other Member States.

Although the Court consists of fifteen Judges, they do not all hear every case. The Court sits either in chambers of three or five Judges[59] or as the full Court, for which the quorum is nine. Thus, even where a case is assigned to the full Court, it is in practice rare for the so-called *grand plenum* of fifteen Judges to be assembled. It is more likely that the *petit plenum* of eleven Judges will deal with it. The formation chosen is in principle determined by the difficulty or importance of the proceedings. The full Court is also used to maintain consistency between the chambers. Before the entry into force of the TEU, there were certain types of case which had to be heard by the Court sitting in plenary session.[60] That requirement has now been removed, although a Member State or a Community institution which is a party to proceedings before the Court may require it to sit in plenary session. That right is exercised relatively infrequently.[61]

The language in which proceedings before the Court take place depends on their nature.[62] In direct actions, that is, actions which start and finish before the Court, the language of the case is in principle chosen by the applicant from a list of twelve procedural languages[63] set out in Article 29(1) of the Rules of Procedure.[64] In references for preliminary rulings, which constitute an episode in proceedings which start and finish in a national court, the language of the case is that of the court which made the reference. The language of the case must be used in written and oral pleadings, although a Member State which intervenes in support of one of the parties in a direct action or submits observations in a reference for a preliminary ruling may use its official language. The Advocate General is entitled to deliver his

[56] See Art 213(1) (ex 157(1)) EC.

[57] See Kennedy, 'Thirteen Russians! The composition of the European Court of Justice' in Campbell and Voyatzi, op cit, ch 4.

[58] France, Italy, Germany, Spain, and the United Kingdom. Until 6 October 2000 Italy will have two Advocates General. See Tridimas, 'The role of the Advocate General in the development of Community law: some reflections' (1997) 34 CMLRev 1349, 1351.

[59] A power conferred on the Court by the TEU to create chambers of seven Judges had not at the time of writing been exercised: see Art 221 (ex 165) EC.

[60] See Art 165, 3rd para, of the EEC Treaty.

[61] See the Court's report on the application of the TEU, *supra*.   [62] See further ch 2.

[63] Danish, Dutch, English, Finnish, French, German, Greek, Irish, Italian, Portuguese, Spanish, and Swedish.

[64] Art 29(2) sets out certain exceptions to that general rule. The most important is that, where the defendant is a Member State or a natural or legal person having the nationality of a Member State, the language of the case is the official language of that State. Where the State concerned has more than one official language, the applicant may choose between them.

Opinion in any of the Court's procedural languages. In practice, the Opinion is normally written in its author's first language. The judgments of the Court and the Opinions of its Advocates General are published in the European Court Reports in all the procedural languages (except Irish). As a matter of practice, the Court uses French as its internal working language. This means that, whatever the language of the case, the pleadings will be translated into French and the draft of the judgment produced in that language before being translated into the language of the case. Ambiguities in other language versions can therefore sometimes be resolved by comparing them with the French version, even though strictly speaking only the version drawn up in the language of the case is authentic.[65]

In proceedings before the European Court of Human Rights in Strasbourg, the judge who is a national of the State party concerned sits as an *ex officio* member.[66] It has been observed that 'it might seem that it would have been more appropriate to exclude a judge who was a national of a State concerned, but the inclusion of the judge of the respondent State has the advantage of ensuring acquaintance with the legal system and the background of the case'.[67] There is no equivalent rule in the case of the Court of Justice. Indeed, the Statutes expressly provide[68] that a party may not apply for a change in the composition of the latter court or of one of its chambers on the ground of the nationality of a Judge or the absence of a Judge of the nationality of the party concerned.

It is sometimes suggested that the members of the Court should be chosen from a list of national nominees by a judicial appointments board composed of very senior members of the judiciaries of the Member States.[69] Such a system, it has been said, would have the advantage of distancing the selection of members from the domestic political process and might ultimately help to break the link between the number of Member States and the number of Judges, which is becoming increasingly impractical the larger the Community gets.[70] In its report on the application of the TEU,[71] the Court acknowledged that 'any significant increase in the number of Judges might mean that the plenary session of the Court would cross the invisible boundary between a collegiate court and a deliberative assembly'. However, it pointed out that 'the presence of members from all the national legal systems on the Court is undoubtedly conducive to harmonious development of Community case-law, taking into account concepts regarded as fundamental in the various Member States and thus enhancing the acceptability of the solutions arrived

---

[65] See Art 31 of the Rules of Procedure. The language regime in the CFI is similar, *mutatis mutandis*, to that which prevails in the Court, although the CFI occasionally uses English as its working language. See generally Art 35 of its Rules of Procedure.

[66] See Art 27 ECHR.

[67] Jacobs and White, *The European Convention on Human Rights* (2nd edn, 1996), p 382.

[68] EC Statute, Art 16; EAEC Statute, Art 16; ECSC Statute, Art 19.

[69] See Koopmans, 'The future of the Court of Justice of the European Communities' (1991) 11 YEL 15, 26.

[70] See the evidence given by Professor Dashwood to the House of Lords Sub-Committee on the 1996 IGC (Session 1994–95, 18th Report), p 259.

[71] *Supra.*

at. It may also be considered that the presence of a Judge from each Member State enhances the legitimacy of the Court.' These points are well taken and it may be doubted whether it would be wise to deprive each Member State of the right to nominate a Judge. The problem of the size of plenary sessions of the Court might perhaps be addressed by leaving the quorum for sittings of the full Court untouched at any future enlargement of the Union.

The idea of involving senior national judges in appointing members of the Court did not commend itself to the House of Lords Select Committee on the European Communities, which said: 'We do . . . have considerable doubts as to whether senior judges within one judicial system are in fact well qualified to pronounce on the relative merits of candidates from another. The task would add considerably to their responsibilities and they would in practice be likely to depend on confidential assessments of competence and character supplied by their own governments.'[72] Notwithstanding the doubts expressed by the Select Committee, it is submitted that the removal of any suspicion, however ill-founded, that members of the Court are being appointed for domestic political reasons would help to reinforce its standing. It may well be that the task of vetting appointments should not be left exclusively in the hands of national judges, but a mixed panel, perhaps consisting of senior national judges and present and former members of the Court itself, should be able to perform the task of selecting candidates from a shortlist drawn up by the Governments of the Member States. Such a procedure, especially if candidates were expected to appear before the panel, would also be more likely than the present system to uncover aspects of a candidate's record which might render him or her unsuitable for appointment.[73]

In a resolution on the functioning of the TEU adopted on 17 May 1995 as part of the preparations for the 1996 IGC,[74] the European Parliament argued that its assent should be required to all nominations to the Court of Justice and the CFI. If that suggestion were taken up, it would introduce the possibility of 'confirmation hearings' on the American model being held before a committee of the Parliament before its assent to individual nominations was given. In its own report on the functioning of the TEU, the Court expressed opposition to the introduction of any such procedure on the ground that prospective appointees would be unable to respond to questions without betraying the discretion they would, if appointed, be required to observe and without prejudging questions they might have to decide in the exercise of their judicial functions. The Court's view that such a procedure would be unacceptable was shared by the House of Lords Select Committee.[75] The Parliament's suggestion was not taken up by the Member States. It is submitted that

---

[72] See its report on the 1996 IGC (Session 1994–95, 21st Report), para 260.

[73] Cf the procedure for the election of judges to the European Court of Human Rights which has applied under Art 22 of the European Convention on Human Rights since the entry into force of the 11th Protocol; Schermers, 'Election of judges to the European Court of Human Rights' (1998) 23 ELRev 568.

[74] See OJ 1995 C151/56, point 23(ii).   [75] Op cit, para 261.

for them to have done so would have been a retrograde step in view of the fre-
quency with which the Parliament is now involved in proceedings before the
Court.

The Court of First Instance and the Future of the Community Judicature

Since at least the late 1970s the workload of the Court of Justice has been giving
cause for concern. It has an adverse effect on the Court's output in two ways. First
of all it causes delay. In 1975, it took the Court on average six months to respond
to a request from a national court for a preliminary ruling and nine months to deal
with a direct action. By 1988, those figures had risen to eighteen months and
twenty-four months respectively.[76] Secondly, the pressure on the Court to deal
with cases as quickly as possible makes it reluctant to carry out detailed investigations into their factual background. It was in an attempt to address these problems
that the Member States made provision in the Single European Act for a court of
first instance to be attached to the Court[77] and in 1988 the Council, acting under
new powers conferred on it by the Treaties, adopted a decision establishing the
Court of First Instance of the European Communities.[78] The Treaties provide that
the judgments of the CFI are to be subject to appeal to the Court of Justice, but
only on points of law. On issues of fact the CFI's judgment is therefore final.
Despite initial fears that the Court of Justice might be overwhelmed by appeals
against rulings of the CFI,[79] the incidence of appeals has, so far at least, been fairly
low.[80] As a result, the CFI at present has the last word in a large majority of the
cases falling within its jurisdiction.

[76] These figures are taken from Millett, op cit, p 2.
[77] Thus the creation of a new institution was not envisaged.
[78] See Decision 88/591, adopted under Art 168a (now 225) of the EC Treaty, Art 32d of the ECSC
Treaty, and Art 140a of the EAEC Treaty. The corrected text of the decision is published at OJ 1989
C215/1. The Court of Justice and the CFI may be referred to collectively as the Community judicature or the Community Courts. See generally Cruz Vilaça, 'The Court of First Instance of the European
Communities: a significant step towards the consolidation of the European Community as a
Community governed by the rule of law' (1990) 10 YEL 1; Due, 'The Court of First Instance' (1988)
8 YEL 1; Kennedy, 'The essential minimum: the establishment of the Court of First Instance' (1989)
14 ELRev 7 and (1990) 15 ELRev 54; Millett, op cit, and 'The new European Court of First Instance'
(1989) 38 ICLQ 811; Schermers, 'The European Court of First Instance' (1988) 25 CMLRev 541;
Toth, 'The Court of First Instance of the European Communities' in White and Smythe (eds), *Current
Issues in European and International Law* (1990), p 19.
[79] See the House of Lords Select Committee on the European Communities, 'A European Court of
First Instance' (Session 1987–88, 5th Report), para 88.
[80] See generally Brown, 'The first five years of the Court of First Instance and appeals to the Court
of Justice: assessment and statistics' (1995) 32 CMLRev 743; Sonelli, 'Appeal on points of law in the
Community system' (1998) 35 CMLRev 871. The proportion of CFI judgments challenged on appeal
is now showing signs of rising.

The CFI began hearing cases at the end of October 1989. Its jurisdiction was initially confined to staff cases, certain proceedings brought by undertakings against the Commission under the ECSC Treaty and competition cases brought by undertakings under the EEC Treaty. In addition, the CFI had jurisdiction where a claim for damages was combined with a claim falling within one of the above categories. These cases represented only a limited proportion of those which the Council was permitted by the Treaties to transfer to it. However, additional transfers in 1993[81] and 1994[82] extended the jurisdiction of the CFI to include all direct actions brought by natural and legal persons.[83] Amendments made to the three Community Treaties at Maastricht gave the Council the power to transfer to the CFI actions brought by Member States or Community institutions. Towards the end of 1998, the Court asked the Council to exercise that power in respect of a limited category of annulment actions brought by Member States with a view to limiting the situations in which challenges to the same act could be brought simultaneously before the Court and the CFI according to the status of the applicant.[84] The Council has no power to transfer to the CFI references for a preliminary ruling made under Article 234 (ex 177) of the EC Treaty or its counterparts in the ECSC and EAEC Treaties.

The CFI consists of fifteen Judges (one from each Member State) appointed for renewable terms of six years. Under the Treaties, each Judge must 'possess the ability required for appointment to judicial office'. As mentioned above, the CFI is not assisted by Advocates General on a permanent basis. However, each Judge[85] may be called upon to perform the function of Advocate General in difficult or complex cases. Only limited use has been made of this possibility. Indeed, it may be doubted whether a member who normally sits as a Judge could be expected to approach a case with the necessary degree of objectivity and detachment if called upon to act as an Advocate General.[86]

Like the Court of Justice, the CFI delivers a single collegiate judgment signed by the Judges who took part in the deliberations. There are no dissenting judgments. The CFI normally sits in chambers of three or five Judges. It is permitted to sit in plenary session where 'the legal difficulty or the importance of the case or special circumstances so justify'.[87] In such circumstances, the CFI must be assisted by an

---

[81] See OJ 1993 L144/21.   [82] See OJ 1994 L66/29.

[83] Thus, actions for annulment or failure to act brought by a natural or legal person against an institution of the Community under Arts 230 (ex 173) or 232 (ex 175) respectively of the EC Treaty, as well as actions brought against the Community for damages under the second paragraph of Art 288 (ex 215) of the EC Treaty, now commence in the CFI.

[84] See *Europe*, 5 February 1999, p 8. At the time of writing, the Court's request had not yet been implemented.

[85] With the exception of the President, who is responsible for directing the judicial business and administration of the CFI.

[86] See Tridimas, 'The role of the Advocate General in the development of Community law: some reflections' (1997) 34 CMLRev 1349, 1384–5.

[87] Rules of Procedure, Art 14.

Advocate General. The possibility of hearing a case in plenary session is used by the CFI relatively rarely.

While the quality of the judgments delivered by the CFI is high and it has undoubtedly succeeded in improving judicial review of complex facts,[88] it has not had the desired effect of speeding up the wheels of justice in the Community.[89] The most that could be said is that the situation would be even worse had the CFI not been set up. By the end of 1998, preliminary rulings were on average taking the Court longer to deliver than before the establishment of the CFI and the length of proceedings before the CFI was itself giving cause for concern. Indeed, in one case the Court quashed part of a ruling made by the CFI on the basis that the proceedings had not been completed within a reasonable time.[90] The CFI has also grown increasingly alarmed[91] at the prospect of having to deal with large numbers of challenges to decisions of the Boards of Appeal established under the Community trade mark regulation.[92] That regulation creates a Community trade mark existing alongside national trade marks but having equal effect throughout the Community. Responsibility for implementing the regulation belongs to OHIM, the Office for Harmonisation in the Internal Market (Trade Marks and Designs). Appeal against decisions of the examiners and the various divisions of OHIM lies to independent Boards of Appeal within OHIM. Decisions of the Boards of Appeal are in turn amenable to judicial review before the CFI.[93]

In an attempt to enable the CFI to cope with its own burgeoning workload, the Court in 1997 proposed that the CFI should be permitted to delegate certain simple cases to a single Judge for decision.[94] It is clear, however, that that proposal

[88] For discussion of the effect of the establishment of the CFI, see Lenaerts, 'The development of the judicial process in the European Community after the establishment of the Court of First Instance' in Clapham (ed), *Collected Courses of the Academy of European Law* (1990), Vol I, Book 1, p 53; Vesterdorf, 'The Court of First Instance of the European Communities after two full years in operation' (1992) 29 CMLRev 897.

[89] Statistics relating to the work of the Community Courts are available on their Website: see http://europa.eu.int/cj/en/stat/index.htm.

[90] See Case C–185/95 P *Baustahlgewebe v Commission*, judgment of 17 December 1998. A period of about five and a half years elapsed between the date on which the application was lodged and the date on which the CFI gave judgment. The Court itself took a further three and half years to deal with the appeal.

[91] See its contribution issued for the purposes of the 1996 IGC, published in 'Proceedings of the Court of Justice and Court of First Instance of the European Communities', No 15/95 (22–6 May 1995).

[92] Reg 40/94, OJ 1994 L11/1. See also Reg 2100/94 on Community plant variety rights, OJ 1994 L227/1.

[93] Such challenges were initially regarded as a form of action for annulment under Art 230 (ex 173) EC: see Jung, 'Proceedings relating to intellectual property rights' in Plender (ed), *European Courts Practice and Precedents* (1997), ch 38, pp 922–3. However, the Court's request, referred to above, that the CFI should be given jurisdiction in some annulment actions brought by Member States envisages that a specific power to deal with trade mark and plant variety right cases should be conferred on the CFI. Cf Arnull, 'The Community judicature and the 1996 IGC' (1995) 20 ELRev 599, 603–4.

[94] The proposal was adopted by the Council on 26 April 1999: see OJ 1999 L114/52. For a detailed examination of the proposal and discussion of the pressures under which the Community Courts are now working, see the House of Lords Select Committee on the European Communities, 'The Court of First Instance: Single Judge' (Session 1997–98, 25th Report).

will only make a relatively small difference to the CFI's ability to deal with cases quickly. Changes of a more fundamental nature to what is known as the judicial architecture of the Union will have to be implemented if the Court and the CFI are to be enabled to deliver judgment within a reasonable time.[95] This apparently prosaic matter has become one of the major preoccupations of the Community Courts. It is something which will need to be considered by the next IGC, since the scope of the changes which could be made without amending the Treaties is limited.

This is not the place for detailed speculation about what might in due course be agreed. However, a brief outline of some possible reforms can be given. First, a significant increase in the number of Judges sitting in the CFI should be considered. This would not give rise to the difficulties, mentioned above, associated with increasing the number of Judges in the Court because the CFI rarely sits in plenary session. Moreover, responsibility for ensuring consistency between the chambers of the CFI belongs, not to the CFI itself, but to the Court in the exercise of its appellate jurisdiction. Secondly, all direct actions, whether brought by a private applicant, a Member State, or a Community institution, might begin in the CFI, leaving the Court to deal mainly with appeals and references for preliminary rulings. Such references are not suitable for transfer to the CFI because of their importance to the proper functioning of the legal order and the impracticality of appeals in what are already interludes in proceedings taking place elsewhere.[96] Thirdly, the right to appeal to the Court might be made exercisable only with the leave of the CFI or of the Court itself. Although such a reform would be out of keeping with the legal traditions of some Member States, where the right to appeal is considered a subjective one belonging to the parties, experience in common law systems shows that it can be an effective way of limiting appeals in cases which are relatively unimportant or which have limited prospects of success. Fourthly, the Court might be permitted to deal with simple cases without an Advocate General. This could either be done automatically where proceedings are assigned to a three-Judge chamber or the decision could be taken by the Court on a case-by-case basis. Finally, consideration should be given to setting up a separate staff tribunal to deal with staff cases, subject to a right to appeal to the CFI on points of law.

Views may admittedly differ about the details of the reforms to the judicial architecture of the Union which are needed. What is incontrovertible is that action to address the logistical problems facing the Community Courts has become pressing.

---

[95] See generally *The Role and Future of the European Court of Justice* (1996), a report by the EC Advisory Board of the British Institute of International and Comparative Law chaired by Lord Slynn; Arnull, 'Refurbishing the judicial architecture of the European Community' (1994) 43 ICLQ 296; Jacqué and Weiler, 'On the road to European Union—a new judicial architecture: an agenda for the intergovernmental conference' (1990) 27 CMLRev 185; Kapteyn, 'The Court of Justice after Amsterdam: taking stock' in Heukels, Blokker and Brus (eds), *The European Union after Amsterdam* (1998), ch 7; Scorey, 'A new model for the Communities' judicial architecture in the new Union' (1996) 21 ELRev 224; van Gerven, 'The role and structure of the European judiciary now and in the future' (1996) 21 ELRev 211.
[96] See the Court's report on the application of the TEU, *supra*; Arnull (1994) 43 ICLQ 296, 307–9.

In the absence of such action, the Member States' commitment to the rule of law, reaffirmed at Amsterdam,[97] will begin to ring rather hollow.

---

[97] See Art 6(1) TEU, as amended by the Treaty of Amsterdam.

Legal foundations

2

The jurisdiction of the Court

The subject of this chapter is the powers expressly conferred on the Court and the approach it has taken to defining their scope. The main focus will be on the Court's jurisdiction under the EC Treaty, since this has been of the greatest practical significance. The Court's jurisdiction under other provisions, such as those of the ECSC Treaty and the TEU, will be touched on where relevant.

Article 220 (ex 164) EC requires the Court to 'ensure that in the interpretation and application of this Treaty the law is observed'. To enable the Court to fulfil that duty, subsequent provisions of the Treaty confer on it a range of specific powers. These include the power, at the suit of the Commission or a Member State, to declare that a Member State has failed to comply with its obligations under the Treaty; to review the legality of certain Community acts; to declare that certain institutions have unlawfully failed to act; to assist national courts called upon to apply provisions of Community law; and to hear claims relating to compensation for damage caused by the institutions of the Community or its servants in the performance of their duties. These powers have not in all respects kept pace with the development of the Community and the Court has sometimes had to deal with the difficult question of how to reconcile its duty under Article 220 with the terms in which its jurisdiction is defined in the Treaty.[1]

The creation of the European Union at Maastricht demonstrated the desire of the Member States to establish a framework for co-operation in certain fields outside the discipline imposed by the three Community Treaties[2] with much weaker supranational elements. Under Titles V and VI[3] on foreign and security policy and (at the outset) justice and home affairs respectively, the role of the Court, along with that of the Commission and the European Parliament, was limited. Article 46 (ex L) of the TEU made it clear that the provisions of the three Community Treaties on the powers of the Court did not apply to Title V of the TEU[4] or (except in very limited circumstances) to Title VI. At Amsterdam, the scope of Title VI of the TEU was significantly extended and new powers were conferred

---

[1] See further Arnull, 'Does the Court of Justice have inherent jurisdiction?' (1990) 27 CMLRev 683.

[2] Which together comprise what is now sometimes known as the first pillar of the Union.

[3] The so-called second and third pillars.

[4] Art 31 of the Single European Act had excluded from the jurisdiction of the Court Title III of that Act, the forerunner to Title V of the TEU.

on the Court to rule on disputes arising out of its application. Article 46 was amended accordingly.[5]

In the discussion which follows, three heads of the Court's jurisdiction which have proved of special importance to the functioning of the legal order will be examined: the enforcement action against Member States, the action for annulment, and the preliminary rulings procedure.

Enforcement actions against Member States

One of the novel features of the Community legal order[6] is the power given to the Commission, an institution independent of the Member States which is required[7] to act in the general interest of the Community, to bring proceedings before the Court against any Member State which fails to fulfil its obligations under the Treaty. Under the EC Treaty, that power derives principally[8] from Article 226 (ex 169),[9] which provides:

If the Commission considers that a Member State has failed to fulfil an obligation under this Treaty, it shall deliver a reasoned opinion on the matter after giving the State concerned the opportunity to submit its observations.

If the State concerned does not comply with the opinion within the period laid down by the Commission, the latter may bring the matter before the Court of Justice.

A corresponding power granted to the Member States under Article 227 (ex 170) EC has been little used in practice.[10] Rulings of the Court under Articles 226 and 227 were originally purely declaratory, Member States simply being required by Article 228 (ex 171) EC to take the steps necessary to comply with the Court's judgment. Since the entry into force of the TEU, the Court has enjoyed the power to impose financial sanctions on Member States which fail to take such steps.[11] That power is discussed below.

---

[5] The Amsterdam version of Art 46 (ex L) also brings within the Court's jurisdiction Title VII (ex VIa), which contains provisions on closer co-operation, and Art 6(2) (ex F(2)), which requires the Union to respect fundamental rights.

[6] See Evans, 'The enforcement procedure of Article 169 EEC: Commission discretion' (1979) 4 ELRev 442, 443, who observes: 'Under traditional international law the enforcement of treaty obligations is a matter to be settled amongst the Contracting Parties themselves.'

[7] Art 213(2) (ex 157(2)) EC.

[8] See also Arts 88(2) (ex 93(2)), 95(9) (ex 100a(4)) and 298 (ex 225) EC. Cf Art 237(d) (ex 180(d)) EC.

[9] See generally Audretsch, *Supervision in European Community Law* (2nd edn, 1986); Brown and Kennedy, *Brown and Jacobs' The Court of Justice of the European Communities* (4th edn, 1994), ch 6; Hartley, *The Foundations of European Community Law* (4th edn, 1998), ch 10; Dashwood and White, 'Enforcement actions under Articles 169 and 170 EEC' (1989) 14 ELRev 388.

[10] At the time of writing, Case 141/78 *France v United Kingdom* [1979] ECR 2923 is the only action under Art 227 (ex 170) to have proceeded to judgment.

[11] See Art 228(2) (ex 171(2)) EC.

The rights and duties of the Commission

Article 226 (ex 169) has proved an important weapon for ensuring compliance by the Member States with their Treaty obligations, but the Court has recognized that it is for the Commission to decide whether to deploy it. If it decides not to institute proceedings, its decision cannot be challenged by a third party with an interest in having the alleged breach established.[12] The Court has been willing to allow the Commission a degree of flexibility in the internal procedure it follows in deciding whether proceedings should be brought. In *Commission v Germany*,[13] it was argued that the proceedings were inadmissible because the issue of the reasoned opinion and the decision to commence proceedings before the Court had been delegated to a single Commissioner instead of having been the subject of a decision by the Commission acting as a college. The Commission explained that, because of the number of infringement proceedings, Commissioners did not have before them draft reasoned opinions when they decided to issue such measures. However, they did have available to them the facts of each case and details of the provisions of Community law which the Commission's services considered to have been breached. They therefore took the decision in principle to issue the reasoned opinion and to commence proceedings before the Court in full knowledge of the essential facts. Drafting of the reasoned opinion then took place at administrative level under the responsibility of the competent Commissioner. The Court ruled that this procedure was acceptable. It was true that the functioning of the Commission was governed by the principle of collegiate responsibility and that therefore 'both the Commission's decision to issue a reasoned opinion and its decision to bring an action for a declaration of failure to fulfil obligations must be the subject of collective deliberation by the college of Commissioners'. However, it was not necessary 'for the college itself formally to decide on the wording of the acts which give effect to those decisions and put them in final form'.[14]

Once proceedings are set in motion, the Court insists on strict compliance by the Commission with the procedural requirements laid down by Article 226 (ex 169). The Court has said that the purpose of the first paragraph of the article is 'to give the Member State an opportunity to justify its position and, as the case may be, to enable the Commission to persuade the Member State to comply of its own accord with the requirements of the Treaty. If this attempt to reach a settlement is unsuccessful, the function of the reasoned opinion is to define the subject-matter of the dispute.'[15] The reasoned opinion should therefore contain 'a coherent statement of the reasons which led the Commission to believe that the State in

---

[12] See eg Case C–191/95 *Commission v Germany*, judgment of 29 September 1998; Case 247/87 *Star Fruit v Commission* [1989] ECR 291.

[13] Ibid. See also Case C–272/97 *Commission v Germany*, judgment of 22 April 1999.

[14] Para 48.

[15] Joined Cases 142 and 143/80 *Amministrazione delle Finanze dello Stato v Essevi and Salengo* [1981] ECR 1413, para 15.

question has failed to fulfil an obligation under the Treaty'.[16] Since the reasoned opinion defines the scope of the proceedings, any subsequent application by the Commission to the Court must be founded on the same grounds and submissions. The Court will not consider a complaint that was not formulated in the reasoned opinion.[17] The reasoned opinion must also lay down a deadline for compliance by the Member State.[18] That deadline determines the relevant date for the purposes of any subsequent proceedings before the Court,[19] for compliance with its obligations by the Member State concerned after the deadline has passed does not prevent the Commission from bringing the matter before the Court. Although the Commission is free to withdraw its action in these circumstances, the Court has said that it retains an interest in continuing with the case since a judgment of the Court 'may be of substantive interest as establishing the basis of a responsibility that a Member State can incur as a result of its default, as regards other Member States, the Community or private parties'.[20]

A case which illustrates strikingly both the extent of the Commission's discretion to pursue proceedings before the Court and its occasional reluctance to withdraw actions which seem to have lost much of their purpose is *Commission v Germany*.[21] In that case, the Commission brought proceedings against Germany for failure to comply with various Council directives on waste. All had been substantially amended or repealed during the administrative or judicial phases of the proceedings. The Court said that it was 'somewhat surprising[,] that the Commission brought its action more than six years after the entry into force of the basic German legislation on the shipment of waste, and did so at a time when the Community had in fact changed its policy in that field along the same lines as those followed by that legislation'.[22] However, the Court ruled that the Commission was entitled to decide when it was appropriate to bring an action. It was not for the Court to review the exercise of that discretion. The Court therefore concluded that the action was admissible.

Given the apparently inexorable increase in the Court's workload and the difficulty it is now experiencing in delivering judgment within a reasonable period of the start of proceedings, one may ask whether this approach, perhaps justified in the early days of the Community's development, should be modified. It may be

---

[16] Case 325/82 *Commission v Germany* [1984] ECR 777, para 8.

[17] See eg Case 186/85 *Commission v Belgium* [1987] ECR 2029, para 13.

[18] See the second paragraph of Art 226 (ex 169).

[19] See eg Case C–362/90 *Commission v Italy* [1992] ECR I–2353.

[20] See Case 39/72 *Commission v Italy* [1973] ECR 101, para 11; Case C–29/90 *Commission v Greece* [1992] ECR I–1971, para 12. On the liability of Member States to private parties for breaches of Community law, see Joined Cases C–6/90 and C–9/90 *Francovich and Others* [1991] ECR I–5357, discussed in ch 5.

[21] Case C–422/92 [1995] ECR I–1097. See also Case C–207/97 *Commission v Belgium*, judgment of 21 January 1999. Cf Case C–362/90 *Commission v Italy* [1992] ECR I–2353, where the Court dismissed an application by the Commission as inadmissible on the basis that, by the expiry of the deadline laid down in the reasoned opinion, the alleged infringement no longer existed.

[22] Para 17. See also the comments of AG Jacobs at pp I–1105–6 and I–1122–3.

contrasted with its attitude in proceedings for failure to act under Article 232 (ex 175) EC. If the respondent institution remedies its inaction after the commencement of proceedings, the Court treats the subject matter of the action as having ceased to exist,[23] notwithstanding the hypothetical possibility that an action for damages might be brought against the institution concerned under the second paragraph of Article 288 (ex 215) EC. It is submitted that this approach should be extended to actions under Article 226, so that compliance by the Member State with its Treaty obligations before the Court gave judgment would be treated as depriving the action of its subject matter even though the deadline laid down in the reasoned opinion had expired. In these circumstances the proceedings may be considered to have served their purpose of securing respect for the Treaty. The potential liability of the delinquent Member State to third parties should be left for another occasion.[24]

Where the Commission decides to make an application to the Court, it bears the burden of proving that the alleged infringement took place. That burden is a heavy one. The Court requires the Commission to indicate the specific complaints on which it is being asked to rule as well as the legal and factual particulars on which those complaints are based.[25] Thus, where a Member State is required by a directive to inform the Commission of the measures it has introduced to comply with it, failure to satisfy that requirement may amount to a breach of Community law, but it will not entitle the Commission to assume that no implementing measures have in fact been adopted.[26] In *Commission v Denmark*,[27] the Commission sought a declaration that Denmark had failed to apply properly a directive on tax exemptions for means of transport temporarily imported from one Member State into another. The Court dismissed the application as inadmissible on the basis that it 'does no more than mention a number of provisions of the directive, certain judgments of the Court and Articles 5 [now 10], 8a [now 18], 95 [now 90] and 189 [now 249] of the Treaty; the application does not give any details of the facts and circumstances which allegedly gave rise to the failure by the Danish authorities to fulfil their obligations'.[28]

If the Commission alleges that an ambiguous provision of national law is inconsistent with Community law, the Court will expect it to give specific examples where the requirements of Community law have not been met. Thus, in *Commission v United Kingdom*[29] the Commission argued that the United Kingdom

---

[23] See eg Case 377/87 *Parliament v Council* [1988] ECR 4017. The issue is discussed by AG Mischo at pp 4041-3.

[24] For a different view, see *The Role and Future of the European Court of Justice* (a report of the EC Advisory Board of the British Institute of International and Comparative Law chaired by Lord Slynn, 1996), p 62.

[25] See Case C–347/88 *Commission v Greece* [1990] ECR I–4747.

[26] See Case 96/81 *Commission v Netherlands* [1982] ECR 1791.

[27] Case C–52/90 [1992] ECR I–2187. See Bieber (1993) 30 CMLRev 1197.   [28] Para 18.

[29] Case C–300/95 [1997] ECR I–2649. Cf Case C–80/92 *Commission v Belgium* [1994] ECR I–1019, where the Commission withdrew a complaint that Art 49 (ex 59) of the Treaty had been infringed, admitting that it had been based on an incorrect reading of the relevant national legislation. The

Consumer Protection Act 1987 failed to give effect properly to a directive on liability for defective products. The United Kingdom pointed out that section 1(1) of
the Act made it clear that its purpose was to give effect to the directive and required
it to be construed accordingly. It maintained that the relevant provision of the Act,
section 4(1)(e), was capable of being interpreted consistently with the directive.
The Court held that the Commission had not succeeded in refuting that argument:[30] '. . . the Court has consistently held that the scope of national laws, regulations or administrative provisions must be assessed in the light of the
interpretation given to them by national courts . . . Yet in this case the Commission
has not referred in support of its application to any national judicial decision which,
in its view, interprets the domestic provision at issue inconsistently with the
Directive.' The United Kingdom courts on the whole have a good record in interpreting national provisions consistently with directives they are designed to implement and this provided a further ground for rejecting the Commission's
application:[31]

. . . there is nothing in the material produced to the Court to suggest that the courts in the
United Kingdom, if called upon to interpret section 4(1)(e), would not do so in the light of
the wording and the purpose of the Directive so as to achieve the result which it has in view
and thereby comply with the third paragraph of Article 189 [now 249] of the Treaty . . .
Moreover, section 1(1) of the Act expressly imposes such an obligation on the national
courts.

The Court concluded that the Commission had failed to make out its allegation
that the Act was inadequate to give effect to the directive.

The responsibilities of the Member States

In the absence of a procedural irregularity or a failure on the part of the
Commission to prove the alleged infringement, or a misunderstanding by the
Commission of what national law or Community law requires, the Court has been
singularly unreceptive to attempts by the Member States to defend themselves
against proceedings under Article 226 (ex 169). The importance attached by the
Court to compliance by the Member States with their obligations under the Treaty
was emphasized in *Commission v Italy*,[32] where it declared:

In permitting Member States to profit from the advantages of the Community, the Treaty
imposes on them also the obligation to respect its rules.
  For a State unilaterally to break, according to its own conception of national interest, the
equilibrium between advantages and obligations flowing from its adherence to the
Community brings into question the equality of Member States before Community law and

---

Commission accepted that the Belgian Government had shown that the contested provisions were compatible with Art 49.

[30] Para 37. [31] Para 38. [32] Case 39/72 [1973] ECR 101, para 24.

creates discriminations at the expense of their nationals, and above all of the nationals of the State itself which places itself outside the Community rules.

Thus, it is no defence that national legislation, although technically incompatible with Community law, is in practice applied in accordance with the requirements of the Treaty. The Court has said that the mere maintenance in force of such legislation 'gives rise to an ambiguous state of affairs by maintaining, as regards those subject to the law who are concerned, a state of uncertainty as to the possibilities available to them of relying on Community law'.[33] The need to avoid this type of uncertainty has also led the Court to refuse to allow Member States to rely on the fact that the provisions of Community law which have been breached are directly effective and may therefore be relied on in the national courts, which, in accordance with the doctrine of the primacy of Community law, are required to accord them precedence over inconsistent provisions of national law.[34] The Court has stated that 'the primacy and direct effect of the provisions of Community law do not release Member States from their obligation to remove from their domestic legal order any provisions incompatible with Community law . . .'.[35]

Nor can Member States rely on a failure by the Community institutions to comply with their own obligations under the Treaty. In *Commission v Luxembourg and Belgium*,[36] the Court said that 'the Treaty is not limited to creating reciprocal obligations between the different natural and legal persons to whom it is applicable . . . [E]xcept where otherwise expressly provided, the basic concept of the Treaty requires that the Member States shall not take the law into their own hands. Therefore the fact that the Council failed to carry out its obligations cannot relieve the defendants from carrying out theirs.' The appropriate remedy for a Member State in such circumstances would be a direct action against the institution in question. Similarly, a Member State may not justify a breach of Community law on the ground that its object was to correct the effects of such a breach by another Member State. The Court made it clear in *Commission v France*[37] that '[a] Member State cannot under any circumstances unilaterally adopt, on its own authority, corrective measures or measures to protect trade designed to prevent[38] any failure on the part of another Member State to comply with the rules laid down by the Treaty'. The Court pointed out that a Member State which considers the action of another Member State incompatible with Community law can take action at the political level, invite the Commission to bring proceedings against that State under Article 226 (ex 169), or take action itself under Article 227 (ex 170). Moreover, reservations or statements made by the Member State concerned in the course of

---

[33] Case 167/73 *Commission v French Republic* [1974] ECR 359, para 41.
[34] On direct effect and primacy, see ch 3.
[35] Case 104/86 *Commission v Italy* [1988] ECR 1799, para 12.
[36] Joined Cases 90 and 91/63 [1964] ECR 625, 631.
[37] Case 232/78 [1979] ECR 2729, para 9.
[38] *Sic*. The French text reads '. . . destinées à obvier à une méconnaissance éventuelle, par un Etat membre, des règles du traité'.

the procedure leading to the adoption of an act which is alleged to have been breached will not be taken into account by the Court, since 'the objective scope of rules laid down by the common institutions cannot be modified by reservations or objections which Member States have made at the time the rules were being formulated'.[39]

The Court pointed out in *Commission v Ireland*[40] that '[i]t is well established in the case-law of the Court . . . that a Member State may not plead internal circumstances in order to justify a failure to comply with obligations and time-limits resulting from Community law. Moreover, it has been held on several occasions . . . that practical difficulties which appear at the stage when a Community measure is put into effect cannot permit a Member State unilaterally to opt out of fulfilling its obligations.' In particular, the Court has made it clear that the obligations arising from the Treaty 'devolve upon States as such and the liability of a Member State under Article 169 [now 226] arises whatever the agency of the State whose action or inaction is the cause of the failure to fulfil its obligations, even in the case of a constitutionally independent institution'.[41] Thus, it is no defence that draft legislation intended to give effect to the requirements of Community law lapsed due to the dissolution of the national parliament.[42]

The Court has even held that a Member State may incur liability under Article 226 (ex 169) as a result of the actions of private individuals where it has not taken appropriate steps to prevent such actions from interfering with the proper functioning of the common market. This was established in *Commission v France*,[43] where the Commission argued that France had breached its Treaty obligations by failing to take effective action to prevent imports of fruit and vegetables from other Member States from being disrupted by acts of violence committed by French farmers. The Court held that the Treaty required the Member States to take all necessary and appropriate measures to ensure that the fundamental principle of the free movement of goods was respected on their territory. Although the Member States had a margin of discretion in determining what measures were most appropriate to eliminate barriers to imports in a given situation, it was the responsibility of the Court to ensure that that margin had not been exceeded. The Court concluded that 'in the present case the French Government has manifestly and persistently abstained from adopting appropriate and adequate measures to put an end to the acts of vandalism which jeopardize the free movement on its territory of

---

[39] Case 39/72 *Commission v Italy* [1973] ECR 101, para 22.

[40] Case C–39/88 [1990] ECR I–4271, para 11.

[41] Case 77/69 *Commission v Belgium* [1970] ECR 237, para 15.

[42] Ibid. See also eg Case 91/79 *Commission v Italy* [1980] ECR 1099. It appears to follow that proceedings under Art 226 (ex 169) could be brought against a Member State if its courts failed to comply with their obligations under the Treaty: see AG Warner in Case 9/75 *Meyer-Burckhardt v Commission* [1975] ECR 1171, 1187. Such proceedings would be highly sensitive: cf Case C–52/90 *Commission v Denmark* [1992] ECR I–2187, para 7.

[43] Case C–265/95 [1997] ECR I–6959. See Muylle, 'Angry farmers and passive policemen: private conduct and the free movement of goods' (1998) 23 ELRev 467.

certain agricultural products originating in other Member States and to prevent the recurrence of such acts'.[44]

The effectiveness of enforcement proceedings

Conscious of the novelty of the procedure established by Article 226 (ex 169), the Court has sought to strike a balance between ensuring respect by the Commission for the procedural requirements laid down in the Treaty and promoting compliance by the Member States with their Community obligations. Notwithstanding the absence in the Treaty in its original form of any form of sanction should a Member State fail to comply with a judgment against it under Article 226, the Court has succeeded in fashioning an effective means of policing the Member States. Indeed, only a small proportion of the cases in which proceedings are instituted proceed to judgment.[45] If the psychological impact of a ruling under Article 226 seemed to diminish during the 1980s and early 1990s, this seems to have been due not to the approach of the Court but to the increased vigour with which the Commission began to pursue infringements of the Treaty, however minor, by the Member States. The Commission's ardour now seems to have dampened somewhat.[46] That may lead to a strengthening of Member States' desire to avoid adverse rulings under Article 226, especially now that the Court has the power, under a second paragraph added to Article 228 (ex 171) at Maastricht, to impose financial sanctions on Member States which fail to comply with rulings against them.[47]

That power was deprived of much of its significance by the Court's ruling in *Francovich and Others*,[48] decided shortly before the TEU was signed, that there was a principle 'inherent in the system of the [EC] Treaty' that Member States which breached their Treaty obligations were liable to compensate individuals who suffered loss as a result. None the less, there remain some situations where the principle of State liability is unlikely to have much practical effect. For example, it is clear from *Francovich* that a Member State which fails to implement a directive adopted in the general interest, but which does not contemplate that rights should be conferred on individuals,[49] does not expose itself to liability in damages. Where

---

[44] Para 65. The Commission was supported in its application by the UK. By a stroke of irony, the judgment was delivered at a time when British farmers were imitating their French colleagues by interfering with imports of beef into the UK, apparently with the acquiescence of the British authorities.

[45] See Gormley (ed), *Kapteyn and VerLoren van Themaat's Introduction to the Law of the European Communities* (3rd edn, 1998), p 453.

[46] Gormley, op cit, p 454.

[47] The power is only exercisable on application by the Commission, which must specify the amount of the financial sanction it considers appropriate. The Commission has issued guidance on the application of Art 228 (ex 171): see its Memorandum on Applying Art 171 of the EC Treaty, OJ 1996 C242/6; Method of Calculating the Penalty Payments Provided for Pursuant to Art 171 of the EC Treaty, OJ 1997 C63/2. For the use initially made by the Commission of its right to propose the imposition of sanctions, see its answer to Written Question E-3278/98, OJ 1999 C135/182. For discussion, see Bonnie, 'Commission discretion under Article 171(2) EC' (1998) 23 ELRev 537. Cf Art 88 ECSC.

[48] Joined Cases C–6/90 and C–9/90 [1991] ECR I–5357. See ch 5.

[49] A possible example is Dir 79/409 on the conservation of wild birds, OJ 1979 L103/1.

the loss suffered by a potential plaintiff is too small to justify the cost of bringing proceedings, or where causation is hard to prove, there may well be no practical possibility that a claim will be brought. Moreover, in some cases, it may be undesirable to leave matters until a willing litigant emerges. In circumstances such as these, the imposition of a financial sanction under Article 228(2) (ex 171(2)) may be particularly apt. This is an area where the Court will have to tread with great sensitivity in the years ahead.

Notwithstanding the Court's generally robust attitude to the application of Article 226 (ex 169), there is one respect in which it has been conspicuous in its restraint. In *Procureur de la République v Waterkeyn*,[50] the Court was asked to clarify the effect produced by a ruling under Article 226 in the legal order of the Member State concerned. The Court might have been expected to say that a national provision declared incompatible with the Treaty in infringement proceedings brought by the Commission could not be enforced in the national courts. Instead it took a more cautious approach, holding that:

if the Court finds in proceedings under Articles 169 [now 226] to 171 [now 228] of the EEC Treaty that a Member State's legislation is incompatible with the obligations which it has under the Treaty the courts of that State are bound by virtue of Article 171 to draw the necessary inferences from the judgment of the Court. However, it should be understood that the rights accruing to individuals derive, not from that judgment, but from the actual provisions of Community law having direct effect in the internal legal order.

In other words, a judgment of the Court under Article 226 does not in itself confer rights on individuals. Such a judgment merely establishes whether or not a given course of conduct by a Member State is compatible with Community law. Where the Court decides that the Member State is in breach of its obligations under a provision of Community law which produces direct effect,[51] the national courts must draw the appropriate consequences and protect rights claimed by individuals under that provision. The ruling of the Court of Justice under Article 226 establishes conclusively that the provision in question has been breached. Moreover, the *Francovich* case makes it clear that a ruling of the Court under Article 226 establishing that a Member State has failed to comply with a provision of Community law, even one that does not have direct effect, may render the State concerned liable to pay compensation to anyone who has thereby suffered loss. However, where the Community rule which has been infringed does not have direct effect and does not satisfy the conditions for the imposition of liability on the defaulting Member State, it seems that the individual is left without a remedy. The explanation for this apparent lacuna appears to be that the rights of individuals should not depend on whether or not the Commission has chosen to bring proceedings under Article 226.[52] The predicament of individuals adversely affected by the breach should in

---

[50] Joined Cases 314 to 316/81 and 83/82 [1982] ECR 4337.
[51] See chs 3 and 4.
[52] Cf Joined Cases C–46/93 and C–48/93 *Brasserie du Pêcheur and Factortame* [1996] ECR I–1029, para 95.

principle be short-lived: action to comply with the Court's judgment must be commenced as soon as it is delivered and completed as soon as possible.[53]

The action for annulment

Introduction

Under Article 230 (ex 173) EC the Court has jurisdiction to review the legality of Community acts. That jurisdiction is essential in view of the extensive legislative powers which the Treaty gives the political institutions, but its scope has been a matter of great controversy. In order to analyse the Court's approach to the application of Article 230, it is necessary to deal with its constituent parts separately, for while the Court has been liberal in some respects, in others it has taken a stricter line.

Article 230 EC, as amended at Maastricht and Amsterdam, provides as follows:

The Court of Justice shall review the legality of acts adopted jointly by the European Parliament and the Council, of acts of the Council, of the Commission, and of the ECB other than recommendations or opinions, and of acts of the European Parliament intended to produce legal effects vis-à-vis third parties.

It shall for this purpose have jurisdiction in actions brought by a Member State, the Council or the Commission on grounds of lack of competence, infringement of an essential procedural requirement, infringement of this Treaty or of any rule of law relating to its application, or misuse of powers.

The Court of Justice shall have jurisdiction under the same conditions in actions brought by the European Parliament, by the Court of Auditors and by the ECB for the purpose of protecting their prerogatives.

Any natural or legal person may, under the same conditions, institute proceedings against a decision addressed to that person or against a decision which, although in the form of a regulation or a decision addressed to another person, is of direct and individual concern to the former.

The proceedings provided for in this Article shall be instituted within two months of the publication of the measure, or of its notification to the plaintiff, or, in the absence thereof, of the day on which it came to the knowledge of the latter, as the case may be.

The first question raised by Article 230 (ex 173) concerns the type of act which is susceptible to review. The Court's approach to that question has been a liberal one. Under the first paragraph, proceedings may be brought against 'acts adopted jointly by the European Parliament and the Council, . . . acts of the Council, of the Commission, and of the ECB other than recommendations or opinions . . .'. According to Article 249 (ex 189) EC, which describes various types of act which

---

[53] See eg Joined Cases 227 to 230/85 *Commission v Belgium* [1988] ECR 1, para 11.

may be adopted under the Treaty, recommendations and opinions 'have no binding force'.[54] The other categories of act mentioned in Article 249 (regulations,
directives, and decisions) do have binding force and are in principle susceptible to
review under Article 230.

The question whether measures adopted by the Council or the Commission
which produce legal effects, but which do not take the form of any of the binding
acts referred to in Article 249 (ex 189), are susceptible to review under Article 230
(ex 173) was considered in the 'ERTA' case,[55] where the Commission sought the
annulment of certain 'conclusions' reached by the Council concerning the negotiating position to be adopted by the Member States in discussions on a European
road transport agreement. The Court stated that 'Article 173 [now 230] treats as
acts open to review by the Court all measures adopted by the institutions which are
intended to have legal force.'[56] The Court said that it would be inconsistent with
the purpose of Article 230, which was to ensure that the law was observed in
accordance with Article 220 (ex 164) EC, 'to limit the availability of this procedure
merely to the categories of measures referred to by Article 189 [now 249]'.[57] It
concluded that '[a]n action for annulment must therefore be available in the case of
all measures adopted by the institutions, whatever their nature or form, which are
intended to have legal effects'.[58]

The value of the approach taken in 'ERTA' in preserving the institutional balance may be illustrated by *France v Commission*.[59] The Commission had withdrawn
a proposal for a directive on pension funds following failure to reach agreement in
the Council. A few days later, it published in the Official Journal a Communication
on the same subject which bore a marked similarity to the withdrawn proposal.
When France sought the annulment of the Communication, the Commission
argued that it was not of a binding nature: it was an interpretative document which
merely spelled out the consequences in a particular context of rules laid down
in the Treaty itself. The Court found, however, that the wording of the
Communication was imperative in nature and that it did more than just clarify the
application of provisions of the Treaty. It constituted 'an act intended to have legal
effects of its own'[60] which the Commission had no power to adopt. The
Communication was therefore annulled by the Court.

[54] Recommendations are not, however, entirely devoid of legal significance: see Case C–322/88
Grimaldi v Fonds des Maladies Professionnelles [1989] ECR 4407; Arnull, 'The legal status of recommendations' (1990) 15 ELRev 318.
[55] Case 22/70 *Commission v Council* [1971] ECR 263. See also Case C–366/88 *France v Commission*
[1990] ECR I–3571.
[56] Para 39.   [57] Para 41.
[58] Para 42. Another important issue addressed by the Court in 'ERTA', that of the external competence of the Community, is addressed in ch 16.
[59] Case C–57/95 [1997] ECR I–1627. See also Case 294/83 *Les Verts v Parliament* [1986] ECR 1339;
Case 34/86 *Council v Parliament* [1986] ECR 2155. *Les Verts* is discussed below. It should be noted that
a provisional measure intended to pave the way for the final decision in a procedure involving several
stages cannot be challenged under Art 230: Case 60/81 *IBM v Commission* [1981] ECR 2639.
[60] Para 23.

In the 'Airport Transit Visas' case,[61] the Court went further. There the applicant sought the annulment pursuant to Article 230 (ex 173) of a joint action adopted by the Council under Article K.3(2) of the Maastricht version of the TEU.[62] The Court rejected the argument of the United Kingdom Government that it had no jurisdiction since the contested act had been adopted outside the framework of the EC Treaty. Article 47 (ex M) of the TEU, which the Court had jurisdiction under Article 46 (ex L) to apply, made it clear that measures such as the contested joint action were not intended to affect the EC Treaty. The Court declared: 'It is therefore the task of the Court to ensure that acts which, according to the Council, fall within the scope of Article K.3(2) of the Treaty on European Union, do not encroach upon the powers conferred by the EC Treaty on the Community.'[63] The decision was essential to prevent the Member States from using the TEU to avoid the decision-making processes laid down in the EC Treaty in fields which fell within the scope of the latter.

The grounds set out in the second paragraph of Article 230 (ex 173) on which the annulment of a Community act may be sought are not applied by the Court in a technical or formalistic manner. Indeed, it has been remarked that 'almost any well substantiated infringement of Community law, other than a really minor one, may be invoked to establish the illegality of a measure and may in principle lead to its annulment. This is a consequence of the fact that the various grounds are drawn up in such wide terms that they encompass amongst themselves almost all conceivable cases of illegality.'[64] It will be apparent that the third ground mentioned, 'infringement of this Treaty or of any rule of law relating to its application', is extremely broad and capable of encompassing the other three. It is under this ground that the Court may strike down measures which fail to comply with general principles of law, such as legal certainty, non-discrimination, or proportionality. The general principles of law are discussed in chapter 6.

The deadline laid down in the fifth paragraph of Article 230 (ex 173) within which proceedings must be brought is relatively short, though it is relaxed somewhat by the Rules of Procedure of the Community Courts. These clarify the moment from which time starts running and allow extra time on account of the distance between Luxembourg and the applicant's home or registered office.[65]

Where an application under Article 230 (ex 173) is successful, the Court declares the contested act void.[66] It cannot order the defendant institution to take any particular steps, but the institution is required by the Treaty to do what is necessary to comply with the judgment.[67] In principle, a declaration by the Court that a measure is void takes effect from the moment the measure was adopted and is good

---

[61] Case C–170/96 *Commission v Council* [1998] ECR I–2763.

[62] Art K.3 (now Art 31) TEU is no longer divided into numbered paragraphs.   [63] Para 16.

[64] Toth, *The Oxford Encyclopaedia of European Community Law* (1990), Vol I, p 282.

[65] Arts 80 and 81 and Annex II of the Rules of Procedure of the Court; Arts 101 and 102 of the Rules of Procedure of the CFI.

[66] Art 231 (ex 174) EC.   [67] Art 233 (ex 176) EC.

against the whole world. However, the second paragraph of Article 231 (ex 174) provides that, where a regulation is declared void, the Court may declare some of its effects definitive. The object of that provision is to avoid the potential threat to legal certainty which might arise from the disappearance of the contested regulation. Where a similar threat to legal certainty was liable to arise from the annulment of a directive, the Court[68] invoked the second paragraph of Article 231 to preserve the effects of the directive until it had been replaced.[69] As Advocate General Jacobs explained, 'to declare a directive void without preserving some or all of its effects might pose as serious a threat to legal certainty as a similar declaration in respect of a regulation . . .'.[70]

There are two aspects of the action for annulment which have proved particularly controversial. One is of largely historical interest, but the other remains of great practical importance. As will become apparent from the discussion which follows, the Court's case law on the two issues tends to be criticized from diametrically opposed perspectives. The issues in question are the position of the European Parliament under Article 230 (ex 173) and the standing of private parties to bring proceedings.

The position of the European Parliament

Before the amendments introduced at Maastricht, Article 230 (ex 173) contained no reference to the European Parliament[71] and the question whether the Parliament could sue (so-called *légitimation active*) or be sued (so-called *légitimation passive*) became the subject of great controversy, particularly after the first set of direct elections in 1979.[72] The Court had no difficulty in allowing the Parliament to benefit from provisions which referred in general terms to the institutions.[73] However, the status of the European Parliament under the original version of Article 230 was considerably more problematic. As the Parliament sought a role in the Community's decision-making processes commensurate with its ambitions, it was inevitable that, in the absence of a Treaty amendment, the issue would have to be resolved by the Court.

---

[68] Following a suggestion of the European Parliament and the Commission and with the support of the Netherlands and United Kingdom Governments.

[69] See Case C–295/90 *Parliament v Council* [1992] ECR I–4193. See the remarks of AG Jacobs at pp I–4227–9. The directive annulled concerned the right of residence for students. See further ch 11.

[70] See p I–4227. The Opinion of AG Jacobs contains a detailed discussion of the issue.

[71] Cf Art 38 ECSC, on which the Court relied in Case 230/81 *Luxembourg v European Parliament* [1981] ECR 255.

[72] See Bradley, 'The variable evolution of the standing of the European Parliament in proceedings before the Court of Justice' (1988) 8 YEL 27; DeLousse, *The European Court of Justice* (1998) pp 97–104.

[73] See eg Case 138/79 *Roquette Frères v Council* [1980] ECR 3333 and Case 139/79 *Maizena v Council* [1980] ECR 3393 (Art 37, EC Statute); Case 13/83 *European Parliament v Council* [1985] ECR 1513 (Art 175 EEC).

Légitimation passive

The question of the Parliament's *légitimation passive* was addressed by the Court in *Les Verts v European Parliament*.[74] The applicant, a political party, sought the annulment of two measures adopted by the Parliament on the reimbursement of expenses incurred by parties taking part in the 1984 elections. It argued that, in the light of Article 164 (now 220), the Court's jurisdiction under Article 173 (now 230) could not be limited to measures adopted by the Council and the Commission without giving rise to a denial of justice. The Parliament did not contest the admissibility of the action, accepting that the Court could, in its capacity as custodian of the law, review the legality of measures other than those adopted by the Council and the Commission.

In agreeing with the parties that the application was admissible, the Court made a series of highly significant statements about the nature of the system established by the Treaty and the importance of judicial review. It began by emphasizing that the Community was based on the rule of law and that neither the Member States nor the institutions could avoid review of whether the measures they adopted were compatible with the Treaty, described by the Court as 'the basic constitutional charter'.[75] The Treaty, it said, 'established a complete system of legal remedies and procedures designed to permit the Court of Justice to review the legality of measures adopted by the institutions'.[76] Although Article 173 (now 230) only mentioned acts of the Council and the Commission, the general scheme of the Treaty was to make a direct action available against any measure adopted by the institutions which was intended to have legal effect. The reason the Parliament was not expressly mentioned in Article 173 was that, in its original form, the Treaty gave it no power to adopt measures intended to have legal effect *vis-à-vis* third parties.[77] The Court concluded:[78]

An interpretation of Article 173 of the Treaty which excluded measures adopted by the European Parliament from those which could be contested would lead to a result contrary both to the spirit of the Treaty as expressed in Article 164 and to its system. Measures adopted by the European Parliament in the context of the EEC Treaty could encroach on the powers of the Member States or of the other institutions, or exceed the limits which have been set to the Parliament's powers, without its being possible to refer them for review by the Court. It must therefore be concluded that an action for annulment may lie against measures adopted by the European Parliament intended to have legal effects *vis-à-vis* third parties.

---

[74] Case 294/83 [1986] ECR 1339.   [75] Para 23.   [76] Ibid.
[77] The motion of censure on the activities of the Commission under Art 201 (ex 144) EC might have been thought to fall within this category but, as AG Mancini explained, 'the political character of that act overshadows its legal character to such a degree that it was inappropriate (or pointless) to provide a right of action against the body competent to adopt it': [1986] ECR 1339, 1351.
[78] Para 25.

Légitimation active

What were the implications of *Les Verts* for the *légitimation active* of the Parliament under Article 173 (now 230)? The Court's departure in that case from the strict wording of the article meant that it could no longer convincingly be maintained that the Parliament had no right to bring annulment proceedings simply because Article 173 did not refer to it. The Court's attempts to resolve this issue involved a remarkable volte-face and underline the difficulty it has experienced in reconciling the wording of Article 173 with the duty imposed on it by Article 164 (now 220).

In the 'Comitology' case,[79] the Parliament sought the annulment under Article 173 (now 230) of a Council decision laying down the procedures for the exercise of implementing powers conferred on the Commission. The Council raised an objection of inadmissibility which the Court decided to deal with without considering the substance of the case. Rejecting the advice of Advocate General Darmon, the Court concluded that 'the applicable provisions, as they stand at present, do not enable the Court to recognize the capacity of the European Parliament to bring an action for annulment'.[80] The Court said that there was no parallel between the capacity to be a defendant and the capacity to be an applicant in annulment proceedings. It was not necessary for the Parliament to be given the right to bring proceedings under Article 173 in order to ensure that its prerogatives were protected. Disregard of the Parliament's prerogatives constituted an infringement of an essential procedural requirement which could be raised in annulment proceedings instituted by someone else. The Court noted that, under Article 155 (now 211), the Commission had a particular responsibility for defending the Parliament's prerogatives and for bringing proceedings under Article 173 for that purpose where these proved necessary. In addition, an infringement of the Parliament's prerogatives during the procedure leading to the adoption of an act could be raised before the national courts and the matter referred to the Court of Justice for a preliminary ruling under Article 177 (now 234).

The Parliament was understandably less than reassured by the Court's claim that the defence of its interests could safely be left in the hands of others. It therefore decided to continue with another case, introduced before 'Comitology' was decided, in which it was seeking the annulment under Articles 146 EAEC and 173 EEC, the terms of which were then identical, of a Council regulation adopted under the EAEC Treaty following the accident in 1986 at the Chernobyl nuclear power station in the Soviet Union.[81] The contested regulation was based on a provision of the EAEC Treaty which empowered the Council to act by qualified majority after consulting the Parliament. The Parliament had asked the Commission to change the legal basis to a provision of the EEC Treaty requiring recourse to the co-operation procedure. Introduced by the Single European Act,[82] that procedure would have given the Parliament an enhanced role in the

---

[79] Case 302/87 *Parliament v Council* [1988] ECR 5615.   [80] Para 28.

[81] Case C–70/88 *Parliament v Council* [1990] ECR I–2041.   [82] See now Art 252 EC.

decision-making process, but the Commission failed to comply with the Parliament's request. The Council again raised an objection of inadmissibility, claiming that the 'Comitology' decision established that the Parliament had no power to bring annulment proceedings under Article 173 EEC or, by implication, under Article 146 EAEC. The Parliament pointed out, however, that in this case it could not rely on the Commission to defend its prerogatives because the two institutions disagreed over the correct legal basis of the disputed regulation. It added that the possibility that proceedings might be brought by private parties on the basis that the Parliament's prerogatives had been infringed was entirely hypothetical.

The Court began by explaining that the admissibility of the action was to be considered under the EAEC Treaty, but that since Article 146 EAEC was the same as Article 173 EEC, this made no practical difference. The 'Comitology' case established that the Parliament could not bring annulment proceedings under either provision. The Court was forced to acknowledge, however, that the alternative means of protecting the Parliament's prerogatives mentioned in that case might sometimes be ineffective. The Parliament could not rely on the hypothetical possibility that proceedings would be started in the national courts or that a Member State or a private party might seek the annulment of a measure which the Parliament considered to have been adopted in breach of its prerogatives. Although the Commission had a duty to ensure respect for those prerogatives, it could not be expected to bring annulment proceedings which it believed to be unfounded.

The existence of these remedies did not therefore provide an absolute guarantee of the Parliament's prerogatives. Those prerogatives constituted one of the elements of the institutional balance created by the Treaties, which obliged the institutions to respect each other's jurisdiction. Any breach of that obligation had to be susceptible to judicial review. Since the Court was responsible under the Treaties for ensuring respect for the law, it had to be able to guarantee respect for the institutional balance and the prerogatives of the Parliament. Although the Court could not include the Parliament among the institutions which had an automatic right to bring annulment proceedings under Articles 173 EEC and 146 EAEC, it had a duty to ensure that the Treaty provisions regulating the relationship between the institutions were fully respected and that the Parliament, like the other institutions, had an effective legal remedy against threats to its prerogatives. The fact that the Treaties contained no provisions conferring on the Parliament the right to bring annulment proceedings might constitute 'a procedural gap',[83] but this could not be allowed to outweigh the fundamental need to ensure respect for the institutional balance created by the Treaties.

The Court concluded that the Parliament had the right to bring proceedings for the annulment of an act adopted by the Council or the Commission where the purpose of the proceedings was to protect the Parliament's prerogatives. Annulment proceedings brought by the Parliament were otherwise subject to the

[83] Para 26.

same conditions as such proceedings instituted by the Council or the Commission. Among the Parliament's prerogatives was the right to participate to the full extent contemplated by the Treaty in the legislative process leading to the adoption of a Community act. Since the Parliament claimed that, in the case of the disputed regulation, it had not been allowed to do so, its prerogatives were in issue. The action was therefore admissible.

It is remarkable that, less than two years after its judgment in 'Comitology', the Court should have been forced to acknowledge that the reasons it gave in that case for denying the Parliament the right to bring annulment proceedings were unconvincing. It is not just the benefit of hindsight that enables one to say that the Commission and the Parliament would not always see eye to eye[84] and that the former could not be expected to defend the interests of the latter where the two were in dispute. The later decision in *Parliament v Council*[85] shows that the Court in 'Chernobyl' intended to sever definitively the link established in 'Comitology' between the right of the Parliament to bring annulment proceedings and the attitude of the Commission. In *Parliament v Council*, the Court summarily dismissed the argument of the United Kingdom Government that the Parliament's right of action arose only where it was not in agreement with the Commission.[86]

Although the Court did not expressly overrule 'Comitology' in 'Chernobyl',[87] it is clear that the two decisions cannot be reconciled, for in the former the Court said that the relevant provisions did not enable the Court to permit the Parliament to bring annulment proceedings. In the latter, that is precisely what the Court allowed the Parliament to do. However, the Court did not depart in 'Chernobyl' from the view it took in 'Comitology' that Article 173 (now 230) did not permit the Parliament to bring annulment proceedings. Indeed, in 'Chernobyl'[88] the Court cited 'Comitology' as authority for that very point. What the Court did in 'Chernobyl' was to create a new right of action, analogous to but separate from the right of the other institutions to bring annulment proceedings, in order to preserve the institutional balance created by the Treaties and enable it to fulfil its task of ensuring respect for the law.[89]

An assessment of the Court's case law

At Maastricht, the Member States amended the text of Article 173 (now 230) to give effect to the Court's decisions in *Les Verts* and 'Chernobyl'.[90] None the less,

[84] Bradley, op cit, p 53, observed that 'the Commission has not shown itself notoriously sensitive to Parliament's interests in the past'.

[85] Case C–295/90 [1992] ECR I–4193 (right of residence for students).

[86] See the Opinion of AG Jacobs at pp I–4222–3.

[87] It was not until later the same year that the Court expressly departed for the first time from one of its previous decisions: see Case C–10/89 *HAG GF* [1990] ECR I–3711. The approach of the Court to judicial precedents is discussed in ch 15.

[88] See paras 12–14.

[89] See further Arnull, 'Does the Court of Justice have inherent jurisdiction?' (1990) 27 CMLRev 683.

[90] The text of Art 230 which is now in force is set out above.

those decisions are regarded by some of the Court's critics as one of the high water marks of its alleged activism. Sir Patrick Neill discussed the two cases (among others) under the heading 'The ECJ extends its own jurisdiction'. He introduced the relevant section of his paper in the following terms: 'In many cases the ECJ has interpreted provisions of the Treaty or "corrected" or "completed" them so as to extend its own jurisdiction as widely as possible. The overall aim has been to assert the omni-competence of the ECJ as a court charged with responsibility for interpreting, upholding or annulling, and enforcing all rules which it deems to form an integral part of the Community legal system.' Of *Les Verts* he observed: 'The effect of this decision was that the ECJ of its own motion altered the language of Article 173 so as to introduce a reference to the European Parliament. The Member States had not made this amendment at the time they altered other Treaty provisions so as to give the Parliament greater powers. Only the Member States can amend the Treaty.' Of the 'Chernobyl' case, Sir Patrick quoted an observation of Professor Hartley that 'it is hard to imagine a clearer example of changing the law while supposedly interpreting it'.[91]

These criticisms seem unpersuasive.[92] Sir Patrick's mention of the alteration of other provisions affecting the Parliament is presumably a reference to the Single European Act which, as we have seen, introduced the co-operation procedure giving the Parliament greater influence in the decision-making process of the Community. It is true that the Member States did not make any corresponding amendments to Article 173, but it is difficult to attach any significance to this since their reasons for failing to do so are not known. They may simply have preferred to leave the question of the Parliament's *légitimation passive* under Article 173 to the Court of Justice. Certainly the Single European Act made no attempt to exclude the conclusion reached in *Les Verts*. Had the Member States considered the result unacceptable, they could have reversed it at Maastricht. However, as we have seen, they took the opposite step of enshrining the Court's decision in the text of the Treaty.

The main consideration underlying the Court's decision in *Les Verts* was not a desire to assert its 'omni-competence' but to ensure that no institution which had acquired the power to adopt acts affecting the legal rights of third parties could escape judicial review.[93] Far from enlarging the powers of the Community at the expense of the Member States, the result was to provide a judicial remedy when the Parliament exceeded the limits of its powers. The value of that remedy to the Council and the Member States was emphasized soon afterwards when the Court gave judgment in an action brought by the Council, supported by the German,

[91] *The Foundations of European Community Law* (4th edn, 1998), p 79. See also Hartley, 'The European Court, judicial objectivity and the constitution of the European Union' (1996) 112 LQR 95, 101; Hartley, *Constitutional Problems of the European Union* (1999), chs 2 and 3.
[92] See the convincing defence of the Court's approach mounted by Keeling, 'In praise of judicial activism. But what does it mean? And has the European Court of Justice ever practised it?' in Curti Gialdino (ed), *Scritti in Onore di G Federico Mancini* (1998) 505, 520–2.
[93] See the Opinion of AG Mancini at [1986] ECR 1339, 1350–1.

French and United Kingdom Governments, against the Parliament for the annulment of the 1986 budget and of the act of the President of the Parliament declaring it finally adopted.[94] The Court, citing *Les Verts*, accepted that the action was
admissible and went on to uphold the Council's claim that the Parliament had acted
in breach of the budgetary procedure laid down in the Treaty in seeking to increase
unilaterally a certain category of expenditure.[95]

The 'Chernobyl' decision was motivated by the related consideration that there
was no point in including in the Treaty detailed rules about the Parliament's prerogatives if those prerogatives could be ignored by the other institutions with
impunity. The Court was again concerned to ensure that the institutions acted
within the limits of their powers, an essential attribute of the rule of law which it
is the Court's duty to uphold.[96]

The standing of private parties

In order to bring proceedings for annulment, an applicant must show that he satisfies the conditions regarding standing laid down in the Treaty. Article 230 (ex 173)
distinguishes three categories of applicant. The Member States, the Council and the
Commission, sometimes called privileged applicants, are presumed to have an
interest in the legality of all Community acts and as a result do not have to establish standing to bring proceedings for annulment. Since Maastricht, the European
Parliament and the European Central Bank and, since Amsterdam, the Court of
Auditors have enjoyed standing where the purpose of the proceedings is to protect
their prerogatives. They may be described as semi-privileged. The third category
comprises natural and legal persons or so-called private applicants, that is, individuals, companies, unincorporated associations, and the like.[97] The members of this
category are often described as non-privileged because the Treaty appears only to
allow them to challenge acts which are, in substance if not in form, decisions which
are either addressed to them or of direct and individual concern to them. The
Treaty does not give such applicants an express right to challenge regulations or
directives.[98]

---

[94] Case 34/86 *Council v Parliament* [1986] ECR 2155. The application was lodged on 11 February
1986. The Single European Act was signed on 17 and 28 February 1986. The sequence of events provides further evidence that no significance should be attached to absence of amendments to Art 173 in
the Single European Act.
    [95] See also Joined Cases 193 and 194/87 *Maurissen and Others v Court of Auditors* [1989] ECR 1045.
    [96] The approach taken by the Court in both *Les Verts* and 'Chernobyl' was not dissimilar to that
taken by the English courts in cognate areas: see Arnull, 'The European Court and judicial objectivity:
a reply to Professor Hartley' (1996) 112 LQR 411, 420–1.
    [97] On the concept of a legal person, see Case T–161/94 *Sinochem Heilongjiang v Council* [1996] ECR
II–695, para 31.
    [98] See generally Albors-Llorens, *Private Parties in European Community Law* (1996).

The Court takes a strict approach

If the Court took a liberal approach on the question of the category of acts susceptible to review and the status of the European Parliament in annulment proceedings, its attitude to the standing of private parties has on the whole been more restrictive. Although in recent years there have been signs of a relaxation in the attitude of the Court, it remains difficult for a non-privileged applicant to establish standing to challenge any act which is not addressed to him.[99] Particularly problematic have been the requirement of a decision and the requirement of individual concern.[100] The copious case law on this issue is impossible to reconcile with the Neill/Hartley view referred to above of a Court determined to extend its own jurisdiction as widely as possible. Indeed, the approach of the Court has justifiably been described as 'the epitome of strict constructionism and of susceptibility to the floodgates argument (the fear of being swamped with cases), which are both regarded as hallmarks of judicial self-restraint'.[101]

Where the contested measure was labelled a regulation, the applicant first had to overcome the hurdle of establishing that it was in substance a decision. The Court recognized that the label was not decisive and that, where the annulment of some only of the provisions of an act was sought, it was the proper classification of those provisions, rather than that of the act as a whole, which mattered.[102] However, a measure which applied to an entire class defined in abstract terms would be seen by the Court as a true regulation even if in practice it was possible to determine the number or even the identity of those affected by it.[103]

The requirement of individual concern is closely related to that of a decision. The Court has stated that '[i]n order for a measure to be of individual concern to the persons to whom it applies, it must affect their legal position because of a factual situation which differentiates them from all other persons and distinguishes them individually in the same way as a person to whom it is addressed'.[104] Where

---

[99] See generally Arnull, 'Private applicants and the action for annulment under Article 173 of the EC Treaty' (1995) 32 CMLRev 7; Neuwahl, 'Article 173, paragraph 4 EC: past, present and possible future' (1996) 21 ELRev 17; Nihoul, 'La recevabilité des recours en annulation introduits par un particulier à l'encontre d'un acte communautaire de portée générale' (1994) 30 RTDE 171; Usher, 'Judicial review of Community acts and the private litigant' in Campbell and Voyatzi (eds), *Legal Reasoning and Judicial Interpretation of Community Law* (1996), 121; Vandersanden, 'Pour un élargissement du droit des particuliers d'agir en annulation contre des actes autres que les décisions qui leur sont adressées' (1995) 31 CDE 535; Waelbroeck and Verheyden, 'Les conditions de recevabilité des recours en annulation des particuliers contre les actes normatifs communautaires' (1995) 31 CDE 399.

[100] The requirement of direct concern has in general proved less of an obstacle: see *Les Verts, supra*, para 31; Case 11/82 *Piraiki-Patraiki v Commission* [1985] ECR 207. Cf Case T–96/92 *CCE de la Société Générale des Grandes Sources and Others v Commission* [1995] ECR II–1213 and Case T–12/93 *CCE de Vittel and others v Commission* [1995] ECR II–1247, discussed by Arnull (1996) 33 CMLRev 319.

[101] Keeling, op cit, p 520.

[102] See eg Joined Cases 16 and 17/62 *Producteurs de Fruits v Council* [1962] ECR 471.

[103] See eg Joined Cases 789 and 790/79 *Calpak v Commission* [1980] ECR 1949.

[104] Case 26/86 *Deutz und Geldermann v Council* [1987] ECR 941, para 9. See also eg Case 25/62 *Plaumann v Commission* [1963] ECR 95, 107; Case 100/74 *CAM v Commission* [1975] ECR 1393, para 19. The test is expressed by the Court in basically the same terms whether the contested measure takes

an applicant could show that he was affected by the contested measure because he
was a member of a class which was closed, both in theory and in practice, at the
time the measure was adopted, he would generally be able to establish individual
concern.[105] However, where the class of persons affected by a measure was potentially an open one, it was much more difficult to do so.[106]

The Court softens its approach

Conscious of the strictness of its case law, the Court in due course began to demonstrate a greater willingness to allow annulment proceedings to be brought by private applicants who enjoyed the right to be heard during an administrative
procedure culminating in the adoption of a Community act. Such procedures are
particularly prominent in three fields: competition, dumping,[107] and State aid.[108]
The Court's traditional approach was especially ill-suited to the second of those
fields, since anti-dumping duties could only be imposed by regulation and such
regulations were in principle legislative in nature, applying to all the traders concerned. It would obviously have been unacceptable if such measures had been
immune to challenge by such traders.[109]

It was perhaps inevitable that the more relaxed approach to the standing of private applicants taken in those fields would eventually affect the Court's stance in
other areas. However, cases where the Court appeared to demonstrate a more liberal approach to standing were characterized by a variety of special features which
cast doubt on their wider application. In *Piraiki-Patraiki v Commission*,[110] for example, the applicants sought the annulment of a Commission decision authorizing
France to restrict imports of cotton yarn from Greece during a specific period. The
Court held that the contested decision was of individual concern to those of the
applicants which, prior to its adoption, had entered into contracts to be performed
while it was in force, in so far as the execution of those contracts was wholly or
partly prevented by its adoption. The Court ruled that the Commission had been
in a position to discover the existence of contracts to be performed during the
period of application of the contested decision. Undertakings which were parties

the form of a regulation or that of a decision, although a measure in the form of a regulation will not
be specifically addressed to anyone.

[105] See eg Joined Cases 41 to 44/70 *International Fruit Company v Commission* [1971] ECR 411, paras
21 and 22. Cf Case 38/64 *Getreide-Import v Commission* [1965] ECR 203; Joined Cases 106 and 107/63
Toepfer v Commission [1965] ECR 405; Case 62/70 *Bock v Commission* [1971] ECR 897; *CAM v
Commission, supra*; Case 88/76 *Exportation des Sucres v Commission* [1977] ECR 709.

[106] See eg Case 97/85 *Deutsche Lebensmittelwerke v Commission* [1987] ECR 2265; Case 1/64
Glucoseries Réunies v Commission [1964] ECR 413.

[107] Dumping takes place when a product is imported into the Community from a non-member
country at a price which is lower than its normal value in that country and the result is to cause injury
to a Community industry. Dumped products may be the subject of anti-dumping duties.

[108] See Arnull, 'Private applicants and the action for annulment under Article 173 of the EC Treaty'
(1995) 32 CMLRev 7, 30–3.

[109] See further Arnull, 'Challenging EC anti-dumping regulations: the problem of admissibility'
(1992) 13 ECLR 73.

[110] Case 11/82 [1985] ECR 207.

to such contracts were therefore individually concerned 'as members of a limited class of traders identified or identifiable by the Commission and by reason of those contracts particularly affected by the decision at issue'. However, the Court attached significance to the fact that Article 130 of the Greek Act of Accession required the Commission to take account of the likely effect the measures it was proposing to authorize would have on such traders. That factor left the implications of the case in other contexts unclear.[111]

The wider implications of the Court's decision in *Les Verts* for natural and legal persons were also unclear. The facts of that case have already been outlined briefly, but it is appropriate to set them out in a little more detail here. The applicant was seeking the annulment of two measures adopted by the European Parliament, in 1982 and 1983 respectively, concerning the reimbursement of election expenses incurred by political groupings taking part in the 1984 European elections. The contested measures affected all groupings participating in those elections, whether or not they were already represented in the Parliament. However, groupings which were already represented took part in the procedure leading to the adoption of the contested measures. The applicant, which was not represented in the Parliament at the time the contested measures were adopted but which intended to contest the 1984 elections, alleged that the measures discriminated in favour of groupings which were already represented. It sought the annulment of those measures under Article 173 (now 230).

Not only did the applicant have to establish that measures adopted by the European Parliament could be challenged under that article, it also had to establish that it was individually concerned by the contested measures. On the basis of the Court's existing case law, this might have seemed an impossible task, since, at the time the contested measures were adopted, political groupings which were not represented in the Parliament but which might wish to contest the 1984 elections, and which would therefore be affected by the measures, could not be identified. In other words, the class to which the applicant belonged was an open one. The only class the members of which could be identified at the time the measures were adopted comprised groupings which were already represented, but they had no interest in mounting a challenge.

Having accepted, as we have seen, that measures adopted by the European Parliament were in principle susceptible to review under Article 173, the Court turned to the question of individual concern. It noted the unprecedented circumstances of the action and said that, because the main measure being challenged concerned 'the allocation of public funds for the purpose of preparing for elections and it is alleged that those funds were allocated unequally, it cannot be considered that only groupings which were represented and which were therefore identifiable at the date of the adoption of the contested measure are individually concerned by

---

[111] Indeed, the Court later held that the reasoning in *Piraiki* did not apply where the defendant institution was not required to enquire into the effect of its action on pre-existing contractual arrangements: Case C–209/94 P *Buralux and Others v Council* [1996] ECR I–615.

it'.[112] The Court concluded that 'the applicant association, which was in existence at the time when the 1982 Decision was adopted and which was able to present candidates at the 1984 elections, is individually concerned by the contested measures'.[113]

Judge Joliet, who was Rapporteur[114] in the case, later observed:[115]

If the Court, in resolving the issue of individual concern, had adhered to the traditional criteria and had ignored the novelty of the situation, that would have produced the paradoxical result of making the action for annulment available to the groupings which had no need of it and denying that remedy to the groupings which did need it. Coming immediately after the declaration that the Community is founded on the rule of law, such a 'denial of justice' would have made a mockery of the reasoning by which the Court arrived at the conclusion that it had jurisdiction to entertain an action for annulment against a measure of the European Parliament.

The ruling in Codorniu: a false dawn?

The Court continued to apply its traditional approach in other contexts,[116] suggesting that *Les Verts* was on this issue confined to its own special facts. Be that as it may, the growing number of cases in which the Court had departed from the conventional test of standing demonstrated the need for that test to be reformed. A decisive break with the Court's earlier case law, on both the requirement of individual concern and that of a decision, appeared to have been made in *Codorniu v Council*,[117] which concerned the validity of a regulation on the description and presentation of sparkling wines. The Court accepted that true regulations could in principle be challenged by non-privileged applicants if they could establish individual concern.[118] The Court held that the applicant was indeed individually concerned because the contested regulation prevented it from using a term which it had registered as a trade mark in 1924 and had traditionally used both before and after that date. That factor, according to the Court, was enough to distinguish the applicant from all other traders affected by the regulation.

Codorniu was the last important ruling to be delivered by the Court of Justice on the standing of private applicants under Article 230 (ex 173) before jurisdiction in such cases was transferred to the CFI.[119] The case was evidently the subject of considerable debate within the Court: it took an unusually long time to decide and the

---

[112] Para 35.

[113] Paras 35 and 37 of the judgment. The Court went on to annul the contested measures.

[114] The Judge Rapporteur is responsible for the general management of a case as it progresses through the various stages of the Court's procedure. One of his main tasks is to draft the judgment.

[115] 'The reimbursement of election expenses: a forgotten dispute' (1994) 19 ELRev 243, 254.

[116] See eg Case 97/85 *Deutsche Lebensmittelwerke v Commission* [1987] ECR 2265.

[117] Case C–309/89 [1994] ECR I–1853. See Waelbroeck and Fosselard (1995) 32 CMLRev 257; Usher, 'Individual concern in general legislation—10 years on' (1994) 19 ELRev 636. The Court's judgment built on its ruling in Case C–358/89 *Extramet Industrie v Council* [1991] ECR I–2501, a dumping case to which AG Lenz attached particular importance.

[118] Direct concern was not at issue in the case.

[119] See Dec 93/350, OJ 1993 L144/21; Dec 94/149 OJ 1994 L66/29.

reasoning was terse, in places even incoherent.[120] None the less, by confirming that a private applicant could challenge a true regulation and apparently relaxing the requirement of individual concern, the judgment seemed to presage a greater willingness on the part of the Court to allow natural and legal persons to bring actions for annulment. It soon became apparent, however, that the CFI was in no hurry to build on the foundations which the Court of Justice appeared to have laid in *Codorniu*. In a series of cases, annulment proceedings brought by private applicants were dismissed as inadmissible by the CFI on the basis of the conventional test of standing.[121] Moreover, any divisions within the Court itself over the *Codorniu* ruling meant that its own approach was liable to be affected by changes in its composition. It may not be without significance that four of the Judges who sat in *Codorniu* had left the Court before the year was out and that Judges from three new Member States took up office early the following year.

In any event, the Court showed no inclination to reinforce the message apparently given in *Codorniu*. In *Asocarne v Council*,[122] the Second Chamber of the Court endorsed the CFI's view that a measure of general application could only be of individual concern to an applicant if its 'specific rights' were adversely affected. That was true of the applicant in *Codorniu* because the contested regulation prevented it from using its trade mark. It was not true of the applicant in *Asocarne* because in the Court's view it was affected only because it was active in the sector covered by the contested act. The Court also took a restrictive approach in *Buralux and Others v Council*,[123] where the Court upheld an Order of the CFI dismissing as inadmissible an application for the annulment of a regulation restricting movements of waste within the Community. The applicants were undertakings engaged in the transport of waste from Germany to France. Although the contested regulation had particularly serious consequences for their business, the Court concluded that the applicants were affected by it 'only in their objective capacity as economic operators in the business of waste transfer between Member States, in the same way as any other operator in that business . . .'.[124] The CFI had therefore been right to hold that they were not individually concerned.

The unwillingness of the Community Courts to sanction any further relaxation in the standing rules applicable to private applicants was confirmed in *Greenpeace and Others v Commission*. In that case the applicants, three associations concerned with the protection of the environment together with a number of individuals, sought the annulment of a Commission decision granting Spain financial assistance towards the construction of two electric power stations in the Canary Islands. The applicants specifically invited the CFI to take a liberal approach on the question of

---

[120] Paras 17 and 18 seem inconsistent with paras 19–22 and the conclusion reached by the Court on the admissibility of the action.

[121] See Arnull, 'Challenging Community acts—an introduction' in Micklitz and Reich (eds), *Public Interest Litigation before European Courts* (1996), 39, 47–51.

[122] Case C–10/95 P [1995] ECR I–4149.

[123] Case C–209/94 P [1996] ECR I–615.   [124] Para 28.

admissibility and to accept that standing could derive not only from purely economic considerations but also from a concern for the protection of the environment. The applicants claimed that in each Member State associations set up for the protection of the environment which were sufficiently representative of the interests of their members, or which satisfied certain formalities, were entitled to challenge administrative decisions alleged to breach rules on environmental protection.[125]

The CFI refused to accept that the standing of the applicants should be assessed by reference to criteria other than those laid down in the case law.[126] It concluded that the individual applicants were affected by the contested measure in the same way as anyone living in, working in, or visiting the area concerned and that they could not therefore be considered individually concerned. The same was true of the applicant associations, since they had been unable to establish any interest of their own distinct from that of their members, whose position was no different from that of the individual applicants. On appeal to the Court,[127] Advocate General Cosmas observed, citing *Buralux*, that[128] '[t]he significance and extent of mitigation by the Court, in *Extramet* and *Codorniu*, of the rigour of the case-law should not . . . be overstated'. His advice that the appeal should be dismissed was followed by the Court, which declared that the approach taken by the CFI was 'consonant with the settled case-law of the Court of Justice'.[129]

An assessment of the current position

The expectations raised by the *Codorniu* case that we were witnessing a decisive break with the restrictive attitude previously adopted by the Court to the standing of private applicants under Article 230 (ex 173) therefore appear to have been dashed. Admittedly it now seems to be established that regulations may in principle be challenged by private applicants. It also seems to have been accepted that a private applicant may challenge a directive, either on the basis that it constitutes a disguised decision[130] or simply that it is of direct and individual concern to the applicant.[131] However, these possibilities are available only in exceptional circumstances. Moreover, the traditional test of individual concern seems to have reasserted itself.

Is this a matter for regret? The answer to that question, it is submitted, is a resounding yes.[132] Any modern polity which purports, like the European

[125] In England, see eg *R v Inspectorate of Pollution, ex parte Greenpeace* [1994] 4 All ER 329 and 352. For discussion of the right of such associations to sue in tort, see Betlem, 'Standing for Ecosystems—Going Dutch' (1995) 54 CLJ 153.

[126] Case T–585/93 [1995] ECR II–2205.   [127] Case C–321/95 P [1998] ECR I–1651.

[128] Ibid., p I–1689.

[129] Para 27. Cf Case C–73/97 P *France v Comafrica and Dole*, judgment of 21 January 1999, where the Court quashed a decision of the CFI and dismissed an application for annulment as inadmissable.

[130] See Case C–298/89 *Gibraltar v Council* [1993] ECR I–3605; *Asocarne, supra*; Case C–408/95 *Eurotunnel and Others v SeaFrance* [1997] ECR I–6315.

[131] See Case T–135/96 *UEAPME v Council* [1998] ECR II–2335.

[132] Although this view is widely shared by academic commentators, it is evidently not shared by a majority of the Judges of the Community Courts. For some arguments against, see Gormley, op cit, p 488; Dashwood (ed), *Reviewing Maastricht: Issues for the 1996 IGC* (1996), 308–11.

Community, to be based on the rule of law must provide a mechanism for subjecting the activities of its legislative and executive bodies to judicial review. The effectiveness of any such mechanism depends to a large extent on the ease with which it may be used by private applicants. There has been a progressive relaxation in standing rules in both common law and civil law jurisdictions.[133] Not only does a more relaxed approach protect the public interest in observance of the law by the administration, it may also be said to promote the proper functioning of the democratic process by facilitating public participation in decision making. Indeed, that an applicant should have standing to challenge governmental acts adversely affecting him may be considered a fundamental right.[134] From this perspective, standing might be seen as an aspect of citizenship. These considerations seem particularly relevant in the context of the European Union as it seeks to become less remote from ordinary people.

Given the essentially open-textured nature of the expression 'direct and individual concern' and the manifest contribution a relaxed approach to standing would make to ensuring that the Community institutions act within the limits of their powers, why has the Court's approach been so restrictive? It seems likely that the Court has been influenced by a number of factors, some connected with the perceived intentions of the authors of the Treaty, some with the Court's own view of the needs of the Community system. One factor mentioned by the Court in an early case[135] is the fact that 'the system . . . established by the Treaties of Rome lays down more restrictive conditions than does the ECSC Treaty for the admissibility of applications for annulment by private individuals'. That consideration seems unconvincing today, when the Community has developed in ways unforeseen by the authors of the Treaty of Rome. Indeed, in other contexts the Court has not regarded comparisons with the ECSC Treaty as helpful in view of the difference in the scope of the two Treaties.[136] Stein and Vining argued[137] that '[t]he Community is a body at the borderline between the federal and the international and in international law the very notion of an individual having independent standing to sue before an international tribunal is little short of revolutionary.' The limited standing conferred by Article 230 (ex 173) on natural and legal persons has also been seen as a reflection of the liberal economic philosophy which underpins much of the Treaty,[138] especially in its original form. Rasmussen regarded the restrictive

[133] See Arnull, 'Private applicants and the action for annulment under Article 173 of the EC Treaty' (1995) 32 CMLRev 7, 8–9.

[134] See Bradley, 'Administrative justice: a developing human right?' (1995) 1 European Public Law 347.

[135] Joined Cases 16 and 17/62 *Producteurs de Fruits v Council* [1962] ECR 471, 478.

[136] Cf Case 6/72 *Europemballage and Continental Can v Commission* [1973] ECR 215, para 22; Case 314/85 *Foto-Frost v Hauptzollamt Lübeck-Ost* [1987] ECR 4199 (see the Opinion of AG Mancini at p 4216).

[137] 'Citizen access to judicial review of administrative action in a transnational and federal context' (1976) 70 AJIL 219, 222 (also published in Jacobs (ed), *European Law and the Individual* (1976), 113). See also Harlow, 'Towards a theory of access for the European Court of Justice' (1992) 12 YEL 213, 227–8.

[138] See Feldman, 'Public interest litigation and constitutional theory in comparative perspective' (1992) 55 MLR 44, 55.

interpretation given by the Court to the expression 'direct and individual concern' as part of a hidden agenda:[139]

. . . the Court arguably has a long term interest in reshaping the judiciary of the Community to allow itself to act more like a high court of appeals of Community law, with the courts and tribunals of the Member States, and any administrative and other Community courts which might be established, acting as courts of first instance. This interest outweighs the citizen's interest in direct access to the Court.

One other consideration seems worth mentioning. This is that a proliferation of direct challenges to Community acts by natural and legal persons, perhaps accompanied by applications for interim measures, could have seriously disrupted the proper functioning of the Community system.[140] This danger was particularly acute during the period when the Council, under the pernicious influence of the Luxembourg Compromise, did not adopt legislation until a consensus had emerged in its support.[141] The increasing maturity of the Community system and, eventually, the demise of the Luxembourg Compromise led the Court to take tentative steps towards a relaxation of the standing requirements. However, another problem had by then begun to assume worrying proportions, namely the increasing difficulty encountered by both the Community Courts in coping with their workload. This seems to have produced a degree of retrenchment. While it may seem wrong in principle that a litigant's right to invoke the jurisdiction of a court of law should depend on factors which are unrelated to the substance of the claim and which may vary with the passage of time, there is no doubt that some national courts take account of similar factors in controlling the right to bring proceedings.[142] It may be observed, however, that, if the Community Courts are indeed motivated by a wish to control their workload, they have not been wholly successful: even though the CFI often dismisses as inadmissible proceedings brought under Article 230 (ex 173), it frequently devotes many pages to analysing the applicant's standing.

If the Community Courts have gone as far as they feel able to, at least for the time being, what are the prospects for a change in the wording of Article 230? In its report on the application of the TEU published in May 1995 as part of the preparations for the 1996 IGC, the Court asked 'whether the right to bring an action for annulment under Article 173 of the EC Treaty . . ., which individuals enjoy only in regard to acts of direct and individual concern to them, is sufficient

---

[139] 'Why is Article 173 interpreted against private plaintiffs?' (1980) 5 ELRev 112, 122.

[140] See Harding, 'The private interest in challenging Community action' (1980) 5 ELRev 354.

[141] A desire to protect the institutions from the disruption which might be caused by excessive recourse to legal proceedings may also have influenced the Court's case law on the action for damages under the second paragraph of Art 288 (ex 215). See eg Joined Cases 83 and 94/76, 4, 15 and 40/77 *HNL and Others v Council and Commission* [1978] ECR 1209, para 5; Arnull, 'Liability for legislative acts under Article 215(2)' in Heukels and McDonnell (eds), *The Action for Damages in Community Law* (1997), ch 7.

[142] See eg *R v Panel on Takeovers and Mergers, ex parte Guinness plc* [1990] 1 QB 146, 177–8, per Lord Donaldson MR.

to guarantee for them effective judicial protection against possible infringements of their fundamental rights arising from the legislative activity of the institutions'.[143] The difficulty with reforming the standing rules along these lines is that it is hard to identify fundamental rights cases without examining their substance. Such a reform would encourage applicants to dress up cases as involving fundamental rights in order to take advantage of the more generous standing rules which would then apply. What is needed is a Treaty amendment making it clear that any binding act, whatever its formal status, can be challenged by a private applicant who is adversely affected by it. Such a test would mark a decisive break with the voluminous and sometimes incoherent case law of the Community Courts on direct and individual concern. However, the standing rules applicable to private parties were left unchanged by the Treaty of Amsterdam[144] and it must be conceded that no significant reforms are likely until a solution has been found to the problem of enabling the Community Courts to cope with their workload.

The preliminary rulings procedure

Introduction

Under Article 234 (ex 177) EC, the Court of Justice has jurisdiction to respond to questions put to it by national courts about the effect of Community law in cases pending before them. In some of the founding Member States,[145] procedures under which national constitutional courts could be asked by lower courts to rule on the validity of certain types of legislation were not unknown. None the less, the insertion of such a procedure, first, in the ECSC Treaty,[146] and then in more developed form in the EC Treaty, was a stroke of genius. By involving the Court of Justice directly in litigation unfolding in the national courts, it permitted the Court to promote the uniform application of the law in a manner which was consistent with the spirit and objectives of the Treaty. It is a truism that a court can only address issues it is called upon to resolve by the parties to a dispute. The preliminary rulings procedure ensured that the Court of Justice was asked to resolve a host of questions of fundamental importance to the functioning of the legal order which might not otherwise have been brought before it. It should not be overlooked, however, that those questions were raised in the first instance by the national courts. The possibility that Community law might grant rights to

[143] See 'Proceedings of the Court of Justice and Court of First Instance of the European Communities', No 15/95 (22–6 May 1995). Cf Alston and Weiler, *The European Union and Human Rights: Final Project Report on an Agenda for the Year 2000* (European University Institute, 1998), para 181.

[144] Indeed, a new provision giving the Court jurisdiction to review the legality of certain acts adopted under Title VI of the TEU confers no standing at all on private parties: see Art 35(6) TEU, discussed below.

[145] Particularly Germany and Italy: see Anderson, *References to the European Court* (1995), pp 5–6.

[146] See Art 41.

individuals which those courts were expected to protect, that it might take precedence over inconsistent provisions of national law,[147] that Member States which failed to respect their Treaty obligations might be liable in damages to individuals who thereby suffered loss,[148] were put to the Court of Justice—directly or indirectly—by judges in the Member States. The answers given by the Court might have been bold and creative, but it is important to remember that it did not conjure them up out of thin air.[149]

Article 234 (ex 177) provides as follows:

The Court of Justice shall have jurisdiction to give preliminary rulings concerning:

(a) the interpretation of this Treaty;
(b) the validity and interpretation of acts of the institutions of the Community and of the ECB;
(c) the interpretation of the statutes of bodies established by an act of the Council, where those statutes so provide.

Where such a question is raised before any court or tribunal of a Member State, that court or tribunal may, if it considers that a decision on the question is necessary to enable it to give judgment, request the Court of Justice to give a ruling thereon.

Where any such question is raised in a case pending before a court or tribunal of a Member State, against whose decisions there is no judicial remedy under national law, that court or tribunal shall bring the matter before the Court of Justice.

Broadly speaking, Article 234 enables any question of Community law to be referred to the Court of Justice at the instance of any national court before which such a question arises. The ruling given by the Court is an interlocutory one: it constitutes a step in the proceedings before the national court which, although bound by it, must proceed to apply it to the facts of the case. It is in this sense that the ruling of the Court of Justice is preliminary.

In one important respect, the Court has interpreted its jurisdiction under Article 234 (ex 177) narrowly. The article might have been read as conferring on it a power to assess the compatibility of provisions of national law with the Treaty and to require the referring court not to apply any which failed to meet with the approval of the Court. Such an interpretation would not have been inconsistent with the terms of Article 234 and might have been seen as both reinforcing Member States' Treaty obligations and strengthening the rights of individuals. However, in a long line of cases the Court has emphasized the limits of its jurisdiction under Article 234. As long ago as 1964, the Court explained in *Costa v ENEL*[150] that the article gave it 'no jurisdiction either to apply the Treaty to a specific case or to decide upon the validity of a provision of domestic law in relation

---

[147] See chs 3 and 4.   [148] See ch 5.
[149] See Edward, 'Judicial activism—myth or reality?' in Campbell and Voyatzi (eds), *Legal Reasoning and Judicial Interpretation of European Law* (1996), ch 3, p 44.
[150] Case 6/64 [1964] ECR 585, 592–3. For a more recent example, see Joined Cases C–332/92, C–333/92 and C–335/92 *Eurico Italia and Others* [1994] ECR I–711, para 19.

to the Treaty, as it would be possible for it to do under Article 169 [now 226]'. The Court added: 'Nevertheless, the Court has power to extract from a question imperfectly worded by the national court those questions which alone pertain to the interpretation of the Treaty.' It is true that the answers given by the Court often leave the national court in little doubt about how the case before it is to be resolved. None the less, it is important to the legitimacy of the system[151] that the final decision is that of the national court. Indeed, the relationship between the Court of Justice and the referring court is co-operative rather than hierarchical in nature and a reference for a preliminary ruling in no sense constitutes an appeal.[152] Rather the proceedings take the form of a dialogue in which the two courts seek a solution to the case in hand which is in harmony with the requirements of Community law.[153]

Who can refer and what can be referred?

In other respects, the Court has construed Article 234 (ex 177) more broadly. Thus, the term 'court or tribunal of a Member State' has been interpreted by the Court of Justice as embracing any national institution exercising a judicial function, even if it does not constitute a court or tribunal for the purposes of its own domestic law.[154] It has also been held that references may be made under Article 234 by courts situated in territories which do not form part of a Member State if the Treaty is applicable there, even if only in part.[155]

It will be observed that Article 234 (ex 177) permits references to be made to the Court of Justice on questions of both validity and interpretation. The article may in this respect be contrasted with its predecessor in the ECSC Treaty, Article 41. According to the latter article: 'The Court shall have sole jurisdiction to give

[151] On legitimacy generally, see ch 16. However, Dehousse, op cit, p 77, points out that the abstract language used by the Court in preliminary rulings 'is generally associated with legislative law-making'.

[152] Thus, there are technically no parties to the proceedings before the Court of Justice: see Case 69/85 *Wünsche v Germany* [1986] ECR 947, para 14. Cf Art 20 of the EC Statute.

[153] See further Slaughter, Stone and Weiler (eds), *The European Courts and National Courts: Doctrine and Jurisprudence* (1998); Weiler, *The Constitution of Europe* (1999), pp 192–5.

[154] See eg Case 36/73 *Nederlandse Spoorwegen v Minister Verkeer en Waterstaat* [1973] ECR 1299 (in particular the Opinion of AG Mayras at pp 1317–20); Case 61/65 *Vaassen v Beamtenfonds Mijnbedrijf* [1966] ECR 261; Case 14/86 *Pretore di Salò v Persons Unknown* [1987] ECR 2545; Case C–54/96 *Dorsch Consult v Bundesbaugesellschaft Berlin* [1997] ECR I–4961; Joined Cases C–69/96 to C–79/96 *Garofalo and Others v Ministero della Sanità* [1997] ECR I–5603; Joined Cases C–9/97 and C–118/97 *Jokela and Pitkäranta*, judgment of 22 October 1998. Cf Case 138/80 *Borker* [1980] ECR 1975; Case 102/81 *Nordsee v Reederei Mond* [1982] ECR 1095; Case C–24/92 *Corbiau v Administration des Contributions* [1993] ECR I–1277; Case C–134/97 *Victoria Film*, judgment of 12 November 1998.

[155] See Case C–355/89 *Barr and Montrose Holdings* [1991] ECR I–3479 (Isle of Man), in particular the Opinion of AG Jacobs at p I–3493–4; Case C–171/96 *Pereira Roque v Lieutenant Governor of Jersey* [1998] ECR I–4607. The UK Government is responsible for the defence and international relations of the Isle of Man and of Jersey. The EC Treaty is applicable there under the conditions referred to in Art 299(6)(c) (ex 227(5)(c)). Cf Case C–337/95 *Parfums Christian Dior v Evora* [1997] ECR I–6013, where it was held that a court common to a number of Member States such as the Benelux Court could make a reference under Art 234 in the same way as the courts or tribunals of any of the States concerned.

preliminary rulings on the validity of acts of the High Authority [now the Commission] and of the Council where such validity is in issue in proceedings brought before a national court or tribunal.' Article 41 does not expressly confer on the Court jurisdiction to give preliminary rulings on the interpretation of the ECSC Treaty or of acts adopted by the Community institutions under it. This led many commentators to assume that it had no such jurisdiction.[156]

In *Busseni*,[157] that view was rejected by the Court. In that case, the Court was asked to give a ruling on the interpretation and effect of a recommendation adopted by the Commission under the ECSC Treaty.[158] The Court decided that it had jurisdiction to answer the questions referred to it. All three Community Treaties gave it the duty of ensuring respect for the law in their interpretation and application. All three established a preliminary rulings mechanism in order to promote the uniform application of Community law and co-operation between the Court of Justice and national courts. The Court pointed to the close link between interpreting a measure and assessing its validity: although Article 41 only referred expressly to questions of validity, such questions could only be answered by interpreting the relevant act. It was true that national courts were less often called upon to apply the ECSC Treaty or measures adopted under it, but co-operation with the Court of Justice was just as necessary as it was in the context of the other Community Treaties 'since the requirement of ensuring uniformity in the application of Community law is equally cogent and equally obvious'.[159] The Court concluded that it would be 'contrary to the objectives and the coherence of the Treaties'[160] to leave responsibility for determining the meaning and scope of rules derived from the ECSC Treaty exclusively in the hands of the national courts, thereby depriving the Court of Justice of any power to ensure they were given a uniform interpretation.

Hartley says the *Busseni* ruling was not justified by the text of the ECSC Treaty,[161] but the reasoning of the Court seems convincing. The failure of the authors of that Treaty to provide expressly for references on matters of interpretation was an oversight which was later rectified in the EEC and EAEC Treaties. The Court's decision to extend the approach laid down in the latter Treaties to the ECSC Treaty did not adversely affect the rights of any third party, but it did enhance the capacity of Article 41 to achieve its objective of ensuring uniformity in the application of the law.

---

[156] See eg Hartley, *The Foundations of European Community Law* (2nd edn, 1988), p 248; Schermers and Waelbroeck, *Judicial Protection in the European Communities* (4th edn, 1987), p 354.

[157] Case C–221/88 [1990] ECR I–495.

[158] ECSC recommendations are similar to EC directives: see Art 14 ECSC.

[159] Para 15.   [160] Para 16.

[161] (1996) 112 LQR 95, 100. See also Hartley, *Constitutional Problems of the European Union* (1999), pp 34–5.

Questions which may be referred under the first paragraph of Article 234 (ex 177) include[162] not only questions on the interpretation of the EC Treaty itself,[163] but also questions on the interpretation of Treaties amending that Treaty[164] or of one of the Treaties of Accession. In addition, the Court has jurisdiction under Article 234 to rule on the interpretation of an international agreement concluded by the Community.[165] Questions may be referred on acts of the Community institutions, such as regulations, directives, and decisions of the Council or Commission and non-binding measures such as recommendations.[166] Article 234 is treated as allowing national courts to ask not only what provisions of Community law mean but also whether they confer rights on individuals which the national courts are bound to protect, that is, whether they produce direct effect.[167]

A problematic issue which the Court has had to confront is whether it has jurisdiction to rule on the effect of provisions of Community law which are applicable in the national proceedings only because their scope has been extended by the Member State concerned. The approach taken by the Court to that question emphasizes the importance it attaches to protecting the uniform application of Community law. In *Dzodzi v Belgium*,[168] Advocate General Darmon took the view that the Court had no jurisdiction to give a ruling where Community law was not applicable in its own right and where the guidance of the Court was being sought essentially to enable the national court to apply provisions of national law. The Court stated, however, that the proper functioning of the Community legal order made it imperative that provisions of Community law should be given a uniform interpretation regardless of the circumstances in which they fell to be applied. It proceeded to deal with the substance of the questions which had been put to it.[169]

The Court seems to have been concerned that, had it declined jurisdiction to give preliminary rulings in these circumstances, parallel lines of national case law might have developed, one concerning the interpretation of provisions of Community law applicable in their own right, the other concerning the interpretation of the same provisions when applicable solely by virtue of national law. The

---

[162] Pursuant to subparagraphs (a) and (b). Subparagraph (c) has not proved to be of any practical significance: see Anderson, op cit, p 59.

[163] The extent to which references can be made on the meaning and effect of Title IV of the EC Treaty is the subject of special provisions: see Art 68 EC, discussed below.

[164] The Court does not have jurisdiction under Art 234 to rule on the interpretation of provisions of the TEU other than those mentioned in Art 46 (ex L): cf Case C–167/94 *Grau Gomis and Others* [1995] ECR I–1023. Special provisions giving the Court a preliminary rulings jurisdiction in relation to Title VI of the TEU were introduced by the Treaty of Amsterdam and are discussed below.

[165] This is so even where the agreement concerned has also been signed by the Member States because it falls partly within their jurisdiction: see Case C–53/96 *Hermès v FHT* [1998] ECR I–3603 (TRIPS Agreement).

[166] See Case C–322/88 *Grimaldi v Fonds des Maladies Professionnelles* [1989] ECR 4407.

[167] See Case 26/62 *Van Gend en Loos v Nederlandse Administratie der Belastingen* [1963] ECR 1, 11. This case is discussed in ch 3.

[168] Joined Cases C–297/88 and C–197/89 [1990] ECR I–3763, followed in Case C–231/89 *Gmurzynska-Bscher v Oberfinanzdirektion Köln* [1990] ECR I–4003.

[169] Which concerned the rules on the free movement of persons.

possibility that cases in the second category might influence cases in the first would in theory have jeopardized the uniform application of Community law. Doubt was none the less cast on the continued applicability of the *Dzodzi* approach by *Kleinwort Benson v City of Glasgow District Council*.[170] In that case, the English Court of Appeal made a reference on the interpretation of the Brussels Convention, which regulates the circumstances in which judgments made by the courts of one Member State have to be recognized and enforced in another Member State.[171] In the United Kingdom, rules based on the Brussels Convention were laid down by the Civil Jurisdiction and Judgments Act 1982 to provide for the allocation of civil jurisdiction between the separate jurisdictions comprising the United Kingdom, namely England and Wales, Scotland, and Northern Ireland. In *Kleinwort Benson*, the Court of Appeal asked the Court of Justice for guidance on the meaning of the Convention so that it could decide whether, under the 1982 Act, the dispute between the parties fell within the jurisdiction of the English or Scottish courts.

The Court of Justice said it had no jurisdiction to answer. The national court had made the reference to enable it to apply, not the Convention, but its national law. Moreover, the 1982 Act, although modelled on the Convention, did not wholly reproduce its terms. The Court concluded that the Act did not render applicable as such the provisions of the Brussels Convention in cases which fell outside the scope of that Convention. Moreover, the Act did not require United Kingdom courts to apply absolutely and unconditionally the interpretation of the Convention supplied by the Court of Justice, but merely to have regard to it when applying provisions of national law modelled on the Convention. Thus any ruling given by the Court would not be binding on the referring court. It was incompatible with the function of the Court under the preliminary rulings procedure for it to give replies which were 'purely advisory and without binding effect'.[172]

Although the circumstances of *Kleinwort Benson* were distinguishable from those of *Dzodzi*, the cases are not easy to reconcile. The possibility that a line of domestic case law might develop on the effect of the Brussels Convention without any direct contribution by the Court of Justice might have been thought to pose a threat to the uniform application of Community law as serious as that which concerned the Court in *Dzodzi*. Moreover, in declining to answer the question referred to it in the former case, the Court was led into an examination of the effect of the 1982 Act, a matter which might have been thought to fall outside its jurisdiction. In *Dzodzi*,[173] the Court declared: 'Where Community law is made applicable by national provisions, it is for the national court alone to assess the precise scope of that reference to Community law.'

[170] Case C–346/93 [1995] ECR I–615.

[171] Since the Convention is an agreement between the Member States rather than an act of the institutions, references to the Court of Justice on its interpretation are not made under Art 234 but under a Protocol to the Convention. This feature of the case has no bearing on the present discussion.

[172] Para 24. See Opinion 1/91 'EEA Agreement' [1991] ECR I–6079, para 61.

[173] Para 41. See also Case 166/84 *Thomasdünger v Oberfinanzdirektion Frankfurt am Main* [1985] ECR 3001, para 11.

However, in two subsequent cases the Court made it clear that *Kleinwort Benson* did not mark a change of direction and that it is confined to situations where a Member State has adapted a solution applied under Community law to suit its own internal requirements. The *Dzodzi* approach continues to apply where a Member State has chosen to align its domestic legislation with Community law so as to apply the same treatment to purely internal situations as that accorded to situations governed by Community law. The cases concerned, *Leur-Bloem v Inspecteur der Belastingdienst/Ondernemingen Amsterdam 2*[174] and *Giloy v Hauptzollamt Frankfurt am Main-Ost*,[175] involved domestic rules on the imposition of tax.[176] The Court reiterated that 'where, in regulating internal situations, domestic legislation adopts the same solutions as those adopted in Community law so as to provide for one single procedure in comparable situations, it is clearly in the Community interest that, in order to forestall future differences of interpretation, provisions or concepts taken from Community law should be interpreted uniformly, irrespective of the circumstances in which they are to apply . . .'.[177]

The *Dzodzi* line of authority was the subject of a searching analysis by Advocate General Jacobs in *Leur-Bloem* and *Giloy*. He did not find convincing the argument that the Court's approach was necessary to ensure the uniform application of Community law:[178]

In such circumstances the threat to the proper application of Community law in the State concerned would at most be only indirect and temporary. It would be clear that any interpretation given to a Community rule by a national court would not be based on a ruling from the Court [of Justice] and that, as soon as that interpretation was applied in a Community context, it would be open to challenge. Moreover, the Court's concern about such remote threats to the uniform application of Community law is difficult to reconcile with the fact that Article 177 [now 234] envisages that Community law will be interpreted and applied primarily by national courts; only in the relatively small number of cases heard by final appeal courts is there an obligation to refer.

The Advocate General came to the following conclusion:[179]

the Court should only rule in cases in which it is aware of the factual and legislative context of the dispute and in which that context is one contemplated by the Community rule. It seems to me that that view is the only one which is consistent with legal principle and with the purpose of Article 177 [now 234]; which guarantees the relevance of the Court's ruling to the determination of the dispute; and which avoids the risk of the Court being asked to interpret a Community rule outside its proper context. It also provides a workable and clear criterion which will provide national courts with the requisite degree of certainty concerning the scope of the Court's jurisdiction.

Advocate General Jacobs was the latest in a line of Advocates General to express reservations about the desirability of responding to questions submitted by national

---

[174] Case C–28/95 [1997] ECR I–4161.
[175] Case C–130/95 [1997] ECR I–4291. See also *Hermès v FHT*, *supra*, paras 31 and 32.
[176] See Betlem (1999) 36 CMLRev 165.   [177] *Giloy*, para 28. Cf *Leur-Bloem*, para 32.
[178] p I–4180.   [179] p I–4187.

courts in these circumstances.[180] The concerns he expressed are compelling. This
is one area where the Court could safely limit its jurisdiction without any adverse
consequences for the proper functioning of the Community legal order.

The discretion conferred on inferior national courts

Under the second paragraph of Article 234 (ex 177), courts and tribunals in the
Member States whose decisions are subject to a judicial remedy under national law
enjoy a discretion in deciding whether or not to ask for a preliminary ruling on
points of Community law they are called on to decide. It is well established that
the national court is in principle the sole judge of whether a preliminary ruling is
necessary and of the relevance of the questions referred. Thus, in *Eurico Italia and
Others*[181] the Court pointed out 'that it has consistently held that it is solely for the
national courts before which actions are brought, and which must bear the responsibility for the subsequent judicial decision, to determine in the light of the special
features of each case both the need for a preliminary ruling in order to enable them
to deliver judgment and the relevance of the questions which they submit to the
Court'. Moreover, the Court made it clear in *Rheinmühlen v Einfuhr- und
Vorratsstelle Getreide*[182] that a national court cannot be deprived of its power to
make a reference by the rulings of superior national courts. [183]

Notwithstanding the breadth of the discretion enjoyed by inferior national
courts under Article 234 (ex 177), a reference will be rejected by the Court where
it is plain that the questions referred are entirely irrelevant to the case pending
before the national court.[184] However, for many years the Court refused in other
circumstances to go behind the decision of the national court to make a reference.
In the *Rheinmühlen* case,[185] for example, the Court declared that 'national courts
have the widest discretion in referring matters to the Court of Justice if they consider that a case pending before them raises questions involving interpretation, or
consideration of the validity, of provisions of Community law, necessitating a decision on their part'.

A fundamental assault on the discretion hitherto enjoyed by the national courts
was mounted in the notorious *Foglia v Novello* cases,[186] where the Court refused to

[180] See also AG Mancini in *Thomasdünger*, AG Darmon in *Dzodzi* and *Gmurzynska-Bscher*, AG
Tesauro in *Kleinwort Benson*.
[181] Joined Cases C–332/92, C–333/92 and C–335/92 [1994] ECR I–711, para 17.
[182] Case 166/73 [1974] ECR 33, paras 4 and 5.
[183] The Treaty does not preclude a decision to refer from remaining subject to the remedies normally available under national law. However, the Court will act on the decision to refer until it has been
formally revoked. See Case 146/73 *Rheinmühlen-Düsseldorf v Einfuhr- und Vorratsstelle Getreide* [1974]
ECR 139, para 3.
[184] Case 126/80 *Salonia v Poidomani* [1981] ECR 1563, 1576–7; Case C–286/88 *Falciola* [1990] ECR
I–191; *Eurico Italia, supra,* para 17.
[185] Case 166/73, *supra,* para 4. See also Joined Cases 36 and 71/80 *Irish Creamery Milk Suppliers
Association v Ireland* [1981] ECR 735, paras 6–8.
[186] Case 104/79 [1980] ECR 745; Case 244/80 [1981] ECR 3045.

entertain a reference made in the context of a collusive action brought in one Member State by parties who were not really in dispute with each other with the intention of challenging the compatibility with the Treaty of the law of another Member State. The Court's judgments in those cases were the subject of heavy criticism[187] and they were subsequently applied with considerable restraint.[188] However, they were given a new lease of life in *Meilicke v ADV/ORGA*,[189] where the Court declined to answer a lengthy and complex series of questions on a company law directive referred to it by a court in Germany. The Court took the view that the questions referred were hypothetical in nature and that the legal and factual background had in any event not been adequately explained. Like those of the *Foglia v Novello* cases, the facts of *Meilicke* were rather odd in that the case seemed to have been constructed by the applicant before the national court in order to test the validity of a theory advanced in a book on company law he had written. Notwithstanding the curious nature of the case, *Meilicke* proved to be the harbinger of a new enthusiasm on the part of the Court for reviewing the circumstances in which references were made.

The Court's new approach was underlined in *Telemarsicabruzzo v Circostel*,[190] where the Vice Pretore di Frascati referred two questions on the compatibility with the Treaty, and in particular the rules on competition, of provisions of Italian law restricting the right of private sector television channels to use certain frequencies. The orders for reference contained very little information about the factual background to the cases or the relevant provisions of Italian law. The Court explained that the need to give a useful ruling in proceedings under Article 234 (ex 177) made it essential for the national judge to define the factual and legislative background to the case, or at least the factual hypotheses on which the questions referred were based. Those requirements were particularly important in the field of competition, characterized as it was by complex legal and factual situations. The Court pointed out that the orders for reference in the instant cases contained no information on these matters. Admittedly, the Court had been able to derive some information from the referring court's file as well as from the written and oral observations which had been submitted in the course of the proceedings. However, this was no more than fragmentary and did not enable the Court, in the absence of sufficient knowledge of the facts at the origin of the main actions, to interpret the Treaty competition rules in the light of those facts pursuant to the referring court's

[187] See eg Barav, 'Preliminary censorship? The judgment of the European Court in *Foglia v Novello*' (1980) 5 ELRev 443; Bebr, 'The existence of a genuine dispute: an indispensable precondition for the jurisdiction of the Court under Art 177 EEC Treaty?' (1980) 17 CMLRev 525 and 'The possible implications of *Foglia v Novello* II' (1982) 19 CMLRev 421.

[188] Cf Case 261/81 *Rau v De Smedt* [1982] ECR 3961; Case C–150/88 *Parfümerie-Fabrik 4711 v Provide* [1989] ECR 3891.

[189] Case C–83/91 [1992] ECR I–4871. See Kennedy, 'First steps towards a European certiorari?' (1993) 18 ELRev 121; Arnull (1993) 30 CMLRev 613.

[190] Joined Cases C–320/90, C–321/90 and C–322/90 [1993] ECR I–393. See Arnull (1994) 31 CMLRev 377.

invitation. In those circumstances, the Court concluded that there were no grounds for ruling on the questions submitted to it.

The judgment in *Telemarsicabruzzo* was delivered by the *grand plenum*[191] and was clearly intended to give a clear message to national judges contemplating making a reference under Article 234 (ex 177): if the background to the case is not clearly set out, the Court will simply decline to give a ruling. That message was subsequently driven home in a series of cases in which inadequately-explained references were dismissed as manifestly inadmissible under the truncated procedure for which provision is made in Article 92 of the Court's Rules of Procedure.[192] In *Zabala Erasun and Others*[193] the Court went further, declining to give a ruling where it considered that a reference, although admissible at the time it was made, should have been withdrawn in the light of later developments.

The overall effect of this line of case law is to place greater emphasis on the circumstances in which references should *not* be made. Is this development welcome?[194] The Court's new approach is clearly influenced by its heavy workload. Cases in which the background has not been clearly set out are particularly time-consuming for the Court and it is clearly entitled to expect national judges to play their part in identifying the issues on which preliminary rulings may properly be sought. However, the *Telemarsicabruzzo* line of authority poses two dangers.

The first is that it may lead the Court to refuse to address a question which the national court in fact needs to resolve in order to give judgment. In these circumstances, the national court is faced with the choice of making a further reference to the Court[195] or deciding the question itself. Where it chooses the latter option, the very risk against which Article 234 (ex 177) is intended to guard—that of divergences in the application of Community law—is heightened. In *Dzodzi*, the Court emphasized the need to ensure the uniform application of every provision of Community law, yet the threat to uniformity is surely greater where the Court refuses to assist a national judge seeking to apply a Community provision which may be directly relevant than where the scope of a Community provision has been enlarged by a Member State.[196]

The second danger posed by the *Telemarsicabruzzo* approach is that national courts will be discouraged from using the preliminary rulings procedure. For many national judges, even in States which have been members of the Union for some

---

[191] For the meaning of this term, see ch 1.

[192] See eg Case C–157/92 *Banchero* [1993] ECR I–1085; Case C–386/92 *Monin Automobiles* [1993] ECR I–2049; Joined Cases C–128/97 and C–137/97 *Testa and Modesti* [1998] ECR I–2181; Case C–361/97 *Nour v Burgenländische Gebietskrankenkasse* [1998] ECR I–3101.

[193] Joined Cases C–422/93, C–423/93 and C–424/93 [1995] ECR I–1567.

[194] See further Anderson, 'The admissibility of preliminary references' (1994) 14 YEL 179; Barnard and Sharpston, 'The changing face of Article 177 references' (1997) 34 CMLRev 1113; O'Keeffe, 'Is the spirit of Article 177 under attack? Preliminary references and admissibility' (1998) 23 ELRev 509.

[195] See eg Case C–428/93 *Monin Automobiles* [1994] ECR I–1707; Case C–387/93 *Banchero* [1995] ECR I–4663.

[196] In his Opinion in *Leur-Bloem* and *Giloy*, AG Jacobs described *Dzodzi* as 'irreconcilable' with the *Telemarsicabruzzo* line of case law: see [1997] ECR I–4161, 4181.

time, a reference to the Court of Justice remains an exceptional event. It is not always easy for a judge who is unfamiliar with Community law and who may not have the benefit of experienced counsel to identify and formulate relevant questions and to set out the background to a case clearly and concisely. This is especially true of judges in new Member States, who face a particularly steep learning curve.[197] It is vital to the healthy development of the Treaty system that such judges should not be discouraged from making references where the guidance of the Court of Justice is genuinely needed.

That said, the limits of the *Telemarsicabruzzo* line of authority should be acknowledged. There are a number of factors which may be said to mitigate the rigour of the Court's current approach. First, it does not exclude the possibility of pursuing before the Court test cases, that is to say, real disputes which have implications for large numbers of people who find themselves in a similar position and which are therefore conducted with special vigour. Cases of this nature have made an important contribution to the development of Community law, notably in the area of equal treatment for men and women, and the Court has never shown any reluctance to deal with them.[198]

Secondly, the Court has continued to deal with some references which might have been thought to fall within the *Telemarsicabruzzo* doctrine. In *Vaneetveld*,[199] for example, the order for reference contained no information about the facts of the case. None the less, Advocate General Jacobs thought that they were clear from the case file and the written observations. Moreover, the issue was in his view a straightforward one and there was no doubt that the answer to the questions would be helpful to the referring court. He did not therefore think it would be appropriate to decline to answer or to reject the reference as inadmissible. The Court agreed:[200]

It is true that the Court has held that the need to arrive at an interpretation of Community law which is useful for the national court requires that court to define the factual and legislative context of the questions, or at least to explain the factual hypotheses on which they are based . . . None the less, that requirement is less pressing where the questions relate to specific technical points and enable the Court to give a useful reply even where the national court has not given an exhaustive description of the legal and factual situation.

The Court concluded that it had enough information to enable it to give a useful answer. Another example is *Leclerc-Siplec v TF1 Publicité and M6 Publicité*,[201] where the parties to the main action were agreed on the correct position under

---

[197] The Court has shown some sensitivity to this factor. In Case C–299/95 *Kremzow v Austrian State* [1997] ECR I–2629, a reference made shortly after Austrian accession by the Austrian Oberster Gerichtshof (Supreme Court) which might have been dismissed as manifestly inadmissible was assigned to a five-Judge Chamber.

[198] See eg Case 69/80 *Worringham and Humphreys v Lloyds Bank* [1981] ECR 767; Case 96/80 *Jenkins v Kingsgate* [1981] ECR 911; Case C–9/91 *Equal Opportunities Commission* [1992] ECR I–4297.

[199] Case C–316/93 [1994] ECR I–763.   [200] Para 13.

[201] Case C–412/93 [1995] ECR I–179, discussed in more detail in ch 7. See also Case C–415/93 *URBSFA and Others v Bosman and Others* [1995] ECR I–4921, discussed in more detail in ch 8.

Community law, but the defendant considered itself obliged to apply the relevant national law until the position had been clarified by the Court of Justice. The Commission argued that, because the parties were not in dispute, the reference was inadmissible, but the Court disagreed. Although it declined to deal with aspects of the question referred which did not relate to the dispute between the parties, it said that the fact that the parties were in agreement as to the result did not make the dispute any less real: other aspects of the question were 'objectively necessary to the outcome of the proceedings'.[202]

These cases suggest that, where the referring court sets out clearly what the case is about and gives a plausible explanation of why it needs an answer to the questions it has referred, the Court will normally proceed to answer them.[203] They perhaps suggest that the criticism attracted by *Telemarsicabruzzo* and its progeny did not fall on entirely deaf ears. However, it remains the case that the Court will not answer questions which are clearly irrelevant or spend time trying to identify what a case is about when this has not been properly explained by the national court.

In late 1996 the Court took the unusual step of publishing a Note for Guidance on References by National Courts for Preliminary Rulings.[204] In that note, the Court attempted to summarize its case law and offered advice on what references should contain. The note was widely circulated and should help to improve the quality of the dialogue between the Court of Justice and the national courts on which the success of the preliminary rulings procedure depends. Further improvement could be brought about if the Court were to be given the right to ask the national court for clarification of its order for reference, a right it currently lacks.[205]

Preliminary rulings on validity

As noted above, Article 234 (ex 177) permits national courts to make references to the Court of Justice not only on matters of interpretation but also on the validity of Community acts.[206] Indeed, the second and third paragraphs of the article do

---

[202] Para 15. Unlike the *Foglia v Novello* cases, the disputed national provision was adopted by the Member State in which the referring court was situated: see AG Jacobs at p I–184.

[203] A suggestion by AG Jacobs in Case C–338/95 *Wiener v Hauptzollamt Emmerich* [1997] ECR I–6495 that national courts should be encouraged to exercise a greater measure of self-restraint before asking for preliminary rulings was not taken up by the Court.

[204] [1997] 1 CMLR 78; (1997) 22 ELRev 55; (1997) 34 CMLRev 1319.

[205] See Koopmans, 'The technique of the preliminary question—a view from the Court of Justice' in Schermers et al (eds), *Article 177 EEC: Experiences and Problems* (1987), 327 at 333; *The Role and Future of the European Court of Justice* (A Report of the EC Advisory Board of the British Institute of International and Comparative Law chaired by Lord Slynn), pp 81–2; Barnard and Sharpston, op cit, pp 1167–8; O'Keeffe, op cit, p 533. Cf Art 96(4) of the Rules of Procedure of the EFTA Court. For general discussion of that court, see Christiansen, 'The EFTA Court' (1997) 22 ELRev 539; Hunnings, *The European Courts* (1996), ch 6.

[206] The Court's jurisdiction under Art 234 to review the validity of Community acts extends to all grounds capable of invalidating them, including incompatibility with a rule of international law: Joined Cases 21 to 24/72 *International Fruit Company v Produktschap voor Groenten en Fruit* [1972] ECR 1219, para 6; Case C–162/96 *Racke v Hauptzollamt Mainz* [1998] ECR I–3655.

not distinguish between questions of interpretation and questions of validity, refer-ring simply to questions of the type mentioned in the first paragraph. While the third paragraph expressly requires courts and tribunals of the Member States against whose decisions there is no judicial remedy in national law to refer to the Court of Justice questions of Community law they are called upon to decide, the Treaty appears to leave inferior courts free to decide for themselves such questions, whether they concern interpretation or validity. Support for that view might be found by comparing Article 234 with Article 41 ECSC which, as we have seen, expressly gives the Court exclusive jurisdiction over questions of validity.[207] However, it would be highly undesirable for a national court to declare a Community act invalid in the absence of a ruling to that effect from the Court of Justice. The decision of the national court would be limited to the State in which it was situated and the contested act would in principle continue to apply in other Member States. The result would be to undermine legal certainty and the uniform application of Community law.

The role of national courts when confronted with a challenge to the validity of a Community act was the subject of a reference to the Court in *Foto-Frost v Hauptzollamt Lübeck-Ost*.[208] The referring court took the view that a Commission decision which had been challenged in the main proceedings might be invalid and requested a preliminary ruling on whether it had jurisdiction to rule on the matter. The referring court expressed the opinion that the answer to that question was 'no' and the Court agreed. Although national courts could reject as unfounded chal-lenges to the validity of Community acts, they did not have the power to declare such acts invalid.[209] According to the Court, Article 234 (ex 177) did not settle the question one way or the other. However, the requirement of uniformity, which it was the purpose of Article 234 to ensure, was 'particularly imperative' when the validity of a Community act was in issue: 'Divergences between courts in the Member States as to the validity of Community acts would be liable to place in jeopardy the very unity of the Comunity legal order and detract from the funda-mental requirement of legal certainty.'[210] The Court pointed out that it had exclus-ive jurisdiction to entertain actions for the annulment of Community acts. The 'coherence of the system of judicial protection established by the Treaty'[211]

---

[207] At least that is how Art 41 was interpreted by the Court in Case C–221/88 *Busseni* [1990] ECR I–495, para 14. An alternative view of Art 41 is that it was designed to prevent such questions from being referred for a preliminary ruling *to national supreme courts* under the mechanisms existing in some Member States on which Art 41 (and later Art 234 EC) is thought to have been modelled.

[208] Case 314/85 [1987] ECR 4199.

[209] The rule is qualified in proceedings before national courts for interim measures: see *Foto-Frost*, para 19; Case C–465/93 *Atlanta Fruchthandelsgesellschaft (I) v Bundesamt für Ernährung und Forstwirtschaft* [1995] ECR I–3761.

[210] Para 15. The uniform application of Community law is evidently also undermined when a national court interprets a provision incorrectly, but the threat is less serious: to interpret a rule assumes an intention to apply it, whereas a declaration that a provision is invalid inevitably causes it not to be applied. See AG Mancini at pp 4218–19.

[211] Para 16.

required that, where the validity of a Community act was challenged before a national court, the power to declare the act invalid should also be reserved to the Court of Justice. The Court added the practical point that, in preliminary ruling proceedings, the institution whose act was challenged would be able to take part.[212] This would not generally be possible in proceedings before a national court, with the result that the question might have to be determined in the absence of representations from the institution most directly concerned.

Although the outcome of the case was consistent with the views of a number of commentators,[213] the judgment in *Foto-Frost* was cited by Sir Patrick Neill in support of his thesis that the Court's overall aim has been to assert its 'omni-competence'. Hartley[214] says the ruling was not justified by the Treaty. There is certainly force in the argument that the terms of Article 234 (ex 177) do not support the view that all national courts, whether or not covered by the third paragraph of the article, are bound to make a reference to the Court where they consider that a challenge to the validity of a Community act might be well founded. However, Advocate General Mancini said that he considered that 'the "eliptical" wording of Article 177 is attributable to a singular but not impossible oversight' on the part of the Treaty's authors.[215] In his view, the textual arguments led to 'such dangerous and anomalous results as to overshadow the undeniable uneasiness which one feels in rejecting them'.[216] The reasons given by the Court for following his advice seem convincing. Both the Advocate General and the Court clearly regarded the consequences of the opposite view as so damaging to the coherence of the Community legal order that they could not be countenanced in the absence of an absolutely explicit indication in the Treaty that that was what its authors intended. The judgment achieves directly what could have been achieved indirectly by laying down strict guidelines for the national courts on the exercise of their discretion to refer in validity cases, something which would clearly have fallen within the jurisdiction of the Court. *Foto-Frost* was, however, a genuinely difficult case. Its allocation to the *grand plenum* and the detailed analysis of the issues in the Opinion of Advocate General Mancini provide a measure of the seriousness with which it was approached by the Court. It is a misunderstanding of the judicial process to suggest that the case could have been resolved simply by applying the language of Article 234 without regard to the consequences. To maintain that the Court was motivated by a desire to extend its own jurisdiction shows a failure to appreciate the nature of the issues at stake.[217]

---

[212] See Art 20 of the EC Statute. See further AG Mancini at p 4219.

[213] See the works cited by AG Mancini at pp 4219–20.

[214] (1996) 112 LQR 95, 100. See also Hartley, *Constitutional Problems of the European Union* (1999), p 34.

[215] See p 4218.

[216] p 4217. The dangers associated with interpreting Art 234 literally in this respect were acknowledged by Hartley in the first edition (1981) of his *The Foundations of European Community Law* at p 266. The book is cited by AG Mancini in *Foto-Frost* at p 4218.

[217] See the comments of Keeling, op cit, pp 523–4.

The *Foto-Frost* case was based on an assumption, not then questioned, that the validity of Community acts could be challenged in the national courts as an alternative to proceedings for annulment before the Court of Justice. Indeed, the Court has sometimes cited the possibility of bringing proceedings in the national courts as a justification for taking a strict view of the standing requirements applicable to private parties under Article 230 (ex 173).[218] However, the view that the validity of Community acts could be challenged before national courts by an unlimited category of applicants without any (or any uniform) time limit was hard to reconcile with the strict standing rules applicable to private applicants under Article 230 and the time limit for bringing proceedings laid down in that article.

In *TWD Textilwerke Deggendorf*,[219] the applicant, a recipient of aid from both Federal and State authorities in Germany, challenged before the national courts the validity of a Commission decision, adopted under Article 88(2) (ex 93(2)) of the Treaty and addressed to the Federal Republic of Germany, declaring the aid unlawful and requiring it to be recovered. Neither the Federal Republic nor the applicant had brought proceedings for the annulment of the decision under Article 230 (ex 173), although the Federal Economics Ministry had specifically drawn the applicant's attention to its right to do so.[220] The Court was asked for a preliminary ruling on the question whether an applicant in those circumstances could contest the validity of the Commission decision in a national court. The Court ruled that considerations of legal certainty prevented a recipient of aid which was the subject of a Commission decision adopted under Article 88 (ex 93) of the Treaty, who could have attacked the decision under Article 230 but who had allowed the deadline laid down in that article to expire, from contesting its legality before the national courts in the context of a challenge to national measures adopted to give effect to it. The Court distinguished earlier case law on the basis that it had not previously been called upon to address the effect in the national courts of the expiry of the deadline for bringing annulment proceedings.[221]

The Court's ruling in *TWD* followed the advice of Advocate General Jacobs, who said that it was only when an applicant's standing to bring annulment proceedings was 'clear beyond doubt'[222] that he should be prevented from challenging the validity of the contested act in the national courts. Otherwise national courts would have to resolve the sometimes difficult question whether the applicant would have had standing under Article 230 (ex 173) had proceedings been

---

[218] See eg Case 307/81 *Alusuisse v Council and Commission* [1982] ECR 3463; Joined Cases 239 and 275/82 *Allied Corporation v Commission* [1984] ECR 1005; Case 97/85 *Deutsche Lebensmittelwerke v Commission* [1987] ECR 2265; Joined Cases 133 to 136/85 *Rau v BALM* [1987] ECR 2289; Case C–209/94 P *Buralux and Others v Council* [1996] ECR I–615; Case C–321/95 P *Greenpeace and Others v Commission* [1998] ECR I–1651.
[219] Case C–188/92 [1994] ECR I–833.
[220] See Case 730/79 *Philip Morris v Commission* [1980] ECR 2671.
[221] It would seem to follow from the Court's ruling that a national court may not declare invalid national provisions which implement a directive on grounds which in effect impugn the validity of the directive. See AG Jacobs in Case C–212/91 *Angelopharm v Hamburg* [1994] ECR I–171, 195–7.
[222] At p I–844.

brought. The view of the Advocate General was reflected in the judgment of the Court, which emphasized that there was no doubt that the applicant could have attacked the Commission's decision under Article 230.[223] The point was confirmed in *Wiljo v Belgian State*[224] where, in a different context, the Court held that the validity of a Commission decision could not be challenged before a national court where the applicant had not sought its annulment in a direct action 'even though it could undoubtedly have done so'.[225]

There is no inconsistency between the rulings in *TWD* and *Foto-Frost*. Where an applicant before a national court is prevented by the former case from challenging the validity of a Community act, the latter case is simply irrelevant. Where *TWD* does not apply, the national court is not permitted[226] to declare the contested act invalid without referring the matter to the Court. None the less, the ruling in *TWD* attracted some misgivings.[227] As Advocate General Jacobs pointed out,[228] however, the preliminary rulings procedure is for a number of reasons a less satisfactory mechanism for reviewing the legality of Community acts than the action for annulment. Unlike proceedings under Article 230 (ex 173), proceedings under Article 234 (ex 177) do not involve a full exchange of pleadings.[229] The opportunity for the Court to investigate the matter depends on the questions formulated by the national court, which may not have any special expertise in the area covered by the contested act. Proceedings in the national courts are likely to involve additional delay and cost. If interlocutory relief is required, there is no guarantee that parallel applications in different Member States will produce the same result.[230] These considerations seem enough to justify the approach taken by the Court,[231] although the continuing confusion surrounding the precise standing test which private applicants must satisfy under Article 230 means that the number of cases affected by *TWD* may be limited.

[223] See paras 14 and 24.

[224] Case C–178/95 [1997] ECR I–585. See also Case C–408/95 *Eurotunnel and Others v SeaFrance* [1997] ECR I–6315.

[225] Para 23. The contested decision was addressed to the applicant. Cf Case C–241/95 *The Queen v Intervention Board for Agricultural Produce, ex parte Accrington Beef and Others* [1996] ECR I–6699, para 15, where the Court ruled that a company could contest the validity in a national court of provisions contained in a regulation because it was 'not obvious' that it could have brought an action against it under Art 230.

[226] Unless the proceedings are interlocutory and the conditions laid down in the *Atlanta* case, *supra*, are met.

[227] See eg Wyatt, 'The relationship between actions for annulment and references on validity after *TWD Deggendorf* in Lonbay and Biondi (eds), *Remedies for Breach of EC Law* (1997), ch 6; AG Tesauro in the *Eurotunnel* case, *supra*, at p I-6328. Cf Tesauro, 'The effectiveness of judicial protection and co-operation between the Court of Justice and the national courts' (1993) 13 YEL 1, 15–16.

[228] At pp I–841-3. See also his Opinion in Case C–358/89 *Extramet Industrie v Council* [1991] ECR I–2501, 2524–5.

[229] See Art 20 of the EC Statute.

[230] Even though the Court has laid down detailed guidelines to be applied by national courts in such cases: see the *Atlanta* case, *supra*.

[231] For a response to some of them, see Nihoul, 'La recevabilité des recours en annulation introduits par un particulier à l'encontre d'un acte communautaire de portée générale' (1994) 30 RTDE 171, 188–93.

Courts of last resort

While most national courts and tribunals enjoy a discretion in deciding whether to make a reference to the Court of Justice, those against whose decisions there is no judicial remedy in national law are, according to the third paragraph of Article 234 (ex 177), under an obligation to do so. That obligation attaches not just to national courts whose decisions are always final, but also to any other national court if there is no judicial remedy against its decision in the instant case.[232]

Whether the obligation imposed on courts covered by the third paragraph of Article 234 (ex 177) was an absolute one was for a long time the subject of controversy. The extent of the obligation was first considered by the Court of Justice in *Da Costa v Nederlandse Belastingadministratie*,[233] where a reference was made by the Tariefcommissie, a Dutch administrative court of last instance in taxation matters, in circumstances which were virtually identical to those of a reference it had made shortly beforehand in the famous case of *Van Gend en Loos v Nederlandse Administratie der Belastingen*.[234] By the time the Court came to deliver judgment in *Da Costa*, it had already decided *Van Gend en Loos* and it therefore took the opportunity to offer the referring court guidance on the scope of the obligation imposed by the Treaty on courts of last resort. The Court explained: 'Although the third paragraph of Article 177 [now 234] unreservedly requires courts or tribunals of a member State against whose decisions there is no judicial remedy under national law—like the Tariefcommissie—to refer to the Court every question of interpretation raised before them, the authority of an interpretation under Article 177 already given by the Court may deprive the obligation of its purpose and thus empty it of its substance. Such is the case especially when the question raised is materially identical with a question which has already been the subject of a preliminary ruling in a similar case.'[235] In other words, although the referring court was in principle covered by the third paragraph of Article 234, there was no need for it to make a reference in *Da Costa*. It could simply have waited and applied the ruling of the Court in *Van Gend en Loos*. Thus, the Court accepted at an early stage in the Community's development that the obligation imposed by the Treaty on national courts of last resort was not an absolute one. None the less, the circumstances mentioned by the Court in which the obligation would not apply were strictly limited: only where the question raised in the new case was *materially identical* with a question which had already been the subject of a *preliminary ruling* by the Court was the obligation removed. This represented such a minor qualification that it was perhaps overshadowed by the the Court's acceptance that a preliminary ruling might have an authority which extended beyond the case in which it was delivered.[236]

[232] See Case 6/64 *Costa v ENEL* [1964] ECR 585; Case 107/76 *Hoffmann-La Roche v Centrafarm* [1977] ECR 957; Joined Cases 35 and 36/82 *Morson and Jhanjan v Netherlands* [1982] ECR 3723. Cf Case C–337/95 *Parfums Christian Dior v Evora* [1997] ECR I–6013.

[233] Joined Cases 28, 29 and 30/62 [1963] ECR 31.   [234] Case 26/62 [1963] ECR 1.

[235] [1963] ECR 31, 38.

[236] See Rasmussen, 'The European Court's *acte clair* strategy in *CILFIT*' (1984) 9 ELRev 242, 249.

Nearly twenty years later, the Court relaxed the obligation imposed on courts of last resort to a much more significant extent. In *CILFIT v Ministry of Health*,[237] the Italian Corte Suprema di Cassazione asked for a preliminary ruling on whether the obligation laid down in the third paragraph of Article 234 (ex 177) was 'conditional on the prior finding of a reasonable interpretative doubt'. This was another way of asking whether the *acte clair* theory applied in this context. According to Advocate General Capotorti, that theory, which originated in the French legal system, meant simply that 'if a provision is unequivocal there is no need to interpret it'.[238] The Advocate General was firmly of the view that the *acte clair* theory had no place in the context of the preliminary rulings procedure: 'Clearly, acceptance of the idea that the obligation to refer a matter to the Court exists only where a reasonable interpretative doubt has arisen would lead to the introduction of a subjective and uncertain factor and might prevent the procedure from attaining its objective, which is . . . to ensure certainty and uniformity in the application of Community law.'[239]

The Court took a more liberal approach. It began by pointing out that all national courts and tribunals had the same discretion in deciding whether a decision on a question of Community law was necessary to enable them to give judgment. It followed that courts of last resort were not obliged to make a reference where the question raised was not relevant, in other words, where 'the answer to the question, regardless of what it may be, can in no way affect the outcome of the case'.[240] Where the question was relevant, the Court made it clear that there was no obligation to refer 'where previous decisions of the Court have already dealt with the point of law in question, irrespective of the nature of the proceedings which led to those decisions, even though the questions at issue are not strictly identical'.[241] This went some way further than *Da Costa*, for national courts were being given the green light to examine the Court's previous case law in order to establish whether the point at issue had *in substance* already been dealt with. They were no longer to be deterred by the nature of the earlier proceedings or the precise content of the questions raised. The extent of that dispensation is sometimes overlooked by those who criticize the strictness of the conditions laid down by the Court of Justice later in the judgment.

Where the point had not previously been dealt with by the Court, the obligation to refer was held not to apply where 'the correct application of Community law is so obvious as to leave no scope for any reasonable doubt'.[242] Before it came to that conclusion, the national court was to ask itself whether the answer to the

---

[237] Case 283/81 [1982] ECR 3415. [238] [1982] ECR 3415, 3435.
[239] [1982] ECR 3415, 3439. [240] Para 10.
[241] Para 14. This applies *a fortiori* 'when the question raised is substantially the same as a question which has already been the subject of a preliminary ruling in the same national proceedings': *Dior v Evora*, supra, para 29. All national courts, including those covered by the third para of Art 234, remain free to bring a matter before the Court of Justice if they consider it appropriate to do so: *CILFIT*, para 15.
[242] Para 21.

question would be equally obvious to the courts of the other Member States and to the Court of Justice. This involved bearing in mind 'the characteristic features of Community law and the particular difficulties to which its interpretation gives rise'.[243] The Court mentioned three features in particular:

(i) that Community legislation was drafted in several languages, all of which were equally authentic. Interpreting a provision of Community law therefore involved comparing the different language versions;

(ii) that Community law used its own terminology and that legal concepts did not necessarily have the same meaning in Community law as in the national laws of the Member States;

(iii) that 'every provision of Community law must be placed in its context and interpreted in the light of the provisions of Community law as a whole, regard being had to the objectives thereof and to its state of evolution at the date on which the provision in question is to be applied'.[244]

It may be noted that the criteria set out by the Court in *CILFIT* are also relevant where courts which are not covered by the third paragraph of Article 234 (ex 177) have to interpret Community law. This is because, where those criteria are satisfied, such courts may properly decline, in the exercise of their discretion, to make a reference. However, it follows from the decision of the Court in *Foto-Frost* that the criteria laid down in *CILFIT* apply only where the question of Community law raised before the national court is one of interpretation. Accordingly, where there is a real possibility in proceedings before a national court of last resort that a Community measure is invalid, the matter must be referred to the Court of Justice.

Although the *CILFIT* decision involved a departure from the strict terms of the Treaty, it is rarely attacked by critics of the Court's alleged activism. This is perhaps due to the fact that the decision is hard to reconcile with the view that the Court has a consistent policy of extending its own jurisdiction as widely as possible.[245] In *CILFIT*, the creative approach adopted to the interpretation of the third paragraph of Article 234 (ex 177) had precisely the opposite effect, allowing national courts of last resort to decide for themselves points of Community law which would otherwise have had to be referred to the Court of Justice. Was the Court wise to depart from the advice of its Advocate General on this issue? The risks inherent in the approach of the Court are evident. The philosophy underlying Article 234 is that, although the parties to a case cannot insist that inferior national courts make a reference, they can, by pursuing the case up to a court of last resort, ensure that relevant points of Community law will not be decided in the absence of guidance from the Court of Justice. The third paragraph of Article 234 is therefore a fail-safe mechanism which helps to guard against the threat to uniform application posed by inferior national courts which decide points of Community law incorrectly without making a reference to the Court of Justice.

---

[243] Para 17.   [244] Para 20.   [245] See Keeling, op cit, pp 524–5.

The capacity of the third paragraph to fulfil that function is jeopardized if the obligation it lays down is not enforced sufficiently strictly.

There are many examples of cases in which national courts of last resort have failed to make references in circumstances where that step ought probably to have been taken.[246] In some of them, the *CILFIT* criteria have been used to give a cloak of legitimacy to the decision not to send the case to Luxembourg.[247] On the whole, however, the criteria seem to be regarded as difficult to satisfy, particularly the one requiring comparison of the different language versions of a provision. Indeed, in one case the criteria were described as 'intimidating to an English judge'.[248] Some observers have therefore advocated that the criteria should be relaxed and national courts of last resort given greater freedom to decide points of Community law for themselves.[249]

It is submitted that these proposals should be treated with extreme caution. It cannot yet be said with confidence that national courts of last resort always apply Community law conscientiously and pay due regard to their obligations under the third paragraph of Article 234 (ex 177). Moreover, the periodic arrival of new Member States brings into the Community system national courts of last resort who have no experience whatsoever of dealing with points of Community law. The Court of Justice should be wary of giving the impression through its case law that the obligation laid down in the third paragraph of Article 234 is not something to be taken seriously. That said, there is perhaps one respect in which the *CILFIT* criteria might be relaxed. Where the parties to a case have not been able to point to a disparity between the different language versions of a provision, it is surely not necessary for a national court of last resort to examine the text of the provision concerned in every one of the growing number of language versions before forming a view of what it means. As long as it is borne in mind that all Community provisions need to be interpreted in the light of their objects and the scheme of the instrument of which they form part, it would be enough for the national court to consult a sample of other language versions.[250] If the uniform application of Community law is not to be undermined, however, any further relaxation of the *CILFIT* criteria could only be contemplated if a provision were to be inserted into

---

[246] See Anderson, *References to the European Court* (1995), pp 167–70.

[247] eg *Re Sandhu, The Times*, 10 May 1985 (HL); judgment of the Bundesgerichtshof of 15 January 1990 and of the Bundesverfassungsgericht of 27 August 1991 referred to by AG Tesauro in Case C–83/91 *Meilicke v ADV/ORGA* [1992] ECR I–4871, 4917 (n 23). See generally Arnull, 'The use and abuse of Article 177 EEC' (1989) 52 MLR 622.

[248] Hodgson J in *R v Secretary of State for Transport, ex parte Factortame* [1989] 2 CMLR 353, 379.

[249] See eg Vaughan and Randolph, 'The interface between Community law and national law: the United Kingdom experience' in Curtin and O'Keeffe (eds), *Constitutional Adjudication in European Community and National Law* (1992), ch 20, p 228; the Slynn Report, *supra*, pp 75–7, which says of the *CILFIT* criteria: 'Compliance with these requirements for *acte clair* is virtually impossible. In practice this test is completely unworkable' (p 76). For a short general discussion, see Anderson, op cit, pp 170–1.

[250] See AG Jacobs in Case C–338/95 *Wiener v Hauptzollamt Emmerich* [1997] ECR I–6495, 6516–17. Cf de la Mare, 'Article 177 in social and political context' in Craig and de Búrca (eds), *The Evolution of EU Law* (1999), ch 6, pp 246–9.

the Treaty giving, say, the Commission the right to refer to the Court a question of Community law which it believes has been decided incorrectly by a national court of last resort without the benefit of guidance from Luxembourg.[251] In the absence of such a provision, there would be no safeguard against abuse of the preliminary rulings procedure by national courts.[252]

The jurisdiction of the Court after the Treaty of Amsterdam

The Treaty of Amsterdam inserted into the EC Treaty a new Title IV (ex IIIa) entitled 'Visas, asylum, immigration and other policies related to free movement of persons'. Title IV gives the Council power to act in a range of areas, some of which previously fell within the scope of the Maastricht version of Title VI of the TEU. Although Title IV of the EC Treaty is located in the first pillar, the extent to which it is subject to oversight by the Court of Justice is limited by Article 68 (ex 73p) EC.[253] National courts of last resort are required by that article to seek preliminary rulings on the interpretation of Title IV and the validity and interpretation of acts of the institutions based on it. Moreover, the Council, the Commission and the Member States are entitled to ask the Court for a ruling on how the provisions of the Title and acts adopted under it should be interpreted.[254] However, lower national courts have no power to ask the Court for preliminary rulings in cases covered by the new Title.

There are precedents for confining the right to refer to higher courts[255] and the result will undoubtedly be to reduce the number of references. However, as the Court itself pointed out in its report on the application of the TEU,[256] there is a

[251] Cf the Slynn Report, supra, p 77–8; Jacobs in Andenas (ed), Article 177 References to the European Court: Policy and Practice (1994), p 30; the Protocols on the interpretation of the Brussels and Rome Conventions. Such a provision was introduced into the Treaty at Amsterdam, but it applies only to Title IV: see Art 68(3), discussed further below.

[252] Such abuse might in theory result in proceedings against the Member State concerned under Art 226 (ex 169): see AG Warner in Case 9/75 Meyer-Burckhardt v Commission [1975] ECR 1171, 1187.

[253] But see Art 67(2) (ex 73o(2)) EC, under which the provisions of Title IV relating to the powers of the Court are to be reviewed, along with the decision-making process applicable, five years after the entry into force of the Treaty of Amsterdam.

[254] Rulings given by the Court in response to such requests do not affect judgments of national courts which have become res judicata: Art 68(3).

[255] See eg the Protocol on the interpretation of the Brussels Convention on jurisdiction and the enforcement of judgments in civil and commercial matters, OJ 1998 C27/28; the First Protocol on the interpretation of the Rome Convention on the law applicable to contractual obligations, OJ 1998 C27/47. In both cases, it is not only courts of last resort who can refer but also other national courts when acting in an appellate capacity. In the case of the Rome Convention Protocol, no obligation to refer is imposed on courts of last resort. Cf the Protocol on the interpretation of the Convention on jurisdiction and the recognition and enforcement of judgments in matrimonial matters ('Brussels II'), OJ 1998 C221/20.

[256] Published in 'Proceedings of the Court of Justice and Court of First Instance of the European Communities', No 15/95 (22–6 May 1995).

price to be paid: the procedure will be less effective in ensuring uniform application and the effective protection of individual rights. Many of those involved in
immigration and asylum cases will not have the resources to pursue them as far as
courts of last resort.[257] The Member States were justifiably concerned about the
possibility that the Court would be inundated by references in the large number of
immigration and asylum cases which come before national courts. However, the
problem of the Court's workload is a more general one, a satisfactory solution to
which is only likely to be found in the context of a general review of the Union's
judicial architecture. No such review was on the agenda at the IGC which resulted
in the Treaty of Amsterdam.

Under Article 68(2) (ex 73p(2)), the Court does not have jurisdiction to rule on
Council measures connected with the removal of controls on the movement of
persons across internal borders 'relating to the maintenance of law and order and
the safeguarding of internal security'.[258] One may ask whether this paragraph is
confined to the Court's preliminary rulings jurisdiction or whether it is more general in scope. It is submitted that the Court's jurisdiction should be regarded as
capable of being limited only by the clearest of language. As a derogation, Article
68(2) should in any event be interpreted strictly. It therefore applies only in cases
covered by Article 68(1). The Court's other powers, notably those it possesses
under Article 230 (ex 173) EC, are accordingly unaffected. As a result, Council
measures taken under Title IV remain fully susceptible to review in annulment
proceedings.

One may also ask whether the *Foto-Frost* principle applies in cases covered by
Title IV. It will be remembered that that principle prevents a national court from
declaring a Community act invalid without referring the question of the act's validity to the Court of Justice. The justification for the principle is the threat to the
uniform application of Community law which would arise if national courts could
declare Community acts invalid without consulting the Court of Justice first.
However, it would be intolerable if parties to national proceedings could not challenge the validity of acts adopted under Title IV without taking their case to a court
of last resort. Even then, the Court of Justice could not be asked to rule on the
validity of a measure falling within the scope of Article 68(2) (ex 73p(2)). The conclusion must therefore be that the *Foto-Frost* principle does not apply in this context and that national courts are free to declare invalid acts adopted under Title IV
(including those covered by Article 68(2)).

The right conferred on the Council, the Commission and the Member States
under Article 68(3) (ex 73p(3)) to ask the Court to rule on the interpretation of the
new rules is based on similar provisions contained in other instruments.[259] While

---

[257] See JUSTICE, 'The jurisdiction of the European Court of Justice in respect of asylum and immigration matters' (May 1997), p 7.

[258] Cf Art 2(1), third indent, of the Protocol integrating the Schengen Acquis into the framework of
the EU, which is annexed to the TEU and the EC Treaty.

[259] See eg the Protocols on the interpretation of the Brussels Convention, the Rome Convention,
and the Brussels II Convention, *supra*.

useful, Article 68(3) seems unlikely to be used frequently. If it were, the object of preventing inferior national courts from referring would be partly defeated. However, it is a potentially useful safeguard against the development of lines of national case law based on an incorrect understanding of Title IV.

Hand in hand with Title IV of the EC Treaty go the revised provisions of Title VI of the TEU, which is renamed 'Provisions on police and judicial cooperation in criminal matters'. Article 35(1) (ex K.7(1)) TEU[260] gives the Court of Justice a preliminary rulings jurisdiction in relation to a range of measures adopted under Title VI, although only at the request of national courts situated in Member States which have declared that they accept the involvement of the Court.[261] There is no provision for such declarations to be revoked once they have been made and they may not be limited to specific instruments. This may mean that Member States which have general reservations about involving the Court will not make declarations even if they would be content in some contexts for the Court to be involved.[262] Under Article 35(3) (ex K.7(3)), Member States may either confine the right to refer to courts and tribunals of last resort or extend it to any court or tribunal.[263] In neither case does the Treaty impose an obligation to refer on courts of last resort, but a declaration (no 10) adopted by the IGC notes that Member States may impose such an obligation as a matter of national law. It is therefore for national law to determine the scope of any such obligation. It follows that the decision of the Court in the *CILFIT* case will apply only to the extent (if any) laid down by national law.[264]

Even where a reference is made from a Member State which has accepted the jurisdiction of the Court, Article 35(5) (ex K.7(5)) prevents the Court from reviewing the validity or proportionality of national police operations or national measures concerned with 'the maintenance of law and order and the safeguarding of internal security'. Like Article 68(2) (ex 73p(2)) EC, Article 35(5) TEU seems iniquitous: both provisions are designed to weaken judicial scrutiny, both pose a serious threat to the uniform application of the law in the Member States to which

[260] Cf the Protocol on the interpretation by the Court of Justice of the Convention on the establishment of a European Police Office ('Europol'), OJ 1996 C299/1; the Protocol on the interpretation of the Brussels II Convention, *supra*; the EEA Agreement, Protocol 34, and the Agreement on the Establishment of a Surveillance Authority and a Court of Justice, Arts 27 and 34.

[261] See Art 35(2). In Opinion 1/91 'EEA Agreement' [1991] ECR I–6079, para 60, the Court accepted that an arrangment of this type was consistent with the Treaty framework then in place.

[262] Under Art 35(4), any Member State, whether or not it has made a declaration accepting the Court's jurisdiction, has the right to submit observations in cases referred under Art 35(1).

[263] As at the entry into force of the Treaty of Amsterdam, Spain had limited the right to refer to courts and tribunals of last resort; Austria, Belgium, Finland, Germany, Greece, Italy, Luxembourg, the Netherlands, Portugal, and Sweden had extended the right to refer to all their courts and tribunals. No declaration had been made by Denmark, France, Ireland, or the United Kingdom. See OJ 1999 C120/24.

[264] As at the entry into force of the Treaty of Amsterdam, Austria, Belgium, Germany, Italy, Luxembourg, the Netherlands, and Spain had expressly reserved the right to impose an obligation to refer on courts of last resort. It is submitted that the *CILFIT* decision *does* apply to Art 68(1) EC, since that provision is a specific application of Art 234.

they apply.[265] That outcome is hard to reconcile with the principles of respect for human rights and fundamental freedoms and the rule of law, which are among those on which the Union is now said to be founded.[266] It seems perverse to limit in this way the jurisdiction of the institution which is best placed to ensure that those principles are respected. However, it is for the Court to define the precise scope of these provisions. There is a potentially important distinction between the two. While Article 68(2) EC deals with measures taken by the *Council*, Article 35(5) TEU is concerned with *national* measures. It may be noted that the Court never (at least in theory) rules directly in reference proceedings on the legality of national measures. What it does is to rule in abstract terms on the requirements of European law, leaving the referring court to apply its ruling to the facts of the case. The practical effect of Article 35(5) may therefore be limited.

As with Article 68 (ex 73p) EC, the question arises whether the *Foto-Frost* principle applies in the context of Article 35 (ex K.7) TEU. The answer once again seems to be that it does not. It is obvious that it could not apply in a Member State which has not accepted the jurisdiction of the Court. For the reasons given above, the *Foto-Frost* principle could not apply either in cases falling within the scope of Article 35(5) or in Member States which have restricted to national courts of last resort the right to refer questions to the Court of Justice. Even in a case brought in a Member State which has extended to all its courts the right to refer, the *Foto-Frost* principle would not be capable of ensuring the uniform application of the law.

The combination of Articles 68 (ex 73p) and 234 (ex 177) EC and Article 35 (ex K.7) TEU is likely to give rise to jurisdictional questions of considerable complexity which national courts and the Court of Justice will need to devote considerable care to unravelling. None the less, the provisions on preliminary rulings introduced at Amsterdam seem on balance to represent a step in the right direction. To the extent that the matters covered by the Title IV (ex IIIa) EC and Title VI TEU previously fell within the scope of the Treaties, they were covered by the Maastricht version of Title VI, which made minimal provision for the involvement of the Court.

Mention should also be made of the last two paragraphs of Article 35 (ex K.7). Article 35(6) is reminiscent of Article 230 (ex 173) EC. It gives the Court jurisdiction to review the legality of 'framework decisions and decisions' adopted under Title VI, but only in actions brought by a Member State or the Commission. In the case of framework decisions, the failure to confer standing on individuals may be thought justified by the nature of that type of act. Article 34(2)(b) (ex K.6(2)(b)) provides that framework decisions, which resemble EC directives, 'shall not entail direct effect'. Since individuals only rarely have standing to challenge directives

[265] Title IV EC does not apply to the UK, Ireland, or Denmark except in the circumstances specified in protocols annexed to the TEU and the EC Treaty.
[266] Art 6(1) TEU provides: 'The Union is founded on the principles of liberty, democracy, respect for human rights and fundamental freedoms, and the rule of law, principles which are common to the Member States.' See ch 6.

under Article 230 EC, it would have been inconsistent to give them an express right to challenge framework decisions. The failure to grant individuals standing to challenge decisions adopted under Title VI is harder to justify. Although it is again provided that decisions of this type 'shall not entail direct effect', they are binding. Moreover, the Council is empowered to adopt the measures necessary to implement them 'at the level of the Union'. The manifest potential of such decisions, and of measures implementing them, to affect the rights and obligations of individuals makes the failure of Article 35(6) to confer on individuals standing to challenge their legality hard to reconcile with some at least of the founding principles of the Union set out in Article 6(1) TEU.

Article 35(7) (ex K.7(7)) is more satisfactory, if only slightly. Subject to certain conditions, this provision gives the Court jurisdiction in disputes between Member States concerning the interpretation or application of acts adopted by the Council under Article 34(2) (ex K.6(2)). It also confers on the Court jurisdiction in disputes between Member States and the Commission over the scope of conventions established under Article 34(2)(d). This to some extent consolidates the rule of law by providing a judicial mechanism for the resolution of disputes which might otherwise have to be settled at the political level.[267] The right which the Commission enjoys to ask the Court to rule on the interpretation or application of conventions established under Article 34(2)(d) is likely to be particularly valuable when the Member State with which it is in dispute has not accepted the jurisdiction of the Court to give preliminary rulings. It is not clear, however, why the Commission's right to ask the Court to intervene does not extend to other acts adopted by the Council under Article 34(2).[268] It is rather as if Article 226 (ex 169) EC were more limited in scope than Article 227 (ex 170).

Notwithstanding their undoubted drawbacks, it is doubtful whether these provisions reflect any general dissatisfaction among the Member States with the way in which the Court discharged its responsibilities in the pre-Amsterdam era. While there are certainly some Member States which would have liked to see some reining in of the Court at Amsterdam,[269] the net result of Title IV (ex IIIa) EC and the revised Title VI of the TEU is to expand its jurisdiction in the areas which those titles cover. Critics of the Court may find solace in its exclusion from cases concerned with law and order and internal security. However, these are areas which involve core responsibilities of the nation State and it comes as no surprise that, at the present stage of European integration, agreement could not be reached on submitting the way such responsibilities are carried out to the scrutiny of the Court. The complexity of the labyrinth created by Title IV EC, Title VI TEU and the

---

[267] See eg the Europol Convention, *supra*, Art 40.

[268] Even where they are the result of a Commission initiative: see Art 34(2) TEU, which enables the Council to act 'on the initiative of any Member State or of the Commission'.

[269] See eg the White Paper entitled 'A Partnership of Nations' published by the UK Government in March 1996 (Cm 3181), paras 36 and 37, and the memorandum on the Court published by the UK the following July.

associated protocols reflects a lack of consensus among the Member States about the desirability of closer integration in the areas they cover. Even where there is some measure of agreement about objectives, the Member States evidently do not always see eye to eye about the most appropriate way of achieving them. Seen in that context, it is not surprising that the provisions on the Court introduced at Amsterdam are somewhat less than satisfactory.[270]

---

[270] See further Albors-Llorens, 'Changes in the jurisdiction of the European Court of Justice after the Treaty of Amsterdam' (1998) 35 CMLRev 1273.

3

The relationship between Treaty provisions and the national laws of the Member States

Although it was inevitable that the Community Treaties—and the EC Treaty in particular—would in due course come into conflict with inconsistent provisions in the national laws of the Member States, they did not say anything about how such conflicts were to be resolved. This could have been taken to imply that the Community Treaties were no different from ordinary treaties, whose effect within the legal order of the contracting parties will depend on a rule of domestic constitutional law.[1] It is true that Article 26 of the Vienna Convention on the Law of Treaties requires the parties to a treaty to implement it in good faith and that Article 27 of that Convention prevents a party from justifying a failure to perform a treaty by reference to its internal law. But the Vienna Convention does not seek to modify the fundamental principle that the application of treaties by domestic courts is governed by domestic law. The result is that the internal effect of a treaty may differ from one contracting party to another. In particular, the question whether a provision of a treaty confers rights on private parties which can be invoked before the national courts, and if so in what circumstances, will receive different answers in different countries. Legal systems may also differ on the question whether treaties take precedence over national law. They may take different approaches to the interpretation of treaties, so that the effect of a provision in a given set of circumstances might vary.

It will be apparent that the constitutional principle that the effect of treaties in national courts depends on domestic law is liable to have adverse consequences for the effectiveness of all international treaties. In the case of the EC Treaty, however, those consequences would be wholly incompatible with the project its authors had in mind. It is of the very essence of a common market that the rules governing its operation should have the same meaning and effect wherever they fall to be applied: an economic regime such as that created by the EC Treaty could not function if an importer in Belgium, France, or the Netherlands[2] could rely in the

---

[1] See Jacobs in Jacobs and Roberts (eds), *The Effect of Treaties in Domestic Law* (1987), p xxiv.

[2] Where treaties which have been ratified by the State automatically become part of the law to be applied by the courts without the need for any separate act of incorporation: see Jacobs and Roberts (eds), *passim*.

national courts on the Treaty prohibition against quantitative restrictions on imports, but an importer in England[3] could not. How could a system ensuring that competition in the internal market is not distorted be ensured if the relevant provisions of the Treaty were interpreted more strictly in Germany[4] than in Denmark?[5]

It was thus apparent from a sympathetic reading of the Treaty that its effect had to be the same throughout the territory of the Member States. Since this result could not be achieved if the relationship between the Treaty and the domestic laws of the Member States was to be determined by reference to the latter, it had to be determined by reference to the former. That this was the intention of the Treaty's authors was supported by two of its provisions, Article 234 (ex 177) and Article 249 (ex 189). Article 234 was examined in the previous chapter. It will be recalled that it makes provision for national courts before which questions of Community law are raised to ask the Court of Justice for guidance on their meaning and effect. As the Court has acknowledged,[6] the purpose of Article 234 is to safeguard the uniform application of Community law. This would be threatened not only if the meaning attributed to particular provisions varied from Member State to Member State, but also if the *effect* of a given provision differed. The inclusion of the procedure in the Treaty therefore implied that the latter issue was a matter of Community law and could not be left to the legal orders of the Member States. As for Article 249, it stipulates that regulations, one of the binding acts which the Community institutions are empowered to adopt, shall be binding in their entirety and directly applicable in each Member State. This means that they take effect in the legal orders of the Member States on their own terms, requiring no national measures of implementation, and that national courts are bound to uphold their terms. It might be suggested that what is true for regulations must necessarily also be true of hierarchically superior norms contained in the Treaty itself.[7] That view was criticized by Professor Hamson, who maintained:

It is clearly the scheme of the Treaty that the very wide obligations undertaken by the parties to the Treaty should be given precision and concrete detail by concerted legislative or administrative action on the part of the Member States or by regulations issued by the Council or the Commission or by both modes of implementation. The draftsman may have meant what he said and may indeed have intended to give to this Subordinate Community legislation, and to it only, direct applicability in the sense of engendering in an individual a right enforceable by action within the national legal system in the very terms in which the right had been defined.[8]

---

[3] Where treaties in principle have no effect unless made part of domestic law.

[4] Where treaties require transformation by domestic law but are then applicable as such.

[5] Where the position is similar to that in the UK.

[6] See Case 166/73 *Rheinmühlen v Einfuhr- und Vorratsstelle Getreide* [1974] ECR 33.

[7] See Lecourt, *L'Europe des Juges* (1976), p 285.

[8] Hamson, 'Methods of Interpretation—A Critical Assessment of the Results' in *Reports of a Judicial and Academic Conference held in Luxembourg on 27–28 September 1976*, II-3, II-16.

But where an obligation undertaken by the parties to the Treaty is given precision and concrete detail in the Treaty itself and further legislation is therefore unnecessary, there seems no good reason for denying to the Treaty the same effect a similar provision would in Hamson's view produce if it were contained in a regulation.

It might be objected that the relationship between Community law and national law is a matter of such fundamental importance that, had the authors of the Treaty intended any radical departure from the traditional model, they would have said so expressly. That view, it is submitted, misunderstands both the nature of international treaties and the role of the Court of Justice in the institutional framework of the Community. As Advocate General Lagrange explained in *Fédération Charbonnière Belgique v High Authority*, 'the common will . . . is in most cases difficult to establish with certainty in the case of documents such as international agreements, which are generally the result of compromises reached with more or less difficulty and in which the obscure or imprecise wording often only conceals fundamental disagreements'.[9] Thus, the absence of a provision in the Treaty regulating a particular matter should not be taken to reflect agreement by the Member States that the matter concerned should be left outside the Treaty's ambit, but simply a lack of consensus among the Member States at the time the Treaty was drafted on whether, and if so how, that matter should be dealt with. If account is then taken of the duty imposed on the Court by Article 220 (ex 164) of the Treaty to ensure observance of the law, it is not unreasonable to infer that the authors of the Treaty intended the Court to bear responsibility for finding solutions to legal controversies for which they had failed to provide which were in keeping with the Treaty's underlying philosophy. *A contrario* reasoning—described by a former Judge of the Court as 'the weakest form of legal argument, as it is based not on the law, but on gaps in the law'[10]—should thus be used with extreme caution in interpreting the Treaty, whatever its value as a technique for making sense of acts of the Community institutions.

The decision in *Van Gend en Loos*

There is a risk that, with the benefit of hindsight, these issues will be presented as clearer than they in fact appeared to be in the years immediately following the signature of the Treaty. Certainly, the answer to the question whether a provision of the Treaty was capable of conferring rights on individuals which national courts had to protect was far from clear to the Tariefcommissie, a Netherlands administrative tribunal having final jurisdiction in revenue cases, which in *Van Gend en*

---

[9] Case 8/55 [1954 to 1956] ECR 245, 277. It will be noted that AG Lagrange thought that this was one of the explanations for the tendency of international courts 'to be more timid than national courts in departing from a literal interpretation . . .'.

[10] Pescatore in Jacobs and Roberts (eds), op cit, p 281.

Loos v Nederlandse Administratie der Belastingen[11] asked the Court of Justice for a preliminary ruling on the matter.[12] At the origin of the dispute before the national
court was the importation into the Netherlands from Germany of a quantity of
urea-formaldehyde. Acting on the basis of the tariff of import duties laid down in
the Tariefbesluit which entered into force on 1 March 1960, the Dutch revenue
authorities applied an *ad valorem* import duty of 8 per cent to the importation in
question. The importer objected: on the date on which the EEC Treaty entered
into force, it claimed, imports of urea-formaldehyde were charged with an import
duty of 3 per cent under the Tariefbesluit of 1947, the nomenclature of which was
taken from a protocol concluded between Belgium, Luxembourg, and the
Netherlands on 25 July 1958 and ratified in the Netherlands by a Law of 16
December 1959. By increasing the import duty on the product in question after
the entry into force of the EEC Treaty, the Netherlands had infringed Article 12
of that Treaty,[13] according to which Member States were to 'refrain from introducing between themselves any new customs duties on imports or exports or any
charges having equivalent effect, and from increasing those which they already
apply in their trade with each other'. The dispute eventually reached the
Tariefcommissie, before which the Dutch authorities maintained that, when the
EEC Treaty entered into force, imports of the product in question would have
been subjected to a duty, not of 3 per cent, but of 10 per cent, so that there had
not in fact been any increase. Without deciding how the product should have been
classified under the 1947 Tariefbesluit, the Tariefcommissie referred two questions
to the Court of Justice. The first asked whether Article 12 conferred on individuals rights which the national courts were bound to protect; the second whether, if
so, Article 12 had been infringed in circumstances such as those of the main action.

   If the Court answered the first question in the affirmative, the result would be a
considerable incursion into the sovereignty of the Member States. Like many other
provisions of the Treaty, Article 12 was addressed to the Member States and contained no express reference to the rights of individuals. If Article 12 were held to
be capable of producing direct effect, the same might be true of many other provisions of the Treaty. In the proceedings before the Court of Justice, observations
were submitted by the parties to the main action, by the Belgian, German and
Dutch Governments and by the European Commission. Only the Commission
supported the position of the importer. The Governments of Belgium and the
Netherlands and the respondent authority contested the very admissibility of the
first question referred to the Court. The Netherlands Government argued that an
alleged infringement of the Treaty by a Member State could only be brought

---

[11] Case 26/62 [1963] ECR 1. It may be noted that the Court's first judgment in an EEC case was
delivered little over a year previously: see Case 7/61 *Commission v Italy* [1961] ECR 317.
[12] The question of direct applicability had been addressed by the Court in Joined Cases 7 and 9/54
Industries Sidérurgiques Luxembourgeoises v High Authority [1954 to 1956] ECR 175, but not in the context of proceedings before the national courts.
[13] Now after amendment Art 25.

before the Court by means of a direct action by the Commission under Article 169 (now 226) of the Treaty or by another Member State under Article 170 (now 227). In any event, the question related, not to the interpretation, but to the application of the Treaty. It therefore fell outside the scope of Article 177 (now 234). According to the Belgian Government, the first question concerned a problem of domestic constitutional law falling within the exclusive jurisdiction of the national court. That court had before it two international treaties, both of which were part of national law. If they turned out to be inconsistent with each other, it would have to decide which one should be given precedence. This would require the referring court to determine whether a national law ratifying a treaty, namely the law of 5 December 1957 ratifying the EEC Treaty, prevailed over another such law adopted subsequently, namely the law of 16 December 1959 ratifying the Brussels Protocol. This was, according to the Belgian Government, a question of national constitutional law falling within the exclusive jurisdiction of the referring court. It had nothing to do with the interpretation of the EEC Treaty. The Commission, however, took the view that the effect of the Treaty could not be determined by national law but only by the Treaty itself. The problem raised by the national court in its first question therefore clearly related to the interpretation of the Treaty.

On the substance of the first question, the importer maintained that Article 12 did indeed have direct internal effect. It made four particular points in support of that submission: first, the article did not require incorporation into the national legislation of the Member States; secondly, it was not dependent on the adoption of further legislation at the Community level; thirdly, although it did not refer directly to the nationals of the Member States, any infringement of it prejudiced the fundamental principles of the Community, against which individuals as well as the Community itself had to be protected; finally, the article was said to be particularly well adapted for direct application by the national courts, which were simply called upon to set aside national provisions introduced in breach of its provisions.

The importer was supported by the Commission, which maintained that the structure of the Treaty showed that it was not intended to be confined to the level of the Member States, nor to fall outside the jurisdiction of the ordinary courts. Moreover, it was imperative that Community law should be applied effectively and uniformly throughout the Community. It followed that the effect of Community law on the national laws of the Member States could only be determined by Community law itself and that national courts were in certain circumstances bound to apply Community law directly, if necessary according it precedence over inconsistent provisions of national law. In the Commission's view, Article 12 was capable of being applied by the national courts as it was clear and complete. The Netherlands, Belgian, and German Governments were resolutely opposed to this approach. They each took the view that Article 12 was intended by the authors of the Treaty to be binding on the international plane only and that it could not be invoked directly in the national courts.

As far as the substance of the case was concerned, only the importer maintained that Article 12 had in fact been breached. The Netherlands and Belgian Governments, supported this time by the Commission, maintained that the importer had made an error in calculating the amount of duty that would have been payable on the entry into force of the Treaty and that there had not in fact been any increase contrary to Article 12.

The Opinion of Advocate General Roemer

Advocate General Roemer gave his Opinion on 12 December 1962. In retrospect, it strikes the reader as remarkably out of step with the prevailing mood among his colleagues at the Court. Had it been followed, the development of the Community might have taken an entirely different course. The Advocate General began by taking a restrictive view of the Court's jurisdiction under Article 177 (now 234) of the Treaty. He argued that the effect of an international treaty depended on the legal force which its authors intended it to have. This was admittedly a question of the interpretation of the relevant provisions and fell within the scope of the Court's powers under Article 177. But it was 'impossible to clarify exhaustively the real legal effects of an international agreement on the nationals of a Member State without having regard to the constitutional law of that Member State.'[14] In other words, the obligations imposed on Member States by the Treaty could be spelled out by the Court, but the effect of the Treaty in the internal legal orders of the Member States was a matter of national law which fell outside the Court's jurisdiction under Article 177. With regard to the substance of the national court's first question, Mr Roemer acknowledged that:

Anyone familiar with Community law knows that in fact it does not just consist of contractual relations between a number of States considered as subjects of the law of nations. The Community has its own institutions, independent of the Member States, endowed with the power to take administrative measures and to make rules of law which directly create rights in favour of and impose duties on Member States as well as their authorities and citizens.

He noted that the EEC Treaty contained provisions which were clearly intended to apply directly in the national systems,[15] such as those relating to competition contained in Articles 85 (now 81) and 86 (now 82). Some provisions were, in the Advocate General's view, designed to produce direct effect at a later stage, such as the provisions on the free movement of persons, services, and capital. But Mr Roemer emphasized that 'many of the Treaty's provisions expressly refer to the *obligations* of Member States'.[16] Those provisions only laid down an obligation on

---

[14] pp 18–19.
[15] Although the English text of the Opinion refers, at p 20, to 'provisions intended to be incorporated in national law', the French text speaks of provisions 'destinées à agir directement sur le droit national': Rec 1963, p 39.
[16] p 20, emphasis in the original.

the part of the Member States, as did certain provisions drafted in a purely declaratory form. By contrast, Mr Roemer pointed out that it was relatively rare to find the terms 'prohibited' or 'prohibition' in the Treaty. Even where these terms were used, he thought it was sometimes clear from the wording or the context that they could not have direct effect. Similarly, where the expression 'incompatible with the Common Market' was used, it did not automatically follow that the provisions concerned had direct effect. The Advocate General concluded that 'large parts of the Treaty contain only obligations of Member States, and do not contain rules having a direct internal effect'.[17] According to Mr Roemer, it was for this reason that the Commission and other Member States had been given the right to institute proceedings before the Court if they considered that a Member State had failed to comply with its obligations under the Treaty.[18]

The Advocate General then turned his attention to the effect of Article 12. He acknowledged that the obligation imposed on Member States by that article was not dependent on the adoption of further measures by the Community institutions, 'which allows us in a certain sense to speak of the direct legal effect of Article 12'.[19] The crucial question, however, was whether this direct effect stopped at the governments of the Member States or whether it could be applied directly by the national courts. Mr Roemer had no doubt that the article did not produce direct effect in this sense. Not only were the Member States the addressees of the provision, it did not contain terms such as 'prohibition', 'inadmissible', or 'without effect' which were to be found in other provisions of the Treaty. 'It is just when a provision is meant to be applied directly . . . that a precise indication of the intended legal effects is indispensable', said the Advocate General.[20] Moreover, in his view the practical application of Article 12 would be very difficult for national courts. To ask them to perform that task could only create uncertainty. In addition, Mr Roemer noted that the relationship between international law and national legislation under the constitutional laws of the Member States was not uniform. However, far from concluding that this factor militated in favour of attributing direct effect to Article 12, the Advocate General came to the opposite conclusion: 'If Article 12 is deemed to have a direct internal effect, the situation would arise that breaches of Article 12 would render the national customs laws ineffective and inapplicable in only a certain number of Member States.'[21] Even in States where international agreements were given precedence over national law, variations in the application of the Treaty might arise which Article 177 (now 234) would do nothing to avoid, being concerned only with the interpretation of the Treaty and not with its compatibility with national law. The Advocate General concluded that Article 12 only contained an obligation on the part of the Member States.[22]

---

[17] p 21.   [18] See Arts 226 (ex 169) and 227 (ex 170) respectively.
[19] The Court used the term 'directly applicable' in this sense in Joined Cases 7 and 9/54 *Industries Sidérurgiques Luxembourgeoises v High Authority* [1954 to 1956] ECR 175.
[20] At p 22.   [21] p 23.
[22] The Advocate General went on to lay down guidelines for the application of Art 12 in case the Court disagreed with him on the question of its direct effect.

The Advocate General's Opinion must have been a great disappointment both to the importer and to the Commission. The model of the Community envisaged by Mr Roemer was one which operated for the most part at the level of the Member States. Only exceptionally would individuals be able to claim rights under the Treaty. The development of the common market would be dependent to a large extent on the adoption of further legislation by the Community institutions.[23] Breaches of the Treaty by the Member States could be rectified only by proceedings under Articles 226 (ex 169) and 227 (ex 170). Not only was it evident that such proceedings would be time-consuming and ill adapted to preventing opportunist infringements of the Treaty by Member States, they imposed a heavy burden on the limited resources of the Commission.

The judgment of the Court

The importer and the Commission need not have worried: Mr Roemer's advice was rejected by the Court, which held that Article 12 produced direct effect and created individual rights which national courts were required to protect. It was infringed, not only where there was an increase in the rate of duty, but also where a rearrangement of the national tariff resulted in the classification of a product under a more highly taxed heading. The argument that the answer to the national court's first question depended not on the interpretation of the Treaty but on the constitutional law of the Netherlands was dismissed by the Court as having no legal foundation. The question referred related to the interpretation of Article 12 'within the context of Community law and with reference to its effect on individuals'.[24] This fell squarely within the scope of its jurisdiction under Article 177 (now 234).

In dealing with the substance of the first question, the Court observed that it was 'necessary to consider the spirit, the general scheme and the wording' of the relevant provisions.[25] With regard to the spirit of the Treaty, the Court noted that its objective was to establish a common market, the functioning of which would be of direct concern to interested parties in the Community. This implied that the Treaty did more than merely create mutual obligations between the contracting States. The preamble to the Treaty, with its reference to the peoples of the Member States, and the establishment of institutions with the power to adopt legislation affecting not only the Member States but also their citizens, supported that implication. Moreover, nationals of the Member States had a role to play in the func-

---

[23] Although at that stage they were functioning broadly as intended by the authors of the Treaty, that was soon to change as a result of the so-called Luxembourg Compromise of January 1966, which prevented a smooth transition to qualified majority voting. See ch 16, below; Wyatt and Dashwood, *European Community Law* (3rd edn, 1993), p 46.

[24] p 11.

[25] The relegation of the wording to third place among the factors to be borne in mind provided an early indication of an approach to the interpretation of Community law that was to become increasingly controversial as the Court grew in stature. See further ch 14.

tioning of the Community through the European Parliament and the Economic and Social Committee. In addition, the preliminary rulings procedure confirmed that Community law could be invoked by individuals before the national courts. These features led the Court to the following conclusion:

. . . the Community constitutes a new legal order of international law for the benefit of which the states have limited their sovereign rights, albeit within limited fields, and the subjects of which comprise not only Member States but also their nationals. Independently of the legislation of Member States, Community law therefore not only imposes obligations on individuals but is also intended to confer upon them rights which become part of their legal heritage. These rights arise not only where they are expressly granted by the Treaty, but also by reason of obligations which the Treaty imposes in a clearly defined way upon individuals as well as upon the Member States and upon the institutions of the Community.[26]

The Court then turned to the general scheme of the Treaty. It noted that, according to Article 9 (now 23), the Community was based upon a customs union, an essential feature of which was the prohibition between Member States of customs duties on imports and exports and of all charges having equivalent effect. Article 9, which was amplified by Article 12, was to be found in a part of the Treaty entitled 'Foundations of the Community': in other words, it was not merely ancillary to some other objective of greater importance but was fundamental to the entire project.[27]

Finally, the Court examined the wording of Article 12, noting that it contained 'a clear and unconditional prohibition which is not a positive but a negative obligation'.[28] Its implementation was not dependent on further action by the national legislatures. These features made it 'ideally adapted to produce direct effects in the legal relationship between Member States and their subjects'. The fact that the article was addressed to the Member States did not in the Court's view imply that their nationals could not rely on it.

The Court concluded the relevant section of its judgment by dismissing the argument put forward by the Belgian, German and Netherlands Governments based on Articles 169 (now 226) and 170 (now 227). Those articles were not to be taken to mean that individuals could not rely on infringements of the Treaty in proceedings before the national courts, for otherwise they would be deprived of direct legal protection of their rights. Moreover, recourse to Articles 169 and 170 might be ineffective if a national measure incompatible with the Treaty had already been introduced. The Court also observed that '[t]he vigilance of individuals concerned to protect their rights amounts to an effective supervision in addition to the

---

[26] p 12. Cf Opinion 1/91 'Agreement creating the European Economic Area' [1991] ECR I–6079, para 21, delivered at the end of 1991, where the Court spoke of the Member States' having limited their sovereign rights 'in ever wider fields'.

[27] The Treaty no longer contains a Part entitled 'Foundations of the Community', but this does not reflect any reduction in the importance of the prohibition on customs duties and charges having equivalent effect.

[28] p 13.

supervision entrusted by Articles 169 and 170 to the vigilance of the Commission and of the Member States'.[29] It followed, said the Court, that 'Article 12 must be interpreted as producing direct effects and creating individual rights which national courts must protect'.[30]

An assessment of the Court's decision

The fundamental importance of the Court's decision in *Van Gend en Loos* is self-evident. Indeed, the case has become so well known among lawyers in the Member States that it is now almost taken for granted. Pescatore, a former Judge at the Court, has gone so far as to describe the direct effect of Community law as 'nothing but the ordinary state of the law',[31] a remark which could hardly have been made on the day the EEC Treaty entered into force. Of course, it is not difficult to devise mechanisms which will in theory ensure the effectiveness of a legal rule. It is infinitely more difficult to gauge whether the climate is one in which the chosen mechanism will be accepted loyally in practice, whether it will be accepted grudgingly, or whether it will be flatly rejected. Only loyal acceptance will ensure that it achieves its intended objective. Rejection out of hand may leave one worse off than before one started. The fact that the direct effect of Treaty provisions is nowadays taken for granted is testimony to the sureness of the Court's touch in the early 1960s: the vision and courage which lay behind that crucial first step should not be allowed to go unnoticed.

Pescatore has said that '[t]he important thing is to see what are the motives underlying this decision. The reasoning of the Court shows that the judges had "une certaine idée de l'Europe" of their own, and that it is this idea which has been decisive and not arguments based on the legal technicalities of the matter.'[32] This observation has been described in one commentary as 'disturbing'.[33] The use of such an adjective seems something of an overreaction. Pescatore was not a member of the Court at the time of the decision in *Van Gend en Loos*. In any event, the 'idea of Europe' which may be said to underlie that decision is inspired by 'the spirit, the general scheme and the wording' of the Treaty, to which the Court expressly made reference.[34] The Court was merely seeking to ensure that the system would work, a consideration which, to borrow a phrase used by Advocate General Warner in another context, runs like 'a golden thread woven into the fabric of all the decisions of the Court'.[35] Pescatore himself goes on to acknowledge

---

[29] p 13.   [30] Ibid.

[31] Pescatore, 'The Doctrine of "Direct Effect": An Infant Disease of Community Law' (1993) 8 ELRev 155, 177. Cf the remarks of AG Jacobs in Case C–316/93 *Vaneetveld* [1994] ECR I–763, 773–4.

[32] (1993) 8 ELRev 155, 157.

[33] See Weatherill and Beaumont, *EC Law* (2nd edn, 1995), p 182, n 142. See also Rasmussen, *On Law and Policy in the European Court of Justice* (1986), p 14.

[34] See p 12 of the judgment.   [35] See Case 24/75 *Petroni v ONPTS* [1975] ECR 1149, 1166.

that 'the Court did not disregard the technical aspect of the matter'[36] in examining the wording of Article 12. The result is a highly persuasive ruling, founded not just on the spirit of the Treaty taken as a whole, but also on the place of Article 12 in its general scheme and on the way in which that provision is phrased.

Some of the points made by the Court in support of its overall conclusion might admittedly be thought less compelling. The reference to Article 177 (now 234) is open to criticism on the basis that a national court might wish to ask the Court of Justice for a preliminary ruling even on provisions of Community law which are not directly effective. An example would be where the effect of a provision of national law depends on the validity and interpretation of Community law. Thus, the existence of Article 177, it might be argued, did not in itself imply that provisions of Community law were capable of producing direct effect.[37] Moreover, the Court failed to acknowledge the distinction drawn by Article 177 between the Treaty and acts of the institutions of the Community. The Treaty itself acknowledges expressly that one category of such acts, namely regulations, are capable of producing direct effect. The interpretation and validity of such an act might depend on the interpretation of the Treaty. It would therefore have been pointless to exclude the latter from the Court's jurisdiction under Article 177, but the fact that the Court may be asked for a preliminary ruling about a given provision by no means implies that that provision is capable of producing direct effect.

Criticism of this nature is not wholly convincing. The Court made it clear in its judgment in *Van Gend en Loos* that the purpose of the preliminary rulings procedure was to secure the uniform interpretation of the Treaty by national courts. But securing uniform interpretation is futile if the provision in question, properly construed, is not given the same effect throughout the Community. The very existence of Article 177 therefore implied that the effect of the Treaty was to be determined by Community law and not by national law. Once that point is established, it is not surprising that the Court should have avoided the lowest common denominator and preferred instead a route that was conducive to the effectiveness of the Treaty and to the proper functioning of the common market. As Pescatore later observed, '[t]he purpose of any legal rule . . . is to achieve some practical aim and it would be running counter to its essential purpose if one handled it in such a way as to render it practically meaningless. Effectiveness is the very soul of legal rules and therefore I think that it is not excessive to say that any legal rule must be at first sight presumed to be operative in view of its object and purpose.'[38] This point was later to receive greater emphasis in the case law and it is perhaps surprising that the Court did not stress it in *Van Gend en Loos*, since it would have

[36] (1993) 8 ELRev 155, 158. Weatherill and Beaumont, op cit, recognize that it is 'possible to construe the *Van Gend en Loos* decision as one that does have textual foundations'.

[37] See, in a slightly different context, Hartley, *The Foundations of European Community Law* (4th edn, 1998), p 201.

[38] Pescatore (1993) 8 ELRev 155, 177. Cf the same author's observations in Jacobs and Roberts (eds), op cit, ch 13.

provided a convincing additional justification for recognizing that provisions of the Treaty might produce direct effect.

The dismissal by the Court of the argument that, by providing special procedures for dealing with breaches of the Treaty by the Member States, Articles 169 (now 226) and 170 (now 227) implied that such breaches could not be raised before the national courts, provides an early example of the Court's determination to give the interests of the Community priority over those of the Member States. It is true that the concept of direct effect has enabled the Court to refrain from developing its powers under Article 226 as vigorously as it might otherwise have been tempted to do. Be that as it may, it is now abundantly clear that, while Article 226 has a useful role to play in policing the application of the Treaty, it would be wholly inadequate to ensure full compliance by the Member States with their Treaty obligations. As for Article 227, it has fallen into almost complete disuse, only one case ever having proceeded to judgment under that provision.[39] It is striking to note, however, that the Court's judgment contains no reference to the procedural guarantees which Articles 226 and 227 offer to Member States who are alleged to have infringed the Treaty, even though the point was specifically raised by the Netherlands Government.[40] The procedure under Article 234 (ex 177) offers Member States far fewer opportunities to defend themselves against an allegation that they have infringed the Treaty.[41] Indeed, in *Foglia v Novello*,[42] the French Government argued that where the compatibility with the Treaty of the law of one Member State is challenged before the courts of another Member State, the rights of defence of the first State were liable to be infringed. That argument appeared to influence the Court in confirming its decision in the first *Foglia* case[43] that it had no jurisdiction to give a ruling on the questions which had been referred to it. The facts of *Van Gend en Loos* were of course different: the relevant Netherlands legislation was being challenged before a Dutch court and the respondent was a public authority, which had ample opportunity to defend its point of view in the domestic proceedings. But where the Member State concerned is not a party to the main action or, as in *Foglia*, the legislation of one Member State is challenged before a court situated in another Member State, the concept of direct effect considerably diminishes the rights of defence of the State whose legislation is in issue. The Court's failure to address this question in its judgment in *Van Gend en Loos* offered the Member States a salutary lesson in the importance it attached to their rights.

---

[39] Case 141/78 *France v United Kingdom* [1979] ECR 2923.   [40] See [1963] ECR 1, 9.
[41] See Art 20, EC Statute.   [42] Case 244/80 [1981] ECR 3045, 3056.
[43] Case 104/79 *Foglia v Novello* [1980] ECR 745.

The direct effect of positive provisions of the Treaty

The negative character of Article 12 (now after amendment Article 25) meant that the Court in *Van Gend en Loos* did not have to ask the national judge to take any coercive measures to ensure that the Netherlands authorities complied with their obligations under the Treaty: the judge was simply asked to deprive of legal effect a provision which was inconsistent with the Treaty. As Hamson explained, all that needed to be done was:

to direct the national court to deal with the matter *as if* the increase [in duty] had not been made . . . At so small a cost the Court will exemplify its power and authority; it will vindicate and enforce the law of the Community; it will enlist to promote that law the energies of individuals in claiming their rights; and it will notably encourage those who are labouring to establish the Community in spite of the recalcitrance and backslidings of some of its component parts. What looks like heroism has evidently a powerful attraction for some types of judicial temperament; and there may be some excuse for a Court's desire to strike a spectacular attitude, especially if the cost appears to be small.[44]

The Court's judgment was, however, carefully worded: it did not say that *because* Article 12 was couched in negative terms it *therefore* had direct effect, but simply that its negative character was one of a number of features which made it 'ideally adapted to produce direct effects . . .'. This more nuanced formulation left open the possibility that Treaty provisions of a positive nature might also have direct effect, although it might admittedly be more difficult to establish.

The implication that positive provisions of the Treaty were in principle capable of producing direct effect was reinforced in *Lütticke v Hauptzollamt Saarlouis*,[45] where the Finanzgericht des Saarlandes asked the Court for a preliminary ruling on the extent to which Article 95 EEC[46] produced direct effect. According to that provision:

No Member State shall impose, directly or indirectly, on the products of other Member States any internal taxation of any kind in excess of that imposed directly or indirectly on similar domestic products.

Furthermore, no Member State shall impose on the products of other Member States any internal taxation of such a nature as to afford indirect protection to other products.

Member States shall, not later than at the beginning of the second stage, repeal or amend any provisions existing when this Treaty enters into force which conflict with the preceding rules.

Thus, the first two paragraphs of Article 95 prevented the Member States forthwith from introducing legislation which contravened the rules contained in those

---

[44] 'Methods of Interpretation—A Critical Assessment of the Results' in *Reports of a Judicial and Academic Conference held in Luxembourg on 27–28 September 1976*, II-3, II-18 (emphasis in the original).
[45] Case 57/65 [1966] ECR 205.　　　　　　　　　　　　　　　[46] See now Art 90 EC.

paragraphs. The third paragraph (now repealed) allowed them until 1 January 1962 to bring into line with the first two paragraphs national legislation already on the statute book when the Treaty entered into force. Article 95 therefore differed from Article 12 in one potentially relevant respect: it imposed a positive obligation on the Member States to act and, by doing so, might have appeared to make the abolition of discriminatory internal taxation dependent on the adoption of appropriate legislation by the national authorities. To have concluded that the article, said by the Court to constitute 'in fiscal matters the indispensable foundation of the Common Market',[47] was not capable of producing direct effect would have seriously reduced its effectiveness. The Court observed that, leaving the third paragraph aside, the clear and unconditional obligation imposed on Member States by the first paragraph was 'complete, legally perfect and consequently capable of producing direct effects on the legal relationships between the Member States and persons within their jurisdiction'.[48] The fact that the article was addressed to the Member States 'does not imply that individuals cannot benefit from it'.[49] The third paragraph simply allowed Member States a period of grace within which to adapt existing national provisions in accordance with the first two paragraphs. Once the second stage of the transitional period came to an end, 'the general rule emerges unconditionally into full force'.[50]

The Court's decision in *Lütticke* caused consternation in Germany and in *Molkerei-Zentrale Westfalen v Hauptzollamt Paderborn*[51] it was asked by the Bundesfinanzhof to reconsider it. The Bundesfinanzhof claimed[52] that to grant individuals a direct remedy before the national courts in the event of an infringement of the Treaty, instead of simply the right to ask the Member State concerned to put an end to the infringement, gave them wider rights than those accorded under Article 169 (now 226) to the Commission. Moreover, the *Lütticke* case was difficult to reconcile with the position of the courts under the German Constitution, according to which it was not their task to compensate for the failure of the competent authorities to adopt the necessary legislation by giving thousands of separate decisions in individual cases. Such decisions would often turn on questions of fact, which the appellate courts would be unable to harmonize.[53] The large number of applications which had already been made to the Finanzgerichte as a result of the ruling in *Lütticke* had therefore given rise to great uncertainty as to the enforceability of German legislation which was allegedly inconsistent with Article 95.

The Court was adamant: there was no parallel between the right of individuals to rely on Community law in the national courts and the powers conferred by the Treaty on the Commission to ensure observance by the Member States with their obligations, since the two had 'different objects, aims and effects':

[47] At p 210.	[48] p 210.	[49] Ibid.	[50] Ibid.
[51] Case 28/67 [1968] ECR 143. See Lecourt, op cit, pp 53–4.
[52] See the Opinion of AG Gand at pp 159–60.
[53] Cf the Sunday trading cases in relation to Art 30 EC, discussed in ch 7.

Every time a rule of Community law confers rights on individuals, those rights, without prejudice to the methods of recourse made available by the Treaty, may be safeguarded by proceedings brought before the competent national courts. Such actions are different from the exercise of the powers conferred on the Community authorities under the Treaty . . . In fact proceedings by an individual are intended to protect individual rights in a specific case, whilst intervention by the Community authorities has as its object the general and uniform observance of Community law'

This conclusion was not affected by the complexity of the position in a particular Member State.

The horizontal direct effect of Treaty provisions

One issue which the Court had not hitherto been called upon to address was whether the Treaty could only be invoked in the national courts in proceedings against a public authority or whether it might also be relied on in national proceedings against a private party. The adjectives 'vertical' and 'horizontal' respectively are sometimes used to describe these two species of direct effect.[54] As we shall see in the next chapter, the distinction assumes particular importance in relation to the extent to which Community legislation in the form of directives is capable of producing direct effect.

The question whether provisions of the Treaty are capable of producing horizontal direct effect was first addressed by the Court in *BRT v SABAM*,[55] a competition case in which the Court considered the effect of Articles 85(1) (now 81(1)) and 86 (now 82) of the Treaty. Basically, these prohibit agreements which distort competition and the abuse of a dominant position respectively, provided trade between Member States is liable to be affected. The Court observed that, because Articles 85(1) and 86 tended 'by their very nature to produce direct effects in relations between individuals, these Articles create direct rights in respect of the individuals concerned which the national courts must safeguard'.[56] Although this was a significant conclusion, it was not surprising. The articles in question were evidently intended to regulate relations between private parties. If they were to have direct effect at all, which Advocate General Roemer in *Van Gend en Loos* appears to have accepted,[57] it had to be in the horizontal sense.

---

[54] These terms derive from a view of the State as a hierarchy, with public bodies on one level and private bodies and individuals on another, lower, level. Where a plaintiff seeks to rely on a rule of Community law against a defendant on another level of the hierarchy, he is said to do so in a vertical direction; when he seeks to do so against someone on the same level of the hierarchy as himself, he is said to do so in a horizontal direction.

[55] Case 127/73 [1974] ECR 51.   [56] Para 16.

[57] See [1963] ECR 1, 20–1. Even this was too much for Professor Hamson: see 'Methods of Interpretation—A Critical Assessment of the Results' in *Reports of a Judicial and Academic Conference held in Luxembourg on 27–28 September 1976*, II-3, II-17.

The Court has, however, reached the same conclusion in relation to other provi-
sions of the Treaty which, although concerned primarily with the actions of Member
States, may find their objectives thwarted by the behaviour of private parties.
Examples are the Treaty provisions on the free movement of persons, the effective-
ness of which may be prejudiced both by measures taken at the level of the Member
States and by measures taken by private bodies. This was recognized in *Walrave v
Union Cycliste Internationale*,[58] in which the Court was asked for a preliminary ruling
in the context of a dispute over the legality under Community law of a rule con-
cerning motor-paced bicycle racing[59] championships, laid down by the Union
Cycliste Internationale, a private body based in Geneva. The Court stated that
Articles 48 (now 39) and 59 (now 49) of the Treaty, concerning the free movement
of workers and the right to provide services respectively, gave effect to the general
Treaty prohibition against discrimination on grounds of nationality. That prohibition was not confined to the activities of public authorities, but extended 'to rules of
any other nature aimed at regulating in a collective manner gainful employment and
the provision of services'.[60] Achieving freedom of movement for persons was one of
the fundamental objectives of the Treaty, yet it would be compromised if the relevant provisions did not apply to the activities of private bodies. The Court added that,
since working conditions were sometimes governed by legislation and sometimes by
agreement between private persons, 'to limit the prohibitions in question to acts of
a public authority would risk creating inequality in their application'.[61]

The decision in *Walrave* represented a significant extension of the Court's case
law on direct effect. Although Articles 81(1) (ex 85(1)) and 82 (ex 86) were evidently intended to regulate the rights of natural and legal persons between themselves, Articles 39 (ex 48) and 49 (ex 59), while not expressly addressed to the
Member States, are concerned principally with the actions of public authorities.[62]
It was, however, clear that the purpose of those provisions would only partly have
been achieved had obstacles to freedom of movement resulting from the activities
of private bodies been held to fall outside their scope. A further consequence, as
the Court acknowledged in *Walrave*, would have been to jeopardize the uniform
application of the Treaty throughout the Community, since its impact would have
been diminished in Member States which chose to allow matters falling within the
scope of the provisions concerned to be regulated by private bodies. The Court
rightly considered such distinctions unacceptable: they prevent the common mar-

---

[58] Case 36/74 [1974] ECR 1405.
[59] For the uninitiated, an explanation of this sport was provided by AG Warner at p 1422.
[60] Para 17.
[61] Para 19. See also Case 13/76 *Donà v Mantero* [1976] ECR 1333; Case C–415/93 *URBSFA and
Others v Bosman and Others* [1995] ECR I–4921. These cases are discussed in more detail in ch 8.
[62] Cf Art 28 (ex 30), which prohibits quantitative restrictions on imports and measures having equivalent effect between Member States and which is generally thought not to have horizontal direct effect.
The reason is not that its legal status renders it incapable of producing such effect, but that as a matter
of substance it applies only to measures taken by Member States. For a brief discussion, see Oliver, *Free
Movement of Goods in the European Community* (3rd edn, 1996), pp 56–60; Jarvis, *The Application of EC
Law by National Courts* (1998), pp 24–5. Art 28 is discussed in ch 7.

ket from functioning properly and allow Member States to deprive individuals of rights which the authors of the Treaty intended them to enjoy and which they do in fact enjoy in other parts of the Community. The point seems self-evident, but, as we shall see in the next chapter, the Court has been prepared to tolerate a distinction of this nature in the case of directives.

The fact that Articles 48 (now 39) and 59 (now 49) of the Treaty simply stated an objective without specifying at whom they were aimed left open the possibility that provisions of the Treaty addressed specifically to the Member States might not be capable of producing horizontal direct effect. Where a provision produces such effect, the result is to impose obligations on individuals. The issue therefore ceases to be one simply of enhancing the effectiveness of the provision in question. In cases where an attempt is made to establish that a provision has vertical direct effect, there may be no doubt that the provision concerned is binding on the State. The question is simply one of the mechanism by which it can be enforced. Where the question is whether a provision produces horizontal direct effect, a different issue is raised: is it fair to subject individuals to obligations which appear to be binding only on the State? This is an issue which will be pursued when the extent to which directives may produce direct effect is considered. In the present context, it is sufficient to note that the fact that a Treaty provision is addressed to the Member States does not prevent it from producing horizontal direct effect. This was established in *Defrenne v SABENA*,[63] a case on Article 119 of the Treaty (now after amendment Article 141). In its original form, the first paragraph of Article 119 provided: 'Each Member State shall during the first stage ensure and subsequently maintain the application of the principle that men and women should receive equal pay for equal work.' In *Defrenne*, the Court held that the article applied not only to the conduct of public authorities but also to contracts between individuals. The Court's contribution to the development of the Community rules on equal treatment for men and women is discussed in more detail in chapter 13.

Treaty provisions not producing direct effect

There are several provisions of the Treaty which have been found by the Court to be incapable of producing direct effect. The reason may be that the provision in question is insufficiently precise or that it depends on the adoption of implementing legislation, either by the Member States or the Community institutions. The Court has also declined to extend its case law on direct effect to the provisions of the ECSC Treaty.

In *Molkerei-Zentrale*,[64] the Court acknowledged that Article 97 of the Treaty (now repealed)[65] was not capable of producing direct effect. That article provided:

---

[63] Case 43/75 [1976] ECR 455.   [64] *Supra.*

[65] Art 97 ceased to be relevant after the Council began the process of harmonizing the national legislation on turnover taxes. See Farmer and Lyal, *EC Tax Law* (1994), pp 79–81.

Member States which levy a turnover tax calculated on a cumulative multi-stage tax system may, in the case of internal taxation imposed by them on imported products or of repayments allowed by them on exported products, establish average rates for products or groups of products, provided that there is no infringement of the principles laid down in Articles 95 and 96.

Where the average rates established by a Member State do not conform to these principles, the Commission shall address appropriate directives or decisions to the State concerned.

There were three reasons why, in the Court's view, that provision was incapable of creating individual rights which could be invoked in the national courts. In the first place, it gave the Member States a discretion which they were free not to make use of. Secondly, where they did decide to make use of it, it was up to them to fix average rates and suitable groups of products. Finally, the second paragraph of the article established a specific remedy, involving the intervention of the Commission, where a Member State fixed average rates which did not conform to the principles laid down in Article 95 (now 90). It followed that, where a Member State which levied a turnover tax based on the cumulative multi-stage tax system had exercised the powers available to it under Article 97, the direct effect of Article 95 had certain limits. Although the national courts had jurisdiction to decide in particular cases whether they were dealing with an average rate for the purposes of Article 97 or internal taxation for the purposes of Article 95, they had no jurisdiction to assess the compatibility of such an average rate with the principles laid down in Article 95. That question fell within the exclusive jurisdiction of the Commission.[66]

In *Casati*,[67] the Court held that the pre-Maastricht Treaty rules on the free movement of capital did not have direct effect since they were not suitable for judicial application in the absence of implementing legislation. According to the first paragraph of Article 67 EEC (now repealed): 'During the transitional period and to the extent necessary to ensure the proper functioning of the common market, Member States shall progressively abolish between themselves all restrictions on the movement of capital belonging to persons resident in Member States and any discrimination based on the nationality or on the place of residence of the parties or on the place where such capital is invested.' Article 69 EEC (also repealed) gave the Council power to 'issue the necessary directives for the progressive implementation of the provisions of Article 67 . . .'. In *Casati*, the Court was asked to rule on the effect of these provisions after the expiry of the transitional period in the context of the prosecution of an individual for exporting banknotes without the requisite authorization. The Council not having taken any steps to liberalize the exportation of banknotes, the Court concluded 'that the obligation contained in Article 67(1) to abolish restrictions on movements of capital cannot be defined, in relation to a specific category of such movements, in isolation from the Council's

---

[66] Cf Case 13/68 *Salgoil v Italy* [1968] ECR 453.   [67] Case 203/80 [1981] ECR 2595.

assessment under Article 69 of the need to liberalize that category in order to ensure the proper functioning of the Common Market'.[68]

The Court has also acknowledged that many of the opening articles of the Treaty are insufficiently precise to produce direct effect.[69] Thus, Article 2 of the Treaty, which sets out the tasks of the Community, does not impose legal obligations on the Member States or confer rights on individuals 'owing to its general terms and its systematic dependence on the establishment of the common market and progressive approximation of economic policies'.[70] The same is true of Article 10 (ex 5), an important provision which states that:

Member States shall take all appropriate measures, whether general or particular, to ensure fulfilment of the obligations arising out of this Treaty or resulting from action taken by the institutions of the Community. They shall facilitate the achievement of the Community's tasks.

They shall abstain from any measure which could jeopardise the attainment of the objectives of this Treaty.

Article 10 may produce significant results when taken in conjunction with other provisions of the Treaty. In *Hurd v Jones*,[71] for example, the Court held that it imposed on the Member States an obligation to refrain from any unilateral measure that would interfere with the system of financing the Community and of apportioning financial burdens between the Member States. It therefore prevented the Member States from imposing domestic taxes on the salaries paid by the European Schools to their teachers where the burden was borne ultimately by the Community budget. None the less, the Court held that Article 5 (now 10) did not produce direct effect in these circumstances, since 'the substance of that obligation is not sufficiently precise'.[72] It was, the Court said, for each Member State to decide how to ensure that the way it taxed teachers at the European Schools did not prejudice the system by which the Community was financed.

While the question of the direct effect of provisions of the EC Treaty arose relatively soon after that Treaty had entered into force, the question whether provisions of the ECSC Treaty might also produce direct effect was not considered in any detail by the Court until the Coal and Steel Community had entered the fifth decade of its existence. The explanation for this lies partly in the limited scope of the ECSC Treaty, which has meant that it has produced far fewer cases than the EC Treaty, and partly in the extensive implementing powers conferred on the Commission, which have meant that the status of the Treaty in the national courts of the Member States has been less controversial.

[68] Para 12.
[69] An exception is Art 12 (ex 6), which prohibits discrimination on the grounds of nationality within the scope of application of the Treaty and which has been held to be directly effective: see Joined Cases C–92/92 and C–326/92 *Collins and Others* [1993] ECR I–5145. Art 12 is discussed in ch 11.
[70] Case 126/86 *Giménez Zaera v Instituto Nacional de la Seguridad Social y Tesorería General de la Seguridad Social* [1987] ECR 3697, para 11.
[71] Case 44/84 [1986] ECR 29, paras 47–8. See further ch 16.   [72] Para 48 of the judgment.

In *Banks*,[73] however, the English Commercial Court asked whether various provisions of the ECSC Treaty, including the competition rules it lays down, had direct effect. Advocate General van Gerven took as his starting point 'the *unity of the Community legal order*',[74] as a result of which he said the Court had always striven to achieve the greatest possible coherence between the EC Treaty and the ECSC Treaty. The features of the former which in *Van Gend en Loos* the Court had regarded as crucial for direct effect were shared by the latter. The differences between the schemes of the two Treaties were of marginal importance by comparison. While it was true that the ECSC Treaty only provided for partial integration, limited to the coal and steel sectors, and that the Commission played a far more prominent role than under the EC Treaty, none the less many provisions of the former Treaty were more detailed than those of the latter. Moreover, unlike most of the provisions of the EC Treaty, many of the rules laid down in the ECSC Treaty were addressed specifically to undertakings: 'In that sense, many provisions of the ECSC Treaty are even better suited to (horizontal) direct effect than those of the EEC Treaty . . .'.[75] The Advocate General concluded that, in determining whether a provision of the ECSC Treaty had direct effect, the same criteria were to be applied as under the EC Treaty. The test was an 'eminently practical' one:

provided and in so far as a provision of Community law is *sufficiently operational* in itself to be applied by a court, it has direct effect. The clarity, precision, unconditional nature, completeness or perfection of the rule and its lack of dependence on discretionary implementing measures are in that respect merely one and the same characteristic feature which that rule must exhibit, namely it must be capable of being applied by a court to a specific case.[76]

The Advocate General concluded that Article 4 of the ECSC Treaty, which prohibits various measures and practices as incompatible with the common market for coal and steel, and the competition rules laid down in Articles 65(1) and 66(7) of that Treaty had direct effect.

Rather strikingly, the Court declined to follow the Opinion of Mr van Gerven. As far as Article 4 of the ECSC Treaty was concerned, the Court noted that it applied by itself only in the absence of more specific rules. Where in a particular case other such rules were applicable, Article 4 could not have direct effect. With regard to Article 65, the Court noted that, by virtue of the second subparagraph of Article 65(4), the Commission had sole jurisdiction, subject to review by the CFI and the Court of Justice, to rule on whether an agreement was compatible with the article. In the Court's view, it followed that 'as long as such incompatibility has not been established by the Commission itself, individuals may not plead, in proceedings before the national courts, that an agreement is incompatible with Article 65'.[77] The Court came to the same conclusion in respect of Article 66(7), which reserves to the Commission the power to find that a dominant position is being used for purposes contrary to the Treaty. The Court concluded: 'The conferral of

---

[73] Case C–128/92 [1994] ECR I–1209.   [74] p I–1233, emphasis in the original.
[75] p I–1236.   [76] p I–1237, emphasis in the original.   [77] Para 17.

sole jurisdiction on the Commission precludes individuals from relying directly on that provision in proceedings before the national courts.'[78]

Although consistent with the text of the relevant provisions, the line taken by the Court was surprising for a number of reasons. In the context of the competition rules applicable to undertakings laid down in the EC Treaty,[79] the Commission's policy is to encourage their enforcement at the national level so that it can concentrate its limited resources on cases 'having particular political, economic or legal significance for the Community'.[80] The Commission had been encouraged to adopt such a policy by both the CFI[81] and by the Court of Justice.[82] Given the Court's emphasis in other contexts on the unity of the Community legal order,[83] it is curious that the Court should have preferred an outcome which leaves the Commission with sole responsibility for enforcing the competition rules of the ECSC Treaty. By exacerbating the administrative burden imposed on the Commission, the effectiveness of those rules is thereby diminished. To paraphrase the language of the Court itself in *Van Gend en Loos*, the vigilance of individuals concerned to protect their rights would have amounted to an effective supervision in addition to the supervision entrusted to the diligence of the Commission.[84]

The Court's decision in *Banks* therefore serves to underline the difference between the EC Treaty and the ECSC Treaty and the central role conferred on the Commission by the latter. The Court may have felt that, given the limited scope and life expectancy of the ECSC Treaty,[85] it was not worth opening a potential Pandora's box by holding its competition rules to be directly effective. Indeed, the fact that the question had not previously been resolved by the Court suggests that the practical importance of the case is limited. None the less, the decision may reflect an unwillingness on the part of the Court to extend the boundaries of the doctrine of direct effect in the post-Maastricht era. This is an issue to which we return in chapter 16.

The doctrine of primacy

It will be apparent from what has been said so far that it is a corollary of the doctrine of direct effect that provisions which enjoy that quality should take precedence over inconsistent provisions of national law. There would be little point in saying that a rule of Community law conferred rights on individuals which national courts were bound to uphold if those rights could be overridden by a contrary rule

---

[78] Para 18.   [79] See ch 12.
[80] See the Commission notice on co-operation between national courts and the Commission in applying Articles 85 and 86 of the EEC Treaty, para 14, OJ 1993 C39/6.
[81] See Case T–24/90 *Automec v Commission* [1992] ECR II–2223.
[82] See Case C–234/89 *Delimitis v Henninger Bräu* [1991] ECR I–935.
[83] See AG van Gerven's Opinion in *Banks* at pp I–1233–4.   [84] Cf [1963] ECR 1, 13.
[85] The ECSC Treaty was concluded for a period of fifty years: see Art 97. By contrast, the EC Treaty was concluded for an unlimited period: see Art 312 (ex 240).

of national law. This aspect of the relationship between Community law and the national laws of the Member States did not need to be addressed by the Court in *Van Gend en Loos* for a very simple reason. As Advocate General Roemer explained,[86] the Netherlands Constitution gave international agreements precedence over national law if they were directly effective. Thus, if the referring court were told that the contested provision of the EEC Treaty conferred rights directly on individuals, that provision would, by virtue of the Netherlands Constitution, automatically take precedence over incompatible rules of national law. It was not therefore necessary for the referring court to raise the issue of precedence expressly or for the Court of Justice to deal with it in its ruling.

The Court did not have to wait long for the issue to be raised directly. In *Costa v ENEL*,[87] the Giudice Conciliatore of Milan referred to the Court a question on the compatibility with various provisions of the EEC Treaty of a Law nationalizing the Italian electricity industry. The question had arisen in the course of a dispute between ENEL, the nationalized electricity company, and a lawyer who had refused to pay a bill for the paltry sum of 1925 lire relating to the supply to him of electricity by ENEL. The amount involved was in inverse proportion to the importance of the issues raised by the case. The Court reiterated its finding in *Van Gend en Loos* that the EEC Treaty had created its own legal system which had become an integral part of the legal systems of the Member States, binding on both those States and on their nationals and which the national courts were bound to apply. It continued:

The integration into the laws of each Member State of provisions which derive from the Community, and more generally the terms and the spirit of the Treaty, make it impossible for the States, as a corollary, to accord precedence to a unilateral and subsequent measure over a legal system accepted by them on a basis of reciprocity. Such a measure cannot therefore be inconsistent with that legal system. The executive force of Community law cannot vary from one State to another in deference to subsequent domestic laws, without jeopardizing the attainment of the objectives of the Treaty set out in Article 5(2) [now 10(2)] and giving rise to the discrimination prohibited by Article 7 [now 12].[88]

The Court noted that, when the Treaty gave the Member States the right to act unilaterally, it did so clearly and precisely. It also pointed out that the Treaty contained a number of provisions which established special authorization procedures for Member States wishing to derogate from the Treaty. Those provisions would, the Court said, be pointless if Member States could avoid their obligations by means of ordinary legislation. Article 189 (now 249), according to which regulations were binding and directly applicable in all Member States, would in the Court's view have been 'quite meaningless if a State could unilaterally nullify its

---

[86] [1963] ECR 1, 20. See also Claes and de Witte, 'Report on the Netherlands' in Slaughter, Stone and Weiler (eds), *The European Court and National Courts—Doctrine and Jurisprudence* (1998), ch 6, p 180.

[87] Case 6/64 [1964] ECR 585.

[88] That is, discrimination on the grounds of nationality. See pp 593–4.

effects by means of a legislative measure which could prevail over Community law'. The Court declared:[89]

It follows from all these observations that the law stemming from the Treaty, an independent source of law, could not, because of its special and original nature, be overridden by domestic legal provisions, however framed, without being deprived of its character as Community law and without the legal basis of the Community itself being called into question.

The transfer by the States from their domestic legal system to the Community legal system of the rights and obligations arising under the Treaty carries with it a permanent limitation of their sovereign rights, against which a subsequent unilateral act incompatible with the concept of the Community cannot prevail. Consequently Article 177 [now 234] is to be applied regardless of any domestic law, whenever questions relating to the interpretation of the Treaty arise.

The Court went on to consider the effect of the provisions of the Treaty mentioned in the Order for Reference.

Rasmussen has referred to *Costa v ENEL* and its progeny as 'cases in which the Court probably pushed its gap-filling activities beyond the proper scope of judicial involvement in society's law and policy making'.[90] That criticism is, in the present writer's view, misplaced. The absence in the Treaty of a provision clearly stating that provisions of Community law were to take precedence over inconsistent provisions of national law should not be taken to imply a consensus among the signatories to the Treaty that this result was not intended. There are various reasons why the authors of the Treaty may have decided not to incorporate the doctrine of primacy expressly. It may have been thought politically unwise to embody such a doctrine explicitly at the outset. It may not have been possible to reach agreement over the wording of an appropriate provision. The six may simply have been divided on whether Community law was to take precedence at all. From this perspective, the absence of a provision saying that it was *not* to have this effect is at least as significant as the absence of a provision saying that it was. It seems probable that the issue was deliberately left obscure, which implies an acceptance that it would eventually have to be resolved by the Court of Justice. Against that background, there can be little dispute that the solution preferred by the Court in *Costa v ENEL* was the only one which was consistent with the scheme of the Treaty.

Costa v ENEL concerned the compatibility with the EEC Treaty of a Law adopted after the entry into force of the Treaty and of a number of presidential decrees issued to give effect to the Law. The Court's reasoning was, however, much broader in scope, implying that Community law would take precedence regardless of the constitutional status under national law of the conflicting domestic norm and regardless of the date on which that norm was adopted, whether before or after the entry into force of the Treaty. That implication was confirmed in *Internationale Handelsgesellschaft v Einfuhr- und Vorratsstelle Getreide*.[91] In that case,

[89] [1964] ECR 585, 594.   [90] Op cit, p 28.   [91] Case 11/70 [1970] ECR 1125.

the Verwaltungsgericht Frankfurt am Main referred to the Court two questions on the validity of a system of export licences and deposits established by a Council regulation on the common organization of the market in cereals and a Commission regulation on import and export licences. The referring court took the view that the contested measures were incompatible with certain fundamental principles contained in the German Constitution which had to be protected within the framework of the Community.

There were three potentially significant differences between *Costa v ENEL* and *Internationale Handelsgesellschaft*. In the latter case, the national provisions in dispute were adopted before the entry into force of the Treaty. Moreover, they had constitutional status. By contrast, the rules of Community law at issue were contained, not in the Treaty itself, but in acts of the Community institutions. None of these factors deterred the Court from ruling that:

Recourse to the legal rules or concepts of national law in order to judge the validity of measures adopted by the institutions of the Community would have an adverse effect on the uniformity and efficacy of Community law. The validity of such measures can only be judged in the light of Community law . . . Therefore the validity of a Community measure or its effect within a Member State cannot be affected by allegations that it runs counter to either fundamental rights as formulated by the constitution of that State or the principles of a national constitutional structure.[92]

Conscious of the momentous nature of that conclusion, the Court went on to acknowledge that 'respect for fundamental rights forms an integral part of the general principles of law protected by the Court of Justice. The protection of such rights, whilst inspired by the constitutional traditions common to the Member States, must be ensured within the framework of the structure and objectives of the Community.'[93] It concluded that the contested provisions did not infringe the Community principle of respect for fundamental rights.

The Court's approach in the *Internationale* case was highly creative. To have accepted that the validity of provisions of Community law could be tested against rules of national law, even those of constitutional status, would have been wholly incompatible with the fundamental principles of the Community legal order which the Court had endeavoured to develop. None the less, the absence in the Treaty of a catalogue of fundamental rights gave rise to a serious risk that national courts which were accustomed to according protection to such rights would simply disregard Community provisions which they considered incompatible with fundamental principles of the domestic legal order. The Court's development of the general principles of Community law, unwritten norms derived from national law and international agreements on which the Member States have collaborated, to ensure protection for fundamental rights within the Community legal order offered a way of reconciling the need to guarantee such protection with the doctrine of

---

[92] [1970] ECR 1125, 1134.   [93] Ibid.

primacy.[94] However, as we shall see, the German courts were initially unpersuaded of the merits of the Court's approach.

The difficulties which can arise where jurisdiction under national law to rule on the constitutionality of a domestic provision belongs to a body other than the referring court were highlighted in *Amministrazione delle Finanze dello Stato v Simmenthal*,[95] a case referred by the Pretore di Susa, Italy. The parties to the main action were in dispute over the compatibility with the EEC Treaty and certain regulations of veterinary and public health fees levied under Italian law on imports of beef and veal. Following a previous ruling by the Court of Justice,[96] the Pretore held that Community law precluded the levying of the disputed fees and ordered the Italian Finance Administration to repay them with interest. The Administration objected on the basis that the Pretore could not simply refuse to apply a national law which he considered to be in conflict with Community law. Until the law in question was amended, the matter had to be brought before the Italian Constitutional Court, which alone had the power to declare the disputed law unconstitutional. Before the Court of Justice could give judgment, the Italian Constitutional Court ruled that some of the provisions of the contested Italian law, including those at issue before the Pretore di Susa, were indeed unconstitutional. The Italian Government, anxious to avoid what might be an inconvenient precedent, therefore sought to persuade the Court that there was no longer any need to answer the questions which had been referred to it. The Court refused to be diverted, simply reiterating its by now well established case law to the effect that a reference under Article 177 (now 234) would be allowed to proceed as long as it had not been withdrawn by the court which made it or quashed on appeal by a superior court.

On the substance of the question which had been put to it, the Court took the opportunity to clarify the emerging doctrine of primacy. The effect of that doctrine, it said, was to 'render automatically inapplicable' provisions of national law which conflicted with provisions of the Treaty and directly effective provisions of Community legislation. Moreover, the doctrine precluded 'the valid adoption of new national legislative measures to the extent to which they would be incompatible with Community provisions'.[97] The Court made it clear that any national measures 'which encroach upon the field within which the Community exercises its legislative power or which are otherwise incompatible with the provisions of Community law' could not be allowed 'any legal effect'.[98] The Court concluded:

. . . a national court which is called upon, within the limits of its jurisdiction, to apply provisions of Community law is under a duty to give full effect to those provisions, if necessary refusing of its own motion to apply any conflicting provision of national legislation, even if

[94] The general principles of Community law and the Court's approach to fundamental rights are considered in more detail in ch 6.
[95] Case 106/77 [1978] ECR 629.
[96] Case 35/76 *Simmenthal v Italian Minister for Finance* [1976] ECR 1871.   [97] Para 17.
[98] Para 18.

adopted subsequently, and it is not necessary for the court to request or await the prior setting aside of such provision by legislative or other constitutional means.[99]

The Court's decision in *Simmenthal* provoked a flurry of comment in the correspondence columns of *The Times*,[100] but the judgment would have come as no surprise to anyone who had been following the Court's case law. It would obviously
have been incompatible with the binding force of directly effective provisions of
Community law for a national court before which such provisions were invoked
to be deprived of jurisdiction to apply them. It is true that in some parts of its judgment the Court referred to the national court's duty to 'set aside' national provisions which conflicted with a rule of Community law.[101] However, the French
text of the judgment[102] made it clear that the Court did not mean to imply that the
national court was expected to quash the inconsistent national provisions. The
operative part of the judgment, quoted above, confirms that the national court
must simply decline to give effect to the inconsistent national rule in the case pending before it. The existence of the incompatibility does not of itself render the
offending provision of national law void.[103] However, to maintain in force national
rules which are incompatible with provisions of Community law constitutes a
breach by the State concerned of its obligations under the Treaty.

The response of the national courts

It would be hard to exaggerate the importance of the doctrines of direct effect and
primacy for the proper functioning of the common market, yet their practical
application depends to a large extent on the goodwill of the national courts.[104]
Their response to the case law of the Court of Justice has not been entirely
positive.[105]

In some Member States, the judges have done their best to comply with the
principles laid down by the Court. An example is the United Kingdom, where, in
the absence of a written constitution, the legislature sought to give effect to the
requirements of Community law by passing the European Communities Act 1972.
That Act was clearly effective to give Community law precedence over earlier legislation, but if it was to satisfy the requirements laid down by the Court it would

[99] Para 24 and the operative part of the judgment.
[100] Sparked off by a letter from Professor P S Atiyah published on 18 April 1978.
[101] See paras 21 and 22.
[102] Which spoke of the national judge '. . . laissant inappliquée toute disposition éventuellement con-
traire de la loi nationale . . .'.
[103] See Joined Cases C–10/97 to C–22/97 *Ministero delle Finanze v IN.CO.GE.'90 and Others*, judgment of 22 October 1998.
[104] See Weiler, 'The Community system: the dual character of supranationalism' (1981) 1 YEL 267,
275–6.
[105] See generally Slaughter, Sweet and Weiler (eds), op cit; de Witte, 'Direct effect, supremacy and
the nature of the legal order' in Craig and de Búrca (eds), *The Evolution of EU Law* (1999), ch 5; Craig
and de Búrca, *EU Law* (2nd edn, 1998), pp 264–95; Hartley, op cit, ch 8.

also have to give Community law precedence over later legislation. Doubts about whether, in the light of the traditional doctrine of the sovereignty of Parliament, it was capable of having that effect were not entirely shared by the courts. In *Macarthys Ltd v Smith*,[106] the Court of Appeal was asked to consider whether the Equal Pay Act 1970, as amended by the Sex Discrimination Act 1975, was compatible with Article 119 EEC[107] on equal pay for men and women. After a reference had been made to the Court of Justice,[108] Lord Denning (with whom Lawton and Cumming-Bruce LJJ agreed) declared:[109]

It is important now to declare—and it must be made plain—that the provisions of Article 119 of the Treaty of Rome take priority over anything in our English statute on equal pay which is inconsistent with Article 119. That priority is given by our own law. It is given by the European Communities Act 1972 itself. Community law is now part of our law: and, whenever there is any inconsistency, Community law has priority. It is not supplanting English law. It is part of our law which overrides any other part which is inconsistent with it.

Lord Denning did not feel the need to explain why the 1972 Act should not be regarded as *pro tanto* repealed to the extent that any subsequent Act introduced provisions which were incompatible with Community law. Lord Bridge was slightly more forthcoming in *R v Secretary of State for Transport, ex p Factortame*, which concerned the compatibility with Community law of provisions on the registration of British vessels contained in Part II of the Merchant Shipping Act 1988. His Lordship explained[110] that the European Communities Act 'has precisely the same effect as if a section were incorporated in Part II of the Act of 1988 which in terms enacted that the provisions with respect to registration of British vessels were to be without prejudice to the directly enforceable Community rights of nationals of any Member State of the EEC'. This approach seems to be of some constitutional significance, for it in effect protects the 1972 Act from implied repeal.[111] As Sir William Wade has pointed out,[112] holding that the terms of the 1972 Act 'are putatively incorporated in the Act of 1988 is merely another way of saying that the Parliament of 1972 has imposed a restriction upon the Parliament of 1988. This is exactly what the classical doctrine of sovereignty will not permit.'

A question which has yet to be resolved by the courts is whether Community law would continue to enjoy precedence as a matter of English law if Parliament passed an Act which was inconsistent with it and which expressly stated that it was to take effect notwithstanding the terms of the European Communities Act. That question was considered by Lord Denning in *Macarthys Ltd v Smith*,[113] where he stated:

---

[106] [1979] 3 CMLR 44.   [107] See now Art 141 EC.
[108] Case 129/79 [1980] ECR 1275.   [109] [1980] 2 CMLR 217, 218.
[110] [1990] 2 AC 85, 140. See also Lord Woolf, 'Droit public—English style' [1995] PL 57, 67.
[111] See Craig, *Administrative Law* (3rd edn, 1994), p 193; Sir John Laws, 'Law and democracy' [1995] PL 72, 89.
[112] 'Sovereignty—revolution or evolution?' (1996) 112 LQR 568, 570.
[113] [1979] 3 CMLR 44, 47. See also the remarks of Lord Diplock in *Garland v British Rail Engineering Ltd* [1983] 2 AC 751, 771.

If the time should come when our Parliament deliberately passes an Act—with the intention of repudiating the Treaty or any provision in it—or intentionally of acting inconsistently with it—and says so in express terms—then I should have thought that it would be the duty of our courts to follow the statute of our Parliament . . . Unless there is such an intentional and express repudiation of the Treaty, it is our duty to give priority to the Treaty.

That is also the view taken by Sir John Laws,[114] but it assumes that the United Kingdom's accession to the Communities did not alter the ultimate legal principle, or rule of recognition, of its legal system. The modification which the classical doctrine of parliamentary sovereignty appears to have undergone as a result of accession suggests that that assumption may no longer be justified.[115] The question may in any event turn out to be largely academic. The marked willingness of the English courts to construe domestic legislation in conformity with the requirements of Community law[116] suggests that, while the United Kingdom purports to remain a Member State, the courts would be extremely loath to find the language used by Parliament sufficiently unequivocal to repudiate the requirements of Community law.

The courts of other Member States, some of which have played a leading role in the political development of the Community and the Union, have openly flouted the case law of the Court. An example is France, where for many years the administrative courts refused to accept the primacy of Community law over inconsistent provisions of national law.[117] The attitude of the administrative courts was all the more striking in that the ordinary courts with jurisdiction in civil and criminal cases were willing to accept the doctrine of primacy.[118] It was not until 1989, in the famous *Nicolo* case,[119] that the Conseil d'Etat, the highest administrative court, appeared to reconcile itself to the doctrine.

The German courts too have at times displayed a marked reluctance to accept the primacy of Community law as laid down by the Court of Justice. The first serious manifestation of that reluctance occurred in the aftermath of the Court's judgment, referred to above, in *Internationale Handelsgesellschaft*. When that judgment was delivered, the Verwaltungsgericht decided to ask the German Federal Constitutional Court, the Bundesverfassungsgericht, for a ruling on the compatibility with the German Constitution of the contested regulations. The Bundesverfassungsgericht noted[120] that the Community lacked a democratically

---

[114] Op cit, p 89.

[115] See further Craig, 'Sovereignty of the United Kingdom Parliament after *Factortame*' (1991) 11 YEL 221; Craig, 'Report on the United Kingdom' in Slaughter, Sweet and Weiler (eds), op cit, ch 7, p 204.

[116] See Arnull, 'Interpretation and precedent in English and Community law: evidence of cross-fertilisation?' in Andenas (ed), *English Public Law and the Common Law of Europe* (1998), ch 6.

[117] See eg the decision of the Conseil d'Etat of 1 March 1968 in *Syndicat Général de Fabricants de Semoules de France* [1970] CMLR 395.

[118] See eg the decision of the Cour de Cassation of 24 May 1975 in *Administration des Douanes v Société des Cafés Jacques Vabre* [1975] 2 CMLR 336.

[119] Judgment of 20 October 1989, [1990] 1 CMLR 173.

[120] Judgment of 29 May 1974, [1974] 2 CMLR 540.

elected parliament to which its legislature was politically responsible. It also drew attention to the absence of a catalogue of fundamental rights which permitted the protection accorded to such rights in the Community legal order to be compared with that accorded under the German Constitution.[121] These features led it to conclude that, in the event of a conflict between Community law and national constitutional law, and in particular with the guarantees of fundamental rights laid down in the Constitution, it was the latter which prevailed. The Bundesverfassungsgericht drew back from the brink, however, by finding that there had been no infringement of the Constitution in the circumstances of the instant case. The rebellion was potentially serious, but it did not last. In the *Wünsche* case,[122] the Bundesverfassungsgericht ruled that developments since *Internationale* meant that the protection accorded to fundamental rights in the Community was essentially comparable to the standards enshrined in the German Constitution. The Bundesverfassungsgericht would therefore no longer exercise its jurisdiction to review the compatibility of Community legislation with those standards and references to it for that purpose would be dismissed as inadmissible. It will be noted, however, that the Bundesverfassungsgericht did not relinquish the jurisdiction it had claimed for itself in *Internationale*, thus leaving open the possibility that it might at some point in the future review its decision not to exercise it.[123]

The Bundesverfassungsgericht unleashed a fresh shot across the bows of the Court of Justice in its *Maastricht* decision,[124] in which complaints were made that ratification by Germany of the TEU would be unconstitutional. The complaints were rejected, but in the course of a long and complex judgment the Bundesverfassungsgericht reiterated its view that it had a general responsibility for guaranteeing that the Community respected the basic rights enshrined in the German Constitution. It also expressed concern about the need for the rights and duties flowing from the Treaties to be defined with sufficient clarity. It observed:[125]

. . . if European institutions or agencies were to treat or develop the Union Treaty in a way that was no longer covered by the Treaty in the form that is the basis for the Act of Accession, the resultant legislative instruments would not be legally binding within the sphere of German sovereignty. The German state organs would be prevented for constitutional reasons from applying them in Germany. Accordingly, the Federal Constitutional Court will review legal instruments of European institutions and agencies to see whether they remain within the limits of the sovereign rights conferred on them or transgress them.

The judgment of the Bundesverfassungsgericht in the *Maastricht* case was highly influential in the wave of litigation which erupted in the German courts following

---

[121] Similar concerns were expressed by the Italian Constitutional Court in *Frontini v Ministero delle Finanze* [1974] 2 CMLR 372, 389.

[122] Judgment of 22 October 1986, [1987] 3 CMLR 225.

[123] See Fröwein (1988) 25 CMLRev 201, 203.

[124] Reported in English as *Brunner v European Union Treaty* [1994] 1 CMLR 57.

[125] [1994] 1 CMLR 57, 89.

the adoption by the Council in 1993 of a regulation establishing a common organ-ization of the market in bananas.[126] That regulation removed Germany's right to import substantial quantities of bananas from non-member countries duty-free. A challenge by Germany to the validity of the regulation before the Court of Justice was rejected,[127] but the ruling of the Court failed to lay to rest the concerns of the German judiciary. Particularly noteworthy was a ruling of the Bundesfinanzhof (Federal Finance Court) of 9 January 1996, where, in the context of an application for interim relief, it was suggested that the regulation might be regarded as incom-patible with GATT rules and as outside the powers of the Community. In view of the judgment of the Bundesverfassungsgericht in the *Maastricht* case, this would mean that the German courts would have to refrain from applying it.[128]

It is hard to believe that the Bundesverfassungsgericht was not influenced in the *Maastricht* decision by the critical remarks directed at the Court of Justice in the early 1990s by several high-ranking German politicians.[129] Paradoxically, the atti-tude of the Bundesverfassungsgericht demonstrates clearly both the need for Community law to take precedence over national law and for the Court of Justice to be the ultimate arbiter of what Community law requires. It is self-evident that, if the national courts arrogate to themselves a power to determine whether Community law is to be treated as binding within their jurisdiction, the political objectives of the Community will rapidly become impossible to achieve.[130] The dangers to which the stance of the Bundesverfassungsgericht is liable to give rise are illustrated all too clearly by the litigation over the banana regulation. As the pre-amble to that regulation explained, the achievement of a single market for bananas was being hampered by the national market organizations which previously existed. It was the purpose of the regulation to replace them with a common organization of the market in order to facilitate the free movement of bananas within the Community and the implementation of common arrangements for trade with third countries. Such an arrangement evidently could not function if the extent to which each Member State was bound by it was determined by its own courts in accordance with their own standards.

Be that as it may, a certain creative tension between the national courts and the Court of Justice is not without its advantages. The decision of the Bundes-verfassungsgericht in the *Internationale* case provided the impetus for the develop-

---

[126] Reg 404/93 OJ 1993 L47/1.   [127] Case C–280/93 *Germany v Council* [1994] ECR I–4973.
[128] See Everling, 'Will Europe slip on bananas? The bananas judgment of the Court of Justice and national courts' (1996) 33 CMLRev 401, 433; Reich, 'Judge-made "Europe à la carte": some remarks on recent conflicts between European and German constitutional law provoked by the banana litiga-tion' (1996) 7 EJIL 103, 110–11; Kokott, 'Report on Germany' in Slaughter, Stone and Weiler (eds), op cit, ch 3, p 117. At the time of writing, the banana saga has not yet reached a conclusion. See fur-ther Peers, 'Taking supremacy seriously' (1998) 23 ELRev 146 and 'Constitutional principles and inter-national trade' (1999) 24 ELRev 185.
[129] See Kapteyn, 'The Court of Justice after Amsterdam: taking stock' in Heukels, Blokker and Brus (eds), *The European Union After Amsterdam* (1998), ch 7, p 140; Weiler, *The Constitution of Europe* (1999), p 217.
[130] This was acknowledged by Everling, op cit, at p 434.

ment by the Court of its case law on the Community principle of respect for fundamental rights. There were serious doubts about the compatibility of the banana regulation with GATT rules and general principles of Community law, notably non-discrimination and fundamental rights, such as the right to property and the freedom to pursue a trade or business, to which the Court may not initially have attached sufficient weight.[131] The attitude of the German courts may subsequently have led it to respond to some of those doubts.[132] But tension can only be creative if those involved maintain a due sense of balance. There are at least two reasons why the Court of Justice should respond where possible to the concerns of the national courts. One is that the values embedded in the legal systems of the Member States may contribute to the healthy development of the Community legal order. The other, more pragmatic, reason is that the proper functioning of the Community depends on the co-operation of the national courts. But they for their part need to recognize the importance of the Court's role as the ultimate arbiter of the meaning and effect of Community law.[133]

---

[131] See Everling, op cit.

[132] See Case C–122/95 *Germany v Council* [1998] ECR I–973; Joined Cases C–364/95 and C–365/95 *T Port v Hauptzollamt Hamburg-Jonas* [1998] ECR I–1023; Peers (1999) 24 ELRev 185.

[133] See further Weiler and Haltern, 'Constitutional or international? The foundations of the Community legal order and the question of judicial Kompetenz-Kompetenz' in Slaughter, Stone and Weiler (eds), op cit, ch 12; Hartley, *Constitutional Problems of the European Union* (1999), pp 152–62.

4

The direct effect of Community legislation

It will be apparent from some of what was said in the previous chapter that direct effect may be produced not only by provisions of the EC Treaty but also by acts of the Community institutions. It is appropriate now to consider in more detail the extent to which such acts may have that effect. It will be recalled that three types of binding act are described in Article 249 (ex 189) EC. The regulation is said to have general application, to be 'binding in its entirety and directly applicable in all Member States'. It may be contrasted with the directive, which, while being binding on the Member States as to the result to be achieved, leaves to the national authorities 'the choice of form and methods'. Thus, both the regulation and the directive are essentially normative in character, but they differ in the mechanism by which they achieve their objectives.[1] The third category of binding act mentioned in Article 249 is the decision, which is said to be 'binding in its entirety upon those to whom it is addressed'. Decisions are therefore more specific in character than either regulations or directives. As the Court explained in *Plaumann v Commission*,[2] '[d]ecisions are characterized by the limited number of persons to whom they are addressed. In order to determine whether or not a measure constitutes a decision one must enquire whether that measure concerns specific persons.'

The date on which the binding acts described in Article 249 enter into force is specified by Article 254 (ex 191) of the Treaty. That article was substantially modified by the TEU. In its original form, it required regulations to be published in the Official Journal of the European Communities and stated that they were to enter into force on the date specified in them or, in the absence of any such date, on the twentieth day after publication. Directives and decisions were not required to be published in the Official Journal (although in practice they often were). The Treaty merely required them to be notified to their addressees and stated that they were

---

[1] Where the institutions have a choice (for example, under Arts 95 (ex 100a) and 308 (ex 235) of the Treaty), a directive may be preferred to a regulation where it is considered desirable for Member States to be permitted to accommodate their national traditions in achieving the objectives in view: see Lauwaars, *Lawfulness and Legal Force of Community Decisions* (1973), pp 63–4; Grabitz in *Thirty Years of Community Law* (1981), pp 88–9. Directives are also considered more in keeping with the principle of subsidiarity: see para 6 of the Protocol on subsidiarity and proportionality annexed to the EC Treaty by the Treaty of Amsterdam. However, because they require implementation by the Member States, directives may be less effective than regulations in achieving uniformity throughout the Community.

[2] Case 25/62 [1963] ECR 95, 107.

to 'take effect upon such notification'. A new version of Article 254 (ex 191) was agreed at Maastricht enlarging the category of acts which had to be published in the Official Journal. All binding acts (regulations, directives and decisions) adopted jointly by the Council and the European Parliament under the procedure referred to in Article 251 (ex 189b)[3] were required to be published. This class of acts did not of course exist prior to the entry into force of the TEU, which introduced Article 251 into the Treaty. The requirement that regulations of the Council and of the Commission should be published was maintained, but a new requirement was introduced that directives of those institutions addressed to all the Member States (in practice virtually all directives) should be published too. This is relevant to the question whether directives may produce direct effect, which is discussed below. As before, all measures which had to be published were to enter into force on the date specified in them or, if no date was specified, on the twentieth day following publication. The position of directives and decisions which did not have to be published was unchanged.

Direct applicability and direct effect

It will be noted that only the regulation is described by Article 249 (ex 189) as directly applicable. The notion of direct applicability denotes that characteristic of regulations which enables them to penetrate directly into the legal orders of the Member States without the need for domestic measures of incorporation.[4] It is a corollary of the regulation's direct applicability that it will also, where capable of being applied by a court in a specific case, produce direct effect. Thus, in *Variola v Amministrazione delle Finanze dello Stato*,[5] the Court, having referred to the description of the regulation in Article 189 (now 249), said: 'Accordingly, owing to its very nature and its place in the system of sources of Community law, a Regulation has immediate effect and, consequently, operates to confer rights on private parties which national courts have a duty to protect.'

The close relationship between the notions of direct applicability and direct effect initially led to a degree of confusion, exacerbated to some extent by the very concise language used by the Court in explaining the effects of regulations. The need to distinguish between the two was underlined by Winter in a seminal article published in 1972.[6] Winter wrote:

---

[3] Sometimes called the co-decision procedure.

[4] See Case 39/72 *Commission v Italy* [1973] ECR 101, para 17; Case 94/77 *Zerbone v Amministrazione delle Finanze dello Stato* [1978] ECR 99, para 23.

[5] Case 34/73 [1973] ECR 981, para 8.

[6] 'Direct applicability and direct effect—two distinct and different concepts in Community law' (1972) 9 CMLRev 425. Cf Bebr, 'Directly applicable provisions of Community law: the development of a Community concept' (1970) 19 ICLQ 257, where the term 'directly applicable' is used in a number of senses.

As the various notions denote different phenomena, it will readily appear that it is danger-ous and unwarranted to use them indiscriminately. It is more and more acknowledged that in the framework of Community Law the term 'direct applicability' should be reserved for the method of incorporation of (secondary) Community Law into the municipal legal order (Art. 189). The problem as to when a Community provision is susceptible of receiving judi-cial enforcement is best described as the question of 'direct effect.'[7]

If direct applicability was synonymous with direct effect and meant that regulations conferred on individuals rights which the national courts were bound to protect, the drafting of Article 249 (ex 189) would suggest that directives and decisions did not possess that quality. While the notions of direct applicability and direct effect are closely related, however, there is in principle a clear difference between them. The case law of the Court establishes that, while direct applicability is a *sufficient* precondition for direct effect, it is by no means a *necessary* precondition.

The distinction drawn by Winter between direct applicability and direct effect provides a conceptual framework within which can be accommodated provisions which confer rights on individuals and those which do not. Bebr suggested that a regulation which required implementation by the Community institutions or by the Member States might be deprived of its character as a regulation because it could no longer be considered directly applicable.[8] If this were correct, it would mean that the institutions could only include in regulations provisions which con-ferred rights directly on individuals. This would evidently be unduly restrictive.[9] The issue was considered by Advocate General Warner in *Galli*.[10] He expressed the view that certain provisions of a regulation at issue in that case 'should be regarded as conferring rights on private persons, whilst others should be regarded as binding Member States only, without conferring such rights'. Referring to Winter's art-icle,[11] Mr Warner argued that such a view should not be considered incompatible with the terms of Article 189 (now 249), which simply ensured that all regulations were automatically incorporated into the law of each Member State without the need for specific measures of incorporation. He went on:

But it does not follow that every provision of every Regulation confers rights on the citizens of Member States that they can rely upon in their national Courts. We are all familiar with national statutes, which unquestionably form part of national law, some provisions of which impose obligations on the State or on public authorities without conferring personal rights on citizens. This must be so too in the case of Community Regulations. Their provisions can have direct effect, in the sense of conferring personal rights, capable of being upheld by national Courts, only in so far as they satisfy the familiar tests laid down by the Court, i.e. the tests of being clear and unconditional, and of requiring no further legislative action for their implementation.

---

[7] Op cit, p 425.   [8] Op cit, pp 290–1.
[9] See Winter, op cit, p 435.   [10] Case 31/74 [1975] ECR 47, 70.
[11] See particularly p 436: 'In every Member State there exists quite a bit of law which is not enforce-able in the courts, because these rules were not meant to give the private individual enforceable rights or because they are too vague or too incomplete to admit of judicial application.'

Thus, where a provision of the Treaty empowers one of the institutions to adopt a regulation in order to achieve a particular objective, the institution enjoys a considerable degree of flexibility. The regulation may contain provisions which confer rights directly on individuals which the national courts must uphold. It may contain provisions which impose obligations on the Member States only. The fact that, under Article 249 (ex 189) of the Treaty, it is directly applicable means that it is immediately binding on its own terms on all those who fall within its field of application and does not depend for its effect on national measures of incorporation.

It is sometimes permissible for Member States to adopt national rules designed to give effect to a Community regulation, but they must exercise great caution if they decide to do so. As the Court explained in *Zerbone*,[12] 'Although it is true that in the event of difficulty of interpretation the national administration may be led to adopt detailed rules for the application of a Community regulation and at the same time to clarify any doubts raised, it can do so only in so far as it complies with the provisions of Community law and the national authorities cannot issue binding rules of interpretation.' In *Commission v Italy*,[13] the Commission brought proceedings against Italy under Article 169 (now 226) on the ground that it had failed to comply with its obligations under two Commission regulations. The principal regulation introduced a system of premiums to encourage the slaughter of dairy cows and the withholding of milk and dairy products from the market. Its object was to reduce the surpluses of such products which then existed. After considerable delay, a decree was adopted which essentially reproduced the provisions of the relevant Community regulations, which were to be 'deemed applicable' in the Italian legal system. The Court stated: 'By following this procedure, the Italian Government has brought into doubt both the legal nature of the applicable provisions and the date of their coming into force.'[14] It went on to emphasize that 'all methods of implementation are contrary to the Treaty which would have the result of creating an obstacle to the direct effect of Community Regulations and of jeopardizing their simultaneous and uniform application in the whole of the Community'.[15] Thus, it is a breach of a Member State's obligations under the Treaty if it purports to implement a regulation in such a way that its entry into force is made to depend on national law or that its status as a source of Community law is concealed. To permit such devices would jeopardize the uniform application of the regulation throughout the Community and prejudice the jurisdiction of the Court of Justice under Article 234 (ex 177) to rule on the validity and interpretation of the regulation at the request of national courts and tribunals.

It may be noted that the term 'direct applicability' in the sense in which it was used by Winter is not apt to describe the Treaties themselves, for they depend for

---

[12] Para 27.
[13] Case 39/72 [1973] ECR 101. Cf Case 93/71 *Leonesio v Italian Ministry for Agriculture and Forestry* [1972] ECR 287.
[14] Para 17.   [15] Ibid.

their effect in the legal orders of the Member States on incorporation in accordance with national law.[16] They did not take effect internally immediately on ratification by the Member States in the absence of a provision of domestic law permitting them to do so. Of course, once ratified, each Member State had an obligation under the Treaties to take the steps necessary at the national level to enable them to enter fully into effect. This meant that individuals had to be given the right to invoke directly effective provisions of the Treaties before the national courts regardless of whether they had been specifically incorporated into national law.

The status of decisions and directives

The questions raised by the internal effects of regulations caused relatively little controversy in comparison with the battle which has waged over the effect of directives in the legal orders of the Member States. Directives have played a crucial role in the process of integration set in motion by the authors of the Treaties. They have been particularly significant as instruments for the harmonization of national laws where disparities between the rules applicable in different Member States could jeopardize the proper functioning of the common market. They were also intended to play an important role in giving effect to the Treaty rules on the four freedoms. The single market programme envisaged the adoption of a vast body of legislation, much of it in the form of directives, in order to secure the completion of the internal market by the end of 1992.[17] Indeed, the Single European Act introduced a new provision, Article 100a,[18] which was designed to facilitate the adoption by the Council of the legislation contemplated. Like Article 100a (now 95), many of the provisions introduced by the TEU giving new legislative powers to the Council spoke in general terms of 'measures' and did not refer specifically to directives,[19] but the emphasis placed by that Treaty on the principle of subsidiarity means that the directive is likely in many cases to be the preferred legislative instrument because it represents less of an intrusion into the 'nooks and crannies of national life'.[20]

A directive is typically addressed to all the Member States and requires them to achieve certain specified objectives within a given deadline. Despite the importance of the instrument as a means of achieving the objectives of the Treaty, however, securing compliance with them by the Member States has been a perennial problem.[21] Sometimes Member States simply fail to adopt the necessary imple-

---

[16] See Winter, op cit, p 438.   [17] See Art 14 (ex 7a) EC.
[18] See now Art 95 EC.
[19] See eg Arts 126(4) (now 149(4)), 128(5) (now 151(5)), 129(4) (now 152(4)). It may be noted that, while the European Central Bank has the power to adopt regulations and decisions, it has no power to issue directives: see Art 110(1) (ex 108a(1)).
[20] See the Protocol on subsidiarity and proportionality agreed at Amsterdam, paras 6 and 7.
[21] See Easson, 'The "direct effect" of EEC directives' (1979) 28 ICLQ 319, 352; Curtin, 'Directives: the effectiveness of judicial protection of individual rights' (1990) 27 CMLRev 709, 709–11.

menting measures by the due date, sometimes the implementing measures adopted are inadequate to satisfy the requirements of the directive. Failure by a Member State to transpose a directive properly can seriously disrupt the proper functioning of the common market. The following question therefore arises: what effects, if any, can directives produce on the rights and obligations of those they are intended to affect in the absence of (adequate) national implementing measures? In short, can directives produce direct effect?

The terms of Article 249 (ex 189) do not provide much assistance in answering that question. If the term direct effect is treated as synonymous with the term direct applicability, the article would suggest that directives cannot have direct effect, since only regulations are described as directly applicable. A Member State which failed to implement a directive properly by the expiry of the deadline laid down in it would expose itself to action by the Commission under Article 226 (ex 169)[22] for the Treaty makes directives binding on the Member States to which they are addressed, but the national courts of the defaulting State could safely ignore the directive. However, it was argued above that there is a distinction between direct applicability and direct effect. It follows that, although it is clear from Article 249 (ex 189) that directives do not possess the former quality, it does not necessarily follow that they do not possess the latter.

Grad v Finanzamt Traunstein

The distinction between direct applicability and direct effect was drawn to the attention of the Court by the Commission in the first case in which the Court gave an indication of its views on the question whether directives could confer rights directly on individuals. In *Grad v Finanzamt Traunstein*,[23] the Finanzgericht München asked for a preliminary ruling on whether a provision contained in a decision in conjunction with a provision contained in a directive created rights for individuals which national courts were required to protect. The decision in question provided that, once a common system of turnover tax had been adopted by the Council and brought into force in the Member States, it was to be applied to the carriage of goods by road, rail, and inland waterway. Once it was brought into force, the common system of turnover tax was to replace any specific taxes to which such carriage of goods was subject. The directive mentioned by the Finanzgericht required the Member States to replace their present systems of turnover tax by the common system of value added tax by 1 January 1970 at the latest, a deadline which was subsequently extended by two years. In the main action, the plaintiff claimed that a tax he had been required to pay on exporting by road a quantity of preserved fruit from Germany to Austria in 1969 was incompatible with these provisions. He said that it did not matter that the common system

---

[22] Or in theory by another Member State under Art 227 (ex 170), but in practice this is a very remote possibility.

[23] Case 9/70 [1970] ECR 825.

of value-added tax had not yet been introduced in all the Member States. Germany had already amended its system of turnover tax in accordance with the requirements of Community law, with the result that it was now bound by the Council's decision.

The Court observed that the question referred to it concerned the combined effect of provisions contained in a directive and a decision, which according to Article 189 (now 249) was binding in its entirety upon those to whom it was addressed. It noted the view of the German Government that the distinction drawn by Article 189 between the effects of regulations on the one hand and directives and decisions on the other ruled out the possibility that the latter categories of instrument might produce direct effect. This was a quality which, in the view of the German Government, was reserved to regulations. The Court did not find that argument persuasive. It explained: '. . . although it is true that by virtue of Article 189, regulations are directly applicable and therefore by virtue of their nature capable of producing direct effects, it does not follow from this that other categories of legal measures mentioned in that article can never produce similar effects'. It went on:

It would be incompatible with the binding effect attributed to decisions by Article 189 to exclude in principle the possibility that persons affected may invoke the obligation imposed by a decision. Particularly in cases where, for example, the Community authorities by means of a decision have imposed an obligation on a Member State or all the Member States to act in a certain way, the effectiveness ('l'effet utile') of such a measure would be weakened if the nationals of that State could not invoke it in the courts and the nationals of that State could not take it into consideration as part of Community law. Although the effects of a decision may not be identical with those of a provision contained in a regulation, this difference does not exclude the possibility that the end result, namely the right of the individual to invoke the measure before the courts, may be the same as that of a directly applicable provision of a regulation.[24]

The Court added that Article 177 (now 234) of the Treaty, which empowered national courts to ask for preliminary rulings on the validity and interpretation of all acts of the Community institutions, implied that such acts could be invoked before the national courts. The crucial question in each case was whether 'the nature, background and wording of the provision in question are capable of producing direct effects in the legal relationships between the addressee of the act and third parties'.[25] In the instant case, the Court concluded that the relevant provisions of the decision and directive in question, taken in conjunction with each other, were capable 'of producing direct effects in the legal relationships between the Member States to which the decision is addressed and those subject to their jurisdiction and of creating for the latter the right to invoke these provisions before the courts'.[26]

---

[24] Para 5.   [25] Para 6.
[26] See the first para of the operative part of the Court's judgment. The ruling was reiterated on two subsequent occasions less than a month later: see Case 20/70 *Lesage v Hauptzollamt Freiburg* [1970] ECR 861; Case 23/70 *Haselhorst v Finanzamt Düsseldorf* [1970] ECR 881.

In rejecting the argument of the German Government and picking up the distinction drawn by the Commission between direct applicability and direct effect, the Court's ruling in *Grad* dealt a fatal blow to the argument that an answer to the question whether directives could confer rights directly on individuals could be found by comparing the description of directives given in Article 189 (now 249) with that of regulations. Although it was clear from Article 189 that neither directives nor decisions were directly applicable, this had no implications for whether or not they could have direct effect.

Although the *Grad* decision was strictly speaking confined to the case of a directive taken in conjunction with a decision, the tenor of the ruling, and in particular the emphasis placed on the need to ensure the effectiveness of Community legislation, suggested that this factor was merely a quirk of the particular case: the logic of the judgment would apply with equal force where a directive or a decision alone was in issue. It may be noted that, in the passage where effectiveness was mentioned, the Court spoke in general terms of the right to invoke provisions contained in directives and decisions before the national courts. Indeed, the Court stated that the direct effect enjoyed by such instruments 'may be the same' as that enjoyed by regulations. Regulations, of course, are capable of producing direct effect in both the vertical and horizontal senses. Did the Court mean to imply that this was also true of directives and decisions? It seems likely that the Court's remarks were intended to be confined to direct effect in the vertical sense. In the following paragraph, it referred explicitly to the need to establish whether the provision in question was 'capable of producing direct effects in the legal relationships *between the addressee of the act and third parties*'.[27] Since a directive can only be addressed to a Member State, such direct effect would be vertical. Decisions, however, may also be addressed to natural and legal persons. It is implicit in the Court's judgment that such a decision could be enforced in the national courts. In that sense, decisions may therefore be said to be capable of producing both vertical and horizontal direct effect. In the case of directives, the tension between the need to ensure the effectiveness of Community acts and the implication, albeit slight, that they could only be enforced in the national courts in the vertical sense was to become increasingly controversial.

SACE v Italian Ministry for Finance

Before the year was out, the Court was asked to consider the effect of a directive in slightly different circumstances. In *SACE v Italian Ministry for Finance*,[28] the plaintiff brought an action before the President of the Tribunale, Brescia, for the repayment of a duty for administrative services it had been required to pay on importing into Italy a quantity of goods from other Member States. There was no doubt that the disputed duty constituted a charge having an effect equivalent to a

---

[27] Para 6, emphasis added.   [28] Case 33/70 [1970] ECR 1213.

customs duty and that it therefore fell within the prohibition contained in Article 9 (now 23) of the Treaty.[29] The question was whether that prohibition could be relied on by SACE in the circumstances of the main action. Article 13(2) of the Treaty (now repealed) required charges having equivalent effect in force between the Member States to be progressively abolished during the transitional period, which ended on 31 December 1969. The timetable for their abolition was to be determined by the Commission by way of directives in the light of the rules laid down in Article 14 (also repealed) in relation to customs duties in the strict sense and the directives issued by the Council under that article. The Council had adopted a so-called Acceleration Decision fixing 1 July 1968 as the date on which all customs duties were to be abolished. On the basis of that decision, the Commission addressed a directive to Italy requiring the duty for administrative services to be abolished for imports from other Member States by the same date. The main action turned on whether that requirement had direct effect and, if so, from what date.

The Court found that, with effect from the end of the transitional period, Articles 9 (now 23) and 13(2) imposed a clear and precise prohibition on exacting charges having an effect equivalent to customs duties which produced direct effect 'in the legal relations between Member States and their subjects'.[30] In order to answer the national court's question, however, it was necessary to consider the combined effect of Articles 9 and 13(2) of the Treaty, the Council's decision and the Commission's directive. The Court found that the fixing by the Commission of a date prior to the end of the transitional period 'has in no way changed the nature of the obligation imposed on Member States by Articles 9 and 13(2)'.[31] That obligation therefore produced direct effect from the earlier date as it would have done at the end of the transitional period. The Commission's directive was not confined to relations between Italy and the Commission, 'but also entails legal consequences of which both the other Member States concerned in its performance and individuals may avail themselves when, by its very nature, the provision establishing this obligation is directly applicable, as are Articles 9 and 13 of the Treaty'.[32] That interpretation, the Court said, was 'all the more imperative' in view of the fact that the Court had ruled that Italy was in breach of the Treaty by continuing to levy the disputed charge after 1 July 1968.[33] The Court concluded that the obligation to abolish the charge laid down in the Commission's directive, in conjunction with Articles 9 and 13(2) of the Treaty and the decision of the Council, produced direct effect in relations between the Member State to whom the directive was addressed and its subjects from 1 July 1968.

---

[29] This had already been established by the Court in proceedings instituted by the Commission under Art 169 (now 226): see Case 8/70 *Commission v Italy* [1970] ECR 961, para 3.

[30] Para 10.   [31] Para 14.

[32] Para 15. Like Winter, the present writer would have preferred the term directly effective.

[33] See Case 8/70, *supra*.

van Duyn v Home Office

Again a directive had produced a decisive effect in a dispute between a Member State and a private party, but again it remained possible to take a minimalist view of the significance of the Court's ruling. After all, the directive concerned had merely fixed the date from which a rule contained in the Treaty was to enter into force. Since the relevant provisions of the Treaty would take direct effect sooner or later in any event, it might not have seemed a major step for the date on which they did so to be brought forward by eighteen months. But the minimalist view was beginning to look a little frayed around the edges. It was in *van Duyn v Home Office*[34] that the Court gave the loose thread in the minimalist case its firmest tug to date. D, a Dutch national, had been refused leave to enter the United Kingdom to take up a post as a secretary with the Church of Scientology, a religious cult of which the British Government disapproved but which it had not proscribed. D sought to rely on the rights conferred on her as a worker by Article 48 (now 39) of the Treaty. According to paragraph 3 of that article, the rights it conferred were 'subject to limitations justified on grounds of public policy, public security or public health'. D maintained that the United Kingdom could not rely on any of those limitations because it had not complied with a Council directive dealing with the circumstances in which they could be invoked.[35] On a reference for a preliminary ruling, the Court was asked whether the directive produced direct effect. The Court declared:

If . . . by virtue of the provisions of Article 189 [now 249] regulations are directly applicable and, consequently, may by their very nature have direct effects, it does not follow from this that other categories of acts mentioned in that Article can never have similar effects. It would be incompatible with the binding effect attributed to a directive by Article 189 to exclude, in principle, the possibility that the obligation which it imposes may be invoked by those concerned. In particular, where the Community authorities have, by directive, imposed on Member States the obligation to pursue a particular course of conduct, the useful effect of such an act would be weakened if individuals were prevented from relying on it before their national courts and if the latter were prevented from taking it into consideration as an element of Community law. Article 177 [now 234], which empowers national courts to refer to the Court questions concerning the validity and interpretation of all acts of the Community institutions without distinction, implies furthermore that these acts may be invoked by individuals in the national courts. It is necessary to examine, in every case, whether the nature, general scheme and wording of the provision in question are capable of having direct effects on the relations between Member States and individuals.[36]

The Court concluded that the relevant provision was indeed capable of having such an effect. Once again, therefore, the Court drew a distinction between direct

---

[34] Case 41/74 [1974] ECR 1337.

[35] Dir 64/221 on the coordination of special measures concerning the movement and residence of foreign nationals which are justified on grounds of public policy, public security or public health, OJ Sp Ed, 1964, p 117. See further ch 10.

[36] Para 12.

applicability and direct effect and emphasized that the 'useful effect' of directives would be enhanced if they were held to be capable of producing direct effect. This time, the Court found support for its view in the binding nature attributed to directives by Article 189 (now 249). It is clear from the final sentence of the passage cited above, however, that the Court was only envisaging vertical, not horizontal, direct effect.

The Court's remarks in *van Duyn* about the direct effect of directives were expressed in general terms, but elsewhere in its judgment the Court also ruled that Article 48 (now 39) of the Treaty had direct effect: it imposed on Member States a precise obligation which did not require any further measures to be adopted either by the Community institutions or by the Member States and which left them no discretion with regard to its implementation. Since the application of the derogations set out in paragraph 3 of the article were subject to judicial control, they did not prevent the rest of the article from producing direct effect.[37] Those who found the idea that directives might produce direct effect difficult to accept might have found in this part of the Court's judgment a way of making the idea more palatable: perhaps it was only when a directive implemented a Treaty provision which was itself directly effective that the directive conferred rights on individuals which the national courts were bound to protect. If this were so, it would mean that the large body of directives for the approximation of national laws which had been adopted did not enjoy this quality. The importance of such directives for the proper functioning of the common market and the ineffectiveness of proceedings under Article 169 (now 226) to enforce timeous compliance with them made this possibility highly unattractive. Moreover, it was a curious position to adopt for those who had sought to rely on the terms of Article 189 (now 249) to deny that any directives might produce direct effect, for it involved differentiating between the effects of particular directives by reference solely to their legal basis, a distinction for which there was no warrant in Article 189.

Nederlandse Ondernemingen v Inspecteur der Invoerrechten en Accijnzen

That the Court would not be willing to draw any such distinction was made clear in *Nederlandse Ondernemingen v Inspecteur der Invoerrechten en Accijnzen*.[38] In that case, the Supreme Court of the Netherlands, the Hoge Raad, asked whether a provision of the second VAT directive produced direct effect. The Court reiterated the reasons it had given in *van Duyn*, to which it referred, for concluding that directives were indeed capable of conferring rights on individuals which national courts were bound to uphold. It added that this was especially so 'when the individual invokes a provision of a directive before a national court in order that the latter shall rule whether the competent national authorities, in exercising the choice which is left

---

[37] Paras 6 and 7.   [38] Case 51/76 [1977] ECR 113.

to them as to the form and the methods for implementing the directive, have kept within the limits as to their discretion set out in the directive'.[39] The basic principle laid down in the relevant provision was subject to certain derogations and exceptions which the Member States had a discretion to determine in the light of other provisions of the directive. As long as a Member State remained within the limits of the discretion conferred on it, its actions could not be the subject of judicial review on the basis of the directive. However, a national court before which the directive was invoked had a duty to examine whether a disputed national measure fell outside the Member State's margin of discretion and could still be considered a legitimate exception to or derogation from the basic principle laid down in the directive. The judgment clearly implied that, where the national court took the view that the Member State concerned had exceeded the bounds of its discretion, it was to apply directly the basic principle laid down in the directive.

The directive at issue in *Nederlandse Ondernemingen* was based on Articles 99 and 100 EEC. Neither of those provisions laid down any substantive rules and they were clearly incapable of producing direct effect themselves. That factor did not, however, prevent the directive from producing that effect. By repeating much of its earlier ruling in *van Duyn*, the Court made it clear that the effect of a directive in the national legal orders was not dependent on its legal basis.

Pubblico Ministero v Ratti

The irrelevance of a directive's legal basis to the question whether it was capable of producing direct effect was confirmed in *Pubblico Ministero v Ratti*,[40] where the Court was asked for a preliminary ruling on the effect of two directives on the approximation of national laws adopted under the enabling provisions of Article 100 EEC. The case gave the Court an opportunity to refine its case law in two important respects. The defendant in the main action was the head of an Italian firm which produced solvents and varnishes. It had packaged those products in accordance with the requirements of two directives, one on the packaging and labelling of solvents, the other on the packaging and labelling of a variety of substances including varnishes. Neither directive had been implemented in Italy and the defendant was prosecuted for failing to comply with the applicable Italian legislation. A novel factor was that, while the deadline for giving effect to the solvents directive had expired at the material time, that for giving effect to the varnishes directive had not. Having been asked by the Pretura Penale, Milan, whether the two directives afforded the defendant a defence to the charges brought against him, the Court began by reiterating its now well established case law on the direct effect of directives. However, it added an additional justification for its view that directives were capable of conferring on individuals rights which the national courts were

---

[39] Para 24.   [40] Case 148/78 [1979] ECR 1629.

bound to uphold and introduced two qualifications to the circumstances in which that would be the case. It stated:

. . . a Member State which has not adopted the implementing measures required by the directive in the prescribed period may not rely, as against individuals, on its own failure to perform the obligations which the directive entails.

It follows that a national court requested by a person who has complied with the provisions of a directive not to apply a national provision incompatible with the directive not incorporated into the internal legal order of a defaulting Member State, must uphold that request if the obligation in question is unconditional and sufficiently precise.'[41]

The qualifications were relatively uncontroversial. Since Member States are not required by the Treaty to achieve the result envisaged by a directive before the expiry of the deadline laid down in it, it would be wrong to pre-empt any choice they might wish to exercise as to the form and methods of implementation by holding that it could have direct effect in advance of that date. Moreover, it is entirely compatible with the Treaty for Member States to continue to apply their national laws unamended up to that point.[42] In the instant case, the result was that the defendant was able to rely on the solvents directive in the national proceedings, but not on the varnishes directive.

The second qualification was that a person invoking a directive before the national courts had to show that he had himself complied with it. This was a condition which the defendant was able to meet, since he had packaged his products in accordance with the requirements of the directives on which he was seeking to rely. The qualification may be considered necessary to prevent the creation of a lacuna: if an individual could rely on a directive with which he had not complied to prevent the application to him of inconsistent national legislation, the result would be that he would escape any regulation at all. In circumstances such as those of the *Ratti* case, this would have meant that the defendant could have packaged and labelled his products as he pleased, a thoroughly undesirable outcome.[43]

The additional justification was of greater significance and has come to be known as a form of estoppel, although it may not resemble very closely the doctrine of estoppel in English law. The idea is that a Member State which has committed a breach of the Treaty by failing to implement a directive by the due date must not be permitted to rely on the unlawful absence of implementing legislation to defeat the claim of an individual which is based directly on the directive. Although in *Ratti* this superficially attractive argument was put forward in addition

---

[41] Paras 22 and 23.

[42] Member States to which a directive is addressed must, however, refrain, during the period laid down for its implementation, from adopting measures liable seriously to compromise the result prescribed: see Case C–129/96 *Inter-Environnement Wallonie v Région Wallonne* [1997] ECR I–7411.

[43] See further Easson, 'EEC directives for the harmonisation of laws: some problems of validity, implementation and legal effects' (1981) 1 YEL 1, 38–9.

to the other arguments on which the Court had hitherto relied,[44] which focused on the binding nature of directives under the Treaty and the need to promote their effectiveness, it is submitted that it came to assume undue prominence in subsequent decisions and led the Court into a cul-de-sac from which it has never really emerged.

Just as *van Duyn* had shown that the existence of a derogation from a Treaty rule allowing Member States a certain margin of discretion did not prevent the rule itself from having direct effect,[45] *Nederlandse Ondernemingen* established that the same was true of directives: because the exercise of a discretion conferred on the Member States by Community law was subject to judicial review, its existence would not prevent a substantive rule from having direct effect once it was established that the limits to the discretionary power had been exceeded. It is therefore apparent that the traditional criteria for direct effect—clarity, unconditionality and the absence of discretion on the part of the institutions and the Member States—are somewhat misleading, even in relation to articles of the Treaty. In relation to directives, they seem singularly inappropriate[46] for a directive is never complete in itself, but always requires implementation by the Member States to whom it is addressed. Indeed, the Court has held that this is so even where the directive in question is directly effective,[47] confirmation, if confirmation were needed, that directives are never directly applicable.[48] Moreover, since Article 249 (ex 189) of the Treaty allows Member States a choice as to the form and methods of implementation, they always enjoy at least a certain degree of discretion in transposing a directive into national law. As Advocate General Warner observed in the *Santillo* case,[49] '[o]f course the width of that choice will depend on the subject-matter and content of the directive, but some element of discretion there will nearly always be'.

Becker v Finanzamt Münster-Innenstadt

The Court's judgment in *Becker v Finanzamt Münster-Innenstadt*[50] contains what has come to be regarded as the classic statement of the circumstances in which directives may produce direct effect. Reiterating both the need to promote the effectiveness of directives and the estoppel argument, the Court declared:

. . . wherever the provisions of a directive appear, as far as their subject-matter is concerned,

---

[44] The shift in emphasis represented by the *Ratti* case is noted by Curtin, 'The province of government: delimiting the direct effect of directives in the common law context' (1990) 15 ELRev 195, 196–7; Prechal, 'Remedies after *Marshall*' (1990) 27 CMLRev 451, 453.

[45] See also Case C–156/91 *Hansa Fleisch v Landrat des Kreises Schleswig-Holstein* [1992] ECR I–5567.

[46] See Easson (1981) 1 YEL 1, 36–7.

[47] See eg Case 104/86 *Commission v Italy* [1988] ECR 1799, para 12; Case 102/79 *Commission v Belgium* [1980] ECR 1473, para 12.

[48] See in the same sense AG Warner in Case 815/79 *Cremonini and Vrankovich* [1980] ECR 3583, 3621. Cf Steiner, 'Direct applicability in EEC law—a chameleon concept' (1982) 98 LQR 229.

[49] Case 131/79 *Regina v Secretary of State for Home Affairs ex p* Santillo [1980] ECR 1585, 1610.

[50] Case 8/81 [1982] ECR 53.

to be unconditional and sufficiently precise, those provisions may, in the absence of implementing measures adopted within the prescribed period, be relied upon as against any national provision which is incompatible with the directive or in so far as the provisions define rights which individuals are able to assert against the State.[51]

It might be thought that the possibility that a provision contained in a directive could be sufficiently precise and unconditional to produce direct effect is incompatible with the very notion of a directive, since Article 249 (ex 189) of the Treaty implies that directives must be flexible enough to leave the Member States some discretion as to how they are implemented.[52] There is, however, no support for that line of argument in the case law of the Court. Indeed, whatever strength such an argument might have had in the early part of the Community's existence, it became untenable once the Single European Act entered into force. The Council's practice of adopting directives which were sufficiently precise to produce direct effect was by then well established and it was clearly envisaged that such directives would play a crucial part in the completion of the internal market by the end of 1992.[53] In so far as the Single European Act embedded that deadline in the Treaty and contemplated greater use of directives, it implicitly endorsed the existing case law of the Court on their legal status. In any event, the freedom given to the Member States by Article 249 (ex 189) is not unlimited. As Advocate General Warner explained in *Enka v Inspecteur der Invoerrechten en Accijnzen*,[54] 'Article 189 of the Treaty, although it leaves to each Member State the choice of the "form and methods" whereby it is to give effect to a directive, does not allow it the choice of not giving effect to the directive at all, or of giving effect to it only in part. On the contrary Article 189 says in terms that a directive "shall be binding, as to the result to be achieved, upon each Member State to which it is addressed". A Member State that fails fully to give effect to a directive is in breach of the Treaty . . .'[55] The freedom of Member States to choose how to transpose a directive is constrained by their duty to ensure that it is implemented in a manner which is calculated to ensure that it is as successful as possible in achieving its objectives.

Can directives have horizontal direct effect?

Notwithstanding isolated cases where the Court has refused to endow particular directives with direct effect,[56] it must be acknowledged that many directives do possess that quality. For some, this was too much to stomach. One outspoken critic

[51] Para 25.
[52] See Lauwaars, *Lawfulness and Legal Force of Community Decisions* (1973), p 30; Easson (1979) 28 ICLQ 319, 344–6; (1981) 1 YEL 1, 10–11; Grabitz in *Thirty Years of Community Law* (1981), pp 85–6.
[53] See the Commission's White Paper entitled 'Completing the Internal Market', COM (85) 310 final.
[54] Case 38/77 [1977] ECR 2203, 2226.
[55] See further Case 102/79 *Commission v Belgium* [1980] ECR 1473; Case 160/82 *Commission v Netherlands* [1982] ECR 4637; Case C–58/89 *Commission v Germany* [1991] ECR I–4983.
[56] See eg Case C–236/92 *Comitato di Coordinamento per la Difesa della Cava and Others* [1994] ECR

of the Court, commenting on the case law summarized in *Becker*, argued that 'the text of Article 189(3) does not offer the Court the slightest justification for ruling the way it did. It went beyond the textual stipulations of that Article leaving behind it a variety of well-merited, legal-interpretative principles.' He added: 'To many a European lawyer this is revolting judicial behaviour.'[57] That view was not without its supporters in the upper reaches of the national judiciaries, where the possibility that directives might have direct effect initially encountered resistance, particularly in France and Germany.[58] The Court cannot have been oblivious to the hostile reaction occasioned by its case law in influential quarters when it turned to the one fundamental issue it had yet to address directly. That was the question whether directives were capable of producing horizontal direct effect, or, to put the question another way, whether they could impose obligations on individuals.

In *Becker*, Advocate General Slynn had expressed the view that it was 'a correct reading of Article 189 [now 249] that a directive, not being addressed to an individual cannot of itself impose obligations on him . . .'.[59] That view appeared to be reflected in the Court's judgment, which referred to 'rights which individuals are able to assert *against the State*'.[60] Moreover, in *Becker* the Court followed its earlier practice of avoiding the term 'direct effect' when discussing the status of directives in proceedings before national courts. This terminological fastidiousness was sometimes said to imply that directives were not capable of producing direct effect in the strict sense, which may be both vertical and horizontal, but only an effect which, although similar, was more limited.[61] On the other hand, the question of horizontal direct effect was not relevant on the facts of *Becker* and it seemed unlikely (although by no means impossible) that the Court would choose to resolve such a hotly debated issue in so oblique a manner. The view that the Court had not intended to exclude the possibility that directives might also define rights which individuals were able to assert against other individuals seemed to be confirmed when it found alternative grounds for disposing of a series of cases in which the point was directly raised.[62]

I–483; Case C–131/97 *Carbonari and Others v Università degli Studi di Bologna and Others*, judgment of 25 February 1999.

[57] Rasmussen, *On Law and Policy in the European Court of Justice* (1986), p 12.

[58] See Plötner, 'Report on France', and Kokott, 'Report on Germany', in Slaughter, Stone and Weiler (eds), *The European Court and National Courts—Doctrine and Jurisprudence* (1998), pp 48–50 (referring to the famous decision of the French Conseil d'Etat of 22 December 1978 in *Minister of the Interior v Cohn-Bendit* [1980] 1 CMLR 543) and p 116 respectively; Hartley, *The Foundations of European Community Law* (4th edn, 1998) pp 238–9 and 244–7; Pescatore, 'The doctrine of "direct effect": an infant disease of Community law' (1983) 8 ELRev 155, 169–70.

[59] At p 81.   [60] Para 25, emphasis added.

[61] See eg Pescatore, op cit, pp 167 and 171; Green, 'Directives, equity and the protection of individual rights' (1984) 9 ELRev 295, 304 and 309. The Court has subsequently used the term 'direct effect' in relation to directives: see eg Case C–188/89 *Foster and others v British Gas plc* [1990] ECR I–3313, para 20; Joined Cases C–6/90 and C–9/90 *Francovich and Others* [1991] ECR I–5357, para 9 and following sub-heading.

[62] See eg Case 129/79 *Macarthys v Smith* [1980] ECR 1275; Case 69/80 *Worringham and Humphreys*

Grasping the nettle

The Court finally chose to confront the issue in *Marshall v Southampton and South-West Hampshire Area Health Authority*,[63] paradoxically a case in which it was not directly relevant. The appellant had been dismissed by her employer, the respondent authority, because she had passed the retirement age applied by the authority to its female employees. The appellant would not have been dismissed had she been a man and she sought to rely on a directive on equal treatment for men and women.[64] Having found that the directive precluded the dismissal of someone in the position of the appellant, the Court turned to the question whether the relevant provision of the directive could be invoked by a litigant in the circumstances of the main action. The respondent authority had been described by the referring court as an 'emanation of the State', but both the authority and the United Kingdom argued that, where the State acted as an employer, it should be treated in the same way as a private employer and that directives were incapable of imposing obligations directly on private bodies.[65] The Court responded to that argument in the following terms:

With regard to the argument that a directive may not be relied upon against an individual, it must be emphasized that according to Article 189 of the EEC Treaty the binding nature of a directive, which constitutes the basis for the possibility of relying on the directive before a national court, exists only in relation to 'each Member State to which it is addressed'. It follows that a directive may not of itself impose obligations on an individual and that a provision of a directive may not be relied upon as such against such a person. It must therefore be examined whether, in this case, the respondent must be regarded as having acted as an individual.

The Court went on to explain that it was irrelevant whether the State was acting as an employer or a public authority: 'In either case it is necessary to prevent the State from taking advantage of its own failure to comply with Community law.'[66] The Court's rejection of that distinction, which would have given rise to some nice problems of definition, would have sufficed to dispose of the case, since the Court was in no doubt that the respondent was a public authority even though it made no formal finding to that effect.[67] It had evidently decided, however, that it was

---

v Lloyds Bank [1981] ECR 767; Case 96/80 *Jenkins v Kingsgate* [1981] ECR 911; Case 12/81 *Garland v British Rail Engineering* [1982] ECR 359; Case 19/81 *Burton v British Railways Board* [1982] ECR 555.

[63] Case 152/84 [1986] ECR 723.

[64] Dir 76/207 on the implementation of the principle of equal treatment for men and women as regards access to employment, vocational training and promotion, and working conditions, OJ 1976 L39/40.

[65] See Dashwood, 'The principle of direct effect in European Community law' (1978) 16 JCMS 229, 243, who proposed 'a distinction between the State acting in the exercise of its *imperium*, where it would be bound as addressee of the directive, and the State acting as a market participant . . . where its position in relation to the directive would be similar to that of any other undertaking'.

[66] Paras 48 and 49.

[67] Indeed, given that responsibility for applying the law to the facts of the case in proceedings under Art 234 (ex 177) belongs to the national court, the Court of Justice had no jurisdiction to make any such finding.

time to end the controversy over the horizontal direct effect of directives. Unfortunately, the ruling is logically incoherent and undesirable as a matter of policy. The detrimental effects it has produced have been exacerbated by the Court's subsequent unwillingness to live with its implications.

The reasoning of the Court in *Marshall*

The judgment in *Marshall* is an object lesson in the dangers of *a contrario* reasoning. It is true that Article 249 (ex 189) only expressly makes directives binding on the Member States, but it does not necessarily follow they are incapable of binding other bodies.[68] In the second *Defrenne* case,[69] the Court declared that 'the fact that certain provisions of the Treaty are formally addressed to the Member States does not prevent rights from being conferred at the same time on any individual who has an interest in the performance of the duties thus laid down'. Indeed, in that case it was held that the provision at issue, Article 119 EEC (now after amendment Article 141 EC), was binding in both the vertical and the horizontal senses. It is also true that Member States should not be able to plead their own default in failing adequately to implement a directive when an individual seeks to rely on it, but this justification, in itself compelling, for according vertical direct effect to directives was not mentioned in the early case law and was introduced in *Ratti* alongside other good reasons for reaching the same result. In *Marshall*, it was elevated to a new status as the decisive factor without any explanation why, when that factor was inapplicable, the other criteria which the Court had previously found sufficient no longer applied.

Perhaps the most serious objection to the Court's reasoning is the importance it attaches to the notion of State. This raises a number of difficulties. One is that it means that the rights of a plaintiff who invokes a directive in a national court may depend exclusively on the status of the defendant. In other words, a person who sues a public authority may find that he enjoys greater rights than a person who sues a private body even though, apart from the status of the defendant, there is no material difference between the two cases.[70] In the *Marshall* case, the United Kingdom drew the Court's attention to the danger of introducing a distinction between the rights of State employees and those of private employees. The Court's response was to observe: 'Such a distinction may easily be avoided if the Member State concerned has correctly implemented the directive in national law.'[71] That remark did less than justice to the nature of the objection: where a directive has

---

[68] See further Barents, 'Some remarks on the "horizontal" effect of directives' in O'Keeffe and Schermers (eds), *Essays in European Law and Integration* (1982), p 97.

[69] Case 43/75 [1976] ECR 455, para 31.

[70] Cf *Duke v GEC Reliance Ltd* [1988] AC 618, an English case where a claim by a woman whose circumstances were in all material respects identical to those of the appellant in *Marshall* failed simply because her employer was not an emanation of the State.

[71] Para 51.

been implemented properly, the question of direct effect simply does not arise because the plaintiff's claim can be based on the national implementing legislation. It is only where the directive has not been properly implemented that the plaintiff is forced to invoke it directly. Here the effect of the Court's case law is to introduce a seemingly arbitrary distinction according to the status of the defendant. It is unconvincing to seek to justify that distinction by reference to a situation which is necessarily hypothetical.

There is another respect in which the effect of the Court's decision is to introduce an arbitrary distinction. The Court seems to have proceeded on the basis that the boundaries of the State were fairly fixed and that there was a Community-wide consensus about where they were to be found. If this was ever the case, it is abundantly clear that it is no longer so. There is no agreement about which activities ought properly to be undertaken by the State and there is a real prospect that bodies will move in and out of State control as the political complexion of the government of the day changes. As Advocate General Mischo emphasized in another context, '[t]he choice of one form or another does not necessarily reflect objective criteria but is often a function of political or historical considerations or even of simple expediency or convenience of management'.[72] In short, the enforceability of a directive may depend not only on the status of the defendant, which may change in accordance with the prevailing political orthodoxy, but also on the defendant's nationality. Given that it is generally one of the purposes of directives to lay down a common core of rules applicable throughout the Member States, this is a result which the Court might have tried harder to avoid.

One argument, not mentioned by the Court, which might have been thought to justify the drawbacks of distinguishing between the public and the private sector is based on the principle of legal certainty. Consider the case of a small employer, struggling to make a profit.[73] There is a considerable body of legislation with which he must comply, some of it introduced to give effect to EC directives. If he is potentially bound by relevant directives, he must ask himself whether they have been implemented. If not, he must consider whether they are capable of producing direct effect. If they have been implemented, he must ask himself whether the national legislation is adequate. If he concludes that it is not, he must ask himself whether the parts of the directive which have not been properly implemented are capable of producing direct effect. In order to answer these questions, he will almost certainly have to seek legal advice. Even his lawyer may have difficulty answering some of them. This, it might be said, is incompatible with the principle of legal certainty, which the Court upholds as a general principle of Community law,[74] because it makes it virtually impossible for our small employer to establish with any degree of certainty what his obligations actually are. Directives should not therefore be capable of producing horizontal direct effect.

---

[72] Case 118/85 *Commission v Italy* [1987] ECR 2599, 2616.
[73] Cf the hypothesis put forward by Easson (1979) 4 ELRev 67, 76.   [74] See ch 6.

One answer to this objection is to say that responsibility for the threat to legal certainty lies with the Member State which has failed to implement the directive concerned. It could be restored simply by the introduction of appropriate national legislation. A different approach was taken by Wyatt, who expressed the view that the argument from legal certainty 'is flawed by its very generality. It does not distinguish between cases where legal certainty is *actually* threatened, and cases where it is not.'[75] He accepted that horizontal direct effect would threaten legal certainty where a private party relied in good faith on national legislation which implemented a directive incorrectly. However, he maintained that legal certainty was not compromised where no national implementing legislation had been adopted and the defendant could not say that he relied in good faith on national law. Here there could be no objection to endowing directives with horizontal direct effect.[76] It may be doubted whether it would be practical to distinguish cases on this basis. Which category would embrace the situation where a Member State has purported to implement a directive, but the national legislation fails to give effect to one of its provisions? Moreover, the distinction would require the plaintiff to perform the difficult task of deciding whether a court was likely to regard the principle of legal certainty as compromised. In any event, the argument from legal certainty has lost much of its force as a result of developments in the Court's case law since *Marshall* was decided.

There were two arguments which were conspicuous by their absence from the Court's ruling in *Marshall*. One was mentioned by Advocate General Slynn, who expressed the view that '[t]o give what is called "horizontal effect" to directives would totally blur the distinction between regulations and directives which the Treaty establishes in Articles 189 [now 249] and 191 [now 254]'.[77] That view, it is submitted, fails to accord sufficient weight to the distinction between direct applicability and direct effect. The essential quality of the regulation is not that it is capable of conferring rights directly on individuals but that it does not require incorporation into the national legal systems in order to enter into force. Likewise, the essential quality of the directive is that it requires implementation by the Member States to which it is addressed. The question whether it confers rights directly on individuals is a separate one, the answer to which does not affect the obligation of addressee Member States to adopt appropriate implementing provisions. Moreover, even where a directive is apt to produce direct effect, it cannot do so until after the deadline for its implementation has expired. As Advocate General Jacobs explained in *Vaneetveld*,[78] '[r]egulations and directives will remain

---

[75] 'The direct effect of Community social law—not forgetting directives' (1983) 8 ELRev 241, 246 (emphasis in the original).

[76] Wyatt went on to argue that legal certainty could in any event be protected by allowing horizontal effect in the case in question and in future cases only. The use by the Court of the prospective ruling is discussed in chs 6 and 13.

[77] At p 734.

[78] Case C–316/93 [1994] ECR I–763, 773. See also AG Lenz in C–91/92 *Faccini Dori v Recreb* [1994] ECR I–3325, 3341–2.

different instruments, appropriate in different situations and achieving their aims by different means, even if it is recognized that in certain circumstances a directive which has not been correctly implemented may impose obligations on certain private entities'.

The second argument concerned the absence in the original version of the EEC Treaty of any requirement that directives be published. As we have seen, before it was amended by the Treaty on European Union, regulations were required by Article 191 to be published in the Official Journal of the Community, but directives were only required to be notified to their addressees. It was sometimes said to be inconceivable that a measure that had not been published should impose obligations on third parties.[79] The argument was never a terribly convincing one, because as a matter of practice directives addressed to all the Member States nearly always were published in the Official Journal. Very few advocates of horizontal direct effect would have objected to denying that quality to a directive which had not been published. The argument was in any event rendered redundant with the entry into force of the Treaty on European Union.

Mitigating factors

The Court's decision in *Marshall* had potentially serious consequences for the rights of individuals and for the uniform application of Community law, but it appeared at the time to be mitigated by two factors. In the first place, national courts were required to interpret their national legislation in accordance with the provisions of any relevant directives. Secondly, the notion of State was widely construed by the Court. The Court subsequently held that, although not capable of producing horizontal direct effect, directives might have certain incidental effects in proceedings between private parties. Moreover, a Member State might in some circumstances be required to compensate individuals who suffered loss where it had failed to implement a directive adequately. It is proposed to consider the duty of construction imposed on national courts, the scope of the notion of State, and the question of incidental effect in the present chapter. Discussion of the potential liability of defaulting Member States in damages is postponed until the following chapter.

The duty of construction

Although the Court had previously encouraged national courts to interpret implementing legislation in the light of directives it was intended to transpose,[80] in *Von Colson and Kamann v Land Nordrhein-Westfalen*[81] the Court elevated that encour-

---

[79] For a short account of the argument, see Easson (1979) 4 ELRev 67, 72. See also AG Lenz in Case C–91/92 *Faccini Dori v Recreb*, supra, p I–3343.
[80] See Case 111/75 *Mazzalai v Ferrovia del Renon* [1976] ECR 657, para 10/11.
[81] Case 14/83 [1984] ECR 1891.

agement to the level of an obligation. One of the issues raised in that case was the compatibility with a directive on equal treatment for men and women of a provision of German law which appeared to limit the amount of compensation which could be awarded to the victims of sex discrimination. The *Von Colson* case was decided on the same day as another case in which the same issue was raised, *Harz v Deutsche Tradax*.[82] However, whereas in the former the defendant was an emanation of the State against which the relevant directive could have been directly invoked, in the latter the defendant was a private company. For the Court to have delivered rulings which led to different outcomes in each case would have been a stark reminder of the discrepancies to which the *Marshall* case was liable to give rise.

The nature of the sanctions available under German law for sex discrimination and the precise effect of the provision concerned were the subject of considerable discussion before the Court. The Court made it clear that it was for the national court to determine the proper interpretation of its national legislation. However, the Court added:

the Member States' obligation arising from a directive to achieve the result envisaged by the directive and their duty under Article 5 [now 10] of the Treaty to take all appropriate measures, whether general or particular, to ensure the fulfilment of that obligation, is binding on all the authorities of Member States including, for matters within their jurisdiction, the courts. It follows that, in applying the national law and in particular the provisions of a national law specifically introduced in order to implement Directive No 76/207, national courts are required to interpret their national law in the light of the wording and the purpose of the directive in order to achieve the result referred to in the third paragraph of Article 189 [now 249].[83]

The duty imposed on national courts was potentially of great importance, but its precise scope was left somewhat obscure. The use of the words 'in particular' in the final sentence of the passage quoted above implied that the duty of construction applied not just to national legislation specifically introduced to implement a directive but to any national law the subject-matter of which overlapped with that of the directive. If this interpretation of the judgment was correct, it would mean that national courts would find themselves constrained to interpret in the light of a relevant directive legislation which was already on the statute book when the directive was adopted.[84] The operative part of the Court's judgment, in which it set out the text of the answers to the questions which had been referred to it, appeared to be more limited. In the operative part, the Court simply stated: 'It is for the national court to interpret and apply *the legislation adopted for the implementation of the directive* in conformity with the requirements of Community law, in so far as it is given discretion to do so under national law.'[85] That statement might

---

[82] Case 79/83 [1984] ECR 1921.

[83] Para 26 of the judgment in *Von Colson*. Cf para 26 of the judgment in *Harz*.

[84] It may also be observed that the Court's remarks were not confined to legislation but were apt to embrace rules laid down by the courts.

[85] Emphasis added. The operative part of the judgment in *Harz* contains a sentence in the same terms.

have been taken to imply that it was only legislation introduced to give effect to a directive that had to be interpreted in accordance with the directive's terms.

The more limited reading of the Court's ruling in *Von Colson* was preferred by Advocate General Slynn in *Marshall*:[86]

It is thus plain that where legislation is adopted to implement a directive, or consequent upon a Treaty obligation, national courts should seek so far as possible to construe the former in such a way as to comply with the latter. To construe a pre-existing statute of 1975 or even 1875 in order to comply with a subsequent directive, which the legislature or executive has not implemented, in breach of its obligation, when it has a discretion as to the form and method to be adopted, is, in my view, wholly different. I am not satisfied that it is a rule of Community law that national courts have a duty to do so—unless it is clear that the legislation was adopted specifically with a proposed directive in mind.

Whilst the logic of this approach was unimpeachable, it risked undermining the effectiveness of the *Von Colson* principle as a mechanism for protecting individual rights and promoting the effectiveness of directives. The limited version of the principle would have left unaffected cases where Member States had simply failed to give effect to directives. Moreover, as Advocate General van Gerven pointed out in the *Barber* case,[87] it may not be easy to determine whether a particular national provision was introduced in order to give effect to a directive. The approach favoured by Advocate General Slynn would have required a distinction to be drawn between cases where a Member State implemented a directive (albeit inadequately) and cases where a Member State failed to introduce implementing legislation because it believed, perhaps in good faith, that its existing legislation was sufficient to meet the directive's requirements. It seems unlikely that the Court intended the *Von Colson* principle to be read in this limited way. It is submitted that the explanation for the terms in which the operative part of the Court's ruling was couched is simply that the Court was adapting the more general statement made earlier in the judgment to the facts of the particular case, which concerned the effect of national legislation adopted to implement the directive concerned.

The *Marleasing* case

It was not until the judgment in the *Marleasing* case[88] that the Court clarified the proper scope of the *Von Colson* principle. *Marleasing* came before the Court by way of a reference for a preliminary ruling by a Spanish court. In the main action, the plaintiff was seeking a declaration that the contract by which the defendant company was established was void. One of the parties to that contract was a third company which was in debt to the plaintiff, which contended that the defendant had been set up solely to put the assets of the third company beyond the reach of its creditors. The plaintiff relied on provisions of the Spanish Civil Code on the valid-

---

[86] At p 733.   [87] Case C–262/88 [1990] ECR I–1889, 1937.
[88] Case C–106/89 [1990] ECR I–4135.

ity of contracts, according to which contracts lacking cause or whose cause was unlawful had no legal effect. In its defence, the defendant invoked a provision of a directive on company law, Article 11 of which contained an exhaustive list of the circumstances in which the nullity of a company could be declared. The list did not include lack of lawful cause, the main ground relied on by the plaintiff. At the material time, however, Spain had not implemented the directive, although it should have done so with effect from its accession to the Community. The Court observed that, since the defendant was not a public authority, the directive could not be enforced directly against it. None the less, the Court stated that it followed from paragraph 26 of the *Von Colson* ruling, that:

in applying national law, *whether the provisions in question were adopted before or after the directive*, the national court called upon to interpret it is required to do so, as far as possible, in the light of the wording and the purpose of the directive in order to achieve the result pursued by the latter and thereby comply with the third paragraph of Article 189 [now 249] of the Treaty.

It follows that the requirement that national law must be interpreted in conformity with Article 11 of Directive 68/151 precludes the interpretation of provisions of national law relating to public limited companies in such a manner that the nullity of a public limited company may be ordered on grounds other than those exhaustively listed in Article 11 of the directive in question.[89]

The Court's judgment in *Marleasing* therefore made it clear that it was the broader version of the duty laid down in *Von Colson* with which national courts were to comply. The date of the national legislation concerned was irrelevant. The only question was whether it overlapped with a directive. If it did, it had to be interpreted in accordance with the directive concerned.[90]

On a superficial reading, the judgment in *Marleasing* might have been thought to represent a strengthening of the duty of construction in another respect. The Court concluded that a national court deciding a case which fell within the ambit of the directive concerned 'is required to interpret its national law in the light of the wording and the purpose of that directive in order to preclude a declaration of nullity of a public limited company on a ground other than those listed in Article 11 of the directive'. That statement might have been taken to imply that the national court was required to interpret its national law so as to produce a particular result regardless of what that law actually said.[91] This, of course, would be tantamount to endowing directives with horizontal direct effect, a quality which the Court had reiterated in *Marleasing* that they did not possess.

---

[89] Paras 8 and 9, emphasis added.

[90] Para 13. It is in relation to directives that the duty of construction has been of particular importance, but it also applies to other requirements of Community law including those laid down in the Treaty: see eg Case 157/86 *Murphy v An Bord Telecom Eireann* [1988] ECR 673, para 11; Case C–165/91 *van Munster v Rijksdienst voor Pensioenen* [1994] ECR I–4661, para 34.

[91] See de Búrca, 'Giving effect to European Community directives' (1992) 55 MLR 215, 223.

It is submitted that the view that the language of the national legislation is no longer relevant is based on a misreading of the judgment in *Marleasing*. The judgment can only be properly understood in the light of the factual context in which it was given. It is clear from the Report for the Hearing that the circumstances in which a declaration of nullity of a company could be granted under Spanish law were unclear. Spanish legislation on public limited companies did not specifically set out the cases of nullity of such companies. According to the legal literature, the matter was governed by the rules of ordinary law, but the application by analogy of those rules was acknowledged to pose a number of difficulties.[92] As Advocate General van Gerven explained:

The national court is thus faced—as I understand it—with a problem concerning the interpretation of company law. The question which arises is to what extent the grounds of nullity under ordinary law can be applied by analogy to public limited companies. It follows, in my view . . . that the requirement that an interpretation must be consistent with a directive precludes the application to public limited companies of the provisions on nullity under ordinary law in such a way as to permit a declaration of nullity of such a company on grounds other than those exhaustively listed in Article 11 of the First Directive.[93]

The case was therefore one in which the effect of the relevant national rules was unclear. In those circumstances, the national court was indeed precluded from interpreting those rules in a manner which produced a result inconsistent with the directive. But it is evident from the circumstances of the case that the Court did not mean to suggest that, in cases where the position under national law was clear, the relevant provisions had to be interpreted *contra legem* to bring them into line with a directive. It is for this reason that, in the general statement of the duty of construction set out in *Marleasing*, the Court makes it clear that the national court is only required to interpret its national law in the light of relevant directives 'as far as possible'.[94]

That this was the correct interpretation of *Marleasing* was confirmed by the Court's subsequent rulings in *Wagner Miret*[95] and *Faccini Dori v Recreb*.[96] In the latter case, the Court explained that, '[i]f the result prescribed by the directive cannot be achieved by way of interpretation . . . Community law requires the Member States to make good damage caused to individuals through failure to transpose a directive',[97] provided certain conditions were met. That statement represented an express acknowledgement by the Court that the language of the relevant national provision would sometimes not admit of an interpretation which was consistent

---

[92] See p I–4137.   [93] p I–4148.

[94] Para 8. This was the view of *Marleasing* taken by Lord Keith in an English case, *Webb v EMO Air Cargo (UK) Ltd* [1992] 4 All ER 929, 940. See also the Opinions of AG van Gerven in Case C–262/88 *Barber* [1990] ECR I–1889, 1937, and in Case C–271/91 *Marshall v Southampton and South West Hampshire Area Health Authority (Marshall II)* [1993] ECR I–4367, 4385–6; Maltby, '*Marleasing*: what is all the fuss about?' (1993) 109 LQR 301.

[95] Case C–334/92 [1993] ECR I–6911, para 22.   [96] *Supra.*

[97] Para 27. See also Case C–192/94 *El Corte Inglés v Blázquez Rivero* [1996] ECR I–1281.

with the directive concerned and that in such cases the party seeking to rely on the directive would have to seek an alternative remedy.

The rule that provisions of national law which are capable of bearing more than one meaning must be interpreted in accordance with any directive dealing with the same subject matter is evidently not the same thing as direct effect: there has to be a national provision before the duty can bite and that provision must to some extent be ambiguous. Moreover, the duty of construction is significantly less effective than the concept of direct effect because of the reliance it places on the willingness of national judges to depart from established national canons of statutory interpretation.[98]

Vertical cases and the duty of construction

In *Von Colson*, *Marleasing*, and *Faccini Dori*, the relevant directives were invoked by private parties. It might have been thought, however, that the duty of construction developed by the Court in those cases was stated broadly enough to enable it to be invoked by public authorities. If this were possible, it might produce the paradoxical result of nullifying the results of a Member State's failure to give effect to a directive. Given that one of the main reasons for the Court's acceptance that directives may produce vertical direct effect was the need to prevent Member States from pleading their own wrong, it is not surprising that this is a result the Court has sought to avoid.

The issue came before the Court in *Kolpinghuis Nijmegen*,[99] where the Court was asked four questions on the effect of a directive under the national law of a Member State which had not yet given effect to it. The issue arose in the following way. A company which ran a café was prosecuted under Dutch law for describing as 'mineral water' a drink which in fact consisted of tap water and carbon dioxide. Before the referring court, the Public Prosecutor relied on a directive which laid down certain conditions which had to be met before water could be marketed as natural mineral water. At the time the alleged offence took place, the directive had not been implemented in the Netherlands, although the deadline for giving effect to it had expired. The questions referred to the Court asked essentially whether a Member State could rely against one of its own nationals on a directive which it had not implemented. The Court reiterated its statement in *Marshall* that a directive could not of itself impose obligations on individuals. It followed that a national authority could not rely, as against an individual, on a directive which had not yet

---

[98] See the comments of Prechal (1990) 27 CMLRev 451, 470–2. For discussion of the approach of the English courts to the interpretation of domestic provisions which overlap with provisions of Community law, see Arnull, 'Interpretation and precedent in English and Community law: evidence of cross-fertilisation?' in Andenas (ed), *English Public Law and the Common Law of Europe* (1998), ch 6, pp. 94–119.

[99] Case 80/86 [1987] ECR 3969. See also Case 14/86 *Pretore di Salò v Persons Unknown* [1987] ECR 2545.

been implemented. The reference to the *Marshall* case should not, however, mislead the observer into thinking that this was a case of horizontal effect. Strictly speaking, as the Commission pointed out,[100] it was a case of inverse vertical effect.[101] However, even if directives were capable of producing horizontal direct effect, it would clearly be unfair to allow a public authority to rely, as against an individual, on the State's failure to comply with its Treaty obligations. The Court went on to explain that the duty of construction laid down in *Von Colson* was 'limited by the general principles of law which form part of Community law and in particular the principles of legal certainty and retroactivity'.[102] The Court concluded that 'a directive cannot, of itself and independently of a law adopted for its implementation, have the effect of determining or aggravating the liability in criminal law of persons who act in contravention of the provisions of that directive'.[103]

The *Kolpinghuis* case was cited in *Arcaro*,[104] where a three-Judge chamber declared that the 'obligation of the national court to refer to the content of the directive when interpreting the relevant rules of its own national law *reaches a limit where such an interpretation leads to the imposition on an individual of an obligation laid down by a directive which has not been transposed . . .*'.[105] It was suggested that the effect of that passage might be to reduce the scope of the duty of construction,[106] but this does not seem to have been the Court's intention. The judgment needed to be understood in the context in which it was delivered. The *Arcaro* case arose out of a prosecution of a businessman for infringing Italian legislation on pollution. It was unclear whether that legislation was consistent with a series of Community directives it was designed to implement. The Court's judgment made it clear that the *Marleasing* principle did not apply where the effect would be to enable *a Member State* to enforce *against an individual* an obligation to which he might not otherwise be subject. Since it is the Member State which is responsible for not having implemented the directive properly (or at all), it would be unconscionable to allow it to escape the consequences of its default in vertical proceedings of this kind. In horizontal proceedings *between individuals*,[107] that consideration is not relevant and the duty of construction continues to apply in its full rigour.

---

[100] See p 3974.   [101] Cf Case C–13/93 *Minne* [1994] ECR I–371.
[102] Para 13.

[103] Para 14. The Court added that it was irrelevant whether or not the deadline for implementing the directive had expired. On the extent to which the duty of construction applies prior to the expiry of the deadline, see AG Jacobs in Case C–156/91 *Hansa Fleisch v Landrat des Kreises Schleswig-Holstein* [1992] ECR I–5567, 5585–7.

[104] Case C–168/95 [1996] ECR I–4705.   [105] Para 42, emphasis added.

[106] See Craig, 'Directives: direct effect, indirect effect and the construction of national legislation' (1997) 22 ELRev 519; Craig and de Búrca, *EU Law* (2nd edn, 1998), 205–6.

[107] eg *Webb v EMO Air Cargo (UK) Ltd* [1995] IRLR 645.

The notion of State

The second factor which limits the repercussions of the *Marshall* decision is the definition given by the Court to the term 'Member State' in Article 249 (ex 189).[108] That definition is evidently crucial, since the Court held that it is upon the Member States to which a directive is addressed that it may impose obligations. In *Marshall*, Advocate General Slynn said:[109]

What constitutes the 'State' in a particular national legal system must be a matter for the national court to decide. However (even if contrary to the trend of decisions in cases involving sovereign immunity where the exercise of imperium is distinguished from commercial and similar activities) as a matter of Community law, where the question of an individual relying upon the provisions of a directive as against the State arises, I consider that the 'State' must be taken broadly, as including all the organs of the State. In matters of employment, which is what Directive 76/207 is concerned with, this means all the employees of such organs and not just the central civil service.

The Court declined to confront the issue directly in its judgment, merely noting that the Court of Appeal had stated in its Order for Reference that the respondent was a public authority. While this left no doubt about the Court's view of the status of the respondent, it offered little guidance to courts and tribunals which might in the future be called upon to determine the status of other bodies. It became increasingly apparent, however, that the concept of 'State' for these purposes was indeed a broad one. In *Johnston v Chief Constable of the Royal Ulster Constabulary*,[110] for example, a reference was made to the Court by an Industrial Tribunal in the context of a dispute between the applicant and the Chief Constable over the effect of Directive 76/207 on equal treatment for men and women. The United Kingdom argued that the directive could not be directly effective in the circumstances because the Chief Constable was constitutionally independent of the State and was involved in the proceedings only in his capacity as an employer. That argument was rejected by the Court, which stated:

As regards an authority like the Chief Constable, it must be observed that, according to the Industrial Tribunal's decision, the Chief Constable is an official responsible for the direction of the police service. Whatever its relations may be with other organs of the State, such a public authority, charged by the State with the maintenance of public order and safety, does not act as a private individual. It may not take advantage of the failure of the State, of which it is an emanation, to comply with Community law.[111]

---

[108] See further Curtin, 'The province of government: delimiting the direct effect of directives in the common law context' (1990) 15 ELRev 195; Prechal, 'Remedies after *Marshall*' (1990) 27 CMLRev 451, 457–62.

[109] At p 735.

[110] Case 222/84 [1986] ECR 1651. Cf Case 271/82 *Auer v Ministère Public* [1983] ECR 2727.

[111] Para 56.

The Court was confronted with a rather less clear-cut situation in *Fratelli Costanzo v Comune di Milano*.[112] That case arose out of a dispute between the applicant and the Municipal Executive Board of Milan. The Board had eliminated a tender submitted by the applicant from a tendering procedure for a public works contract, which was awarded to another company. The national court asked the Court of Justice for guidance on the effect of a directive on the award of public works contracts. It wanted to know in particular whether administrative and municipal authorities were under the same obligations as national courts to apply the relevant provisions of the directive and to refrain from applying provisions of national law which were inconsistent with them. The Court reiterated that provisions contained in a directive which were unconditional and sufficiently precise bound all the authorities of the Member States. It continued:[113]

It would moreover be contradictory to rule that an individual may rely upon the provisions of a directive which fulfil the conditions defined above in proceedings before the national courts seeking an order against the administrative authorities, and yet to hold that those authorities are under no obligation to apply the provisions of the directive and refrain from applying provisions of national law which conflict with them. It follows that when the conditions under which the Court has held that individuals may rely on the provisions of a directive before the national courts are met, all organs of the administration, including decentralized authorities such as municipalities, are obliged to apply those provisions.

A body's status as a public authority will not, however, prevent it from relying on a directive itself in proceedings against the State in the strict sense, as *Ufficio Distrettuale delle Imposte Dirette di Fiorenzuola d'Arda and Others v Comune di Carpaneto Piacentino and Others*[114] demonstrates. That case arose out of a dispute between the Italian tax authorities and a number of local authorities over their liability to VAT. In order to resolve the dispute, a number of questions were referred to the Court on the meaning and effect of the Sixth VAT Directive. The Court said that bodies governed by public law, 'which, in this context must be assimilated to individuals', could rely on the directive to oppose the application of a national provision making them subject to VAT. The *Carpaneto* decision attracted a certain amount of criticism, since it seemed to indicate that the status of a party might vary according to the context. One commentator remarked that the notion of State had become a concept 'à contenu variable'.[115]

Although the relevant part of the Court's judgment is perhaps not happily expressed, it is submitted that the criticism to which it has been subject is misplaced. In the previous paragraph, the Court had referred to its ruling in *Becker*, where it spoke of 'rights which individuals are able to assert against the State'. It is submitted that, in assimilating a public body to an individual, the Court was merely say-

---

[112] Case 103/88 [1989] ECR 1839.   [113] Para 31.
[114] Joined Cases 231/87 and 129/88 [1989] ECR 3233.
[115] Manin, 'L'invocabilité des directives: quelques interrogations' (1990) 26 RTDE 670, 685. See also Emmert and Pereira de Azevedo, 'L'effet horizontal des directives. La jurisprudence de la CJCE: un bateau ivre?' (1993) 29 RTDE 503, 512.

ing that such a body might also be able to assert rights laid down in directives against the State. The reason for that conclusion is simply that, where a directive is invoked in proceedings before a national court, the status of the *plaintiff* is not relevant to the question whether the directive has direct effect. Thus it is not correct to say that the notion of State, which is used to determine the status of the *defendant*, is variable in content.

It was inevitable that the Court would eventually have to define in more general terms the types of body that fell within the notion of State within the meaning of Article 249 (ex 189). Decisions which were closely related to the facts of particular cases did not provide national courts with enough guidance to obviate the need for a preliminary ruling to be sought each time the status of a new body fell to be established. In *Foster and Others*,[116] Advocate General van Gerven sought to deal with the problem in more general terms. The case turned on whether the appellants could rely directly on Directive 76/207 in proceedings against British Gas plc, the successor to their former employer, the British Gas Corporation. At the material time, the Corporation was responsible for developing and maintaining a system of gas supply in Great Britain and had a monopoly of the supply of gas. The members of the Corporation were appointed by the Secretary of State, who had the power to give the Corporation directions and instructions in relation to various matters, including the allocation of funds. The Corporation was required to submit to the Secretary of State periodic reports on the exercise of its functions and had the right, with the consent of the Secretary of State, to submit proposed legislation to Parliament. In 1986, the Corporation was privatized and its rights and liabilities transferred to British Gas plc, the respondent in the main proceedings.

In the Court of Appeal, Lord Donaldson MR, with whom Nourse and Mann LJJ agreed, said that the question whether the notion of State embraced a nationalized industry such as the Corporation was 'a mixed question of European law and national law'.[117] It was, he argued, for European law to determine the types of bodies which constituted the State for the purposes of the direct effect of directives and for English law to determine the proper classification of any particular body in accordance with the criteria laid down by the Court of Justice. His Lordship took the view that the *Marshall* and *Johnston* cases 'establish that, as a matter of European law, the Directive gives rise to legal rights in employees of the State itself and of any organ or emanation of the State, an emanation of the State being understood to include an individual public authority charged by the State with the performance of any of the classic duties of the State, such as the defence of the realm or the maintenance of law and order within the realm'.[118] He concluded that the Corporation did not fall within that category. The appellants appealed to the House of Lords, which referred the matter to the Court of Justice.

According to Advocate General van Gerven, the *Marshall* and *Johnston* cases showed that a Member State, and any public body charged with responsibilities by

[116] Case C–188/89 [1990] ECR I–3313.   [117] [1988] IRLR 354, 355.   [118] Ibid.

the State from which it derived its authority, was not permitted to benefit from the State's failure to give effect to the directive in question. The existing case law left no doubt that the expression 'public body', which the Court used interchangeably with terms such as 'emanation of the State', 'organ of the State', 'public authority', and 'State authority',[119] was to be understood very broadly: 'all bodies which pursuant to the constitutional structure of a Member State can exercise any authority over individuals fall within the concept of "the State". In that respect it is immaterial how that authority (which I shall call public authority) is organized and how the various bodies which exercise that authority are related . . . there is no need for any criterion of delegation or control by other public authorities.'[120] The question was whether that case law could be extended to a public undertaking such as the Corporation which exercised no authority in the strict sense over individuals. The Advocate General concluded that individuals could rely on an unconditional and sufficiently precise provision of a directive:

against a person or body, in this case a public undertaking, in respect of which the State (understood as any body endowed with public authority, regardless of its relationship with other public bodies or the nature of the duties entrusted to it) has assumed responsibilities which put it in a position to decisively influence the conduct of that person or body in any manner whatsoever (other than by means of general legislation) with regard to the matter in respect of which the relevant provision of a directive imposes an obligation which the Member State has failed to implement in national law.[121]

The Advocate General made it clear that it was for the national courts to apply that test in particular cases, but he left little doubt that, in his view, the Corporation fell within the class of bodies against which directives could be directly enforced.

The Court began by rejecting a challenge to its jurisdiction raised by the United Kingdom on the basis that it was not for the Court of Justice but for the national courts to determine whether a directive could be enforced against a body such as the Corporation. The Court made it clear that it had jurisdiction 'to determine the categories of persons against whom the provisions of a directive may be relied on. It is for the national courts, on the other hand, to decide whether a party to proceedings before them falls within one of the categories so defined.'[122] That conclusion, which was in accordance with the views of both Advocate General van Gerven and Lord Donaldson in the Court of Appeal, was incontrovertible. The question referred by the House of Lords essentially asked the Court to define the term 'Member State' as used in Article 189 (now 249) of the Treaty, since the *Marshall* decision took as its starting point the fact that it is only upon the Member States to which they are addressed that the Treaty makes directives binding. The proper interpretation of a term used in an article of the Treaty is self-evidently a matter which falls within the jurisdiction of the Court of Justice. Moreover, as Advocate General van Gerven pointed out, '[i]f the Court itself did not lay down a basis in Community law, the result would be a complete lack of uniformity

---

[119] See p I–3330.   [120] p I–3339.   [121] p I–3340.   [122] Para 15.

among the Member States with regard to the direct effect of provisions of direct-ives'.[123]

As far as the substance of the case was concerned, the Court observed that it had held on a number of occasions that the provisions of a directive could in principle be relied upon 'against organizations or bodies which were subject to the author-ity or control of the State or had special powers beyond those which result from the normal rules applicable to relations between individuals'.[124] However, that was as far as it went by way of general definition, its answer to the question referred to it being closely linked to the facts of the case. The Court stated:[125]

a body, whatever its legal form, which has been made responsible, pursuant to a measure adopted by the State, for providing a public service under the control of the State and has for that purpose special powers beyond those which result from the normal rules applicable in relations between individuals *is included in any event among* the bodies against which the provisions of a directive capable of having direct effect may be relied upon.

When it came to apply that ruling, the House of Lords did not resist the clear implication that the Corporation did indeed constitute a public body for these purposes.[126]

It is important to note that the passage quoted above was not intended by the Court to be an exhaustive definition of the notion of State for the purposes of the direct effect of directives. It was merely intended to offer the House of Lords enough guidance to enable it to decide the instant case. That the statement in ques-tion was not designed to perform any broader function is clear from the words 'is included in any event among', emphasized above. The Court was saying that, whatever the position might be in cases involving other bodies, a body with the characteristics enumerated constituted an emanation of the State.[127]

Pressure for change

The increasing complexity of establishing the status of directives in national proceedings led to pressure for the Court to reconsider its case law to the effect that such acts could not have horizontal direct effect. A leading proponent of a *revirement* in the Court's approach was Advocate General van Gerven, who first expressed reservations about the *Marshall* ruling in his Opinion in the *Barber*

---

[123] p I–3332.

[124] Para 18. Curiously, the Court went on to state that it had held in *Marshall* that a directive could be relied on against public authorities providing public health services: see para 19. This is, of course, incorrect. In *Marshall* the Court was not called upon to determine the status of the respondent author-ity and merely acquiesced in the classification accorded to it by the referring court.

[125] Para 20. Emphasis added.   [126] [1991] ICR 463, [1991] 2 CMLR 217.

[127] The ruling does not therefore exclude the possibility that British Gas plc, established as a result of the privatization of the Corporation, might also constitute an emanation of the State. Cf the English cases of *Rolls Royce plc v Doughty* [1992] ICR 538 and *NUT and Others v St Mary's Church of England Junior School and Others* [1997] 3 CMLR 630.

case.[128] One of the many issues considered by the Advocate General in that case was whether the applicant could rely directly on an unimplemented directive in proceedings against his former employer, the Guardian Royal Exchange Assurance Group, which was not an emanation of the State.

The Advocate General said that the real question was not whether the directive imposed obligations on the applicant's former employer, 'but whether Mr Barber can rely as against the Guardian on the failure of a Member State which is in default to comply with *its* obligation to implement Community law, if Mr Barber's rights had been impaired thereby [emphasis in the original]'. Conversely, was it permissible for a private body to profit from a Member State's default in order to deprive an individual of an advantage which Community law intended him to enjoy?[129] The Advocate General noted that the Court's case law allowed individuals to rely on a Member State's default in failing to transpose a directive against independent public bodies which bore no responsibility themselves for the failure of the State concerned to implement the directive. 'Does that case-law have to be extended', he asked, 'in the sense that even an individual who is in no way connected with the public authorities may not derive any advantage in his relations with other individuals from a Member State's default and must therefore refrain from relying on a (statutory or contractual) provision which is contrary to the directive? It cannot be ruled out that the *nemo auditur [propriam turpitudinem allegans]*[130] principle (or doctrine of estoppel) may be interpreted as a general prohibition on taking advantage of another's default, *once* that principle is endowed with such a wide effect, as in the aforesaid case-law, that it no longer relates to a "personal" default on the part of the Member State in its capacity as *law*maker (emphasis in the original)'. The Advocate General did not propose that this further step be taken in the instant case, which he thought could be resolved on the basis of an article of the Treaty which produced both vertical and horizontal direct effect, namely Article 119 (now 141), laying down the principle that men and women should receive equal pay for equal work. None the less, he pointed out that endowing directives with horizontal direct effect would avoid several problems:

the unequal treatment of employers in the public and private sectors (an economic problem) and above all of workers employed by public or private employers (a social problem) would be eliminated as a result, and awkward problems of delimitation would be avoided, in connection with the term 'State', between the public sector and the private sector, problems which are further aggravated by the fact that workers employed by the same public utility institution or undertaking may, depending on whether it is privatised or nationalized, find themselves at one moment in the private sector and at the next in the public sector.

In *Marshall II*,[131] Advocate General van Gerven repeated his view that 'the coherence of the Court's case-law would benefit if the Court were now also to confer

---

[128] Case C–262/88 [1990] ECR I–1889, 1938–9.
[129] The Advocate General called this 'third-party effect' or *Drittwirkung*: see p I–1938, n 44.
[130] No one may bring a claim which is based on his own turpitude.
[131] Case C–271/91 *Marshall v Southampton and South West Hampshire Area Health Authority* [1993] ECR I–4367.

horizontal direct effect on sufficiently precise and unconditional provisions of Directives'.[132] He was joined in his campaign for a departure from *Marshall I* by Advocate General Jacobs who, in *Vaneetveld*,[133] expressed the view that the anomalies to which the former case had given rise justified a different approach.

In *Faccini Dori v Recreb*,[134] the *grand plenum* reviewed the question whether directives might have horizontal direct effect. That case concerned the right of an Italian consumer to cancel a contract concluded with a private company away from the company's business premises. Such a right was conferred on consumers by a directive adopted in 1985, but at the material time Italy had not taken any steps to transpose it into national law even though the deadline for its implementation had expired. One of the issues referred to the Court by the Giudice Conciliatore di Firenze was whether the directive was capable of having direct effect between individuals once the deadline for its implementation had expired.

As Advocate General Lenz explained in his Opinion, the Court asked all the Member States to express a view on whether or not directives could have horizontal direct effect. Only Greece was in favour of departing from the Court's existing case law. Even the Commission argued that that case law should be followed. However, Advocate General Lenz aligned himself with the growing body of opinion which favoured a new approach. He emphasized the damage caused to the proper functioning of the internal market by Member States who failed to implement directives correctly and the contribution which horizontal direct effect would make to equalizing conditions of competition throughout the Member States. In a concession to the requirements of legal certainty, however, the Advocate General proposed that the existing case law be maintained as far as the past (apparently including the instant case) was concerned, but that for the future directives should be recognized as capable of producing horizontal direct effect. The Court was unmoved, ruling that 'in the absence of measures transposing the directive within the prescribed time-limit consumers cannot derive from the directive itself a right of cancellation as against traders with whom they have concluded a contract or enforce such a right in a national court'.[135]

Where the Commission and nearly all the Member States are unanimous in their view of how a question of such fundamental importance should be answered, it is perhaps unsurprising when the Court follows them. Given the force of the arguments pointing the other way and the distinguished sources from which they emanated, however, the reader cannot fail to be struck by the paucity of the reasons given by the Court for refusing to depart from its existing case law. Although the Court devoted twelve paragraphs of its judgment to the question of direct

---

[132] p I–4387, emphasis in the original. See also van Gerven, 'The horizontal effect of directive provisions revisited: the reality of catchwords' in Curtin and Heukels (eds), *Institutional Dynamics of European Integration* (Vol II) (1994), p. 335.

[133] Case C–316/93 [1994] ECR I–763. See also Manin, op cit; Emmert and Pereira de Azevedo, op cit.

[134] Case C–91/92 [1994] ECR I–3325.   [135] Para 30.

effect, only one contained anything new. In paragraph 24, the Court said that
the effect of extending its case law on the vertical direct effect of directives 'to the
sphere of relations between individuals would be to recognize a power in the
Community to enact obligations for individuals with immediate effect, whereas it
has competence to do so only where it is empowered to adopt regulations'.

That short sentence contrived both to beg the question and to misrepresent the
consequences of endowing directives with the capacity to produce horizontal
direct effect. It begged the question because whether the Community has competence to enact obligations for individuals with immediate effect by means other than
regulations depends on the effects of directives, which was precisely the question
the Court had been asked to resolve. Perhaps more importantly, however, the
effect of conferring on directives the capacity to produce horizontal direct effect
would not be 'to recognize a power in the Community to enact obligations for
individuals with immediate effect'. First of all, there was no suggestion that directives should produce horizontal direct effect before the period prescribed for their
implementation had passed. Secondly, it is never the purpose of a directive to
achieve its objectives directly, because directives always require implementation by
the Member States. It is only where the system malfunctions that direct effect
comes into play. Even then, the delinquent State remains obliged to give effect to
the directive concerned and retains the discretion conferred on it by Article 249
(ex 189) as to the form and methods of doing so. The reader searches the judgment
of the Court in vain for an explanation of why the estoppel principle is relevant in
cases involving public bodies which have no power or responsibility for implementing directives. Although the referring court was reminded of the duty of construction, there was no acknowledgement by the Court of the shortcomings of that
duty as a means of protecting the rights of individuals and safeguarding the uniform
application of Community law.

The incidental effect of directives

A series of cases decided after *Faccini Dori* might have been thought to cast doubt
on the proposition that directives could not have horizontal direct effect. Perhaps
the best known is *CIA Security v Signalson and Securitel*,[136] where the plaintiff
argued, in proceedings before the Belgian courts, that the defendants had libelled
it by claiming that an alarm system it marketed did not comply with the Belgian
legislation on security systems. The defendants replied that the plaintiff was marketing an alarm system which had not been approved and should be restrained from
carrying on business. Under a Community directive on technical standards, the relevant national legislation should have been notified to the Commission prior to its
introduction. The national court asked for guidance on the consequences where

---

[136] Case C–194/94 [1996] ECR I–2201. Cf Case C–226/97 *Lemmens*, judgment of 16 June 1998.

that requirement had not been respected. The Court held that a breach of the obligation to notify rendered national technical regulations inapplicable, with the result that they could not be enforced against individuals.

The Court appeared to take a similar approach in two other cases. In *Pafitis and Others v TKE and Others*,[137] the Court held that a directive on company law precluded national legislation under which the capital of a bank constituted in the form of a public limited company and which was in financial difficulty could be increased by an administrative measure, without a resolution of the general meeting. In *Ruiz Bernáldez*,[138] the Court held that certain directives on motor insurance required Member States to ensure that the use of vehicles was covered by insurance which enabled third-party victims of accidents to be compensated. An insurer was therefore precluded from relying on provisions of national law or contractual clauses to avoid paying compensation for damage caused to third parties by the insured vehicle.

Each of these cases involved the imposition on a private party of some sort of burden derived from a directive. In *CIA Security*, the relevant directive undermined, potentially fatally, the position of the defendants. In *Pafitis*, the relevant directive deprived the new shareholders of their status as such and of their right to participate in the general meeting of the bank. In *Ruiz Bernáldez*, the relevant directive led to the imposition on the insurer of an obligation to compensate a third-party victim of an accident caused by the insured. Were these decisions perhaps to be interpreted as a departure from the case law denying that directives may produce horizontal direct effect?[139]

It seems clear that the Court did not intend them to be interpreted in that way, for the Court expressly reaffirmed *Faccini Dori* in *El Corte Inglés v Blázquez Rivero*,[140] a case decided just five days before *Pafitis*. Moreover, in *CIA Security*, Advocate General Elmer observed that, while the directive in question imposed a number of obligations on Member States, it did not 'aim to impose duties on individuals and therefore no question arises as to whether the Directive should have direct effect as far as individuals' obligations are concerned'.[141] The Advocate General said it would be 'unsatisfactory and incomprehensible' if Community law sought 'to prevent a Member State from prosecuting an individual who had not complied with a non-notified technical provision, but on the other hand would debar the same individual from relying on the same circumstance in a case against a competitor who had stated that the individual in question had conducted himself unlawfully . . .'.[142]

The principle underlying the more recent case law therefore seems to be that, where a directive has not been implemented by the due date, private parties may

---

[137] Case C–441/93 [1996] ECR I–1347.   [138] Case C–129/94 [1996] ECR I–1829.
[139] See further Lackhoff and Nyssens, 'Direct effect of directives in triangular situations' (1998) 23 ELRev 397; Hilson and Downes, 'Making sense of rights: Community rights in EC law' (1999) 24 ELRev 121; Ellis, *EC Sex Equality Law* (2nd edn, 1998), pp 31–4.
[140] Case C–192/94 [1996] ECR I–1281.   [141] p I–2227.
[142] Ibid. Cf Lord Hoffmann in *R v Secretary of State, ex parte Seymour-Smith* [1997] 2 CMLR 904, 909.

not benefit from a breach by the State of the requirements which the directive lays down.[143] Thus, in *CIA Security*, the defendants were seeking to rely on national legislation adopted by the State in the exercise of its *imperium* which did not comply with substantive provisions of the relevant directive.[144] In *Pafitis*, the first of several disputed increases in the capital of the bank was effected by a temporary administrator appointed by the Governor of the Bank of Greece. The administrator's appointment, and his decision ordering that shares be allotted to the new shareholders, were subsequently ratified by a Greek Law adopted pursuant to a Presidential Decree. In both cases, the Member State concerned had taken positive measures after the adoption of the directive in question which were incompatible with its substantive requirements. The effect of the Court's decisions was to prevent individuals from relying on those measures. The 'incidental effect' produced by directives in these circumstances may require some reappraisal of the extent to which they affect individuals, but it is not the same as horizontal direct effect in the strict sense: where the State simply fails to implement a directive, it remains the case that the directive will not impose obligations on individuals.[145] The *Ruiz Bernáldez* case was slightly different and seems to have involved a misinterpretation by the national court of first instance of the position under domestic law.[146] The Court's ruling simply ensured that the relevant national legislation was interpreted in a manner consistent with the applicable directives.[147]

Conclusion

The Court may initially have been deterred from endowing directives with horizontal direct effect by the hostile reaction from some senior national courts which greeted its case law establishing that directives might have vertical direct effect. Not for the first time the Court's timidity produced considerable imagination as the Court sought to attenuate some of the drawbacks of allowing directives to produce direct effect in one direction only. The result is a body of case law of considerable complexity which may itself be considered damaging to legal certainty. However, it now seems highly unlikely that there will be any fundamental change in the position in the absence of an amendment to the Treaty. In the present climate, no such amendment is likely to be forthcoming. Indeed, provisions introduced at Amsterdam state expressly that certain types of measure[148] adopted under the amended Title VI of the Treaty on European Union 'shall not entail direct effect'.[149] Whether those provisions are apt to exclude the duty of construction or the principle of State liability remains to be seen.

[143] Cf AG van Gerven in *Barber, supra*.   [144] Cf Slot (1996) 33 CMLRev 1035, 1049–50.
[145] See *El Corte Inglés, supra*.   [146] See AG Lenz at p I–1834.
[147] See para 4 of the judgment.
[148] One of which, the framework decision, resembles the EC directive.
[149] See Art 34(2) (ex K.6) TEU.

5

European rights, national remedies

It was argued in chapter 3 that, although the concepts of direct effect and primacy may not have been expressly spelled out, they were nevertheless implicit in the system created by the Treaties. Be that as it may, once the concepts had been recognized by the Court of Justice, a host of ancillary problems began to arise. The basic issue can be simply put: what does Community law actually require a national court to do to protect the rights the Court of Justice says it is bound to uphold? Must it award damages to those whose rights have been infringed and who have thereby suffered loss? If so, how are they to be calculated? Are such claims subject to a period of limitation and, if so, how long is it? Does Community law have anything to say about awards of interest, the burden of proof, injunctions?[1] The Court has not adopted a consistent policy on questions of this nature and some of its case law is as a result difficult to reconcile. Three phases can be identified. In the initial phase, the Court laid down the basic principles to be applied, but showed considerable restraint in using them to interfere with national procedural rules. In the second phase, the Court adopted a much more interventionist stance in which greater emphasis was given to the need to ensure the effective protection of Community rights. The consequences of the Court's interventionism were in some respects ill-judged and we now seem to have entered a third phase in which there is evidence of retrenchment. It may be doubted whether the Court has yet found the right balance between upholding rights conferred by Community law and respecting national rules of procedure, although the case law seems to be moving in broadly the right direction. None the less, the lack of consistency in the Court's approach and the fine distinctions it has drawn between apparently similar cases have created great uncertainty.

---

[1] On these and related issues, see generally Brealey and Hoskins, *Remedies in EC Law* (2nd edn, 1998); Lewis, *Remedies and the Enforcement of European Community Law* (1996); Lonbay and Biondi (eds), *Remedies for Breach of EC Law* (1997); Prechal, *Directives in European Community Law* (1995), chs 8, 9, 12, and 13; Steiner, *Enforcing EC Law* (1995); van Gerven, 'Bridging the gap between Community and national laws: towards a principle of homogeneity in the field of legal remedies?' (1995) 32 CMLRev 679; Caranta, 'Judicial protection against Member States: a new *jus commune* takes shape' (1995) 32 CMLRev 703.

The initial phase: judicial restraint

The principle of national procedural autonomy

The basic principle laid down in the first phase, which remains the Court's starting point, is that of national procedural autonomy. That principle was developed in a series of cases concerning charges imposed by Member States in breach of the Treaty. The essential question was whether Community law required such charges to be repaid or whether it merely entitled traders to resist demands for their payment. The question arose in *Rewe v Landwirtschaftskammer Saarland*,[2] where a claim had been brought in the German courts for the repayment (with interest) of charges which the Court of Justice had found in an earlier case[3] to have an effect equivalent to customs duties within the meaning of Article 13(2) EEC (now repealed), a provision having direct effect. The respondents accepted that the charges were unlawful, but rejected the appellants claim for a refund on the basis that the time limits laid down by German law had not been observed. The case came before the Court of Justice under Article 177 (now 234) of the Treaty and Advocate General Warner summarized the essential issue as follows:[4] '[W]here a Member State has, in breach of Community law, exacted from a trader a charge having an effect equivalent to a customs duty, either on imports from or on exports to another Member State, may that State, in proceedings brought in its own Courts by that trader for recovery of the amount unlawfully charged, plead a limitation period prescribed by its own national law?'

A positive answer to that question might have meant that rights conferred on individuals by the Treaty would be rendered nugatory. It might have seemed inconsistent to say on the one hand that national law could not directly contradict provisions of Community law having direct effect if effectively the same result could be achieved indirectly by national rules of procedure. Advocate General Warner did not find that line of argument convincing. He stated:[5]

Where Community law confines itself to forbidding this or that kind of act on the part of a Member State and to saying that private persons are entitled to rely on the prohibition in their national Courts, without prescribing the remedies or procedures available to them for that purpose, there is really no alternative to the application of the remedies and procedures prescribed by national law. The plaintiffs submitted that to allow national law to apply in such circumstances was to allow it to override Community law. I do not think that that is a correct description of the situation. I see it as a situation in which Community law and national law operate in combination, the latter taking over where the former leaves off, and working out its consequences.

---

[2] Case 33/76 [1976] ECR 1989.
[3] Case 39/73 *Rewe-Zentralfinanz v Landwirtschaftskammer Westfalen-Lippe* [1973] ECR 1039.
[4] At p 2000.   [5] At p 2003.

Given that there was no Community procedural law applicable in cases such as this, the Advocate General thought that '[t]he reductio ad absurdum of the plaintiffs' argument is that an action brought by them for restitution of the levies in question could not be dismissed by the competent national Court on any procedural ground whatever, not even, for instance, want of prosecution'.[6]

The Opinion of Advocate General Warner was followed by the Court, but only up to a point. The Court declared:[7] '. . . in the absence of Community rules on this subject, it is for the domestic legal system of each Member State to designate the courts having jurisdiction and to determine the procedural conditions governing actions at law intended to ensure the protection of the rights which citizens have from the direct effect of Community law . . .'. However, the Court added two conditions. The first may be referred to as the principle of equivalence.[8] According to that principle, the procedural conditions laid down by national law 'cannot be less favourable than those relating to similar actions of a domestic nature'. The second condition may be referred to as the principle of effectiveness: procedural conditions laid down by national law would not be applicable if their effect was to make it 'impossible in practice to exercise the rights which the national courts are obliged to protect'.[9] In a case such as this, the Court made it clear that both conditions were satisfied. The laying down of a reasonable period of limitation was, it said, 'an application of the fundamental principle of legal certainty protecting both the tax-payer and the administration concerned'.

Similar issues were raised in *Comet v Produktschap voor Siergewassen*,[10] where the plaintiff in the main action asked the national court to allow it to set off levies imposed in breach of Community law against other amounts claimed by the defendant. The defendant argued that the plaintiff could no longer impugn the contested levies or claim their reimbursement because it had failed to institute proceedings within the period prescribed by national law. The case was decided on the same day as *Rewe*, the Court giving a ruling in similar terms.

The application of the principle of national procedural autonomy

The approach taken by the Court in *Rewe* and *Comet* was followed in *Just v Ministry for Fiscal Affairs*,[11] which arose out of a dispute between a trader and the Danish authorities over the recovery of duty paid on imported spirits which the Court had

---

[6] At p 2004.   [7] Para 5.

[8] This is the term now used by the Court: see eg Case C–261/95 *Palmisani v INPS* [1997] ECR I–4025, para 27. It is sometimes known as the principle of non-discrimination: see eg Oliver, 'Enforcing Community rights in the English courts' (1987) 50 MLR 881.

[9] As we shall see, later cases applied a slightly less strict test, referring to national rules making 'excessively difficult the exercise of rights conferred by Community law': see eg Joined Cases C–430/93 and C–431/93 *van Schijndel and van Veen v SPF* [1995] ECR I–4705, para 17.

[10] Case 45/76 [1976] ECR 2043 Cf Case 177/88 *Pigs and Bacon Commission v McCarren* [1979] ECR 2161.

[11] Case 68/79 [1980] ECR 501.

held in a previous case[12] to be incompatible with Article 95 of the EEC Treaty, which prevents Member States from imposing internal taxes of a discriminatory or protective nature on products from other Member States. It seemed that under Danish law the recovery of charges which had been unlawfully levied was not permitted where the charges concerned had been passed on to the plaintiff's customers. The Danish Government claimed that was precisely what had happened in this case. As a result, it said, to refund the disputed charges would constitute unjust enrichment. The Court held that Community law did not require an order for the recovery of charges which had been unlawfully imposed to be granted in such circumstances. There was therefore nothing 'to prevent national courts from taking account in accordance with their national law of the fact that it has been possible for charges unduly levied to be incorporated in the prices of the undertaking liable for the charge and to be passed on to the purchasers'.[13]

The ruling in *Just* was consistent with the principles laid down in *Rewe* and *Comet*, to which the Court referred. However, two aspects of the case give cause for concern.[14] First, the Court found that the contested Danish legislation was discriminatory and protective in nature, yet the effect of its ruling was that Denmark was able to breach Article 95 (now 90) with impunity. Member States would have been more likely to take their obligations under the article seriously if they had known that they would not be able to profit from any breach. Did it not amount to the unjust enrichment of the Danish State to allow it to retain charges which it had imposed in breach of Community law? Secondly, the approach of the Danish Government, accepted by the Court, was based on the assumption that the breach of Article 95 (now 90) had not caused the plaintiff any loss. That assumption seems unfounded, since it may be supposed that if the charges had not been passed on the plaintiff's products would have been cheaper and its sales correspondingly higher. Indeed, this seems implicit in the Court's finding that the disputed Danish legislation was protective in its effect.[15]

The *Just* decision exemplifies the Court's nervousness in dealing with such cases during the initial phase. The Court seems to have been intimidated by two factors. The first was the emphasis placed by the Danish Government on the serious financial consequences if it were to be required to refund the disputed charges, given that the limitation period applicable under Danish law to claims for refunds was five years.[16] The Court also seems to have been struck by the lack of any uniformity of approach among the laws of the Member States in such cases.[17] Those considerations were reiterated in *Denkavit Italiana*,[18] a case concerning the refund of charges having an effect equivalent to customs duties, where a similar approach was

[12] Case 171/78 *Commission v Denmark* [1980] ECR 447.   [13] Para 26.
[14] See further Oliver, op cit, at pp 889–90.
[15] See further AG Mancini in Case 199/82 *San Giorgio* [1983] ECR 3595, 3624–6; AG Tesauro in Joined Cases C–192/95 to C–218/95 *Comateb and Others v Directeur Général des Douanes et Droits Indirects* [1997] ECR I–165, 176–8. These cases are discussed below.
[16] See para 21.   [17] See para 22.   [18] Case 61/79 [1980] ECR 1205.

taken.[19] The Court observed in that case that the 'Member States involved may be faced with a heavy accumulation of claims when certain national tax provisions have been found to be incompatible with the requirements of Community law'.[20]

The principle of national procedural autonomy was applied in a different context in *Roquette v Commission*,[21] where the question arose whether a trader was entitled to interest when charges which had been levied in breach of Community law were reimbursed by the national authorities. The Court simply said that '[i]n the absence of provisions of Community law on this point, it is currently for the national authorities, in the case of reimbursement of dues improperly collected, to settle all ancillary questions relating to such reimbursement, such as any payment of interest'.[22] The same approach was taken in *Express Dairy Foods*.[23] The plaintiff in the main action claimed reimbursement from the Intervention Board for Agricultural Produce of sums paid by way of monetary compensatory amounts (MCAs) on exports of powdered whey under various Commission regulations, one of which had subsequently been declared invalid by the Court.[24] The plaintiff also sought to recover interest. The Board said that it was bound to collect the MCAs payable under the regulations which had not been declared invalid and to apply the remaining regulation until it was declared invalid by the Court. On a reference for a preliminary ruling, the Court ruled that the other regulations were also invalid in so far as they fixed MCAs in respect of trade in powdered whey. However, it held that the remaining issues in dispute between the parties fell within the jurisdiction of the national courts. They were responsible for settling all ancillary questions relating to the reimbursement of charges which had been improperly imposed, 'such as the payment of interest, by applying their domestic rules regarding the rate of interest and the date from which interest must be calculated'.[25]

The issue of who has standing to invoke a breach of Community law in the national courts was one which the Court of Justice was also content to leave to domestic law. That issue arose in the case of the so-called 'Butter-buying cruises'.[26] Various shipping undertakings organized *Butterfahrten* from ports in Germany on the Baltic coast. The cruises lasted no more than eight hours and sailed from the maritime customs zone into territorial waters or the high seas outside German territory. Sometimes they stopped briefly at Danish ports where passengers were allowed to disembark. During the cruises passengers could buy various goods. Provided they did not exceed certain limits, no tax was charged when the goods were imported into Germany. Moreover, as the goods left the geographical territory of the Community, export refunds and MCAs were sometimes granted. The cruises had an adverse effect on the trade of wholesalers and retailers established in

[19] See also Case 811/79 *Ariete* [1980] ECR 2545; Case 826/79 *MIRECO* [1980] ECR 2559; Case 130/79 *Express Dairy Foods* [1980] ECR 1887.
[20] Para 24.   [21] Case 26/74 [1976] ECR 677.   [22] Para 12.
[23] Case 130/79 [1980] ECR 1887.
[24] See Case 131/77 *Milac v Hauptzollamt Saarbrücken* [1978] ECR 1041.
[25] Para 17.   [26] Case 158/80 *Rewe v Hauptzollamt Kiel* [1981] ECR 1805.

Germany along the Baltic coast. In proceedings before the German courts, a challenge was mounted to the practice of the customs authorities in permitting the goods concerned to clear customs free of tax.

The case was referred to the Court for a preliminary ruling. The Court ruled that passengers on butter-buying cruises were only entitled to import into Germany any goods purchased free of tax in certain limited circumstances. Three of the national court's questions were designed to establish whether a person who was adversely affected by national rules which were incompatible with Community law, or by the application of an unlawful Community measure, could bring proceedings in the national courts to have the measures concerned declared inapplicable. The referring court explained that such a person would have a right of action in German law. The Court replied[27] that the Treaty:

> . . . was not intended to create new remedies in the national courts to ensure the observance of Community law other than those already laid down by national law. On the other hand the system of legal protection established by the Treaty, as set out in Article 177 [now 234] in particular, implies that it must be possible for every type of action provided for by national law to be available for the purpose of ensuring observance of Community provisions having direct effect, on the same conditions concerning the admissibility and procedure as would apply were it a question of ensuring observance of national law.

The significance of the Court's remark in 'Butter-buying cruises' that the Treaty was not intended to create new remedies should not be exaggerated. It may be noted that the Court was not being asked to create a new remedy in that case, but simply whether a remedy available under national law had to be provided to a claimant seeking to rely on Community law. Of greater importance was the Court's subsequent observation that 'every type of action provided for by national law' had to be available to ensure observance of Community provisions. It is that statement which is reproduced in the operative part of the ruling,[28] not the reference to the creation of new remedies. Moreover, the judgment in 'Butter-buying cruises' had to be read in the light of the *Simmenthal* case,[29] decided less than four years previously. The effect of that case was that national courts could not be required to wait for a ruling from a higher court before they refused to apply a provision of national law which was incompatible with Community law. The result was that those who considered their rights under Community law to have been breached had a right of action in the ordinary courts which they would not have enjoyed had their claim been based exclusively on domestic law. It therefore seems that the Court wished to emphasize in 'Butter-buying cruises' that, although national courts would not be required to invent new remedies, they might have to adapt to the requirements of Community law the circumstances in which an exist-

---

[27] Para 44.   [28] See para 7.
[29] Case 106/77 [1978] ECR 629. See ch 3, *supra*; Prechal, *Directives in European Community Law* (1995), pp 155–8 and 185–7.

ing remedy—damages or interim relief, for example—was granted.[30] The assumption underlying the Court's approach was that all developed legal systems would have a sophisticated array of remedies which could if necessary be adapted to the requirements of Community law.

A right to damages?

Perhaps surprisingly, the question of the liability of the Member States in damages for breaches of Community law to those who suffered loss as a result arose only incidentally in the initial phase of the case law, although it was later to assume great importance. The Treaties are silent on the matter, although it might be thought that such liability is a corollary of primacy and direct effect, in that the payment of damages may in some circumstances be the only way of upholding an individual's rights under Community law. This point was clearly explained by Advocate General Léger in the much later case of *The Queen v MAFF, ex parte Hedley Lomas*:

An action for damages against the State for breach of Community law constitutes the indispensable adjunct to the principle laid down in the *Simmenthal* judgment . . . that domestic legislation that is contrary to Community law is inapplicable. To make good the consequences of the application of that legislation in the past is to annul the effects of that application and, ultimately, to render that legislation inapplicable in the past, or to draw the consequences of such inapplicability for the past.

Just as individuals are protected by the fact that the courts or the administration may disapply legislation, so they must also be protected by reparation of the damage which they have incurred through the application of legislation which ought to have remained a dead letter.[31]

There are isolated remarks in the Court's early case law which are consistent with this view. In *Humblet v Belgium*,[32] a case decided under the ECSC Treaty, the Court remarked: '. . . if the Court rules in a judgment that a legislative or administrative measure adopted by the authorities of a Member State is contrary to Community law, that Member State is obliged, by virtue of Article 86 of the ECSC Treaty,[33] to rescind the measure in question and to make reparation for any

---

[30] Cf AG Tesauro in Joined Cases C–46/93 and C–48/93 *Brasserie du Pêcheur and Factortame* [1996] ECR I–1029, 1093–5; Schockweiler, 'La responsibilité de l'autorité nationale en cas de violation du droit communautaire' (1992) 28 RTDE 27, 47–8. *Brasserie du Pêcheur and Factortame* is discussed below.

[31] Case C–5/94 [1996] ECR I–2553, 2572. Later in the same Opinion, the Advocate General remarked: 'Respect for primacy requires not only that legislation contrary to Community law should be disapplied. It requires also that damage resulting from its application in the past should be made good': see p I–2580.

[32] Case 6/60 [1960] ECR 559, 569.

[33] That article is the counterpart of Art 10 (ex 5) EC. The first two paragraphs provide:
'Member States undertake to take all appropriate measures, whether general or particular, to ensure fulfilment of the obligations resulting from decisions and recommendations of the institutions of the Community and to facilitate the performance of the Community's tasks.
Member States undertake to refrain from any measures incompatible with the common market . . .'

unlawful consequences which may have ensued'. The view that Member States which breach Community law may be liable in damages is also supported by a number of cases brought by the Commission against Member States under Article 226 (ex 169) EC. Member States which have complied with their obligations after the expiry of the deadline laid down in the Commission's reasoned opinion but before the Court has given judgment have sometimes argued that the proceedings have become devoid of purpose and that there is no need for the Court to give a decision. As we saw in chapter 2, the Court has consistently rejected that argument on the basis that a ruling of the Court 'may be of substantive interest as establishing the basis of a responsibility that a Member State can incur as a result of its default, as regards other Member States, the Community or private parties'.[34] That formula suggests that a Member State in breach of its obligations may be liable not only to individuals but also to other Member States and to the Community itself.[35] Some of these potentially far-reaching possibilities have yet to be explored even today.

The issue of State liability was addressed directly by the Court in *Russo v AIMA*,[36] which arose out of a dispute between an Italian producer of durum wheat and the State intervention agency. Some of the questions referred to the Court concerned the position of traders whose rights had been infringed by unlawful State interference in the machinery of price formation prescribed by the common organization of the market in cereals. According to the operative part of the Court's ruling:[37] 'If an individual producer has suffered damage as a result of the intervention of a Member State in violation of Community law it will be for the State, as regards the injured party, to take the consequences upon itself in the context of the provisions of national law relating to the liability of the State.' The language used by the Court in its reasoning was slightly different. There the Court said that, if damage is caused to an individual by an infringement of Community law by the State, 'the State is liable to the injured party [for] the consequences in the context of the provisions of national law on the liability of the State'.[38] Both formulations contained an essential ambiguity:[39] did the relevant provisions of national law determine *whether* liability arose in such circumstances or merely the *way* in which proceedings against the State were to be pursued? That ambiguity was also evident in the Opinion of Advocate General Reischl, who observed: '. . . when the other prerequisites under the particular national law are present, a claim for damages may lie against the Member State which has not fulfilled its obligations under the Treaty'.[40]

---

[34] The quotation is taken from Case 39/72 *Commission v Italy* [1973] ECR 101, para 11, the first occasion on which the Court made this point. For a subsequent example, see Case C–29/90 *Commission v Greece* [1992] ECR I–1971, para 12.

[35] The latter possibility was noted by AG Léger in *Hedley Lomas, supra*, at p I–2573, n 69.

[36] Case 60/75 [1976] ECR 45.   [37] Para (c).   [38] Para 9.

[39] See Barav, 'Damages in the domestic courts for breach of Community law by national public authorities' in Schermers, Heukels and Mead (eds), *Non-Contractual Liability of the European Communities* (1988), p 149 at p 156.

[40] At p 62.

The issue was clearly one which merited further clarification. However, although a number of cases did arise in the national courts in which the question of the State's liability in damages for breaches of Community law arose,[41] rather surprisingly the Court was not asked for further guidance until the landmark case of *Francovich* reached it at the beginning of 1990. This apparent reticence on the part of the national courts has been attributed[42] to the principle of direct effect and the duty of consistent interpretation enunciated in the *Van Colson* case. These factors undoubtedly reduced the number of potential claims for compensation by enabling individuals to invoke provisions of Community law at an early stage.[43]

The need for legislation

A major problem with entrusting the enforcement of Community law rights to the legal systems of the Member States is the lack of uniformity which inevitably results. It is too much to expect that different States from different legal traditions will all take the same approach on questions such as causation, remoteness, interim relief, limitation, the measure of damages. It follows that the rights conferred on individuals by Community law may be protected more effectively in some Member States than in others.[44] In principle, this problem could be resolved by the adoption of legislation at Community level harmonizing the conditions under which actions for the enforcement of Community rights may be brought in the national courts. In the first *Rewe* case, the Court observed:[45] 'Where necessary, Articles 100 [now 94] to 102 [now 97] and 235 [now 308] of the Treaty enable appropriate measures to be taken to remedy differences between the provisions laid down by law, regulation or administrative action in the Member States if they are likely to distort or harm the functioning of the Common Market.' It was only '[i]n the absence of such measures of harmonization' that rights conferred by Community law were to be exercised before the national courts in accordance with the conditions laid down by national law.

The invitation to the Community legislature to act, repeated in the *Comet* case, was not taken up. In *Express Dairy Foods*,[46] the Court repeated its belief that

[41] See e.g. the well known English case of *Bourgoin SA v Ministry of Agriculture* [1986] 1 QB 716. For a general survey, see Green and Barav, 'Damages in the national courts for breach of Community law' (1986) 6 YEL 55.

[42] See Schockweiler (1992) 28 RTDE 27, 38.

[43] Other considerations which may have played a part in keeping the issue in the domestic forum were the widespread belief that the matter was to be determined by national law and a reluctance among some national judges to make use of the preliminary rulings procedure.

[44] See generally Bridge, 'Procedural aspects of the enforcement of European Community law through the legal systems of the Member States' (1984) 9 ELRev 28; Himsworth, 'Things fall apart: the harmonisation of judicial procedural protection revisited' (1997) 22 ELRev 291; Oliver, op cit, pp 894–7.

[45] Para 5.

[46] Case 130/79 [1980] ECR 1887, para 12. See also Opinion 1/94 'WTO' [1994] ECR I–5267, para 104.

legislation was necessary in stronger terms:[47] 'In the regrettable absence of Community provisions harmonizing procedure and time limits the Court finds that this situation entails differences of treatment on a Community scale. It is not for the Court to issue general rules of substance or procedural provisions which only the competent institutions may adopt.' It will be recalled that the *Express Dairy* case involved an action for the recovery of charges imposed by the United Kingdom intervention agency on behalf of the Community under various regulations which subsequently turned out to be invalid. The Court explained what sort of legislation it considered necessary in circumstances such as those:

The rules to be adopted should involve equal treatment as regards conditions of form and substance in which traders may contest Community charges imposed upon them and claim their recovery in the event of undue payment together with a similar harmonization of the conditions in which the administrative authorities of the Member States, acting on behalf of the Community, impose the said charges and, where appropriate, recover financial benefits which have been irregularly granted.

One of the questions submitted to the Court concerned the issue whether a plaintiff was entitled to recover the disputed charge in full where it had been passed on to subsequent purchasers. According to the Commission, an affirmative answer to that question would have resulted in the plaintiff enjoying what were described as 'windfall profits'.[48] The Court pointed out,[49] citing the *Denkavit Italiana* case,[50]

that the protection of rights guaranteed in the matter by the Community legal order does not require the grant of an order for the recovery of charges improperly levied in conditions such as would involve an unjustified enrichment of assigns and that from the point of view of Community law there is therefore nothing to prevent national courts from taking account in accordance with their national law of the fact that it has been possible for charges unduly levied to be incorporated in the prices of the undertaking liable for the charge to be passed on to the purchasers of the products in question . . .

That conclusion reinforced the Court's plea for the matter to be regulated by legislation, because it was by no means clear that the national law applicable contained any principle of unjust enrichment analogous to that invoked in *Denkavit Italiana* and *Just* which would have enabled the defendant to resist the plaintiff's claim.[51] Thus, a plaintiff might succeed in England but fail in Italy or in Denmark on precisely the same facts.

There are now a number of measures laying down, in more or less detail, rules dealing with the remedies available in particular contexts.[52] However, notwith-

---

[47] See also the Opinion of AG Capotorti at p 1910.   [48] See [1980] ECR 1887, 1895.
[49] Para 13.   [50] Case 61/79 [1980] ECR 1205.   [51] See [1980] ECR 1887, 1891–3.
[52] See generally Steiner, *Enforcing EC Law* (1995), pp 56–9. Particularly noteworthy are Dir 89/665 on the co-ordination of the laws, regulations and administrative provisions relating to the application of review procedures to the award of public supply and public works contracts, OJ 1989 L395/33, and Dir 92/13 co-ordinating the laws, regulations and administrative provisions relating to the application of Community rules on the procurement procedures of entities operating in the water, energy, transport and telecommunications sectors, OJ 1992 L76/14. See further Haguenau, *L'application effective du droit*

standing the Court's repeated exhortations, it remains the case that there is no Community legislation dealing in general terms with the protection of Community rights in the national courts.[53] The absence of such legislation was undoubtedly one of the factors which induced the Court to take greater responsibility than it had perhaps originally intended for formulating a set of uniform principles which the national rules on remedies must satisfy where Community rights are in issue. The minimalist approach taken by the Court in *Rewe* and *Comet* was stated to apply only in the absence of Community legislation on the subject of remedies. A growing realization on the part of the Court that the type of harmonizing legislation it was envisaging in those cases was not likely to be adopted in the foreseeable future, if at all, led it to take a more creative approach to provisions concerning remedies, even if apparently limited in scope, which were to be found in legislative acts concerned principally with laying down substantive rules.

A provision which was to assume special significance in this respect was Article 6 of Directive 76/207 on equal treatment for men and women as regards access to employment, vocational training and promotion and working conditions.[54] According to that provision, 'Member States shall introduce into their national legal systems such measures as are necessary to enable all persons who consider themselves wronged by failure to apply to them the principle of equal treatment within the meaning of Articles 3, 4 and 5 to pursue their claims by judicial process after possible recourse to other competent authorities.'[55] The seemingly innocuous terms of Article 6 of Directive 76/207 have been interpreted by the Court with great boldness and creativity and have provided the basis for a principle of effective judicial protection which is of general application. One explanation for this development is that Article 6 of Directive 76/207 lies at the confluence of two related concerns which have assumed the utmost importance in the Court's case law: the need to make Community law effective on the one hand, the promotion of equal treatment for men and women on the other.[56] The Court's new approach may also have been attributable to the continued unwillingness of some Member States to

communautaire en droit interne (1995), pp 497–537. Cf Recommendation R(84)15 on public liability adopted by the Committee of Ministers of the Council of Europe on 18 September 1984 with a view to achieving greater unity between its members.

[53] For discussion of the work which has been done by the political institutions to draw up such legislation, see Haguenau, op cit, pp 539–68.

[54] OJ 1976 L39/40.

[55] Similar provisions may be found in a number of cognate measures: see Dir 75/117 relating to the application of the principle of equal pay for men and women, OJ 1975 L45/19, Art 2; Dir 79/7 on the progressive implementation of the principle of equal treatment for men and women in matters of social security, OJ 1979 L6/24, Art 6; Dir 86/378 on the implementation of the principle of equal treatment for men and women in occupational social security schemes, OJ 1986 L225/40, Art 10; Dir 86/613 on the application of the principle of equal treatment between men and women engaged in an activity, including agriculture, in a self-employed capacity, and on the protection of self-employed women during pregnancy and motherhood, OJ 1986 L359/56, Art 9; Dir 92/85 on the safety and health at work of pregnant workers and workers who have recently given birth or are breastfeeding, OJ 1992 L348/1, Art 12.

[56] Equal treatment for men and women is discussed in more detail in ch 13.

implement directives properly and timeously. The case law on Article 6 belongs to the second phase of the Court's jurisprudence.

The second phase: judicial interventionism

An end to restraint?

Early intimations that the restraint evident in the Court's early case law would not last indefinitely came with its decision in *San Giorgio*.[57] Between 1974 and 1977, the plaintiff in the main action was required in breach of Community law to pay health inspection charges on the importation into Italy of dairy products from other Member States. Under Italian law, a person was not entitled to repayment in these circumstances when the charge in question had been passed on. Moreover, the charge was presumed to have been passed on when the goods to which it related were transferred unless documentary proof to the contrary was produced. The Court made it clear that this was going too far. Whilst reiterating the approach taken in *Just*, it emphasized that 'any requirement of proof which has the effect of making it virtually impossible or excessively difficult to secure the repayment of charges levied contrary to Community law would be incompatible with Community law'.[58] Once it was established that a charge had been imposed in breach of Community law, the national court had to be free to decide whether it had been passed on without being hampered by presumptions or rules of evidence which systematically placed upon the taxpayer the burden of establishing that this was not the case.[59] The Court also took the opportunity to make it clear that the principles of effectiveness and equivalence laid down in *Rewe* and *Comet* were cumulative, not alternative. Thus, it was irrelevant that the same rules as to proof applied to claims for the repayment of charges levied in breach of national law: 'the requirement of non-discrimination laid down by the Court cannot be construed as justifying legislative measures intended to render any repayment of charges levied contrary to Community law virtually impossible, even if the same treatment is extended to taxpayers who have similar claims arising from an infringement of national tax law'.[60]

[57] Case 199/82 [1983] ECR 3595. Cf Case C–377/89 *Cotter and McDermott* [1991] ECR I–1155, where the Court refused to allow a Member State to justify a breach of a directive on equal treatment for men and women by reference to the principle of unjust enrichment. For a brief comment, see Craig and de Búrca, op cit, p 225, n 27. See also Case C–212/94 *FMC and Others v Intervention Board for Agricultural Produce and Another* [1996] ECR I–389; Case C–188/95 *Fantask and Others v Industriministeriet* [1997] ECR I–6783.

[58] Para 14. On the right to restitution of unlawful charges, see further Barav, 'La répétition de l'indu dans la jurisprudence de la Cour de Justice des Communautés Européennes' (1981) CDE 507; Hubeau, 'La répétition de l'indu en droit communautaire' (1981) RTDE 442; Smith, 'A European concept of *conditio indebiti*' (1982) 19 CMLRev 269; Tatham, 'Restitution of charges and duties levied by the public administration in breach of European Community law: a comparative analysis' (1994) 19 ELRev 146.

[59] See also Joined Cases 331, 376 and 378/85 *Bianco and Girard v Directeur Général des Douanes et Droits Indirects* [1988] ECR 1099.

[60] Para 17. See also Case C–208/90 *Emmott* [1991] ECR I–4269, discussed below.

The right to effective protection under Directive 76/207

If *San Giorgio* sowed the seeds of a new phase in the case law, they were to germinate spectacularly in the development by the Court of a far-reaching right to effective protection. The existence of such a right began to emerge in *Von Colson and
Kamann v Land Nordrhein-Westfalen*,[61] where the significance of Article 6 of
Directive 76/207 became apparent. A male prison administered by the defendant
Land had refused to engage the plaintiffs as social workers because they were
women. Instead male candidates were appointed who were in other respects less
well qualified. The referring court concluded that the plaintiffs had been subjected
to discrimination on grounds of sex. When it considered the sanctions to be
imposed on the employer, however, it encountered a difficulty. It took the view
that, under German legislation which purported to implement Directive 76/207,
the Land was only liable to pay damages in respect of any loss caused to the plaintiffs as a result of their expectation that they would not suffer discrimination. The
referring court concluded that, under German law, it could only order the reimbursement of any expenses they had incurred in applying for the job. This would
generally be a nominal sum only and the Court was asked whether compensation
of that order was compatible with the requirements of the directive. In particular,
the referring court wished to know whether the directive required the imposition
on the employer of an obligation to engage a job applicant who had been subjected
to discrimination on grounds of sex.

The Court declared that it followed from Article 6:[62]

. . . that Member States are required to adopt measures which are sufficiently effective to
achieve the objective of the directive and to ensure that those measures may in fact be relied
on before the national courts by the persons concerned. Such measures may include, for
example, provisions requiring the employer to offer a post to the candidate discriminated
against or giving the candidate adequate financial compensation, backed up where necessary
by a system of fines. However the directive does not prescribe a specific sanction; it leaves
Member States free to choose between the different solutions suitable for achieving its
objective.

The Court went on to make it clear that real equality of opportunity could not be
achieved without an appropriate system of sanctions. That followed from the purpose of the directive and also, more specifically, from Article 6 which constituted
an acknowledgement that candidates for a post who had been discriminated against
enjoyed rights which could be invoked before the national courts. The Court
explained:[63]

Although . . . full implementation of the directive does not require any specific form of sanction for unlawful discrimination, it does entail that that sanction be such as to guarantee real
and effective judicial protection. Moreover it must also have a real deterrent effect on the

---

[61] Case 14/83 [1984] ECR 1891.   [62] Para 18.   [63] Para 23.

employer. It follows that where a Member State chooses to penalize the breach of the prohibition of discrimination by the award of compensation, that compensation must in any
event be adequate in relation to the damage sustained.

National provisions limiting the right to compensation to a purely nominal amount
could not therefore be considered adequate to give effect to the directive.

The Court then considered whether the directive was in this respect precise
enough to be relied on in the national courts. On this point, the Court's ruling was
at first sight less encouraging to the plaintiffs. The Court declared that 'the directive does not include any unconditional and sufficiently precise obligation as regards
sanctions for discrimination which, in the absence of implementing measures
adopted in good time may be relied on by individuals in order to obtain specific
compensation under the directive, where that is not provided for or permitted
under national law'.[64] However, that conclusion proved not to be fatal to the plaintiffs' chances of success. The national court's view of the sanctions available under
German law in cases of sex discrimination was challenged by the German
Government. The effect of the relevant national law was evidently a matter for the
referring court, but the Court of Justice made it clear that the national court had a
duty to interpret its national law in the light of the requirements of the directive.[65]

The reference in *Von Colson* to the obligation of Member States to ensure that
the rights which the directive was intended to confer received 'real and effective
judicial protection' was to prove highly significant. Its implications began to
emerge in *Johnston v Chief Constable of the Royal Ulster Constabulary*.[66] In that case,
the Court was asked for a preliminary ruling on the compatibility with Directive
76/207 of the Chief Constable's refusal to renew the claimant's contract as a member of the RUC full-time Reserve or to allow her to be trained in the handling and
use of firearms. One of the issues raised by the case was the effect of the Sex
Discrimination (Northern Ireland) Order, which gave effect in the province to
Directive 76/207. According to Article 53(1) of that Order, none of its provisions
prohibiting discrimination were to 'render unlawful an act done for the purpose of
safeguarding national security or of protecting public safety or public order'.
Moreover, by virtue of Article 53(2), 'a certificate signed by or on behalf of the
Secretary of State and certifying that an act specified in the certificate was done for
a purpose mentioned in paragraph (1) shall be conclusive evidence that it was done
for that purpose'. In the proceedings before the referring court, the Chief
Constable had produced a certificate issued by the Secretary of State under Article
53(2). One of the questions which arose before the Court of Justice was the effect
of that certificate, if any, on the claimant's right to rely on the directive.

The United Kingdom Government maintained that Article 6 of the directive did
not mean that every question which might arise in the application of the directive

---

[64] Para 27.
[65] The ambit of the national courts' duty to interpret their national law in the light of relevant directives is explored in more detail in ch 4.
[66] Case 222/84 [1986] ECR 1651.

had to be open to judicial review, even where national security and public safety were involved. Article 53(2) of the Sex Discrimination Order was, it said, merely a rule of evidence of a type which was quite common in national procedural law. Its rationale was that national security and public safety were matters which could only be assessed satisfactorily by a politician. That apparently sophisticated argument was inconsistent with the right to an effective judicial remedy embodied in Article 6 of the directive and it was roundly rejected by the Court. It followed from that article, said the Court, 'that the Member States must take measures which are sufficiently effective to achieve the aim of the directive and that they must ensure that the rights thus conferred may be effectively relied upon before the national courts by the persons concerned'.[67] The Court declared that a provision like Article 53(2) of the Sex Discrimination Order 'allows the competent authority to deprive an individual of the possibility of asserting by judicial process the rights conferred by the directive. Such a provision is therefore contrary to the principle of effective judicial control laid down in Article 6 of the directive.'[68]

The Court took a further step in developing Article 6 of Directive 76/207 in *Marshall II*.[69] There it was asked whether that article permitted Member States to fix an upper limit to the amount of compensation payable to the victims of sex discrimination and whether it required compensation to include an award of interest. The Court ruled that an upper limit on the amount of compensation which could be awarded was not consistent with Article 6, 'since it limits the amount of compensation *a priori* which is not necessarily consistent with the requirement of ensuring real equality of opportunity through adequate reparation for the loss and damage sustained as a result of discriminatory dismissal'.[70] The Court added that 'full compensation for the loss and damage sustained as a result of discriminatory dismissal cannot leave out of account factors, such as the effluxion of time, which may in fact reduce its value. The award of interest, in accordance with the applicable national rules, must therefore be regarded as an essential component of compensation for the purposes of restoring real equality of treatment.'[71] Moreover, although Article 6 left Member States free to choose among the various different ways in which the objectives of the directive could be achieved, once they had

---

[67] Para 17.

[68] Para 20. Like *San Giorgio*, the ruling in *Johnston* also demonstrated the Court's willingness to interfere with national rules of evidence: Art 53(2) of the Sex Discrimination Order described a certificate issued by the Secretary of State as 'evidence' and was treated as a rule of evidence by the UK Government. Cf Case 109/88 *Handels- og Kontorfunktionærernes Forbund i Danmark v Dansk Arbejdsgiverforening, acting on behalf of Danfoss* [1989] ECR 3199, para 14, another sex discrimination case, where the Court said that national rules on the burden of proof might have to be adjusted where necessary for the effective implementation of the principle of equality. *Danfoss* is discussed in more detail in ch 13.

[69] Case C–271/91 *Marshall v Southampton and South-West Hampshire AHA* [1993] ECR I–4367. See Curtin (1994) 31 CMLRev 631; Moore (1993) 18 ELRev 533. Cf Case C–180/95 *Draehmpaehl v Urania Immobilienservice* [1997] ECR I–2195.

[70] Para 30.   [71] Para 31.

opted for a particular solution, individuals enjoyed a directly effective right to
ensure that it satisfied the requirements of effectiveness and deterrence.

The Court's ruling in *Marshall II* was in some respects a surprising one. True, in
Johnston the Court said that Article 6 of Directive 76/207 conferred on individuals
a directly effective right to some form of judicial remedy. However, in *Von Colson*,
the Court held that it did not prescribe specific penalties enabling individuals to
obtain remedies other than those laid down by national law. Unlike the applicant
in *Johnston*, the applicant in *Marshall II* did have a remedy under national law. The
question was whether it was sufficiently effective: that was precisely the question
which the Court said in *Von Colson* could not be answered with sufficient precision by reference to Article 6 for a claimant to be able to invoke directly effective
rights. Advocate General van Gerven acknowledged that, on the basis of the
Court's existing case law, a victim of discrimination could not rely on Article 6 in
order to have a national limit on the amount of compensation which could be
awarded set aside by the national courts. None the less, he thought that case law
had now been 'overtaken' by intervening decisions in other contexts which had
clarified the critieria which had to be taken into account by the Member States in
laying down an appropriate system of sanctions:

> The judgment in *Johnston* holds, in connection with the obligation stipulated by Article 6 to
> provide for effective *judicial protection*, that Article 6 has direct effect . . . I take the view that
> the *requirement to impose sanctions* laid down by Article 6 . . . now also has direct effect as
> against the Member States, on the ground that the principles of Community law on which
> that requirement is based, [have] in the meantime likewise been defined sufficiently precisely
> in the Court's case-law . . .[72]

It will also be recalled that, in both *Roquette* and *Express Dairy Foods*, the Court said
that whether or not an applicant was entitled to interest was in principle an ancillary question to be settled by national law. Those cases were of course concerned
with claims for the recovery of levies which had been imposed unlawfully, whereas
Marshall II was an action for compensation for loss suffered as a result of an unlawful act. None the less, as Oliver LJ pointed out in the English case of *Bourgoin SA
v Ministry of Agriculture*,[73] 'A claim for damages is . . . essentially no different in kind
from a claim for the reimbursement of unlawfully levied moneys which the cases
treat as an adjunct to the right created in the individual by the directly effective provision of the Treaty.' Of course, effective judicial protection cannot be secured if
the national courts have no power to award interest. It would therefore seem that
Roquette and *Express Dairy Foods* were on this point also to be regarded as having
been overtaken by subsequent developments. It may be noted that both decisions
purported to apply only in the then state of development of Community law.[74]

---

[72] pp I–4386–7, emphasis in the original.
[73] [1986] 1 QB 716, 765. See also para 41 of the Opinion of AG Mischo in *Francovich*.
[74] See *Roquette*, para 12 ('. . . it is currently for the national authorities . . .'); *Express Dairy Foods*, para
17 ('. . . it is at present for the national authorities . . .').

A general right to effective protection

The full significance of the *Johnston* ruling was perhaps that it was not confined to Article 6 of Directive 76/207. In the course of its judgment, the Court remarked that[75] '[t]he requirement of judicial control stipulated by that article reflects a general principle of law which underlies the constitutional traditions common to the Member States. That principle is also laid down in Articles 6[76] and 13[77] of the European Convention on Human Rights . . .' That remark implied that the right to an effective judicial remedy embodied in Directive 76/207 was not dependent on Article 6 for its existence: if that right reflected a general principle of law, it might arguably be implicit in any Community provision which envisaged that rights should be conferred on individuals. The Court could look to the constitutional traditions of the Member States and to the European Convention for guidance on the ambit of the right.

Further evidence of the general nature of the right to effective judicial protection came with the Court's decision in *UNECTEF v Heylens*,[78] a case on the free movement of workers. The Court was asked whether a decision of a national authority refusing to recognize the equivalence of a diploma held by a worker who was a national of another Member State, thereby preventing him from practising his profession in the host State, had to be open to judicial challenge and to state the reasons on which it was based. The Court answered 'yes' to both questions. The fundamental nature of the right of free access to employment conferred on workers by the Treaty meant, it said, that 'the existence of a remedy of a judicial nature against any decision of a national authority refusing the benefit of that right is essential in order to secure for the individual effective protection for his right'.[79] The Court made it clear that the right to effective protection, particularly in an area as fundamental as the free movement of workers, imposed on the competent national authority an obligation to inform the individual concerned of the reasons for its decision so that he could defend his Treaty rights under the best possible conditions. There were no specific provisions on remedies similar to Article 6 of Directive 76/207 relevant in the circumstances of the *Heylens* case. None the less, the Court referred to its statement in *Johnston* that the requirement of an effective remedy reflected a general principle of Community law. The case therefore provides support for the view that that requirement is inherent in the rights conferred on individuals by Community law and arises independently of specific legislative provisions. That view is confirmed by the judgment in *Vlassopoulou*,[80] a case on the freedom of establishment, where the Court followed the line it had taken in *Heylens*.[81]

---

[75] Para 18.   [76] Right to a fair trial.   [77] Right to an effective remedy.
[78] Case 222/86 [1987] ECR 4097.   [79] Para 14.
[80] Case C–340/89 [1991] ECR I–2357.   [81] These cases are discussed in more detail in ch 9.

The decisions in *Johnston* and *Heylens* were cited by the Court in *Verholen and Others*,[82] where it used the right to effective judicial protection to justify a greater willingness to interfere with national rules on standing than had been evident in 'Butter-buying cruises'. The Court was asked whether a married man could rely on Directive 79/7 when he was affected by a discriminatory national provision concerning his spouse, even if she was not a party to the proceedings. The Court's decision in the 'Butter-buying cruises' case might have suggested that a person's standing to invoke a rule of Community law before the national courts was one of the procedural issues which it was for national law to determine. However, in *Verholen*, the Court took a more interventionist approach. It pointed out that the right to rely on Directive 79/7 was not confined to those who came within its personal scope, but extended to anyone who had 'a direct interest in ensuring that the principle of non-discrimination is respected as regards persons who are protected'.[83] In a case such as the present, the Court held that an individual who bore the effects of a discriminatory national provision concerning his spouse was entitled to rely on Directive 79/7 if his spouse came within the scope of the directive. The reasoning of the Court, drawing on its case law in a variety of different contexts, underlined the pervasive character of the right to effective judicial protection:[84]

While it is, in principle, for national law to determine an individual's standing and legal interest in bringing proceedings, Community law nevertheless requires that the national legislation does not undermine the right to effective judicial protection (see the judgments in [*Johnston* and *Heylens*]) and the application of national legislation cannot render virtually impossible the exercise of the rights conferred by Community law (judgment in [*San Giorgio*]).

The duties of Member States

The cases discussed up to this point were concerned principally with the remedies available to individuals who claimed that their rights under the Treaty had been infringed. A corollary of the principles developed by the Court is that Member States have a duty to act to prevent infringements of Community law so that the rights of individuals or the Community interest in general are not prejudiced. This is implicit in the *Von Colson* case, although the dispute there focused on the remedies available to the social workers concerned, who claimed they had been subjected to discrimination on grounds of sex. In *Commission v Greece*,[85] the focus was on the duty of Member States to act against infringements of Community law. An investigation by the Commission had led it to conclude that a fraud on the Community budget had been perpetrated with the complicity of Greek civil servants and that a

---

[82] Joined Cases C–87/90, C–88/90 and C–89/90 [1991] ECR I–3757. Cf Case C–77/95 *Züchner v Handelskrankenkasse (Ersatzkasse) Bremen* [1996] ECR I–5689; Waddington, 'The Court of Justice fails to show its caring face' (1997) 22 ELRev 587.

[83] Para 23.   [84] Para 24.   [85] Case 68/88 [1989] ECR 2965.

number of senior Greek officials had made false statements in order to conceal it. In infringement proceedings against Greece under Article 169 (now 226) of the Treaty, the Commission argued that the Member States were required by Article 5 (now 10) of the Treaty to penalize anyone who infringed Community law in the same way that they penalized those who infringed national law. That argument was upheld by the Court, which observed that, where Community legislation did not specifically lay down any penalties for its infringement or referred for that purpose to national law, Article 5 required the Member States 'to take all measures necessary to guarantee the application and effectiveness of Community law'.[86] The Court went on:[87]

For that purpose, whilst the choice of penalties remains within their discretion, they must ensure in particular that infringements of Community law are penalized under conditions, both procedural and substantive, which are analogous to those applicable to infringements of national law of a similar nature and importance and which, in any event, make the penalty effective, proportionate and dissuasive.

Moreover, the national authorities must proceed, with respect to infringements of Community law, with the same diligence as that which they bring to bear in implementing corresponding national laws.

In the present case, the Greek authorities did not appear to have taken any proceedings against those involved in the fraud. The Commission's submissions on this point were therefore upheld.

The importance of this ruling was underlined by the Commission in a notice published in the Official Journal.[88] The Commission declared that it considered the principles laid down by the Court to be of importance 'in safeguarding Community law in general, and in combating fraud in particular' and undertook to ensure that the Member States fulfilled their obligations as defined by the Court. The Commission added that it took the view that the principles set out by the Court 'apply not only where Community rules make no specific provision for penalties, but also where Community instruments carry provisions dealing with certain consequences of failure to comply with the rules they contain'.

An approach similar to that adopted in *Commission v Greece* was taken by the Court in two infringement actions against the United Kingdom which again raised the question of the way Member States were required to deal with infringements of Community law. The first[89] concerned the adequacy of the UK legislation giving effect to Directive 77/187 on safeguarding employees' rights in the event of transfers of undertakings, businesses or parts of businesses.[90] One of the Commission's complaints was that the sanctions laid down by national law for failure on the part of a transferor or transferee to comply with their obligation to consult and inform employee representatives were not a sufficient deterrent for employers because of various restrictions on the amount of compensation which an

---

[86] Para 23. [87] Paras 24 and 25. [88] OJ 1990 C147/3.
[89] Case C–382/92 *Commission v United Kingdom* [1994] ECR I–2435. [90] OJ 1977 L61/26.

employer could be ordered to pay. That complaint was upheld by the Court, which observed:

> Where a Community directive does not specifically provide any penalty for an infringement or refers for that purpose to national laws, regulations and administrative provisions, Article 5 [now 10] of the Treaty requires the Member States to take all measures necessary to guarantee the application and effectiveness of Community law. For that purpose, while the choice of penalties remains within their discretion, they must ensure in particular that infringements of Community law are penalized under conditions, both procedural and substantive, which are analogous to those applicable to infringements of national law of a similar nature and importance and which, in any event, make the penalty effective, proportionate and dissuasive . . .[91]

The same observation is to be found in the Court's judgment,[92] delivered on the same day, in infringement proceedings against the United Kingdom for failing to transpose correctly various provisions of Directive 75/129 relating to collective redundancies.[93] These cases confirm not only that the right to an effective remedy is inherent in the Treaty—that much was already clear—but also that the Member States are under a positive duty to ensure that Community law can be properly enforced within their territory, either by the State itself or by individuals who claim that their rights have been infringed.

Limitation periods

The Court's concern to ensure the proper transposition of directives led it to adopt a particularly interventionist approach in the controversial case of *Emmott*.[94] The Court was asked whether a Member State which had not correctly transposed a directive could prevent an individual from relying on it before the national courts on the ground that a time-limit laid down in national law had expired. The conduct of the Member State concerned was almost completely lacking in merit and the Court was induced to lay down a principle which came to be widely regarded as excessively broad. It was eventually persuaded to reappraise the position and in the process began to attach greater value to national rules of procedure.

The *Emmott* case arose from Ireland's failure to implement Directive 79/7 on equal treatment for men and women in matters of social security[95] within the prescribed deadline, which expired on 23 December 1984. E was a married woman with two children. As from December 1983, she had been in receipt of a disability benefit under Irish social security legislation. Had she been a man, she would have

---

[91] Para 55. The Court cited the *Greece* case, discussed above, and Case C–7/90 *Vandevenne* [1991] ECR I–4371.
[92] Case C–383/92 *Commission v United Kingdom* [1994] ECR I–2479, para 40.
[93] OJ 1975 L48/29.
[94] Case C–208/90 [1991] ECR I–4269. See Szyszczak (1992) 29 CMLRev 604.
[95] OJ 1979 L6/24.

been entitled to a higher amount of benefit. In a case decided in March 1987,[96] the Court held that the prohibition against discrimination on the grounds of sex laid down in Article 4(1) of the directive had direct effect and that, in the absence of proper implementing legislation, women were entitled to have applied to them the same rules as those applicable to men. When E became aware of that ruling, she entered into correspondence with the Minister for Social Welfare with a view to obtaining, with effect from 23 December 1984, the same amount of benefit as that paid to a married man in the same situation. The Minister replied that, since the directive was still the subject of litigation in the national courts, no decision could yet be taken. In 1988, E was given leave to apply for judicial review in order to recover the benefits to which she claimed to be entitled. The Minister responded that, by virtue of national law, the proceedings were now out of time.

On a reference for a preliminary ruling by the High Court of Ireland, the Court began by reiterating that laying down reasonable time limits for bringing proceedings was in principle acceptable. It emphasized, however, that 'account must nevertheless be taken of the particular nature of directives'.[97] The Court reminded Member States that they were required to ensure the full application of directives in a clear and precise manner, so that individuals could ascertain the full extent of the rights they were intended by the directive to enjoy and, if necessary, rely on those rights before the national courts. The only way in which the necessary degree of legal certainty could be achieved, the Court said, was by transposing the directive properly into national law. It concluded:[98] 'It follows that, until such time as a directive has been properly transposed, a defaulting Member State may not rely on an individual's delay in initiating proceedings against it in order to protect rights conferred upon him by the provisions of the directive and that a period laid down by national law within which proceedings must be initiated cannot begin to run before that time.'

The ruling in *Emmott* had potentially far-reaching implications. The open-textured nature of many Community directives meant that even Member States who did their best to comply with their obligations could never be entirely certain that their implementing legislation would not subsequently turn out to be inadequate. It is true that, where the Court gives an unexpected interpretation to a directive, it may be persuaded to limit the so-called temporal effect of its ruling. Where it employs this device,[99] only the plaintiff in the case in hand, and others who have brought equivalent proceedings, are able to rely on the ruling in respect of periods preceding the date on which it was delivered. However, such a limit is only imposed by the Court in exceptional cases. Where it declines to do so, the *Emmott* ruling implied that individuals who were prejudiced by defective implementing legislation would be able to bring claims dating back to the expiry of the deadline laid down in the directive, however long ago that might have been. As we shall see,

[96] Case 286/85 *McDermott and Cotter v Minister for Social Welfare and Attorney-General* [1987] ECR 1453.
[97] Para 17.   [98] Para 23.   [99] See further chs 6 and 13.

these implications were to lead the Court to confine the *Emmott* rule to wholly exceptional cases of which *Emmott* itself may well remain the only example.

Interim protection

Notwithstanding its far-reaching implications, *Emmott* was not the most dramatic inroad into national procedural autonomy perpetrated by the Court in the interventionist phase of its case law. A strong candidate for that distinction is *Factortame I*,[100] which concerned interim relief. The right to an effective remedy in principle implies that an individual should be able to ask a court to grant interim relief to protect his position while his rights under Community law are established. In the absence of any right to seek such relief, and a concomitant power on the part of the national courts to grant it, an individual's rights under the Treaty might be rendered nugatory, for they would effectively be held in abeyance while their content was being determined. A right to damages once final judgment had been given might not constitute adequate redress. Moreover, the effective suspension of Community law during the intervening period might result in the frustration of the policy underlying it.

The right of an individual seeking to rely on Community law before the national courts to interim relief to protect his position while the extent of his rights was being clarified was upheld in dramatic circumstances in *Factortame I*. The appellants in the main proceedings were British companies whose directors and shareholders were mostly Spanish nationals. They had brought proceedings for judicial review in the English courts against the Secretary of State for Transport in which they challenged the legality of the Merchant Shipping Act 1988. That Act altered the system governing the registration of British shipping vessels to combat a practice known as quota hopping, whereby vessels flying the British flag but lacking any genuine link with the United Kingdom acquired the right to fish against the quotas allocated to the United Kingdom under the common fisheries policy. The 1988 Act provided for the establishment of a new register in which all British fishing vessels had to be registered. By virtue of section 14, a fishing vessel only qualified for registration if it was British-owned and managed from the United Kingdom by a qualified person or company. This meant: (a) a British citizen resident and domiciled in the United Kingdom, or (b) a company incorporated in the United Kingdom and having its principal place of business there, at least 75 per cent of whose shares were owned by qualified persons or companies and at least 75 per cent of whose directors were qualified persons. The fishing vessels belonging to the appellants had been registered as British under the statutory regime previously in force, but they were unable to satisfy all the conditions for registration in the new register. They therefore faced the prospect of being deprived of the right to fish against the British quota.

The appellants brought proceedings in the Divisional Court in which they argued that the relevant provisions of the 1988 Act were incompatible with various provisions of Community law and asked for interim relief to protect their position until final judgment was given. The Divisional Court[101] stayed the proceedings and made a reference to the Court of Justice on the substance of the case.[102] It also ordered that, by way of interim relief, the application of the relevant provisions of national legislation should be suspended as regards the applicants. The Secretary of State appealed against the Divisional Court's decision to grant interim relief. The Court of Appeal held[103] that the English courts had no power under national law to suspend, even on an interim basis, the application of Acts of Parliament whose incompatibility with the requirements of Community law had not been definitively established. The Divisional Court's interim order was therefore set aside. The appellants appealed to the House of Lords.[104] The House accepted that the appellants were liable to suffer irreparable damage if interim relief were refused. However, their Lordships held that national law did not permit the award of an interim injunction against the Crown. They also held that there was a presumption that an Act of Parliament was compatible with the requirements of Community law until the contrary had been established. As a matter of national law, the House therefore concluded that the appellants were not entitled to interim relief. However, the Court of Justice was asked whether Community law required or permitted such relief to be granted and, if so, in what circumstances.[105]

Advocate General Tesauro explained that the purpose of interim protection was 'to ensure that the time needed to establish the existence of the right does not in the end have the effect of irremediably depriving the right of substance, by eliminating any possibility of exercising it; in brief, the purpose of interim protection is to achieve that fundamental objective of every legal system, the effectiveness of judicial protection. Interim protection is intended to prevent so far as possible the damage occasioned by the fact that the establishment and existence of the right are not fully contemporaneous from prejudicing the effectiveness and the very purpose of establishing the right . . .'[106] The Advocate General did not believe that national courts were entitled to give priority to national legislation merely because it had not yet been shown to be incompatible with Community law: 'That would be tantamount to saying that the right conferred by ordinary legislation may receive

---

[100] Case C–213/89 [1990] ECR I–2433. [101] [1989] 2 CMLR 353.

[102] In Case C–221/89 *R v Secretary of State for Transport, ex parte Factortame II* [1991] ECR I–3905, the Court held essentially that the Act was incompatible with the Treaty. That ruling was largely followed in Case C–246/89 *Commission v United Kingdom* [1991] ECR I–4585, in which the compatibility of aspects of the Act with Community law was the subject of proceedings by the Commission under Article 169 (now 226) of the Treaty. In the course of those proceedings, the Commission was awarded interim measures by the Court of Justice requiring the UK to suspend the application of part of the Act: see [1989] ECR 3125. The UK adopted the Merchant Shipping Act 1988 (Amendment) Order 1989 (SI 1989 No 2006) in order to comply with that requirement.

[103] [1989] 2 CMLR 353. [104] [1989] 3 CMLR 1.

[105] For a discussion of that question prior to the ruling of the Court of Justice, see Barav, 'Enforcement of Community rights in the national courts: the case for jurisdiction to grant an interim relief' (1989) 26 CMLRev 369.

[106] At p I–2457.

interim protection, whereas protection is denied to the right conferred by the Community, or in any event higher-ranking, provision, on the basis of the presumption of validity in favour of that legislation; as if the same presumption, which after all is nothing other than "putative", did not also avail the provision having precedence.'[107]

The Court's judgment was short and to the point. It pointed out that directly effective rules of Community law had to be fully applied by the Member States from the moment they entered into force and that such rules rendered conflicting provisions of national law automatically inapplicable. Responsibility for protecting the rights derived by individuals from directly effective provisions of Community law belonged to the national courts. Those courts could not be deprived by national law of the power to set aside national rules which might stop Community law from producing full force and effect, even if only on a temporary basis. These points were clear from the Court's existing case law. The Court concluded:[108]

It must be added that the full effectiveness of Community law would be just as much impaired if a rule of national law could prevent a court seised of a dispute governed by Community law from granting interim relief in order to ensure the full effectiveness of the judgment to be given on the existence of the rights claimed under Community law. It follows that a court which in those circumstances would grant interim relief, if it were not for a rule of national law, is obliged to set aside that rule.

That interpretation was reinforced, the Court said, by the preliminary rulings procedure, the effectiveness of which would be reduced if a national court which had stayed the proceedings pending before it and made a reference to the Court of Justice were not able to grant interim relief pending the Court's ruling.

Did the Court's ruling require the House of Lords to create a new remedy?[109] Advocate General Tesauro, the essence of whose Opinion was followed by the Court, observed that the solution he was proposing did not amount to the imposition of remedies or judicial procedures different from those already provided for in domestic law. In the Advocate General's view, it merely implied that such remedies or procedures had to be used to secure the observance of Community provisions having direct effect, on the same conditions concerning admissibility and procedure as those applicable where observance of national law was concerned.[110] There seems little doubt that the Court agreed with this view: it was merely asking the House of Lords to set aside a national obstacle to the grant of an existing remedy which was necessary to ensure that the rights of the plaintiffs under Community law were protected.

It might be said that the problem for the national courts in *Factortame* was not that there was an obstacle to the grant of interim relief, but that they simply had no power to grant such relief against the Crown.[111] It was not therefore enough to ask

---

[107] At p I–2461.   [108] Para 21.   [109] Cf the 'Butter-buying cruises' case, *supra*.
[110] At p I–2462.   [111] See Toth (1990) 27 CMLRev 573, 586.

the House of Lords to set aside an obstacle. It had to be told to devise a remedy where none previously existed. However, subsequent case law confirms that the Court did not intend its ruling to be construed narrowly. In *Zuckerfabrik Süderdithmarschen and Zuckerfabrik Soest*,[112] the Court offered a summary of the effect of *Factortame*. It did not refer to the setting aside of obstacles to the grant of a remedy available in national law. It simply said that it had held in that case that a national court in the position of the House of Lords 'had to be able to grant interim relief and to suspend the application of the disputed national legislation until such time as it could deliver its judgment on the basis of the interpretation given [by the Court of Justice] in accordance with Article 177 [now 234]'.[113]

In the event, the House of Lords declined to engage in minute textual analysis of the language used by the Court and proceeded on the basis that the ruling gave it the power to grant the relief sought by the plaintiffs. The result was that, in proceedings against the Crown, individuals seeking to assert rights under Community law enjoyed greater protection than individuals seeking to assert rights based on national law. This anomaly was widely regarded as unsatisfactory and, in *M v Home Office*,[114] a contempt case, the House of Lords held that as a matter of national law interim relief was available against the Crown. Lord Templeman observed:[115] '. . . the argument that there is no power to enforce the law by injunction or contempt proceedings against a minister in his official capacity would, if upheld, establish the proposition that the executive obey the law as a matter of grace and not as a matter of necessity, a proposition which would reverse the result of the Civil War'. Critics of the Court's alleged activism were not quick to praise it for its contribution to this wholly desirable reform in the English law of remedies.[116]

The ruling of the House of Lords in the *M* case confirmed the open-textured nature of the relevant United Kingdom legislation[117] and suggested an alternative basis on which the Court of Justice in *Factortame* might have secured essentially the same result. It could simply have applied a variant of the *Marleasing* principle, that is to say, imposed a duty on the House of Lords to construe its national law in a way which maximized the protection available to individuals seeking to rely on rights conferred under the Treaty. On balance, however, the line taken by the Court seems preferable. A *Marleasing*-type ruling would have required the House of Lords to reopen a question of national law which it had settled earlier in the same proceedings and would have depended for its effect in other cases on the existence of a relevant but ambiguous provision of national law.

[112] Joined Cases C–143/88 and C–92/89 [1991] ECR I–415.

[113] Para 19 of the judgment in *Zuckerfabrik*.

[114] [1993] 3 WLR 433. Cf *Woolwich Building Society v IRC* [1993] AC 70, 177, per Lord Goff, who observed, citing the decision of the Court of Justice in *San Giorgio*, that '. . . it would be strange if the right of the citizen to recover overpaid charges were to be more restricted under domestic law than it is under European law'. See Beatson, 'Restitution of taxes, levies and other imposts: defining the extent of the *Woolwich* principle' (1993) 109 LQR 401.

[115] At p 437.

[116] For a more detailed account, see Craig, *Administrative Law* (3rd edn, 1994), pp 726–31.

[117] The Supreme Court Act 1981.

It will be recalled that one of the questions referred to the Court of Justice by the House of Lords in *Factortame* asked what criteria were to be applied by a national court in deciding whether or not to grant interim protection of rights claimed under the Treaty if Community law gave it the power to do so. The Court of Justice conspicuously failed to answer that question. Advocate General Tesauro had proposed a ruling modelled on *Rewe* and *Comet*. In the absence of Community harmonization, he said, it was for national law to determine the procedure and pre-conditions for granting such relief, on condition that national law did not make it impossible to secure the interim protection of rights based on Community law and that such rights were not treated less favourably in this respect than similar rights based on national law. That was essentially the approach taken by the House of Lords, which applied the guidelines laid down by Lord Diplock in *American Cyanamid Co v Ethicon Ltd*.[118] The House was influenced in its decision to grant the relief sought by the decision in *Bourgoin*,[119] which it was assumed would prevent the applicants from recovering damages even if their arguments on the substance of the case were upheld by the Court of Justice.[120] As we shall see, that assumption turned out to be erroneous. Thus, the question of interim relief might in the end have been irrelevant due to the possibility that the applicants in fact had an adequate remedy in damages.

An alternative to the approach suggested by Advocate General Tesauro on this question would have been to lay down criteria modelled on those applied by the Court of Justice itself in deciding whether to grant interim measures[121] in a direct action. That was the line taken by the Court in a subsequent case concerning interim relief, *Zuckerfabrik Süderdithmarschen and Zuckerfabrik Soest*.[122] The essential point at issue in that case was whether, and if so in what circumstances, a national court could suspend the operation, not of national legislation, but of a Community regulation. The Court of Justice observed that, although it had exclusive jurisdiction to declare the regulation invalid,[123] the rights of individuals to challenge regulations in the national courts would be compromised if they could not be suspended pending a ruling on their validity from the Court of Justice. National courts could therefore grant interim relief to suspend the application of a Community act pending a preliminary ruling on its validity in the same circumstances as the Court itself awarded interim relief in actions for annulment. It proceeded to spell out in some detail precisely what those conditions were.[124]

---

[118] [1975] AC 396. See [1990] 3 CMLR 375, 393–9, per Lord Goff. Cf the views of Lord Jauncey at pp 399–406.

[119] [1986] 1 QB 716.

[120] See [1990] 3 CMLR 375, 395 (per Lord Goff) and 406 (per Lord Jauncey).

[121] Under Arts 242 (ex 185) and 243 (ex 186) EC.

[122] Joined Cases C–143/88 and C–92/89 [1991] ECR I–415. See Schermers (1992) 29 CMLRev 133.

[123] See Case 314/85 *Foto-Frost v Hauptzollamt Lübeck-Ost* [1987] ECR 4199.

[124] See para 33 of the judgment. The Court refined the conditions in Case C–465/93 *Atlanta Fruchthandelsgesellschaft (I) v Bundesamt für Ernährung und Forstwirtschaft* [1995] ECR I–3761.

In the course of its ruling, the Court referred to its decision in *Factortame* and declared:[125] 'The interim legal protection which Community law ensures for individuals before national courts must remain the same, irrespective of whether they contest the compatibility of national legal provisions with Community law or the validity of secondary Community law, in view of the fact that the dispute in both cases is based on Community law itself.' That statement suggests that the conditions for the grant of interim relief by national courts laid down in *Zuckerfabrik* apply both to cases like *Factortame*, where provisions of national law are said to be incompatible with Community law, and to those where provisions of Community law are said to be unlawful, like *Zuckerfabrik* itself. In both types of case, the uniform application of Community law, the importance of which was emphasized by the Court in *Zuckerfabrik*, is liable to be jeopardized if the conditions under which interim relief is available differ according to the applicable national law.

Why then did the Court not spell out those conditions in *Factortame*? That question is very difficult to answer. It is certainly true that to give a national court the power to suspend an act of its own legislature has greater symbolic importance than empowering such a court to suspend a Community act. The Court was undoubtedly conscious that the case raised issues that went to the heart of the English doctrine of parliamentary sovereignty. The brevity of the Court's response to the questions submitted by the House of Lords shows that the Court did not wish to go any further than absolutely necessary. The Court may also have felt that the facts of the case were such that any threat to the uniform application of Community law was minimal. The *Zuckerfabrik* case was perhaps not as constitutionally delicate as *Factortame*. Moreover, there the Court was anxious to avoid the real danger that national courts might suspend the application of Community acts on an interim basis without asking for a preliminary ruling on their validity and without taking due account of the Community interest. That would have posed a serious threat to the uniform application of Community law and made it imperative that the conditions on which interim relief could be granted should be spelled out by the Court.

The principle of State liability

The vigorous development of the right to an effective remedy suggested that, if given the opportunity, the Court would confirm that a Member State which failed to comply with its obligations under the Treaty would be liable in damages to anyone who suffered loss as a result. The issue arose directly in two cases, *Francovich and Others*,[126] referred to the Court by Italian Preture concerning the consequences of Italy's failure to implement Directive 80/987 on the protection of employees in the event of the insolvency of their employer.[127] That failure had been recorded by the Court in infringement proceedings brought by the Commission.[128] The

---

[125] Para 20.
[127] OJ 1980 L283/23.
[126] Joined Cases C–6/90 and C–9/90 [1991] ECR I–5357.
[128] Case 22/87 *Commission v Italy* [1989] ECR 143.

purpose of the directive was to guarantee employees a minimum level of protection if their employer became insolvent. In particular, it made provision for claims for unpaid wages to be met. The plaintiffs in the main proceedings had been unable to recover the wages owed to them from their insolvent employers and sought to enforce their rights under the directive against the Italian State or, in the alternative, compensation. Two main questions were referred to the Court. First, could the directive be enforced in the national courts against the State in the absence of implementing measures? In other words, did the directive have direct effect? If not, was the State liable to make good loss and damage suffered by individuals as a result of its failure to transpose the directive?

The Court found that the directive was insufficiently precise to produce direct effect[129] and it therefore had to confront the question of the existence and scope of a State's liability for loss and damage resulting from breach of its obligations under Community law. That question, the Court said, was to be considered 'in the light of the general system of the Treaty and its fundamental principles'.[130] The Court reiterated that the Treaty had created its own legal system, which was integrated into the legal systems of the Member States and the rules of which their courts were required to uphold. The system created by the Treaty affected not only States but also their nationals, imposing on them burdens but also giving them rights 'which become part of their legal patrimony'.[131] The Court emphasized that national courts had a particular duty to ensure that rights conferred on individuals by Community law were protected.[132] It went on:[133]

The full effectiveness of Community rules would be impaired and the protection of the rights which they grant would be weakened if individuals were unable to obtain redress when their rights are infringed by a breach of Community law for which a Member State can be held responsible.

The possibility of obtaining redress from the Member State is particularly indispensable where, as in this case, the full effectiveness of Community rules is subject to prior action on the part of the State and where, consequently, in the absence of such action, individuals cannot enforce before the national courts the rights conferred upon them by Community law.

It follows that the principle whereby a State must be liable for loss and damage caused to individuals as a result of breaches of Community law for which the State can be held responsible is inherent in the system of the Treaty.

The Court found further support for that conclusion in Article 5 (now 10) of the Treaty. The 'appropriate measures' which that article required the Member States to take to ensure fulfilment of their obligations included 'the obligation to nullify the unlawful consequences of a breach of Community law'.[134] It followed, the

---

[129] This was a slightly surprising conclusion. For speculation as to the Court's motives, see Steiner, 'From direct effects to *Francovich*: shifting means of enforcement of Community law' (1993) 18 ELRev 3, 9.

[130] Para 30.   [131] Para 31. The Court referred to *Van Gend en Loos* and *Costa v ENEL*.

[132] Para 32. The Court mentioned *Simmenthal* and *Factortame*.   [133] Paras 33–5.

[134] Para 36. The Court referred to its decision in *Humblet v Belgium*, discussed above.

Court declared, 'that it is a principle of Community law that the Member States are obliged to make good loss and damage caused to individuals by breaches of Community law for which they can be held responsible'.[135]

The Court went on to consider the conditions under which the liability of the State arose. These depended, the Court said, 'on the nature of the breach of Community law giving rise to the loss and damage'.[136] Where the breach consisted, as in the present case, of failure to implement a directive, there were three conditions which had to be met. First, the directive should envisage the grant of rights to individuals. Second, the provisions of the directive had to make it possible to identify the content of those rights. Third, there had to be a causal link between the failure of the State to comply with its obligations and the loss suffered by the injured party. Where those conditions were satisfied, individuals had 'a right founded directly on Community law'[137] to obtain reparation. The Court added that reparation was to be made on the basis of national law on liability. Referring to *Russo*, *Rewe*, and 'Butter-buying cruises', the Court explained that the absence of Community legislation on the matter meant that it was for each Member State to designate the competent courts and to lay down the procedural rules applicable, but that the familiar principles of equivalence and effectiveness had to be respected. In the present case, the failure of the State concerned to comply with its obligations had been confirmed by a judgment of the Court. The directive contemplated the grant to employees of a right to the payment of unpaid wages, the content of which could be identified from the directive itself. The referring court was therefore required to protect the right of employees to obtain reparation for the loss they had suffered as a result of the State's failure to transpose the directive in accordance with its national rules on liability.[138]

The importance of this ruling is self-evident[139] and it possesses a number of striking features. One is that the Court felt able to deduce a principle of State liability

---

[135] Para 37.   [136] Para 38.   [137] Para 41.

[138] By a cruel stroke of irony, it appears that Mr Francovich was not himself entitled to any compensation: see Case C–479/93 *Francovich v Italian Republic* [1995] ECR I–3843.

[139] The literature on *Francovich* and its aftermath is extensive. See eg Beatson and Tridimas (eds), *New Directions in European Public Law* (1998); Barav, 'State liability in damages for breach of Community law in the national courts' in Heukels and McDonnell (eds), *The Action for Damages in Community Law* (1997), ch 20; Convery, 'State liability in the United Kingdom after *Brasserie du Pêcheur*' (1997) 34 CMLRev 603; Craig, '*Francovich*, remedies and the scope of damages liability' (1993) 109 LQR 595; Craig, 'Once more unto the breach: the Community, the State and damages liability' (1997) 105 LQR 67; Curtin, 'State liability under Community law: a new remedy for private parties' (1992) 21 ILJ 74; Harlow, '*Francovich* and the problem of the disobedient State' (1996) 2 ELJ 199; Lewis and Moore, 'Duties, directives and damages in European Community law' [1993] PL 151; Plaza Martin, 'Furthering the effectiveness of EC directives and the judicial protection of individual rights thereunder' (1994) 43 ICLQ 26; Ross, 'Beyond *Francovich*' (1993) 56 MLR 55; Steiner, 'From direct effects to *Francovich*: shifting means of enforcement of Community law' (1993) 18 ELRev 3; Szyszczak, 'European Community law: new remedies, new directions?' (1992) 55 MLR 690; Van den Bergh and Schäfer, 'State liability for infringement of the EC Treaty: economic arguments in support of a rule of "obvious negligence" ' (1998) 23 ELRev 552; van Gerven, 'Bridging the unbridgeable: Community and national tort laws after *Francovich* and *Brasserie*' (1996) 45 ICLQ 507; Waelbroeck, 'Treaty violations and liability of Member States: the effect of the Francovich case law' in Heukels and McDonnell, op cit, ch 17.

from the general scheme of the Treaty in the absence of any express provision. Indeed, in *Brasserie du Pêcheur and Factortame*[140] the German Government argued that a right to damages could only be created by legislation. That argument was rejected by the Court, which declared that the existence and extent of the principle of State liability were questions of Treaty interpretation which fell within its jurisdiction. Since the Treaty did not deal expressly with the consequences of a breach of Community law by a Member State, it was for the Court to rule on the matter 'in accordance with generally accepted methods of interpretation, in particular by reference to the fundamental principles of the Community legal system and, where necessary, general principles common to the legal systems of the Member States'.[141] The Court pointed out that, under the second paragraph of Article 215 (now 288) of the Treaty, the non-contractual liability of the Community itself was based on the general principles common to the laws of the Member States. That provision reflected, it said, 'the general principle familiar to the legal systems of the Member States that an unlawful act or omission gives rise to an obligation to make good the damage caused' and the obligation of public authorities 'to make good damage caused in the performance of their duties'.[142] The Court added: 'in many national legal systems the essentials of the legal rules governing State liability have been developed by the Courts'.[143]

The reference in *Francovich* to the *Russo* case is significant, since it suggests that the Court was seeking essentially to remove an ambiguity in that judgment by clarifying that the right to reparation was founded directly on Community law and that it was only the implementation of that right that was left to national law. This would explain the otherwise startling failure of the Court to accede to the request of the Italian Government that the temporal effect of its ruling should be limited. In that respect, the Court departed from the advice of Advocate General Mischo, who noted that several Member States had ascribed to the relevant case law a much more restricted scope than he proposed to give it. The Advocate General remarked:[144]

It was reasonable for the Member States to consider that they could incur liability for infringement of a rule of Community law only on the basis of the provisions of national law, and that they could not incur such liability in respect of failure to implement a directive which did not give rise to direct effect. In those circumstances, overriding considerations of legal certainty preclude legal situations which have exhausted all their effects in the past from being called into question where that might have very considerable financial consequences for the Member States.

---

[140] Joined Cases C–46/93 and C–48/93 [1996] ECR I–1029. See Emiliou, 'State liability under Community law: shedding more light on the *Francovich* principle?' (1996) 21 ELRev 399; Oliver (1997) 34 CMLRev 635.

[141] Para 27.   [142] Para 29.

[143] Para 30. See also Schockweiler, 'Le régime de la responsabilité extra-contractuelle du fait d'actes juridiques dans la Communauté européenne' (1990) 26 RTDE 27. Schockweiler was a member of the formation which decided both *Brasserie du Pêcheur and Factortame* and *Francovich* itself.

[144] At p I–5400.

The Court's power to limit the effects in time of its judgments in suitable cases was by then well established. The financial implications of its ruling for the Member States were evidently incontrovertible. The explanation for its failure to heed the Advocate General's advice on this point seems to be that the Court merely felt it was clarifying what was already implicit in its previous decisions. One of the Judges who took part in the case has described it as the final and logical culmination of a line of cases affirming and developing the principles of the special nature of the Community legal order, of primacy and of direct effect.[145]

The Court's judgment in *Francovich* suggested that the question whether or not the rule of Community law alleged to have been breached was directly effective was not relevant to the question of the State's liability in damages. This was confirmed in *Brasserie du Pêcheur and Factortame*,[146] where the Court said that, where a Member State infringed a directly effective provision of Community law, 'the right to reparation is the necessary corollary of the direct effect of the Community provision whose breach caused the damage sustained',[147] since otherwise 'the full effectiveness of Community law would be impaired'.[148] None the less, it is where the plaintiff is unable to rely directly on a provision of Community law that the principle of State liability is particularly important. The provision's failure to produce direct effect might be due to its lack of precision or, in the case of a provision contained in a directive, to the private status of the defendant. In the latter situation, the plaintiff would have to bring fresh proceedings against the State in order to recover damages for the loss occasioned by its failure to implement the directive, but the Court evidently regards the principle of State liability as an important weapon in the hands of those upon whom directives contemplate that rights should be conferred. This is clear from *Faccini Dori*,[149] where the Court reaffirmed that directives were not capable of producing horizontal direct effect, but specifically drew the referring court's attention to the obligation of a Member State to make good damage caused to individuals through failure to transpose a directive. The Court also made it clear that the directive at issue in that case 'is undeniably intended to confer rights on individuals and it is equally certain that the minimum content of those rights can be identified by reference to the provisions of the directive alone'.[150]

The Court's reference to *Francovich* in *Faccini Dori* might have been thought surprising, in that the Italian State does not seem to have been a party to the main action and the referring court was not therefore in a position to apply the principle of State liability. The Court seems to have been anxious to emphasize that, although directives might not produce horizontal direct effect, there were other ways in which the rights of individuals might be protected. In fact, the Court's

---

[145] Schockweiler (1992) 28 RTDE 27, 46: 'L'arrêt *Francovich* constitue l'aboutissement final et logique d'une évolution jurisprudentielle qui a affirmé et développé les principes de la spécificité de l'ordre juridique communautaire, de la primauté et de l'effet direct du droit communautaire.'

[146] *Supra.*   [147] Para 22.   [148] Para 20.

[149] Case C–91/92 [1994] ECR I–3325.   [150] Para 28.

judgment, whilst underlining the importance of *Francovich* in cases where an unimplemented directive envisages the imposition of obligations on private parties, also
made it clear that the principle of State liability was a remedy of last resort which
came into play only '[i]f the result prescribed by the directive cannot be achieved
by way of interpretation' in accordance with the ruling in *Marleasing*.[151] Later case
law was to lay down fairly strict conditions which had to be satisfied if a successful
claim was to be brought. That case law belongs to the third phase.

The third phase: redressing the balance?

The *Emmott*, *Factortame*, and *Francovich* cases represented the apotheosis of the
Court's enthusiasm for interfering with national procedural autonomy in the name
of the effective protection of Community law rights. It gradually became apparent
that the Court was becoming reluctant to interfere further with the balance
between the Member States and those seeking to rely on Community law. A
reassessment by the Court of the importance of national procedural rules and the
interests they were designed to serve subsequently led to something of a renaissance
in the principle of national procedural autonomy.

The demise of *Emmott*

The Court's new conservatism was perhaps most strikingly evident in the line of
cases which finally led to the demise of the *Emmott* doctrine, at least in the broad
form in which it was originally enunciated by the Court. It will be recalled that the
Court stated in that case that a Member State could not rely on a national limitation period to prevent an individual from pursuing a claim based on a directive
unless and until the directive had been properly implemented. One of the problems with the Court's ruling was that it was explicitly based on 'the particular
nature of directives', yet its underlying rationale—the need to protect legal certainty—seemed to apply equally where national law was inconsistent with provisions of the Treaty or Community acts other than directives. Another problem was
that the *Emmott* rule could expose a Member State to claims dating back many years
even if its default had only recently become apparent.

  The Court's unwillingness to extend the *Emmott* rule first became apparent in
Steenhorst-Neerings,[152] where the applicant sought to rely on Article 4(1) of
Directive 79/7 in order to secure the payment under Dutch legislation of a benefit for incapacity for work with effect from 23 December 1984. The Court was
asked whether Community law precluded the application of a national rule,

---

[151] Para 27. See also to the same effect Case C–334/92 *Wagner Miret v Fondo de Garantía Salarial*
[1993] ECR I–6911, para 22.
[152] Case C–338/91 [1993] ECR I–5475. See Sohrab (1994) 31 CMLRev 875.

invoked by the respondent, according to which benefit was payable no earlier than one year before the date of the claim. The Commission argued that the *Emmott* principle was applicable. Advocate General Darmon agreed. He was not convinced by the argument that, in the absence of a limit on the backdating of claims, individuals would be able to claim benefits several years after their entitlement arose. That could only happen if there had been a prolonged failure by the respondent Member State to implement the directive. It would be unjust, said the Advocate General, to make the intended beneficiary of the rights conferred by the directive bear the burden of that failure because of the expiry of the time limits laid down in national procedural law.[153]

The Court was not convinced. *Emmott*, it said, was distinguishable. First, the Court pointed out that, unlike a rule of domestic law fixing time limits for bringing actions, the rule at issue in the present case did not affect the right of individuals to rely on the directive. It merely limited the retroactive effect of claims. The purpose of the rule at issue in *Emmott* was to ensure that the legality of administrative decisions could not be challenged indefinitely. That consideration could not be allowed to prevail over the rights conferred on individuals by directives. The aim of the contested rule restricting the retroactive effect of claims for benefit was quite different. That rule was designed to make it possible to ensure that the claimant was in fact eligible for benefit and to establish the claimant's degree of incapacity, which could well vary over time. It also reflected the need to preserve financial balance in a scheme in which claims submitted by insured persons during a given year in principle had to be covered by contributions collected during the same year. The Court therefore held that Community law did not preclude the application of a national rule according to which benefits for incapacity for work were payable no earlier than one year before the date of the claim where the competent Member State had not yet properly transposed the directive into national law.

The judgment in *Steenhorst-Neerings* was followed in *Johnson*,[154] where both Advocate General Gulmann and the Court rejected an attempt to distinguish the former case. Again the issue, referred by the English Court of Appeal, was the compatibility with Directive 79/7 of a rule of national law limiting the period prior to the bringing of a claim for benefit in respect of which arrears of benefit were payable where the directive had not been properly implemented. The Court pointed out that '. . . the solution adopted in *Emmott* was justified by the particular circumstances of the case, in which a time-bar had the result of depriving the applicant of any opportunity whatever to rely on her right to equal treatment under the directive'.[155] However, the Court went on, the rule at issue in *Steenhorst-Neerings* did not affect the right of individuals to rely on the directive. It merely limited the retroactive effect of claims for benefit. The Court concluded that '. . . the national rule which adversely affects Mrs Johnson's action before the Court of

---

[153] Para 29 of the Opinion.   [154] Case C–410/92 [1994] ECR I–5483.   [155] Para 26.

Appeal is similar to that at issue in *Steenhorst-Neerings*. Neither rule constitutes a bar to proceedings; they merely limit the period prior to the bringing of the claim in respect of which arrears of benefit are payable.'[156]

The Court may have been influenced in *Steenhorst-Neerings* and *Johnson* by a reluctance to intervene too strongly in the increasingly controversial area of social security,[157] but its attempt to distinguish *Emmott* was not wholly convincing, for it is not at all clear that the rule at issue there entirely excluded the claimant's rights under the directive. The issue in all three cases was the claimant's right to arrears of benefit. There was no doubt that each of them could if necessary rely on the directive to claim benefit for the future.[158] It was in due course to become clear, however, that *Steenhorst-Neerings* and *Johnson* represented merely the first stage in a *revirement* that was to leave *Emmott* very much confined to its facts. The scope of the rule laid down in that case was raised again in a series of cases assigned to Advocate General Jacobs, whose Opinions subjected the underlying rationale of the rule to close scrutiny. It is in his Opinion in *Fantask and Others v Industriministeriet*[159] that the most detailed analysis of the *Emmott* rule is to be found, although much of the ground was laid in his Opinion in *Denkavit Internationaal and Others v Kamer van Koophandel en Fabrieken voor Midden-Gelderland and Others*.[160] Because of the view it took on the substance of the case, the Court did not address the effect of the *Emmott* rule in *Denkavit*, but its rulings in the other cases made it clear that the scope of that rule was now very limited.

In *Fantask*, several companies were seeking to rely on a directive concerning indirect taxes on the raising of capital in support of a claim to the repayment of certain charges levied on them by the Danish authorities. One of the questions raised by the referring court asked whether the time limit for bringing proceedings could start to run before the directive had been properly implemented. A number of Member States which submitted observations in the case argued that the principle laid down in *Emmott* had been stated too broadly and they encountered a sympathetic response from Advocate General Jacobs, who observed:[161] 'my main reservations about a broad view of the *Emmott* ruling are that it disregards the need, recognized by all legal systems, for a degree of legal certainty for the State, particularly where infringements are comparatively minor or inadvertent; it goes further than is necessary to give effective protection to directives; and it places rights under directives in an unduly privileged position by comparison with other Community rights'.

---

[156] Para 30. The Court deals with the claimant's attempt to distinguish *Steenhorst-Neerings* at paras 31–5. See also the Opinion of AG Gulmann at pp 5492–6.

[157] See further Sohrab (1994) 31 CMLRev 875; Cousins, 'Equal treatment and social security' (1994) 19 ELRev 123, 142–5.

[158] This was pointed out by the applicant in *Johnson*: see the Opinion of AG Gulmann at p I–5496.

[159] Case C–188/95 [1997] ECR I–6783.

[160] Case C–2/94 [1996] ECR I–2827. See also Case C–90/94 *Haahr Petroleum v Åbenrå Havn and Others* [1997] ECR I–4085; Joined Cases C–114/95 and C–115/95 *Texaco and Olieselskabet Danmark* [1997] ECR I–4263.

[161] p I–6811.

The Advocate General added that a broad view of the *Emmott* rule could not be reconciled with the approach to national time limits which had been taken in the *Steenhorst-Neerings* and *Johnson* cases. The distinction drawn by the Court in those cases between the types of limit applicable there and that applicable in *Emmott* was, he thought, unconvincing: '. . . a five-year time-limit for instituting proceedings, if applied to recurring taxes or benefits, could equally be viewed as a rule limiting to five years the extent to which a claim may relate back. Conversely, a rule, such as that in *Johnson*, which limits entitlement to benefits to a period not exceeding 12 months prior to a claim, could equally be viewed as a time-limit barring claims in respect of a particular period after 12 months; although in most cases the application of such a time-limit will merely reduce the amount of benefit paid, it will lead to complete denial of the claim in all cases in which entitlement to benefit has ceased 12 months before the claim is made.'[162]

In any event, the Court's reasoning in *Emmott* would on the face of things prevent a Member State from relying on either type of time limit since both permitted a Member State to resist claims relating to periods in which a directive had not been properly implemented. Advocate General Jacobs did not object to the outcome in *Emmott*, but thought the case should be understood as establishing that a Member State could not rely on a limitation period where it was in default 'both in failing to implement a directive and in obstructing the exercise of a judicial remedy in reliance upon it, or perhaps where the delay in exercising the remedy is in some other way due to the conduct of the national authorities'.[163] The Advocate General added that the conduct of the Member State in *Emmott* was aggravated by the applicant's vulnerability as an individual dependent on social welfare.

Less than a month after Advocate General Jacobs delivered his Opinion in *Fantask*, the Court gave judgment in *Haahr Petroleum* and *Texaco*, where the applicants were seeking to rely, not on directives which had not been correctly implemented, but on provisions of the Treaty and of free-trade agreements concluded by the Community with non-member countries. A Court committed to the *Emmott* rule might have been willing to extend it to such provisions. Instead the Court said that it was 'only because of the particular nature of directives and having regard to the specific circumstances of that case' that the Court had come to the conclusion it reached in *Emmott*. That conclusion did not apply where the applicant was relying on the Treaty or a free-trade agreement.[164] In *Fantask* itself, the Court implicitly acknowledged that the attempt to distinguish *Emmott* in *Steenhorst-Neerings* and *Johnson* was not entirely convincing and that Member States were not automatically precluded from relying on national limitation periods where claims were brought against them under directives which had not been properly implemented. Referring *inter alia* to the *Rewe* and *Comet* cases, the Court made it clear that, as long as the principles of equivalence and effectiveness were

---

[162] p I–6812.   [163] p I–6816.

[164] See *Haahr Petroleum v Åbenrå Havn and Others, supra,* paras 52–3; *Texaco and Olieselskabet Danmark, supra,* paras 48–9.

satisfied, the setting of reasonable time limits for bringing proceedings was compatible with Community law because it promoted legal certainty. The apparently contrary ruling in *Emmott* 'was justified by the particular circumstances of that case . . .'.[165]

There can therefore now be no doubt that the Court has retreated from the extreme form of the *Emmott* rule. The line of cases in which this outcome has been produced illustrates the renaissance of the principle of national procedural autonomy and the Court's renewed commitment to the principles of equivalence and effectiveness as the appropriate vehicles for ensuring the effectiveness of Community law. It may also be said to demonstrate a willingness on the part of the Court to respond to criticism and to acknowledge its own fallibility.

Can a national court be prevented from raising points of Community law of its own motion?

Further evidence of a readiness during this period to reappraise the importance of national rules of procedure may be found in the Court's decision in *van Schijndel and van Veen v SPF*.[166] That case arose out of a dispute before the Netherlands courts over whether the applicants could be compelled to join the occupational pension scheme for members of their profession or whether they were free to make their own pension arrangements. In appeal proceedings against judgments given by national courts of first instance, the position of the defendant pension fund was upheld. The applicants brought an appeal in cassation before the Netherlands Supreme Court, the Hoge Raad, where they sought to rely for the first time on the argument that compulsory membership of the fund was incompatible with the Treaty competition rules. The Hoge Raad found that the applicants were seeking to rely in support of that argument on various facts and circumstances which had not been established by the lower courts. Under Netherlands law, they were not entitled to raise new arguments at this stage of the proceedings if they required further examination of the facts. Although the courts were sometimes required to raise points of law of their own motion, they were not entitled in proceedings such as these to go outside the facts on which the claim had originally been based. Notwithstanding these restrictions, did Community law require the Hoge Raad to allow the applicants to pursue their claim based on the Treaty?

The Court reiterated the familiar principles of national procedural autonomy, equivalence, and effectiveness. In order to apply those principles, it said,[167]

each case which raises the question whether a national procedural provision renders application of Community law impossible or excessively difficult must be analysed by reference

---

[165] Para 51.
[166] Joined Cases C–430/93 and C–431/93 [1995] ECR I–4705. Cf Case C–72/95 *Kraaijeveld and Others v Gedeputeerde Staten van Zuid-Holland* [1996] ECR I–5403.
[167] Para 19.

to the role of that provision in the procedure, its progress and its special features, viewed as a whole, before the various national instances. In the light of that analysis the basic principles of the domestic judicial system, such as protection of the rights of the defence, the principle of legal certainty and the proper conduct of procedure, must, where appropriate, be taken into consideration.

The limitation imposed by national law on the arguments which could be raised before the Hoge Raad in the present case was in the Court's view 'justified by the principle that, in a civil suit, it is for the parties to take the initiative, the court being able to act of its own motion only in exceptional cases where the public interest requires its intervention. That principle reflects conceptions prevailing in most of the Member States as to the relations between the State and the individual; it safeguards the rights of the defence; and it ensures proper conduct of proceedings by, in particular, protecting them from the delays inherent in the examination of new pleas.'[168]

The case is a notable one because, notwithstanding the importance of the Treaty provisions invoked by the applicants, the Court was not prepared to interfere with 'the basic principles of the domestic judicial system'. The Court was clearly influenced in the conclusion it reached by the Opinion of Advocate General Jacobs, who observed:[169]

if the view were taken that national procedural rules must always yield to Community law, that would . . . unduly subvert established principles underlying the legal systems of the Member States. It would go further than is necessary for effective judicial protection. It could be regarded as infringing the principle of proportionality and, in a broad sense, the principle of subsidiarity, which reflects precisely the balance which the Court has sought to attain in this area for many years. It would also give rise to widespread anomalies, since the effect would be to afford greater protection to rights which are not, by virtue of being Community rights, inherently of greater importance than rights recognized by national law.

Although the result might be some divergence in the way in which Community law was applied, this was 'a consequence of the variety of the national legal systems themselves'.[170]

The significance of *van Schijndel* was perhaps obscured by another case decided on the same day in which the Court arrived at an apparently inconsistent result. *Peterbroeck v Belgian State*[171] also raised the legality of a domestic restriction on the power of a national court to consider of its own motion the issue of the compatibility of municipal law with Community law. The case arose out of a dispute between a Belgian limited liability partnership and the Belgian State over the former's tax liability. The partnership lodged a complaint with the competent Regional Director of Direct Contributions over a charge to tax. The complaint was for the most part rejected, whereupon the partnership brought proceedings before the Cour d'Appel, Brussels, where it sought to rely for the first time on the right

---

[168] Para 21. [169] See pp I–4715–16. [170] At p I–4719.
[171] Case C–312/93 [1995] ECR I–4599.

of establishment laid down in Article 52 (now 43) of the Treaty. Under Belgian law, a taxpayer had the right to rely on arguments which had not been invoked in the original complaint or raised by the Director of his own motion provided they were submitted within sixty days of the lodging by the Director with the Cour d'Appel of the contested decision and case file. That time limit had expired when the partnership first sought to rely on Article 52. The Cour d'Appel was not entitled to examine of its own motion issues which the taxpayer could no longer raise because the sixty-day limit had expired. Was that limit compatible with Community law?

The circumstances of the case were undoubtedly similar to those of *van Schijndel*, in that a rule of national law prevented a national court from considering of its own motion a claim based on Community law. Advocate General Jacobs proposed a similar result: because the time limit satisfied the principle of equivalence and the time limit was not unreasonable, the taxpayer having had ample opportunity to raise the Community law point at an earlier stage in the proceedings, Community law did not require it to be disregarded. The Court took a different view. While accepting that the sixty-day limit was not objectionable in itself, it drew attention to three features of the procedure in question. First, since the Director belonged to the national tax authorities, he did not constitute a court or tribunal for the purposes of Article 177 (now 234).[172] That meant that the Cour d'Appel was the first court in the procedure which could make a reference to the Court of Justice for a preliminary ruling. Secondly, the sixty-day period had expired by the time of the hearing before the Cour d'Appel. Thirdly, it appeared that no other national court would be able to consider of its own motion the compatibility of the disputed national measure with Community law at a later stage of the proceedings. These features of the procedure were regarded by the Court as interfering with the proper functioning of the preliminary rulings procedure. It therefore declared that a procedural rule such as that at issue in the main action was incompatible with Community law.

The *van Schijndel* and *Peterbroeck* decisions are not easy to reconcile. It has been powerfully argued[173] that the national rule at issue in the former case posed as serious a threat to the operation of the preliminary rulings procedure as the rule at issue in the latter. In particular, it appears from the account of the national background given in the Advocate General's Opinion[174] and the judgment in *van Schijndel* that none of the courts which had dealt with the case could under national law have raised the Community law point of their own motion. Perhaps the distinction is simply that the applicants in *van Schijndel* had missed too many opportunities to invoke Community law to complain about the procedural limits applicable in proceedings before the Hoge Raad.

---

[172] See Case C–24/92 *Corbiau v Administration des Contributions* [1993] ECR I–1277; ch 2, *supra*.

[173] See de Búrca, 'National procedural rules and remedies: the changing approach of the Court of Justice' in Lonbay and Biondi (eds), *Remedies for Breach of EC Law* (1997), ch 4.

[174] See pp I–4709–10.

The judgment in *Peterbroeck* contains the same passages as *van Schijndel* on the principle of procedural autonomy and was interpreted as heralding a more intrusive approach by the Court to the appraisal of national procedural rules. The statement in both cases[175] about how to go about establishing whether such rules complied with the principles of equivalence and effectiveness was criticized as imprecise and liable to produce an increase in the number of references to the Court.[176] With the benefit of hindsight, however, *Peterbroeck* may perhaps be seen as standing slightly apart from the main body of case law on the principle of national procedural autonomy and as concerned mainly with preserving the integrity of the preliminary rulings procedure.[177] It was *van Schijndel* which had the greater implications for national rules of procedure and it suggested, not that the Court was becoming more interventionist, but that it would henceforward attach greater importance to the interests which such rules were designed to protect.

The conditions under which State liability arises

The *Francovich* decision left unanswered the question whether the liability of the delinquent State was strict or whether some degree of knowledge that it was acting in breach of the requirements of Community law had to be established by the plaintiff. A related question was whether the case law of the Court on the non-contractual liability of the Community itself under the second paragraph of Article 288 (ex 215) was relevant. In *Francovich*, Advocate General Mischo took the view that:[178]

. . . it would seem appropriate that the grant of damages by a national court for breach of Community law by a Member State should be subject to the same conditions as the grant of damages by the Court of Justice for infringement of that same Community law by a Community institution. That would make it possible to avoid a situation where, pursuant to Community law, a Member State might incur liability for breach of Community law by one of its authorities in circumstances where the non-contractual liability of the Community for breach of Community law by one of its institutions would not arise. That seems to me to be particularly necessary inasmuch as the rules laid down in this regard by the Court on the basis of the second paragraph of Article 215 of the Treaty are said to flow from the general principles common to the laws of the Member States.

A similar approach was taken by the majority of the Court of Appeal in the *Bourgoin* case.[179] Others doubted the appropriateness in this context of the case law on Article 288 (ex 215). Schockweiler[180] pointed out that to transpose the case law of

---

[175] *Peterbroeck*, para 14; *van Schijndel*, para 19.

[176] See Hoskins, 'Tilting the balance: supremacy and national procedural rules' (1996) 21 ELRev 365. Cf Prechal, 'Community law in national courts: the lessons from *van Schijndel*' (1998) 35 CMLRev 681.

[177] Cf Jacobs, 'Enforcing Community rights and obligations in national courts: striking the balance' in Lonbay and Biondi (eds), *supra*, ch 3, p 32.

[178] At p I–5395–6.   [179] *Supra*.   [180] (1992) 28 RTDE 27, 49.

the Court under that article to the situation where a Member State breaches
Community law would in some Member States mean applying a stricter test than
that applicable under their national law.[181] This, he said, would be particularly
paradoxical given that Community law has a status higher than that of national law:
it would be strange if it were more difficult to recover compensation for breach of
a rule which was hierarchically superior. Schockweiler also observed that the
restrictive conditions laid down in the Court's case law on Article 288 (ex 215)
concerned acts of a legislative nature adopted in fields where the institutions
enjoyed a discretion. Those conditions could only be transposed to legislative acts
adopted by the Member States, in respect of which most Member States did not
recognize that any liability in damages might arise.

Schockweiler's second point was developed by Advocate General Léger in *The
Queen v MAFF, ex parte Hedley Lomas*,[182] where he pointed out that a State might
incur liability for a breach of Community law regardless of the status in national
law of the body to which the damage was attributable:[183]

Consequently, the liability of the State acting in its legislative capacity cannot be *excluded* a
priori. Nor is it possible, when a breach of Community law is at issue, to make the State *qua*
legislator subject to more restrictive or more severe liability rules than the State *qua* execu-
tor and which would not comply with the requirements of Community law. If a Member
State only had to let an act be passed by the national Parliament in order to avoid an action
in damages, laying down a Community standard for governing such actions would be futile.

Since, where a breach of Community law has occurred, the obligation of a Member State
to pay damages is a question of Community law, the arising of that obligation and the
requirements of Community law relating to the action to obtain the damages cannot be
made subject to questions concerning the allocation of powers between legislative, regulatory, administrative and judicial organs, *which by definition are governed by domestic law*.

Schockweiler thought that the best solution to this problem would be for the
Community legislature to lay down common rules as to the circumstances in which
State liability arose. The Council's record made such legislation unlikely and the
Court was itself soon asked for guidance on the conditions under which the liabil-
ity of the State arose. In *Brasserie du Pêcheur and Factortame*,[184] it made it clear that
those conditions should not in principle differ from those governing the liability of
the Community: '[t]he protection of the rights which individuals derive from
Community law canot vary depending on whether a national authority or a
Community authority is responsible for the damage'.[185]

The *Brasserie du Pêcheur and Factortame* cases concerned claims for damages arising out of breaches by Member States of Treaty provisions which gave them a wide

---

[181] It may be noted that the conditions laid down in *Zuckerfabrik Süderdithmarschen, supra*, appear to
have made it more difficult in some Member States to obtain the suspension of national measures: see
AG Léger in *Hedley Lomas, infra*, p I–2588.
[182] Case C–5/94 [1996] ECR I–2553. See Oliver (1997) 34 CMLRev 666.
[183] p I–2582, emphasis in the original.
[184] Joined Cases C–46/93 and C–48/93 [1996] ECR I–1029.
[185] Para 42.

discretion. The Court declared that, in such circumstances, Community law conferred on the plaintiffs a right to damages where three conditions were met. The first was that the rule infringed had to be intended to confer rights on individuals. Secondly, the infringement had to be sufficiently serious in the sense that the defendant had manifestly and gravely disregarded the limits on its discretion. The Court mentioned various factors which the national courts might take into consideration in establishing whether a breach was to be regarded as sufficiently serious: 'the clarity and precision of the rule breached, the measure of discretion left by that rule . . ., whether the infringement and the damage caused was intentional or involuntary, whether any error of law was excusable or inexcusable, the fact that the position taken by a Community institution may have contributed towards the omission, and the adoption or retention of national measures or practices contrary to Community law'.[186] A prior judgment of the Court establishing the breach was not essential, but 'a breach of Community law will clearly be sufficiently serious if it has persisted despite a judgment finding the infringement in question to be established, or a preliminary ruling or settled case-law of the Court on the matter from which it is clear that the conduct in question constituted an infringement'.[187] The third condition was that there had to be a direct causal link between the breach of the obligation resting on the State and the damage sustained by the injured parties. The application of those conditions was in principle a matter for the competent national court, but the Court of Justice went on to give clear guidance as to the extent to which they were satisfied in the instant cases. The Court also made it clear that the organ of the State whose behaviour lay at the origin of the breach of Community law was irrelevant, even if it was a legislative body: 'the obligation to make good damage caused to individuals by breaches of Community law cannot depend on domestic rules as to the division of powers between constitutional authorities'.[188]

In *The Queen v MAFF, ex parte Hedley Lomas*,[189] another case concerning an alleged breach of the Treaty, the Court said that, if at the time it committed the infringement, the defendant State 'was not called upon to make any legislative choices and had only considerably reduced, or even no, discretion, the mere infringement of Community law may be sufficient to establish the existence of a sufficiently serious breach'. Thus, where a Member State fails to take any of the measures necessary to give effect to a directive on time, it commits a sufficiently serious breach of Community law for liability in damages to arise if the directive concerned satisfies the conditions laid down in *Francovich*.[190] By contrast, the incorrect transposition of a directive will not amount to a sufficiently serious breach of Community law where the Member State concerned acts in good faith and the

---

[186] Para 56.   [187] Para 57.   [188] Para 33.

[189] Case C–5/94 [1996] ECR I–2553, para 28.

[190] See Joined Cases C–178/94, C–179/94, C–188/94, C–189/94 and C–190/94 *Dillenkofer and Others v Federal Republic of Germany* [1996] ECR I–4845, paras 26–7; Oliver (1997) 34 CMLRev 675.

directive is reasonably capable of bearing the construction put upon it by the State concerned.[191]

It is undoubtedly true that the effect of this body of case law was to impose on certain Member States liability in damages to which they would not have been subject under their national law. However, the Court's acceptance that Member States should not be liable in damages for infringing Community law in circumstances in which the Community itself would not be so liable limited the exposure of the Member States because of the restrictive terms in which the Court has defined the extent of the Community's liability under the second paragraph of Article 288 (ex 215). As we have seen, it was by no means self-evident that the Court would transpose the conditions developed in cases concerning the liability of the Community to cases concerning the liability of Member States. That it chose to do so demonstrates a degree of restraint which contrasts with its boldness in *Francovich*.

The incidental effect of the principle of State liability

A further illustration of the Court's renewed confidence in the principle of national procedural autonomy is provided by its decision in *The Queen v Secretary of State for Social Security, ex parte Sutton*.[192] The issue in that case was whether a person was entitled to interest on arrears of benefit which had been withheld in breach of Directive 79/7 on equal treatment for men and women in matters of social security. The applicable national legislation did not provide for the payment of interest, but Article 6 of that directive provides: 'Member States shall introduce into their national legal systems such measures as are necessary to enable all persons who consider themselves wronged by failure to apply the principle of equal treatment to pursue their claims by judicial process, possibly after recourse to other competent authorities.' It is virtually identical to Article 6 of Directive 76/207, which the Court held in *Marshall II* required interest to be paid on compensation awarded for a discriminatory dismissal. It might therefore have been thought that interest also had to be paid where benefits had been wrongly withheld. However, the Court took a different view. The judgment in *Marshall II* had been concerned with interest on a sum designed to compensate for the loss and damage suffered by a person who had been dismissed because of her sex. By contrast, the present case concerned the right to receive interest on social security benefits. Such benefits were not designed to compensate the recipient for loss or damage, so the Court's reasoning in *Marshall II* did not apply.[193] The payment of interest on arrears of benefits could

---

[191] See Case C–392/93 *The Queen v H M Treasury, ex parte British Telecommunications* [1996] ECR I–1631, discussed by Oliver (1997) 34 CMLRev 658; Joined Cases C–283/94, C–291/94 and C–292/94 *Denkavit Internationaal and Others v Bundesamt für Finanzen* [1996] ECR I–5063.

[192] Case C–66/95 [1997] ECR I–2163. See Ward, 'New frontiers in private enforcement of EC directives' (1998) 23 ELRev 65.

[193] This is presumably the distinction between *Marshall II* on the one hand and *Steenhorst-Neerings* and *Johnson* on the other, cases which are not at first sight easy to reconcile. See Fitzpatrick and Szyszczak, 'Remedies and effective judicial protection in Community law' (1994) 57 MLR 434; Coppel,

not be considered an essential element of the right to non-discriminatory treatment under Directive 79/7.

The distinction drawn by the Court seems less than wholly convincing. The purpose of making an award of interest where a sum of money has been wrongly withheld is to put the creditor in the position he would have been in had the debtor complied with his legal obligations. It also prevents the debtor from profiting from his unlawful failure to pay on time the amount due by using or investing the money until the creditor enforces payment. In short, interest may be said to encourage the prompt payment of moneys due and to provide the creditor with some protection against the adverse consequences of the debtor's default. These considerations seem relevant whether the amount due represents compensation for a wrongful act or a benefit to alleviate the consequences of the social predicament in which the recipient finds himself. Indeed, the case for awarding interest in the latter case may be thought stronger due to the precarious financial position of the recipient. It will be recalled, however, that the payment of interest was originally regarded by the Court as an ancillary matter to be dealt with by national law.[194] It must be conceded that there is no reason for treating someone deprived of benefit in breach of Community law more favourably than someone deprived of benefit in breach of some rule of domestic law. Provided the principle of equivalence is satisfied, the absence of a right to interest cannot be said to render the enforcement of the rights conferred by Community law excessively difficult.

Somewhat paradoxically, the Court used the principle of State liability, one of the most striking recent developments in its case law, to reinforce its restrictive conclusion on the payment of interest. The applicant had argued that she was entitled by virtue of the principle of State liability to compensation equivalent to the amount by which the benefit paid to her had been eroded by inflation. The Court concluded that it was for the national court to assess whether and to what extent the applicant was entitled to reparation for the loss she claimed to have suffered as a result of the breach of Community law by the Member State concerned. Thus, the Court contemplated that the outcome might be the same as it would have been had the applicant been entitled to interest under Directive 79/7. However, the route chosen by the Court gave the national court more influence over whether that outcome materialized.

The Court had employed a similar tactic in *Comateb and Others v Directeur Général des Douanes et Droits Indirects*,[195] decided a few months previously. There the Court

'Time up for *Emmott?*' (1996) 25 ILJ 153. Cf Case C–180/95 *Draehmpaehl v Urania Immobilienservice* [1997] ECR I–2195, decided on the same day as *Sutton*, where the incompatibility of the disputed national rules with the principle of equivalence seems to have been decisive.

[194] See eg Case 26/74 *Roquette v Commission* [1976] ECR 677; Case 130/79 *Express Dairy Foods* [1980] ECR 1887.

[195] Joined Cases C–192/95 to C–218/95 [1997] ECR I–165. See Biondi and Johnson, 'The right to recovery of charges levied in breach of Community law: no small matter' (1998) 4 European Public Law 313. Cf Case C–343/96 *Dilexport v Amministrazione delle Finanze dello Stato*, judgment of 9 February 1999.

was called upon to consider whether the rule preventing a trader from recovering an unlawfully levied charge if it had been passed on to the trader's customers applied where the trader was legally obliged to pass the charge on. As we have seen, such rules are based on the idea that a trader would be unjustly enriched if he were permitted to recover from the State a charge which he had passed on to his customers. Advocate General Tesauro found that view unconvincing: 'I do not in fact believe it can be right to describe as unjust enrichment the profit derived by an individual from the reimbursement of a charge unduly required and levied by the authorities. More especially, I do not believe that the State, which itself has actually obtained unjust enrichment by levying—for years, even—an unlawful charge, may then specifically rely on a principle of that kind to refuse to repay the sums unduly paid.'[196] Whether or not the charge had been passed on by the trader was in the view of the Advocate General irrelevant, 'as presumably he was then obliged to reduce his profit margin or accept a reduction in the volume of his sales'.[197]

The Court was not prepared to abandon its well established case law in the way suggested by Advocate General Tesauro. A Member State was, it said, entitled to resist repayment of a charge imposed in breach of Community law 'where it is established that the charge has been borne in its entirety by someone other than the trader and that reimbursement of the latter would constitute unjust enrichment'.[198] It followed that 'if the burden of the charge has been passed on only in part, it is for the national authorities to repay the trader the amount not passed on'.[199] The Court acknowledged, however, that a trader might suffer damage as a result of incorporating a charge in the price of his goods. It therefore observed, somewhat cryptically, 'that where domestic law permits the trader to plead such damage in the main proceedings, it is for the national court to give such effect to the claim as may be appropriate'.[200] The Court added that 'traders may not be prevented from applying to the courts having jurisdiction, in accordance with the appropriate procedures of national law, and subject to the conditions laid down in [*Brasserie du Pêcheur and Factortame*], for reparation of loss caused by the levying of charges not due, irrespective of whether those charges have been passed on'.[201]

The judgment in *Comateb* is not in all respects easy to interpret. Like *Sutton*, the Court seemed to give back with one hand what it had taken away with the other. Advocate General Tesauro had alluded to the possibility that the principle of State liability might assist a trader who was prevented from recovering an unlawfully levied charge because it had been passed on to his customers. He wondered, however, 'whether it would not be a great deal simpler—and not only for the trader concerned—to recognize that the latter is entitled to reimbursement of the sum unduly paid'.[202] It will be noted that in *Comateb*, unlike *Sutton*, the Court expressly contemplated the possibility that reliance on the principle of State liability might entail separate proceedings before a different national court. This possibility might have been thought incompatible with the principle of effectiveness on the basis that

---

[196] p I–177.   [197] Ibid.   [198] Para 27.   [199] Para 28.   [200] Para 33.
[201] Para 34.   [202] p I–178.

it would render vindication of the applicant's Community rights excessively diffi-cult. It appears, however, that the Court did not wish to interfere with the domes-tic allocation of responsibilities among national courts by requiring them to deal with claims which would normally fall outside their jurisdiction. This approach is not lacking in merit. As Advocate General Jacobs pointed out in *Fantask*,[203] it 'ensures that claims are properly categorized and brought in the appropriate courts in accordance with appropriate substantive and procedural conditions, in particu-lar time-limits'. It provides further evidence of the importance now once again attached by the Court to the principle of national procedural autonomy.

An assessment of the Court's current approach

The above discussion is not intended to suggest that there has been a wholesale retreat by the Court back to the restrained stance it tended to adopt in the 1970s and early 1980s. There are several cases from what is identified here as the third phase of the case law in which the Court has declared certain types of national pro-cedural rule incompatible with Community law. Among the more noteworthy are two cases on sex discrimination.[204] *Magorrian and Cunningham v EHSSB and DHSS*[205] concerned the situation of female employees who had been excluded from membership of their employer's occupational pension scheme. The Court found that the exclusion of employees in the position of the applicants was con-trary to Article 119 (now 141) of the Treaty on equal pay for men and women[206] and that they were therefore entitled to additional benefits. The referring court asked whether Community law precluded the application in these circumstances of a national rule which prevented a woman in an equal pay case from recovering any money in respect of a period earlier than two years before the date on which proceedings were brought. *Steenhorst-Neerings* and *Johnson* might have suggested a negative answer to that question, but the Court thought those cases were distin-guishable. The present case was concerned not with the retroactive award of ben-efits but membership of a pension scheme which conferred a future entitlement to additional benefits: unlike the disputed rules in *Steenhorst-Neerings* and *Johnson*, the rule at issue here limited the extent to which the applicants' service record could be taken into account in order to calculate the additional benefits payable even after the date of the claim. Such a rule struck at the very essence of the rights conferred on the applicants by Community law and was incompatible with the principle of effectiveness.

---

[203] *Supra*, p I–6815.
[204] See also Case C–212/94 *FMC and Others v Intervention Board for Agricultural Produce and Another* [1996] ECR I–389; *Fantask, supra*.
[205] Case C–246/96 [1997] ECR I–7186.
[206] There is a large body of case law dealing with the effect of Art 141 on pensions. For a more detailed discussion, see ch 13.

Essentially the same rule came before the Court in *Levez v Jennings (Harlow Pools) Ltd*,[207] where the applicant, a woman, discovered after leaving her job with the respondent that she had been paid less than her male predecessor even though the work they had both done was the same. The respondent had deliberately misled the applicant about the level of her predecessor's pay and, by the time she found out about the disparity, she was prevented by a national limitation period from claiming arrears of pay for the first seven months during which she had held the post. The Employment Appeal Tribunal, London, asked the Court whether the right to equal pay laid down by Community law precluded the application of the national limitation period. The Court accepted that the period laid down was not in itself objectionable. However, it took the view that to allow an employer to rely on it in circumstances such as these would be incompatible with the principle of effectiveness: 'Application of the rule at issue is likely, in the circumstances of the present case, to make it virtually impossible or excessively difficult to obtain arrears of remuneration in respect of sex discrimination. It is plain that the ultimate effect of this rule would be to facilitate the breach of Community law by an employer whose deceit caused the employee's delay in bringing proceedings for enforcement of the principle of equal pay.'[208]

The United Kingdom Government argued that the applicant could in fact have claimed full compensation in the County Court, where the contested rule would not have applied. The Court alluded to the possibility that proceedings before the County Court might entail additional costs and delay by comparison with proceedings before the Industrial Tribunal. It concluded that the existence of an alternative remedy made no difference if it was 'likely to entail procedural rules or other conditions which are less favourable than those applicable to similar domestic actions'.[209] It was for the national court to determine whether that was so.

Where a national procedural rule constitutes a serious impediment to the enforcement of Community law rights and cannot reasonably be justified by principles such as legal certainty or the proper conduct of proceedings,[210] the Court therefore remains willing to step in. The national rules at issue in both *Magorrian and Cunningham* and *Levez* were incompatible with the principle of effectiveness because they threatened to undermine the very essence of the applicants' rights.[211] In less extreme cases, the overall approach of the Court has become more finely balanced than hitherto, attaching greater weight to the interests served by national rules of procedure. What is the explanation for the Court's apparent retreat from the more interventionist stance it took in some cases decided in the late 1980s and early 1990s? One is that the *Emmott* case was widely seen as having gone too far and the process of subjecting the Court's reasoning there to detailed scrutiny led to

---

[207] Case C–326/96, judgment of 1 December 1998.   [208] Para 32.   [209] Para 53.
[210] See para 33 of the judgment in *Levez*.
[211] Cf Case C–185/97 *Coote v Granada Hospitality Ltd* [1998] 3 CMLR 958.

a clearer understanding of the role and importance of national rules of procedure. Another is that the more detailed enumeration of the Community's powers in the TEU might, at least in the immediate aftermath of Maastricht, have made the Court less willing than previously to compensate for the shortcomings of the legislature. This is an issue to which we return in chapter 16.

6

General principles of law and fundamental rights

The way in which the Court of Justice exercises its jurisdiction under the Treaties is profoundly influenced by the general principles of Community law, a body of unwritten principles used by the Court to supplement the Treaties and acts of the institutions.[1] The development of general principles as a source of law represents one of the Court's most remarkable and inspired initiatives, not only filling in the inevitable gaps which emerged in the Treaty framework but also allowing the Court to draw on national law, thereby ensuring that Community law reflects the basic legal values of the Member States.

The notion of 'general principles of Community law' is now mentioned in Article 6(2) (ex F(2)) of the TEU,[2] but the textual justification in the EC Treaty for recourse to such principles was originally limited. There is no equivalent in the Community legal order of Article 38(1)(c) of the Statute of the International Court of Justice, which requires that court to apply the 'general principles of law recognised by civilised nations'. None the less, there was some basis for thinking that the authors of the Treaty envisaged that the Court might sometimes look beyond its four corners in resolving disputes with which it was confronted. An express reference to general principles may be found in the second paragraph of Article 288 (ex 215), according to which the non-contractual liability of the Community is to be determined in accordance with 'the general principles common to the laws of the Member States'. The reference in Article 220 (ex 164) to 'the law',[3] unless nothing more than 'a pious aspiration or a harmless piece of padding',[4] must have been intended to embrace something more than the law expressly laid down by or under the Treaty itself. Similarly, Article 230 (ex 173) mentions as one of the grounds on which Community acts may be declared void 'infringement of this Treaty *or of any rule of law relating to its application*' (emphasis added), evidently something different from infringement of the Treaty.

---

[1] See generally Tridimas, *The General Principles of EC Law* (1999); Usher, *General Principles of EC Law* (1998); Arnull, *The General Principles of EEC Law and the Individual* (1990); Hartley, *The Foundations of European Community Law* (4th edn, 1998), ch 5.

[2] Which reflects the case law of the Court on fundamental rights. See further below.

[3] French: 'le respect du droit'.

[4] Keeling, 'In praise of judicial activism. But what does it mean? And has the European Court of Justice ever practised it?' in Curti Gialdino (ed), *Scritti in Onore di G Federico Mancini* (1998), p 505 at p 521.

In formulating general principles, the Court draws inspiration from the constitutional traditions common to the Member States and from international treaties on which the Member States have collaborated or of which they are signatories. An example of such a treaty which has special significance in the Community legal order is the European Convention on Human Rights. As we shall see, the European Convention is treated as supplying guidelines on the fundamental rights protected by the Court of Justice as an integral part of the general principles of law.[5] The approach taken by the Court when having recourse to the national laws of the Member States has been described by a former Judge as follows:[6]

There is complete agreement that when the Court interprets or supplements Community law on a comparative law basis it is not obliged to take the minimum which the national solutions have in common, or their arithmetic mean or the solution produced by a majority of the legal systems as the basis of its decision. The Court has to weigh up and evaluate the particular problem and search for the 'best' and 'most appropriate' solution. The best possible solution is the one which meets the specific objectives and basic principles of the Community . . . in the most satisfactory way.

That passage was cited by Advocate General Slynn in *AM & S v Commission*,[7] where he went on to explain that '[s]uch a course is followed not to import national laws as such into Community law, but to use it as a means of discovering an *unwritten* principle of Community law'. Thus, once a principle derived from national law is incorporated into Community law, it acquires a life of its own independent of its national origins. In *AM & S*, the Court held that Regulation 17 on the application of the Treaty competition rules[8] was to be interpreted as protecting, subject to certain conditions, the confidentiality of written communications between lawyer and client. The principle of such protection was generally recognized in the legal systems of the Member States, although its scope varied and there was no express provision on the matter in the Treaty or in Regulation 17.[9]

Although it might seem paradoxical, a third source of general principles is the Treaties themselves.[10] The Court sometimes treats a particular provision as reflecting a general principle which can be applied outside the scope of the provision concerned. An example is *Brasserie du Pêcheur and Factortame*[11] where, in response to an argument that a principle of State liability could only be laid down by legislation and not by judicial decision, the Court declared: 'The principle of the non-contractual liability of the Community expressly laid down in Article 215 [now

---

[5] See eg Case C–260/89 *ERT* [1991] ECR I–2925, paras 41–5.

[6] H Kutscher, 'Methods of interpretation as seen by a Judge at the Court of Justice', p I–29, *Judicial and Academic Conference*, Luxembourg, 1976.

[7] Case 155/79 [1982] ECR 1575, 1649 (emphasis in the original).

[8] OJ Sp Ed 1959–62, p 87. The *AM & S* case and Reg 17 are discussed in more detail in ch 12.

[9] See also Case 17/74 *Transocean Marine Paint v Commission* [1974] ECR 1063, para 15, where, on the basis of a survey of the national laws of the Member States by AG Warner, the Court acknowledged the existence of a 'general rule that a person whose interests are perceptibly affected by a decision taken by a public authority must be given the opportunity to make his point of view known'.

[10] See Usher, op cit, ch 2.

[11] Joined Cases C–46/93 and C–48/93 [1996] ECR I–1029, para 29.

288] of the Treaty is simply an expression of the general principle familiar to the legal systems of the Member States that an unlawful act or omission gives rise to an obligation to make good the damage caused. That provision also reflects the obligation on public authorities to make good damage caused in the performance of their duties.' Another example is Article 34(2) (ex 40(3)) EC, according to which the common organization of agricultural markets 'shall exclude any discrimination between producers or consumers within the Community'. The Court has held that the prohibition of discrimination laid down in that provision 'is merely a specific enunciation of the general principle of equality which is one of the fundamental principles of Community law'.[12]

General principles of law may be invoked not only as a ground for annulment under Article 230 (ex 173) and in actions for damages under the second paragraph of Article 288 (ex 215), but also in interpreting written rules of Community law. Such principles are binding on both the Community institutions and on the Member States when they act within the scope of Community law.[13] In order to illustrate more clearly the effect such principles are capable of producing, it is appropriate to examine a number of them in greater detail.

Specific principles

Legal certainty

A general principle of wide application is that of legal certainty.[14] That principle played an important part in the Court's reasoning in the *Foto-Frost* case,[15] where, despite the contrary suggestion given by the terms of Article 234 (ex 177) EC, the Court ruled that national courts had no power to declare Community acts invalid. The principle of legal certainty has a number of aspects,[16] one of the most important of which is that, as the Court explained in *Ireland v Commission*,[17] 'Community legislation must be certain and its application foreseeable by those subject to it.'

---

[12] Joined Cases 124/76 and 20/77 *Moulins Pont-à-Mousson v Office Interprofessionnel des Céréales* [1977] ECR 1795, para 16.

[13] See eg Case 316/86 *Hauptzollamt Hamburg-Jonas v Krücken* [1988] ECR 2213, para 22; Case C–260/89 *ERT* [1991] ECR I–2925, paras 41–5. Conversely, 'the Court may not rule on an alleged breach of the general principles of Community law in the case of a dispute which is not connected in any way with any of the situations contemplated by the Treaty provisions': Case C–361/97 *Nour v Burgenländische Gebietskrankenkasse* [1998] ECR I–3101, para 19.

[14] The principle is not, however, an absolute one; its application must be combined with that of the principle of legality: see Joined Cases 42 and 49/59 *SNUPAT v High Authority* [1961] ECR 53, 87, where the Court said that the question which of those principles should prevail in any given case depends on a comparison of the public and private interests at stake.

[15] Case 314/85 [1987] ECR 4199, discussed in ch 2.

[16] eg the principles of legitimate expectations, non–retroactivity, and vested rights. Legitimate expectations and non–retroactivity are discussed below. See further Usher, op cit, ch 4; Hartley, op cit, pp 142–7.

[17] Case 325/85 [1987] ECR 5041, para 18.

That case concerned an application for the annulment of a Commission decision failing to charge certain expenditure incurred by the applicant to the European Agricultural Guidance and Guarantee Fund, Guarantee Section. In finding the contested decision void, the Court observed that the requirement of legal certainty 'must be observed all the more strictly in the case of rules liable to entail financial consequences, in order that those concerned may know precisely the extent of the obligations which they impose on them'.[18]

In *Commission v Italy*,[19] the Court pointed out that 'the principles of legal certainty and the protection of individuals require, in areas covered by Community law, that the Member States' legal rules should be worded unequivocally so as to give the persons concerned a clear and precise understanding of their rights and obligations and enable national courts to ensure that those rights and obligations are observed'. The Court found that the ambiguous nature of certain Italian legislation on value-added tax lay at the root of an administrative practice which was incompatible with the Sixth VAT Directive and that Italy was therefore in breach of its Treaty obligations. It is for the same reason that, as we have seen, it is no defence in proceedings brought under Article 226 (ex 169) EC that national legislation which is inconsistent with Community law is not in practice applied[20] or that the provisions of Community law in question produce direct effect in any event.[21]

Although judgments of the Court on the interpretation of a Community rule generally take effect from the date on which the rule concerned entered into force, the Court recognized in *Defrenne v SABENA*[22] that the principle of legal certainty might sometimes justify restricting the temporal effect of a ruling. In the *Defrenne* case, the Court recognized for the first time the direct effect of Article 119 (now 141) EC, which lays down the principle that men and women should receive equal pay for equal work.[23] Citing 'important considerations of legal certainty', however, the Court concluded that the direct effect of the article could not be invoked in support of claims relating to periods which preceded the date of the judgment, except in the case of those who had already brought proceedings. We shall come across other examples of cases in which the Court has limited the temporal effect of its judgments in this way, although they were all in some way exceptional. In deciding whether to impose such a limit, the Court takes account of two main factors: (a) what are the practical consequences likely to be if it fails to limit the temporal effect of its ruling; and (b) have those who are liable to be affected by the ruling been led to believe that the legal position was different from that declared by the Court?[24] It may be noted that the financial consequences which might ensue for a Member State from a ruling of the Court cannot in themselves justify

---

[18] Ibid.   [19] Case 257/86 [1988] ECR 3249, para 12.

[20] See eg Case C–58/90 *Commission v Italy* [1991] ECR I–4193, para 12.

[21] See eg Case 104/86 *Commission v Italy* [1988] ECR 1799, para 12.

[22] Case 43/75 [1976] ECR 455.   [23] See further ch 13.

[24] See AG Jacobs in Case C–163/90 *Administration des Douanes et Droits Indirects v Legros and Others* [1992] ECR I–4625, 4651.

limiting its temporal effect.[25] None the less, the imposition of such limits has proved controversial. The technique is discussed in more detail in chapter 13.

Legitimate expectations

One aspect of the principle of legal certainty which has produced particularly important practical effects is the principle of the protection of legitimate expectations.[26] In *CNTA v Commission*,[27] an action for damages under the second paragraph of Article 215 (now 288), the Court declared that a trader could legitimately expect that, for transactions into which he had entered irrevocably, no unforeseeable alteration would occur which might have the effect of causing him inevitable loss. The Community would be liable to pay compensation if, in the absence of an overriding matter of public interest, it failed to respect that expectation.

Interpreted too broadly, the principle of legitimate expectations would constitute an excessive fetter on the law-making institutions of the Community and the Court has therefore subjected the principle to some common-sense limitations. Thus, the Court has made it clear that 'a wrongful act on the part of the Commission or its officials, and likewise a practice of a Member State which does not conform with Community rules, is not capable of giving rise to legitimate expectations on the part of an economic operator who benefits from the situation thereby created'.[28] Similarly, the principle of legitimate expectations cannot be invoked to challenge a Community measure likely to harm the applicant's interests if a 'prudent and discriminating trader' would have foreseen its adoption.[29] Thus, the Court has held that traders cannot have a legitimate expectation that an existing situation will continue when the Community institutions have a discretionary power to alter it. That is especially true in areas like the common agricultural policy, which involve constant adjustments in the light of changes in the economic situation.[30]

However, even in the context of the common agricultural policy it may sometimes be possible to overcome these limitations. This is dramatically demonstrated by a series of cases which arose out of the Community's efforts to limit milk production.[31] The cases illustrate both the scope of the principle of the protection of legitimate expectations and the capacity of general principles of law to invalidate Community acts and ground a claim in damages against the institutions. At the risk

---

[25] See eg Case C–137/94 *R v Secretary of State for Health, ex parte Richardson* [1995] ECR I–3407, para 37.

[26] The origins of the principle can be traced to the German law principle of *Vertrauensschutz*: see Usher, op cit, p 54; Hartley, op cit, p 145.

[27] Case 74/74 [1975] ECR 533.

[28] Case 316/86 *Hauptzollamt Hamburg-Jonas v Krücken* [1988] ECR 2213, para 23.

[29] See eg Case 265/85 *Van den Bergh en Jurgens v Commission* [1987] ECR 1155, para 44; Case 246/87 *Continentale Produkten-Gesellschaft v Hauptzollamt München-West* [1989] ECR 1151, para 17.

[30] See eg Case C–353/92 *Greece v Council* [1994] ECR I–3411, para 44.

[31] See generally Cardwell, *Milk Quotas* (1996).

of some oversimplification, the background may be summarized as follows.[32] A Council regulation adopted in 1977 introduced a system of 'non-marketing premiums' which were paid to producers who undertook not to market milk and milk products for a specified period. The system did not prove sufficiently effective in curbing milk production, so in 1984 the Council adopted further regulations imposing a levy on quantities of milk delivered in excess of a reference quantity (or quota) calculated by reference to the amount delivered by the producer concerned during a particular calendar year. A producer who did not deliver any milk during that reference year because he had entered into a non-marketing undertaking under the 1977 regulation could not be certain that he would obtain a reference quantity under the levy system. In *Mulder I*,[33] a reference for a preliminary ruling, the Court held that the regulations concerning the levy on milk were invalid because they infringed the principle of legitimate expectations. The Court observed that where a producer 'has been encouraged by a Community measure to suspend marketing for a limited period in the general interest and against payment of a premium he may legitimately expect not to be subject, upon the expiry of his undertaking, to restrictions which specifically affect him precisely because he availed himself of the possibilities offered by the Community provisions'.[34]

In its judgment in *Mulder I*,[35] the Court accepted that a producer who had voluntarily ceased production for a given period could not legitimately expect to be able to resume production under conditions identical to those which applied previously. The Council therefore sought a way of accommodating the legitimate expectations of producers who had given non-marketing undertakings within the framework of the levy system. Accordingly, in 1989 it adopted a further regulation providing essentially that producers who had not, pursuant to a non-marketing undertaking given under the 1977 regulation, delivered any milk during the relevant reference year were to receive a special reference quantity equal to 60 per cent of the quantity of milk delivered during the twelve months preceding the month in which the application for the non-marketing premium was made. In *Spagl*,[36] also a reference for a preliminary ruling, the Court found that the reduction of 40 per cent applied to producers who had entered into non-marketing undertakings substantially exceeded the rates of reduction applicable to producers whose reference quantities were fixed on the basis of milk deliveries actually made during the relevant reference year. The application of such a high rate of reduction therefore amounted to a restriction which specifically affected producers in the former

---

[32] For a somewhat fuller account of the background and subsequent developments, see AG Léger in Case C–127/94 *R v MAFF, ex parte Ecroyd* [1996] ECR I–2731, 2735–40.

[33] Case 120/86 *Mulder v Minister van Landbouw en Visserij* [1988] ECR 2321.

[34] Para 24. See also Case 170/86 *von Deetzen v Hauptzollamt Hamburg-Jonas* [1988] ECR 2355. Cf Case C–63/93 *Duff and Others v Minister for Agriculture and Food, Ireland, and the Attorney General* [1996] ECR I–569.

[35] Para 23.

[36] Case C–189/89 [1990] ECR I–4539; see also Case C–217/89 *Pastätter* [1990] ECR I–4585; Case C–44/89 *von Deetzen II* [1991] ECR I–5119.

category precisely because of the undertakings they had given under the 1977 regulation. The Court concluded that 'the contested 60% rule likewise infringes the legitimate expectations which the producers concerned were entitled to entertain as to the limited nature of their undertakings'.[37] The contested provision was therefore declared void.

These cases produced a flood of claims for damages against the Community under the second paragraph of Article 215 (now 288). The first to be decided were those brought by the applicants in *Mulder II*,[38] where the claims were in part upheld, a rare example of a successful claim for damages against the Community in respect of an unlawful *legislative* act. The Court observed:[39] 'in so far as it failed completely, without invoking any higher public interest, to take account of the specific situation of a clearly defined group of economic agents . . . the Community legislature manifestly and gravely disregarded the limits of its discretionary power . . .'. It had thereby committed a serious breach of a superior rule of law, one of the conditions which must be satisfied to fix the Community with non-contractual liability for a legislative act.[40] The Court added that the complete exclusion of the producers concerned from the allocation of a reference quantity, which had the effect of preventing them from resuming the marketing of milk when their non-marketing undertaking expired, could not be regarded as foreseeable or as 'falling within the bounds of the normal economic risks inherent in the activities of a milk producer'.[41]

By contrast, the Court held that the introduction of the 60 per cent rule did not give rise to non-contractual liability because the breach of the principle of the protection of legitimate expectations found in *Spagl* was not sufficiently serious to produce that result. Unlike the 1984 rules, it could not be said that the Council had failed to take account of the situation of producers who had given non-marketing undertakings when it introduced the 60 per cent rule. In adopting the 1989 regulation following the rulings in *Mulder I* and *von Deetzen*, the Court said that 'the Community legislature made an economic policy choice with regard to the manner in which it was necessary to implement the principles set out in those judgments'.[42] The 60 per cent rule represented an attempt by the Council to preserve

[37] Para 29.

[38] Joined Cases C–104/89 and C–37/90 *Mulder and Others v Council and Commission* [1992] ECR I–3061. See Heukels (1993) 30 CMLRev 368; van Gerven, 'Non-contractual liability of Member States, Community institutions and individuals for breaches of Community law with a view to a common law for Europe' (1994) 1 MJ 6, 25–32.

[39] Para 16.

[40] See Case 5/71 *Zuckerfabrik Schöppenstedt v Council* [1971] ECR 975; Arnull, 'Liability for legislative acts under Article 215(2) EC' in Heukels and McDonnell (eds), *The Action for Damages in Community Law* (1997), ch 7.

[41] Para 17. The number of producers involved led the Council to adopt a regulation in order to facilitate the settlement of claims: see Reg 2187/93 providing for an offer of compensation to certain producers of milk and milk products temporarily prevented from carrying on their trade, OJ 1993 L196/6; Cardwell, op cit, ch 2.

[42] Para 21.

the fragile stability which had been achieved in the milk products sector while at the same time striking a balance between all the producers concerned. 'Accordingly,' the Court observed, 'the Council took account of a higher public interest, without gravely and manifestly disregarding the limits of its discretionary power in this area.'[43]

Non-retroactivity

Although no general rule against the retroactive effect of Community acts is to be found in the Treaties, the Court has developed such a rule as an aspect of the principle of legal certainty in general and the principle of the protection of legitimate expectations in particular. The Opinion of Advocate General Warner in *IRCA v Amministrazione delle Finanze dello Stato*[44] shows that the position which has evolved though the case law of the Court is very similar to that which prevails in the national laws of several Member States. Thus, as a matter of interpretation, Community acts are presumed by the Court not to be retroactive. Where it is clear that a Community act was intended by the legislature to have retroactive effect, its validity may thereby be cast into doubt. The Court has made it clear 'that in general the principle of legal certainty precludes a Community measure from taking effect from a point in time before its publication and that it may be otherwise only exceptionally, where the purpose to be achieved so demands and where the legitimate expectations of those concerned are duly respected'.[45] In *Racke v Hauptzollamt Mainz*,[46] the Court accepted that a regulation extending the system of monetary compensatory amounts to wine imported into the Community from third countries with effect from a date which preceded slightly the regulation's publication was valid in view of the need to avoid disturbances in the Community wine market. The Court noted that, on the date when the new amounts took effect, the Commission had taken special steps to bring them to the attention of those affected. By contrast, in *Meiko-Konservenfabrik v Germany*,[47] the Court held that the Commission had acted unlawfully in retroactively imposing a fixed deadline by which contracts between producers and processors of fruit and vegetables had to be forwarded to it in order to qualify for aid.

The Court applies the principle of non-retroactivity with particular strictness in the field of criminal law. In *Regina v Kirk*,[48] the master of a Danish fishing vessel was prosecuted for infringing a United Kingdom measure prohibiting vessels registered in Denmark from fishing within the United Kingdom's twelve-mile coastal zone. The disputed events took place between 1 and 25 January 1983. On the

---

[43] Ibid.   [44] Case 7/76 [1976] ECR 1213, 1236–9.
[45] Joined Cases 212 to 217/80 *Amministrazione delle Finanze dello Stato v Salumi* [1981] ECR 2735, para 10.
[46] Case 98/78 [1979] ECR 69. See also Case 246/87 *Continentale Produkten-Gesellschaft v Hauptzollamt München-West* [1989] ECR 1151; Case C–331/88 *Fedesa and Others* [1990] ECR I–4023.
[47] Case 224/82 [1983] ECR 2539.   [48] Case 63/83 [1984] ECR 2689.

latter date, the Council adopted a regulation on the conservation and management of fishery resources, Article 6(1) of which permitted Member States, with effect from 1 January 1983, to derogate in certain circumstances from the principle of non-discrimination on grounds of nationality. It was argued that the contested United Kingdom measure fell within the scope of the authorization granted retrospectively to the Member States by the Council's regulation. That argument was rejected by the Court:[49]

> Without embarking upon an examination of the general legality of the retroactivity of Article 6(1) of that regulation, it is sufficient to point out that such retroactivity may not, in any event, have the effect of validating *ex post facto* national measures of a penal nature which impose penalties for an act which, in fact, was not punishable at the time at which it was committed. That would be the case where at the time of the act entailing a criminal penalty, the national measure was invalid because it was incompatible with Community law.

The Court said that the principle that penal provisions could not have retroactive effect was common to the Member States and was enshrined in Article 7 of the European Convention on Human Rights: 'it takes its place among the general principles of law whose observance is ensured by the Court of Justice'.[50]

Notwithstanding the strength of the presumption developed by the Court against the retroactive application of Community acts, the so-called retroactive application of its own judgments has attracted criticism.[51] The objection here is that, when the Court interprets a provision of Community law, the interpretation in principle takes effect as from the moment the provision concerned entered into force, however long ago that may be. This is not, however, an example of true retroactivity. As Sir Patrick Neill acknowledged in his paper on judicial activism, the same approach is taken by English courts: 'When an English court interprets a provision in a statute it decides what the meaning of the provision is and what it always has been from the moment when the material part of the statute came into effect.' In the memorandum on the Court tabled by the United Kingdom at the IGC in July 1996, the approach of the Court of Justice was acknowledged to be 'in accordance with a general jurisprudential principle'. Moreover, as we have seen, the Court on occasion limits the temporal effect of its rulings in recognition of the inconvenience that may be caused where a provision of Community law is given an unexpected interpretation. As mentioned above, the imposition by the Court of a limit on the temporal effect of its rulings also attracts criticism.[52] There are those who say that the Court should not impose such limits in the absence of express authorization. Some object to the imposition of such a limit in particular cases, or to the failure of the Court to impose any such limit in others. Views may legitimately differ as to when it is appropriate to limit the temporal effect of a ruling. However, the very existence of the device shows a willingness on the part of the Court to curtail the effect which its judgments, like those of national courts, would normally be expected to produce.

[49] Para 21.
[51] See eg 'A Partnership of Nations', Cm 3181, para 37.
[50] Para 22.
[52] See further ch 13.

Proportionality

Described by the Court in an early case[53] as 'a generally accepted rule of law', the principle of proportionality is derived from the German principle of *Verhältnismäss-igkeit*.[54] It imposes a general limitation on the exercise by both Community and national authorities of the powers conferred upon them by Community law by requiring the measures they adopt to be in proportion to their ultimate object-ives.[55] The importance of the principle is underlined by the third paragraph of Article 5 (ex 3b) EC, introduced at Maastricht, according to which '[a]ny action by the Community shall not go beyond what is necessary to achieve the objectives of this Treaty'. The Treaty of Amsterdam annexed to the EC Treaty a Protocol on the Application of the Principles of Subsidiarity and Proportionality in order to 'establish the conditions' for their application (both being enshrined in Article 5) and 'with a view to defining more precisely the criteria for applying them and to ensure their strict observance and consistent implementation by all institutions'. However, the Protocol is concerned more with the principle of subsidiarity than with the principle of proportionality, which is well established in the case law of the Court.[56]

In *Fedesa and Others*,[57] the Court explained that it had 'consistently held that the principle of proportionality is one of the general principles of Community law. By virtue of that principle, the lawfulness of the prohibition of an economic activity is subject to the condition that the prohibitory measures are appropriate and neces-sary in order to achieve the objectives legitimately pursued by the legislation in question; when there is a choice between several appropriate measures recourse must be had to the least onerous, and the disadvantages caused must not be dispro-portionate to the aims pursued.' Lord Diplock put it rather more directly in *R v Goldstein*:[58] 'In plain English it means "you must not use a steam hammer to crack a nut, if a nutcracker would do." ' Thus, the principle is infringed if the restrictions imposed by a particular measure, or the harm it causes, outweigh the importance of the objective in view.

A straightforward case in which the principle of proportionality was applied is *Rau v De Smedt*.[59] There the Court held that national legislation requiring mar-garine to be packaged in cube-shaped blocks in order to prevent it from being con-fused with butter constituted an unlawful restriction on trade between Member States. Although legislation designed to avoid confusion in the mind of the con-sumer was in principle legitimate, the Court took the view that '[c]onsumers may

---

[53] Case 8/55 *Fédération Charbonnière Belgique v High Authority* [1954–56] ECR 245, 299.

[54] See Hartley, op cit, p 148; Tridimas, op cit, p 89.

[55] For detailed analysis, see Emiliou, *The Principle of Proportionality in European Law* (1996); Ellis (ed), *The Principle of Proportionality in the Laws of Europe* (1999); de Búrca, 'The principle of proportionality and its application in EC law' (1993) 13 YEL 105; Tridimas, op cit, chs 3 and 4.

[56] Subsidiarity is discussed in ch 16.

[57] Case C–331/88 [1990] ECR I–4023, para 13.   [58] [1983] 1 WLR 151, 155.

[59] Case 261/81 [1982] ECR 3961.

in fact be protected just as effectively by other measures, for example by rules on labelling, which hinder the free movement of goods less'.[60] Many other examples are given elsewhere in this book of the application of the principle of proportionality. It has been used to particularly useful effect by the Court in controlling recourse by the Member States to the Treaty derogations from the fundamental principles of freedom of movement[61] in the context of both goods and people[61] and in relation to attempts to justify measures which, although neutral in appearance, adversely affect one sex more than the other.[62]

It may be noted that the intensity with which the principle is applied by the Court may vary according to the importance of rules at issue in the scheme of the Treaty and the extent of any discretion they confer on the competent authorities. Thus, in *Fedesa* itself, the Court was asked for a preliminary ruling on the validity of a directive prohibiting the use in livestock farming of certain substances having a hormonal action. It was argued that the directive was incompatible with the principle of proportionality in three respects. The first was that prohibiting the use of the hormones concerned was an inappropriate way of attaining the directive's aim of removing distortions of competition and barriers to trade caused by disparities in the applicable national laws. The directive, it was said, was impossible to apply in practice and could lead to the creation of a black market. Secondly, if the directive was also intended to allay the fears of consumers, that objective could be met by disseminating information and advice. Thirdly, it was said that the financial cost to the traders affected outweighed any benefits which were likely to flow from the directive in terms of the general interest. The Court responded to those arguments by observing that 'in matters concerning the common agricultural policy the Community legislature has a discretionary power which corresponds to the political responsibilities given to it by Articles 40 [now 34] and 43 [now 37] of the Treaty. Consequently, the legality of a measure adopted in that sphere can be affected only if the measure is manifestly inappropriate having regard to the objective which the competent institution is seeking to pursue . . .'[63] The Court took the view that the contested directive could not be regarded as manifestly inappropriate: a more limited form of prohibition might also have led to the emergence of a black market and could require costly control measures, the effectiveness of which might be doubtful. The Council was entitled to take the view that, having regard to the requirements of health protection, the removal of barriers to trade and distortions of competition could not be achieved simply by the dissemination of information and the labelling of meat. The Court added that the importance of the objectives being pursued was 'such as to justify even substantial negative financial consequences for certain traders'.[64] It concluded that the principle of proportionality had not been infringed.

By contrast, in *Bilka v Weber von Hartz*[65] the Court was asked whether the exclusion of part-time employees, most of whom were women, from an occupational

---

[60] Para 17.   [61] See in particular chs 7 and 10.   [62] See ch 13.
[63] Para 14.   [64] Para 17.   [65] Case 170/84 [1986] ECR 1607.

pension scheme was compatible with Article 119 (now 141) of the Treaty, which requires men and women to be paid equal pay for equal work. The respondent employer argued that the excluding part-timers from the pension scheme was objectively justified by the need to make full-time work more attractive, thereby ensuring staff cover at unpopular times. The Court ruled that the employer's argument could only succeed if it were established that the means it had chosen 'correspond to a real need on the part of the undertaking, are appropriate with a view to achieving the objective in question and are necessary to that end'.[66]

A strict proportionality test was also applied in the context of the free movement of goods in *Familiapress v Bauer Verlag*.[67] There the issue was whether a national rule preventing the importation of periodicals containing prize competitions was proportionate to the aim of maintaining press diversity. The Court said that the application of the proportionality test was a matter for the national court, but it set out a number of detailed matters concerning the national press market concerned which the national court would have to investigate in order to determine whether the contested national legislation was proportionate.

Non-discrimination or equality

The Court has recognized a general principle of non-discrimination or equality as 'one of the fundamental principles of Community law',[68] requiring 'that similar situations shall not be treated differently unless differentiation is objectively justified'.[69] In *Sermide v Cassa Conguaglio Zucchero*,[70] the Court recognized that the principle of non-discrimination may also be infringed by treating in the same way two situations which are essentially different without objective justification. In that case, the Court was asked for a preliminary ruling on the validity of two regulations concerned with a quota system imposed on producers of sugar. It was alleged that the method laid down for calculating the levies payable by manufacturers who produced quantities of sugar in excess of the quotas allocated to them placed Southern European producers at a disadvantage in relation to Northern European producers. The Court observed that 'the various elements in the common organization of the markets, such as protective measures, subsidies, aid and so on, may not be differentiated according to region or according to other factors affecting production or consumption except by reference to objective criteria which ensure a proportionate division of the advantages and disadvantages for those concerned

---

[66] Para 37. The Court has not, however, been entirely consistent in the intensity with which it applies the principle of proportionality in the context of equal treatment for men and women. See further ch 13.

[67] Case C–368/95 [1997] ECR I–3689.

[68] For detailed analysis, see Dashwood and O'Leary (eds), *The Principle of Equal Treatment in EC Law* (1997).

[69] Joined Cases 124/76 and 20/77 *Moulins Pont-à-Mousson v Office Interprofessionnel des Céréales* [1977] ECR 1795, paras 16 and 17.

[70] Case 106/83 [1984] ECR 4209.

without distinction between the territories of the Member States'.[71] The Court found that the method of calculation adopted was objectively justified and that the argument that it arbitrarily placed a particular category of producers at a disadvantage had not been made out.

The Community rules on equality of treatment prohibit not only overt (or direct) discrimination but also covert (or indirect) forms of discrimination which in practice lead to the same result. Thus, in *Commission v Ireland*[72] the Commission alleged that certain Irish measures designed to conserve fish stocks discriminated against the fishing fleets of other Member States. The contested measures were based on apparently objective factors, such as the size and power of boats. However, there were hardly any boats in the Irish fleet which exceeded the limits laid down, whereas the fleets of certain other Member States were seriously handicapped by the measures. The Court found that they involved indirect discrimination on grounds of nationality.

The general principle of equality is regarded by the Court as having been given specific expression in several provisions of Community law which expressly prohibit certain forms of discrimination.[73] Discrimination on the grounds of nationality, for example, is prohibited within the scope of the Treaty by the first paragraph of Article 12 (ex 6); we have seen that the common organization of agricultural markets is required by Article 34(2) (ex 40(3)) to 'exclude any discrimination between producers or consumers within the Community'; as already mentioned, Article 141 (ex 119) lays down the principle that men and women should receive equal pay for equal work. The prohibition contained in Article 12 (ex 6) is reiterated *inter alia* in Articles 39(2) (ex 48(2)), 43 (ex 52), and 49 (ex 59), which concern respectively the free movement of workers, the right of establishment, and the freedom to provide services. As a *lex generalis*, Article 12 (ex 6) in principle 'applies independently only to situations governed by Community law in respect of which the Treaty lays down no specific prohibition of discrimination'.[74] Moreover, Article 12 operates only within the Treaty's sphere of application. Thus, in *Grado and Bashir*[75] the Amtsgericht Reutlingen asked the Court whether it was compatible with Article 12 for a public prosecutor to refuse to use the courtesy title 'Herr' in criminal proceedings against a national of another Member State where that title was used in similar proceedings against German nationals. The referring court had not provided any evidence that Community law in general, or the rules on freedom of movement in particular, were applicable. The Court concluded that the article did not therefore seem to be relevant. Where it does apply, however, the first paragraph of Article 12 produces direct effect[76] and has been held to prohibit

---

[71] Para 28.   [72] Case 61/77 [1978] ECR 417.
[73] See eg Joined Cases 201 and 202/85 *Klensch v Secrétaire d'Etat* [1986] ECR 3477, para 9; Case C–13/94 *P v S and Cornwall County Council* [1996] ECR I–2143, para 18.
[74] Case C–18/93 *Corsica Ferries* [1994] ECR I–1783, para 19.
[75] Case C–291/96 [1997] ECR I–5531.
[76] Joined Cases C–92/92 and C–326/92 *Collins and Others* [1993] ECR I–5145.

discrimination in a variety of contexts,[77] some of which are examined in chapter 11.

The Treaty of Amsterdam supplemented Article 12 with a new provision, Article 13 (ex 6a), which authorizes the Council, within the limits of the powers conferred upon the Community by the Treaty, to 'take appropriate action to combat discrimination based on sex, racial or ethnic origin, religion or belief, disability, age or sexual orientation'. Unlike Article 12, Article 13 does not itself prohibit the forms of discrimination to which it refers. It is not therefore capable of producing direct effect. Moreover, the Court has used the article to support a ruling that, in the absence of Council action based on it, discrimination based on sexual orientation is not covered by Community law.[78] The Court does not therefore appear to regard Article 13 as an expression of the general principle of equality.[79]

Fundamental rights

The general principles of law considered so far have undoubtedly produced an important impact on the way in which Community law is applied. However, that impact has for the most part been confined to technical 'lawyer's law'. Of greater controversy and political significance has been the use by the Court of the notion of general principles of law to ensure protection for fundamental rights in the Community and the Union. The importance of the Court's contribution in this area is such that it merits examination at somewhat greater length.

Although the EC Treaty has always contained provisions prohibiting discrimination on grounds of nationality and requiring equal pay for men and women, it did not originally refer to fundamental rights in a general sense. It is sometimes said that the reason for that omission is that the primarily economic objectives of the Treaty in its original form made such a catalogue unnecessary.[80] That explanation is not entirely convincing: even without the benefit of hindsight, it is hard to believe that the authors of the Treaty failed to foresee that fundamental rights issues might arise when the rules on matters such as the free movement of persons and competition fell to be applied in concrete cases. It is perhaps more likely that the Member States could not reach agreement on the subject.[81]

---

[77] See eg Case C–357/89 *Raulin* [1992] ECR I–1027; Case 186/87 *Cowan v Trésor Public* [1989] ECR 195.

[78] See Case C–249/96 *Grant v South-West Trains* [1998] ECR I–621, para 48. This case is discussed in more detail in ch 13.

[79] On the potential of Art 13, see More, 'The principle of equal treatment: from market unifier to fundamental right?' in Craig and de Búrca (eds), *The Evolution of EU Law* (1999), ch 14, pp 547–8.

[80] See eg the House of Lords Select Committee on the European Communities, *Human Rights Re-examined* (Session 1992–93, 3rd Report, HL Paper 10), para 3.

[81] See Clapham, 'A human rights policy for the European Community' (1990) YEL 309, 358–9. Cf Dauses, 'The protection of fundamental rights in the Community legal order' (1985) 10 ELRev 398, 399–400.

Whatever the reason for the omission, it caused particular controversy in
Germany, where the question whether Community law took precedence over the
fundamental rights enshrined in the *Grundgesetz,* or Basic Law, was the subject of
a lively debate which in due course reached the Court of Justice through the preliminary rulings mechanism. The Court proceeded to develop a remarkable body
of case law which gave the Community a firm fundamental rights basis while at the
same time preserving the coherence of the Community legal order and demon-
strating its capacity to absorb the basic values of the national legal systems.

The general principle of respect for fundamental rights

The first indication of the Court's approach came in *Stauder v Ulm,*[82] where the
Verwaltungsgericht Stuttgart asked whether a Commission decision on the sale of
cut-price butter to the recipients of certain social welfare benefits required beneficiaries to disclose their names to retailers. The Court took the view that the disputed provision did not require the names of beneficiaries to be disclosed where
their entitlement could be established in other ways. The Court observed that
'[i]nterpreted in this way the provision at issue contains nothing capable of prejudicing the fundamental human rights enshrined in the general principles of
Community law and protected by the Court'.[83] Thus the Court acknowledged for
the first time that it would protect fundamental rights as general principles of law.
In the absence of a catalogue of such rights in the Treaty, however, it was not at
that stage clear which rights would be regarded by the Court as fundamental.

A partial answer to that question was given in *Internationale Handelsgesellschaft v
Einfuhr- und Vorratsstelle Getreide,*[84] where the Verwaltungsgericht Frankfurt am
Main put it to the Court that the provisions of certain regulations were invalid
because they were inconsistent with several principles of German constitutional
law which had to be protected in the Community legal order. The Court made it
clear that 'the validity of a Community measure or its effect within a Member State
cannot be affected by allegations that it runs counter to either fundamental rights
as formulated by the constitution of that State or the principles of a national constitutional structure'.[85] The Court conceded, however, that it was necessary to
examine whether 'any analogous guarantee inherent in Community law' had been
disregarded. It went on: 'In fact, respect for fundamental rights forms an integral
part of the general principles of law protected by the Court of Justice. The protection of such rights, whilst inspired by the constitutional traditions common to the
Member States, must be ensured within the framework of the structure and objectives of the Community.'[86] The Court concluded that the disputed provisions did

---

[82] Case 29/69 [1969] ECR 419.   [83] Para 7.   [84] Case 11/70 [1970] ECR 1125.
[85] Para 3.   [86] Para 4.

not violate any right of a fundamental nature.[87] In *Nold v Commission*,[88] an action for annulment brought by a German undertaking under the ECSC Treaty, the Court added that 'international treaties for the protection of human rights on which the Member States have collaborated or of which they are signatories, can supply guidelines which should be followed within the framework of Community law'.[89] The applicant in *Nold* sought to rely *inter alia* on the European Convention on Human Rights.[90] All the Member States are parties to that Convention and it is now treated by the Court as having 'special significance' in the Community legal order.[91]

The Court's case law on fundamental rights affects not only acts of the Community institutions but also national rules which fall within the scope of Community law. Where, for example, a Community act imposes an obligation on a Member State, its scope may be affected by the fundamental rights upheld by the Court. Thus, in *Rutili v Minister for the Interior*,[92] the Court observed that restrictions imposed by regulation and directive of the Council on the right of a Member State to limit the movements of a national of another Member State were a 'specific manifestation'[93] of a principle enshrined in certain provisions of the European Convention on Human Rights. Similarly, in *Johnston v Chief Constable of the Royal Ulster Constabulary*,[94] the Court held that a provision of a directive on equal treatment for men and women requiring a judicial remedy to be given to victims of discrimination reflected a general principle of law underlying the constitutional traditions of the Member States and enshrined in the European Convention. That principle led the Court to conclude that the national authorities were not entitled to deprive individuals of their right to a judicial remedy.

The Member States must also respect the fundamental rights protected by the Court when acting in pursuance of powers granted under Community law. This

---

[87] For the domestic sequel, see *Internationale Handelsgesellschaft v Einfuhr- und Vorratsstelle für Getreide und Futtermittel* ('Solange I') [1974] 2 CMLR 540, where the Bundesverfassungsgericht ruled that the safeguards provided by Community law for fundamental rights were inadequate and that Community acts were therefore subject to the fundamental rights guarantees contained in the Grundgesetz. In that case, however, those guarantees were held not to have been infringed. The Bundesverfassungsgericht never in fact found any such infringement. It eventually accepted that the Community legal order offered adequate protection for fundamental rights and that it was no longer necessary to review Community acts for compliance with the guarantees of such rights contained in the Grundgesetz: see *Wünsche Handelsgesellschaft* ('Solange II') [1987] 3 CMLR 225; Hartley, op cit, pp 237–8.

[88] Case 4/73 [1974] ECR 491, para 13.

[89] The Court's reference to international treaties 'on which the Member States have collaborated or of which they are signatories' seems to be attributable to the fact that, at the time the act disputed in that case was adopted, the Convention had not been ratified by France. The lawfulness of a decision is to be determined by reference to the circumstances prevailing at the time of its adoption: see eg Joined Cases 15 and 16/76 *France v Commission* [1979] ECR 321, para 7. See further Schermers and Waelbroeck, *Judicial Protection in the European Communities* (5th edn, 1992), p 39.

[90] Cf Case 44/79 *Hauer v Land Rheinland-Pfalz* [1979] ECR 3727, paras 17–19; Case 222/84 *Johnston v Chief Constable of the Royal Ulster Constabulary* [1986] ECR 1651, para 18.

[91] See Case C–260/89 *ERT* [1991] ECR I–2925, para 41; Case C–299/95 *Kremzow v Austrian State* [1997] ECR I–2629, para 14.

[92] Case 36/75 [1975] ECR 1219.   [93] Para 32.   [94] *Supra*, para 18.

emerges from the decision in *Wachauf v Bundesamt für Ernährung und Forstwirtschaft*,[95] which concerned a dispute over a tenant farmer's right to compensation for abandoning milk production under national rules based on a Community regulation. The competent national authority had refused to compensate the tenant since his application did not have the consent of his landlord, as required by the relevant national rules. The referring court observed that, if a lessee were unable to take advantage of the compensation system without the consent of the lessor and the lessor, as in the present case, had never engaged in milk production or contributed to the setting up of the farm, the lessee would be deprived without compensation of the fruits of his labour, which would be incompatible with his constitutional rights. The Court accepted that Community rules which 'had the effect of depriving the lessee, without compensation, of the fruits of his labour and of his investments in the tenanted holding would be incompatible with the requirements of the protection of fundamental rights in the Community legal order. Since those requirements are also binding on the Member States when they implement Community rules, the Member States must, as far as possible, apply those rules in accordance with those requirements.'[96] The Court concluded that the relevant Community regulations left the competent national authorities enough discretion to apply them in a manner which was consistent with the fundamental rights of the tenant.

In addition, the Member States must comply with the fundamental rights protected by the Court when invoking exceptions and derogations for which Community law provides. This was made clear in *ERT*,[97] which concerned the compatibility with various provisions of the Treaty of a national system of exclusive television rights. The Member State concerned sought to rely on Articles 56 (now 46) and 66 (now 55) of the Treaty, which allow Member States to derogate from the Treaty rules on services 'on grounds of public policy, public security or public health'. It had been suggested that the contested national provisions were incompatible with the right to freedom of expression embodied in Article 10 of the European Convention. The Court declared:[98]

where a Member State relies on the combined provisions of Articles 56 and 66 in order to justify rules which are likely to obstruct the exercise of the freedom to provide services, such justification, provided for by Community law, must be interpreted in the light of the general principles of law and in particular of fundamental rights. Thus the national rules in question can fall under the exceptions provided for by the combined provisions of Articles 56 and 66 only if they are compatible with the fundamental rights the observance of which is ensured by the Court.

The application of that test was left to the referring court.

[95] Case 5/88 [1989] ECR 2609.   [96] Para 19. See the Opinion of AG Jacobs at p 2629.
[97] Case C–260/89 [1991] ECR I–2925. See also Case C–368/95 *Familiapress v Bauer Verlag* [1997] ECR I–3689, in which the Court held that, where a Member State seeks to rely on mandatory or overriding requirements to justify national rules liable to obstruct the free movement of goods, it must show that the general principles of Community law, and in particular the principle of respect for fundamental rights, are satisfied. The *Familiapress* case is discussed later in this chapter.
[98] Para 43.

The growing willingness of the Court to review national measures for compliance with the general principle of respect for fundamental rights reflects its policy of consolidating respect for such rights in the Community while at the same time avoiding the fragmentation which would result from the application of divergent national standards. Where a Member State implements a Community rule, it seems 'self-evident', as Advocate General Jacobs put it in *Wachauf*,[99] that it must comply with the standard imposed by the Court on the Community legislator, who has no power to require or permit the national authorities to depart from that standard. It must be regarded as implicit in Community provisions to which Member States are required to give effect that the Community principle of respect for fundamental rights is to be upheld. Where Member States seek to rely on derogations from Community rules, it would be bizarre if Community law permitted them to do so in circumstances which involved an infringement of a fundamental right. The Court clearly cannot allow national provisions on fundamental rights to be applied since these, where they exist at all, will vary from one Member State to another. Moreover, the scope of the Treaty cannot be determined by national law. Thus, in this context also it is right that the Court should require compliance with the general principle of respect for fundamental rights.[100]

It is important to note the limits to this case law. It follows from what has already been said that the Court has no jurisdiction to consider the compatibility with the fundamental rights it upholds of national legislation falling outside the scope of Community law.[101] Thus, in *Kremzow v Austrian State*,[102] the Court declined to answer a number of questions referred to it by the Austrian Oberster Gerichtshof (Supreme Court) concerning the effect of the European Convention in proceedings arising out of the conviction of an Austrian national for murder and unlawful possession of a firearm. The Court observed that the appellant's situation was 'not connected in any way with any of the situations contemplated by the Treaty provisions on freedom of movement for persons'[103] and that the national provisions under which he had been convicted 'were not designed to secure compliance with rules of Community law'.[104] The approach of the Court reflects the boundary between the jurisdiction of the Community and that of the Member States.

[99] [1989] ECR 2609, 2629.
[100] See further Weiler and Lockhart, ' "Taking rights seriously" seriously: the European Court and its fundamental rights jurisprudence—Part I' (1995) 32 CMLRev 51, 74–8. That article is a reply to Coppel and O'Neill, 'The European Court of Justice: taking rights seriously?' (1992) 29 CMLRev 669, where a different view is taken. The second part of the article by Weiler and Lockhart is published at (1995) 32 CMLRev 579.
[101] See Case 12/86 *Demirel v Stadt Schwäbisch Gmünd* [1987] ECR 3719; Case C–159/90 *Society for the Protection of Unborn Children Ireland v Grogan and Others* [1991] ECR I–4685. *Grogan* is discussed later in this chapter and in ch 9. For an analysis of *Demirel* from a fundamental rights perspective, see Weiler, 'Thou shalt not oppress a stranger (Ex 23:9): on the judicial protection of the human rights of non-EC nationals' in Schermers et al (eds), *Free Movement of Persons in Europe* (1993), p 248 at pp 255–67.
[102] Case C–299/95 [1997] ECR I–2629.   [103] Para 16.   [104] Para 17.

A bold attempt to extend the jurisdiction of the Community was made by Advocate General Jacobs in *Konstantinidis*,[105] where a Greek national who worked in Germany as a self-employed masseur and assistant hydrotherapist[106] objected to the way in which his name was transcribed into Roman characters in the register of marriages at the Registry Office in Altensteig. The Advocate General said there was a principle of law which the Court was responsible for upholding which protected, within the scope of Community law, an individual's dignity, moral integrity and sense of personal identity. That principle was violated if an individual was compelled without a very good reason to abandon or modify his name. In the view of Advocate General Jacobs:[107]

a Community national who goes to another Member State as a worker or self-employed person under Articles 48 [now 39], 52 [now 43] or 59 [now 49] of the Treaty is entitled not just to pursue his trade or profession and to enjoy the same living and working conditions as nationals of the host State; he is in addition entitled to assume that, wherever he goes to earn his living in the European Community, he will be treated in accordance with a common code of fundamental values, in particular those laid down in the European Convention on Human Rights. In other words, he is entitled to say 'civis europeus sum' and to invoke that status in order to oppose any violation of his fundamental rights.

The Court's approach was less sweeping.[108] National rules on the transcription of Greek names into Roman characters were 'incompatible with Article 52 [now 43] of the Treaty only in so far as their application causes a Greek national such a degree of inconvenience as in fact to interfere with his freedom to exercise the right of establishment enshrined in that article'.[109] Such an interference would occur if the spelling which the individual concerned was required to use 'is such as to modify its pronunciation and if the resulting distortion exposes him to the risk that potential clients may confuse him with other persons'.[110] The limited scope of the Court's ruling, confined to the economic freedoms conferred by the EC Treaty, emphasizes its caution about extending further the field within which Member States must comply with the Community principle of respect for fundamental rights.

The Court has also made it clear that, even in cases falling within the scope of Community law, the fundamental rights it upholds are not absolute. In the *Wachauf* case, the Court said that the fundamental rights it recognized had to be considered in relation to their social function: 'Consequently, restrictions may be imposed on the exercise of those rights, in particular in the context of a common organization of a market, provided that those restrictions in fact correspond to objectives of

---

[105] C–168/91 [1993] ECR I–1191.

[106] And who therefore fell within the scope of Art 52 (now 43) EC, which concerns the right of establishment.

[107] At pp I–1211–12.

[108] In Case C–2/92 *Bostock* [1994] ECR I–955, 971, n 12, AG Gulmann described the view expressed by AG Jacobs in *Konstantinidis* as 'too far-reaching'.

[109] Para 15.   [110] Para 16.

general interest pursued by the Community and do not constitute, with regard to the aim pursued, a disproportionate and intolerable interference, impairing the very substance of those rights.'[111] The omission of that passage from the judgment in *ERT* led two commentators to suggest that there were 'two standards in operation—one standard for Community acts, another standard for individual Member States' acts derogating from Community law'.[112] That suggestion seems misconceived.[113] Both cases involved the scope of the Community principle of respect for fundamental rights, the application of which invariably involves the balancing of competing interests. There is nothing unusual about the Community principle in this respect: as Weiler and Lockhart observe,[114] 'human rights by their nature are rarely, if at all, absolute. Their very definition almost invariably involves a balance between competing interests of the individual on the one hand, and the general interest of society on the other, or of one individual and competing interests of others.' Thus, in *ERT* it was incumbent upon the national court entrusted with the application of the principles laid down by the Court of Justice to carry out the balancing exercise in determining whether the disputed national provisions were compatible with Community law. It is clear from the Court's ruling that, if the national court had concluded, having balanced the various interests at stake, that those provisions were inconsistent with the right to freedom of expression, it would have been required to strike them down. Similarly, had the Court of Justice come to the conclusion that the Community rules at issue in *Wachauf* were incompatible with the Community principle of respect for fundamental rights, it would have declared those rules invalid. It may be noted that the interpretation given by the Court in that case to the provisions concerned reflected the concerns of the referring court and may well have been unwelcome to the Council and the Commission.[115]

The response of the Member States and the other institutions

The developing case law of the Court of Justice in due course prompted steps by the other institutions and the Member States to underline the Community's

[111] Para 18. See also Case 44/79 *Hauer v Land Rheinland-Pfalz* [1979] ECR 3727; Case C–280/93 *Germany v Council* [1994] ECR I–4973; Case C–84/95 *Bosphorus v Minister for Transport, Energy and Communications, Ireland and the Attorney General* [1996] ECR I–3953; Case C–368/96 *The Queen v The Licensing Authority established by the Medicines Act 1968, ex parte Generics (UK) Ltd*, judgment of 3 December 1998. Cf Case C–2/92 *Bostock* [1994] ECR I–955, where the Court refused to extend the reasoning in *Wachauf* to a situation where the tenant had surrendered his lease. The two cases are not easy to reconcile: see Weiler and Lockhart, op cit, Part II, pp 605–17.
[112] Coppel and O'Neill, op cit, p 684.
[113] It may be noted that in *Bostock, supra*, decided after the article by Coppel and O'Neill was published, the matter was left to be decided under national law alone. Even though the case fell within the scope of Community law, no substantive principle of that law had been infringed. See also *Konstantinidis, supra*, another case decided after the publication of Coppel and O'Neill's article.
[114] Op cit, Part II, (1995) 32 CMLRev 579, 585.
[115] See AG Jacobs, [1989] ECR 2609, 2630; Weiler and Lockhart, op cit, Part II, p 590–1.

political commitment to respect for fundamental rights. In 1977, the European Parliament, the Council and the Commission issued a Joint Declaration stressing 'the prime importance' they attached to the protection of fundamental rights and referring expressly to the European Convention. In their Declaration on Democracy made in Copenhagen in 1978, the Heads of Government of the Member States associated themselves with the Joint Declaration of the previous year and solemnly declared 'that respect for and maintenance of representative democracy and human rights in each Member State are essential elements of membership of the European Communities'.[116]

With the signature of the Single European Act in 1986 came the first reference in a Community Treaty to fundamental rights, the preamble referring to the fundamental rights recognized in the constitutions and laws of the Member States, the European Convention, and the European Social Charter.[117] A stronger commitment was given in the TEU, which contained a series of provisions reflecting an increased awareness at the political level of the need for the Union to demonstrate the importance attached to fundamental rights.[118] The most prominent was Article F(2) (now 6(2)),[119] according to which '[t]he Union shall respect fundamental rights, as guaranteed by the European Convention for the Protection of Human Rights and Fundamental Freedoms signed in Rome on 4 November 1950 and as they result from the constitutional traditions common to the Member States, as general principles of Community law'. That provision thus extended to the Union as a whole part of the law applicable under the first pillar. Article L (now 46) of the TEU initially excluded Article F(2) (now 6(2)) from the jurisdiction of the Court of Justice, but that exclusion was removed by the Treaty of Amsterdam, which extended the jurisdiction of the Court under the Community Treaties to 'Article 6(2) with regard to action of the institutions . . .'.

Since the EC Treaty was signed, there has therefore been a steady expansion in the extent to which the Court of Justice is prepared to intervene to ensure protection for fundamental rights. There has undoubtedly also been a corresponding increase in political awareness of the importance of acting—and being seen to act—in accordance with such rights. However, those developments could not disguise

[116] Both the Joint Declaration and the Declaration on Democracy are published in an appendix to the report of the House of Lords Select Committee on the European Communities entitled 'Human Rights Re-examined' (Session 1992–93, 3rd Report).
[117] It was in the same year that the Bundesverfassungsgericht ruled that the protection of fundamental rights in the Community legal order was sufficient to meet the standards laid down in the Grundgesetz and that it would no longer hear challenges to Community acts on the basis that those standards had not been met: see *Wünsche Handelsgesellschaft* [1987] 3 CMLR 225; Hartley, op cit, pp 236–40.
[118] See generally Neuwahl and Rosas (eds), *The European Union and Human Rights* (1995); Twomey, 'The European Union: three pillars without a human rights foundation' in O'Keeffe and Twomey (eds), *Legal Issues of the Maastricht Treaty* (1994), ch 8.
[119] See also Art 177(2) (ex 130u(2)) EC; Art 11(1) (ex J.1(2)), fifth indent, TEU; the Maastricht version of Art K.2(1) TEU. Evidence of the impact of Arts F(2) (now 6(2)) and J.1(2) (now 11(1)) may be found in Council Decision 94/776/EC appointing an ombudsman for Mostar for the duration of the European Union administration of Mostar, OJ 1994 L312/34.

the fact that the transfer of competence involved in acceding to the Community—and now the Union—caused a corresponding diminution in the jurisdiction of the organs of the European Convention on Human Rights, in the sense that matters which were previously resolved at national level were dealt with after accession by the institutions of an entity which was not itself subject to the control mechanisms established by the Convention. This came to be seen in some quarters as incompatible with the oft-proclaimed commitment of the Community and the Union to respect for fundamental rights.

Accordingly the Commission, with the support of the European Parliament, began to float the idea of accession to the European Convention by the Community itself, so that its institutions would be subject to the review mechanisms set up under the Convention in the same way as the Member States. In 1979 the Commission published a memorandum[120] advocating accession in which it suggested that a legal basis for taking that step might be found in Article 235 (now 308) EC.[121] That article provides:

If action by the Community should prove necessary to attain, in the course of the operation of the common market, one of the objectives of the Community and this Treaty has not provided the necessary powers, the Council shall, acting unanimously on a proposal from the Commission and after consulting the European Parliament, take the necessary measures.

The Commission's memorandum was the subject of a report by the House of Lords Select Committee on the European Communities, which took the view that '[t]he immediate practical gains of accession are likely to be limited, the benefits being largely indirect and to some extent symbolic'.[122] It pointed out that the use of Article 235 (now 308) as the legal basis for accession was contested and thought that amendments to the Treaty would be necessary to enable accession to take place.[123] The Select Committee concluded that there were more pressing demands on the Community's resources. That negative response to the Commission's memorandum was echoed in the Council and no concrete steps ensued.

However, the Commission remained convinced that accession would be beneficial and in 1990 it reignited the debate by issuing a Communication in which it asked the Council for authority to begin negotiations. The Commission observed that 'no matter how closely the Luxembourg Court monitors human rights, it is not the same as scrutiny by the Strasbourg Court, which is outside the Community legal system and to which the constitutional courts and supreme courts of the Member States are subject'. The Commission maintained that the ramifications of accession would be limited to matters which fell within the Community's field of

---

[120] 'Memorandum on the accession of the European Communities to the Convention for the Protection of Human Rights and Fundamental Freedoms', *Bulletin of the European Communities*, Supplement 2/79.

[121] And, in the case of the Coal and Steel Community and Euratom, Arts 95 ECSC and 203 EAEC respectively.

[122] 'Human Rights' (Session 1979–80, 71st Report), p xvi, para 32.

[123] Ibid, p xv, para 31(i)(a), and p xxviii, para 29.

competence: the legal systems of the Member States would be affected only as regards the scope of a Community legal act and accession would have no bearing on the effects of the Convention in other areas. Thus, accession would not result in any new obligations for the Member States of the Community. It would simply give their citizens better protection against Community measures which might infringe their fundamental rights. The Commission envisaged Community accession not only to the Convention itself but also to each of the Protocols which had been added to it in so far as they were relevant to the field of application of Community law. Although some of the Protocols had not been accepted by all the Member States, the Commission's view was that any Member State which had not accepted a particular Protocol would be unaffected by Community accession as far as national law was concerned. With regard to the legal basis for accession, the Commission repeated its view that recourse to Article 235 (now 308) (and the corresponding provisions of the other Treaties) would be justified. The Commission's Communication was the subject of a further report by the House of Lords Select Committee, which remained of the view that the benefits of accession would be limited and that the Community had more pressing tasks.[124] However, influenced by the references to fundamental rights and to the European Convention in both the Single European Act and the TEU (which had been signed but had yet to enter into force), the Select Committee was now 'inclined to the view that the Council could make use of the powers in Article 235 so far as EEC accession is concerned'.[125]

The Commission's request for negotiating directives led the Council in 1994 to ask the Court of Justice under Article 228(6) (now 300(6)) EC whether accession by the Community to the European Convention on Human Rights would be compatible with the EC Treaty. The intervention of the Court was once again to have a crucial bearing on subsequent developments. Article 228(6) (now 300(6)) enables the Council, the Commission or a Member State to obtain the opinion of the Court on the compatibility with the Treaty of an agreement with a third State or an international organization which is 'envisaged'.[126] Several Governments argued before the Court that the Council's request was premature. There was consensus that the only possible legal basis for accession was Article 235 (now 308) which required the Council to act unanimously, but the Member States were not agreed on the desirability of accession. Even if such agreement were in principle to be reached, various approaches to the extent of any accession by the Community and to the institutional difficulties which would be raised might be contemplated. No agreement could therefore be described as 'envisaged' within the meaning of Article 228(6) (now 300(6)).

[124] See 'Human Rights Re-examined' (Session 1992–93, 3rd Report), p 41, paras 104 and 105. The Commission's Communication is published as an appendix to the report.

[125] Ibid, p 37, para 87. The Committee agreed with the Commission that the accession of Euratom could be effected under Art 203 EAEC, but thought that Art 95 ECSC could not be used as the basis for accession by the Coal and Steel Community.

[126] See further ch 16.

The response of the Court to those objections[127] linked the admissibility of the request with the substance. The Court observed that Article 228(6) (now 300(6)) was intended to avoid the complications that might arise if the Court found an agreement incompatible with the Treaty after it had been concluded. In order to establish whether the lack of firm information about the precise terms of any accession agreement affected the admissibility of the Council's request, the Court distinguished between two problems that would be raised by accession. These were (a) the *competence of the Community* to conclude an agreement to accede; and (b) the *compatibility of any such agreement with the EC Treaty*, in particular with its provisions relating to the jurisdiction of the Court.

With regard to the question of competence, the Court reiterated[128] that it was in the interests of the Community institutions and of all the States concerned, both members and non-members, to have that question clarified from the outset. All that was necessary was that the purpose of the agreement envisaged should be known before negotiations commenced. In this particular case, the Court said that 'the general purpose and subject-matter of the Convention and the institutional significance of such accession for the Community are perfectly well known'.[129] It did not matter that the Council had not yet adopted a decision to open negotiations. The question of accession was 'on the Council's agenda'[130] and it envisaged the possibility of negotiating and concluding an agreement. Its request for an Opinion appeared to have been prompted, the Court said, 'by the Council's legitimate concern to know the exact extent of its powers before taking any decision on the opening of negotiations'.[131] The Court concluded that the request was therefore admissible in so far as it concerned the question of the Community's competence to conclude an agreement of the type in question.

As regards the compatibility of any accession agreement with the Treaty, the Court had previously accepted that the Community was competent to submit itself to the jurisdiction of a court established by an international agreement in order to rule on the interpretation and application of its provisions.[132] However, in order to decide whether accession to the Convention would be compatible with the rules contained in the Treaty, particularly Articles 164 (now 220) and 219 (now 292)[133] concerning the jurisdiction of the Court, the Court said it would need sufficient information on 'the arrangements by which the Community envisages submitting to the present and future judicial control machinery established by the Convention'.[134] Since no detailed information had been provided as to *how* the Community was to be subjected to the jurisdiction of an international court,

---

[127] See Opinion 2/94 [1996] ECR I–1759. Cf *Grant v South-West Trains*, *supra*, discussed in ch 13.

[128] See Opinion 1/78 'International Agreement on Natural Rubber' [1979] ECR 2871.

[129] Para 12.   [130] Para 14.   [131] Ibid.

[132] See Opinion 1/91 'Agreement Creating the European Economic Area' [1991] ECR I–6079, para 40.

[133] 'Member States undertake not to submit a dispute concerning the interpretation or application of this Treaty to any method of settlement other than those provided for therein.'

[134] Para 20.

the Court said it was not in a position to give an opinion on the compatibility of Community accession to the Convention with the rules of the Treaty.

In examining the Community's competence to accede, the Court drew attention to the first paragraph of Article 3b (now 5) EC, according to which the Community is to act 'within the limits of the powers conferred upon it by this Treaty and of the objectives assigned to it therein'. The Court said that it followed from that provision that the Community was based on the principle of conferred powers, a principle which applied in both the internal and the external spheres. This meant that the Community only had those powers which had been conferred on it, either expressly or by implication. The Court reiterated that, wherever the institutions of the Community enjoyed internal powers for the purpose of achieving a given objective, 'the Community is empowered to enter into the international commitments necessary for attainment of that objective even in the absence of an express provision to that effect'.[135] However, no provision of the Treaty gave the institutions any general power to enact rules on human rights or to conclude international conventions in that field.

The Commission had been supported by the Parliament and a number of Governments in arguing that a legal basis for accession to the European Convention could be found in Article 235 (now 308) of the Treaty. They maintained that the protection of fundamental rights was a 'transverse' or 'horizontal' objective to be pursued by the Community in the exercise of all its activities and that such protection was essential for the proper functioning of the common market. However, several other Governments disputed the legitimacy of recourse to Article 235 as the legal basis for accession and their doubts were shared by the Court of Justice.

The Court made some general observations about Article 235 (now 308) before considering whether it could be used as a basis for accession by the Community to the Convention. It declared that the article, 'being an integral part of an institutional system based on the principle of conferred powers, cannot serve as a basis for widening the scope of Community powers beyond the general framework created by the provisions of the Treaty as a whole and, in particular, by those that define the tasks and the activities of the Community'.[136] In particular, the article could not be used as a basis for the adoption of provisions whose effect would in substance be to amend the Treaty. The Court went on to note that respect for fundamental rights had been emphasized in a variety of declarations made by the Member States and the Community institutions, in the Single European Act and in the TEU. Fundamental rights also formed an integral part of the general principles of law upheld by the Court. It continued:[137]

Respect for human rights is therefore a condition of the lawfulness of Community acts. Accession to the Convention would, however, entail a substantial change in the present

---

[135] Para 26. The Court referred to Opinion 2/91 'ILO Convention No 170 Concerning Safety in the Use of Chemicals at Work' [1993] ECR I–1061, para 7.
[136] Para 30.   [137] Paras 34 and 35.

Community system for the protection of human rights in that it would entail the entry of the Community into a distinct institutional system as well as the integration of all the provisions of the Convention into the Community legal order.

Such a modification of the system for the protection of human rights in the Community, with equally fundamental institutional implications for the Community and the Member States, would be of constitutional significance and would therefore be such as to go beyond the scope of Article 235. It could be brought about only by way of Treaty amendment.

The Court therefore concluded that, as Community law then stood, the Community lacked competence to accede to the Convention.

The Court's Opinion was delivered just before the opening of the 1996 IGC and it placed the ball firmly back in the court of the Member States: if they really thought accession by the Community to the European Convention was desirable, they had an ideal opportunity at the IGC to make the necessary amendments to the Treaty. However, accession would also mean negotiating changes to the Convention itself, which is at present open only to Members of the Council of Europe[138] and whose procedures would have to be adapted to accommodate the Community. In addition, further consideration of the *extent* to which the Community should bind itself, and the consequences of any disparities between the obligations of the Community and those of individual Member States, would be required.[139] Although some Member States were in favour of reversing the Court's Opinion in the new treaty, it was evident from the proceedings before the Court that several Member States took a different view. In the event, as we shall see, a different approach was taken to ensuring respect for fundamental rights in the Community and the Union. That outcome might have been seen as vindicating the cautious approach taken by the Court: the lack of consensus among the Member States as to the desirability of Community accession to the Convention showed the wisdom of the Court's decision not to take upon itself responsibility for resolving the issue.

Opinion 2/94 undoubtedly disappointed some observers, who believed that accession to the Convention would both reinforce the protection of fundamental rights in the Community and have symbolic value.[140] It did not, however, follow from the Court's Opinion that Article 308 (ex 235) could not be used as the basis for other steps, short of accession, to consolidate protection for fundamental rights in the Community. The Court's description of respect for human rights as 'a condition of the lawfulness of Community acts' seemed to imply an acceptance that the protection of fundamental rights was one of the Community's objectives which it was necessary to attain in the course of the operation of the common market. Article 308 might therefore be used as the basis for a horizontal Council measure

---

[138] Art 59(1) of the Convention. Membership of the Council of Europe is in turn open only to European States: Art 4, Statute of the Council of Europe.

[139] See the House of Lords Select Committee's 1992 Report, *supra*, paras 63–8 and 101–3.

[140] See JUSTICE, 'Judging the European Union: Judicial Accountability and Human Rights' (1996), pp 13–14; Gaja (1996) 33 CMLRev 973; Waelbroeck (1996) CDE 549; Burrows, 'Question of Community accession to the European Convention determined' (1997) 22 ELRev 58. Cf *Matthew v United Kingdom*, judgment of 18 February 1999 (European Court of Human Rights).

on fundamental rights applicable to all activities carried out within the scope of the Treaty, such as a regulation laying down a Community catalogue of such rights.[141] At the international level, Article 308 might in principle be used as the basis for Community accession to international treaties for the protection of fundamental rights which have a less developed supervisory mechanism than the European Convention.[142] The article might also provide the foundation for an agreement with the Contracting Parties to the Convention establishing a formal system for the exchange of information concerning judgments of the Luxembourg and Strasbourg Courts along the lines of the EEA Agreement.[143] None of these steps would be of constitutional significance within the meaning of the Court's Opinion because they would not entail any substantial modification of the existing mechanism for protecting fundamental rights in the Community. Whether any of them would command unanimous support in the Council is, however, another matter. One innovation, suggested by some of the Governments which submitted observations to the Court in Opinion 2/94, which might be of value would be an agreement permitting the Luxembourg and Strasbourg Courts to ask each other for preliminary rulings. However, it should be remembered that, unlike the Community system in which the uniform application of the law is of the utmost importance, primary responsibility for protecting the rights and freedoms enshrined in the Convention lies with the Contracting States: the machinery of protection established by the Convention is a subsidiary one.[144] In any event, such an agreement could only be concluded pursuant to an amendment to the Treaty since it would clearly have constitutional implications, at least if the rulings were to be binding on the referring court.[145]

What are the implications of the Court's Opinion for other provisions of the Treaty which confer legislative powers on the Community institutions? It may be

[141] See Lenaerts, 'Fundamental rights to be included in a Community catalogue' (1991) 16 ELRev 367. The adoption of such a catalogue may be undesirable as a matter of principle: even if agreement could be reached on its content, it could have the effect of undermining the Convention. See the House of Lords Select Committee's 1980 report, paras 21–3 and 33, and its 1992 report, paras 39 and 76. Toth observes that the adoption of a Community catalogue of fundamental rights 'would probably be the worst possible scenario', but argues that, in the light of Opinion 2/94, the Community lacks competence to enact such a catalogue without a Treaty amendment: 'The European Union and human rights: the way forward' (1997) 34 CMLRev 491, 501–2.

[142] See eg the European Social Charter; the International Covenant on Economic, Social and Cultural Rights; the International Covenant on Civil and Political Rights; the Convention against Torture and Other Cruel, Inhuman or Degrading Treatment or Punishment. In 1984, the European Parliament proposed that the Union should consider acceding to the first three of those instruments as well as to the European Convention: see Art 4(3) of its draft Treaty establishing the European Union, OJ 1984 C77/33; Capotorti, Hilf, Jacobs and Jacqué, *The European Union Treaty* (1986), pp 39–44.

[143] Cf Art 106 of the EEA Agreement. Similar systems have been established in relation to the Brussels and Lugano Conventions on jurisdiction and the enforcement of judgments and the Rome Convention on the law applicable to contractual obligations.

[144] See eg *Handyside v United Kingdom*, Series A No 24, (1979–80) 1 EHRR 737, para 48.

[145] This would be necessary as far as the rulings of the Court of Justice are concerned: see Opinion 1/91, *supra*, para 61, where the Court said its function as conceived by the Treaty was 'that of a court whose judgments are binding'.

noted that the Court did not say that the Community had no express or implied powers to adopt rules on fundamental rights, but merely that it has no *general* power to enact such rules. Taken together with the Court's acknowledgement that Community acts must respect human rights as a condition of their lawfulness, the implication would seem to be, not only that Community acts adopted under specific powers must avoid infringing such rights, but that such powers can be used as the basis for provisions which are specifically designed to protect them.[146] If this is correct, Articles 18(2) (ex 8a(2)) and 22 (ex 8e), second paragraph, of the Treaty might be used as the basis for measures concerning fundamental rights in connection with citizenship of the Union; similarly, Article 40 (ex 49) of the Treaty might be used as the basis for such measures in the field of freedom of movement for workers. That conclusion would seem to be reinforced by the difficulty of distinguishing clearly between protecting fundamental rights and avoiding their infringement.

The Treaty of Amsterdam

Although the Treaty of Amsterdam failed to reverse Opinion 2/94, it did seek to reinforce the protection of fundamental rights in the Union in other ways. A new Article 6(1) (ex F(1)) TEU read: 'The Union is founded on the principles of liberty, democracy, respect for human rights and fundamental freedoms, and the rule of law, principles which are common to the Member States.' This elevated to the body of the TEU a number of principles previously mentioned in its preamble and had the potential to endow them with a constitutional status superior to that of other principles, in particular those relating to the functioning of the common market.

The importance of the principles referred to in Article 6(1) was underlined in two ways. First, Article 49 (ex O) restricted the right to apply for membership of the Union to '[a]ny European State which respects the principles set out in Article 6(1)'. Secondly, a procedure was introduced for suspending the rights of Member States which were found to be in 'serious and persistent breach' of those principles. Under Article 7 (ex F.1) TEU, the Council, meeting in the composition of Heads of State or Government, has the power to determine the existence of such a breach. Once such a determination has been made, the Council[147] has the power to

---

[146] The Court has accepted that co-operation agreements concluded under Art 181 (ex 130y) EC may, by virtue of Art 177(2) (ex 130u(2)), contain provisions concerning respect for human rights: see Case C–268/94 *Portuguese Republic v Council* [1996] ECR I–6177. Cf Reg 975/1999 laying down the requirements for the implementation of development co-operation operations which contribute to the general objective of developing and consolidating democracy and the rule of law and to that of respecting human rights and fundamental freedoms, OJ 1999 L120/1; Reg 976/1999 laying down the requirements for the implementation of Community operations, other than those of development co-operation, which, within the framework of Community co-operation policy, contribute to the general objective of developing and consolidating democracy and the rule of law and to that of respecting human rights and fundamental freedoms in third countries, OJ 1999 L120/8.

[147] Here the Treaty does not specify the composition.

suspend certain of the Members State's rights arising under the TEU, including that State's voting rights in the Council. The Court has not expressly been given juris-diction over acts of the Council under Article 7 but it has a potentially important role in policing compliance with the principles set out in Article 6(1). According to a new Article 309(1) (ex 236(1)) EC, where a decision has been taken to sus-pend the voting rights of a Member State under Article 7(2) TEU, its voting rights are automatically suspended under the EC Treaty as well. Moreover, a Council determination under Article 7(1) TEU of the existence of a serious and persistent breach gives the Council the power under Article 309(2) to suspend the delinquent State's rights under the EC Treaty as well. Where the Council exercises its power under Article 309(2) EC, its decision will clearly be reviewable in annulment pro-ceedings under Article 230 (ex 173) EC. In such proceedings, the applicant may allege that the procedural requirements laid down in Article 309(4) have not been followed or (more controversially) that the determination made by the Council under Article 7(1) TEU was unlawful. A claim of the latter sort would make it hard for the Court to avoid examining whether the Council was justified in concluding that the State concerned was guilty of a serious and persistent breach of any of the principles referred to in Article 6(1).

Even if the Council does not exercise its power under Article 309(2), a Council decision under Article 7(2) to suspend the delinquent State's rights under the TEU might still be reviewable under Article 230 (ex 173) because of the automatic sus-pension of that State's voting rights under the EC Treaty which ensues. Although taken outside the Community system, the decision of the Council produces legal effects within it. If the decision does not comply with Article 7 TEU, that conse-quence would be incompatible with Article 47 (ex M) TEU, according to which Article 7 does not affect the EC Treaty.[148] The Court invoked Article M (now 47) in the 'Airport Transit Visas' case,[149] in which the applicant sought the annulment pursuant to Article 173 (now 230) EC of a joint action adopted by the Council under the TEU. In the course of finding the action admissible, the Court observed that it was responsible for ensuring that acts said to be based on the TEU did not encroach upon the powers conferred on the Community by the EC Treaty.

It may be useful to remind both existing and future Member States that mem-bership of the Union requires constant vigilance to ensure that the principles men-tioned in Article 6(1) (ex F(1)) are respected, not just at the moment of accession but on a permanent basis. There is no mechanism in either the EC or the Euratom Treaties for suspending the rights of Member States which fail to comply with the economic and social principles on which those Treaties are based. Only in Article 88 ECSC do comparable powers exist where a Member State fails to comply with its obligations in the economic field. Those powers have never been exercised and if Article 7 (ex F.1) TEU and its counterparts in the other Treaties likewise fall into

---

[148] Where the requirements of Art 7 are satisfied, that article must be regarded as a *lex specialis* in rela-tion to Art 47.

[149] Case C–170/96 *Commission v Council* [1998] ECR I–2763.

disuse, that will provide some measure of their success. However, the heaviness of the procedure prescribed by these provisions and the potentially damaging consequences of invoking them make them weapons of last resort. They will do little to reinforce the protection afforded to individuals in concrete cases. That is one of the reasons why an amendment to the Treaties to permit the accession of the Community or the Union to the European Convention continues to be advocated.

An assessment of the Court's contribution

Reaction to the development by the Court of the general principle of respect for fundamental rights has been mixed. Hartley, for example, comments: 'it is probably fair to say that the conversion of the European Court to a specific doctrine of human rights has been as much a matter of expediency as conviction' and speaks of the need for the Court 'to take action to head off a possible "rebellion" ' by the German courts.[150] That view seems somewhat churlish. Whatever the authors of the Treaty might have thought, by the time the Court gave judgment in *Stauder v Ulm* it had become apparent that the application of the Treaty could give rise to situations in which fundamental rights recognized by the Member States might be jeopardized. The same was true of fundamental rights enshrined in international treaties like the European Convention which had been signed by the Member States. For the Court to have disregarded such rights would have been unacceptable on grounds of both principle and pragmatism. It would have meant accepting that the Community institutions were not constrained in the exercise of their legislative powers by considerations of fundamental rights. That would have dealt a potentially fatal blow to the legitimacy of the Community legal order. The solution devised by the Court to this dilemma was ingenious: it equipped the Community with a uniform standard of fundamental rights distinct from yet inspired by the constitutional traditions of the Member States and international treaties to which the Community was not itself a party. Thus, Community law was able to reflect the basic values of the Member States without the coherence of the system being called into question. This was a remarkable achievement. The later case law requiring the Member States to respect the Community principle of respect for fundamental rights when acting within the scope of the Treaties was an essential but natural development of the Court's earlier decisions. Although that development was liable to bring the Court into conflict with the Member States in potentially delicate situations,[151] the Court has balanced the issues involved with extraordinary skill, going with the grain of national legal traditions and leaving a good deal to the discretion of the national courts.

The Court's talent for equilibration is clearly illustrated by its decision in *Familiapress v Bauer Verlag*, the facts of which have already been briefly described.

[150] Op cit, pp 132–3.
[151] See Mancini and Keeling, 'From *CILFIT* to *ERT*: the constitutional challenge facing the European Court' (1991) 11 YEL 1, 11–12.

It will be recalled that the case concerned the compatibility with the Treaty rules on the free movement of goods of a national law preventing the sale of periodicals containing prize competitions. It was argued before the Court that the aim of the contested legislation was to maintain press diversity and that as a result it was justified. The Court was therefore confronted with a dilemma: preserving the diversity of the press was in itself an important objective, but it was capable of being used to undermine the free movement of goods, one of the fundamental principles of the common market. How could these apparently conflicting requirements be reconciled? The Court declared that '[m]aintenance of press diversity may constitute an overriding requirement justifying a restriction on free movement of goods. Such diversity helps to safeguard freedom of expression, as protected by Article 10 of the European Convention on Human Rights and Fundamental Freedoms, which is one of the fundamental rights guaranteed by the Community legal order . . .'[152] However, in order to be regarded as legitimate, it had to be established that the national legislation was proportionate to the aim of maintaining press diversity. It also needed to be borne in mind that a prohibition on the sale of certain publications could detract from freedom of expression. It was for the national court to examine these questions by studying the relevant national press market and considering a range of factors set out by the Court in some detail. Thus, the circle was squared. The fundamental importance of the interest invoked by the Member State concerned was recognized by the Court but its application was confined to cases where it could genuinely be regarded as threatened. It was not the Court itself but the national court which was to establish whether or not this was so. In performing that task, the national court was to apply detailed criteria laid down by the Court.

None the less, the acid test must be a substantive one: how effective a guardian of fundamental rights has the Court proved itself to be? It may be noted at the outset that, in the *Maastricht* decision, the Bundesverfassungsgericht again accepted that protection for fundamental rights under the EC Treaty was in principle adequate to satisfy the standards of the Grundgesetz.[153] It is also worth emphasizing that the Court has never knowingly disregarded a relevant provision of the European Convention or refused to follow the case law of the Strasbourg Court. Cases where that Court has subsequently adopted a view of the Convention's scope which differs from that taken by the Court of Justice are rare.

An example which is sometimes cited in this context is *Hoechst v Commission*,[154]

---

[152] Case C–368/95 [1997] ECR I–3689, para 18. On the concept of overriding or mandatory requirements, see further ch 7.

[153] See *Brunner v European Union Treaty* [1994] 1 CMLR 57, 79, 81–2; Everling, 'The Maastricht judgment of the German Federal Constitutional Court and its significance for the development of the European Union' (1994) 14 YEL 1; Herdegen, 'Maastricht and the German Constitutional Court: constitutional restraints for an "ever closer union" ' (1994) 31 CMLRev 235; Foster, 'The German constitution and EC membership' [1994] PL 392; MacCormick, 'The Maastricht-Urteil: sovereignty now' (1995) 1 ELJ 259; Zuleeg, 'The European constitution under constitutional constraints: the German scenario' (1997) 22 ELRev 19. The *Brunner* case is discussed in more detail in ch 3.

[154] Joined Cases 46/87 and 227/88 [1989] ECR 2859. See ch 12.

a competition case concerning the scope of the Commission's investigatory powers.[155] The Court of Justice held that Article 8(1) of the Convention, which provides that everyone has the right to respect for his private and family life, his home
and his correspondence, did not extend to business premises, noting that there was
no case law of the Strasbourg Court on the subject.[156] The Court of Human Rights
subsequently ruled[157] that Article 8(1) did in fact extend to professional or business
premises and found that it had been infringed by a search of a lawyer's office. None
the less, in *Hoechst* the Court of Justice went on to recognize that protection against
arbitrary or disproportionate intervention constituted a general principle of
Community law and to set out various conditions which the Commission had to
meet when carrying out investigations. Given the derogation laid down in Article
8(2) of the Convention,[158] it may be doubted whether the practical result would
have been much different had the Court accepted that Article 8(1) was applicable.

The scope of the Commission's investigatory powers in competition cases was
also challenged in *Orkem v Commission*,[159] where the question arose whether an
undertaking under investigation had the right to remain silent. The applicant
sought to rely on Article 6 of the Convention, which embodies the right to a fair
trial, but the Court of Justice said that 'neither the wording of that article nor the
decisions of the European Court of Human Rights indicate that it upholds the right
not to give evidence against oneself'.[160] The Court of Human Rights subsequently
held[161] that Article 6 did indeed embody a right to remain silent and not to incriminate oneself. However, the Court of Justice went on in *Orkem* to hold that the
rights of the defence, which it described[162] as 'a fundamental principle of the
Community legal order', prevented the Commission from compelling an undertaking 'to provide it with answers which might involve an admission on its part of
the existence of an infringement [of the Treaty competition rules] which it is
incumbent upon the Commission to prove'.[163] There may admittedly be room for
argument over whether the rights of the defence under EC law have precisely the
same scope as the right not to incriminate oneself under Article 6 of the
Convention, but any discrepancy is likely to be marginal. Far from suggesting a lack

---

[155] See further Wils, 'La compatibilité des procédures communautaires en matière de concurrence
avec la Convention européenne des droits de l'homme' (1996) 32 CDE 329, 352; Waelbroeck and
Fosselard, 'Should the decision-making power in EC antitrust procedures be left to an independent
judge? The impact of the European Convention on Human Rights on EC antitrust procedures' (1994)
14 YEL 111.

[156] The Court of Justice was criticized for failing to refer to the judgment of the Strasbourg Court
delivered earlier the same year in the *Chappell* case, Series A No 152, (1990) 12 EHRR 1: see Clapham,
'A human rights policy for the European Community' (1990) 10 YEL 309, 337–8.

[157] See *Niemietz v Germany*, Series A No 251, (1993) 16 EHRR 97.

[158] 'There shall be no interference by a public authority with the exercise of this right except such
as is in accordance with the law and is necessary in a democratic society in the interests of national security, public safety or the economic well-being of the country, for the prevention of disorder or crime,
for the protection of health or morals, or for the protection of the rights and freedoms of others.'

[159] Case 374/87 [1989] ECR 3283. See Wils, op cit, p 345; ch 12, *infra*.

[160] Para 30.   [161] See *Funke v France*, Series A No 256, [1993] 1 CMLR 897.

[162] Para 32.   [163] Para 35.

of sensitivity on the part of the Court to questions of fundamental rights, the case shows the Court's willingness to protect such rights even where it believes that the European Convention offers no assistance.

Perhaps the most controversial example of an apparent conflict between Community law and the Convention is the *Grogan* case,[164] where the Court of Justice was asked about the compatibility with the Treaty rules on services of a national restriction on the publication of information concerning the availability of abortion facilities lawfully provided in another Member State. The Court held that such a restriction fell outside the scope of the relevant provisions of the Treaty where those performing the abortions were not involved in distributing the information. Since the relevant national legislation did not come within the ambit of Community law, the Court said it had no jurisdiction to assess its compatibility with fundamental rights. In *Open Door and Dublin Well Woman v Ireland*,[165] the Court of Human Rights subsequently held that an injunction granted by the Irish Supreme Court in similar circumstances restraining the applicants from imparting or receiving information about abortion facilities available abroad amounted to a breach of Article 10 of the Convention concerning freedom of expression.

These cases were cited by a former President of the Court of Human Rights to illustrate an alleged difference in the approach taken by the two Courts and what he called the inherent weaknesses of *la solution prétorienne* to the problem of ensuring the protection of fundamental rights in the Union.[166] It is submitted that the criticism implicit in those remarks is misplaced. Because the circumstances of the *Grogan* case fell outside the scope of the Treaty, the Court of Justice lacked jurisdiction to apply the Convention. It did not therefore express any view about the effect of Article 10. The restrictive view taken by the Court of Justice of the scope of the Treaty rules on services might well have been motivated by a desire to avoid considering a question on the effect of the Convention which was pending before the Court of Human Rights.[167] But there is no overlap, and consequently no inconsistency, between the rulings of the two Courts.

Indeed, it would be a mistake to assume that the Court of Human Rights invariably takes a more progressive approach than the Court of Justice to questions of fundamental rights. The Strasbourg Court has consistently refused to accept that the right to respect for private and family life entitles post-operative transsexuals to have their new gender officially recognized.[168] By contrast, the Luxembourg

---

[164] Case C–159/90 *Society for the Protection of Unborn Children Ireland v Grogan and Others* [1991] ECR I–4685. See generally de Búrca, 'Fundamental human rights and the reach of EC law' (1993) 13 OJLS 283; Phelan, 'Right to life of the unborn v promotion of trade in services: the European Court of Justice and the normative shaping of the European Union' (1992) 55 MLR 670; O'Leary, 'The Court of Justice as a reluctant constitutional adjudicator: an examination of the abortion case' (1992) 16 ELRev 138.

[165] Series A No 246, (1993) 15 EHRR 244.

[166] See Ryssdal, 'Human Rights in the European Union' in *The Developing Role of the European Court of Justice* (European Policy Forum/Frankfurter Institut, August 1995), p 9, at pp 11–12.

[167] Cf the Report for the Hearing in *Grogan* at p I–4687 and the Opinion of AG van Gerven at p I–4727.

[168] See eg *Sheffield and Horsham v United Kingdom* (1999) 27 EHRR 163.

Court has held that to dismiss a transsexual for a reason related to a gender reassignment is incompatible with the Community rules on equal treatment for men and women.[169] The contrast between the approach of the two Courts is revealing, since the provisions of the Convention would seem more suitable for protecting the rights of transsexuals than those relied on by the Court of Justice.

Thus, the Court of Justice, through the concept of the general principles of law, has provided the Community with a firm fundamental rights foundation. As the authors of *The European Union and Human Rights: Final Project Report on an Agenda for the Year 2000* acknowledged,[170] '[t]he European Court of Justice deserves immense credit for pioneering the protection of fundamental human rights within the legal order of the Community when the Treaties themselves were silent on this matter. It has been the Court that has put in place the fundamental principles of respect for human rights which underlie all subsequent developments.'[171] As we have seen, at Maastricht the Member States enshrined the case law of the Court in the TEU and made it applicable to the Union as a whole.[172] The Court's ruling, in Opinion 2/94, that the Community lacked competence to accede to the European Convention led to the introduction in the Treaty of Amsterdam of far-reaching new provisions designed to enhance the protection afforded to fundamental rights in the Union. The Court has a potentially important role to play in the application of those provisions.

This is not to say that the present position could not be improved. The report referred to above and the accompanying agenda[173] advocate a series of further steps, including the appointment of a Commissioner with special responsibility for human rights, the establishment of a European Human Rights Monitoring Agency and accession to the European Convention, even if this necessitates a Treaty amendment, as well as to the European Social Charter. These proposals merit detailed consideration by the Member States and the institutions of the Union. But it is unlikely that the Union would have reached this stage if the Court had not taken that small first step in *Stauder v Ulm*.

---

[169] See Case C–13/94 *P v S and Cornwall County Council* [1996] ECR I–2143. See further ch 13.

[170] The report, published by the European University Institute, Florence, in 1998, was one of the results of a project funded by the European Commission to mark the 50th anniversary of the adoption of the Universal Declaration of Human Rights. Its authors are Professors Philip Alston and Joseph Weiler.

[171] Para 175 of the report.   [172] See Art 6(2) (ex F(2)).

[173] 'Leading by example: a human rights agenda for the European Union for the year 2000'.

Substantive law

7

The free movement of goods

At the core of the common market contemplated by the EEC Treaty lay the free movement of goods. The Treaty contained provisions designed to eliminate various forms of obstacle to imports and exports which States, left to their own devices, might seek to erect. Thus, Articles 9 to 16 EEC[1] were concerned with the elimination between Member States of customs duties on imports and exports and charges having equivalent effect. Article 9 (now 23) was originally the first provision of Part Two of the Treaty entitled 'Foundations of the Community', a fact to which the Court attached some significance in *Van Gend en Loos*, as we have seen. Since the entry into force of the TEU, the EC Treaty no longer contains a Part bearing that title, a reflection of the increased importance now accorded to other policies, some of which were not mentioned in the Treaty in its original form. There is no doubt, however, that the free movement of goods remains one of the cornerstones of the Community system.[2]

Alongside the Treaty prohibition on customs duties and charges having equivalent effect went Articles 30 to 36,[3] which were concerned with the elimination of quantitative restrictions on imports and exports between Member States and all measures having equivalent effect. It is with those provisions that the present chapter is mainly concerned. They have made a major contribution to realizing one of the Treaty's principal objectives, namely 'to unite national markets in a single market having the characteristics of a domestic market'.[4] Notwithstanding (or perhaps because of) their importance, the application of the Treaty provisions on quantitative restrictions has proved more problematic than that of the rules on customs duties. Although the Court has played a major role in defining the ambit of the provisions concerned, it has had considerable difficulty in pursuing a clear and consistent policy towards their interpretation and application. This is doubtless due in part to the somewhat vague terms in which they are couched. It may also be attributable to ambivalence about, or fluctuating attitudes towards, the extent to which the Court should use those provisions to restrict the freedom of the Member States

---

[1] See now Arts 23–5 EC.

[2] The Treaty also made provision for the adoption of a common customs tariff governing trade between the Member States and third countries, a fundamental plank of the customs union on which the Community was based. See now Arts 23 (ex 9) and 26 (ex 28) EC.

[3] See now Arts 28–30 EC.

[4] Case 207/83 *Commission v United Kingdom* ('Origin Marking') [1985] ECR 1201, para 17.

to regulate matters which are only loosely connected with the free movement of goods.[5]

The main prohibition is contained in Article 28 (ex 30), which states: 'Quantitative restrictions [QRs] on imports and all measures having equivalent effect [MEE] shall be prohibited between Member States.' Articles 31 and 32 (now repealed) laid down standstill rules preventing the Member States from introducing any new QRs or MEE and 'from making more restrictive the quotas[6] and measures having equivalent effect existing at the date of the entry into force of this Treaty'. Member States were also required to abolish all such quotas (and, presumably, MEE)[7] by the end of the transitional period, that is to say by the end of 1969. Article 33 (also repealed) then set out a mechanism designed to ensure their progressive abolition by that date. A parallel prohibition concerning exports is contained in Article 29 (ex 34(1)), according to which: 'Quantitative restrictions on exports, and all measures having equivalent effect, shall be prohibited between Member States.' By virtue of Article 34(2) (now repealed), any such measures in existence when the Treaty entered into force were to be abolished by the end of the first stage of the transitional period (31 December 1961).

The scope of Article 28 (ex 30)

One striking feature of Article 28 (ex 30) is its disarming simplicity. In *Ianelli v Meroni*,[8] the Court noted that the prohibition it contained was 'mandatory and explicit' and that 'its implementation does not require any subsequent intervention of the Member States or Community institutions'. The Court deduced that it therefore had direct effect as from the end of the transitional period. However, the apparent clarity of Article 28 (ex 30) is in fact an illusion. An obvious difficulty is the Treaty's failure to define the crucial terms 'quantitative restriction' and 'measure having equivalent effect'. It was doubtless assumed that the former notion was familiar in international trade law, but this could not be said of the latter. As Gormley points out,[9] '[w]hilst the notion of quantitative restrictions had been taken from the Liberalisation Code of the OEEC, that of measures having equivalent effect was entirely original to the EEC Treaty, there being no direct equivalent in the GATT or any previous trade Treaty'.

One way of interpreting Article 28 (ex 30) might have been to apply the *ejusdem generis* rule, treating the notion of MEE as confined to national measures which

---

[5] For detailed discussion from a constitutional perspective of the Court's approach to Art 28 (ex 30), see Poiares Maduro, *We the Court: the European Court of Justice and the European Economic Constitution* (1998).

[6] The terms 'quantitative restriction' and 'quota' seem to have been used interchangeably. In the *Dassonville* case, *infra*, AG Trabucchi described the two concepts as 'identical': [1974] ECR 837, 858.

[7] See Oliver, *Free Movement of Goods in the European Community* (3rd edn, 1996), p 71, n 2.

[8] Case 74/76 [1977] ECR 557, para 13.

[9] *Prohibiting Restrictions on Trade within the EEC* (1985), p 10.

singled out imports for special treatment and which made it more difficult for them to penetrate the market of the country concerned than domestically produced goods. Alternatively, it might have been said that any national measure which impeded imports had an effect equivalent to a QR. Taken to its extreme, that view would have rendered the concept of the MEE capable of embracing customs duties and charges of equivalent effect, fiscal measures, and a whole range of national rules concerning the characteristics of products and the circumstances in which they could be sold. In the context of the Treaty, this would clearly have gone too far, for there were provisions dealing expressly with customs duties and charges of equivalent effect and with internal taxation.[10] These were evidently to be considered *leges speciales* excluding application of the *lex generalis* which was Article 30. That was the view taken in *Ianelli v Meroni*,[11] where the Court said that '[h]owever wide the field of application of Article 30 [now 28] may be, it nevertheless does not include obstacles to trade covered by other provisions of the Treaty . . . Thus obstacles which are of a fiscal nature or have equivalent effect and are covered by Articles 9 to 16 [now 23-5] and 95 [now 90] of the Treaty do not fall within the prohibition in Article 30 [now 28].'[12] This left a potentially broad category of national rules which might none the less be regarded as constituting MEE.

During the transitional period, the scope of the notion of the MEE was the subject of a lively debate.[13] There were essentially three currents of opinion. The most restrictive was that only measures which discriminated directly against imports (so-called 'distinctly applicable' measures) were to be considered as having an effect equivalent to quantitative restrictions. At the other end of the spectrum were those who regarded the question of discrimination as irrelevant: on this view, any measure which restricted inter-State trade was in principle to be considered a MEE unless it could be justified under Article 30 (ex 36), which sets out various grounds of derogation from Article 28 (ex 30). There was a variety of intermediate approaches which charted a course somewhere between these two extremes. One proponent of such an approach was the Commission itself which, on the eve of the end of the transitional period, adopted Directive 70/50 on the abolition of MEE which were not covered by other provisions adopted under the EEC Treaty.[14] Directive 70/50 was based on Article 33(7) of the Treaty (now repealed), which required the Commission to issue directives on the abolition by Member States of 'any measures *in existence when this Treaty enters into force* which have an effect equivalent to quotas'.[15] Article 1 of the directive made it clear that it was intended to apply only to measures 'which were operative at the date of entry into force of the EEC Treaty'. Since the second paragraph of Article 32 (now repealed) required all such measures to be abolished by the end of the transitional period anyway, it might

[10] See Art 90 (ex 95).   [11] *Supra*, para 9.
[12] The relationship between Art 28 (ex 30) and the Treaty rules on State aids is more problematic. It appears that both sets of rules are capable of applying simultaneously: see Oliver, op cit, pp 83–6.
[13] For useful surveys of the early literature, see Oliver, op cit, pp 90–2; Gormley, op cit, chap 2.
[14] OJ Eng Sp Ed, 1970 (I), p 17, adopted on 22 December 1969.   [15] Emphasis added.

have been thought that the useful life of the directive would be limited. Although it is now technically redundant and could not in any event bind the Court,[16] as an indication of the Commission's views its significance extended beyond national measures in existence when the Treaty entered into force. It has been referred to by the Court in a number of cases in which it has been called upon to decide how far the notion of MEE extends.

Article 2 of the directive was concerned with distinctly applicable measures. According to Article 2(1), the directive covered 'measures, other than those applicable equally to domestic or imported products, which hinder imports which could otherwise take place, including measures which make importation more difficult or costly than the disposal of domestic production'. Article 2(3) set out a lengthy illustrative catalogue of the types of measure envisaged. According to Article 3:

This directive also covers measures governing the marketing of products which deal, in particular, with shape, size, weight, composition, presentation, identification or putting up and which are equally applicable to domestic and imported products, where the restrictive effect of such measures on the free movement of goods exceeds the effects intrinsic to trade rules. This is the case, in particular, where:

— the restrictive effects on the free movement of goods are out of proportion to their purpose;
— the same objective can be attained by other means which are less of a hindrance to trade.

That provision made it clear that the Commission did not subscribe to the narrow view of the scope of Article 28 (ex 30). Measures which did not discriminate between domestic and imported products were in principle capable of constituting MEE. Some light on the circumstances in which the effect of such measures on the free movement of goods might exceed 'the effects intrinsic to trade rules' was provided by the preamble to the directive, which referred to the effects 'normally inherent in the disparities between rules applied by Member States in this respect'. Thus, the Commission seemed to envisage that restrictions on the free movement of goods which resulted simply from differences in the marketing rules applicable in the State of origin and the State of import would not constitute MEE. However, the position would change if the rules of the latter State did not comply with the principle of proportionality, in other words where the purpose of the rules, albeit in itself legitimate, could be attained just as effectively by other means which were less of a hindrance to trade. In brief, national measures which impeded inter-State trade might constitute MEE if they were unreasonable, notwithstanding the fact that they applied equally to domestic products and to imports. Interpreted in this way, Directive 70/50 may be seen as containing the seeds of the rule of reason which was to germinate in the Court's case law some years later.

---

[16] See Gormley, op cit, p 12.

The *Dassonville* formula

In *Procureur du Roi v Dassonville*[17] decided in 1974, the Court offered a definition of its own of the notion of a MEE. The case was referred to the Court in the course of criminal proceedings which had been brought in Belgium against two traders who had imported into that country a consignment of Scotch whisky which they had lawfully acquired in France. The operation entailed an infringement of Belgian law because the two traders did not have a certificate of origin issued by the British customs authorities. During the proceedings before the Court, it emerged that it would have been very difficult for them to obtain such a certificate, although they would have been able to do so relatively easily had they imported the whisky directly from the United Kingdom.

The Court said that a requirement that an importer in circumstances such as these should be in possession of a certificate of authenticity constituted a MEE. It offered the following definition of that notion:[18] 'All trading rules enacted by Member States which are capable of hindering, directly or indirectly, actually or potentially, intra-Community trade are to be considered as measures having an effect equivalent to quantitative restrictions.' That statement (hereafter referred to as 'the *Dassonville* formula') was remarkable for its breadth. It was implicit in the language used by the Court that it was the effect of a national measure rather than its form which counted. Moreover, by acknowledging that an indirect or potential effect on trade might be enough, the Court indicated that it was not necessary to adduce direct evidence of an alteration in the pattern of trade in order to establish an infringement of Article 28 (ex 30). The term 'trading rules' might have been used to limit the formula, but it subsequently became clear that this had not been the Court's intention, for in later cases the term 'measures' was used instead.[19]

It will also be noted that the formula contained no reference to the idea of discrimination. The omission seems to have been deliberate: Advocate General Trabucchi regarded Article 28 (ex 30) as capable of applying to national measures which were non-discriminatory[20] and the contested national provisions appear to have been applicable to all spirits, whether imported or domestically produced. However, the Court attached significance to the fact that the requirement they laid down was more difficult to satisfy if the goods in question were imported into Belgium from a third country.[21] Because they were capable of disadvantaging imports, the disputed national rules could therefore be regarded as indirectly discriminatory. The ruling consequently made it clear that Article 28 (ex 30) was capable of applying to national rules which did not discriminate directly against imports (often described as 'indistinctly applicable'), but failed to resolve the

---

[17] Case 8/74 [1974] ECR 837.   [18] Para 5.

[19] See eg Joined Cases C–267 and C–268/91 *Keck and Mithouard* [1993] ECR I–6097, para 11 ('. . . any measure . . .').

[20] See p 859.   [21] See also AG Trabucchi at p 863.

question whether it also applied to national measures which were genuinely non-discriminatory.[22] That question was to come back to haunt the Court.

Notwithstanding the breadth of the *Dassonville* formula, the following paragraph of the judgment[23] offered a hint as to where the outer limits of the prohibition laid down in Article 28 (ex 30) were to be found. The Court said:

In the absence of a Community system guaranteeing for consumers the authenticity of a product's designation of origin, if a Member State takes measures to prevent unfair practices in this connexion, it is however subject to the condition that these measures should be reasonable and that the means of proof required should not act as a hindrance to trade between Member States and should, in consequence, be accessible to all Community nationals.

That statement suggested that a reasonable measure taken by a Member State to prevent consumers from being misled might not be caught by Article 28 (ex 30) even if it hindered intra-Community trade. This approach, clearly influenced by Article 3 of Directive 70/50, which had been cited by Advocate General Trabucchi, heralded a major development in the case law, for the interests of consumers were not mentioned in Article 30 (ex 36) of the Treaty, the only derogation from Article 28 (ex 30) which had hitherto been recognized.

In *Dassonville*, the Court spoke of intra-Community trade in general terms without distinguishing between imports and exports. This suggested that the formula applied to both Article 28 (ex 30) and Article 29 (ex 34), but it subsequently became clear that the scope of the latter was more limited. In *Groenveld v Produktschap voor Vee en Vlees*,[24] the Court declared that Article 29 (ex 34) concerned 'national measures which have as their specific object or effect the restriction of patterns of exports and thereby the establishment of a difference in treatment between the domestic trade of a Member State and its export trade in such a way as to provide a particular advantage for national production or for the domestic market of the State in question at the expense of the production or of the trade of other Member States'. It has been remarked that '[t]here is undeniably a certain inelegance in attributing a significantly narrower meaning to the notion of measures having an effect equivalent to quantitative restrictions in Article 34 than

---

[22] The term 'indistinctly applicable' is sometimes used to describe national rules which are neither directly nor indirectly discriminatory, sometimes in the more limited sense of not directly discriminatory. Thus, in Joined Cases 60 and 61/84 *Cinéthèque v Fédération Nationale des Cinémas Français* [1985] ECR 2605, 2609, AG Slynn spoke of the question whether Art 28 (ex 30) applied to 'a measure even if it is not applied only to imports but is "indistinctly applicable" to imports and national products and if it cannot be said to be discriminatory'. See further Marenco, 'Pour une interprétation traditionnelle de la notion de mesure d'effet équivalent à une restriction quantitative' (1984) 20 CDE 291, 332 and 334 (at n 53).

[23] Para 6.

[24] Case 15/79 [1979] ECR 3409, para 7. See also Case 155/80 *Oebel* [1981] ECR 1993, para 15; Joined Cases 141 to 143/81 *Holdijk* [1982] ECR 1299, para 11; Case 237/82 *Jongeneel Kaas v Netherlands* [1984] ECR 483, para 22; Case C–203/96 *Dusseldorp and Others v Minister van Volkhuisvesting, Ruimtelijke Ordening en Milieubeheer* [1998] ECR I–4075, para 40.

in the closely related Article 30'.[25] The explanation is presumably that Member States are less likely to impede exports than imports.[26]

The effect of *Dassonville*

The prohibition laid down in Article 28 (ex 30), as interpreted by the Court in *Dassonville*, has ensnared a variety of national measures which, although discriminatory (at least in substance), might have been thought far removed from the idea of a quantitative restriction on imports. An example is the 'Buy Irish' case.[27] The Irish Government had taken a series of measures designed to promote Irish products. These included encouraging the use of the 'Guaranteed Irish' symbol for products made in Ireland and the organization by a body called the Irish Goods Council of a system for investigating complaints about products carrying the symbol. They also included an extensive publicity campaign organized by the Irish Goods Council in favour of Irish goods. The Commission argued that these measures were incompatible with Article 28 (ex 30).

In its defence, the Irish Government pointed out that the Irish Goods Council was a company limited by guarantee: it could in no sense be considered a public body. Its purpose was to encourage Irish industry to co-operate and the Government's involvement was limited to providing financial assistance and moral support. However, the Court found that the activities of the Council were attributable to the Irish Government, which appointed its Management Committee, covered the greater part of its expenses from public funds, and had defined the aims and the broad outlines of its campaign to promote Irish products.

The Court also brushed aside arguments that Article 28 (ex 30) had not been infringed because the case did not involve any binding measures emanating from a public authority and figures showed that the activities of the Council had been ineffective. The Council's contested activities, the Court said, amounted 'to the establishment of a national practice, introduced by the Irish Government and prosecuted with its assistance, the potential effect of which on imports from other Member States is comparable to that resulting from government measures of a binding nature'.[28] It was irrelevant that the actions of the Council were not binding since they had the capacity to influence the conduct of traders and consumers and thereby to frustrate the aims of the Community.

A similarly robust approach to the application of Article 28 (ex 30) was taken in the 'Origin Marking' case,[29] where the Commission sought a declaration that the

---

[25] Dashwood, 'The Cassis de Dijon line of authority' in Bates et al (eds), *In Memoriam J D B Mitchell* (1983), p 157.

[26] See Keeling, 'The free movement of goods in EEC law: basic principles and recent developments in the case law of the Court of Justice of the European Communities' (1992) 26 The International Lawyer 467, 468. See also Dashwood, ibid.

[27] Case 249/81 *Commission v Ireland* [1982] ECR 4005.   [28] Para 27.

[29] Case 207/83 *Commission v United Kingdom* [1985] ECR 1201.

United Kingdom had failed to fulfil its obligations by prohibiting the retail sale of certain goods unless they were marked with or accompanied by an indication of their origin. The Court rejected an argument put forward by the United Kingdom that the disputed national measure fell outside the scope of Article 28 (ex 30) because it applied to both imported and national products alike and had an uncertain, if not non-existent, effect on trade between Member States. The Court accepted the argument of the Commission that retailers would tend to ask wholesalers to supply them with goods which were already origin-marked in order to avoid the need to indicate the origin of the goods separately. Wholesalers would make similar requests of manufacturers. The Court observed: 'The effects of the contested provisions are therefore liable to spread to the wholsale trade and even to manufacturers.'[30] The Court also took the view 'that the purpose of indications of origin or origin-marking is to enable consumers to distinguish between domestic and imported products and that this enables them to assert any prejudices which they may have against foreign products'. This made the sale in one Member State of goods produced in another more difficult, thereby impeding the creation of a single market.[31]

Even where the national law of a Member State appears on its face to comply with Article 28 (ex 30), there will be a breach of the prohibition laid down in that article if the practice does not match up to the appearance. In *Commission v France*,[32] the Commission had received a complaint from a leading British manufacturer of postal franking machines which had encountered various bureaucratic obstacles in seeking approval for the sale of its machines in France. The Court observed:[33]

The fact that a law or regulation such as that requiring prior approval for the marketing of postal franking machines conforms in formal terms to Article 30 of the EEC Treaty [now Article 28 EC] is not sufficient to discharge a Member State of its obligations under that provision. Under the cloak of a general provision permitting the approval of machines imported from other Member States, the administration might very well adopt a systematically unfavourable attitude towards imported machines, either by allowing considerable delay in replying to applications for approval or in carrying out the examination procedure, or by refusing approval on the grounds of various alleged technical faults for which no detailed technical explanations are given or which prove to be inaccurate.

The Court pointed out that, if the Treaty prohibition against MEE did not apply to such practices, it would lose much of its useful effect.

The Court might very well have concluded its judgment at that point, but in what seems to have been a concession to a minority view it went on to say that an administrative practice had to 'show a certain degree of consistency and generality' in order to constitute a MEE. Whether a practice was to be considered sufficiently

---

[30] Para 16. The Court noted that this tendency had been confirmed by complaints received by the Commission.

[31] The Court went on to find that the disputed measure was not justified on the ground of consumer protection and that it was therefore caught by the prohibition laid down in Art 28 (ex 30): see below.

[32] Case 21/84 [1985] ECR 1355.   [33] Para 11.

general to fall foul of Article 28 (ex 30) depended on 'whether the market concerned is one on which there are numerous traders or whether it is a market, such as that in postal franking machines, on which only a few undertakings are active. In the latter case, a national administration's treatment of a single undertaking may constitute a measure incompatible with Article 30 [now 28].'[34] The Court concluded that France had infringed Article 28 (ex 30) by refusing without proper justification to approve postal franking machines from another Member State.

The qualification added by the Court to its basic statement of principle seems too broad.[35] One can readily accept that isolated, inadvertent lapses by individual officials from the requirements of the Treaty should not necessarily entail the responsibility of the State concerned under Article 226 (ex 169). However, it is not obvious why treatment such as that meted out to the complainant in this case should be considered lawful if the trader affected is merely one of many competitors who are active on the market (although in those circumstances the Commission might well decline to pursue the matter under Article 226). Be that as it may, the Court's judgment confirms that in principle the innocent appearance of a national provision will not avail a Member State if it is not in practice applied in a manner which conforms with the requirements of the Treaty.

The capacity of Article 28 (ex 30) to close gaps in other provisions of Community law is illustrated by the 'Dundalk Water Supply' case.[36] The Commission sought a declaration under Article 226 (ex 169) that Ireland had infringed Article 28 (ex 30) by (a) permitting the inclusion in the contract specification for a scheme to improve Dundalk's drinking water supply of a clause providing that certain pipes should comply with an Irish standard, and (b) rejecting a tender providing for the use of pipes manufactured to an alternative standard which offered the same guarantees of safety, performance, and reliability. The contract in question fell outside the scope of the relevant directive on procedures for the award of public works contracts[37] and the Irish Government argued that it was concerned essentially with the performance of work, with the result that it fell to be appraised under the Treaty rules on services rather than goods. The Court was unreceptive, observing that 'the fact that a public works contract relates to the provision of services cannot remove a clause in an invitation to tender restricting the materials that may be used from the scope of the prohibition set out in Article 30 [now 28]'.[38]

The Court proceeded to examine whether the disputed clause was liable to impede imports of pipes into Ireland. It noted that the clause might discourage from tendering traders who produced or used pipes which did not comply with the Irish standard even if they complied with another equivalent standard. It also pointed out that the only undertaking which could supply pipes which complied with the specified standard was in fact Irish, so that the disputed clause had the

---

[34] Para 13.
[36] Case 45/87 *Commission v Ireland* [1988] ECR 4929.
[38] Para 17.

[35] See Oliver, op cit, p 78.
[37] Dir 71/305, OJ 1971 L 185/5.

effect of restricting the supply of pipes for the Dundalk scheme to Irish manufacturers. More significantly, the Court noted that the essence of the Commission's complaint was that the Irish authorities had refused unlawfully to verify whether pipes which did not conform to the requisite Irish standard nevertheless met the same technical requirements. The Court pointed out that, had it included in the disputed clause the words 'or equivalent' after the reference to the Irish standard,[39] 'the Irish authorities could have verified compliance with the technical conditions without from the outset restricting the contract only to tenderers proposing to utilise Irish materials'.[40] The Court therefore concluded that Ireland had failed to fulfil its obligations under Article 28 (ex 30).

The 'Dundalk Water Supply' case shows that in some circumstances a Member State may find itself required by Article 28 (ex 30) to assess the extent to which products manufactured in compliance with standards other than its own none the less meet the same technical requirements. It finds a parallel in the case law on the free movement of persons, where the Court has held that a Member State may have to appraise the qualifications and experience of a migrant in order to establish whether he or she can be required to acquire further qualifications before being admitted to a particular trade or profession.[41] In terms of promoting freedom of movement, this approach is less effective than the concept of compulsory mutual recognition which the Court has applied in some situations. As we shall see, that concept means essentially that a Member State may be obliged to grant access to a product which has been lawfully marketed in its Member State of origin. In terms of the burden imposed on the Member State of importation, however, the 'Dundalk' approach imposes greater practical demands, for it requires the State concerned to carry out an assessment of the product concerned. It is therefore capable of providing a useful incentive to the Member States to adopt a *communautaire* outlook in cases where laying down some sort of standard is objectively necessary. They cannot automatically reject products which do not comply with their own standards but must ask themselves what guarantees those standards are designed to give and whether equivalent guarantees are offered by products which satisfy different standards (or even no standards at all). This approach therefore has the capacity to change the mindset of national officials in a way which forcing them to accept imported products is unlikely to achieve.

In all of the cases which have just been discussed, the disputed national measures and practices discriminated against imported products, either directly, as in the 'Buy Irish' and 'Postal Franking Machines' cases, or indirectly, as in the 'Origin Marking' and 'Dundalk Water Supply' cases. However, notwithstanding the discriminatory character of the disputed measures, they were not, in form at least, concerned directly with intra-Community trade, nor did they necessarily have the effect in practice of impeding imports from other Member States: in the 'Buy Irish'

---

[39] As envisaged by Dir 71/305 where it applied.   [40] Para 22.

[41] See Case 222/86 *Unectef v Heylens* [1987] ECR 4097; Case C–340/89 *Vlassopoulou* [1991] ECR I–2357. Those cases are discussed in ch 9.

case, the activities of the Irish Goods Council did not prevent a decline in the share of the Irish market held by goods produced in Ireland.[42] These factors did not deter the Court from finding that Article 28 (ex 30) had been infringed.

What is a 'measure'?

The Court has also taken a broad view of the type of conduct for which the State is to be held responsible. The fact that the Irish Goods Council was technically a company limited by guarantee did not enable the Irish Government to escape responsibility for the Council's actions. In the 'Dundalk Water Supply' case, the Irish Government did not bother to challenge the Commission's view that it was responsible for the acts of the Dundalk Urban District Council, the promoter of the scheme for augmenting Dundalk's drinking water supply.

In *Apple and Pear Development Council v Lewis*,[43] the Court was asked to consider the compatibility of the applicant Council's activities *inter alia* with Article 28 (ex 30). The Council was established by the competent Minister by statutory instrument made under an Act of Parliament. The precise functions of the Council were laid down by the Minister in accordance with the more general indications given in the parent Act and he appointed the Council's members. The activities of the Council were financed by a charge imposed on growers in England and Wales. One of its functions was to advertise apples and pears in general and English and Welsh apples and pears in particular. Referring to the 'Buy Irish' case, the Court said that a publicity campaign designed to promote domestic products could fall within the prohibition contained in Article 28 (ex 30) if it had the support of a public authority. A body having the characteristics of the Council, the Court continued, 'cannot under Community law enjoy the same freedom as regards the methods of advertising used as that enjoyed by producers themselves or producers' associations of a voluntary character'.[44] In particular, it had 'a duty not to engage in any advertising intended to discourage the purchase of products of other Member States or to disparage those products in the eyes of consumers. Nor must it advise consumers to purchase domestic products solely by reason of their national origin.'[45] However, the Court accepted that a body like the Council could highlight the qualities of fruit grown in the Member State concerned and promote the sale of certain varieties, even if they were typical of national production.

This broad approach to the concept of a 'measure' within the meaning of Article 28 (ex 30) was continued in *The Queen v Royal Pharmaceutical Society of Great Britain, ex parte Association of Pharmaceutical Importers*.[46] In that case the Council of the respondent Society, the professional body for pharmacists in Great Britain, had published a statement drawing attention to its ethical rule which normally

---

[42] See para 22 of the judgment.
[43] Case 222/82 [1983] ECR 4083.
[44] Para 17.
[45] Para 18.
[46] Joined Cases 266 and 267/87 [1989] ECR 1295. See also Case C–292/92 *Hünermund and Others* [1993] ECR I–6787, discussed below.

prevented a pharmacist from substituting any other product for a product specifically named in a doctor's prescription, even where the therapeutic effect of the other
product was believed to be identical. The Council took the opportunity to underline that that rule applied 'to imported medicines as well as those produced for the
United Kingdom market'. Following publication of the Society's statement and the
simultaneous application of a National Health Service (NHS) rule requiring pharmacists to supply the precise products specified in prescriptions, parallel imports of
medicines bearing a brand name which differed from that of the equivalent product authorized in the United Kingdom virtually ceased. The members of the applicant Association carried out parallel imports of pharmaceutical products from other
Member States and brought proceedings in the English courts challenging both the
Society's statement and the NHS rule.

The referring court specifically asked whether Article 28 (ex 30) covered a measure adopted by a professional body such as the Society. The Court's answer was
affirmative: '. . . measures adopted by a professional body, such as the Pharmaceutical Society of Great Britain, which lays down rules of ethics applicable to the
members of the profession and has a committee upon which national legislation has
conferred disciplinary powers that could involve removal from the register of
persons authorized to exercise the profession, may constitute "measures" within
the meaning of Article 30 of the EEC Treaty'.[47]

Article 30 (ex 36)

General considerations

In the *Pharmaceutical Society* case, the Court went on to find that the disputed measures were justified under Article 30 (ex 36) of the Treaty on grounds of the protection of public health. It is therefore convenient at this point to consider in
general terms how the Court has applied that provision. Article 30 (ex 36) provides
as follows:

The provisions of Articles 28 [ex 30] and 29 [ex 34] shall not preclude prohibitions or restrictions on imports, exports or goods in transit justified on grounds of public morality, public
policy or public security; the protection of health and life of humans, animals or plants; the
protection of national treasures possessing artistic, historic or archaeological value; or the
protection of industrial and commercial property. Such prohibitions or restrictions shall not,
however, constitute a means of arbitrary discrimination or a disguised restriction on trade
between Member States.

Only the most ardent advocate of free trade would have maintained that the prohibition laid down in Article 28 (ex 30) should apply without qualification and the
authors of the Treaty recognized that circumstances might arise in which obstacles

[47] Para 16.

to inter-State trade resulting from national laws might serve a legitimate purpose. Under the scheme of the Treaty, such obstacles are to be removed, not by the application of Article 28 (ex 30), but by the adoption of legislation harmonizing national requirements and ensuring that any legitimate purpose the obstacles were intended to achieve is protected at a Community level. Where such legislation is adopted and it is intended to be exhaustive, its effect will be to exclude recourse by the Member States to Article 30 (ex 36), which will be considered superseded by the provisions of the legislation.[48] As the Court explained in *Centre d'Insémination de la Crespelle v Coopérative de la Mayenne*,[49] 'where . . . Community directives provide for the harmonization of the measures necessary to ensure *inter alia* the protection of animal and human health and establish Community procedures to check that they are observed, invoking Article 36 [now 30] is no longer justified and the appropriate checks must be carried out and protective measures adopted within the framework outlined by the harmonizing directive'.

Whether a particular directive is intended to exclude recourse to Article 30 (ex 36) in this way is a question of interpretation. In the *Centre d'Insémination de la Crespelle* case, the French Government sought to rely on Article 30 (ex 36) to justify certain restrictions on the free movement of bovine semen. The Court examined three relevant Community directives and concluded 'that health conditions in intra-Community trade in bovine semen have not yet been fully harmonized at Community level in relation to the State for which the semen is destined. Member States may therefore rely on health grounds in impeding the free movement of bovine semen, provided that the restrictions on intra-Community trade are in proportion to the aim in view.'[50] The Court concluded that national rules requiring importers of semen from another Member State to deliver it to an approved insemination or production centre were compatible with Community law. It was for the national courts to make sure that the way in which approved centres operated did not entail discrimination against imported semen.

The balance struck by the Court between the prohibition laid down in Article 28 (ex 30) and the derogations contained in Article 30 (ex 36) would evidently have a crucial impact on the success of the former in securing the free movement of goods. Like other derogations from fundamental rules, the Court has held that Article 30 (ex 36) is to be interpreted strictly. Thus, in the 'Irish Souvenirs' case, the Irish Government sought to rely on Article 30 (ex 36) in an attempt to show that certain restrictions on the free movement of goods were justified on grounds of consumer protection and fairness in commercial transactions between producers. The Court said that, as a derogation from the basic rule that obstacles to the free movement of goods between Member States were to be eliminated, Article 30

---

[48] See Oliver, op cit, pp 187–9.

[49] Case C–323/93 [1994] ECR I–5077, para 31 (with references to earlier case law). See also *The Queen v MAFF, ex parte Hedley Lomas* [1996] ECR I–2553, paras 18–19; Case C–1/96 *R v MAFF, ex parte Compassion in World Farming* [1998] ECR I–1251, para 47.

[50] Para 35.

(ex 36) was to be strictly construed. The exceptions laid down in it could not therefore be extended to cases other than those specifically laid down. Since Article 30
(ex 36) did not mention the protection of consumers or the fairness of commercial
transactions, it could not be invoked by the Irish Government.

The Court has made it clear that Article 30 (ex 36) 'is not designed to reserve
certain matters to the exclusive jurisdiction of Member States but only permits
national laws to derogate from the principle of the free movement of goods to the
extent to which such derogation is and continues to be justified for the attainment
of the objectives referred to in that article'.[51] Thus, cases on the application of
Article 30 (ex 36) do not turn on the extent of the Member States' *jurisdiction* to
deal with a particular problem, but on the extent to which the problem concerned
justifies derogating from the principle of the free movement of goods. It follows
that a Member State which seeks to rely on Article 30 (ex 36) must comply with
the principle of proportionality. The Court's case law also establishes that it must
be able to show that it is not seeking to do so for economic reasons.

For example, in *Evans Medical and Macfarlan Smith*,[52] a case concerning the
importation into the United Kingdom of a consignment of diamorphine originating in the Netherlands, the Court was asked whether a Member State was entitled
under Article 30 (ex 36) to refuse a licence for the importation of a narcotic drug
from another Member State on the grounds that such importation would threaten
the survival of the only licensed manufacturer of the drug in the first State and jeopardize supplies of the drug for medical purposes. The Court reiterated 'that Article
36 [now 30] relates to measures of a non-economic nature'. It therefore ruled that
a measure which restricted intra-Community trade could not be justified 'by a
Member State's wish to safeguard the survival of an undertaking'.[53] The Court
accepted that the need to ensure reliable supplies of a drug for essential medical purposes could, under Article 30 (ex 36), justify a barrier to intra-Community trade
where the health and life of humans would otherwise be jeopardized. However, it
emphasized 'that the derogation provided for in Article 36 [now 30] cannot apply
to national rules or practices if the health and life of humans can be as effectively
protected by measures less restrictive of intra-Community trade'.[54] The introduction of a tendering scheme had been mentioned as a way of reconciling the need
to ensure reliability of supplies with the principle of the free movement of goods
between Member States. The Court ruled that the Community legislation applicable to the awarding of public contracts entitled a contracting authority which
wished to obtain diamorphine 'to award the contract on the basis of the tendering
undertakings' ability to provide reliable and continuous supplies to the Member
State concerned'.[55]

---

[51] Case 251/78 *Denkavit Futtermittel v Minister für Ernährung, Landwirtschaft und Forsten* [1979] ECR
3369, para 14.
[52] Case C–324/93 [1995] ECR I–563.   [53] Para 36.   [54] Para 38.   [55] Para 50.

Public policy and public security

A notable feature of the case law in this area is that the Court has not always applied Article 30 (ex 36) as strictly as its rhetoric sometimes suggests. In *Campus Oil Limited v Minister for Industry and Energy*,[56] the Court addressed a number of the issues referred to above—the effect of Community legislation on the applicablilty of Article 30 (ex 36), the relevance of economic considerations, the principle of proportionality—before concluding that a MEE could be justified on the ground of public security. The case concerned the compatibility with Articles 28 (ex 30) and 30 (ex 36) of Irish rules requiring importers of petroleum products to purchase a certain proportion of their requirements from a State-owned company which operated a refinery in Ireland at prices fixed by the competent Minister. Under a 1982 Order made by the competent Minister for the purpose of maintaining fuel supplies, anyone importing certain petroleum products was required to purchase a proportion of their requirements from the Irish National Petroleum Corporation at a price fixed by the Minister taking account of the Corporation's costs. The Corporation's share capital was owned by the Irish State and its function was to improve the security of oil supplies in Ireland. In 1982, the Corporation had acquired Ireland's only refinery, situated at Whitegate, after its previous owners, four major oil companies, had announced their intention to close it. The acquisition of the refinery was intended to maintain a domestic refining capacity and reduce reliance on supplies from abroad, thereby safeguarding supplies of petroleum products in Ireland. The purpose of the obligation to purchase laid down in the 1982 Order was to ensure that the refinery could dispose of its products.

The first question addressed by the Court was whether a national measure such as the Order constituted a MEE for the purposes of Article 28 (ex 30). Because such a measure obviously had a restrictive effect on imports of refined oil, the Court gave an affirmative answer to that question. It was irrelevant that crude oil had to be imported into Ireland in order for refined oil to be produced. The Court also brushed aside an unconvincing argument advanced by the Irish Government to the effect that oil was not covered by Article 28 (ex 30) because of its importance. The Court observed that goods could not be considered exempt from the fundamental principle of the free movement of goods merely because they were 'of particular importance for the life or the economy of a Member State'.[57]

The Court then turned to the application of Article 30 (ex 36). It approached this question in three stages: (a) was there any Community legislation on maintaining oil supplies which might have the effect of excluding recourse by the Member States to Article 30 (ex 36)? (b) if not, was a national measure such as the 1982 Order capable of falling within any of the grounds of justification set out in

[56] Case 72/83 [1984] ECR 2727. Cf Case C–367/89 *Richardt and 'Les Accessoires Scientifiques'* [1991] ECR I–4621.
[57] Para 17.

Article 30 (ex 36)? (c) if so, was the contested system apt to attain its objective and did it comply with the principle of proportionality?

As to the first stage, the Court observed that the Community had taken certain precautionary measures to deal with interruptions in supplies of crude oil and petroleum products. The Member States were, for example, required by directive to maintain minimum stocks of ninety days' average consumption. The Court acknowledged that the measures taken by the Community legislature reduced the risk of Member States being deprived of essential supplies, but said that 'there would none the less still be real danger in the event of a crisis'.[58] It concluded that the Community measures were insufficient to give a Member State like Ireland 'an unconditional assurance that supplies will in any event be maintained at least at a level sufficient to meet its minimum needs. In those circumstances, the possibility for a Member State to rely on Article 36 [now 30] to justify appropriate complementary measures at national level cannot be excluded, even where there exist Community rules on the matter.'[59] The Community system for ensuring that oil would be available in a crisis seemed relatively comprehensive and it may be noted that the Court did not challenge its exhaustiveness. As Currall notes,[60] the reason given for permitting continued recourse to Article 30 (ex 36) did not relate to the particular Community measure in issue but was general in scope. He observes: 'It is difficult to imagine that any directive (or any national measure, for that matter) could give an unconditional assurance that the interest in question would be protected in all circumstances: no such standards are possible in human affairs. If such a standard were required of harmonisation directives, it is clear that recourse to Article 36 [now 30] would still be possible, so that the value of the harmonisation would be largely lost.'

Of the grounds of justification set out in Article 30 (ex 36), the Court said that only the concept of public security was relevant. It declared 'that petroleum products, because of their exceptional importance as an energy source in the modern economy, are of fundamental importance for a country's existence since not only its economy but above all its institutions, its essential public services and even the survival of its inhabitants depend upon them. An interruption of supplies of petroleum products, with the resultant dangers for the country's existence, could therefore seriously affect the public security that Article 36 [now 30] allows States to protect.'[61] The Court reiterated that Member States were not entitled to evade their obligations under Article 28 (ex 30) 'by pleading the economic difficulties caused by the elimination of barriers to intra-Community trade'.[62] However, once it had been shown that a measure was justified on grounds of public security, the fact that it also made it possible to achieve other objectives of an economic nature

---

[58] Para 30.   [59] Para 31.

[60] 'Some aspects of the relation between Articles 30–36 and Article 100 of the EEC Treaty, with a closer look at optional harmonisation' (1984) 4 YEL 169, 189. See also Gormley, op cit, pp 137–8; Oliver, op cit, p 189.

[61] Para 34.   [62] Para 35.

did not exclude the application of Article 30 (ex 36). This is not an unreasonable view to take, but it does mean that the Court must be alert to prevent Member States dressing up measures designed to achieve essentially economic objectives in the clothes of Article 30 (ex 36).[63]

As for the necessity and proportionality of the contested measure, the Court accepted that a State which had its own refining capacity could enter into long-term contracts with oil-producing countries for the supply of crude oil which offered a guarantee of supplies in the event of a crisis. Such a State would be less exposed than it would be if it could only meet its needs by purchasing crude oil on the open market. However, the Court underlined that Member States could only rely on Article 30 (ex 36) 'if no other measure, less restrictive from the point of view of the free movement of goods, is capable of achieving the same objective'.[64] In circumstances such as those of the present case, the Court said that a Member State could legitimately require importers 'to cover a certain proportion of their needs by purchases from a refinery situated in its territory at prices fixed by the competent minister on the basis of the costs incurred in the operation of that refinery, if the production of the refinery cannot be freely disposed of at competitive prices on the market concerned'.[65] The Court went on to explain that:

> The quantities of petroleum products covered by such a system must not exceed the minimum supply requirement without which the public security of the State concerned would be affected or the level of production necessary to keep the refinery's production capacity available in the event of a crisis and to enable it to continue to refine at all times the crude oil for the supply of which the State concerned has entered into long-term contracts.

It was for the national court to establish whether the disputed measure satisfied those requirements.

The conclusion reached in *Campus Oil* may seem surprising in view of the protectionist effect which the Court found the disputed measure produced. By authorizing unilateral action against a threat which the Community legislature had sought to deal with on a collective basis, the Court risked making the Community rules ineffective.[66] It has also been doubted whether it was necessary to have a refinery in Ireland in order to refine oil supplied under long-term contracts: it might have been possible to ensure continuity of supply by making use of refineries situated abroad.[67] The case is a striking example of the Court's willingness in exceptional circumstances to uphold the right of Member States to take action which undermines fundamental principles of the Treaty. The ruling in *Campus Oil* was not, however, entirely favourable to the interests of the Member States. The concept of public policy, referred to in one of the referring court's questions, was

---

[63] See Gormley, op cit, p 138.

[64] Para 44.

[65] Para 51.

[66] See Gormley, op cit, pp 137–8.

[67] See Marenco, 'La giurisprudenza communitaria sulle misure di effetto equivalente a una restrizione quantitativa (1984–1986)' [1988] Il Foro Padano IV, 166, cited by Oliver, op cit, p 201, n 2.

peremptorily dismissed by the Court as 'not pertinent'.[68] Interpreted broadly, that concept would be capable of embracing a plethora of considerations, including all the other grounds of justification mentioned in Article 30 (ex 36). An English judge once remarked that public policy was 'a very unruly horse and when once you get astride of it, you never know where it will carry you'.[69] The way the Court dealt with the concept in *Campus Oil* demonstrated that it was aware of these dangers.

In another case decided just over six months later, the Court again dismissed an attempt by a Member State to rely on the concept of public policy, though in less robust terms than those it had employed previously. The case was *Cullet v Leclerc*[70] and it concerned the compatibility with *inter alia* Article 28 (ex 30) of minimum prices fixed by the French authorities for the sale of petrol and diesel to consumers. The Court held that the disputed national rules were caught by Article 28 (ex 30), reiterating its established case law to the effect that State systems of price control, 'if applicable to domestic products and imported products alike, do not in themselves constitute measures having an effect equivalent to a quantitative restriction but may have such an effect when the prices are fixed at a level such that imported products are placed at a disadvantage compared to identical domestic products, either because they cannot profitably be marketed on the conditions laid down or because the competitive advantage conferred by lower cost prices is cancelled out . . .'.[71]

In seeking to rely on Article 30 (ex 36) to justify the disputed rules, the French Government sought to rely on the protection of public policy and public security, arguing that the introduction of unrestricted competition among retailers might provoke violent disorder. In response to that argument, the Court said that the French Government had not established that it would not be able, 'using the means at its disposal',[72] to deal with any repercussions for public order and security entailed by bringing the disputed rules into line with the requirements of the Treaty. That response was adequate to dispose of the point, but it implied that very serious disorder which is beyond the capacity of a Member State to contain might in principle justify a failure to comply with the principle of the free movement of goods. The potential consequences of this line of argument are serious, as Advocate General VerLoren van Themaat emphasized:[73]

If road-blocks and other effective weapons of interest groups which feel threatened by the importation and sale at competitive prices of certain cheap products or services, or by immigrant workers or foreign businesses, were accepted as justification, the existence of the four fundamental freedoms of the Treaty could no longer be relied upon. Private interests groups

---

[68] Para 33. In Case 177/83 *Kohl v Ringelhan & Rennett* [1984] ECR 3651, para 19, the Court rejected a suggestion that the concept of public policy embraced considerations of consumer protection. In the *Henn and Darby* case, *infra*, the concept of public policy was mentioned by the referring court but dismissed by the AG Warner as 'irrelevant' ([1979] ECR 3795, 3825) and ignored by the Court.

[69] Burrough J in *Richardson v Mellish* (1824) 2 Bing 229, 252, cited by AG Slynn in *Campus Oil* at p 2767.

[70] Case 231/83 [1985] ECR 305.   [71] Para 23 (with references to earlier case law).
[72] Para 33.   [73] At p 312.

would then, in the place of the Treaty and Community (and, within the limits laid down in the Treaty, national) institutions, determine the scope of those freedoms. In such cases, the concept of public policy requires, rather, effective action on the part of the authorities to deal with such disturbances.

That view now seems to have been accepted by the Court. In *Commission v France*,[74] it held that France had breached its Treaty obligations by failing to prevent the free movement of fruit and vegetables from being obstructed by acts of violence committed by private individuals.

Public morality

By its very nature, Article 30 (ex 36) may require the Court to enquire into delicate matters touching the very soul of a Member State. The Court has on occasion shown signs of an unwillingness to interfere with a State's assessment of what local conditions require. An example is *Regina v Henn and Darby*,[75] where the Court was called upon for the first time to consider the concept of public morality within the meaning of Article 30 (ex 36). It also elucidated the meaning of the second sentence of that article. The case arose out of the prosecution of the defendants for contravening a prohibition laid down in United Kingdom customs legislation on the importation of indecent or obscene articles. The charge related to six films and seven magazines of Danish origin. The defendants argued that the legislation under which they were being prosecuted was incompatible with Article 28 (ex 30) and the House of Lords asked the Court of Justice for guidance on two matters: whether legislation of the type in dispute was caught by Article 28 (ex 30) and, if so, whether it was justified under Article 30 (ex 36).

The answer to the first question was obviously 'yes' and the issue would not be worth dwelling on had the English Court of Appeal not found that Article 28 (ex 30) did not apply to an absolute prohibition on the importation of certain goods because such a prohibition was not concerned with quantity.[76] As Advocate General Warner pointed out,[77] that view was inconsistent with the case law of the Court[78] and with the language of Article 30 (ex 36), which refers to '*prohibitions* or

---

[74] Case C-265/95 [1997] ECR I-6959. See ch 2. The Court's decision led to action by the Council and the Member States to underline the importance of the free movement of goods for the proper functioning of the internal market: see Reg 2679/98 on the functioning of the internal market in relation to the free movement of goods among the Member States, OJ 1998 L337/8; Resolution of the Council and of the Representatives of the Governments of the Member States, meeting within the Council, on the free movement of goods, OJ 1998 L 337/10. Cf the decision of the House of Lords in *R v Chief Constable of Sussex, ex parte International Trader's Ferry Ltd* [1999] 1 CMLR 1320.
[75] Case 34/79 [1979] ECR 3795. See Catchpole and Barav, 'The public morality exception and the free movement of goods: justification of a dual standard in national legislation?' (1980/1) LIEI 1.
[76] See [1978] 1 WLR 1031.   [77] At p 3820.
[78] See eg Case 2/73 *Geddo v Ente Nazionale Risi* [1973] ECR 865, para 7: 'The prohibition on quantitative restrictions covers measures which amount to a total or partial restraint of, according to the circumstances, imports, exports or goods in transit.'

restrictions on imports . . .'.[79] Moreover, it could not be reconciled with the purpose of Article 28 (ex 30) since a total prohibition is more harmful to the free
movement of goods than a partial restraint. The Court made it clear in its ruling
that a law such as that in issue constituted a quantitative restriction on imports
within the meaning of Article 28 (ex 30).[80]

The main part of the Court's judgment was concerned with the question whether
such legislation could be justified on grounds of public morality for the purposes of
Article 30 (ex 36). The defendants maintained that the legislation could not be justified because the United Kingdom did not have a consistent policy on indecent or
obscene articles, the law applicable in the different constituent parts of the United
Kingdom on this matter being slightly different. Nowhere in the United Kingdom,
it was said, was pornography treated as severely internally as it was when imported.
As Advocate General Warner explained,[81] nowhere in the United Kingdom was the
mere possession (that is, possession otherwise than with a view to sale) of pornographic articles an offence. In England and Wales, articles which, although indecent
or obscene, did not tend to deprave and corrupt those exposed to them could be
sold provided they were not exhibited or sold in a public place. Moreover, they
could be sent by private carrier, though not by post. In England and Wales, even
material which did tend to deprave and corrupt could be published if this was for
the public good on certain specified grounds. According to the defendants, the
absolute prohibition on importation therefore constituted arbitrary discrimination
for the purposes of the second sentence of Article 30 (ex 36).

Advocate General Warner said that the two sentences of Article 30 (ex 36)
should be read together: 'The second sentence of Article 36 [now 30] is intended,
in my opinion, to make it clear that a prohibition or restriction that constitutes "a
means of arbitrary discrimination or a disguised restriction on trade between
Member States" cannot be "justified" within the meaning of that word in the first
sentence.'[82] The Advocate General maintained that it might be difficult to say
whether Article 30 (ex 36) could be invoked where the importation of an obscene
book published in another Member State was prohibited where it was lawfully on
sale in England because its publication was considered to be for the public good.
However, that difficult question probably did not arise here, since the material in
question was so obscene that it was treated in the same way under United Kingdom
law whether it was of domestic or foreign origin. 'Perhaps the only difference lies
in the fact that the "mere possession" of pornography, however "hard", is not forbidden in the United Kingdom.'[83]

The Advocate General concluded[84] that 'the test must in each case be whether
any element of discrimination inherent in the prohibition or restriction on imports

---

[79] Emphasis added.

[80] And not a measure having equivalent effect thereto, as it had been described by the House of
Lords. As AG Warner pointed out, '[a] total prohibition is a quantitative restriction, the quantity being
zero': see p 3822.

[81] See pp 3824–5.   [82] See p 3826.   [83] p 3829.   [84] At p 3831.

under consideration is, in all the circumstances, reasonable. This it will not be if its effect is disproportionate to any legitimate purpose pursued, be that purpose to prevent, guard against or reduce the likelihood of breaches of the internal law of the Member State concerned, or to avoid excessive administrative burdens and public expenditure, or both. Where the Member State concerned is so constituted that there are variations in the laws of different parts of it, that in my opinion is a factor—it may be an important factor—to be taken into account in applying the test.' He did not think a problem arose where someone imported a large quantity of material which was so obscene that it could not be published or distributed anywhere in the United Kingdom without a criminal offence being committed: 'No one can suppose that a man who imports such material in bulk does so only for his private delectation, so that . . . there is no element of discrimination in the prohibition of such an importation.'[85]

Two points may be made about the Advocate General's analysis. First, the situation of the obscene book published abroad which is lawfully on sale in the State into which it is sought to be imported is not difficult at all. Allowing the book in poses no threat to the public morality of the importing State, rather the reverse. If sale of the book when published in England is deemed conducive to the public good, then the same must be true of the same book when published abroad. To prohibit the importation of the latter edition would clearly amount to arbitrary discrimination.

Secondly, it may be doubted whether a restriction on the free movement of goods which discriminates against imports in an otherwise arbitrary manner could normally be saved by the need to avoid undue administrative burdens or public expenditure. These sound like economic considerations which the Court has said cannot justify recourse to Article 30 (ex 36). The willingness of the State concerned to shoulder the cost and administrative burden of ensuring that imports and domestic products are treated even-handedly provides one measure of the importance it attaches to the interest the restriction concerned is designed to protect. If the burden is considered too great, it is not unreasonable to expect the State to abandon the restriction on imports and rely on internal controls which apply to both imported and domestic goods. This view is supported by the judgment in *de Peijper*,[86] cited by Advocate General Warner, where the Court said: 'Article 36 [now 30] cannot be relied on to justify rules or practices which, even though they are beneficial, contain restrictions which are explained primarily by a concern to lighten the administration's burden or reduce public expenditure, unless, in the absence of the said rules or practices, this burden or expenditure clearly would exceed the limits of what can reasonably be required.' The qualification at the end of that statement was evidently intended by the Court to apply only in exceptional circumstances and that is certainly how it should be understood, otherwise there would be considerable scope for abuse. How is the Court to gainsay an assertion

[85] p 3831.   [86] Case 104/75 [1976] ECR 613, para 18.

by a Member State that a given measure was the only one that was administratively practicable or which could be implemented at reasonable cost?

In its judgment in *Henn and Darby*, the Court acknowledged that in principle it was 'for each Member State to determine in accordance with its own scale of values and in the form selected by it the requirements of public morality in its territory'.[87] In principle, a Member State was entitled to prohibit the importation from other Member States of indecent or obscene articles and to apply the prohibition to the whole of its national territory, notwithstanding any variations between the laws applicable in its constituent parts. As to the question whether the contested legislation fell foul of the second sentence of Article 30 (ex 36), the Court had this to say:[88]

> this provision . . . is designed to prevent restrictions on trade based on the grounds mentioned in the first sentence of Article 36 [now 30] from being diverted from their proper purpose and used in such a way as either to create discrimination in respect of goods originating in other Member States or indirectly to protect certain national products. That is not the purport of a prohibition, such as that in force in the United Kingdom, on the importation of articles which are of an indecent or obscene character. Whatever may be the differences between the laws on this subject in force in the different constituent parts of the United Kingdom, and notwithstanding the fact that they contain certain exceptions of limited scope, these laws, taken as a whole, have as their purpose the prohibition, or at least, the restraining, of the manufacture and marketing of publications and articles of an indecent or obscene character. In these circumstances it is permissible to conclude, on a comprehensive view, that there is no lawful trade in such goods in the United Kingdom. A prohibition on imports which may in certain respects be more strict than some of the laws applied within the United Kingdom cannot therefore be regarded as amounting to a measure designed to give indirect protection to some national product or aimed at creating arbitrary discrimination between goods of this type depending on whether they are produced within the national territory or another Member State.

On the facts of the case, there was of course no question of the disputed legislation having been designed to protect domestically produced pornography. The whole thrust of the legal framework was to discourage the production and distribution of pornography, whatever its origin. The United Kingdom Government had expressly rejected any suggestion that the legislation was '*aimed at* creating arbitrary discrimination' in the sense of that being one of the objectives it was intended to achieve. Advocate General Warner took the view, however, that it was unnecessary to enquire into the intentions of those who enacted the disputed measure, since such an enquiry would in most cases be 'impracticable, and indeed unrealistic'.[89] The suggestion in the judgment that the Court did not share that view is

---

[87] Para 15. The Court proceeded to refer to 'the *powers reserved* to the Member States by the first sentence of Article 36 [now 30]' (emphasis added), but it is evident from the remainder of the judgment that it was not intending to imply that the exercise by Member States of the discretion conferred on them by that article was unlimited. See the remarks of AG Warner at p 3828 and of Gormley, op cit, at p 127.

[88] Para 21.   [89] p 3827.

unfortunate. More fundamentally, the Court's statement that there was 'no lawful trade in such goods in the United Kingdom' goes too far: there was a lawful trade in material which, although indecent or obscene, did not tend to deprave and corrupt and in material which did have that tendency but which, despite its obscenity, was deemed conducive to the public good.[90] It may well have been unlikely that the films and magazines which were the subject of the relevant charge would have fallen into either of those categories,[91] but that was a matter for the national court to determine. The Court's ruling goes too far in suggesting that the disputed legislation was in all circumstances justified under Article 30 (ex 36).

Advocate General Warner drew a parallel in *Henn and Darby*[92] with the case law of the Court on the public policy proviso to the Treaty rules on the free movement of workers.[93] In *van Duyn v Home Office*,[94] the Court accepted that a Member State could prevent a national of another Member State from taking up employment with an organization based on its territory which it considered socially harmful, even though the activities of the organization itself were not restricted and nationals of the first State were free to join and to work for it. It was evidently illogical to maintain that a Member State's public policy could be threatened by a national of another Member State who merely wished to do something which its own nationals were perfectly free to do. In *Adoui and Cornuaille v Belgium*,[95] the Court appeared to recognize the illogicality, ruling that the proviso could only be invoked by a Member State which took 'genuine and effective measures' to combat behaviour of the type in question when perpetrated by its own nationals. The *Adoui and Cornuaille* case was cited by Advocate General Slynn in *Conegate v H M Customs & Excise*,[96] a goods case where the Court distanced itself from the approach it had taken in *Henn and Darby*.

The appellant had imported from Germany into the United Kingdom through Heathrow Airport in London various consignments of life-size inflatable dolls and other erotic articles. The United Kingdom customs authorities took the view that the articles concerned were indecent or obscene and that their importation was therefore prohibited. The forfeiture of the goods concerned was later ordered by a court. On appeal, the appellant argued that the forfeiture of the goods in question was incompatible with Article 28 (ex 30) and could not be justified under Article 30 (ex 36). It submitted that there was a lawful trade in such goods in the United Kingdom since the manufacture and marketing of erotic articles was not generally prohibited. A number of questions were referred to the Court of Justice, the first

---

[90] A point made by Oliver, op cit, p 196, and by Gormley, op cit, pp 127–8.

[91] An agreed statement of facts accompanying the Order for Reference contained a description of the material which is quoted by AG Warner at p 3819. Gormley, op cit, p 126, notes that 'by pretty well any view the materials involved were of a nature which might well revolt the average man on the Clapham omnibus'.

[92] See p 3828. [93] See ch 10. [94] Case 41/74 [1974] ECR 1337.

[95] Joined Cases 115 and 116/81 [1982] ECR 1665, para 9.

[96] Case 121/85 [1986] ECR 1007, 1011.

of which asked whether there was a lawful trade in certain articles within the meaning of *Henn and Darby* where the articles in question:

may be manufactured and marketed within the Member State of importation, subject only to

(i) an absolute prohibition on their transmission by post
(ii) a restriction on their public display
(iii) a system of licensing of premises for their sale to customers aged 18 years and over, in certain areas of the Member State and which licensing system in no way affects the substantive law on indecency or obscenity in that Member State.

The United Kingdom noted that, while that question correctly stated the legal position in England and Wales and in Northern Ireland, the position in Scotland and the Isle of Man was stricter. It argued that 'a State which is comprised of different constituent parts and which allows differences to subsist in the legislation applicable thereto but which nevertheless has a common customs régime, must of necessity bring that régime into line with the most rigorous internal rules'.[97] That argument clearly went too far, since it would have meant that access to the entire United Kingdom market could be denied to a product which could not lawfully be sold in the Isle of Man, which is not part of the United Kingdom[98] and which enjoys a special status under the Treaty.[99] Even if the unusual position of the Isle of Man were left aside, it would have been inimical to the free movement of goods if a Member State could exclude from the most important part of its territory an imported product which could lawfully be marketed there on the ground that it could not be so marketed in another part of its territory which was less economically significant.

The Court of Justice was rightly unwilling to be distracted by the law applicable in areas other than that into which the disputed goods had been imported. It defined the general problem raised by the referring court's first question as being 'whether a prohibition on the importation of certain goods may be justified on grounds of public morality where the legislation of the Member State concerned contains no prohibition on the manufacture or marketing of the same products within the national territory'.[100] Following its approach in *Adoui and Cornuaille*, the Court declared:[101]

although Community law leaves the Member States free to make their own assessments of the indecent or obscene character of certain articles, it must be pointed out that the fact that goods cause offence cannot be regarded as sufficiently serious to justify restrictions on the free movement of goods where the Member State concerned does not adopt, with respect to the same goods manufactured or marketed within its territory, penal measures or other serious and effective measures intended to prevent the distribution of such goods in its territory.

[97] Para 9 of the judgment.
[98] The position of the Isle of Man under the EC Treaty is discussed by AG Jacobs in Case C–355/89 *Barr and Montrose Holdings* [1991] ECR I–3479.
[99] See Art 299(6)(c) (ex 227(5)(c)).   [100] Para 13.   [101] Para 15.

The Court said it was not its responsibility to decide whether the manufacture or marketing of the goods in question was prohibited within the United Kingdom. Where a State was comprised of a number of constituent parts, each with their own internal legislation, it was necessary to take all the relevant rules into account. In order for the State concerned to be able to rely on Article 30 (ex 36), it was not necessary for it to show that the manufacture and marketing of the products concerned was prohibited throughout all its constituent parts provided it was 'possible to conclude from the applicable rules, taken as a whole, that their purpose is, in substance, to prohibit the manufacture and marketing of those products'.[102] In this case, the Court noted that the referring court had in its first question carefully defined the substance of the national rules whose compatibility with the Treaty it wished to determine. The Court made it clear that the restrictions to which the national court had referred could not 'be regarded as equivalent in substance to a prohibition on manufacture and marketing'.[103] In effect, therefore, the Court found that the contested national legislation constituted a means of arbitrary discrimination within the meaning of the last sentence of Article 30 (ex 36).[104]

Both *Henn and Darby* and *Conegate* illustrate the Court's extreme sensitivity when dealing with issues such as the right of Member States to act in the interests of public morality. The latter case repaired much of the damage done by the former by striking a more judicious balance between the prerogatives of the Member States and the principle of the free movement of goods. However, even there the Court did not really deal satisfactorily with the dilemma posed by internal rules which vary in their severity from one region of a Member State to another. The test it laid down, involving identifying the purpose in substance of the applicable national rules taken as a whole, leaves a good deal to the discretion of the national court. It is submitted that the Court would have been justified in saying that, if a given product may lawfully be manufactured or marketed anywhere within the Member State of importation, that State may not rely on Article 30 (ex 36) to exclude imports of similar products from other Member States. As the Court made clear in *Conegate*,[105] that view would not prevent a Member State from subjecting imports to the same restrictions on marketing as those which apply to similar domestic products. That the Court did not take this approach demonstrates the importance it sometimes accords to the rights of the Member States, even in an area as fundamental as the free movement of goods.

Industrial and commercial property

The Court has had to confront difficulties of a different order in dealing with the exception in Article 30 (ex 36) relating to 'the protection of industrial and

---

[102] Para 17.   [103] Para 18.
[104] See Oliver, op cit, p 197. Cf Gormley, 'The answer, my friend, is blowing in the wind . . .' (1986) 11 ELRev 443, 447.
[105] Para 21.

commercial property'. Such property, often referred to by the compendious term 'intellectual property', may take a variety of forms of which the most common are patents, trade marks and copyright. Intellectual property plays an important role in fostering and promoting innovation but, being normally granted by national law, is liable to partition the common market along national lines and thereby threaten the free movement of goods.[106] That threat could be removed by replacing the national systems of intellectual property with a Community system conferring rights valid throughout the territory of the Member States. Progress towards the achievement of that objective has, however, been slow.[107]

Article 295 (ex 222) EC provides that '[t]his Treaty shall in no way prejudice the rules in Member States governing the system of property ownership'. That provision shows that the Treaty was not designed to abolish national systems of intellectual property. However, had Article 295 (ex 222) been intended to remove such property from the scope of Article 28 (ex 30), the reference in Article 30 (ex 36) to 'industrial and commercial property' would have been unnecessary. That reference confirms that intellectual property legislation may constitute a MEE, but that its application may sometimes be justified. It has fallen to the Court to carry out the difficult task of drawing the line between legitimate and illegitimate reliance on national intellectual property rights. It has on the whole performed that task with great skill.

Basic principles

The basic principles applied by the Court were laid down in *Deutsche Grammophon v Metro*.[108] In that case, a German record manufacturer sought to restrain the sale in Germany of records it had manufactured for distribution in France. The records concerned had been supplied by the manufacturer to its Paris subsidiary. They subsequently found their way to Germany, where they were bought by M and sold at a price below that fixed by the manufacturer for that country. The manufacturer

---

[106] Assignments and licences of intellectual property may also fall within the scope of Art 81 (ex 85) EC: see eg Case 40/70 *Sirena v Eda* [1971] ECR 69; Case 258/78 *Nungesser v Commission* [1982] ECR 2015; Case 193/83 *Windsurfing International v Commission* [1986] ECR 611. The way in which intellectual property rights can be exercised may in addition be affected by Art 82 (ex 86) EC. Arts 81 and 82 played a particularly prominent role in the early cases. See Goyder, *EC Competition Law* (3rd edn, 1998), chs 13 and 16, pp 351–67. Arts 81 and 82 are considered in ch 12.

[107] Though not non-existent: see Reg 40/94 on the Community trade mark, OJ 1994 L11/1; Reg 2100/94 on Community plant variety rights, OJ 1994 L227/1. The latter is discussed by Millett, 'The Community system of plant variety rights' (1999) 24 ELRev 230. The Agreement Relating to Community Patents (OJ 1989 L401/1), which incorporated the 1975 Community Patent Convention, now seems unlikely to enter into force: see House of Lords Select Committee on the European Communities, 'The Community patent and the patent system in Europe' (Session 1997–98, 26th Report). In 1988, the Council adopted an important directive to approximate the laws of the Member States relating to trade marks: see Dir 89/104, OJ 1989 L40/1, considered below. Note also Dir 92/100 on rental right and lending right and on certain rights related to copyright in the field of intellectual property, OJ 1992 L346/61. The validity of Art 1(1) of that directive was upheld in Case C–200/96 *Metronome Musik v Music Point Hokamp* [1988] ECR I–1953. See Travers, 'Rental rights and the specific subject-matter of copyright in Community law' (1999) 24 ELRev 171.

[108] Case 78/70 [1971] ECR 487.

relied on German legislation which conferred on the manufacturers of sound recordings an exclusive right of reproduction and distribution related to copyright.[109] The case was eventually referred to the Court of Justice, which was asked whether it would be consistent with Community law to uphold the manufacturer's claim.

In its decision, the Court laid down three principles which were to form the basis of subsequent developments. First, it said that 'although the Treaty does not affect the *existence* of rights recognized by the legislation of a Member State with regard to industrial and commercial property, the *exercise* of such rights may nevertheless fall within the prohibitions laid down by the Treaty'.[110] The distinction drawn by the Court between the existence and the exercise of intellectual property rights has attracted criticism.[111] It is sometimes said that to limit the circumstances in which a right can be exercised, and therefore to reduce its commercial value, is tantamount to diminishing the very substance of the right. However, the distinction is implicit in the Treaty: Article 30 (ex 36) makes it clear that reliance on national intellectual property rights will sometimes, but not always, fall foul of Article 28 (ex 30). In other words, while Article 28 (ex 30) does not have the effect of rendering national systems of intellectual property invalid,[112] it does impose limits on the extent to which they can be invoked where the consequence would be to interfere with the free movement of goods. The distinction drawn by the Court between the existence and the exercise of a right is a convenient way of making this point.[113]

The second principle laid down by the Court in *Deutsche Grammophon* was that of 'specific subject-matter': 'Although it permits prohibitions or restrictions on the free movement of products, which are justified for the purpose of protecting industrial and commercial property, Article 36 [now 30] only admits derogations from that freedom to the extent to which they are justified for the purpose of safeguarding rights which constitute the specific subject-matter of such property.'[114] As Advocate General Jacobs explained in *HAG GF*,[115] this principle 'is an essential concomitant of the existence/exercise dichotomy, because it makes it possible to determine, in relation to each type of intellectual property, the circumstances in which the exercise of the right will be permissible under Community law'.

The Court proceeded to indicate the existence of a principle of exhaustion which prevents the holder of an intellectual property right from using it to prevent

---

[109] On copyright in the usual sense, see Joined Cases 55 and 57/80 *Musik-Vertrieb Membran v GEMA* [1981] ECR 147; Case 158/86 *Warner Brothers and Another v Christiansen* [1988] ECR 2605; *Metronome Musik, supra.*

[110] Para 11, emphasis added.

[111] See eg Craig and de Búrca, *EU Law* (2nd edn, 1998), pp 1027–8; Jarvis, *The Application of EC Law by National Courts: the Free Movement of Goods* (1998), pp 295–6.

[112] That would be inconsistent with Art 295 (ex 222).

[113] See AG Jacobs in Case C–10/89 *HAG GF* [1990] ECR I–3711, pp I–3728 and 3730; Goyder, op cit, p 302.

[114] Para 11 of the judgment.   [115] *Supra* at p I–3730.

the importation of a product marketed in another Member State by the holder or
with his consent. The Court stated in *Deutsche Grammophon*: 'If a right related to
copyright is relied upon to prevent the marketing in a Member State of products
distributed by the holder of the right or with his consent on the territory of another
Member State on the sole ground that such distribution did not take place on the
national territory, such a prohibition, which would legitimize the isolation of
national markets, would be repugnant to the essential purpose of the Treaty, which
is to unite national markets into a single market.'[116]

Specific subject matter and exhaustion

These basic principles provided the framework for the cases which were to come
before the Court in the years which followed. Two issues in particular would
require further clarification: first, which particular rights constituted the specific
subject matter of the range of intellectual property recognized by the national laws
of the Member States; secondly, when was the holder of an intellectual property
right to be regarded as having consented to the distribution of a protected product
in another Member State?

If the *Deutsche Grammophon* case had concerned a rather esoteric form of intellectual property, the Court was called upon to define the specific subject matter or
more mainstream forms of such property in the *Centrafarm* cases. SD, an American
company, owned patents in the Netherlands and the United Kingdom relating to
a medicine. The medicine was protected by the trade mark 'Negram', which was
owned in the United Kingdom by SW, a subsidiary of SD, and in the Netherlands
by W, a subsidiary of SW. C acquired a quantity of the drug concerned in England,
where it had been placed on the market by SW under licence from SD, and
imported it into the Netherlands. There, without the agreement of SD, C marketed it under the trade mark 'Negram'. C's object was to take advantage of a considerable price differential, the price of the medicine concerned in the United
Kingdom being half its price in the Netherlands. SD brought proceedings in the
Netherlands courts for an order restraining C from infringing its patent. W sought
an order restraining C from infringing its 'Negram' trade mark. Both cases were
referred to the Court of Justice.

In *Centrafarm v Sterling Drug*,[117] the Court offered the following definition of the
specific subject matter of a patent: '. . . the guarantee that the patentee, to reward
the creative effort of the inventor, has the exclusive right to use an invention with
a view to manufacturing industrial products and putting them into circulation for
the first time, either directly or by the grant of licences to third parties, as well as
the right to oppose infringements'. In *Centrafarm v Winthrop*,[118] the specific subject
matter of a trade mark was defined by the Court in the following terms: '. . . the
guarantee that the owner of the trade mark has the exclusive right to use that trade

---

[116] Para 12. For a fuller statement of the principle, see eg Case 144/81 *Keurkoop v Nancy Kean Gifts*
[1982] ECR 2853, para 25.
[117] Case 15/74 [1974] ECR 1147, para 9.   [118] Case 16/74 [1974] ECR 1183, para 8.

mark, for the purpose of putting products protected by the trade mark into circulation for the first time . . .'. That guarantee was intended to protect the owner 'against competitors wishing to take advantage of the status and reputation of the trade mark by selling products illegally bearing that trade mark'.

The *Sterling Drug* and *Winthrop* cases suggested that the definition of the specific subject matter of a particular form of intellectual property was a matter of Community law to be laid down by the Court of Justice. From a theoretical point of view, that seems inescapable: if the Member States were free to determine the specific subject matter of intellectual property rights granted by their own legislation, the effect of the Treaty might in effect be determined by national law. It is therefore a matter of some surprise to find the Court taking precisely that position is certain later cases, where it has shown a marked reluctance to scrutinize the scope of the rights granted by national law. In *CICRA and Another v Renault*,[119] for example, the Court was asked for a ruling on the effect of the Treaty in the context of a dispute between several independent manufacturers of spare parts for cars and a car manufacturer, which had registered a protective right in the design for spare parts intended for its own cars. The applicants in the main action sought a declaration that the protective rights held by the respondent were void in so far as they related to spare parts having no intrinsic aesthetic value of their own. The Court was asked whether the Treaty prevented the owner of such a protective right from using it to prevent the export to another Member State of spare parts made by third parties.[120] The Court declared that, 'with respect to the protection of designs and models, in the present state of Community law and in the absence of Community standardization or harmonization of laws the determination of the conditions and procedures under which such protection is granted is a matter for national rules. It is for the national legislature to determine which products qualify for protection, even if they form part of a unit already protected as such.'[121] The power to prevent the manufacture and sale of products incorporating the protected design constituted, the Court said, the substance of the owner's exclusive right. 'To prevent the application of the national legislation in such circumstances would therefore be tantamount to challenging the very existence of that right.'[122]

This line of case law clearly allows the Member States a considerable margin of discretion.[123] The Court's reluctance to intervene is in marked contrast to the other heads of justification laid down in Article 30 (ex 36), where the actions of the Member States' have been subjected to much closer scrutiny. The Court's reticence seems to be attributable to at least two factors. One is an understandable unwillingness to engage in a process of redefining the range of intellectual property rights granted under the national laws of the Member States. Another is a wariness

---

[119] Case 53/87 [1988] ECR 6039. See also Case 238/87 *Volvo v Veng* [1988] ECR 6211.

[120] The Court was also asked for a ruling on the effect of Art 82 (ex 86) EC.

[121] Para 10. See also *Keurkoop v Nancy Kean Gifts, supra*; Case 35/87 *Thetford and Another v Fiamma and Others* [1988] ECR 3585; Case C–317/91 *Deutsche Renault v Audi* [1993] ECR I–6227.

[122] Para 11.   [123] See Oliver, op cit, pp 255–61; Jarvis, op cit, pp 326–34.

in the light of Article 295 (ex 222) of the Treaty about being seen to undermine the existence of such rights. The solution to the problem lies in the adoption of legislation to approximate the laws of the Member States relating to intellectual property.[124] The specific subject matter of the form of intellectual property in question would then be established by reference to the terms of the relevant legislation, as interpreted in the last resort by the Court of Justice. The extent of the problem should not, however, be overstated. It has been observed that the approach of the Court has not led to widespread abuse by the national courts.[125] In any event, the second sentence of Article 30 (ex 36)[126] enables the Court to intervene in the most egregious cases.

The Court's reference in the *Sterling Drug* and *Winthrop* cases to the exclusive right to market the protected product for the first time indicated the importance it attached to the principle of exhaustion, which it proceeded to develop. In the *Sterling Drug* case,[127] it emphasized that a derogation from the principle of the free movement of goods could not be justified 'where the product has been put onto the market in a legal manner, by the patentee himself or with his consent, in the Member State from which it has been imported, in particular in the case of a proprietor of parallel patents'. The Court added:[128]

In fact, if a patentee could prevent the import of protected products marketed by him or with his consent in another Member State, he would be able to partition off national markets and thereby restrict trade between Member States, in a situation where no such restriction was necessary to guarantee the essence of the exclusive rights flowing from the parallel patents.

The application of the exhaustion principle has given rise to special problems in the context of patents. One is that a product which is patentable in one Member State may not be patentable in another. The question then arises whether the owner of the patent in the first State can use it to oppose imports from the second State, on the basis that he has not 'consented' to the marketing of the product there. An early case in which this issue arose was *Parke, Davis v Centrafarm*,[129] where the holder of Netherlands patents for an antibiotic sought to prevent the importation of the product concerned from Italy, where medicaments were not patentable and it was therefore freely available. The Court held that, in circumstances such as these, the Treaty did not preclude reliance on the patents held in the State of importation. The judgment concentrates mainly (though not exclusively) on the Treaty competition rules and is somewhat opaque, having been delivered before the basic ana-

---

[124] See eg in relation to trade marks Dir 89/104, OJ 1989 L40/1. That directive is considered further below.

[125] Jarvis, op cit, p 333.

[126] See the *Thetford* case, *supra*, para 16; the *Audi* case, *supra*, para 21; Case C–3/93 *IHT Internationale Heiztechnik v Ideal Standard* [1994] ECR I–2789, para 19.

[127] Para 11. Cf the *Winthrop* case, para 10.

[128] Para 12. Para 11 of the *Winthrop* judgment is in similar terms.

[129] Case 24/67 [1968] ECR 55.

lytical framework had been formulated in the *Deutsche Grammophon* case. However, in the *Sterling Drug* case, the Court made it clear that an obstacle to the free movement of goods 'may be justified on the ground of protection of industrial property where such protection is invoked against a product coming from a Member State where it is not patentable and has been manufactured by third parties without the consent of the patentee . . .'.[130]

The position is different where it is the holder of the patent in the State of importation who has placed the product on the market in a Member State where it is not patentable. In *Merck v Stephar and Exler*,[131] the Court held that, if the patent holder decides to take that step, 'he must then accept the consequences of his choice as regards the free movement of the product within the Common Market'.[132] Otherwise, the result would be to 'bring about a partitioning of the national markets which would be contrary to the aims of the Treaty'.[133] In *Merck and Others v Primecrown and Others* and *Beecham v Europharm*,[134] an unsuccessful attempt was made to persuade the Court to reconsider the rule in *Merck v Stephar and Exler*. The Court did, however, add the proviso that, 'where a patentee is legally bound under either national law or Community law to market his products in a Member State, he cannot be deemed, within the meaning of the ruling in *Merck*, to have given his consent to the marketing of the products concerned. He is therefore entitled to oppose importation and marketing of those products in the State where they are protected.'[135]

The rule laid down in *Merck v Stephar and Exler* was invoked in *Pharmon v Hoechst*,[136] where the owner of Netherlands and United Kingdom patents in respect of a medicine known as 'frusemide' sought to prevent an importer from marketing a consignment of it in the Netherlands. The consignment had been purchased from a third party which had manufactured it under a compulsory licence granted in accordance with the legislation in force in the United Kingdom. It was argued by the importer that someone taking out a patent in the United Kingdom accepted the whole body of legislation applicable there and all the consequences which that implied, including the possibility that a parallel licence might be granted. However, the Court focused on the lack of consent on the part of the patentee in circumstances such as these:

> where, as in this instance, the competent authorities of a Member State grant a third party a compulsory licence which allows him to carry out manufacturing and marketing operations which the patentee would normally have the right to prevent, the patentee cannot be deemed to have consented to the operation of that third party. Such a measure deprives the patent proprietor of his right to determine freely the conditions under which he markets his products.[137]

---

[130] *Supra*, para 11.
[131] Case 187/80 [1981] ECR 2063.
[132] Para 11.
[133] Para 13.
[134] Joined Cases C–267/95 and C–268/95 [1996] ECR I–6285.
[135] *Primecrown*, para 50.
[136] Case 19/84 [1985] ECR 2281.
[137] Para 25.

He was therefore entitled to prevent the importation and marketing of products manufactured under a compulsory licence in order to protect the substance of the exclusive rights conferred on him by his patent.[138]

The definition given by the Court in *Centrafarm v Winthrop* of the specific subject matter of trade marks was subsequently refined in *Hoffmann-La Roche v Centrafarm*,[139] where the problems posed by repackaging were raised. HLR owned a particular trade mark in several Member States. C purchased a product covered by the trade mark in one Member State and sold it in another Member State, where prices were higher, after repackaging it and re-affixing HLR's trade mark to the new packaging. This process was necessary because the product was sold in packages containing different quantities in the two Member States. However, under the law of the State of importation it involved an infringement of HLR's trade mark. The question referred to the Court was essentially whether Community law prevented HLR from relying on its trade mark to oppose the imports of the product.

In order to answer that question, the Court said that 'regard must be had to the essential function of the trade-mark, which is to guarantee the identity of the origin of the trade-marked product to the consumer or ultimate user, by enabling him without any possibility of confusion to distinguish that product from products which have another origin'. The Court explained that the trade mark holder's right to prevent 'any use of the trade-mark which is likely to impair the guarantee of origin so understood is therefore part of the specific subject-matter of the trade-mark right'.[140] The holder was consequently entitled, under the first sentence of Article 30 (ex 36), to prevent an importer from affixing the trade mark to new packaging without the holder's permission. However, where the repackaging was not capable of affecting adversely the original condition of the product,[141] it might amount to a disguised restriction on trade between Member States within the meaning of the last sentence of Article 30 (ex 36) for a trade mark holder to rely on his trade mark to oppose the importation of repackaged products from another Member State. Otherwise, the Court explained, the trade mark holder would be able to partition the common market along national lines by marketing the same product in different packages in different Member States. The Court concluded that the owner of a trade mark could not prevent the marketing in one Member State of a repackaged product to which the mark had lawfully been applied in another Member State where four conditions were satisfied. These were:[142] (i) 'that the use of the trade-mark right by the proprietor, having regard to the marketing system which he has adopted, will contribute to the artificial partitioning of the markets between

---

[138] Cf Case 434/85 *Allen and Hanburys v Generics* [1988] ECR 1245, which concerned a patent granted under UK legislation and endorsed 'licences of right'.

[139] Case 102/77 [1978] ECR 1139.   [140] Para 7.

[141] eg where the product has been marketed in packaging consisting of two layers and the repackaging affects only the external layer, leaving the internal layer intact.

[142] See para 14 of the judgment. See also Case 1/81 *Pfizer v Eurim-Pharm* [1981] ECR 2913.

Member States'; (ii) 'that the repackaging cannot adversely affect the original condition of the product'; (iii) 'that the proprietor of the mark receives prior notice of the marketing of the repackaged product'; and (iv) 'that the new packaging carries a statement identifying the undertaking responsible for the repackaging'.

The trade marks directive

The case law of the Court on exhaustion and repackaging was enshrined in the first Council directive on the approximation of the laws of the Member States relating to trade marks, Directive 89/104,[143] which was adopted under Article 100a (now 95) of the EC Treaty. Article 7 of the directive provides:

1. The trade mark shall not entitle the proprietor to prohibit its use in relation to goods which have been put on the market in the Community under that trade mark by the proprietor or with his consent.[144]
2. Paragraph 1 shall not apply where there exist legitimate reasons for the proprietor to oppose further commercialization of the goods, especially where the condition of the goods is changed or impaired after they have been put on the market.

The relationship between Directive 89/104 and Articles 28 (ex 30) and 30 (ex 36) of the Treaty was considered in *Bristol-Myers Squibb and Others v Paranova*,[145] another repackaging case in which Article 7(2) was in issue. Advocate General Jacobs took the view that, because the Community legislature had adopted specific provisions dealing with the effects of trade marks, a solution to the case should be sought in the first instance in those provisions. That did not, however, mean that Articles 28 (ex 30) and 30 (ex 36) ceased to be relevant:

On the contrary, the Directive must be interpreted in the light of the Treaty provisions. If there were any conflict between them and the Directive, the conflict would have to be resolved by giving precedence to the Treaty provisions, which are a primary source of law. Clearly a directive adopted under Article 100a [now 95] of the Treaty for the purpose of approximating the laws of the Member States could not derogate from the fundamental rules of the Treaty on the free movement of goods. Certainly a directive could not legitimize obstacles to trade between Member States which would otherwise be contrary to Articles 30 [now 28] and 36 [now 30] of the Treaty.[146]

That view is reflected in the judgment.[147] The Court observed that both Article 7 of the directive and Article 30 (ex 36) of the Treaty were 'intended to reconcile the fundamental interest in protecting trade mark rights with the fundamental

---

[143] OJ 1989 L40/1.

[144] Art 7(1) does not apply to products put on the market in non-member countries: Case C–355/96 *Silhouette International v Hartlauer* [1998] 2 CMLR 953. See Alexander, 'Exhaustion of trade mark rights in the European Economic Area' (1999) 24 ELRev 56.

[145] Joined Cases C–427/93, C–429/93 and C–436/93 [1996] ECR I–3457. See also Joined Cases C–71/94, C–72/94 and C–73/94 *Eurim-Pharm v Beiersdorf* [1996] ECR I–3603; Case C–232/94 *MPA Pharma v Rhône-Poulenc Pharma* [1996] ECR I–3671. Cf Case C–349/95 *Loendersloot v Ballantine* [1997] ECR I–6227, which concerned the relabelling of alcoholic drinks.

[146] p I–3486.   [147] See paras 24–8.

interest in the free movement of goods within the common market, so that those two provisions, which pursue the same result, must be interpreted in the same way'.[148] On the particular issue of repackaging, the Court explained that its case law on the effect of Article 30 (ex 36) was to 'be taken as the basis for determining whether, under Article 7(2) of the directive, a trade mark owner may oppose the marketing of repackaged products to which the trade mark has been reaffixed'.[149] The Court proceeded to reiterate and expand upon the conditions laid down in the *Hoffmann-La Roche* case. In particular, it made it clear that: (i) the importer was not required to indicate on the new packaging that the product had been repackaged without the authorization of the trade mark owner. An indication of that nature 'could be taken to imply . . . that the repackaged product is not entirely legitimate';[150] (ii) the presentation of the repackaged product must not be 'liable to damage the reputation of the trade mark and of its owner; thus, the packaging must not be defective, of poor quality, or untidy';[151] and (iii) the importer had to notify the trade mark owner before the repackaged product was put on sale and, if requested, supply him with a specimen of the repackaged product. The Court added, however, that the importer did not have to show that the trade mark owner had deliberately sought to partition the market artificially, thereby creating a disguised restriction on trade between Member States. It was enough for the importer to show that the repackaging did not impair the essential function of the trade mark.[152]

The case law on repackaging indicates the lengths to which the Court has gone to reconcile the interests of the owners of trade marks with the principle of the free movement of goods. The approach of the Court has been necessary to prevent trade mark holders from using different national rules and practices on packaging to partition the common market. The Court has formulated a detailed set of principles to be applied in establishing whether repackaging by an undertaking other than the holder of the trade mark may be treated as an infringement. The elaborate conditions laid down in the case law stand in stark contrast to the brevity of Article 7(2) of Directive 89/104.

The importance of trade marks in the Court's case law

To the extent that the judgment in *Bristol-Myers Squibb* makes it easier for a trade mark holder to oppose parallel imports of repackaged products, the case marks a further step in the rehabilitation of trade marks as a form of intellectual property important enough in some cases to justify precedence over the principle of free movement. Evidence of the somewhat dismissive view originally taken of trade marks by the Court may be found in *Sirena v Eda*,[153] where it declared:

---

[148] Para 40.   [149] Para 41.   [150] Para 72.   [151] Para 79.

[152] See para 57. Cf Case 3/78 *Centrafarm v American Home Products Corporation* Case 3/78 [1978] ECR 1823.

[153] Case 40/70 [1971] ECR 69, para 7. See also AG Dutheillet de Lamothe at pp 87–8.

The exercise of a trade-mark right is particularly apt to lead to a partitioning of markets, and thus to impair the free movement of goods between States which is essential to the Common Market. Moreover, a trade-mark right is distinguishable in this context from other rights of intellectual property, inasmuch as the interests protected by the latter are usually more important, and merit a higher degree of protection, than the interests protected by an ordinary trade-mark.

That view of the value of trade marks and the dangers they posed to the proper functioning of the common market reached its apotheosis in the notorious case of *Van Zuylen v Hag (HAG I)*,[154] in which the Court laid down the doctrine of common origin. The case arose out of a dispute concerning the right to use the trade mark 'HAG', which was registered in Germany in 1907 in the name of HAG AG, a German company which invented the first process for decaffeinating coffee. The following year HAG AG registered the HAG mark in Belgium and Luxembourg. In 1927 HAG AG set up a subsidiary in Belgium, Café HAG, to which it later assigned its Belgian and Luxembourg trade marks. In 1944, the assets of Café HAG were sequestrated by the Belgian authorities as enemy property and sold to the Van Oevelen family. Some years later, the right to use the HAG trade mark in Belgium and Luxembourg was assigned to a company called Van Zuylen Frères, which sought to rely on the mark to prevent the sale in Luxembourg of coffee exported by HAG AG under its German HAG trade mark.

The dispute eventually reached the Court of Justice, which ruled that a trade mark owner could not in circumstances such as these rely on its trade mark to prevent imports: '. . . to prohibit the marketing in a Member State of a product legally bearing a trade mark in another Member State, for the sole reason that an identical trade mark having the same origin exists in the first state, is incompatible with the provisions providing for free movement of goods within the Common Market'.[155] The Court's very brief reasoning emphasized the need to avoid partitioning the common market but attached little importance to protecting the essential function of a trade mark, that of guaranteeing to the consumer the origin of the product bearing the mark. In *Terrapin v Terranova*,[156] the Court said that, in circumstances such as those of *HAG I*, 'the basic function of the trade-mark to guarantee to consumers that the product has the same origin is already undermined by the subdivision of the original right'. However, as Advocate General Jacobs pointed out in *HAG GF (HAG II)*,[157] the essential function of the HAG trade mark was undermined, not by its fragmentation in 1944, but by the Court's judgment in *HAG I*.

In the *HAG II* case, the tables were reversed. HAG AG sought to rely on its German HAG mark to restrain imports from Belgium into Germany of coffee bearing the HAG mark by the successors in title of Van Zuylen Frères. That attempt might have seemed to be precluded by *HAG I*, but the Court was persuaded by a coruscating Opinion by Advocate General Jacobs to reconsider that

---

[154] Case 192/73 [1974] ECR 731.
[156] Case 119/75 [1976] ECR 1039, para 6.
[155] Para 15.
[157] Case C–10/89 [1990] ECR I–3711, 3735.

ruling and abandon the doctrine of common origin. The Court acknowledged that trade marks were 'an essential element in the system of undistorted competition which the Treaty seeks to establish and maintain. Under such a system, an undertaking must be in a position to keep its customers by virtue of the quality of its products and services, something which is possible only if there are distinctive marks which enable customers to identify those products and services. For the trade mark to be able to fulfil this role, it must offer a guarantee that all goods bearing it have been produced under the control of a single undertaking which is accountable for their quality.'[158] Although the marks at issue had a common origin, since the date of the expropriation they had each offered a guarantee within their fields of application that the marked products came from a single source and it was not relevant that they had once belonged to the same proprietor. The Court concluded that, in circumstances such as these, each of the trade mark owners was entitled to oppose the importation and marketing, in the Member State where the mark belonged to him, of goods originating from the other proprietor, 'in so far as they are similar products bearing an identical mark or one which is liable to lead to confusion'.[159]

In *IHT Internationale Heiztechnik v Ideal Standard*,[160] the Court held that the reasoning in *HAG II* also applied where the ownership of a trade mark was divided voluntarily by contractual assignment. These decisions elevate trade marks to the status enjoyed by other forms of intellectual property under the Treaty rules on the free movement of goods. They demonstrate that the Court is not blind to the important role that intellectual property plays in the modern economy and that, even after the Single European Act, it is prepared in appropriate cases to accord such property precedence over the dictates of the internal market. The way to make that market function properly is not by undermining the essential function of intellectual property rights but by approximating the laws of the Member States and introducing intellectual property rights having effect throughout the Community. These steps have both been taken in relation to trade marks.[161] At a more general level, *HAG II* shows that the Court does not consider itself infallible and that it is prepared to depart from previous rulings where convinced that they were wrongly decided.[162]

Non-discriminatory barriers to trade and the rule of reason

So far the discussion has concentrated mainly on the problems raised by national measures which in some way discriminated against imports. It will be recalled that

---

[158] Para 13.   [159] Para 19.   [160] Case C–9/93 [1994] ECR I–2789.
[161] See Dir 89/104, *supra*, and Reg 40/94 on the Community trade mark, *supra*.
[162] The significance of the case from the point of view of judicial precedent is considered in ch 15.

the question whether Article 28 (ex 30) was capable of catching national rules which applied equally to domestic goods and to imports but which nevertheless hindered intra-Community trade was the subject of considerable debate during the early years of the Community's existence. The Court's ruling in *Dassonville* suggested that those who had argued that the question of discrimination was irrelevant were correct: the important question was whether or not the disputed national rule interfered with the free movement of goods. That suggestion was confirmed by the Court in the famous 'Cassis de Dijon' case,[163] which gave rise to a line of case law so far-reaching in its effects that the Court was finally led, in one of its most remarkable and controversial decisions, to qualify the *Dassonville* formula itself.

The facts of 'Cassis de Dijon' were simple enough. The plaintiff in the main action applied to the competent German authorities for permission to import a consignment of the eponymous liqueur originating in France. Permission was denied because the product was not strong enough: under German law, fruit liqueurs such as Cassis de Dijon could only be marketed in Germany if they had a minimum alcohol content of 25 per cent. The alcohol content of Cassis de Dijon, which was freely available in France, was between 15 and 20 per cent. The plaintiff took the view that the German rules on the minimum alcohol content of fruit liqueurs constituted a MEE prohibited by Article 28 (ex 30) and the dispute was referred to the Court of Justice. In a passage pregnant with implications, the Court declared:[164]

In the absence of common rules relating to the production and marketing of alcohol . . . it is for the Member States to regulate all matters relating to the production and marketing of alcohol and alcoholic beverages on their own territory.

Obstacles to movement within the Community resulting from disparities between the national laws relating to the marketing of the products in question must be accepted in so far as those provisions may be recognized as being necessary in order to satisfy mandatory requirements relating in particular to the effectiveness of fiscal supervision, the protection of public health, the fairness of commercial transactions and the defence of the consumer.

The German Government had sought to justify its rules on the minimum alcohol content of alcoholic beverages on two grounds. First, it was said that the proliferation of such beverages with a low alcohol content needed to be avoided because they created a tolerance to alcohol more easily than beverages with a higher alcohol content. This risible argument was given short shrift by the Court, which noted that there was a wide range of low- and medium-stength alcoholic beverages available in Germany and that many of the stronger beverages available there were usually drunk in diluted form. The German Government's second argument was little more convincing than the first. Because alcohol constituted the most expensive ingredient of alcoholic beverages, the disputed rules were said to be necessary to prevent the consumer from being misled about the true alcoholic content of a

[163] Case 120/78 *Rewe v Bundesmonopolverwaltung für Branntwein* [1979] ECR 649.
[164] Para 8.

beverage. Furthermore, said the German Government, if Article 28 (ex 30) were interpreted as allowing products to circulate freely merely because they complied with the rules in force in the State of production, the effect would be to impose the most liberal requirements of any of the Member States as a common Community standard. The Court pointed out, however, that if the real reason for the disputed rules was to protect consumers, it was disproportionate: 'it is a simple matter to ensure that suitable information is conveyed to the purchaser by requiring the display of an indication of origin and of the alcohol content on the packaging of products'.[165] The Court evidently regarded the disputed rules as protectionist: the main effect of such rules, it observed, was 'to promote alcoholic beverages having a high alcohol content by excluding from the national market products from other Member States which do not answer that description'.[166] It concluded that there was no valid reason why an alcoholic beverage such as Cassis de Dijon which had been lawfully produced and marketed in one Member State should not be placed on the market in any other Member State. Rules such as those in dispute were therefore contrary to Article 28 (ex 30).

In a case decided the following year, *Gilli and Andres*,[167] the Court applied the new approach, sometimes called the 'rule of reason', in the context of a prosecution of two traders in Italy for having in their possession for commercial purposes apple vinegar made in Germany containing acetic acid not derived from the acetic fermentation of wine, which was an offence under Italian law. On a reference for a preliminary ruling, the Court, repeating some of the language used in 'Cassis de Dijon', observed:[168] 'It is only where national rules [relating to the production, distribution and consumption of a product],[[169]] *which apply without discrimination to both domestic and imported products*, may be justified as being necessary in order to satisfy imperative requirements . . . that they may constitute an exception to the requirements arising under Article 30 [now 28].' It was common ground that apple vinegar was harmless and that the receptacles used by the defendants were clearly labelled with an indication of their contents. The Court concluded that there was therefore 'no factor justifying any restriction on the importation of the product in question from the point of view either of the protection of public health or of the fairness of commercial transactions or of the defence of the consumer'.[170] Rules such as those in dispute were therefore incompatible with Article 28 (ex 30).

The Court's ruling that Article 28 (ex 30) could apply to obstacles to the free movement of goods which resulted simply from the fact that the rules relating to the marketing of a product in the State of importation were not the same as those in force in the State of origin was of the utmost significance.[171] It seemed to bring

---

[165] Para 13. The Court subsequently held that national rules requiring a product's origin to be indicated might themselves be caught by Art 28 (ex 30): Case 207/83 *Commission v United Kingdom* [1985] ECR 1201, *supra*.

[166] Para 14.   [167] Case 788/79 [1980] ECR 2071.

[168] Para 6, emphasis added.   [169] See para 5 of the judgment.   [170] Para 8.

[171] See Dehousse, *The European Court of Justice* (1998), pp 84–8. Oliver, op cit, p 93, acknowledges that 'Cassis de Dijon' 'constituted a major landmark in the Court's case law on Article 30', but says it

a much wider category of national measure within the ambit of Article 28 (ex 30) and had profound implications for the Commission's programme of harmonization. This was acknowledged by the Commission in a Communication issued in late 1980.[172] It had previously been thought that obstacles to trade caused by disparities between the technical and commercial requirements laid down in different Member States could only be eliminated by Community legislation harmonizing those requirements. Not only was this an immensely laborious and time-consuming process, it ran the risk of abolishing distinctive national products, which in themselves were entirely harmless, and replacing them with unappealing alternatives—Euro-beer, Euro-bread, Euro-sausages, and such like. The 'Cassis de Dijon' decision showed that such far-reaching legislation was unnecessary to ensure the free movement of goods. The Communication accordingly announced that '[t]he Commission's work of harmonization will henceforth have to be directed mainly at national laws having an impact on the functioning of the common market where barriers to trade to be removed arise from national provisions which are admissible under the criteria set by the Court'.[173]

The relationship between the rule of reason and Article 30 (ex 36)

Alongside the expansion in the perceived scope of the prohibition laid down in Article 30, the Member States were at the same time offered greater possibilities of justifying measures which appeared to hinder imports. Notwithstanding its insistence that Article 30 (ex 36) was to be strictly construed, the Court seemed to introduce an additional category of interests, the so-called 'mandatory requirements',[174] by reference to which obstacles to intra-Community trade resulting from disparities between national laws on the marketing of products might be justified. Moreover, by introducing the list of those requirements with the words 'in particular', the Court made it clear that the catalogue it was putting forward was not exhaustive but merely illustrative. In subsequent cases, the Court added to the list the protection of the environment,[175] the maintenance of press diversity[176] and the need to avoid undermining the financial balance of national social security systems.[177] Curiously, one of the requirements mentioned by the Court—the protection of public health—was mentioned in Article 30 (ex 36), which perhaps suggested that the mandatory requirements did not have the same effect or perform the same function as that article. It was, however, clear from the way in which the

would be wrong to describe it as revolutionary: 'Rather it has brought together in a new form strands that were to be found in various earlier cases.'

[172] Communication from the Commission concerning the consequences of the judgment given by the Court of Justice on February 20, 1979 in Case 120/78 ('Cassis de Dijon'), OJ 1980 C256/2.

[173] For subsequent developments, see Oliver, op cit, chs XII and XIII. Cf Dehousse, op cit, p 92.

[174] Referred to as 'imperative' or 'overriding' requirements in some later cases.

[175] See Case 302/86 *Commission v Denmark* [1988] ECR 4607, para 9.

[176] See Case C–368/95 *Familiapress v Bauer Verlag* [1997] ECR I–3689, para 18.

[177] See Case C–120/95 *Decker v Caisse de Maladie des Employés Privés* [1998] ECR I–1831, para 39.

Court dealt with the German Government's attempts to justify the disputed rules that a Member State wishing to invoke one of the mandatory requirements would have to show that the principle of proportionality had been respected.

The reference to the notion of discrimination in *Gilli and Andres* suggested that it was only indistinctly applicable national rules that were capable of benefiting from the mandatory requirements recognized by the Court in 'Cassis de Dijon'. That suggestion was confirmed in the 'Irish Souvenirs' case,[178] where the Commission sought a declaration that Irish rules requiring souvenirs of Ireland manufactured abroad to bear an indication of their country of origin or the word 'foreign' were incompatible with Article 28 (ex 30). The Irish Government argued that the disputed rules were justified on grounds of consumer protection and fairness in commercial transactions between producers. Referring *inter alia* to its rulings in 'Cassis de Dijon' and *Gilli and Andres*, the Court acknowledged that those grounds had been recognized as mandatory requirements, but underlined that they could only be invoked in relation to measures which did not discriminate between domestic and imported goods. The rules concerned in the present case, it said, 'are not measures which are applicable to domestic products and to imported products without distinction but rather a set of rules which apply only to imported products and are therefore discriminatory in nature, with the result that the measures in issue are not covered by the decisions cited above which relate exclusively to provisions that regulate in a uniform manner the marketing of domestic products and imported products'.[179]

Had the judgment ended at that point, it would have been clear that the mandatory requirements could only be relied upon to justify non-discriminatory national rules. However, the force of the judgment was somewhat weakened by the fact that the Court went on to consider an argument of the Irish Government that the disputed rules were discriminatory in appearance only, there being an essential difference between home-produced and imported souvenirs. In the course of examining (and rejecting) that argument, the Court was led into considering whether the disputed rules were justified in the interests of consumers and fair trading. However, subsequent case law[180] showed that the Court did not thereby intend to qualify its earlier assertion that the mandatory requirements could not be used to save discriminatory restrictions on imports.

The 'Irish Souvenirs' case also offered a clue as to the difference between the mandatory requirements and the grounds of justification mentioned in Article 30 (ex 36). The Court remarked[181] that it was necessary to examine the Irish Government's attempt to rely on the interests of consumer protection and fairness

---

[178] Case 113/80 *Commission v Ireland* [1981] ECR 1625.   [179] Para 11.
[180] eg Case 177/83 *Kohl v Ringelhan & Rennett* [1984] ECR 3651, para 14; Case C–21/88 *Du Pont de Nemours Italiana* [1990] ECR I–889, para 14 (both citing 'Irish Souvenirs'); Case 207/83 *Commission v United Kingdom* ('Origin Marking') [1985] ECR 1201, paras 19–20. See also Dashwood, 'The Cassis de Dijon line of authority' in Bates et al (eds), *In Memoriam J D B Mitchell* (1983), p 145, at pp 154–5; Oliver, op cit, pp 112–13.
[181] At para 9. See also Case 434/85 *Allen and Hanburys v Generics* [1988] ECR 1245, para 35.

in commercial transactions to establish whether it could be said that the disputed rules 'are not measures having an effect equivalent to quantitative restrictions on imports . . .'. In *Kohl v Ringelhan & Rennett*,[182] the Court, referring to the 'Irish Souvenirs' case, said that considerations of consumer protection 'may in certain circumstances be taken into account in establishing whether national measures applicable without distinction to domestic and imported products are caught by the prohibitions laid down in Article 30 [now 28]; they cannot, however, serve to justify restrictions on imports under Article 36 [now 30]'. This seemed to imply that the mandatory requirements were regarded as defining the scope of the prohibition laid down in Article 28 (ex 30); they were not considered justifications or derogations like the grounds referred to in Article 30 (ex 36). Thus, an indistinctly applicable national rule on the marketing of a particular product which was necessary to ensure the protection of the consumer would *fall outside the scope of Article 28 (ex 30) entirely.* By contrast, where a Member State successfully invoked Article 30 (ex 36), it did not thereby establish that the disputed national rule was not caught by Article 28 (ex 30), simply that, although caught by that article, it was none the less justified. This meant that a Member State which was unsuccessful in invoking the mandatory requirements could in theory then seek to rely on Article 30 (ex 36).[183] This approach enabled the mandatory requirements to be reconciled with the case law to the effect that Article 30 (ex 36) was to be interpreted strictly since they were not regarded as extending the grounds of justification laid down in that article. Indeed, the doctrine born in 'Cassis de Dijon' echoed Article 3 of Commission Directive 70/50, according to which, it will be recalled, the concept of MEE extended to 'measures governing the marketing of products . . . which are equally applicable to domestic and imported products, where the restrictive effect of such measures on the free movement of goods exceeds the effects intrinsic to trade rules'.[184]

The distinction drawn in the previous paragraph between the mandatory requirements and Article 30 (ex 36) might be thought to be one without a difference: it is not obvious what practical difference it would make whether a national rule were considered outside the scope of Article 28 (ex 30) or caught by that article but justified. The artificiality of the distinction may be illustrated by *Aragonesa de Publicidad Exterior and Publivía*.[185] The appellant companies had been fined for

---

[182] *Supra*, para 19. See also Joined Cases 60 and 61/84 *Cinéthèque v Fédération Nationale des Cinémas Français* [1985] ECR 2605, para 26, where the Court said it had no power to examine the compatibility with the European Convention on Human Rights of national legislation which fell within the jurisdiction of the national legislator because, although restrictive of trade, it was justified under the rule of reason. The Court appeared to depart from that position in *Familiapress, supra*. See ch 6.

[183] See Case C–362/88 *GB-INNO-BM* [1990] ECR I–667, para 19; Marenco, 'Pour une interprétation traditionnelle de la notion de mesure d'effet équivalent à une restriction quantitative' (1984) CDE 291, 339.

[184] Oliver, op cit, p 110, points out that the presumption of legality embodied in Art 3 of the directive seems to have been reversed by the Court, so that the burden of proof now lies with the Member State seeking to justify a measure restricting trade.

[185] Joined Cases C–1/90 and C–176/90 [1991] ECR I–4151. See also Case 216/84 *Commission v France* ('Milk Substitutes') [1988] ECR 793, para 7; Case C–332/89 *Marchandise and Others* [1991] ECR I–1027, paras 18–19.

infringing restrictions imposed by Catalan law on the advertising of beverages having an alcoholic strength of more than 23 degrees. The appellants argued that the
restrictions were incompatible with Article 28 (ex 30) because they made it more
difficult for beverages originating in other Member States to be marketed. There
was no real doubt that the restrictions were capable of constituting a MEE within
the meaning of Article 28 (ex 30) and the Court so held. Argument concentrated
on whether the restrictions could be justified in the interests of public health and,
if so, on what basis.

Unlike the appellants, Advocate General van Gerven took the view that the disputed restrictions were non-discriminatory and were justified on the ground of
protecting public health. As has already been noted, that ground is mentioned in
both Article 30 (ex 36) and 'Cassis de Dijon'. The Advocate General therefore proceeded to consider which should be applied in the instant case. On grounds of strict
logic, one might have thought that the latter should be applied, since if a measure
falls outside the scope of Article 28 (ex 30) there can be no question of applying
Article 30 (ex 36). Advocate General van Gerven took a more pragmatic approach,
noting that the question had 'little if any practical import, since the conditions governing the applicability of the "Cassis de Dijon" doctrine and of Article 36 [now
30] are the same (absence of harmonization, examination of the criteria of necessity and proportionality, prohibition of arbitrary discrimination or disguised restriction on trade)'.[186] Having examined other cases in which the question whether
non-discriminatory rules impeding trade could be justified on public health
grounds, the Advocate General expressed the view that 'under its current case-law,
the Court is correct to have direct recourse to Article 36 [now 30] where one of
the grounds of justification mentioned in that article is raised. Indeed it seems to
me curious to rely on an unwritten "imperative requirement" of public health
when the public health justification is expressly provided for in a provision of written law.'[187]

The Court broadly speaking followed the advice of Advocate General van
Gerven, observing:[188]

The protection of public health is expressly mentioned amongst the grounds of public interest which are set out in Article 36 [now 30] and enable a restriction on imports to escape the
prohibition laid down in Article 30 [now 28]. In those circumstances, since Article 36 [now
30] also applies where the contested measure restricts only imports, whereas according to the
Court's case-law the question of imperative requirements for the purposes of the interpretation of Article 30 [now 28] cannot arise unless the measure in question applies without distinction to both national and imported products, it is not necessary to consider whether the
protection of public health might also be in the nature of an imperative requirement for the
purposes of the application of Article 30 [now 28].

---

[186] p I–4177. See also Oliver, op cit, p 112, who notes that, in 'Cassis de Dijon', the Court said that
the mandatory requirements applied only in the absence of common rules.
[187] p I–4178.   [188] Para 13.

The Court said it was therefore necessary to consider whether the legislation in issue was 'of such a nature as to protect public health' and, if so, whether it was proportionate to its objective. It went on to find that both questions merited an affirmative answer.

The passage cited above is in one respect unfortunately worded, in that the Court had recognized on a number of previous occasions[189] that the protection of public health constituted a mandatory requirement for the purposes of the 'Cassis de Dijon' doctrine. The last clause of the above passage seems to cast doubt on whether that remains the case. However, it is clear that, since that interest is specifically referred to in Article 30 (ex 36) and that article can be used to justify both discriminatory and non-discriminatory obstacles to trade, the question whether the interests of public health also constitute a mandatory requirement has no practical importance. Instead of saying that the mandatory requirements define the scope of Article 28 (ex 30), we might as well say simply that non-discriminatory obstacles to intra-Community trade benefit from an extended category of derogations. This is of course incompatible with the view that Article 30 (ex 36) is to be strictly construed, but to seek to conceal that incompatibility by denying that the mandatory requirements are derogations amounts to little more than sophistry. This view was confirmed in *Familiapress*,[190] where the Court held, departing from its decision in *Cinéthèque*,[191] that a Member State invoking a mandatory requirement had to comply with the Community principle of respect for fundamental rights. Since that principle applies to the Member States only when they act within the scope of Community law,[192] it follows that the mandatory requirements do not have the effect of taking a case outside the ambit of Article 28 (ex 30).

What is a discriminatory rule?

The appellants in the *Aragonesa* case had maintained that the disputed advertising restrictions were discriminatory. They argued that, although the Catalan law made no formal distinction between domestic and imported alcoholic beverages, most such beverages produced in Catalonia had an alcoholic strength of less than 23 degrees. The restrictions were therefore said to be protective in their effect and contrary to the second sentence of Article 30 (ex 36). That argument raised an argument of principle about the circumstances in which national rules might be considered discriminatory for the purposes of Article 28 (ex 30), for the Catalan restrictions on advertising affected alcoholic beverages produced in other parts of Spain in the same way as such beverages produced in other Member States. The question whether rules which favoured a particular region of a Member State were to be considered discriminatory was addressed by the Court in *Du Pont de Nemours Italiana*,[193] which concerned the compatibility with Article 28 (ex 30) of Italian

---

[189] eg in 'Cassis de Dijon' itself and *Gilli and Andres*, para 6.   [190] *Supra.*
[191] *Supra.*   [192] See ch 6.   [193] Case C–21/88 [1990] ECR I–889.

rules which reserved a proportion of public supply contracts to firms established in the Mezzogiorno. The Court pointed out that a system which favoured goods produced in a particular region of a Member State impeded intra-Community trade by preventing public bodies from obtaining some of their supplies from other Member States. It made no difference that the system affected in the same way 'products manufactured by undertakings from the Member State in question which are not situated in the region covered by the preferential system and . . . products manufactured by undertakings established in other Member States'.[194] As the Court emphasized:[195]

> although not all the products of the Member State in question benefit by comparison with products from abroad, the fact remains that all the products benefiting by the preferential system are domestic products . . . the fact that the restrictive effect exercised by a State measure on imports does not benefit all domestic products but only some cannot exempt the measure in question from the prohibition set out in Article 30 [now 28].

In the *Aragonesa* case, the Court reiterated that approach but, in accordance with the Opinion of Advocate General van Gerven, rejected on the facts the appellants' argument that the Catalan advertising restrictions tended to favour locally-produced beverages. The Court noted that 'those restrictions affect both products, in not inconsiderable quantities, originating in the part of the national territory to which they apply and products imported from other Member States'.[196] The Court was called upon to deal with the issue in rather more difficult circumstances in the 'Belgian Waste' case.[197] The conclusion reached by the Court there highlights its ambivalence about what it means when it describes a national measure as 'discriminatory' for the purposes of the 'Cassis de Dijon' doctrine.

The 'Belgian Waste' case concerned the compatibility with Community law of a Decree of the Walloon Regional Council which was designed to prevent the build-up of waste in Wallonia, to encourage recycling, and to make arrangements for waste disposal. To those ends, the Decree contained a prohibition on the storage, tipping or dumping in Wallonia of waste originating in other Member States or other regions of Belgium. The Commission sought a declaration under Article 226 (ex 169) of the Treaty that the Decree was incompatible with two directives on waste and with Articles 28 (ex 30) and 30 (ex 36) of the Treaty to the extent that it prohibited the dumping in Wallonia of waste from other Member States.

In so far as the Decree applied to hazardous waste, the Court found that the prohibition it laid down was incompatible with a directive on the trans-frontier shipment of hazardous waste, which was intended to introduce a comprehensive system for the disposal of such waste and which did not permit the Member States to introduce a blanket prohibition on shipments of it. As far as non-hazardous waste

---

[194] Para 12.

[195] Para 13. See also Joined Cases C–277/91, C–318/91 and C–319/91 *Ligur Carni* [1993] ECR I–6621, para 37.

[196] Para 25.   [197] Case C–2/90 *Commission v Belgium* [1992] ECR I–4431.

was concerned, the Court found that the contested Decree was not precluded by the other directive relied on by the Commission. It therefore turned to the question whether the Belgian rules contravened Article 28 (ex 30) in so far as they covered non-hazardous waste.

It was common ground that recyclable and reusable waste which had an intrinsic commercial value constituted 'goods' for the purposes of the Treaty and therefore fell within the scope of Article 28 (ex 30). However, the Belgian Government argued that waste which could not be recycled or reused was not covered by Article 28 (ex 30). The question whether such waste constituted goods within the meaning of the Treaty was examined at some length by Advocate General Jacobs, who underlined the practical difficulties of distinguishing between the two categories of waste. The Advocate General said that in his opinion the concept of goods included 'any movable physical object to which property rights or obligations attach (and which can therefore be valued in monetary terms, whether positive or negative). If the exercise of such rights, or the fulfilment of such obligations, involves the selection of a method of disposal, and if the method selected entails the movement of the object between Member States, national provisions restricting such movement fall to be examined under Articles 30 [now 28] to 36 [now 30] of the Treaty.'[198] The Court agreed, observing that 'waste, whether recyclable or not, is to be regarded as "goods" the movement of which, in accordance with Article 30 [now 28] of the Treaty, must in principle not be prevented'.[199]

The crux of the case, in so far as non-hazardous waste was concerned, was whether or not the contested Decree could be justified. Advocate General Jacobs had concluded that it could not. The directive on hazardous waste excluded recourse to Article 30 (ex 36).[200] While the other directive invoked by the Commission did not have that effect, the Advocate General took the view that:

it is not in any event open to Belgium to rely on Article 36 [now 30] in order to restrict imports of non-dangerous waste. According to well-established case-law, Article 36 [now 30] must be interpreted restrictively . . . and I therefore do not think it is possible to adopt a wide interpretation of the 'human health' exception so as to permit restrictions on substances which do not threaten health or life but at the most 'the quality of life'. Nor is it possible to rely on the 'mandatory requirements' exceptions to Article 30 [now 28], which include the protection of the environment . . . Those exceptions can be invoked only for measures which are not discriminatory. But the measure in question, which favours waste produced in one region of a Member State, is plainly not indistinctly applicable to domestic and imported products.

Despite the force of the Advocate General's analysis, the Court took a different view. It found that the contested Decree was 'justified by imperative requirements

---

[198] p I–4465.   [199] Para 28.

[200] At least as regards the categories of waste to which it applied. In the view of AG Jacobs, a global ban on imports from other Member States of dangerous waste which fell outside the scope of the directive, while in principle capable of justification under Art 30 (ex 36), was 'neither necessary nor proportionate': p I–4457.

of environmental protection'[201] and rejected the suggestion that the Decree discriminated against waste originating in other Member States. It accepted that the mandatory requirements could only be taken into account in the case of measures which applied without distinction to domestic and imported products, but maintained that, 'in assessing whether or not the barrier in question is discriminatory, account must be taken of the particular nature of waste'.[202] It pointed out that Article 174(2) (ex 130r(2)) of the Treaty enshrined the principle that environmental damage should be rectified at source. This meant that each region had a responsibility to ensure that its own waste was disposed of as close as possible to the place where it was produced in order to reduce to a minimum the transport of waste. That principle was consistent with an international convention to which the Community was a signatory.[203] The Court declared: 'It follows that having regard to the differences between waste produced in different places and to the connection of the waste with its place of production, the contested measures cannot be regarded as discriminatory.'[204]

It is clear from the Court's reasoning that it was not intending to depart from its previous decisions to the effect that mandatory requirements can only be invoked in relation to national measures which are non-discriminatory: had it intended to do so, it would not have needed to show that the contested Decree was non-discriminatory.[205] Be that as it may, the Court's conclusion on the question of discrimination is wholly unconvincing, Advocate General Jacobs having demonstrated beyond argument that the Decree discriminated against waste which did not originate in Wallonia. That view was reinforced by the fact that the Decree provided for exceptions to be made in the case of waste originating in other parts of Belgium in accordance with agreements between Wallonia and other regions. A power contained in the Decree to grant derogations in the case of waste produced abroad was much more limited in scope. Thus, the Decree systematically treated waste produced in Belgium more favourably than waste produced in other Member States.[206]

Why did the Court adopt a conclusion so lacking in logic? It seems to have considered it important to find a way of reconciling the principles embodied in Article 174(2) (ex 130r(2)) of the Treaty and the Community's international commitments with the requirements of Article 28 (ex 30). Since the purpose of the Walloon Decree was evidently to protect the environment and that purpose had been recognized as a mandatory requirement, all that needed to be done to square the circle was to find the Decree indistinctly applicable. But Advocate General Jacobs had suggested a way which did not entail discrimination in which the principle that

---

[201] Para 32.   [202] Para 34.
[203] The Basel Convention of 22 March 1989 on the control of transboundary movements of hazardous wastes and their disposal.
[204] Para 36.   [205] See Craig and de Búrca, op cit, p 604.
[206] Cf *Du Pont de Nemours Italiana, supra.*

environmental damage should be rectified at source could be reconciled with the free movement of goods:[207]

> a provision applying throughout a region of a Member State, requiring waste to be disposed of within its locality of generation, might be said to be indistinctly applicable. Such a provision would prevent the exportation of locally produced waste to another locality or another Member State in exactly the same way that it prevented the disposal of waste coming from another State or locality. Such a measure might moreover be justified in terms of the need to reduce the amount of waste in transit and to limit the areas used for waste disposal.

That approach would not have saved the contested Decree. If that was an overriding consideration, the Court might have pressed into service the notion of public policy mentioned in Article 30 (ex 36). Although the Court has rightly sought to prevent that potentially broad notion from being invoked too frequently,[208] it is submitted that the interests of environmental protection are sufficiently important to justify being included in it. It is true that there is a certain inelegance in including the same interest among the mandatory requirements and the list of exceptions in Article 30 (ex 36), but the protection of public health has belonged to both categories since 'Cassis de Dijon', as we have seen. Reliance on the notion of public policy might also have been said to cast doubt on the oft-repeated dictum that Article 30 (ex 36) is to be interpreted strictly. However, as has been pointed out above, that dictum cannot in any event be taken at face value. The course chosen by the Court—that of describing as white something which was evidently black— was infinitely worse.

The 'Belgian Waste' case raises two further issues of a more general nature. The first concerns the more liberal treatment accorded by the Court to indistinctly applicable restrictions on trade. This is in itself unexceptionable: discrimination against the products of another Member State may be considered inimical to the very foundations of the common market established by the Treaty,[209] a view reflected in the second sentence of Article 30 (ex 36). But the Court could have ensured that discriminatory national rules were in practice treated more strictly by the rigorous application of that sentence and through the principle of proportionality. Instead it chose the less flexible device of the rule of reason. That device implies that the mandatory requirements are less mandatory than the exceptions contained in Article 30 (ex 36): the latter are so important that they can justify even discriminatory national rules, which normally attract particular severity. But that view is difficult to sustain. Whatever may have been the position when the Treaty was drawn up, is the protection of national treasures really more important today than the protection of the environment, the protection of plant health more important than the protection of the consumer,[210] the protection of industrial and commercial property more important than the effectiveness of fiscal supervision? The answer to those questions must be that it depends on the circumstances, but

---

[207] p I–4467.   [208] See above.   [209] See Craig and de Búrca, op cit, p 630.
[210] See Oliver, op cit, p 112.

the 'Cassis de Dijon' doctrine is too inflexible to allow the circumstances to be taken into account. Thus, when in the 'Belgian Waste' case the Court wanted to say that the interests of environmental protection were important enough to justify even a discriminatory national measure, it was forced to deny that the measure concerned in fact possessed that quality.[211] Resort to such legerdemain is unnecessary where, even though the contested national rule is concerned in a general sense with the protection of the environment, it happens to be possible to invoke one of the grounds mentioned in Article 30 (ex 36).[212]

Secondly, the 'Belgian Waste' case draws attention to a certain vagueness about what the Court means when it describes a national measure as discriminatory or distinctly applicable. In the 'Origin Marking' case,[213] the United Kingdom argued that its rules requiring certain goods to carry an indication of their origin were applicable without distinction to domestic and imported products and that they were justified in the interests of consumer protection, a mandatory requirement. That argument was rightly rejected by the Court, which observed that the disputed rules were 'applicable without distinction to domestic and imported products only in form because, by their very nature, they are intended to enable the consumer to distinguish between those two categories of products, which may thus prompt him to give his preference to national products'.[214] The rules were therefore caught by Article 28 (ex 30) because they made it harder to market imports than domestically-produced goods and could not be justified on any ground recognized by Community law.

The 'Origin Marking' case shows that, in order to benefit from the mandatory requirements laid down in 'Cassis de Dijon', a national measure must not merely be *formally* non-discriminatory, it must apply without any distinction whatsoever to both domestic and imported products. That test was certainly not satisfied by the Walloon Decree at issue in the 'Belgian Waste' case, but there are grounds for doubting whether it was satisfied by the contested German rules in 'Cassis de Dijon' itself. A producer established in a large country like Germany or France is likely to be concerned mainly with ensuring that its goods can be marketed there. Cassis de Dijon complied with French law and was lawfully marketed in France. German law was different and the disparity between the two legal regimes impeded the free movement of goods. But just as cassis produced in France met the requirements of French law, so liqueurs produced in Germany could have been expected to comply with the requirements of German law. If they did not, they would have

[211] Cf Case C–203/96 *Dusseldorp and Others v Minister van Volkhuisvesting, Ruimtelijke Ordening en Milieubeheer* [1998] ECR I–4075, para 44, another case on environmental protection, where the Court declined to rule out recourse to the doctrine of mandatory requirements in the context of Art 29 (ex 34), even though that article only applies to national measures which are discriminatory. See the discussion by AG Jacobs at p I–4102.
[212] Cf Case C–67/97 *Bluhme* [1999] 1 CMLR 612 (national measure prohibiting the keeping of bees of certain species in a particular place justified on the ground of the protection of health and life of animals).
[213] Case 207/83 *Commission v United Kingdom* [1985] ECR 1201.   [214] Para 20.

excluded themselves from their most readily accessible market. So the German rules which prevented cassis from being marketed in Germany were more likely to be satisfied by German liqueurs than by liqueurs produced in other Member States. To borrow the language of the Court in the 'Origin Marking' case, they were applicable without distinction to domestic and imported products only in form. The same is true, *mutatis mutandis*, of the Italian rules at issue in *Gilli and Andres*: vinegar produced in Italy would have been most unlikely to contain acetic acid not derived from the acetic fermentation of wine. Such rules should only have been capable of justification, if at all, under Article 30 (ex 36) of the Treaty. It was not until later that Article 28 (ex 30) was in practice applied to genuinely non-discriminatory national measures. That development ultimately led the Court to seek ways of restricting the scope of the article, as we shall see.

Testing the limits of Article 28 (ex 30)

It was not long after 'Cassis de Dijon' before the vagaries of litigation threw up some striking examples of how broad the prohibition laid down in Article 28 (ex 30) had become. *Oosthoek's Uitgeversmaatschappij*[215] concerned the compatibility with that article of a Dutch law restricting the circumstances in which businesses could offer potential customers free gifts as an inducement to purchase their products. O marketed in several Member States a range of encyclopaedias and offered to subscribers a free dictionary, atlas or small encyclopaedia. In proceedings against it for infringement of the relevant Dutch law, it sought to rely on Article 28 (ex 30) and a reference was made to the Court of Justice. The Court declared:[216]

Legislation which restricts or prohibits certain forms of advertising and certain means of sales promotion may, although it does not directly affect imports, be such as to restrict their volume because it affects marketing opportunities for the imported products. The possibility cannot be ruled out that to compel a producer either to adopt advertising or sales promotion schemes which differ from one Member State to another or to discontinue a scheme which he considers to be particularly effective may constitute an obstacle to imports even if the legislation in question applies to domestic products and imported products without distinction.

However, the Court went on to find legislation such as that in issue justified on grounds of consumer protection and fair trading.

The *Oosthoek* case was cited by the Court in *Buet and Another v Ministère Public*, which concerned the compatibility with Article 28 (ex 30) of a French prohibition on canvassing in connection with the sale of educational material. B was the manager of a company whose representatives went to the homes of potential customers in order to sell them English-language teaching materials. This technique accounted for 90 per cent of the company's turnover. The Court found that a

---

[215] Case 286/81 [1982] ECR 4575.   [216] Para 15.

prohibition on canvassing such as that laid down by French law was to be regarded as an obstacle to imports, but that it was justified on the ground of consumer protection. The Court pointed out that, in order to benefit from one of the mandatory requirements, a national measure 'must be proportionate to the goals pursued, and if a Member State has at its disposal less restrictive means of obtaining [sic] the same goals, it is under an obligation to make use of them'.[217] Those tests were satisfied in this case. An obvious alternative to a ban on canvassing was to give purchasers the right to cancel contracts concluded in their own home. However, purchasers of educational material were particularly vulnerable to the blandishments of salesmen and an ill-considered purchase could cause long-term damage. A Member State might therefore justifiably conclude that a right of cancellation did not confer adequate protection and that a ban on canvassing at private dwellings was necessary.

Similarly, in *GB-INNO-BM*[218] the Court was asked to consider the compatibility with Article 28 (ex 30) of a national rule on advertising which prevented sales offers involving a temporary price reduction from stating the duration of the offer or referring to previous prices. The case arose out of proceedings in the Luxembourg courts against a Belgian supermarket chain, GB-INNO-BM, some of whose stores were near the border with Luxembourg. GB-INNO-BM had distributed advertising leaflets in Belgium and Luxembourg which were said by an association representing Luxembourg traders to be unlawful under Luxembourg law. It was apparent that the distribution of the leaflets in Belgium was lawful.

A preliminary argument was that Article 28 (ex 30) was irrelevant since the case was concerned solely with advertising and did not involve the movement of goods between Member States, GB-INNO-BM only selling its products in Belgium. In rejecting that argument, the Court reiterated that legislation which affected marketing opportunities was capable of restricting the volume of trade. It took the opportunity to emphasize that the benefit of Article 28 (ex 30) was not confined to the world of business:

Free movement of goods concerns not only traders but also individuals. It requires, particularly in frontier areas, that consumers resident in one Member State may travel freely to the territory of another Member State to shop under the same conditions as the local population. That freedom for consumers is compromised if they are deprived of access to advertising available in the country where purchases are made.[219]

It had been argued that the disputed legislation was justified on the ground of consumer protection, but the Court understandably found unconvincing the quaintly

[217] Case 382/87 [1989] ECR 1235, para 11.
[218] Case C–362/88 [1990] ECR I–667. Cf Case C–241/89 *SARPP* [1990] ECR I–4695 (Art 28 (ex 30) precluded the application to imports of national provisions prohibiting any allusion in the advertising of artificial sweeteners to the word 'sugar' or to the physical, chemical, or nutritional properties of sugar); Case C–126/91 *Yves Rocher* [1993] ECR I–2361 (application to imported catalogues and brochures of national law prohibiting eye-catching price comparisons incompatible with Art 28 (ex 30)).
[219] Para 8.

paternalistic view that the interests of consumers could be protected by *denying* them access to information. National rules of the type in dispute were therefore found to be caught by Article 28 (ex 30).

The measures at issue in these cases were regarded as capable of justification under the rule of reason because the Court treated them as involving non-discriminatory obstacles to trade.[220] However, like the rules challenged in 'Cassis de Dijon' and *Gilli and Andres*, the measures in question in *Oosthoek*, *Buet*, and *GB-INNO-BM* could have been regarded as discriminatory in that they required businesses to adjust marketing techniques developed in one country to the requirements of another country's rules. Businesses established in the second country could have been expected to ensure that their marketing techniques already complied with the rules in force there. It was the very difference in the impact of the national rules in question on the two categories of business which rendered those rules capable of impeding imports. In an important—but then heterodox—article published in 1984, Marenco argued that the notion of discrimination, broadly defined, remained essential to the application of the prohibition contained in Article 28 (ex 30).[221]

However, in due course cases started to emerge in which, although Article 28 (ex 30) was found to be applicable, it was difficult to detect any element of discrimination, however broadly that troublesome notion was understood. An example is *Cinéthèque v Fédération Nationale des Cinémas Français*,[222] which concerned the compatibility with Article 28 (ex 30) of national legislation on the distribution of films. Under French law, no film being shown in cinemas could at the same time be sold or hired to the public on video for private use until the expiry of a period of twelve months. The purpose of the legislation was to ensure the continued viability of the film industry, which was heavily dependent on box-office takings. French courts had granted injunctions on the basis of the legislation concerned preventing the applicants in the main actions from selling and distributing two films on video before the expiry of the twelve-month embargo. The injunctions were challenged by the applicants on the basis that the legislation in question restricted the marketing of imported videos and was therefore incompatible with Article 28 (ex 30).

The Commission maintained that the contested legislation unquestionably hindered imports of video recordings which had been lawfully produced and marketed in other Member States, although it thought that such restrictions on the free

---

[220] Cf Joined Cases C–34/95, C–35/95 and C–36/95 *KO v De Agostini and TV-Shop* [1997] ECR I–3843, paras 44–6, where the Court implied that a municipal rule on selling arrangements applying to all traders operating within the national territory was to be treated as non-discriminatory even if it had a greater impact on products imported from other Member States.

[221] See 'Pour une interprétation traditionnelle de la notion de mesure d'effet équivalant à une restriction quantitative' (1984) 20 CDE 291. Note in particular his observations on 'Cassis de Dijon' and *Gilli and Andres* at pp 306–7 and on *Oosthoek* at p 308. For further discussion, see Poiares Maduro, op cit, chs 2 and 3.

[222] Joined Cases 60 and 61/84 [1985] ECR 2605.

movement of goods might be justified on cultural grounds. Advocate General Slynn preferred a different approach:

> . . . in an area in which there are no common Community standards or rules, where a national measure is not specifically directed at imports, does not discriminate against imports, does not make it any more difficult for an importer to sell his products than it is for a domestic producer, and gives no protection to domestic producers, then in my view, *prima facie*, the measure does not fall within Article 30 [now 28] even if it does in fact lead to a restriction or reduction of imports.[223]

Article 28 (ex 30), he said, could not have been intended to grant film distributors in other Member States more favourable conditions than domestic distributors, who would be unable to rely on it because it did not apply in situations which were purely internal to a Member State.[224] He concluded that the disputed provisions were not covered by Article 28 (ex 30). Had he come to a different view on that point, he would have been prepared to accept that the provisions in question might be justified under the 'Cassis de Dijon' doctrine as necessary for the maintenance of the film industry and the supply of films to the consumer, which he considered a legitimate objective.

The Court followed the second course proposed by Advocate General Slynn. Although a system such as that in dispute did not give national producers any advantage over producers in other Member States,

> the application of such a system may create barriers to intra-Community trade in video-cassettes because of the disparities between the systems operated in the different Member States and between the conditions for the release of cinematographic works in the cinemas of those States. In those circumstances a prohibition of exploitation laid down by such a system is not compatible with the principle of the free movement of goods provided for in the Treaty unless any obstacle to intra-Community trade thereby created does not exceed that which is necessary in order to ensure the attainment of the objective in view and unless that objective is justified with regard to Community law.[225]

In the circumstances of this case, the Court considered those conditions satisfied: '. . . a national system which, in order to encourage the creation of cinematographic works irrespective of their origin, gives priority, for a limited initial period, to the distribution of such works through the cinema, is so justified'.[226]

By contrast, in the 'Milk Substitutes' case,[227] the Court found that a French ban on the importation and sale of substitutes for milk powder and concentrated milk was contrary to Article 28 (ex 30). The prohibition on the marketing of milk substitutes also covered domestic products, but the Court said that the application of

---

[223] p 2611.
[224] Cf *Oosthoek, supra,* para 9: '. . . the application of the Netherlands legislation to the sale in the Netherlands of encyclopaedias produced in that country is in no way linked to the importation or exportation of goods and does not therefore fall within the scope of Articles 30 and 34 of the EEC Treaty'. The concept of the purely internal situation is considered in more detail in relation to the free movement of workers: see ch 8.
[225] Para 22.   [226] Para 23.   [227] Case 216/84 *Commission v France* [1988] ECR 793.

national legislation to products imported from other Member States was compatible with the Treaty only if it could be justified under Article 30 (ex 36) or the rule of reason.[228] The Court did not think that any of the suggested grounds of justification had been made out.

It is hard to detect any element of discrimination in either of these cases. Importers were not being asked to change their product specifications or marketing methods to secure access to the State of importation; they were merely being subjected to the same restrictions as their domestic competitors. It is true that in the 'Milk Substitutes' case the disputed French legislation conferred protection on milk products, but France is not the only Member State which produces milk.[229] *Cinéthèque* was the more significant of the two cases, however, because the effect on trade of the measure at issue there was more remote. That case proved to be the harbinger of a series of cases in which attempts were made to rely on Article 28 (ex 30) in circumstances where the alleged obstacle to imports was extremely indirect.

In a prescient article published in 1989, White, a member of the Commission's Legal Service, argued that, as a result of the way in which the Court's case law was developing, 'complainants seeking to attack State measures will become ever more courageous in their interpretation of Article 30 [now 28] and the point will eventually come where the Court of Justice is obliged to address its attention to defining more clearly the limits of this provision rather than creating new fields of application'.[230] White rejected Marenco's thesis, that the crucial question was whether the national measure was discriminatory, as undesirable as a matter of principle and inconsistent with the case law of the Court. Instead he advocated that a distinction be drawn between national rules concerning the characteristics of imported products and those concerning the circumstances in which imported products could be sold. Rules falling within the former category would in principle be caught by Article 28 (ex 30), those falling within the latter category would not:

> as the judgment of the Court in *Cassis de Dijon* clearly shows, Member States are not entitled to require that imported products have the same *characteristics* as are required of, or are traditional in, domestic products unless this is strictly necessary for the protection of some legitimate interest. There is not, however, the same need to require the rules relating to the *circumstances* in which certain goods may be *sold or used* in the importing Member State to be overridden for this purpose as long as imported products enjoy *equal access* to the market of the importing Member State compared with national goods.[231]

Some support for this approach could be found in a line of cases decided by the Court which had hitherto been generally regarded as anomalous.[232] In *Oebel*,[233]

---

[228] Para 7. The Court treated both classes of exception as having the same effect. See the discussion of the *Aragonesa* case, *supra*.

[229] See Oliver, op cit, p 94.

[230] 'In search of the limits to Article 30 of the EEC Treaty' (1989) 26 CMLRev 235, 238.

[231] p 246, emphasis in the original.

[232] See eg Gormley, op cit, p 252; Oliver, op cit, p 94.   [233] Case 155/80 [1981] ECR 1993.

the Court was asked for guidance on the compatibility with Articles 28 (ex 30) and 29 (ex 34) of a German rule which, in order to protect workers in small and medium-sized bakeries, prohibited the transport and delivery of baker's wares to consumers or retail outlets before 5.45 a.m. The prohibition applied to all producers, whether established in Germany or in other Member States. Because it prevented producers in other Member States from delivering their wares in time to consumers and shops in Germany (and vice versa), it was said to be incompatible with Articles 28 (ex 30) and 29 (ex 34). The Court took a different view:[234]

> If such rules are confined to transport for delivery to individual consumers and retail outlets only, without affecting transport and delivery to warehouses or intermediaries, they cannot have the effect of restricting imports or exports between Member States. In this case, indeed, trade within the Community remains possible at all times, subject to the single exception that delivery to consumers and retailers is restricted to the same extent for all producers, wherever they are established. Under these circumstances, such rules are not contrary to Articles 30 [now 28] and 34 [now 29] of the Treaty.

Since the Court acknowledged that intra-Community trade was restricted and the 'Cassis de Dijon' case had established that, in the case of Article 28 (ex 30) if not that of Article 29 (ex 34),[235] it regarded the question of discrimination as irrelevant, it might have been expected to find that the disputed prohibition constituted an obstacle to the free movement of goods requiring justification. Curiously the Court had accepted earlier in its judgment that a complementary prohibition on working before 4 a.m. in the bread and confectionary industry constituted 'a legitimate element of economic and social policy, consistent with the objectives of public interest pursued by the Treaty'.[236] However, the restrictions on transport and delivery did not need justification, since even to the extent that they applied to imports they fell entirely outside the scope of Article 28 (ex 30).

Similarly, in *Blesgen v Belgium*,[237] the Court held that Article 28 (ex 30) did not apply to a ban on stocking and selling certain spirits in places open to the public. Although the ban was evidently capable of reducing imports of the spirits to which it applied, the Court said that Article 28 (ex 30) did not cover 'a legislative provision concerning only the sale of strong spirits for consumption on the premises in all places open to the public and not concerning other forms of marketing the same drinks. It is to be observed in addition that the restrictions placed on the sale of the spirits in question make no distinction whatsoever based on their nature or origin. Such a legislative measure therefore has no connection with the importation of the products and for that reason is not of such a nature as to impede trade between Member States.'[238] The same applied to the ancillary restrictions on the stocking of spirits. It is striking that, although the purpose of the disputed rules was to combat alcoholism, as in *Oebel* the Court did not require them to be justified.

---

[234] Para 20.   [235] See the *Groenveld* case, *supra*, cited in *Oebel* at para 15. Cf *Dusseldorp*, *supra*.
[236] Para 12.   [237] Case 75/81 [1982] ECR 1211.   [238] Para 9.

Again, in *Direction Générale des Impôts v Forest*,[239] the Court was asked to consider the compatibility with Article 28 (ex 30) of national legislation providing for
the allocation to mills of an annual milling quota, which could not in principle be
exceeded, for common wheat to be processed into flour. The Court observed that
the legislation did not affect imports of flour from other Member States. It continued: '. . . even though a restriction on the quantities of wheat which may be milled
may prevent millers from buying wheat, millers are free to buy imported wheat to
cover part or all of their requirements. It therefore appears that such a system of
quotas at the level of flour production in fact has no effect on wheat imports and is
not likely to impede trade between Member States.'[240] The Court did not explain
why the chance that millers might have purchased more imported wheat in the
absence of the quota system did not suffice to bring it within the scope of Article
28 (ex 30).

Less surprising was the decision in *Krantz*,[241] decided after the publication of
White's article, where the Court was asked whether Article 28 (ex 30) applied to
a national rule authorizing the tax authorities to seize certain goods found on a taxpayer's premises, even if the goods concerned belonged to a supplier in another
Member State. The Court noted that the national rule in question applied equally
to domestic and imported goods and was not designed to regulate inter-State trade.
It continued: 'the possibility that nationals of other Member States would hesitate
to sell goods on instalment terms to purchasers in the Member State concerned
because such goods would be liable to seizure by the collector of taxes if the purchasers failed to discharge their Netherlands tax debts is too uncertain and indirect
to warrant the conclusion that a national provision authorizing such seizure is liable
to hinder trade between Member States'.[242] Article 28 (ex 30) did not therefore
cover such a rule.

In the same year as *Krantz* the Court gave judgment in *Quietlynn and Richards*,[243]
where it was asked whether provisions prohibiting the sale of lawful sex articles
from unlicensed sex shops were compatible with Article 28 (ex 30). Citing its judgments in *Oebel* and *Blesgen*, the Court noted that legislation such as that in dispute
applied without distinction to imported and domestic products. It did not lay down
an absolute ban on the sale of the products to which it applied, but merely regulated the way in which they could be distributed. Moreover, 'the marketing of
products imported from other Member States is not rendered any more difficult
than that of domestic products'.[244] The Court also declared that the disputed provisions had 'no connection with intra-Community trade', since the products covered by them could be marketed through licensed sex shops and other channels.[245]
The Court concluded that those provisions were not intended to regulate the

---

[239] Case 148/85 [1986] ECR 3449.   [240] Para 19.
[241] Case C–69/88 [1990] ECR I–583.   [242] Para 11.
[243] Case C–23/89 [1990] ECR I–3059.   [244] Para 9.
[245] The Court mentioned mail order and shops which did not have to be licensed because sex articles accounted for only an insignificant proportion of their sales.

movement of goods between Member States and were not therefore such as to impede intra-Community trade. The question of justification was not addressed in the judgment.

The demise of the *Dassonville* formula?

White represented the Commission in *Quietlynn and Richards* and the Court's decision might have been seen as endorsing the views he had advanced in his 1989 article: the disputed national provisions did not relate to the characteristics of the products to which they applied but to the circumstances in which they could be sold. Moreover, they were truly non-discriminatory in that the restrictions they imposed affected imports and domestic products in exactly the same way. However, the apparently anomalous nature of this approach was underlined by another case decided less than a year before *Quietlynn and Richards* in which the views of White, who again represented the Commission, seemed to be comprehensively rejected. The case, *Torfaen Borough Council v B & Q PLC*,[246] was the first in a series in which the Court was called upon to consider the compatibility with Article 28 (ex 30) of national rules restricting Sunday trading. The issues raised by the case were deceptive in their simplicity and the difficulty the Court experienced in dealing with them marked the beginning of the end for the *Dassonville* formula in the broad sense in which it had come to be widely understood.

The Sunday trading cases

The *Torfaen* case arose out of a challenge by a large retailer to the compatibility with Article 28 (ex 30) of the restrictions on Sunday trading contained in section 47 of the United Kingdom Shops Act 1950. That section, which applied only to England and Wales, required shops to close on Sundays except for the purposes of transactions listed in the fifth schedule to the Act. The effect of that schedule was bizarre in the extreme. It permitted the sale of fish and chips on a Sunday from an Indian takeaway but not from a fish and chip shop. High street newsagents could open on Sundays for the sale of pornographic magazines but not the Bible. B & Q was a large do-it-yourself store which was prosecuted by the Council, which had responsibility under the Act for enforcing section 47 in its district, for selling goods on Sundays which were not authorized under the fifth schedule. In its defence, B & Q argued that many of the goods it sold on Sundays were imported from other Member States. If it had to close on that day, much of the trade lost would not be recovered during the rest of the week. Section 47 therefore had the effect of reducing the volume of imports from other Member States into England and Wales and

---

[246] Case C–145/88 [1989] ECR 3851. Four of the five Judges who sat in *Torfaen* also sat in *Quietlynn and Richards*. The juxtaposition of the two cases is underlined by Gormley, 'Recent case law on the free movement of goods: some hot potatoes' (1990) 27 CMLRev 825, 829.

was as a result incompatible with Article 28 (ex 30). A reference was made to the Court of Justice.

In view of the then prevailing trend of the case law, the Court might have been expected to respond as follows. According to *Dassonville*, Article 28 (ex 30) caught all national measures which were capable of hindering, directly or indirectly, actually or potentially, trade between Member States. A measure such as the Shops Act which affected imports and domestically produced goods in the same way would, however, be compatible with Article 28 (ex 30) if it could be justified as necessary to satisfy a mandatory requirement. None of the mandatory requirements which had hitherto been recognized by the Court seemed apt to apply to a measure like the Shops Act, but the category of mandatory requirements was not closed. However, even if it were to be extended, it would have to be shown that the disputed measure was suitable for achieving its aims and that it went no further than was absolutely necessary to do so. A more controversial alternative would have been to adopt the approach subsequently taken in *Quietlynn and Richards*, in other words to say that the disputed measure treated imports in the same way as domestic goods, neither of which were the subject of an absolute prohibition on sale. It was to be considered unconnected with inter-State trade, which it was not designed to regulate, and therefore fell outside the scope of Article 28 (ex 30).

A potential difficulty with the second approach was that the referring court had found that the disputed legislation had actually reduced the defendant's total sales and that about 10 per cent of the goods it sold came from other Member States. As Advocate General van Gerven pointed out,[247] '[t]he Court is therefore asked to assume that there is a causal link between the contested legislation and the reduction in imports; such a link was not found in the *Oebel, Blesgen* or *Forest* cases'. That factor need not have caused the Court undue difficulty. It was self-evident that the measures at issue in those cases were at least capable of impeding imports and the Court has never required evidence of an *actual* effect on imports before Article 28 (ex 30) can apply. In *Quietlynn and Richards*, the Court was also asked to assume a reduction in sales of imported material,[248] yet this did not prevent it from applying the *Oebel/Blesgen* line of cases.

Advocate General van Gerven also expressed unease about the first approach, involving what he described[249] as 'a "mechanical" application' of the *Dassonville* formula. In the Advocate General's view, the great disadvantage of that approach was 'that the Court will inevitably have to decide in an increasing number of cases on the reasonableness of policy decisions of Member States taken in the innumerable spheres where there is no question of direct or indirect, factual or legal discrimination against, or detriment to, imported products. The question may arise

---

[247] p 3868.

[248] See the referring court's first question; Keeling, 'The free movement of goods in EEC law: basic principles and recent developments in the case law of the Court of Justice of the European Communities' (1992) 26 The International Lawyer 467, 477.

[249] At p 3879.

whether excessive demands would not then be put on the Court, which would be confronted with countless new "mandatory requirements" and grounds of justification.'[250]

The Advocate General therefore sought ways of defining and limiting the scope of Article 28 (ex 30). He argued that the article was automatically applicable to national rules which 'screened off' a national market. However,

[i]f the national rule at issue merely increases the difficulty in penetrating the national market, the prohibition in Article 30 [now 28] is applicable only if it appears from the entire legal and economic context that the economic interweaving of national markets sought by the Treaty is thereby threatened. In such a case, the compartmentalization of the market should be made sufficiently probable by a number of quantitative factors which show that the application of the rule makes it more difficult to penetrate the market, thereby rendering the market so inaccessible (expensive, unprofitable) that it must be feared that the majority of imported goods will disappear from the market.[251]

Whatever the theoretical merits of that approach, it would have left too much to the discretion of the national courts to be workable in practice[252] and it did not commend itself to the Court. Without mentioning either *Dassonville* or 'Cassis de Dijon', the Court said that it was necessary to consider whether, having regard to their aim, rules such as those in dispute, which applied to imported and domestic products alike, were justified under Community law. Referring to its judgment in *Oebel*, the Court said that national rules concerning the opening hours of retail premises constituted a legitimate part of economic and social policy which was consistent with the objectives of the Treaty: 'Such rules reflect certain political and economic choices in so far as their purpose is to ensure that working and non-working hours are so arranged as to accord with national or regional socio-cultural characteristics, and that, in the present state of Community law, is a matter for the Member States.'[253] The Court added that such rules were 'not designed to govern the patterns of trade between Member States'.[254] Referring to Article 3 of Directive 70/50, the Court explained that it was then necessary to establish whether 'the effects of such national rules exceed what is necessary to achieve the aim in view'.[255] That was a question of fact to be determined by the national court.

On a theoretical level, the terseness of the Court's reasoning in *Torfaen* made it difficult to situate the decision within its existing case law on Article 28 (ex 30). However, although the Court did not use the expression 'mandatory (or imperative) requirements', the better view seemed to be that the decision represented an application of the 'Cassis de Dijon' doctrine: the disputed legislation, being non-discriminatory, would not be caught by Article 28 (ex 30) if it could be justified as necessary to accord with national or regional sociocultural characteristics, a

---

[250] p 3880.   [251] p 3878.
[252] See Mortelmans, 'Article 30 of the EEC Treaty and legislation relating to market circumstances: time to consider a new definition?' (1991) 28 CMLRev 115, 127; Oliver, op cit, p 97.
[253] Para 14.   [254] Ibid.   [255] Para 15.

consideration which constituted a new mandatory requirement.[256] It was possible
to argue, however, that, because Sunday trading rules are less restrictive of trade
than the measures at issue in 'Cassis de Dijon', the Court intended to introduce a
lower standard of justification for such rules.[257] There was virtually universal agreement that, whatever the Court meant, it had performed a lamentable job in
explaining its approach. Moreover, a serious practical difficulty soon began to
emerge: national courts called upon to apply the Court's ruling were reaching different conclusions about the purpose of the Shops Act and about whether it satisfied the principle of proportionality. Thus, section 47 was found to be enforceable
in Torfaen but not in Shrewsbury and Atcham.[258]

While the English courts were struggling to apply the ruling in *Torfaen*, the
Court gave two further rulings on Sunday trading, this time in connection with
French and Belgian legislation respectively which restricted the employment of
workers on Sundays. In *Conforama and Others*[259] and *Marchandise and Others*,[260] the
Court declared that 'the restrictive effects on trade which may stem from such rules
do not seem disproportionate to the aim pursued'. The Court did not trouble to
explain why it had decided to perform itself a task which in *Torfaen* it had expressly
said was the responsibility of the national courts. In *Council of the City of
Stoke-on-Trent and Another v B & Q*,[261] the House of Lords asked the Court
whether its decisions in *Conforama* and *Marchandise* meant that Article 28 (ex 30)
did not apply to rules such as those at issue in *Torfaen*. If this was not the case, the
Court was also asked on what basis national courts were to establish whether such
rules were excessively restrictive of intra-Community trade. In its judgment, the
Court acknowledged that the answer to the question whether a particular measure
was compatible with Community law 'cannot be allowed to vary according to the
findings of fact made by individual courts in particular cases'.[262] In determining
whether a national rule satisfied the principle of proportionality, the Court said it
was necessary to consider whether any restrictive effects it produced on the free

[256] This was the view taken by the present author: see 'What shall we do on Sunday?' (1991) 16
ELRev 112.
[257] See Keeling, op cit, p 480. Cf the views of AG van Gerven in Case C–306/88 *Rochdale BC v
Anders* [1992] ECR I–6457, 6477–9, and Joined Cases C–267 and C–268/91 *Keck and Mithouard* [1993]
ECR I–6097, 6121, and those of AG Tesauro in Case C–292/92 *Hünermund and Others* [1993] ECR
I–6787, 6806–7.
[258] See *Torfaen BC v B & Q plc* [1990] 3 CMLR 455, where s 47 was found compatible with Art 28
(ex 30), and *B & Q Ltd v Shrewsbury and Atcham BC* [1990] 3 CMLR 535, where it was found that the
objective of the Shops Act could be achieved by other means which would be less restrictive of inter-
State trade. For a useful summary of the variety of conclusions reached by English courts on the compatibility of the Shops Act with Art 28 (ex 30) in the light of the Court's ruling, see Steiner, 'Drawing
the line: uses and abuses of Article 30 EEC' (1992) 29 CMLRev 749, 760–2.
[259] Case C–312/89 [1991] ECR I–997, para 12.
[260] Case C–332/89 [1991] ECR I–1027, para 13.
[261] Case C–169/91 [1992] ECR I–6635. See also Case C–306/88 *Rochdale BC v Anders* [1992] ECR
I–6457; Case C–304/90 *Reading BC v Payless DIY* [1992] ECR I–6493; Arnull, 'Anyone for tripe?'
(1993) 18 ELRev 314.
[262] Para 14.

movement of goods 'are direct, indirect or purely speculative and whether those effects do not impede the marketing of imported products more than the marketing of national products'.[263] On the basis of those considerations, the Court concluded that Article 28 (ex 30) did not apply to national legislation which prohibited retailers from opening on Sundays.

The conclusion of this protracted saga—that section 47 of the Shops Act was compatible with Article 28 (ex 30)—was widely thought to be unobjectionable.[264] It may, however, be thought that the Court failed to examine closely enough the purpose which a measure like the Act was intended to serve. It might be possible to identify the purpose of a measure laying down a complete prohibition on Sunday trading or of a measure which, while prohibiting Sunday trading in principle, permitted exceptions in certain objectively justified cases. But where, as in the case of the fifth schedule to the Shops Act, the list of exceptions is almost entirely arbitrary, it becomes much more difficult to say what the purpose of the measure is. If the purpose is this, why can this product be sold on Sundays but not that one? Where the purpose of the measure cannot be established, it becomes impossible to describe it as necessary to reflect national or regional sociocultural characteristics. Even if the purpose can be established, those seeking to enforce the measure might be expected to explain why the sale of one product has to be prohibited in order to achieve that purpose when the sale of another does not. The Court's unwillingness to address these issues reflected a feeling that the Shops Act simply had nothing to do with the free movement of goods.

The ruling in *Keck and Mithouard*

The judgment in *Stoke-on-Trent* suggested that the Court was on the verge of a new departure in its case law, for it showed that it would not be difficult to justify an indistinctly applicable national rule which, although in principle caught by Article 28 (ex 30), produced only an indirect or purely speculative effect on the free movement of goods. The ruling indicated that the notion of discrimination, hitherto relevant only to the grounds on which a national measure might be justified, was in future to assume a much larger role in establishing whether Article 28 (ex 30) had been infringed. The Court's ruling might cause the observer to feel some sympathy for Advocate General van Gerven. In *Torfaen*, he suggested a new approach but his advice was rejected. The Court's judgment was terse and unhelpful, but was reasonably capable of being interpreted as a conventional application of previous case law. The continued validity of the conventional approach seemed to be confirmed by the rulings in *Conforama* and *Marchandise*. Thus, in *Stoke-on-Trent* Advocate General van Gerven declared that in the light of those cases 'it is clearly

---

[263] Para 15.

[264] Even Gormley, an outspoken critic of the Court's failure to apply the *Dassonville* formula coupled with the rule of reason, seemed to regard the argument of the Sunday traders as lacking in 'integrationist merit': see (1990) 27 CMLRev 141, 150.

established that the Court's broad *Dassonville* and *Cassis-de-Dijon* formula continues to apply with undiminished scope'.[265] It was in that case that the Court chose
to suggest that this was no longer so.[266]

The *Stoke-on-Trent* case was merely a foretaste of what was to come. In *Keck and
Mithouard*[267] the Court finally pulled the rabbit out of the hat. That case concerned
the compatibility with Article 28 (ex 30) of national legislation prohibiting resale
at a loss. The defendants were the managers of supermarkets situated in France near
the German border. They were prosecuted for selling beer and coffee at a loss,
which was an offence under French law. In their defence, they sought to rely on
Article 28 (ex 30). Advocate General van Gerven thought that a prohibition against
resale at a loss was capable of hindering inter-State trade within the meaning of the
Dassonville formula. Selling at a loss was a method of promoting sales and, since
Oosthoek, the Court had treated national legislation restricting certain means of sales
promotion as capable of falling within Article 28 (ex 30). Moreover, the contested
legislation was capable of affecting trade between Member States. It was true that
it did not prevent manufacturers from selling at a loss, but it prevented a retailer
from launching an imported product on the French market by selling it at a loss
without the help of its foreign manufacturer. The same potential obstacle to
imports would arise where an importer of a product from another Member State
found himself in competition with a domestic manufacturer who, unlike the
importer, would be free to sell at a loss. Since the disputed legislation was indistinctly applicable, the question therefore arose whether it could be justified under
the 'Cassis de Dijon' doctrine. The referring court had suggested that it might be
justified on the grounds of consumer protection and the protection of healthy and
fair competition. The Advocate General accepted that a prohibition on resale at a
loss might be capable of justification on those grounds, but thought that the disputed legislation was too broad in scope, since it prevented such resale even where
there was no threat to the consumer or to fair competition. He mentioned in particular selling at a loss to launch a new product or penetrate a new market or to dispose of surplus stock. Since resale at a loss was also prevented by the disputed
legislation in these circumstances, that legislation could not be justified and was
therefore caught by Article 28 (ex 30).

The reasoning of the Advocate General might well have been thought unimpeachable. It corresponded broadly with the view put forward by the Commission
(not this time represented by White), which maintained that legislation such as that
in dispute was caught by Article 28 (ex 30) and could not be justified. However,
the chamber to which the case had been assigned decided to refer it to the full
Court. In a second Opinion delivered some months later, the Advocate General
modified the conclusion he had reached. The facts of the present cases were, he

---

[265] [1992] ECR I–6457, 6471.

[266] But see AG van Gerven's discussion of *Stoke-on-Trent* in *Keck and Mithouard, infra*, pp I–6122–3.

[267] Joined Cases C–267 and C–268/91 [1993] ECR I–6097. See the very full discussion of the case
and its aftermath in Oliver, op cit, pp 100–10.

said, unconnected with the hypotheses on the basis of which he had argued in his
first Opinion that the application of a prohibition on resale at a loss would be unjustified. He therefore suggested that the Court answer the questions which had been
referred to it by saying that, *in the circumstances of the main actions*, the application of
legislation prohibiting resale at a loss was compatible with Article 28 (ex 30).

When an Advocate General gives more than one Opinion in the same case and
they differ as to the result, the Court is like an orchestra without a conductor. Its
reasoning in *Keck and Mithouard* owed little to the advice it had received from
Advocate General van Gerven. The Court began by reiterating the *Dassonville* formula (although it did not mention that case by name). It noted that it was not the
purpose of national legislation prohibiting resale at a loss to regulate inter-State
trade. It acknowledged that, by depriving businesses of a method of sales promotion, such legislation was capable of reducing sales of products from other Member
States. This in itself was not sufficient, however, to enable the legislation to be
described as a MEE. The Court then said that '[i]n view of the increasing tendency
of traders to invoke Article 30 [now 28] of the Treaty as a means of challenging any
rules whose effect is to limit their commercial freedom even where such rules are
not aimed at products from other Member States, the Court considers it necessary
to re-examine and clarify its case-law on this matter'.[268] Traders are of course perfectly entitled to invoke Article 28 (ex 30) where the Court's case law suggests it
might have been breached. If the Court had failed to make clear where the limits
of Article 28 (ex 30) were to be found, it had no one to blame but itself.[269] Having
referred to its decision in 'Cassis de Dijon', the Court then declared:[270]

However, contrary to what has previously been decided, the application to products from
other Member States of national provisions restricting or prohibiting certain selling arrangements is not such as to hinder directly or indirectly, actually or potentially, trade between
Member States within the meaning of the *Dassonville* judgment . . ., provided that those provisions apply to all affected traders operating within the national territory and provided that
they affect in the same manner, in law and in fact, the marketing of domestic products and
of those from other Member States.

Where those conditions are fulfilled, the application of such rules to the sale of products
from another Member State meeting the requirements laid down by that State is not by
nature such as to prevent their access to the market or to impede access any more than it
impedes the access of domestic products. Such rules therefore fall outside the scope of Article
30 [now 28] of the Treaty.

This passage was evidently designed to mark a deliberate retreat from the position
as it had hitherto been understood.[271] The suggestion in *Stoke-on-Trent* that the

---

[268] Para 14.

[269] This was acknowledged by Due, who was President of the Court when *Keck and Mithouard* was
decided: see '*Dassonville* revisited or no cause for alarm?' in Campbell and Voyatzi (eds), *Legal Reasoning
and Judicial Interpretation of European Law* (1996), p 19 at p 27.   [270] Paras 16–17.

[271] See generally Weatherill, 'After *Keck*: some thoughts on how to clarify the clarification' (1996)
33 CMLRev 885; Picod, 'La nouvelle approche de la Cour de justice en matière d'entraves aux
échanges' (1998) 34 RTDE 169.

notion of discrimination was henceforth to assume greater importance was resoundingly confirmed. However, the Court's failure to specify the cases it now considered to have gone too far was profoundly unsatisfactory.[272] It is clear from a subsequent ruling of the Court[273] that national legislation on the closure of shops on Sundays is no longer regarded as caught by Article 30 where it does not affect the marketing of products from other Member States any differently from the marketing of domestic products. Few will shed tears at the demise of the pre-*Keck and Mithouard* case law to the effect that such legislation needed to be justified. But if the Court also intended to overrule cases like *Oosthoek*, *Buet*, and *GB-INNO-BM*, its decision can only be regarded as retrograde. The irony of taking such a step so soon after the completion of the single market did not go unremarked.[274]

Moreover, the Court's reasoning seemed contradictory. The Court had reiterated at the outset that 'any measure which is capable of directly or indirectly, actually or potentially, hindering intra-Community trade' constituted a MEE.[275] It then acknowledged that legislation such as that in issue was capable of restricting the volume of imported products sold in a Member State. None the less, the Court concluded that such legislation, provided it affected imports and domestic goods in the same way, did not even indirectly or potentially hinder trade. The Court would have done better to abandon the pretence that it was still adhering to the *Dassonville* formula and simply state that national rules restricting selling arrangements were not caught by Article 28 (ex 30) where they did not impede the access of imported products to the market of a Member State any more than they impeded the access of national products.

It is also strange that the Court should have chosen *Keck and Mithouard* to effect such a fundamental *revirement* in its case law. Unlike rules on Sunday trading, the legislation preventing resale at a loss was purely economic in character and did not seem to involve any particularly sensitive areas of national culture or morals. Had the Court been really anxious to avoid condemning it as contrary to Article 28 (ex 30), it could have found it justified on grounds of fairness in commercial transactions or (less convincingly) consumer protection. Alternatively, it might simply have reiterated that Article 30 did not apply to situations which were purely internal to a single Member State.[276]

[272] Cf the Opinion of AG Tesauro in Case C–292/92 *Hünermund and Others* [1993] ECR I–6787, 6813.

[273] Joined Cases C–69/93 and C–258/93 *Punto Casa and PPV* [1994] ECR I–2355. Cf Joined Cases C–418/93, C–419/93, C–420/93, C–421/93, C–460/93, C–461/93, C–462/93, C–464/93, C–9/94, C–10/94, C–11/94, C–14/94, C–15/94, C–23/94, C–24/94 and C–332/94 *Semeraro Casa Uno Srl and Others v Sindaco del Comune di Erbusco and Others* [1996] ECR I–2975. See also Joined Cases C–401/92 and C–402/92 *Tankstation 't Heukske and Boermans* [1994] ECR I–2199.

[274] Waelbroeck, 'L'arrêt *Keck et Mithouard*: les conséquences pratiques' (1994) JTDE 160, cited in Oliver, op cit, p 107.

[275] See also Joined Cases C–277/91, C–318/91 and C–319/91 *Ligur Carni* [1993] ECR I–6621, para 35. The Court regarded the measure at issue in that case as bearing more heavily on imports: see para 38.

[276] See Gormley, 'Reasoning renounced? The remarkable judgment in *Keck & Mithouard*' (1994) EBLR 63, 66; *Oosthoek*, supra, para 9.

The approach preferred by the Court must have given considerable satisfaction to Marenco and particularly White, whose views were substantially endorsed. It also seems to have been influenced by the Opinion of Advocate General Tesauro in *Hünermund*, which was delivered less than a month previously. In that case, the Court was asked whether a professional rule preventing pharmacists from advertising certain products outside their pharmacies was caught by Article 28 (ex 30). The Advocate General was highly critical of the Court's case law on the subject: it was inconsistent and in some cases too broad. He took the view that it had the effect of encouraging traders to attack an ever larger category of national measures which restricted their commercial freedom and invited the Court to distance itself expressly from some of its previous case law.[277] He took the view that, in the absence of any obstacle to the free movement of the products concerned within the Community or disparity between the laws of the Member States concerned, the concept of MEE did not extend to national rules which were capable of reducing imports purely because of their effect on sales. In its judgment, the Court followed the line it had taken in *Keck and Mithouard*, which had in the meantime been decided. The relevant section of its judgment started with a ritual but now largely meaningless incantation of the *Dassonville* formula but ended with the observation that a national measure such as that in issue which affected all products regardless of their origin and which applied to all pharmacists within the jurisdiction of a professional body did not affect the marketing of products from other Member States any more than that of national products. Such a measure was not therefore caught by Article 28 (ex 30).

Restrictions on advertising can have a serious effect on the interpenetration of national markets envisaged by the Treaty.[278] Indeed, in *Hünermund* the Court accepted[279] that the contested measure, like that at issue in *Keck and Mithouard*, was capable of reducing sales of imported products. In the light of that finding, it is an abuse of language to say, as the Court did, that such a measure is not capable, indirectly or potentially, of hindering intra-Community trade. However, it may be noted that the measure at issue in *Hünermund* did not stop pharmacists from selling the products concerned, nor did it lay down a complete ban on advertising them: they could be sold in other retail outlets which were in principle free to advertise them.[280] Moreover, as Advocate General Tesauro pointed out,[281] the gravamen of the applicants' complaint was not that imports were being impeded but that pharmacists were being placed at a disadvantage by comparison with other traders selling the same products. Any adverse effect produced by the disputed legislation on the free movement of goods might therefore have been considered insignificant.

---

[277] Unlike the Court in *Keck and Mithouard*, AG Tesauro was prepared to mention specific cases: see p I–6813. Did the Court's failure to do so mean that it agreed or disagreed with his view of them?

[278] For discussion of the role of advertising, see AG Jacobs in Case C–412/93 *Leclerc-Siplec v TF1 Publicité* and *M6 Publicité* [1995] ECR I–179, 186–7.

[279] See para 20.

[280] See the Report for the Hearing, p I–6791.

[281] At p I–6814.

Does Article 28 (ex 30) perhaps only apply where the effect of a national measure on inter-State trade is appreciable? That question is addressed below.

What are selling arrangements?

One of the Court's main objectives in *Keck and Mithouard* seems to have been to introduce a degree of certainty into the law relating to the free movement of goods: only in this way could the troublesome tendency of traders continually to test the limits of Article 28 (ex 30) be curbed. The Court sought to achieve that objective by introducing the distinction between requirements to be met by goods themselves (the Court mentioned by way of example requirements relating to 'designation, form, size, weight, composition, presentation, labelling, packaging')[282] and 'national provisions restricting or prohibiting certain selling arrangements'.[283] Since it was in relation to the latter class of national measure that the decision marked a new departure, the Court might have been expected to offer a definition of the concept of a selling arrangement, but none was forthcoming. In *Hünermund*, Advocate General Tesauro referred to such matters as *who* may sell a product and *where*, *when*, and *how* this is permitted.[284] However, it is far from clear that the distinction is workable.[285] In *Verband Sozialer Wettbewerb v Clinique Laboratories and Estée Lauder*,[286] the Court was asked for guidance on the effect of Article 28 (ex 30) in the context of an attempt by a trade association to prevent, on the basis of German rules on unfair competition and consumer protection, the marketing in Germany of cosmetics under the name 'Clinique'. The argument was that consumers might be misled into believing that the products in question had medicinal qualities. However, they were presented as cosmetics and were not sold in Germany in pharmacies but in perfumeries and the cosmetics departments of large stores. The Court found that '[t]he clinical or medical connotations of the word "Clinique" are not sufficient to make that word so misleading as to justify the prohibition of its use on products marketed in the aforesaid circumstances'.[287] Article 28 (ex 30) would therefore be infringed by a national rule which prevented such products from being imported and sold.

The judgment makes it clear that the disputed national rules, relating as they did to the designation of the products affected, were regarded by the Court as laying down requirements to be met by the goods themselves. However, as Oliver pointed out,[288] 'the idea that the name under which a product is sold constitutes one of its inherent characteristics is by no means unassailable: there is a fine line indeed between restrictions on the use of allegedly misleading names and

---

[282] *Keck and Mithouard*, para 15.   [283] Ibid, para 16.
[284] At p I–6803. Cf White, op cit, p 247, who refers to cases relating to 'where, when, by whom, or how [a product] may be sold or used or at what price it may be sold'.
[285] See Reich, 'The "November revolution" of the European Court of Justice: *Keck, Meng* and *Audi* revisited' (1994) 31 CMLRev 459, 471–2 and 486.
[286] Case C–315/92 [1994] ECR I–317.   [287] Para 23.   [288] Op cit, p 102.

restrictions on advertising and promotion . . .'. Reich, who was strongly critical of the distinction drawn by the Court, observed that '[t]oday's marketing mix derives from a uniform concept of product presentation, advertising and sales promotion . . .'.[289] That view seems to be borne out by the *Familiapress* case,[290] where the Court was asked to consider the compatibility with Article 28 (ex 30) of national legislation preventing the sale of periodicals containing prize competitions. The Member State concerned said that Article 28 (ex 30) was not applicable because offering readers the opportunity to take part in competitions was merely a way of promoting sales. It therefore constituted a selling arrangement for the purposes of the judgment in *Keck and Mithouard*. That argument was rejected by the Court on the basis that the contested national legislation 'bears on the actual content of the products, in so far as the competitions in question form an integral part of the magazine in which they appear'.[291] The fact remains, however, that the inclusion of prize competitions in many of the periodicals affected would have been incidental to their main purpose. It seems arbitrary for a practice designed essentially to boost sales to be treated as within the scope of Article 28 (ex 30) simply because it happens to affect the content of the products concerned.

Nous ne regrettons rien

The dangers inherent in the Court's new approach were underlined by Advocate General Lenz in *Commission v Greece* ('Infant Formula'),[292] where the Commission sought a declaration under Article 226 (ex 169) EC that Greece had infringed Article 28 (ex 30) by requiring that processed milk for infants should in principle only be sold by pharmacies.[293] The Advocate General observed:[294]

Admittedly, a sales monopoly effectuated by a State measure is a selling arrangement, but it is capable of guiding and channelling sales. This compulsorily excludes other sales channels, which is certainly capable of adversely affecting imports. Since the use in certain circumstances of proven distribution systems is forbidden, this makes product marketing more onerous and more expensive, which has a direct effect on imports. The development of new manners of marketing may in these circumstances prove more difficult for foreign manufacturers than for domestic ones, who are familiar with conditions on the home market. Rules governing the marketing of a product or a group of products generally are more intensive in their effects than rules governing general conditions of sale.

He concluded that the contested legislation constituted a MEE and dismissed the attempts of the Greek Government to show that it was justified by the need to protect the health of infants.

The Court declined to follow the advice of Advocate General Lenz, maintaining that Article 28 (ex 30) was inapplicable in these circumstances because the

[289] Op cit, p 471.   [290] *Supra.*   [291] Para 11.
[292] Case C–391/92 [1995] ECR I–1621.
[293] There was an exception for municipalities which did not possess a pharmacy.
[294] At p I–1629 (footnotes omitted).

disputed rules amounted to selling arrangements within the meaning of *Keck and Mithouard* and the conditions laid down in that case were satisfied. The Commission had pointed out that Greece did not produce any infant formula, a fact which Advocate General Lenz had considered significant: 'since *in fact only* the marketing of products from other Member States is affected, the measure must be categorized as a measure having equivalent effect'.[295] The Court took a different view:[296]

> The application of Article 30 [now 28] of the Treaty to a national measure for the general regulation of commerce, which concerns all the products concerned without distinction according to their origin, cannot depend on such a purely fortuitous factual circumstance, which may, moreover, change with the passage of time. If it did, this would have the illogical consequence that the same legislation would fall under Article 30 [now 28] in certain Member States but fall outside the scope of that provision in other Member States.

The Court said that the position would be different where the legislation in issue protected similar or competing domestic products, but that that was not the case here. It therefore concluded that the contested legislation fell outside the scope of Article 28 (ex 30).

It is submitted that the legislation at issue in the 'Infant Formula' case was no less inimical to the free movement of goods than that at issue in *Clinique Laboratories*. The 'illogicality' of making the applicability of Article 28 (ex 30) depend on whether or not the Member State concerned actually produced the product in question would, in the pre-*Keck and Mithouard* era, have been resolved by saying, not that it applied in neither case, but that it applied in both. The latter result, it is submitted, is better calculated to promote the free movement of goods, although it is admittedly not one the Court could have been expected to reach so soon after *Keck and Mithouard*.

Advocate General Lenz was not the first Advocate General to seek to divert the Court from the path on which it had set out. Unease at the reasoning of the Court in *Keck and Mithouard* was also expressed by Advocate General Jacobs in *Leclerc-Siplec v TFI Publicité and M6 Publicité*,[297] which arose out of a challenge, based *inter alia* on Article 28 (ex 30), by a distributor of petrol and other fuels in France to a French rule preventing the distribution sector from advertising on television. One of the purposes of the rule was to protect France's regional daily press by increasing its advertising revenue. Advocate General Jacobs said that he considered the Court's reasoning in *Keck and Mithouard* unsatisfactory for two reasons. First, it was 'inappropriate to make rigid distinctions between different categories of rules, and to apply different tests depending on the category to which different rules belong'.[298] Measures affecting selling arrangements might create serious obstacles to trade, he said, and he gave the example of a rule permitting certain products to be sold exclusively in a limited number of small shops in a Member

---

[295] See p I–1630, emphasis in the original. [296] Para 17.
[297] Case C–412/93 [1995] ECR I–179. [298] p I–194.

State. Such a rule 'would be almost as restrictive as an outright ban on importation and marketing'.[299] Advocate General Jacobs's second objection was that the Court's new approach effectively introduced a test of discrimination in relation to selling arrangements. Such a test he thought inconsistent with the aims of the Treaty: 'If an obstacle to inter-State trade exists, it cannot cease to exist simply because an identical obstacle affects domestic trade.'[300]

In the view of the Advocate General, the guiding principle was 'that all undertakings which engage in a legitimate economic activity in a Member State should have unfettered access to the whole of the Community market, unless there is a valid reason for denying them full access to a part of that market'. The appropriate test for determining whether Article 28 (ex 30) applied was accordingly whether there was 'a substantial restriction on that access', in other words a *de minimis* test.[301] Such a test would not be applicable to measures which discriminated against imports for they were prohibited by Article 28 (ex 30) *per se*, even where their effect on trade was only slight. Moreover, he thought that rules laying down requirements which goods must meet (the first category mentioned by the Court in *Keck and Mithouard*) inevitably created a substantial barrier to trade. Restrictions on selling arrangements, however, would also be caught by Article 28 (ex 30), even if non-discriminatory, where they were liable substantially to restrict access to the market. In the Advocate General's view, the measure at issue in the present case, like that at issue in *Keck and Mithouard*, could not be said to have a substantial impact on access to the market. It therefore fell outside the scope of Article 28 (ex 30).[302]

The Court declined to adopt the reasoning suggested by Advocate General Jacobs and simply applied the *Keck and Mithouard* formula. The disputed legislation concerned selling arrangements for the purposes of that case because it prohibited 'a particular form of promotion (televised advertising) of a particular method of marketing products (distribution)'.[303] Although the legislation was capable of reducing sales, it did not prevent distributors from using other forms of advertising. It therefore fell outside the scope of Article 28 (ex 30).

If the result in *Leclerc-Siplec* was unexceptionable, one can only regret that the Court did not take the opportunity to bring some restrictions on selling arrangements back within the scope of Article 28 (ex 30). Whether a *de minimis* test can play a useful role in defining the ambit of that article is controversial. In *Hünermund*, Advocate General Tesauro said that in his view such a test would be very difficult, if not impossible, to apply in the context of the free movement of goods because

---

[299] White would probably assimilate such a rule to a prohibition: op cit, p 258, where he gives the example of a national rule stipulating that cigarettes may only be sold on Christmas Day.
[300] p I–194.   [301] p I–195.
[302] Cf Joined Cases C–34/95, C–35/95 and C–36/95 *KO v De Agostini and TV-Shop* [1997] ECR I–3843, where it was argued that television advertising was the only effective form of advertising available. There is an apparent contradiction in the English text of that judgment between paras 40, 44, and 45 on the one hand and para 47 (which also appears in the operative part) on the other. However, comparison with the French text reveals this to be due to a mistranslation.
[303] Para 22.

of the difficulty of proving that hypothetical effects might be substantial in character.[304] As Advocate General Jacobs acknowledged in *Leclerc-Siplec*, a *de minimis* test has in some cases been ruled out by the Court: in *Prantl*, for example, the Court said that, for national measures to be caught by Article 28 (ex 30), it was not necessary 'that they should have an appreciable effect on intra-Community trade'.[305] However, the Court's approach on this point, as on so many others in this context, has not been consistent. In *Krantz*,[306] it will be recalled, it stated that the possibility that the contested national provision would discourage traders in other Member States from selling goods to purchasers in the Netherlands was 'too uncertain and indirect' for the provision to be regarded as liable to hinder trade. Similarly, in the *Stoke-on-Trent* case,[307] the Court said that, in assessing whether a national rule satisfied the principle of proportionality, it was necessary to examine whether any effect it had on trade was 'direct, indirect or purely speculative'. Thus, the Court has in some contexts examined (or required the national courts to examine) the extent of a measure's effect, actual or potential, on trade.

Conclusion

It is submitted that the search for a simple test which distinguishes national measures which pose a genuine threat to the free movement of goods from others which only erect indirect obstacles to imports is unlikely to be successful.[308] The demands of certainty and effectiveness can, in this context at least, only to a limited extent be reconciled. If the *Dassonville* formula and the 'Cassis de Dijon' doctrine tended to give priority to the latter consideration, *Keck and Mithouard* represented an attempt to reinforce the former, but it served only to undermine both. It is going too far to say that restrictions on selling arrangements, even if applicable in the same way to domestic goods and to imports, can *never* hinder trade between Member States. In any event, national courts do not seem to find the new approach much

---

[304] This he described as a '*probatio diabolica*': see [1993] ECR I–6787, 6811. A similar view is taken by Oliver, op cit, pp 109–10.

[305] Case 16/83 [1984] ECR 1299, para 20. Cf Case C–126/91 *Yves Rocher* [1993] ECR I–2361, para 21. In *Leclerc-Siplec*, AG Jacobs referred, at p I–197, to a number of other cases which are often understood as reiterating the same point, but they all say not only that it is irrelevant that any hindrance to imports may be slight but also that it is irrelevant that imported products can be marketed in other ways: see eg Case 103/84 *Commission v Italy* [1986] ECR 1759, para 18. It is clear from *Keck and Mithouard* that the latter factor is no longer irrelevant; the continued irrelevance of the former factor can therefore no longer be taken for granted.

[306] Case C–69/88 [1990] ECR I–583, para 11.

[307] Case C–169/91 [1992] ECR I–6635, para 15.

[308] In Case C–120/95 *Decker v Caisse de Maladie des Employés Privés* [1998] ECR I–1831, the Court somewhat surprisingly held that national rules under which a domestic social security institution refused to reimburse the cost of a pair of glasses purchased from an optician in another Member State were caught by Art 28 (ex 30). A parallel case on the freedom to provide services, Case C–158/96 *Kohll v Union des Caisses de Maladie* [1998] ECR I–1931, is discussed in ch 9. For a very radical proposal, see Poiares Maduro, op cit, pp 173–4.

easier to apply than the old one. There are three particular reasons why the Court's attempt to set clear limits to the scope of Article 28 (ex 30) in *Keck and Mithouard* was unsuccessful and they are worth reiterating briefly here. First, the Court was unwilling to abandon the *Dassonville* formula, although it can clearly no longer be taken at face value. Secondly, although the Court made it clear that it was departing from some of its earlier case law, it did not specify the decisions which were no longer to be regarded as authoritative. Thirdly, it failed to define the crucial concept of selling arrangements.

Traders and national courts must clearly be given some guidance on what constitutes a MEE and it is submitted that a *de minimis* test has a useful role to play. Measures which discriminate against imports should not be capable of benefiting from such a test,[309] but it should apply to all non-discriminatory national measures which are capable of hindering intra-Community trade, whether directly or indirectly. In order for a *de minimis* test to function properly, it would be imperative for the Court to indicate clearly to national courts, in cases referred to it, the circumstances in which the test was to be considered satisfied. The Sunday trading débâcle was due in large measure to the Court's failure in the *Torfaen* case to give the national courts adequate guidance on the application of the principle of proportionality. A *de minimis* test would admittedly be hard to apply in some cases, but it does not a priori seem any more difficult to employ than that principle.

In *Leclerc-Siplec* Advocate General Jacobs suggested a number of factors that might be relevant in assessing the impact of a national measure, such as the range of goods to which it applied, the extent to which the marketing of the goods affected was impeded and whether the effect of the measure was 'direct or indirect, immediate or remote, or purely speculative and uncertain'.[310] Those factors are all susceptible to analysis by legal means: it would not be desirable for the Court to require the production of empirical evidence of the concrete effect of a particular measure on the movement of goods, because such evidence would often be extremely difficult to acquire. It might also be relevant to ask whether the contested measure concerns the product itself or merely the arrangements for selling it, for measures which fall into the former category seem generally more likely to have a significant effect on trade. However, it would not be sensible to rule out the application of a *de minimis* test entirely in the case of product-related measures,[311] because this would be too rigid an approach: a national rule on, say, the presentation of a product which does not hinder trade to any appreciable extent may be no more inimical to the free movement of goods than a rule restricting selling arrangements which only has an indirect or speculative effect on imports.

In *Hünermund*, Advocate General Tesauro observed[312] that the case gave the Court the opportunity to explain whether Article 28 (ex 30) was concerned with liberalizing intra-Community trade or more generally with promoting the free exercise of commercial activities in each Member State. It is clear from the Court's

---

[309] See AG Jacobs in *Leclerc-Siplec*, p I–196.   [310] See p I–196.
[311] Cf AG Jacobs in *Leclerc-Siplec* at pp I–196–7.   [312] [1993] ECR I–6787, 6800.

ruling that it sees the former as the purpose of the article. The case law of which *Hünermund* forms a part is hard to reconcile with the notion of a Court which is forever expanding its own competence and that of the Community at the expense of the Member States.

8

The free movement of workers

It is a fundamental component of the system envisaged by the EC Treaty that workers should be able to move freely from one Member State to another. That objective is spelled out in Article 39 (ex 48), according to the second paragraph of which freedom of movement for workers is to entail 'the abolition of any discrimination based on nationality between workers of the Member States as regards employment, remuneration and other conditions of work and employment'. That paragraph suggests that the rights contemplated are economic in scope: the worker's right is limited to travel in connection with employment. That suggestion is supported by the third paragraph of Article 39 (ex 48), which specifies certain more detailed rights which workers are to enjoy, namely the rights 'to accept offers of employment' and 'to move freely within the territory of Member States' for the purpose of accepting such offers, 'to stay in a Member State for the purpose of employment' and 'to remain in the territory of a Member State after having been employed in that State . . .'.

The Treaty lays down two derogations to which the rights it confers on workers are subject. Article 39(3) (ex 48(3)) entitles the Member States to impose limitations on those rights where this is 'justified on grounds of public policy, public security or public health', sometimes called the 'public policy proviso'. Article 39(4) (ex 48(4)) states that the article does not apply 'to employment in the public service'. These derogations are discussed in more detail in chapter 10.

The authors of the Treaty envisaged that the bare bones of Article 39 (ex 48) would be fleshed out by regulations and directives and a considerable body of legislation has been adopted to give effect to the Treaty.[1] Regulation 1612/68 on freedom of movement for workers within the Community, adopted by the Council under Article 40 (ex 49) of the Treaty,[2] spells out some of the implications of the prohibition against discrimination on grounds of nationality laid down in Article 39(2) (ex 48(2)) and contains important provisions on the families of workers. Article 1(1) of the Regulation confirms the suggestion in Article 39(2) of the Treaty that rights of free movement are enjoyed only by nationals of the Member States. Although a broad construction of the words 'workers of the Member States' in Article 39(2) might have brought within the scope of the Treaty workers who were nationals of third countries but who were lawfully employed in a Member State,

[1] The Commission has proposed significant changes to some of the legislation: see COM(1998) 394 final.

[2] OJ Sp Ed, 1968 (II), p 475.

this is not a line the Court has chosen to follow.[3] Moreover, despite the theoretical attractions of a Community definition of nationality, the Court has accepted that the question whether someone possesses the nationality of a Member State is to be determined by the law of that State.[4]

Directive 68/360 on the abolition of restrictions on movement and residence,[5] also adopted by the Council under Article 40 (ex 49), sets out the administrative requirements which Member States are entitled to require workers and their families who are seeking to exercise their rights under Regulation 1612/68 to meet. Regulation 1251/70 on the right of workers to remain in the territory of a Member State after having been employed there was adopted by the Commission pursuant to Article 39(3)(d) (ex 48(3)(d)) of the Treaty. It gives nationals of a Member State who have been employed in another Member State and members of their families the right in certain circumstances to remain permanently in the territory of the second State after the employment concerned comes to an end.

By virtue of Article 42 (ex 51), the Council was placed under an obligation to adopt measures alleviating the adverse social security consequences which might ensue when a worker moved from one Member State to another.[6] In awarding social security benefits, each Member State was to be required to take account of periods during which the worker was resident in other Member States where those periods were regarded by the latter as giving rise to a right to benefit. This is known as the principle of aggregation, a term actually used in Article 42. Moreover, benefits to which a worker was entitled were to be payable throughout the Community, as long as the beneficiary was resident in a Member State (not necessarily the one paying the benefit). This is known as the principle of exportability.[7]

---

[3] See further Oliver, 'Non-Community nationals and the Treaty of Rome' (1985) 5 YEL 57; Weiler, 'Thou shalt not oppress a stranger (Ex 23:9): on the judicial protection of the human rights of non-EC nationals—a critique', Alexander, 'Free movement of non-EC nationals: a review of the case-law of the Court of Justice', and Hoogenboom, 'Free movement and integration of non-EC nationals and the logic of the internal market', in Schermers et al (eds), *Free Movement of Persons in Europe* (1993), pp 248, 485 and 497 respectively.

[4] See Case C–369/90 *Micheletti and Others* [1992] ECR I–4239 (Member State not entitled to deprive national of another Member State of Treaty rights on ground that he also possessed nationality of a non-member country). Note also the declaration on nationality agreed at Maastricht.

[5] OJ Sp Ed, 1968 (II), p 485.

[6] See Reg 1408/71 on the application of social security schemes to employed persons, to self-employed persons and to members of their families moving within the Community and Reg 574/72 laying down the procedure for implementing Reg 1408/71. Both regulations have been subject to frequent amendment. Updated versions were published as Reg 2001/83, OJ 1983 L230/6, but that regulation has itself subsequently been amended.

[7] Since their extension to self-employed persons, Regs 1408/71 and 574/72 have been based on Art 308 (ex 235) as well as Art 42 (ex 51), which both require the Council to act unanimously. That requirement was identified as an obstacle to reform by the High Level Panel on the Free Movement of Persons chaired by Mrs Simone Veil in a report presented to the Commission on 18 March 1997 (see p 49). Although the Treaty of Amsterdam amended Art 42 (ex 51) so that the procedure referred to in Art 251 (ex 189b) (co-decision) now applies, the Council is exceptionally required to act unanimously throughout that procedure. Moreover, Art 42 (ex 51) remains confined to workers and no changes were made to Art 308 (ex 235). None the less, the enhanced involvement of the European Parliament may induce the Council to take a more flexible approach to reforms such as those suggested by the High Level Panel.

The Treaty chapter on workers and the legislation adopted to give effect to it placed considerable responsibility on the shoulders of the Court to make the system work. A way had to be found of protecting the rights of Member States under Article 39(3) and (4) (ex 48(3) and (4)) without undermining the very objectives of Article 39; the legislation adopted under Articles 40 (ex 49) and 42 (ex 51) was to give rise to a host of problems which the Court would be called upon to resolve. The Court would also have to compensate for the failure of the Treaty's authors to define the term worker. In undertaking these tasks, the Court has not followed a wholly consistent line. Whilst it has in the main sought to promote freedom of movement, it has on occasion failed to satisfy expectations it was itself partly responsible for creating.

The economic emphasis of the Treaty in its original form was fundamentally altered by the TEU. New provisions on education,[8] vocational training,[9] culture[10] and economic and social cohesion[11] changed the legal context in which the rules on the free movement of persons were to be applied by underlining the importance of political and social factors. The tension liable to be created between factors such as these and the existing rules on the free movement of workers may be illustrated by a case decided before the TEU was signed, *Groener v Minister for Education and the City of Dublin Vocational Education Committee*.[12] G, a Netherlands national, worked on a temporary basis as a part-time art teacher at a college in Dublin run by the defendant Committee. She applied for a permanent full-time post as a lecturer in art at the college. Under Irish law, candidates for such posts could only be appointed if they held a certificate of proficiency in the Irish language or an equivalent qualification recognized by the defendant Minister. The Minister also had the power to exempt candidates from abroad from the requirement to demonstrate a knowledge of Irish where there were no other fully qualified candidates for the post. G was unable to obtain the requisite qualifications in the Irish language and the Minister refused to grant her an exemption because there were other fully qualified candidates for the post.

G brought proceedings in which she maintained that the rules making appointment to the post concerned conditional upon knowledge of Irish were contrary to Article 39 (ex 48) and Regulation 1612/68. The last subparagraph of Article 3(1) of that regulation permits the Member States to lay down conditions for employment within their territories 'relating to linguistic knowledge required by reason of the nature of the post to be filled'. Art and most other subjects were taught in English in colleges such as the one in which G was seeking employment, so that, as the referring court put it, knowledge of the Irish language was 'not required to discharge the duties attached to the post'. However, under the Irish Constitution, Irish was the national language and first official language of the State and Irish Governments had for many years followed a policy of promoting the use of Irish

---

[8] Art 149 (ex 126) EC.   [9] Art 150 (ex 127) EC.   [10] Art 151 (ex 128) EC.
[11] Arts 158 (ex 130a) to 162 (ex 130e) EC.
[12] Case C–379/87 [1989] ECR 3967. See McMahon (1990) 27 CMLRev 129.

as a way of expressing national identity and culture. The Court accepted that a policy of that kind was in principle compatible with the Treaty. It continued:[13]

The importance of education for the implementation of such a policy must be recognized. Teachers have an essential role to play, not only through the teaching which they provide but also by their participation in the daily life of the school and the privileged relationship which they have with their pupils. In those circumstances, it is not unreasonable to require them to have some knowledge of the first national language.

It follows that the requirement imposed on teachers to have an adequate knowledge of such a language must, provided that the level of knowledge required is not disproportionate in relation to the objective pursued, be regarded as a condition corresponding to the knowledge required by reason of the nature of the post to be filled within the meaning of the last subparagraph of Article 3(1) of Regulation No 1612/68.

The Court went on to emphasize the duty of Member States to comply with the principle of non-discrimination. This precluded in particular 'the imposition of any requirement that the linguistic knowledge in question must have been acquired in the national territory'.[14]

Notwithstanding the importance attached by the Court to respect for the principles of proportionality and non-discrimination, the outcome of the case was in many ways surprising. As a derogation from the fundamental principle of freedom of movement for workers, the last subparagraph of Article 3(1) should in principle have been interpreted strictly, as Advocate General Darmon acknowledged.[15] Construed in that way, it would have been natural to regard it as confined to posts where knowledge of a given language was necessary to enable the duties they involved to be performed. The argument for limiting the scope of the derogation in this way might have been considered particularly strong in the case of a language like Irish, knowledge of which is more likely to be possessed by Irish nationals than by the nationals of other Member States and which is not widely taught outside Ireland.[16]

The consequence of this line of reasoning, however, would have been to undermine attempts by national governments to defend and promote minority languages, which are widely regarded as one of Europe's riches.[17] The Court's willingness to protect a policy such as that adopted by the Irish Government from the strict requirements of rules as fundamental to the Community system as those relating to the free movement of workers demonstrates the importance it attaches to preserving the national identities of the Member States. The sensitivity manifested by the Court was endorsed at Maastricht, where new provisions agreed by the Member States required the Union to 'respect the national identities of its Member States'[18]

---

[13] Paras 20 and 21.   [14] Para 23.   [15] See p 3980.

[16] The Opinion of AG Darmon implies that Irish could not be studied in the Netherlands, although courses were apparently available in a limited number of other parts of the Community: see p 3984.

[17] See AG Darmon at pp 3981-2; report of the High Level Panel on the Free Movement of Persons, ch V.

[18] Art 6(3) (ex F(1)) TEU.

and imposed on the Community a duty to 'contribute to the flowering of the cultures of the Member States, while respecting their national and regional diversity . . .'.[19]

The change in emphasis which resulted from the amendments agreed at Maastricht perhaps emerged even more clearly from the insertion into the EC Treaty of a new Part Two entitled 'Citizenship of the Union' (Articles 17 to 22 (ex 8 to 8e)).[20] According to Article 17(1) (ex 8(1)), anyone holding the nationality of a Member State is a citizen of the Union. The resonance of the concept of citizenship is reflected in an amendment made to Article 17(1) at Amsterdam to make it clear that '[c]itizenship of the Union shall complement and not replace national citizenship'. Some of the new rights introduced by the provisions on citizenship were relatively minor,[21] although Article 18(1) (ex 8a(1)) may prove to be of greater significance. That provision states that '[e]very citizen of the Union shall have the right to move and reside freely within the territory of the Member States, subject to the limitations and conditions laid down in this Treaty and by the measures adopted to give it effect'. Article 18(2) (ex 8a(2)) gives the Council a power to facilitate the exercise of the rights mentioned in paragraph 1.

The language of Article 18(1) (ex 8a(1)) does not make it clear whether it is intended to add to the rights conferred on Community nationals by Articles 39 to 55 (ex 48 to 66) of the Treaty or whether it confers any rights on citizens of the Union in the absence of action by the Council under Article 18(2) (ex 8a(2)). Early cases in which Article 18 (ex 8a) was considered by the Court suggested that the answer to both questions was 'no'.[22] Subsequently, however, the Court started to attach greater significance to Article 18(1) (ex 8a(1)). The cases concerned are considered in chapter 11.

---

[19] Art 151(1) (ex 128(1)) EC.

[20] See O'Leary, *The Evolving Concept of Community Citizenship* (1996); Closa, 'The concept of citizenship in the Treaty on European Union' (1992) 29 CMLRev 1137; O'Leary, 'Nationality law and Community citizenship: a tale of two uneasy bedfellows' (1992) 12 YEL 353; O'Keeffe, 'Union citizenship', and Closa, 'Citizenship of the Union and nationality of Member States', in O'Keeffe and Twomey (eds), *Legal Issues of the Maastricht Treaty* (1994), pp 87 and 109 respectively; Shaw, 'The many pasts and futures of citizenship in the European Union' (1997) 22 ELRev 554. Cf Plender, 'An incipient form of European citizenship' in Jacobs (ed), *European Law and the Individual* (1976), p 39.

[21] In accordance with arrangements adopted by the Council, citizens of the Union residing in Member States other than their own have the right to vote and stand as a candidate at municipal elections and elections to the European Parliament in the Member State in which they are resident under the same conditions as nationals of that State: Art 19 (ex 8b) EC. See further Dir 93/109, OJ 1993 L329/34, and Dir 94/80, OJ 1994 L368/38. Citizens of the Union are also entitled to protection by the diplomatic or consular authorities of any Member State in the territory of third countries in which their own Member State is not represented: Art 20 (ex 8c).

[22] See eg Case C–193/94 *Skanavi and Chryssanthakopoulos* [1996] ECR I–929; Joined Cases C–64/96 and C–65/96 *Land Nordrhein-Westfalen v Uecker* and *Jacquet v Land Nordrhein-Westfalen* [1997] ECR I–3171.

Discrimination and the material scope of Article 39 (ex 48)

As might have been expected, the prohibition against discrimination on the grounds of nationality laid down in Article 39(2) (ex 48(2)) has been construed broadly by the Court as embracing not just direct or overt, but also indirect or covert, discrimination. However, the prohibition does not preclude differences in the treatment accorded to situations which are not comparable. Two cases on national income tax legislation indicate its potential scope. The cases are significant because, unlike indirect taxation,[23] the Treaty does not contain any provisions expressly regulating the imposition of direct taxes by the Member States or conferring on the institutions of the Community express authority to harmonize them.[24] It might therefore have been thought that national legislation on the matter was unaffected by Article 39 (ex 48). The Court has predictably rejected that conclusion but at the same time taken care to ensure that established principles of international tax law were not upset by clumsy application of the principle of equal treatment.

In *Biehl*,[25] a German national who had lived and worked for a time in Luxembourg challenged the refusal of the Luxembourg tax authorities to refund income tax which had been over-deducted by his employer before he moved to Germany. That refusal was based on a provision of Luxembourg law confining the right to a refund of tax to those who were resident in Luxembourg throughout the year. The taxpayer challenged the refusal before the Luxembourg Conseil d'Etat, which asked the Court for a ruling on the compatibility of the disputed Luxembourg rule with the requirements of Community law and particularly Article 39 (ex 48) of the Treaty.

The Court, noting that Article 39(2) (ex 48(2)) prohibited discrimination based on nationality between workers of the Member States with regard to remuneration, observed: 'The principle of equal treatment with regard to remuneration would be rendered ineffective if it could be undermined by discriminatory national provisions on income tax.'[26] The Court then reiterated its well established case law to the effect that the Community rules on equality of treatment prohibited not only direct discrimination, but also 'all covert forms of discrimination which, by the application of other criteria of differentiation, lead to the same result'.[27] This was a case where a rule which appeared to be applicable irrespective of the taxpayer's

---

[23] See Arts 90 (ex 95) to 93 (ex 99) EC.

[24] Indeed, recourse to Art 95 (ex 100a) in the fiscal field is expressly excluded: see Art 95(2).

[25] Case C–175/88 [1990] ECR I–1779. Cf Case C–18/95 *Terhoeve v Inspecteur van de Belastingdienst Particulieren/Ondernemingen Buitenland*, judgment of 26 January 1999.

[26] Para 12. The Court referred to the requirement, laid down in Art 7(2) of Reg 1612/68, that workers who are nationals of a Member State should enjoy in the territory of the host State the same tax advantages as national workers. Art 7(2) is considered in more detail below.

[27] Para 13. See also Case 152/73 *Sotgiu v Deutsche Bundespost* [1974] ECR 153, para 11.

nationality in fact operated to the disadvantage of taxpayers who were nationals of other Member States, because they were more likely to leave Luxembourg or to take up residence there during the course of the year. The Court rejected an attempt to justify the disputed legislation by reference to the need to avoid distorting the system of progressive taxation. The point was that a taxpayer who spread his income among more than one State might be taxed at a more favourable rate than a taxpayer who earned all his income in Luxembourg. The Court pointed out that that argument disregarded the situation of the temporarily resident taxpayer who did not earn anything in the country he had left or to which he had moved. Such a taxpayer might find himself taxed in Luxembourg at a higher rate than a taxpayer who was resident there all the year round, but would still have no right to a refund of tax which had been over-deducted by his employer. The disputed national legislation could not be saved by a discretionary procedure which temporarily resident taxpayers could invoke with a view to having their position reviewed because it did not oblige the tax authorities to rectify the position.

A later case illustrates the difficulties that may sometimes arise in deciding whether apparently similar situations are genuinely comparable. In *Schumacker*,[28] another tax case where the *Biehl* decision was applied, the Court was asked for guidance to help the national court assess the compatibility with Article 39 (ex 48) of certain provisions of German tax law under which the treatment accorded to a taxpayer depended on whether or not he was resident within the national territory. Taxpayers who were resident enjoyed certain advantages, such as the right to split their income with their spouses with a view to reducing the rate at which it was taxed and the right to claim certain reliefs and rebates in the light of their personal and family circumstances. The Court noted that, under international tax law, the overall taxation of individuals was in principle a matter for the State of residence, which was where most of the taxpayer's income normally arose and which was better able to take account of the taxpayer's personal circumstances. Advocate General Léger explained the rationale behind that principle:[29]

The logic of the distinction between residents and non-residents is clear: by choosing to reside in a particular State, a person assumes the obligation to contribute to the costs of public administration and the public services made available to him by that State. It is therefore logical that that State should tax the entirety of his income, on a comprehensive basis. It is also that State, where the taxpayer has focused his family life, which will grant him allowances and reliefs. There is a personal link between the taxpayer and his State of residence . . . Thus, clearly, tax law draws a distinction between residents and non-residents because they are not, objectively, in the same situation. That distinction, moreover, is to be found at the heart of the OECD model double taxation convention on income and capital.

Thus, Article 39 (ex 48) did not in principle prohibit national legislation which treated non-residents less favourably than residents in the same employment. However, in this case the non-resident received no significant income in his State

---

[28] Case C–279/93 [1995] ECR I–225.   [29] At pp I–234-235.

of residence, with the result that that State was not in a position to take account of his personal circumstances in applying its own tax legislation. Was this situation compatible with Article 39? Advocate General Léger emphasized the practical importance of the question: 'frontier workers—in very many cases—receive all their income in the State where they are employed. They are therefore, in that respect, in a situation wholly comparable with that of residents. Can the distinction between residents and non-residents be invoked against them when, objectively, they are for tax purposes *in the same situation as residents*?'[30] The Advocate General thought the answer to that question was no and the Court agreed, observing:[31]

There is no objective difference between the situations of such a non-resident and a resident engaged in comparable employment, such as to justify different treatment as regards the taking into account for taxation purposes of the taxpayer's personal and family circumstances.

In the case of a non-resident who receives the major part of his income and almost all his family income in a Member State other than that of his residence, discrimination arises from the fact that his personal and family circumstances are taken into account neither in the State of residence nor in the State of employment.

The principle of equal treatment therefore required the State of employment to take account in such a case of the personal circumstances of a foreign non-resident to the same extent as those of resident nationals and to grant him the same tax benefits.

The Court did not think this would give rise to administrative difficulties, because a Council directive[32] had put in place ways of obtaining information from the tax authorities of another Member State. In any event, Germany granted frontier workers who were resident in the Netherlands but worked in Germany the advantages accorded to workers who were resident in Germany provided they earned 90 per cent of their income there. There seemed no reason why similar treatment should not be accorded to frontier workers resident in Belgium. The Court went on to add that Article 39 (ex 48) also required equal treatment at the procedural level. Thus, a refusal to make available to non-resident Community nationals annual adjustment procedures which were available to resident nationals and which could lead to a refund of tax which had been overpaid constituted unjustified discrimination.[33]

It has been observed that the Court's underlying caution in tax matters led it to adhere in *Schumacker* 'to an analysis based on discrimination rather than restriction of freedom of movement'.[34] In the controversial *Bosman* case,[35] the Court focused

---

[30] At p I–240, emphasis in the original.   [31] Paras 37 and 38.

[32] Dir 77/799 concerning mutual assistance by the competent authorities of the Member States in the field of direct taxation, OJ 1977 L336/15.

[33] In other cases the Court has accepted that national tax rules which operate to the disadvantage of migrants may be justified. See further below.

[34] Farmer, 'Article 48 EC and the taxation of frontier workers' (1995) 20 ELRev 310, 315. See also the report of the High Level Panel on the Free Movement of Persons, ch IV.

[35] Case C–415/93 *URBSFA and Others v Bosman and Others* [1995] ECR I–4921. The case was the subject of an avalanche of comment. See in particular Weatherill (1996) 33 CMLRev 991; Martín, 'Redefining obstacles to the free movement of workers' (1996) 21 ELRev 313.

instead on the question whether, leaving aside any question of discrimination on grounds of nationality, a worker's right to freedom of movement had been restricted. However, both *Bosman* and the tax cases have in common that they illustrate the extensive material scope of Article 39 (ex 48)[36] and the Court's willingness to countenance national measures on grounds other than those mentioned expressly in the Treaty.

Bosman concerned the effect of Article 39 (ex 48) on the rights of professional footballers to change clubs when their contracts expired. The profound consequences which the case had for the way in which professional football is organized in the Member States give it a strong claim to be considered one of the most momentous ever to come before the Court, although some of the legal issues it raised were, by the time it fell to be decided, relatively straightforward. B, a Belgian, was a professional footballer employed by RC Liège. When his contract expired, he was offered a new contract for one season at a fraction of his previous salary. B refused to sign and was put on the transfer list. A French club, US Dunkerque, eventually agreed with RC Liège to purchase B for a fee which would become payable when the French football authorities had received a transfer certificate from their counterparts in Belgium in accordance with regulations laid down by FIFA, the world governing body, which was an association governed by Swiss law. It was up to RC Liège to initiate this process by asking the Belgian football authorities to send the transfer certificate to France. However, after it had reached agreement with US Dunkerque it started to have doubts about the latter's solvency and therefore failed to ask for the certificate to be dispatched. As a result, the proposed transfer fell through. Moreover, RC Liège then suspended B and he was unable to play for an entire season.

B began legal proceedings claiming, *inter alia*, declarations that the transfer rules laid down by the football authorities and nationality rules limiting the number of foreign players a club could field were unlawful, as well as damages for the losses he had suffered. He was awarded an injunction requiring RC Liège and the Belgian governing body to refrain from impeding his engagement by other clubs, but there was circumstantial evidence that B was subsequently boycotted by a large number of European clubs. Eventually, the proceedings reached the Court d'Appel, Liège, which referred the following deceptively simple questions to the Court of Justice:

Are Articles 48 [now 39], 85 [now 81] and 86 [now 82] of the Treaty of Rome of 25 March 1957 to be interpreted as:

(i) prohibiting a football club from requiring and receiving payment of a sum of money upon the engagement of one of its players who has come to the end of his contract by a new employing club;

---

[36] See further Johnson and O'Keeffe, 'From discrimination to free movement: recent developments concerning the free movement of workers 1989–1994' (1994) 31 CMLRev 1313; Martin, 'Réflexions sur le champ d'application matériel de l'article 48 du traité CE' (1993) CDE 555.

(ii) prohibiting the national and international sporting associations or federations from including in their respective regulations provisions restricting access of foreign players from the European Community to the competitions which they organise?

Articles 81 and 82 EC are the main competition rules applicable to undertakings laid down in the Treaty,[37] but they were not considered by the Court in *Bosman*, which answered the questions referred solely on the basis of Article 39. The questions gave rise to a series of fundamental issues about the scope of that article. First, to what extent was sport subject to its requirements? Second, did the article affect the conduct of private bodies, particularly if based outside the Community? Did it matter that B's nationality had not affected the way he had been treated? To the extent that Article 39 did in principle apply, were there any derogations on which the defendants in the main proceedings could rely?

The *Bosman* case was not the first in which the Court had been called upon to consider some of the questions mentioned in the previous paragraph. In *Walrave v Union Cycliste Internationale*,[38] the Court had held that sport was covered by Community law where it constituted an 'economic activity'[39] and that the Treaty prohibition against discrimination on grounds of nationality was not confined to the actions of public bodies, since otherwise the effectiveness of the Treaty rules would be compromised and 'inequality in their application'[40] might be created. The Court concluded that several provisions of the Treaty, including Article 39 (ex 48), applied to the rules of a sporting organization based outside the Community in so far as it governed legal relations which could be located within the Community. Moreover, in *Donà v Mantero*,[41] it had been held that the activities of professional footballers constituted an economic activity for these purposes and that they were therefore covered by the Treaty rules on freedom of movement. The Court followed those decisions in *Bosman*, ruling that Article 39 applied to rules laid down by sporting associations which determined the terms on which professional sportsmen could engage in gainful employment.[42] It rejected an argument that a more permissive approach should now be taken because of the introduction at Maastricht of provisions, mentioned above, designed to 'contribute to the flowering of the cultures of the Member States'.[43] The alleged similarity between sport and culture was irrelevant, the Court said, because the referring court's questions concerned 'the scope of the freedom of movement of workers guaranteed by Article 48 [now 39], which is a fundamental freedom in the Community system'.[44] The point is perhaps not well made, for the Court was being invited to temper the effect of Article 39 where too rigorous an application of its requirements might have the effect of weakening the cultural heritage of the Member States. The Court was surely right, however, to reject any suggestion that the provisions on culture,

---

[37] See further ch 12.   [38] Case 36/74 [1974] ECR 1405.   [39] Para 4.
[40] Para 19. It will be recalled that the Court was not persuaded of the force of that argument in the context of the horizontal direct effect of directives. See ch 4.
[41] Case 13/76 [1976] ECR 1333.   [42] Paras 87 and 116.
[43] See Art 151(1) (ex 128(1)) EC.   [44] Para 78.

which do not refer directly to sport, could have the effect of curtailing so basic a provision as Article 39 in circumstances such as these.[45] That view was accepted by the Member States at Amsterdam, when a declaration emphasizing the social significance of sport was issued but no attempt made in the Treaty which was agreed there to shelter sport from the substantive requirements of Community law.

In the light of the conclusion that Article 39 (ex 48) was applicable, it was inevitable that the Court would find that the rules limiting the numbers of foreign players which clubs were entitled to field in official matches were in principle caught by it. The Court brushed aside the argument that those rules did not actually restrict the employment of foreign players, observing: 'In so far as participation in such matches is the essential purpose of a professional player's activity, a rule which restricts that participation obviously also restricts the chances of employment of the player concerned.'[46] It was in relation to the transfer rules that the Court went further than in previous decisions in ruling that they fell within the scope of Article 39 notwithstanding their indistinctly applicable character. The Court declared that '[p]rovisions which preclude or deter a national of a Member State from leaving his country of origin in order to exercise his right to freedom of movement . . . constitute an obstacle to that freedom even if they apply without regard to the nationality of the workers concerned'.[47] As Advocate General Lenz pointed out, the transfer rules made it more difficult for players to leave their clubs even after the expiry of their contracts and thereby restricted their freedom of movement. It could make no difference that movement between clubs within the same Member State was subject to similar restrictions.

In the circumstances of the *Bosman* case, the force of that argument was considerable. However, the case law on the free movement of goods shows that, once the scope of a prohibition on freedom of movement is extended to non-discriminatory restrictions, a vast range of measures only indirectly related to freedom of movement may have to be justified if they are to escape the reach of the prohibition concerned. That danger was recognized by Advocate General Lenz, who emphasized that the *Bosman* case was concerned with access to the employment market, where a broad rule was appropriate. Rules concerned, not with access, but merely with the exercise of an occupation were different and could be treated more leniently. The Advocate General gave the following example in an attempt to clarify the distinction:[48]

The question has just been raised again whether a professional league should for instance have 16, 18 or more clubs. It is perfectly plain that the number of clubs available affects a player's chances of finding employment with a club. The smaller the number of clubs, the more difficult it is likely to be as a rule to find employment. Nevertheless, provisions of *that* nature do not appear to me to raise doubts with respect to Article 48 [now 39]. They do not concern the possibility of access for foreign players as such, but the exercise of the occupation.

---

[45] Cf the *Groener* case, *supra*.   [46] Para 120.   [47] Para 96.   [48] At p I–5011.

The distinction drawn by the Advocate General between access to and the exercise of an occupation calls to mind the distinction drawn by the Court in *Keck and Mithouard*[49] in the context of Article 28 (ex 30) EC between rules on the requirements which goods themselves must meet and rules relating to the circumstances in which they may be sold. Indeed, an attempt was made in *Bosman* to rely on that case, but without success. The Court said that the transfer rules were not comparable to rules on selling arrangements for goods because they directly affected players' access to the employment market in other Member States. Unlike its Advocate General, however, the Court did not distinguish rules having that effect from rules concerning the exercise of an occupation. The Court's remarks may therefore be interpreted as emphasizing the immediacy of the impact of the contested rules on the freedom of movement of players rather than as endorsing the perhaps unduly rigid dividing-line drawn by Advocate General Lenz and the decision in *Keck and Mithouard*.

If that interpretation is correct, the outcome is desirable: it avoids the danger that rules posing a real threat to freedom of movement will be upheld merely because they are regarded as relating to the exercise of an occupation rather than access to it. There is, however, another danger to which this approach is liable to give rise, namely that it will be difficult for national courts to decide whether Article 39 (ex 48) is applicable in cases involving non-discriminatory obstacles to freedom of movement without making a reference to the Court of Justice. Two aspects of the *Bosman* ruling accentuate that difficulty. The first is that it will not be easy for a national judge to decide whether a rule has a sufficiently immediate effect on freedom of movement to be caught by Article 39. The second is the Court's acceptance that the transfer rules would not be caught by Article 39 if it could be shown that they 'pursued a legitimate aim compatible with the Treaty and were justified by pressing reasons of public interest'.[50] The parallel with the 'Cassis de Dijon' doctrine in relation to Article 28 (ex 30) is self-evident and the danger, mentioned by Advocate General van Gerven in the *Torfaen* case,[51] that the Court will be asked to decide on the reasonableness of national policy decisions in an infinite range of situations, is as real in the case of workers as it was in the case of goods before the decision in *Keck and Mithouard*. *Bosman* itself is a good example. The Court examined (but rejected)[52] the argument that the transfer rules were justified by the need to maintain 'a balance between clubs by preserving a certain degree of equality and uncertainty as to results' and to encourage 'the recruitment and training of young players', aims which the Court accepted as legitimate.[53] These are tasks which it is

---

[49] Joined Cases C–267/91 and C–268/91 [1993] ECR I–6097.

[50] Para 104. The Court added that 'application of those rules would still have to be such as to ensure achievement of the aim in question and not go beyond what is necessary for that purpose'.

[51] Case C–145/88 [1989] ECR I–3851, 3880.

[52] Although it did limit the temporal effect of its ruling that the transfer rules were incompatible with Art 39.

[53] See para 106.

to be hoped the Court will remain willing to undertake, for otherwise the effectiveness of Article 39 would be undermined.

For the sake of completeness, it should be noted that the Court also examined
whether the nationality clauses were justified, but again concluded that they were
not.[54] Although those clauses were by definition discriminatory, the judgment
should not be taken to imply that the 'pressing reasons of public interest' to which
the Court referred earlier extended to such obstacles to freedom of movement. The
relevant section of the Court's judgment should rather be regarded as an application to the particular facts of *Bosman* of its earlier ruling in *Donà*[55] that the Treaty
rules on the free movement of persons and services did not apply to rules 'excluding foreign players from participation in certain matches for reasons which are not
of an economic nature, which relate to the particular nature and context of such
matches and are thus of sporting interest only, such as, for example, matches
between national teams from different countries'.[56]

The personal scope of Article 39 (ex 48)

The Court has taken a similarly broad view of the personal scope of Article 39 (ex
48). In view of the presence in the Treaty of specific provisions dealing with the
rights of the self-employed, any lawyer with a passing acquaintance with labour law
would probably assume that the term 'worker' connotes some sort of employment
relationship, in other words an arrangement whereby an individual agrees to carry
out certain tasks under the direction of someone else in return for payment.
Support for that assumption would be found in Article 1(1) of Regulation 1612/68,
which refers to an 'activity as an employed person'. This has broadly speaking been
the approach taken by the Court, which has said that the concept of worker 'must
be defined in accordance with objective criteria which distinguish the employment
relationship by reference to the rights and duties of the persons concerned. The
essential feature of an employment relationship . . . is that for a certain period of
time a person performs services for and under the direction of another person in
return for which he receives remuneration.'[57] So a person working full-time for an
employer and earning enough to support himself clearly constitutes a worker for
the purposes of Article 39.

But what of part-timers, trainees, or those whose pay is very low? Here the
Court has been adventurous, emphasizing two things: first, that the term 'worker'

---

[54] On this point, it declined to limit the temporal effect of its judgment: 'In the light of the *Walrave*
and *Donà* judgments, it was not reasonable for those concerned to consider that the discrimination
resulting from those clauses was compatible with Article 48 [now 39] of the Treaty' (para 146).

[55] *Supra*, para 14.

[56] See the Opinion of AG Lenz in *Bosman* at pp I–4976–84.

[57] Case 66/85 *Lawrie-Blum v Land Baden-Württemberg* [1986] ECR 2121, para 17. That definition
does not necessarily extend to Reg 1408/71: Case C–85/96 *Martínez Sala v Freistaat Bayern* [1998] ECR
I–2691, para 31.

defines the scope of one of the fundamental freedoms granted by the Treaty and must not be interpreted restrictively; and secondly, that the term must be defined at the level of the Community, for otherwise the Member States would be able to alter its meaning at will. Thus, in *Levin*, the Court observed that 'whilst part-time employment is not excluded from the field of application of the rules on freedom of movement for workers, those rules cover only the pursuit of effective and genuine activities, to the exclusion of activities on such a small scale as to be regarded as purely marginal and ancillary'.[58] In *Kempf v Staatssecretaris van Justitie*,[59] a case concerning a part-time music teacher of German nationality who worked in the Netherlands, the Court declared that a person in 'effective and genuine' part-time employment did not fall outside the scope of Article 39 (ex 48) 'merely because the remuneration he derives from it is below the level of the minimum means of subsistence and he seeks to supplement it by other lawful means of subsistence'.[60] Provided the effective and genuine nature of the work was established, the Court said it made no difference whether the worker's additional resources derived from private means[61] or, as in this case, from the public purse. A similarly broad approach was taken in *Lawrie-Blum v Land Baden-Württemberg*,[62] where a British national was seeking to qualify as a teacher in Germany and sought to rely on Article 39 to gain admission to a period of preparatory service which was necessary for employment as a teacher in the State school system and also, in practice, in private schools. The Court noted:[63]

during the entire period of preparatory service the trainee teacher is under the direction and supervision of the school to which he is assigned. It is the school that determines the services to be performed by him and his working hours and it is the school's instructions that he must carry out and its rules that he must observe. During a substantial part of the preparatory service he is required to give lessons to the school's pupils and thus provides a service of some economic value to the school. The amounts which he receives may be regarded as remuneration for the services provided and for the duties involved in completing the period of preparatory service.

Such trainees constituted workers for the purposes of Article 39. It was irrelevant that they gave lessons for only a few hours a week and were paid less than qualified teachers.

As a rule, a person loses his status as a worker once the employment relationship has come to an end.[64] However, the Court has accepted that in certain circumstances the rights conferred on migrant workers by Community law do not depend on the continued existence of an employment relationship. This issue has arisen in cases involving migrant workers who have sought to pursue full-time courses of education in the host State and to claim, on the basis of their status as a worker

---

[58] Para 17. [59] Case 139/85 [1986] ECR 1741. [60] Para 14.
[61] See eg Case 53/81 *Levin v Staatssecretaris van Justitie* [1982] ECR 1035.
[62] Case 66/85 [1986] ECR 2145. See also Case C–357/89 *Raulin* [1992] ECR I–1027; Case C–3/90 *Bernini* [1992] ECR I–1071.
[63] Para 18. [64] See *Martínez Sala v Freistaat Bayern, supra*, para 32.

within the meaning of Article 39 (ex 48), various financial advantages made available by that State to its own nationals. In *Lair v Universität Hannover*[65] it was held that a national of a Member State who had been employed in another Member State and subsequently ceased employment in order to pursue a university course in the second State retained his status as a worker if there was a link between the course and his previous occupation. Even that link was not required, the Court said, where the migrant had become unemployed involuntarily and needed to undergo retraining in another field. Moreover, the migrant does not lose his status as a worker even if he allows a certain period of time to elapse between stopping work and commencing his studies.[66]

The limits of Article 39 (ex 48) were reached in *Bettray v Staatssecretaris van Justitie*,[67] which concerned a German national employed in the Netherlands under social legislation intended to provide employment for those who were unable to work under normal conditions. The Court ruled that a national of another Member State employed under a scheme in which the activities carried out were 'merely a means of rehabilitation or reintegration' did not constitute a worker for the purposes of Article 39, since the activities of such a person could not be considered effective and genuine.[68] The Court's decision in *Bettray* underlines the economic rather than social focus of the rights conferred by Article 39, for the activities concerned doubtless seemed effective and genuine to the person carrying them out.[69] None the less, it is only because the Court's case law on the meaning of the term 'worker' has generally been so liberal that the more restrictive approach taken in *Bettray* causes surprise. The expansive approach of the Court was in due course to lead it into difficulty.

It will be observed that Article 39 (ex 48) does not in terms say anything about whether the unemployed have a right to travel in search of work. It would seem odd to exclude such people from the benefit of the article: in a true common market, people should be able to travel to where the jobs are and conferring on individuals a right to do so would help to demonstrate in a concrete way the value to them of the Treaty project. All the same, the wording of Article 39 seems only to envisage movement by workers who have already secured employment in another Member State.

The issue was considered by the Member States when, on the same day, the Council adopted Regulation 1612/68 and Directive 68/360. Recorded in the Council minutes was a declaration to the effect that a national of a Member State

---

[65] Case 39/86 [1988] ECR 3161. See also Case C–357/89 *Raulin* [1992] ECR I–1027.

[66] See Case C–3/90 *Bernini* [1992] ECR I–1071, para 21.

[67] Case 344/87 [1989] ECR 1621. Cf Case 196/87 *Steymann v Staatssecretaris van Justitie* [1988] ECR 6159.

[68] Para 17.

[69] It may be noted that the Amsterdam Treaty introduced a provision authorizing the Council to take action to combat discrimination based on disability: see Art 13 (ex 6a) EC. That provision is unlikely to be treated by the Court as affecting the scope of Art 39 (ex 48): cf Case C–249/96 *Grant v South-West Trains* [1998] ECR I–621, discussed in ch 13.

moving to another Member State in search of work there was to be allowed to stay in the second State for a minimum period of three months, provided he did not become a burden on the social welfare system of that State. Regulation 1612/68 itself contained, in Articles 1 and 5, provisions which were consistent with a right to move in search of work, but neither that regulation nor Directive 68/360 unequivocally conferred such a right on the nationals of the Member States. The absence of any such provision suggests that the Member States could not agree on whether a right to move in search of work was inherent in Article 39 (ex 48) or, if it was not, should be created by act of the Council. Further evidence of a lack of consensus on this issue is to be found in Article 69 of Regulation 1408/71,[70] which provides that an unemployed person who is entitled to benefits in one Member State and who goes to another Member State in order to look for work retains his right to benefit in the first State for a maximum period of three months. That provision seems to have been intended to encourage the unemployed to take advantage of the possibility presented by the Council's 1968 declaration by reducing the risk that a migrant would become dependent on the social welfare system of the host State before the period of three months had expired. However, Regulation 1408/71 did not (and, because of its legal basis, probably could not) confer on individuals a right to freedom of movement where none otherwise existed.

If there was an assumption among some Member States that the unemployed had no right to freedom of movement under Article 39 (ex 48), it eventually started to become apparent that that assumption was unlikely to be shared by the Court. In *Royer*, the Court referred to the right of a national of a Member State to enter another Member State '. . . *to look for* or pursue an occupation or activities as employed or self-employed persons . . .'[71] and in *Levin* it observed that 'the rules relating to freedom of movement for workers also concern persons who pursue *or wish to pursue* an activity as an employed person . . .'[72] These remarks might have been considered inconclusive because in both cases they appeared incidental to the Court's reasoning. In *Centre Public d'Aide Sociale de Courcelles v Lebon*,[73] the Court made it clear that those who moved in search of employment were entitled to equal treatment as regards access to employment under Article 39 and Regulation 1612/68. The Court's reasoning in *Lebon* was somewhat terse, but in *Antonissen*[74] it considered the issue in more detail. There the Court held that 'Article 48(3) [now 39(3)] must be interpreted as enumerating, in a non-exhaustive way, certain rights benefiting nationals of Member States in the context of the free movement of workers and that that freedom also entails the right for nationals of Member States to move freely within the territory of the other Member States and to stay there for the purposes of seeking employment.'[75] Otherwise the chances that an unemployed national of a Member State would find work in another Member State would be jeopardized, thereby rendering Article 39(3) 'ineffective'.[76]

---

[70] *Supra.*   [71] Case 48/75 [1976] ECR 497, para 31 (emphasis added).
[72] Para 16 (emphasis added).   [73] Case 316/85 [1987] ECR 2811.
[74] Case C–292/89 [1991] ECR I–745.   [75] Para 13.   [76] Para 12.

The Court found support for that interpretation of Article 39 (ex 48) in Regulation 1612/68, Articles 1 and 5 of which it said 'presuppose that Community nationals are entitled to move in order to look for employment, and hence to stay, in another Member State'.[77] That conclusion led the Court to consider whether the right of a Community national to stay in another Member State while looking for work lasted indefinitely or whether the host State was entitled to impose a temporal limitation on it. The Court dismissed the declaration made on the adoption of Regulation 1612/68 and Directive 68/360 as devoid of legal significance since it was not referred to in the acts concerned. Regulation 1408/71 was also irrelevant in the Court's view because there was 'no necessary link between the right to employment benefit in the Member State of origin and the right to stay in the host State'.[78] According to the Court, the essential requirement was that the person concerned should be given a reasonable time to familiarize himself with employment prospects in the host State. It concluded that that State was entitled to require him to leave its territory '(subject to appeal) if he has not found employment there after six months, unless the person concerned provides evidence that he is continuing to seek employment and that he has genuine chances of being engaged'.[79] Six months was the period laid down by the national rules at issue in the main proceedings.[80]

The rights of migrant workers

Once a person has established that he is a worker within the meaning of Article 39 (ex 48), he can in principle claim a panoply of substantive and procedural rights under the legislation adopted by the Council. One provision which has been interpreted by the Court in a particularly expansive way is Article 7(2) of Regulation 1612/68, according to which a worker who is a national of a Member State shall enjoy, in the territory of other Member States, 'the same social and tax advantages as national workers'. An early case in which the Court sought to define the scope of Article 7(2) was *Ministère Public v Even*.[81] The Court's decision in that case illustrates its propensity for making broad statements of principle which it holds inapplicable in the instant case but which can be built on in subsequent cases. E, a French national resident in Belgium, claimed an early retirement pension without reduction paid to Belgian nationals who served in the allied forces during the Second World War and who were in receipt of a war service invalidity pension. He was in receipt of such a pension under French legislation. The Court held that E could not rely on Regulation 1408/71 because it did not extend to the benefit in question. It then considered whether that benefit constituted a social advantage

[77] Para 14.   [78] Para 20.   [79] Para 22.
[80] The domestic background to, and consequences of, the *Antonissen* case were discussed by the House of Lords in *Chief Adjudication Officer v Wolke* [1997] 1 WLR 1640, [1998] 1 All ER 129.
[81] Case 207/78 [1979] ECR 2019.

for the purposes of Article 7(2) of Regulation 1612/68. The Court observed that 'the advantages which this regulation extends to workers who are nationals of other Member States are all those which, whether or not linked to a contract of employment, are generally granted to national workers primarily because of their objective status as workers or by virtue of the mere fact of their residence on the national territory and the extension of which to workers who are nationals of other Member States therefore seems suitable to facilitate their mobility within the Community'.[82] That broad statement was not, however, wide enough to embrace a benefit based on a scheme of national recognition which was designed for the advantage of national workers who had rendered service to their own country in wartime.

The *Even* formula was repeated in *Ministère Public v Mutsch*,[83] where the applicant was more successful. M was a Luxembourg national resident in a German-speaking part of Belgium. On the basis of Article 7(2) of Regulation 1612/68, he sought to rely on a provision of Belgian law entitling Belgian nationals resident in German-speaking areas to use German in certain court proceedings. The right claimed by M had no connection with his employment and was unlikely to have any effect on the willingness of nationals of other Member States to seek employment in Belgium. The Court none the less held that it constituted a social advantage within the meaning of Article 7(2). Recognizing the special importance of protecting the linguistic rights and privileges of individuals, the Court observed:[84]

The right to use his own language in proceedings before the courts of the Member State in which he resides, under the same conditions as national workers, plays an important rôle in the integration of a migrant worker and his family into the host country, and thus in achieving the objective of free movement for workers.

Another striking illustration of the Court's willingness to use Article 7(2) to promote freedom of movement is provided by its decision in *Netherlands v Reed*.[85] R, an unmarried British national, was the partner of W, also an unmarried British national, who was employed in the Netherlands. R applied for a Netherlands residence permit and sought to rely on Article 10(1)(a) of Regulation 1612/68, which confers on the spouses of migrant workers the right to install themselves with the worker concerned in the territory of the host State. Although R and W were not married, R argued that the term 'spouse' should be construed in the light of legal and social developments as extending to unmarried partners. Anxious not to interpret the regulation in a way which would be out of step with social developments in at least some of the Member States, the Court was not prepared to accept that argument and concluded that the term 'spouse' in Article 10 covered married partners only. However, it was the policy of the Netherlands to permit its own nationals to bring to the Netherlands partners of foreign nationality and this was enough

---

[82] Para 22.
[83] Case 137/84 [1985] ECR 2681. Cf Case C–274/96 *Bickel and Franz*, judgment of 24 November 1998, discussed in ch 11.
[84] Para 16.   [85] Case 59/85 [1986] ECR 1283. See para 28.

to bring Article 7(2) of Regulation 1612/68 into play. The Court observed that 'it must be recognized that the possibility for a migrant worker of obtaining permission for his unmarried companion to reside with him, where that companion is not a national of the host State, can assist his integration in the host State and thus contribute to the achievement of freedom of movement for workers'. That possibility therefore constituted a social advantage for the purposes of Article 7(2), with the result that a Member State which offered such a possibility to its own nationals could not refuse to offer it to workers who were nationals of other Member States.

The decision in *Reed* illustrates well the creative use to which the Court has been prepared to put Article 7(2) of Regulation 1612/68, but it is important to note that it did not reflect any view on the part of the Court of the importance of the institution of marriage. Indeed, its conclusion on the scope of Article 10 of the regulation was based on the Court's acceptance that questions of that nature were for the Member States to resolve. All the Court took exception to was a national policy which had the effect of treating marriage as more important in the case of foreigners than in the case of nationals of the State concerned. It was that element of discrimination which was liable to discourage freedom of movement and led the Court to intervene.

The Court's willingness to interpret Article 7(2) broadly has on occasion enabled it to take a strict view of the scope of Regulation 1408/71 while at the same time giving a ruling favourable to a migrant worker. An example is *Hoeckx v Openbaar Centrum voor Maatschappelijk Welzijn Kalmthout*.[86] H, a Netherlands national resident in Belgium, challenged the refusal of the Belgian authorities to grant her a minimum assistance allowance. That refusal was based on H's failure to satisfy the condition laid down by Belgian law that claimants should have been resident in Belgium for the previous five years. The Court was asked whether the refusal to pay the benefit in these circumstances was contrary to the equal treatment rules laid down in either Regulation 1408/71 or Regulation 1612/68.

Regulation 1408/71 contains in Article 4(1) a list of the branches of social security to which it applies and the Court said that, in order to come within the scope of the regulation, national legislation had to cover one of the risks mentioned. Since an allowance of the type claimed by H was general in nature, it could not be classified under any of the branches of social security mentioned in Article 4(1) and was not therefore covered by Regulation 1408/71. However, the Court found that the contested benefit constituted a social advantage for the purposes of Article 7(2) of Regulation 1612/68 and could not therefore be denied 'to a migrant worker who is national of another Member State and is resident within the territory of the State paying the benefit, nor to his family'.[87] Moreover, the residence requirement, an additional condition imposed on workers who were nationals of other Member States, was discriminatory and could not therefore be imposed.

[86] Case 249/83 [1985] ECR 973. See also Case 261/83 *Castelli v ONPTS* [1984] ECR 3199; Case 122/84 *Scrivner v Centre Public d'Aide Sociale de Chastre* [1985] ECR 1027.
[87] Para 22.

The Court's reasoning in *Hoeckx* was of more than merely technical importance and was less adventurous than it might at first sight appear. The principle of exportability, mentioned in Article 42 (ex 51) of the Treaty, applies only to social security benefits which are covered by Regulation 1408/71: it does not extend to social advantages within the meaning of Article 7(2) of Regulation 1612/68. Member States are not therefore required to extend such advantages to those who have left the national territory.[88] It may also be noted that, while Regulation 1408/71 has been extended to the self-employed, Regulation 1612/68 is confined to workers and their families. Thus, while Article 7(2) of the latter regulation was adequate to entitle H to the benefit she was seeking, the practical consequences of the Court's ruling were less extensive than might have been the case had it based its decision on Regulation 1408/71.

Regulation 1612/68 also contains important provisions on workers' families. Article 10, on the right of a spouse and certain other family members to install themselves in the host State with the worker to whom they are related, has already been mentioned. It may be noted that the Court has held that a spouse's right to remain in the host State subsists as long as his or her marriage to the worker concerned has not been terminated, even where the couple live separately and intend to divorce at a later date.[89] It is convenient now to consider briefly the Court's approach to the interpretation of Article 12 of Regulation 1612/68, which confers important rights on the children of migrant workers. Article 12 provides as follows:

The children of a national of a Member State who is or has been employed in the territory of another Member State shall be admitted to that State's general educational, apprenticeship and vocational training courses under the same conditions as the nationals of that State, if such children are residing in its territory.

Member States shall encourage all efforts to enable such children to attend these courses under the best possible conditions.

An early case in which the Court was asked for guidance on the scope of that provision was *Michel S v Fonds National de Reclassement Social des Handicapés*,[90] in which the handicapped son of an Italian worker who had been employed in Belgium until his death claimed the benefit of Belgian legislation on the rehabilitation of the handicapped. Although the Court rejected the argument that such legislation amounted to a social advantage within the meaning of Article 7(2) of Regulation 1612/68,[91] it held that it was covered by Article 12. The Court regarded that conclusion as dictated by the need to ensure the integration of the worker's family into the host State, an objective mentioned in the preamble to Regulation 1612/68.

---

[88] But cf Case C–57/96 *Meints v Minister van Landbouw, Natuurbeheer en Visserij* [1997] ECR I–6689.

[89] See Case 267/83 *Diatta v Land Berlin* [1985] ECR 567. The spouse in that case was not a national of a Member State and would presumably have lost her rights under Reg 1612/68 on divorce. Cf Case C–370/90 *Singh* [1992] ECR I–4265, where the spouse was not divorced when he attempted to re-enter the Member State of which his wife was a national.

[90] Case 76/72 [1973] ECR 457.

[91] The narrow view it took of the scope of that provision was later abandoned.

The Court's judgment contained a clear indication of its willingness to interpret Article 12 broadly:[92]

The fact that the abovementioned Article 12 does not expressly refer to educational arrangement provided in favour of such children, is not to be understood as denoting the intention to exclude these arrangements from the scope of the Regulation, but is explained by the difficulty of mentioning all hypotheses exhaustively, especially those of an exceptional character, in view of which it is necessary to guarantee the equality of nationals of all the Member States, in order to ensure that the right of freedom of movement can be exercised to its full extent.

A remarkable illustration of the breadth of Article 12 is provided by the decision in *Echternach and Another v Minister for Education and Science*,[93] in which the Court was asked for guidance on its effect in the context of proceedings brought by two German students against the refusal of the competent Netherlands authorities to award them grants for the purposes of further study. One of the applicants, M, had arrived in the Netherlands, where his father worked, at the age of five and received his primary and secondary education there. When M began his studies at technical college, his father was transferred to Germany, where he moved with his family. M found, however, that his Netherlands diplomas were not recognized in Germany, so he returned to the Netherlands to continue his studies there. The Court rejected the argument of the Netherlands Government that, because his father no longer worked in the Netherlands, a student such as M could not be considered a member of a Community worker's family. The Court also considered it irrelevant that M had left the Netherlands in order to settle in Germany with his parents and had only later returned to live in the Netherlands. The integration of the members of a worker's family into the society of the host State would in the Court's view be hindered if a student in these circumstances were unable to rely on Article 12 so as to complete his education. Such a student therefore retained his status as a member of a worker's family. The Court emphasized that Article 12 extended to all forms of education, whether vocational or general, and reiterated that it applied 'not only to the rules relating to admission itself, but also to general measures intended to facilitate educational attendance'.[94] It followed that the children of Community workers 'must be eligible for study assistance from the State in order to make it possible for them to achieve integration in the society of the host country. That requirement applies *a fortiori* where the persons covered by the provisions of Community law in question are students who arrived in the host country even before the age at which they had to attend school.'[95]

The broad personal and material scope which has been attributed to Article 39 (ex 48) together with the extensive rights conferred on migrant workers and mem-

---

[92] Para 15.
[93] Joined Cases 389 and 390/87 [1989] ECR 723. Cf Case C–308/89 *di Leo* [1990] ECR I–4185; Case 235/87 *Matteucci v Communauté Française of Belgium* [1988] ECR 5589.
[94] Para 33. See Case 9/74 *Casagrande v Landeshauptstadt München* [1974] ECR 773, para 9.
[95] Para 35.

bers of their families by the Council give rise to possibilities which go some way beyond what the authors of the Treaty are likely to have contemplated. To take a hypothetical example, is a national of a Member State who moves to another Member State in search of work entitled to take his family with him? If he finds in the host State that his skills are inadequate to enable him to find work, can he claim financial assistance from the host State to enable him to attend a full-time course of retraining? While he is undergoing retraining, are his children entitled to financial assistance from the host State to enable them to attend educational courses? Notwithstanding its generally expansive approach to the scope of the Community rules, the Court has baulked at these far-reaching possibilities and has imposed certain limits on the requirements of Community law in circumstances such as these. Even though the policy considerations underlying those limits might seem compelling, their logic has not always been self-evident from a legal point of view, perhaps suggesting that the Court has not been entirely consistent in the balance it has struck between the rights of migrants and those of the Member States.

The Court made it clear in *Centre Public d'Aide Sociale de Courcelles v Lebon*[96] that someone falling within the personal scope of Article 39 (ex 48) might not enjoy the full range of rights which that article, and the legislation adopted by the Council under Article 40 (ex 49), were capable of conferring. One of the questions raised by the case was whether a person moving in search of work could rely on Article 7(2) of Regulation 1612/68. In principle the answer to that question should have been 'yes'. There only appears to be one category of persons covered by Article 39, namely workers, all of whom seem to be entitled to claim the benefit of Regulation 1612/68. However, the Court rejected that view:[97]

The right to equal treatment with regard to social and tax advantages applies only to workers. Those who move in search of employment qualify for equal treatment only as regards access to employment in accordance with Article 48 [now 39] of the EEC Treaty and Articles 2 and 5 of Regulation 1612/68.

The language used by the Court might have been taken to imply that those who move in search of work are not workers for the purposes of Article 39 (ex 48) although they enjoy rights to freedom of movement and non-discrimination under that article and can rely on certain provisions of Regulation 1612/68 (though not Article 7(2)). The terms of the judgment in *Antonissen* are consistent. As we have seen, in that case the Court examined in more detail the rights of those moving in search of work but again avoided describing such people as workers, referring instead to the 'rights benefiting nationals of Member States in the context of the free movement of workers'.[98]

However, in *Martínez Sala v Freistaat Bremen*[99] the Court said that 'a person who is genuinely seeking work must . . . be classified as a worker'. It therefore seems

---

[96] Case 316/85 [1987] ECR 2811.   [97] Para 26. Cf, however, *Martínez Sala, supra*, para 34.
[98] Case C–292/89 [1991] ECR I–745, para 13.
[99] *Supra*, para 32. See O'Leary, 'Putting flesh on the bones of European Union citizenship' (1999) 24 ELRev 68.

that there are some categories of worker who enjoy less extensive protection under the Treaty than others. Support for that view may be found in *Brown v Secretary of State for Scotland*,[100] where the Court was asked for a preliminary ruling in the context of a dispute over the respondent's refusal to award the applicant a student grant. The applicant was born in France in 1966 to a British father and a French mother who had gone to France the previous year after having worked in the United Kingdom. The applicant had dual French and British nationality and received his primary and secondary education in France. However, he moved to the United Kingdom after taking his *baccalauréat* and worked for just over eight months in employment described by the referring court as 'pre-university industrial training'. Shortly after his employment came to an end, he began a degree course in electrical engineering.

Among the issues which the Court was asked to consider was whether the applicant was a worker within the meaning of Article 7(2) of Regulation 1612/68 and, if not, whether he could rely on Article 12 of that regulation. The Court gave an affirmative answer to the first question: the term worker in Article 7(2) included 'a national of another Member State who enters into an employment relationship in the host State for a period of eight months with a view to subsequently undertaking university studies there in the same field of activity and who would not have been employed by his employer if he had not already been accepted for admission to university'.[101] The Court then reiterated that a maintenance grant awarded to a university student constituted a social advantage for the purposes of Article 7(2).[102] At this point, things were looking good for the applicant, but the Court then abruptly changed direction. It did not follow 'that a national of a Member State will be entitled to a grant for studies in another Member State by virtue of his status as a worker where it is established that he acquired that status exclusively as a result of his being accepted for admission to university to undertake the studies in question. In such circumstances, the employment relationship, which is the only basis for the rights deriving from Regulation No 1612/68, is merely ancillary to the studies to be financed by the grant.'[103] Such a person was not entitled under Article 7(2) to a maintenance grant from the host State. Nor could someone in the position of the applicant claim any rights under Article 12 of Regulation 1612/68, since that provision 'grants rights only to a child who has lived with his parents or either one of them in a Member State whilst at least one of his parents resided there as a worker. It cannot therefore create rights for the benefit of a worker's child who was born after the worker ceased to work and reside in the host State.'[104]

The applicant in *Brown* would presumably have been able to claim a maintenance grant on the basis of Article 12[105] had his parents postponed their move to France until shortly after his birth. He might have been forgiven for thinking this a rather arbitrary distinction. Moreover, it is not entirely fanciful to suggest that the

---

[100] Case 197/86 [1988] ECR 3205.   [101] Para 23.

[102] The Court referred to *Lair, supra*, decided on the same day as *Brown*. Cf *Bernini, supra*.

[103] Para 27.   [104] Para 30.   [105] Cf *Echternach* and *di Leo, supra*.

Court's approach is capable of deterring nationals of the Member States from exercising the rights to freedom of movement conferred on them by the Treaty. To
that extent, it seems inconsistent with the spirit of the ruling in *Singh*, where—
admittedly in slightly different circumstances—the Court underlined the importance of permitting the spouse and children of a migrant 'to enter and reside in the
territory of his Member State of origin under conditions at least equivalent to those
granted them by Community law in the territory of another Member State'.[106] A
more fundamental objection to the ruling in *Brown* is the illogicality of holding
someone in the position of the applicant to be a worker within the meaning of
Article 7(2) of Regulation 1612/68 and then, without a scintilla of textual justification, denying him the advantages which that provision confers. What the Court
should really have said was that someone in the applicant's situation did not constitute a worker, but this would no doubt have involved too much of a departure
from well-established case law. The case illustrates how an apparently progressive
approach by the Court on some questions may lead it to adopt a restrictive
approach on others, in order to redress the balance between the various interests
involved.

Wholly internal situations

Notwithstanding the broad approach which the Court has generally taken to the
scope, both material and personal, of Article 39 (ex 48), it has drawn the line at situations which may be described as internal to a Member State, in other words
where the claimant has never exercised his or her rights of free movement under
the Treaty and is seeking to rely on the Treaty against the Member State of which
he or she is a national. There is a parallel here with Articles 81 (ex 85) and 82 (ex
86), the principal competition rules applicable to undertakings, which apply only
where trade between Member States is affected, but in the case of those provisions
the requirement is spelled out in the Treaty. This is not the case with Article 39
and the Court's insistence that that article does not apply to internal situations has
produced some odd results. Changes in the Treaty context have rendered it
increasingly anomalous: the objective of creating a properly functioning internal
market laid down in the Single European Act; the introduction of the concept of
citizenship of the Union by the Maastricht Treaty;[107] the establishment of an area
of freedom, security and justice for which provision was made in the Amsterdam
Treaty.[108] The case law on internal situations is therefore a striking example of a

---

[106] Case C–370/90 [1992] ECR I–4265, para 20.

[107] In Joined Cases C–64/96 and C–65/96 *Land Nordrhein-Westfalen v Uecker* and *Jacquet v Land
Nordrhein-Westfalen* [1997] ECR I–3171, para 23, the Court stated: 'it must be noted that citizenship of
the Union, established by Article 8 [now 17] EC, is not intended to extend the scope *ratione materiae* of
the Treaty also to internal situations which have no link with Community law'.

[108] See Title IV (ex IIIa) EC and Title VI TEU, discussed in ch 11.

context in which the Court has been content to let the Member States make the running.

The origins of the doctrine may be traced to *Regina v Saunders*,[109] a case decided in 1979. S was a British national who apparently came from Northern Ireland. She pleaded guilty in the Bristol Crown Court to a charge of theft and was bound over on condition that she proceed to Northern Ireland and keep out of England and Wales for three years. S did not comply with that condition and was subsequently arrested in Wales and brought back before the Crown Court. At that point, the question was raised whether S was a worker for the purposes of Article 39 (ex 48) and, if so, whether the binding over order infringed her rights under that article. On a reference to the Court of Justice for a preliminary ruling, Advocate General Warner argued[110] that Community law did not affect restrictions on the freedom of movement of individuals imposed by criminal courts in the ordinary course of the administration of justice. However, an order made by a criminal court in order to secure the deportation of a person or his banishment from a substantial part of the territory of the Member State to which the court in question belonged would, in the view of the Advocate General, be caught by Article 48 unless it was justified on grounds of public policy or public security. It was for the referring court to decide into which category its own order fell.

The Court took a different approach. It accepted that, while Article 39 (ex 48) might require Member States to change the rules applicable to their own nationals, it did not 'aim to restrict the power of the Member States to lay down restrictions, within their own territory, on the freedom of movement of all persons subject to their jurisdiction in implementation of domestic criminal law.'[111] The Court went on:[112]

The provisions of the Treaty on freedom of movement for workers cannot therefore be applied to situations which are wholly internal to a Member State, in other words, where there is no factor connecting them to any of the situations envisaged by Community law.

The application by an authority or court of a Member State to a worker who is a national of that same State of measures which deprive or restrict the freedom of movement of that worker within the territory of that State as a penal measure provided for by national law by reason of acts committed within the territory of that State is a wholly domestic situation which falls outside the scope of the rules contained in the Treaty on freedom of movement for workers.

The Court was evidently anxious to avoid interfering in the sentencing policies of national courts. It may also have taken the view that to apply Article 39 (ex 48) to wholly internal situations would have brought too many disputes within its scope, but that the distinction drawn by Advocate General Warner between the different types of restriction on freedom of movement that might be imposed by national courts was too imprecise to be helpful. However, the test devised by the Court

---

[109] Case 175/78 [1979] ECR 1129.   [110] At p 1144.   [111] Para 10.
[112] Paras 11 and 12.

seems no less satisfactory. True, it has enabled the Court to dispose quickly of cases that had no real connection with the functioning of the common market. Thus, in *Moser v Land Baden-Württemberg*[113] the Court dismissed as wholly internal a dispute between the applicant, a German national, and the respondent Land over the Land's refusal to allow the applicant to complete the training necessary to become a teacher in Germany on the basis that his loyalty to the German Basic Law was in doubt. The referring court had taken the view that the Land's attitude might deprive the applicant of the chance of working as a teacher in other Member States, but the Court observed: 'A purely hypothetical prospect of employment in another Member State does not establish a sufficient connection with Community law to justify the application of Article 48 [now 39] of the Treaty.'[114]

However, in other cases the *Saunders* rule has produced anomalies. In *Morson and Jhanjan v State of the Netherlands*[115] M and J, who were nationals of Surinam, had come to the Netherlands as tourists and taken up residence there with their children, who were nationals of that State and on whom they were dependent. They applied for residence permits and, since their children were in employment in the Netherlands, they sought to rely on Article 10(1)(b) of Regulation 1612/68, which gives 'dependent relatives in the ascending line of the worker' the right to install themselves with him irrespective of their own nationality. Unfortunately for M and J, Article 10(1) applies only where 'a worker who is a national of one Member State . . . is employed in the territory of another Member State'. The Court therefore concluded that the case had no factor linking it with any of the situations governed by Community law, since the workers on whom M and J were dependent had never exercised their right to freedom of movement within the Community.

The outcome would clearly have been different had those workers been nationals of, or resident in, another Member State for they would clearly then have been covered by Article 10(1) of the regulation. It would also have been different had M and J taken up residence with their children in another Member State and they had all then sought to return to the Netherlands. In *Singh*,[116] the Court held that a Member State had to grant leave to enter and reside in its territory to the spouse, of whatever nationality, of a national of that State who had gone, with the spouse, to another Member State in order to work there and who returned to the first State in order to pursue an economic activity. The Court observed:

[113] Case 180/83 [1984] ECR 2539. See also Case C–332/90 *Steen v Deutsche Bundespost* [1992] ECR I–341.
[114] Para 18.
[115] Joined Cases 35 and 36/82 [1982] ECR 3723. See also Joined Cases C–297/88 and C–197/89 *Dzodzi* [1990] ECR I–3763.
[116] Case C–370/90 [1992] ECR I–4265. Cf Case C–112/91 *Werner v Finanzamt Aachen-Innenstadt* [1993] ECR I–429, an Art 43 (ex 52) case, where the Court held that the fact that a self-employed person lived in a Member State which was not his own was not enough to trigger the application of the Treaty when he had obtained his qualifications in the Member State of which he was a national, had always practised his profession there, and was subject to the tax legislation of that State.

A national of a Member State might be deterred from leaving his country of origin in order to pursue an activity as an employed or self-employed person as envisaged by the Treaty in the territory of another Member State if, on returning to the Member State of which he is a national in order to pursue an activity there as an employed or self-employed person, the conditions of his entry and residence were not at least equivalent to those which he would enjoy under the Treaty or secondary law in the territory of another Member State.

Although the Court in *Singh* only referred expressly to the spouse and children of a migrant worker, the logic of the above passage applies equally to dependent relatives in the ascending line, who are covered by the same provision—Article 10(1)—of Regulation 1612/68. It does not of course apply directly in the circumstances of a case like *Morson and Jhanjan*, but the Court's decision in that case might have the effect of encouraging some Member State nationals to exercise their rights to freedom of movement in order to enhance the rights enjoyed by members of their families. Even if the Commission was right in that case when it argued that a Member State was entitled to prevent its nationals from abusing the right to freedom of movement to avoid the application of its national law,[117] such cases might in practice prove hard to identify and any steps taken by the Member State concerned would have to avoid prejudicing those who were genuinely seeking to take advantage of the rights conferred on them by the Treaty.

Similar difficulties arise as a result of the *Bosman* ruling, where the Court reiterated its case law on the inapplicability of Article 39 (ex 48) to situations which are wholly internal to a Member State. Although the Court made it clear that the circumstances of that case, involving the transfer of a Belgian player from a club in Belgium to one in France, could not be classified as wholly internal, it seems clear that the ruling does not apply to domestic transfers. This could encourage clubs to concentrate on other Member States when searching for new players or to arrange for a player from a club in the same Member State to move temporarily to one in another Member State before arriving at the true purchaser in order to avoid having to pay a transfer fee.[118] It is clearly undesirable that the functioning of the common market should be distorted in this way. If the Court is not prepared to abandon the doctrine of the wholly internal situation, a better approach might have been to exclude from Article 39 at least certain types of non-discriminatory national rule[119] and to apply a rule of remoteness to those that remained within its scope.

Administrative obstacles to freedom of movement

The legislation adopted by the Council under Article 40 (ex 49) EC includes various provisions concerning the formalities with which migrant workers must

[117] See p 3730.
[118] These possibilities are explored by Weatherill (1996) 33 CMLRev 991, 1019–26, who points out that such an arrangement might in principle be caught by Art 81 (ex 85) EC.
[119] Cf the suggestion of AG Lenz in *Bosman*.

comply in order to avail themselves of the rights of free movement conferred by the Treaty. The most important set of such provisions is to be found in Directive 68/360 on the abolition of restrictions on movement and residence within the Community for workers of Member States and their families.[120] Article 3 of that directive requires Member States to allow nationals of other Member States and certain members of their families[121] 'to enter their territory simply on production of a valid identity card or passport' (Article 3(1)). Visas may only be demanded from members of the migrant's family who are not nationals of a Member State and even then such persons are to be accorded 'every facility for obtaining any necessary visas' (Article 3(2)). Article 4 requires Member States to grant the right of residence to migrant workers and members of their families on production of certain specified documents and to issue to them a residence permit as proof of their right of residence. Rules are laid down as to the scope, renewal and withdrawal of the residence permit. However, it is made clear in Article 5 of the directive that '[c]ompletion of the formalities for obtaining a residence permit shall not hinder the immediate beginning of employment under a contract concluded by the applicants'. Moreover, Article 8 lists certain categories of worker whose right of residence in their territory Member States are to recognize without issuing a residence permit. By virtue of Article 10, Member States may only derogate from the directive on grounds of public policy, public security or public health.

Inevitably it fell to the Court to determine the rights of migrants who failed to protect their position by recourse to the arrangements put in place under Directive 68/360. The Court has been firm in regarding the directive as concerned purely with formalities and in refusing to allow its provisions to undermine the substance of the rights conferred by the Treaty. One of the leading cases on the significance of failing to comply with the requirements of the directive is *Royer*,[122] where the Court made it clear that the Treaty and the legislation adopted by the Council under Article 40 (ex 49) directly conferred rights to freedom of movement on certain nationals of the Member States and members of their families and that those rights were acquired independently of the issue of a residence permit by the host State. The permit was to be regarded 'not as a measure giving rise to rights but as a measure by a Member State serving to prove the individual position of a national of another Member State with regard to provisions of Community law'.[123] Member States were obliged, the Court said, to issue a residence permit to a person who, by producing the documents specified in Directive 68/360, could prove that he came within the personal scope of the directive. It followed that 'the mere failure by a national of a Member State to complete the legal formalities concerning access, movement and residence of aliens does not justify a decision ordering

---

[120] OJ Sp Ed 1968 (II), p 485.

[121] ie those to whom Reg 1612/68 applies.

[122] Case 48/75 [1976] ECR 497. See also Joined Cases 389 and 390/87 *Echternach and Another v Minister for Education and Science* [1989] ECR 723, paras 24–6.

[123] Para 33. Cf *Martínez Sala, supra*.

expulsion'.[124] Nor could such a failure in itself be considered a breach of public policy or public security.

The Court has accepted that Member States may impose reasonable penalties on migrants who fail to comply with the formalities prescribed or permitted by Community law, provided they are not 'so severe as to cause an obstacle to the freedom of entry and residence provided for in the Treaty'.[125] Moreover, it was accepted in *Royer* that Member States were entitled to adopt rules on the control of foreigners and to enforce them by sanctions falling short of expulsion. In doing so, however, Member States must comply with the principles of proportionality and non-discrimination, as the Court made clear in *Watson and Belmann*.[126] In that case, criminal proceedings had been brought in Italy against a British national who had spent several months there, and an Italian national who had provided her with accommodation, for failing to report her presence in Italy as required by Italian law. The penalties laid down for infringements of the legislation concerned were severe and the Court was asked whether such legislation constituted discrimination based on nationality and a restriction on the free movement of persons. The Court accepted that Member States were entitled to require nationals of other Member States to report their presence to the national authorities and to penalize failure to do so, but emphasized that the penalty had to be 'comparable to those attaching to infringements of provisions of equal importance by nationals'.[127] Member States were not entitled to impose 'a penalty so disproportionate to the gravity of the infringement that it becomes an obstacle to the free movement of persons'.[128] Thus, to deport someone protected by Community law would be unlawful because deportation 'negates the very right conferred and guaranteed by the Treaty'.[129]

This line of case law reflects an attempt by the Court to balance the requirements of the Treaty rules on freedom of movement with the desire of Member States to monitor the comings and goings of aliens. The outcome is not entirely satisfactory. The Court's conclusion that the right to freedom of movement did not depend on compliance with the formalities laid down in Directive 68/360 was entirely in accordance with the tenor of the directive[130] and the terms of Article 39 (ex 48) itself, which refers to the right of workers to move freely within the territory of Member States. However, the Court's willingness to accept that a Member State could require the nationals of other Member States exercising their right to free-dom of movement to comply with the host State's legislation on the movement of aliens, even in the absence of any threat to the public policy or public security of the host State, lacks any basis in the Treaty. Such legislation is inherently discrim-

---

[124] Para 38.

[125] Case 8/77 *Sagulo, Brenca and Bakhouche* [1977] ECR 1495, para 12. See also Case 157/79 *Regina v Pieck* [1980] ECR 2171.

[126] Case 118/75 [1976] ECR 1185. See also Case C–265/88 *Criminal Proceedings against Messner* [1989] ECR I–4209.

[127] Para 21.   [128] Ibid.   [129] Para 20.   [130] See in particular Arts 4(2) and 5.

inatory and seems (particularly to observers who are not accustomed to being required to carry identity cards) liable to hinder the integration of migrant workers and their families into the life of the host State, a consequence which in other contexts[131] the Court has sought to avoid.

The Court has even accepted that Member States are entitled to apply such legislation at the frontier, notwithstanding the requirement laid down in Article 3(1) of Directive 68/360 that Member States must allow persons within the personal scope of the directive to enter their territory 'simply on production of a valid identity card or passport'. In *Commission v Belgium*,[132] the Commission sought a declaration under Article 226 (ex 169) EC that Belgium had infringed the Treaty by imposing checks—albeit only sporadically—on the entry into its territory of nationals of other Member States who were already legally resident there to see whether they were carrying their residence or establishment permit, as required by Belgian law. The Court accepted that the only precondition that Member States were entitled to impose on entry into their territory by those enjoying rights to freedom of movement under the Treaty was production of a valid identity card or passport in accordance with Directive 68/360 and the equivalent directive for the self-employed, Directive 73/148.[133] In particular, the public policy proviso could not be used to justify the systematic imposition of additional formalities at the frontier. However, the Court observed that the controls at issue 'are not a condition for the exercise of the right of entry into Belgian territory and it is undisputed that Community law does not prevent Belgium from checking, within its territory, compliance with the obligation imposed on persons enjoying a right of residence under Community law to carry their residence or establishment permit at all times, where an identical obligation is imposed upon Belgian nationals as regards their identity card'.[134] In these circumstances, the Court considered the disputed controls acceptable, although it made it clear that it would have taken a different view had they been carried out 'in a systematic, arbitrary or unnecessarily restrictive manner'.[135]

It is unclear whether the remarkably tolerant attitude manifested by the Court towards administrative controls imposed by Member States on nationals of other Member States will be affected by the Amsterdam Treaty, which envisages the progressive establishment of an area of freedom, security, and justice in which controls on persons crossing internal borders are abolished and common standards and procedures on the crossing of the external borders of the Member States are laid down.[136] On the one hand, it might be said that, in order to establish an area of total freedom of movement within the external frontiers of the Community, controls on the movement of aliens which are laid down by national law and applied within the territory of a Member State should no longer be tolerated. On the other hand, it might be said that the importance of such controls would be reinforced if

[131] See eg the case law on Art 7(2) of Reg 1612/68, *supra*.   [132] Case 321/87 [1989] ECR 997.
[133] OJ 1973 L172/14, Art 3(1).   [134] Para 12.   [135] Para 15.
[136] See Title IV (ex IIIa) of the EC Treaty, in particular Art 62 (ex 73j).

border controls were completely removed. The Court's case law to date suggests that the latter argument is likely to prevail in the absence of intervention by the Council, particularly since the new Title does not apply in the same way to all the Member States.[137]

---

[137] See the Protocols annexed to the TEU and the EC Treaty making special arrangements for the UK, Ireland, and Denmark.

9

The right of establishment and freedom to provide services

The authors of the Treaty did not envisage that the benefits of the common market would be confined to workers. Article 3(b) EEC in its original form referred to the abolition of obstacles to freedom of movement for *persons*, a broader term than workers, and also for services. Those terms were repeated in the definition of the internal market contained in Article 14 (ex 7a) EC, which was inserted by the Single European Act. The Treaty rules on workers were therefore supplemented by chapters on the right of establishment and the freedom to provide services. Those chapters placed considerable responsibility for achieving their objectives on the Council, but the difficulties experienced by the Council in passing the requisite legislation led the Court to intervene in a bold and imaginative manner and the Treaty rules on services have come to adopt a central place in the law regulating the common market.

The right of establishment is the subject of Articles 43 (ex 52) to 48 (ex 58) EC. The basic rule is laid down in Article 43, the first paragraph of which originally provided that 'restrictions on the freedom of establishment of nationals of a Member State in the territory of another Member State shall be abolished[1] by progressive stages in the course of the transitional period. Such progressive abolition shall also apply to restrictions on the setting up of agencies, branches, or subsidiaries by nationals of any Member State established in the territory of any Member State.' Article 44(1) (ex 54(1)) originally required the Council to draw up a general programme for the abolition of existing restrictions on freedom of establishment within the Community setting out 'the general conditions under which freedom of establishment is to be attained in the case of each type of activity and in particular the stages by which it is to be attained'. Under the following paragraph, the general programme was to be implemented by Council directive. Article 47(1) (ex 57(1)) imposed on the Council a particular responsibility for issuing directives 'for the mutual recognition of diplomas, certificates and other evidence of formal qualifications'; Article 47(2) (ex 57(2)) required the Council, before the end of the transitional period, to issue directives for the coordination of national provisions concerning the activities of self-employed persons.

The Treaty envisaged two derogations from the right of establishment. Article 46(1) (ex 56(1)) resembled Article 39(3) (ex 48(3)) in the case of workers. It

---

[1] Art 43 now uses the term 'prohibited'.

provided: 'The provisions of this Chapter and measures taken in pursuance thereof shall not prejudice the applicability of provisions laid down by law, regulation or administrative action providing for special treatment for foreign nationals on grounds of public policy, public security or public health.'[2] An additional derogation was to be found in the first paragraph of Article 45 (ex 55): 'The provisions of this Chapter shall not apply, so far as any given Member State is concerned, to activities which in that State are connected, even occasionally, with the exercise of official authority.' Although worded differently, that provision was the counterpart of Article 39(4) (ex 48(4)), which excluded 'employment in the public service' from the provisions of Article 39 (ex 48). Both derogations are discussed in more detail in the next chapter.

If Article 43 (ex 52) contemplated the permanent integration of the migrant into the economy of the host State, the chapter on services (Articles 49–55 (ex 59–66)) was designed to facilitate economic activities which involved a more transient involvement with the host State. According to the original text of the first paragraph of Article 49 (ex 59), restrictions on freedom to provide services within the Community were to be abolished[3] within the Community during the transitional period 'in respect of nationals of Member States who are established in a State of the Community other than that of the person for whom the services are intended'. The Treaty gave no definition of 'services', but did say in the first paragraph of Article 50 (ex 60) that the chapter applied to services which were 'normally provided for remuneration, in so far as they are not governed by the provisions [of the Treaty] relating to freedom of movement for goods, capital and persons'. Like the chapter on establishment, Article 52 (ex 63) originally required the Council to draw up a general programme for the abolition of existing restrictions on freedom to provide services within the Community and to issue directives to implement the general programme. Restrictions which had not yet been abolished were to be applied by the Member States 'without distinction on grounds of nationality or residence to all persons providing services within the meaning of the first paragraph of Article 59 [now 49]'. By virtue of Article 55 (ex 66), Articles 45 (ex 55) to 48 (ex 58) were also to apply to the Chapter on services.

Two preliminary points may be made about these provisions before examining the way they have been interpreted by the Court of Justice. First, the Treaty set a deadline of the end of the transitional period—31 December 1969—for the abolition of restrictions on both the right of establishment and the freedom to provide services. The main device for ensuring that that deadline was met was to be the directive, which it was the Council's responsibility to adopt. The directive was to be used to secure the abolition of existing restrictions, the coordination of national laws and the mutual recognition of qualifications. The General Programmes for the abolition of restrictions on freedom of establishment[4] and freedom to provide

---

[2] The Council was to issue directives for the coordination of such provisions before the end of the transitional period: Art 56(2) (now 46(2)).

[3] Art 49 now uses the term 'prohibited'.   [4] OJ, Sp Ed, Second Series, IX, p 7.

services[5] contemplated by the Treaty were adopted by the Council in 1961, but the pernicious influence of the Luxembourg Compromise of 1966 meant that, by the end of the transitional period, much remained to be done. Progress began to be made in 1973, when the Council adopted Directive 73/148 on the abolition of restrictions on movement and residence within the Community for nationals of Member States with regard to establishment and the provision of services.[6] That directive largely parallels Directive 68/360 in the case of workers. The following year saw the adoption of Directive 75/34 concerning the right of nationals of a Member State to remain in the territory of another Member State after having pursued therein an activity in a self-employed capacity.[7] That directive grants self-employed persons rights similar to those conferred on workers by Regulation 1251/70.[8] There is no equivalent in the context of the self-employed of Regulation 1612/68, however, and real progress towards the mutual recognition of qualifications was not made until the end of the 1980s.[9]

The second preliminary point is that, although national rules which discriminated against the citizens of other Member States would be particularly inimical to the attainment of the objectives of the Treaty, neither the rules on establishment nor those on services seemed to be confined to such rules, at least once the transitional period had ended. This much was clear from the text of Article 43 (ex 52), which, in its original form, simply stated that 'restrictions on the freedom of establishment . . . shall be abolished'. The article went on to make it clear that the right of establishment included (but was not therefore limited to) 'the right to take up and pursue activities as self-employed persons and to set up and manage undertakings . . . under the conditions laid down for its own nationals by the law of the country where such establishment is effected'. Similarly, Article 49 (ex 59) in its original form spoke of abolishing restrictions on the freedom to provide services in a general sense. The reference in the second paragraph of Article 50 (ex 60) to a provider of services temporarily pursuing his activities 'in the State where the service is provided, under the same conditions as are imposed by that State on its own nationals' might have seemed to limit the Treaty rules to the abolition of discrimination, but that interpretation was apparently contradicted by Article 54 (ex 65), which provided: 'As long as restrictions on freedom to provide services have not been abolished, each Member State shall apply such restrictions without distinction on grounds of nationality or residence to all persons providing services within the meaning of the first paragraph of Article 49.' In other words, Article 49 did indeed contemplate the abolition of both discriminatory and non-discriminatory

---

[5] OJ, Sp Ed, Second Series, IX, p 3.   [6] OJ 1973 L172/14.

[7] OJ 1975 L14/10.

[8] The difference in the nature of the acts concerned seems to be attributable to their legal bases and the institutions which adopted them. See also Dir 90/365 on the right of residence for employees and self-employed persons who have ceased their occupational activity, OJ 1990 L180/28.

[9] See Dir 89/48 on a general system for the recognition of higher-education diplomas awarded on completion of professional education and training of at least three years' duration, OJ 1989 L19/16. That directive is discussed below.

restrictions. This was to have been achieved by the end of the transitional period, a deadline which the Treaty assumed would be met. In the meantime, remaining restrictions were to be applied in a non–discriminatory manner.[10]

The distinction between establishment and services

Why did the Treaty contain separate chapters on establishment and services? If the substantive rules were so similar, it would surely have been more convenient to deal with both in the same chapter. One reason seems to be that the Treaty has traditionally regarded persons and services as separate factors of production.[11] Within the former category, there are obvious distinctions between employees and the self-employed which justify separate treatment. A second reason is that, at the time the Treaty was drawn up in the 1950s, the distinction between establishment and services probably seemed reasonably clear, because the slowness of travel and communication made it hard for anyone other than a frontier-dweller to carry on business in more than one State at the same time.[12] Nowadays electronic methods of communication give businesses options that were simply not available in the past and the borderline between establishment and services has consequently become more difficult to draw. A further reason is that establishment implies a greater degree of integration into the economy of the host State than the provision of services. This may mean that national rules which seem reasonable when applied to someone seeking to establish themselves in a State which is not their own may appear excessive if that State seeks to enforce them against someone who only wishes to provide services there on a temporary basis. As Advocate General Jacobs put it in *Säger*, '[i]t does not seem unreasonable that a person establishing himself in a Member State should as a general rule be required to comply with the law of that State in all respects. In contrast, it is less easy to see why a person who is established in one Member State and who provides services in other Member States should be required to comply with all the detailed regulations in force in each of those States. To accept such a proposition would be to render the notion of a single market unattainable in the field of services.'[13] The view that a Member State might legit-imately impose more onerous conditions on those seeking to establish themselves in its territory than on those wishing merely to provide services there was endorsed

---

[10] See the Opinion of AG Warner in Case 52/79 *Procureur du Roi v Debauve* [1980] ECR 833, 870–2. The extent to which this analysis is reflected in the case law of the Court is considered below.

[11] See eg Arts 3(1)(c) and 14 (ex 7a).

[12] A point made by Edward, 'Establishment and services: an analysis of the insurance cases' (1987) 12 ELRev 231, 252–3.

[13] Case C–76/90 [1991] ECR I–4221, 4234. AG Jacobs thought that, at least in some circumstances, services were more closely related to goods than establishment. Evidence of the economic link between goods and services may be found in the annexes to the Agreement establishing the World Trade Organization, which was considered by the Court of Justice in Opinion 1/94 [1994] ECR I–5267. See generally Eeckhout, *The European Internal Market and International Trade: A Legal Analysis* (1994), ch 1.

by the Court in the 'Tourist Guide' cases, where it declared that 'the Member State cannot make the performance of the services in its territory subject to observance of all the conditions required for establishment; were it to do so the provisions securing freedom to provide services would be deprived of all practical effect'.[14]

The extent of a person's right to do business in another Member State without complying with local rules may therefore depend on whether he falls within the scope of Article 43 (ex 52) or Article 49 (ex 59). The distinction which is in principle drawn by the Court between the two reflects some of the factors mentioned above. The question was discussed in some detail in *Gebhard v Consiglio dell'Ordine degli Avvocati e Procuratori di Milano*,[15] which arose out of a dispute concerning the right of a German national who was entitled to practise as a *Rechtsanwalt* in Germany to practise in Italy from his own chambers under the title *avvocato*. The Court began by noting that the Treaty chapters on workers, the right of establishment and services were mutually exclusive. The first was not relevant on the facts and the third was subordinate to the second.[16] The Court noted that a person— natural or legal—could be established in more than one Member State: a company might set up an agency, branch, or subsidiary in another Member State, a member of a profession might establish a second professional base.[17] The Court said that the concept of establishment was therefore 'a very broad one, allowing a Community national to participate, on a stable and continuous basis, in the economic life of a Member State other than his State of origin and to profit therefrom, so contributing to economic and social interpenetration within the Community in the sphere of activities as self-employed persons'.[18] By contrast, the chapter on services envisaged the pursuit of activities by the provider on a temporary basis. The question whether particular activities were to be considered temporary was 'to be determined in the light, not only of the duration of the provision of the service, but also of its regularity, periodicity or continuity. The fact that the provision of services is temporary does not mean that the provider of services within the meaning of the Treaty may not equip himself with some form of infrastructure in the host Member State (including an office, chambers or consulting rooms) in so far as such infrastructure is necessary for the purposes of performing the services in question.'[19] The Court took the view that the circumstances of this case fell within the scope of the chapter on establishment. The applicant, it said, 'pursues a professional activity on a stable and continuous basis in another Member State where he holds

[14] Case C–154/89 *Commission v France* [1991] ECR I–659, para 12. See also Case C–180/89 *Commission v Italy* [1991] ECR I–709, para 15; Case C–198/89 *Commission v Greece* [1991] ECR I–727, para 16. These cases are discussed in more detail below.
[15] Case C–55/94 [1995] ECR I–4165. See also Case C–70/95 *Sodemare and Others v Regione Lombardia* [1997] ECR I–3395, discussed below.
[16] See Art 50 (ex 60), first para.
[17] The Court referred to Case 107/83 *Ordre des Avocats au Barreau de Paris v Klopp* [1984] ECR 2971, where a German lawyer was denied admission to the Paris Bar because he had retained chambers in Düsseldorf. An *avocat* was permitted to open chambers in one place only. The Court found that in these circumstances there was an infringement of Art 43 (ex 52).
[18] Para 25.   [19] Para 27.

himself out from an established professional base to, amongst others, nationals of that State'.[20]

The wording of the Court's judgment suggests that it is only in exceptional circumstances that a person who equips himself 'with some form of infrastructure in the host Member State' will be considered covered by the chapter on services rather than that on establishment. That was certainly the view taken by Advocate General Léger[21] and it is supported by the judgment of the Court in the 'Insurance' case,[22] which concerned the compatibility with the Treaty of various restrictions imposed by German law on the right of insurance companies in other Member States to provide services in Germany. The Court emphasized that 'an insurance undertaking of another Member State which maintains a permanent presence in the Member State in question comes within the scope of the provisions of the Treaty on the right of establishment, even if that presence does not take the form of a branch or agency, but consists merely of an office managed by the undertakings own staff or by a person who is independent but authorized to act on a permanent basis for the undertaking, as would be the case with an agency'.[23] This is a very broad definition indeed of the notion of establishment and it means that a Community national who carries on business in another Member State risks being subject to many of the requirements of that State as soon as he establishes a permanent presence there.[24] It is by no means clear where the line between maintaining a permanent presence and equipping oneself with some form of infrastructure within the meaning of *Gebhard* is to be drawn. The upshot is to give the Court a considerable degree of flexibility in appraising the rights of individuals and the powers of Member States to regulate the pursuit of economic activities on their own territory.

Because the chapter on services is liable to impinge significantly on the prerogatives of the Member States, the Court has sometimes treated activities as covered by the chapter on establishment instead even in the absence of any form of permanent presence in the host State. In *van Binsbergen*,[25] for example, the Court made it clear that a person established in one Member State, whose activities are entirely or principally directed towards another Member State, may be treated by that State *as if he were established there* where his purpose in establishing himself in the first State was to avoid rules of conduct applicable in the second State. The Court applied that principle in *TV10*,[26] which arose out of an attempt by a Member State to apply restrictive provisions of its legislation on broadcasting to a broadcaster established in another Member State whose activities were mainly directed towards the first

---

[20] Para 28.   [21] See p I–4175.

[22] Case 205/84 *Commission v Germany* [1986] ECR 3755. See Dehousse, *The European Court of Justice* (1998), pp 88–90. Cf Case C–118/96 *Safir v Skattemyndigheten i Dalarnas Län* [1998] ECR I–1897.

[23] Para 21.

[24] See Edward, 'Establishment and services: an analysis of the insurance cases' (1987) 12 ELRev 231, 254.

[25] Case 33/74 [1974] ECR 1299, para 13. See also the 'Insurance' case, *supra*, para 22.

[26] Case C–23/93 [1994] ECR I–4795.

State. The contested legislation was designed to pursue objectives of cultural policy which the Court had found, in a series of previous cases, to be legitimate. It
concluded that such a broadcaster could be treated as established in the first State if
it had intended to avoid the rules applicable there by establishing itself in the second State. The approach taken by the Court in cases of this nature is a creative one
which prevents the provisions of the Treaty from being abused in order to avoid
justifiable attempts by Member States to regulate commercial activities in their own
territories. It provides clear evidence of the Court's sensitivity to the legitimate
concerns of Member States and its willingness to curtail the rights of individuals
where necessary to ensure that those concerns are met.

Compensating for the failings of the Council: the question of direct effect

The Court was called upon to consider the consequences of the Council's failure
to implement its General Programmes by the end of the transitional period in
Reyners v Belgium,[27] a case on the right of establishment. A Netherlands national
who held a legal diploma giving the right to take up the profession of *avocat* in
Belgium had been denied the right to do so because of his nationality. Advocate
General Mayras observed that the problem of securing freedom of establishment for
lawyers 'is one of those which have, since the coming into force of the Treaty,
given rise to the most lively controversies and the most marked divergencies
between the Bars and between the national Governments, to the point where
action by the Community organs has been paralysed and no positive measure has
until now been able to be taken to free the activities of the *avocat* at a Community
level'.[28] However, the Court was not willing to allow the inability to reach agreement of the parties concerned (some with vested interests) to interfere with the
attainment of a fundamental objective of the Treaty. It declared that, from the end
of the transitional period, Article 43 (ex 52) 'had the character of a provision which
is complete in itself and legally perfect'.[29] The adoption of directives by the
Council was intended to facilitate the achievement of the objective of Article 43,
but the absence of such directives could not deprive that article of any effect at all:
'In laying down that freedom of establishment shall be attained at the end of the
transitional period, Article 52 [now 43] thus imposes an obligation to attain a precise result, the fulfilment of which had to be made easier by, but not made dependent on, the implementation of a programme of progressive measures.'[30] Thus, once
the transitional period had expired, directives were no longer necessary to give
effect to the Treaty prohibition against discrimination on grounds of nationality,
which the Treaty itself required the national courts to uphold. Directives were not,
however, entirely irrelevant: they 'preserve an important scope in the field of

[27] Case 2/74 [1974] ECR 631.   [28] At p 658.   [29] Para 12.   [30] Para 26.

measures intended to make easier the effective exercise of the right to freedom of establishment'.[31] They would therefore continue to be needed to realize the right of establishment where obstacles resulted simply from differences in the national laws, themselves perfectly reasonable, regulating particular trades and professions.

Six months later, the Court gave judgment in *van Binsbergen v Bedrijfsvereniging Metaalnijverheid*,[32] in which the approach taken in the *Reyners* case was extended to Articles 49 (ex 59) and 50 (ex 60). A person chosen by the appellant to act as his legal representative in proceedings before a Netherlands court where representation by a lawyer was not compulsory found his capacity to continue doing so challenged when he moved his home from the Netherlands to Belgium during the proceedings. Under Netherlands law, only those established in the Netherlands could act as legal representatives before the court concerned. The Court declared that the restrictions which Articles 49 and 50 required to be abolished included 'all requirements imposed on the person providing the service by reason in particular of his nationality or of the fact that he does not habitually reside in the State where the service is provided, which do not apply to persons established within the national territory or which may prevent or otherwise obstruct the activities of the person providing the service'.[33] The Court acknowledged that special provisions might be acceptable where necessary to ensure observance of professional rules which were objectively justified. That was not so in circumstances such as these: the activity in question was essentially unregulated and the requirements of the administration of justice could be met by requiring legal advisers to have an address for service in the Netherlands.[34] Moreover, at least in relation to obstacles such as these, Articles 49 and 50 had direct effect:

. . . as regards at least the specific requirement of nationality or of residence, Articles 59 [now 49] and 60 [now 50] impose a well-defined obligation, the fulfilment of which by the Member States cannot be delayed or jeopardized by the absence of provisions which were to be adopted in pursuance of powers conferred under Articles 63 [now 52] and 66 [now 55].[35]

The timing of these decisions should not pass unremarked. The 1960s had been a decade of contrasts. The Court of Justice had attacked its task with gusto, laying down the twin doctrines of primacy and direct effect which were to have such a profound effect on the legal shape of the Community.[36] The Council, however, had been unable or unwilling to follow the Court's lead, allowing the transitional period to expire with much still to be done to complete the common market. From the Court's deliberation room at the beginning of the 1970s, the task must have seemed clear: to save the project from failure by compensating, within the spirit of the Treaty, for the failure of the Council to fulfil the responsibilities with which it

---

[31] Para 31.   [32] Case 33/74 [1974] ECR 1299.   [33] Para 10.
[34] It may be doubted whether even that requirement would be justified in the modern world, where documents can be transmitted by fax and e-mail.
[35] Para 26.   [36] See ch 3.

had been entrusted. The Court was aided in this endeavour by evidence in the Treaty itself, notably in its preamble, of what its authors had envisaged and by a certain imprecision in some of the language in which the Treaty was couched. In particular, the Treaty in its original form tended not to spell out the consequences if a deadline it laid down was not respected.[37] The year 1974 was one in which the Court made a particularly major contribution to completing the common market: less than a month after the *Reyners* case was decided, the Court gave judgment in *Dassonville* which, as we saw in chapter 7, gave a broad scope to one of the other cornerstones of the common market, Article 28 (ex 30).

The beneficiaries of the Treaty

Although undoubtedly adventurous, the Court's case law on establishment and services should not be considered unduly activist. It is worth emphasizing that, like Article 39 (ex 48) in the case of workers, Articles 43 (ex 52) and 49 (ex 59) do not apply in purely internal situations.[38] This is a significant limitation on their scope. The Court's willingness to countenance it may perhaps be justified by the language of the latter articles, which do seem to envisage some element linking two or more Member States in order for them to apply. However, it was pointed out in chapter 8 that confining the Treaty rules on freedom of movement to purely internal situations accords a significance to national borders which may be thought hard to reconcile with the notion of an internal market. None the less, the limitation of the Treaty rules to activities which are not confined to a single Member State does not mean that they cannot be invoked by someone against the Member State of which he is a national. Thus, in *van Binsbergen* the fact that the applicant was of Dutch nationality did not prevent him from relying on Articles 49 (ex 59) and 50 (ex 60) to resist the application to him of the relevant provision of Netherlands law. The case was not a purely internal one because at the material time the applicant was resident in Belgium.[39]

Cases in which someone seeks to rely on the Treaty rules against his own Member State in circumstances which are not purely internal have in practice been relatively unusual. Not surprisingly, the Treaty rules have most often been invoked where the law of one Member State hinders the right of another Member State's

[37] Cf the declaration adopted at the time of the signature of the Single European Act, in which the Member States stated that '[s]etting the date of 31 December 1992 does not create an automatic legal effect'. That date was embodied in what is now Art 14 of the Treaty and the Member States seemed to have wished to prevent the Court from treating it in the same way as the expiry of the transitional period. See further Schermers, 'The effect of the date 31 December 1992' (1991) 28 CMLRev 275; Toth, 'The legal status of the declarations annexed to the Single European Act' (1986) 23 CMLRev 803.

[38] See eg Case 115/78 *Knoors v Secretary of State for Economic Affairs* [1979] ECR 399, para 24; *Debauve, supra*, para 9.

[39] See also Case 39/75 *Coenen v Sociaal-Economische Raad* [1975] ECR 1547; *Knoors, supra*; Case C–19/92 *Kraus v Land Baden-Württemberg* [1993] ECR I–1663. The *Kraus* case is discussed below.

nationals to establish themselves or to provide a service. In such cases, the Court
has taken a characteristically flexible approach to the scope of the Treaty rules. That
flexibility has been particularly evident in the context of Article 49 (ex 59).
Although that article only expressly contemplates that the persons providing the
service will wish to move to another Member State, the Court held in *Luisi and
Carbone v Ministero del Tesoro*[40] that a recipient of services 'may go to the State in
which the person providing the service is established'. This, the Court said, was the
'necessary corollary' of the provider's right to travel to the Member State of the
recipient.[41] It went on to specify that '. . . tourists, persons receiving medical treatment and persons travelling for the purpose of education or business' were to be
regarded as recipients of services in this sense. The Italian Government had argued
that Articles 49 and 50 (ex 60) only applied to activities which were defined in
advance, in other words that the particular service in question and who was going
to provide it had to be identified at the time the recipient attempted to exercise his
right to freedom of movement. Support for that view was to be found in the
Opinion of Advocate General Trabucchi in *Watson and Belmann*, who had
observed that, if Article 49 were interpreted broadly, 'namely, by including all
those who are likely to be recipients of services . . ., the practical effect is to extend
the right of freedom of movement to all nationals of the Member States because
everyone is actually or potentially a recipient of services. This does not accord with
the wording of Article 59 [now 49] and is inconsistent with the very structure of
the Treaty, which provides for freedom of movement in respect of specific categories of professional or trade activities.'[42] In *Luisi and Carbone*, however,
Advocate General Mancini took the view that to adopt his predecessor's approach
and remove from the scope of Article 49 a sector as economically important as
tourism would undermine the pre-eminent position the article was intended to
have in the process of integration. That argument found favour with the Court,
whose judgment was not limited in the way suggested by the Italian Government.

The effect of the decision in *Luisi and Carbone* may be illustrated by *Cowan v
Trésor Public*.[43] C, a British national, was assaulted at the exit from a Metro station
during a visit to Paris. When it proved impossible to identify the perpetrators, C
applied for compensation under the Code de Procédure Pénale, but his application
was turned down because he did not hold a residence permit and no reciprocal
agreement on the matter had been concluded with the United Kingdom. C sought
to rely on what is now Article 12 EC which, '[w]ithin the scope of application of
this Treaty', prohibits discrimination on the grounds of nationality. The Court held
that, as a tourist, C was a recipient of services and that the circumstances of the case

---

[40] Joined Cases 286/82 and 26/83 [1984] ECR 377.   [41] Para 10.
[42] Case 118/75 [1976] ECR 1185, 1204.
[43] Case 186/87 [1989] ECR 195. Cf Case 293/83 *Gravier v City of Liège* [1985] ECR 593, where the
applicant put forward an argument based on her alleged status as a recipient of services. The argument
is considered by AG Slynn at pp 602–4. The Court decided the case on other grounds. *Cowan* and
Gravier are discussed in more detail in ch 11.

therefore fell within the scope of the Treaty. Although the contested national provisions did not directly interfere with C's freedom of movement and were not connected with any services he might have consumed in his capacity as a tourist, the
Court declared:

> When Community law guarantees a natural person the freedom to go to another Member
> State the protection of that person from harm in the Member State in question, on the same
> basis as that of nationals and persons residing there, is a corollary of that freedom of move-
> ment. It follows that the prohibition of discrimination is applicable to recipients of services
> within the meaning of the Treaty as regards protection against the risk of assault and the right
> to obtain financial compensation provided for by national law when that risk materializes.

In the 'Tourist Guide' cases, the Court was called upon to consider whether Article
49 (ex 59) was confined to the situation where the person providing the service in
question was established in a Member State other than that of the recipient. The
cases arose out of challenges by the Commission to the national laws of several
Member States which restricted the rights of guides from other Member States to
accompany groups of tourists in the countries being visited and to comment on
places of interest. The Court identified two possible provisions of services in this
situation: 'A tour company established in another Member State may itself employ
guides. In that case it is the tour company that provides the service to tourists
through its own guides. A tour company may also engage self-employed tourist
guides established in that other Member State. In that case, the service is provided
by the guide to the tour company.'[44] The Court then considered whether these
activities fell within the scope of Article 49. It observed:[45]

> Although Article 59 [now 49] of the Treaty expressly contemplates only the situation of a
> person providing services who is established in a Member State other than that in which the
> recipient of the service is established, the purpose of that Article is nevertheless to abolish
> restrictions on the freedom to provide services by persons who are not established in the
> State in which the service is to be provided . . . It is only when all the relevant elements of
> the activity in question are confined within a single Member State that the provisions of the
> Treaty on freedom to provide services cannot apply . . .

The Court concluded that Article 49 was applicable in all cases where services were
offered in a Member State other than that in which the provider was established.
It did not matter where the recipients were established.

In *Alpine Investments*,[46] the Court was asked whether Article 49 (ex 59)
was applicable to a national provision which restricted the right of a company
established in one Member State to contact potential clients, sometimes established

---

[44] Case C–154/89 *Commission v France* [1991] ECR I–659, para 6. See also Case C–180/89
Commission v Italy [1991] ECR I–709, para 5; Case C–198/89 *Commission v Greece* [1991] ECR I–727,
para 5.

[45] *France*, para 9. See also *Italy*, para 8; *Greece*, para 9.

[46] Case C–384/93 [1995] ECR I–1141. Cf Case C–288/89 *Collectieve Antennevoorziening Gouda*
[1991] ECR I–4007; Case C–353/89 *Commission v Netherlands* [1991] ECR I–4069; Case C–76/90 *Säger*
[1991] ECR I–4221.

in other Member States, by telephone without their prior consent to offer them various financial services. There were two potential difficulties with the view that Article 49 applied in circumstances such as these. The first was that, at the time the telephone calls were made, no services were actually being provided: only some of those contacted would instruct the company to enter into transactions on their behalf. Although the Court did not cite the case in its judgment, that difficulty seemed to have been resolved in *Luisi and Carbone* and the Court noted that there did not have to be an identifiable recipient at the time the offer was made in order for Article 49 to bite. The second difficulty was that, in the scenario envisaged by the referring court, neither the provider nor the recipient would move from the States in which they were established. That difficulty did not detain the Court for long either, the judgment noting that the provision of services by a person established in one Member State to a recipient established in another Member State fell within the express terms of Article 49.[47]

The notion of a restriction on the rights conferred by the Treaty

The *Reyners* and *van Binsbergen* cases provide examples of national rules which directly impeded the freedom of the applicants to carry on business. The need to find a way of bringing the rules concerned within the scope of the relevant provisions of the Treaty notwithstanding the absence of the directives contemplated by those provisions was therefore compelling. The same might be said of *Thieffry v Conseil de l'Ordre des Avocats à la Cour de Paris*,[48] where the Paris Bar Council refused to admit a Belgian advocate who held a Belgian degree of Doctor of Laws on the basis that he did not hold a French law degree. That conclusion had been reached even though the applicant's Belgian degree had been recognized by a French university as equivalent to a French law degree and the applicant had passed the French qualifying examination for the profession of advocate. The Conseil de l'Ordre maintained that it could only be required to recognize foreign diplomas as equivalent to French diplomas where the appropriate directives had been adopted under Article 47 (ex 57) and that no such directives yet existed for the profession of advocate. Referring to the General Programme, the Court held, however, that such a requirement derived in some circumstances directly from Article 43 (ex 52): the absence of directives under Article 47 could not be used to deny a person the right to establish himself in a Member State other than his own where that right could be secured by applying the relevant national rules in accordance with the

---

[47] Which prohibits restrictions on the provision of services by 'nationals of Member States who are established in a State of the Community other than that of the person for whom the services are intended'. Cf Case C–118/96 *Safir v Skattemyndigheten i Dalarnas Län* [1998] ECR I–1897.

[48] Case 71/76 [1977] ECR 765. See also Case 11/77 *Patrick v Ministre des Affaires Culturelles* [1977] ECR 1199.

objectives of the Treaty. The circumstances of a case such as this involved an unjustified restriction on the freedom of establishment.

With the benefit of hindsight it is easy to underestimate the difficulty of these early cases. It is therefore worth underlining the inventiveness of the Court in finding a solution which gave effect to the clear policy of the Treaty's authors even though they had been over-optimistic about the Council's ability to deliver the legislation which would have made such inventiveness unnecessary. In later cases the Court applied the Treaty rules to national provisions which, although restrictive, were less directly related to the freedoms contemplated by the Treaty. Those cases dramatically demonstrated the potential reach of the Treaty rules, but they involved less of a creative leap than the early cases which paved the way for subsequent developments.

An example is *Steinhauser v City of Biarritz*,[49] where the City of Biarritz refused to allow S, a professional artist of German nationality who was resident there, to tender for a rented lock-up used for the exhibition and sale of craft products. Under the Conditions of Tender, only French nationals were allowed to submit tenders. Referring to the *Thieffry* case and to the Council's General Programme, the Court found:[50]

> that any practice or rule adopted by a local authority of a Member State which discriminates against nationals of other Member States falls within the prohibition laid down by Article 52 [now 43] of the Treaty. Moreover, it must be emphasized that freedom of establishment, as provided for by that article, includes the right not only to take up activities as a self-employed person but also to pursue them in the broad sense of the term. The renting of premises for business purposes furthers the pursuit of an occupation and therefore falls within the scope of Article 52 of the EEC Treaty.

An equally broad view was taken in *Commission v Italy*,[51] in which the Commission challenged the compatibility with *inter alia* Articles 43 (ex 52) and 49 (ex 59) of the Treaty of Italian rules which only permitted Italian nationals to purchase or lease housing built or renovated with public funds or to obtain reduced-rate mortgages. The Italian Government argued that Article 49 could have no bearing on the disputed legislation because that article only affected those who did not have a permanent presence in the host State. The Court did not consider that point decisive. Articles 43 and 49, it said, were 'intended to secure the benefit of national treatment for a national of a Member State who wishes to pursue an activity as a self-employed person in another Member State and they prohibit all discrimination on grounds of nationality resulting from national or regional legislation and preventing the taking up or pursuit of such an activity'.[52] The pursuit of an occupation did not merely require access to commercial premises but also access to housing. Even someone who remained established in his State of origin 'may be led to pursue his occupational activities in another Member State for such an extended period that

---

[49] Case 197/84 [1985] ECR 1819.   [50] Para 16.   [51] Case 63/86 [1988] ECR 29.
[52] Para 13.

he needs to have permanent housing there'.[53] The Court concluded that both Articles 43 and 49 had been infringed.

As we saw earlier, although the Court has accepted that setting up some form of infrastructure in the host State is not necessarily incompatible with the provision of services under Article 49, there is a very fine line between that situation and becoming established in the host State. When it comes to housing, however, it seems that access to private accommodation on a permanent basis cannot in itself have the effect of transferring a case from the ambit of Article 49 to that of Article 43. This demonstrates a remarkably broad approach on the part of the Court to the scope of the Treaty rules.

The Court took a similar approach in *Commission v Greece*,[54] where Greek legislation prohibiting the acquisition by foreigners of immoveable property situated in border regions, and restricting the rights which could be granted over such property to foreigners, was found to be incompatible with Articles 39 (ex 48), 43 (ex 52) and 49 (ex 59) of the Treaty. Whatever technical difficulties had to be overcome in *Commission v Italy*, the decision in that case made the result in *Commission v Greece* almost inevitable.[55] It is, moreover, a result which is entirely consonant with the notion of a common market in which people have the right to move freely for the purpose of pursuing an economic activity, a notion which has been fundamental to the very idea of the Community since the Treaty of Rome was signed. However, the Court's decision in the Greek case caused consternation in Denmark,[56] whose legislation restricted the rights of foreigners to acquire second homes there. Accordingly, at Maastricht agreement was reached on a protocol to limit the effect of the rules on freedom of movement as interpreted by the Court. The protocol in question, which was annexed by the TEU to the EC Treaty, provides: 'Notwithstanding the provisions of this Treaty, Denmark may maintain the existing legislation on the acquisition of second homes.'[57] It is extremely rare for the Member States to insert in the Treaty a limitation on the case law of the Court: as we have seen elsewhere, Treaty amendments giving effect to the Court's case law are more common. The protocol on property in Denmark constitutes a potentially worrying precedent, for it derogates from the *acquis communautaire* in an area of fundamental importance to the proper functioning of the common market. It did not, however, prevent the Danish electorate from rejecting the TEU in a referendum held on 2 June 1992.[58]

---

[53] Para 19.   [54] Case 305/87 [1989] ECR 1461.

[55] The straightforward nature of the case is indicated by the length of the Advocate General's Opinion (less than five pages), the fact that the Greek Government did not seriously contest the alleged infringements (see Opinion, p 1469), and the assignment of the case to a formation of only seven Judges.

[56] Although Denmark had not seen fit to intervene in the case.

[57] See also Art 2(3) of Dir 90/365, according to which the directive is not to affect 'existing law on the acquisition of second homes'.

[58] The result was reversed in a second referendum held on 18 May 1993. See further Curtin and Van Ooik, 'Denmark and the Edinburgh Summit: Maastricht without tears' in O'Keeffe and Twomey (eds), *Legal Issues of the Maastricht Treaty* (1994), p 349.

The mutual recognition of qualifications

One area in which the adoption of directives co-ordinating the requirements laid down by national law might have seemed essential is the mutual recognition of qualifications. In the absence of recognition by the competent authorities of the host State that a qualification held by a migrant was equivalent to the corresponding qualification awarded in that State, as in *Thieffry*, it seemed hard for the Court to intervene. After all, the Court is not qualified to assess whether a diploma granted in one Member State provides evidence of the same level of expertise as a diploma granted in another Member State. However, acceptance of that view would have seriously weakened the capacity of the Treaty to achieve freedom of movement for the self-employed and the Court, by a bold and creative stroke, has rejected it.

Initial indications that the restrictive view of the scope of the Treaty put forward in the preceding paragraph was unlikely to commend itself to the Court came in *Unectef v Heylens*,[59] a case on Article 39 (ex 48) but which had profound implications for both workers and the self-employed. H was a Belgian national who held a Belgian football-trainer's diploma. He secured a post as trainer of a French professional football team. Under French law, a person who wished to practise the occupation of football trainer in France had to be the holder of a French football-trainer's diploma or a foreign diploma which had been recognized by a government minister as equivalent. An application by H to have his Belgian diploma recognized as equivalent to the corresponding French diploma was unsuccessful and, when H continued in his new post, a private prosecution was brought against him by the French union of football trainers. The Court of Justice was asked whether the relevant provision of French law constituted a restriction on freedom of movement for workers.

The Court accepted that, as long as the conditions of access to a particular occupation had not been harmonized, the Member States were 'entitled to lay down the knowledge and qualifications needed in order to pursue it and to require the production of a diploma certifying that the holder has the relevant knowledge and qualifications'.[60] However, the Court reiterated[61] that, when it was possible under national law for the equivalence of foreign diplomas to be recognized, a Member State could not deny the practical benefit of freedom of movement to a person subject to Community law merely because no directive on the mutual recognition of the relevant qualifications had yet been adopted. The Court concluded that 'the procedure for the recognition of equivalence must enable the national authorities to assure themselves, on an objective basis, that the foreign diploma certifies that its holder has knowledge and qualifications which are, if not identical, at least equivalent to those certified by the national diploma'.[62] The Court added that any

---

[59] Case 222/86 [1987] ECR 4097.
[60] Para 10.
[61] See the *Thieffry* and *Patrick* cases, *supra*.
[62] Para 13.

decision of the national authorities refusing to recognize the equivalence of the foreign diploma had to be properly reasoned and amenable to judicial review in order to secure for the individual effective protection of his right to freedom of movement.

Heylens was a natural but significant extension of *Thieffry*, for the Court was now asserting a power to interfere in the process by which the equivalence of a foreign diploma was assessed by the competent national authorities. A further step was taken in *Vlassopoulou*.[63] V was a Greek national and a qualified Greek lawyer. She also held a German doctorate in law and had been working for a number of years with a firm of German lawyers where she gave advice on matters of Greek law and Community law. In due course she applied to the competent Ministry for admission as a German lawyer. Her application was turned down on the basis that she did not hold the qualifications prescribed by German law. Article 43 (ex 52) of the Treaty, she was told, did not entitle her to practise in Germany on the basis of the professional qualifications she had obtained in Greece. V's challenge to the Ministry's decision eventually reached the Bundesgerichtshof, which asked the Court of Justice for guidance on the effect of Article 43 in these circumstances.

V faced a number of obstacles to the success of her claim which might have proved insurmountable. The requirements laid down by German law for admission to the legal profession did not discriminate (at least overtly) on the grounds of nationality: V would have been treated in exactly the same way had she been German. Moreover, not only had her Greek qualifications not been recognized as equivalent to the corresponding German qualifications, there appeared to be no formal procedure for according such recognition. In any event, V was not relying solely on her Greek qualifications but also on her German doctorate and her practical experience of working in a German law firm. There was no doubt, however, that Member States were entitled to restrict access to the legal profession to those who were appropriately qualified and that the conditions of access to that profession had not yet been harmonized.

Without itself making any substantive assessment of V's qualifications and experience, the Court succeeded in overcoming each of those obstacles. The Court observed that 'even if applied without any discrimination on the basis of nationality, national requirements concerning qualifications may have the effect of hindering nationals of the other Member States in the exercise of their right of establishment guaranteed to them by Article 52 [now 43] of the EEC Treaty. That could be the case if the national rules in question took no account of the knowledge and qualifications already acquired by the person concerned in another Member State.'[64] It followed, according to the Court, that:

a Member State which receives a request to admit a person to a profession to which access, under national law, depends upon the possession of a diploma or a professional qualification must take into consideration the diplomas, certificates and other evidence of qualifications

---

[63] Case C–340/89 [1991] ECR I–2357.   [64] Para 16.

which the person concerned has acquired in order to exercise the same profession in another Member State by making a comparison between the specialized knowledge and abilities certified by those diplomas and the knowledge and qualifications required by the national rules.[65]

The Court then set out a number of requirements with which the process of comparing the applicant's qualifications was required to comply. In particular, the Court stated that if it were found that the foreign diploma corresponded only partly to the equivalent national diploma, the host State was entitled to require the migrant to show that he or she had acquired the missing knowledge and qualifications. However, the national authorities had to establish whether that requirement was satisfied by attendance at a course of study in the host State or by the acquisition of practical experience there. They also had to ask whether such experience could be regarded as satisfying, wholly or partly, any requirement that the applicant complete a period of training prior to admission.

The decision of the Court went considerably further than *Thieffry* and even than *Heylens*. The former did not require the competent French authorities to take any positive steps to assess the equivalence of the applicant's qualifications, since that issue had already been resolved. All it did was to require that equivalence to be recognized. The latter was concerned principally with the mechanism used by the competent authority to assess the equivalence of the applicant's qualifications, although it clearly implied that the substance of an adverse decision taken at the end of a properly conducted procedure might be challenged if it did not satisfy the requirements of the Treaty as interpreted by the Court. *Vlassopoulou*, however, appeared to require national authorities to set up a procedure to assess the equivalence of qualifications awarded in another Member State where one did not already exist and to examine the extent to which any disparities were compensated for by additional training or practical experience. It implied that applications had to be examined on a case-by-case basis, since the combination of formal qualifications, additional training and practical experience is almost infinitely variable.

Directive 89/48

The Court was no doubt encouraged in the approach it took in *Vlassopoulou* by the adoption by the Council of Directive 89/48 on a general system for the recognition of higher-education diplomas awarded on completion of professional education and training of at least three years' duration,[66] although it was not in force at the material time. Directive 89/48 marked a major departure from the slow and painstaking approach previously adopted of trying to secure agreement on directives harmonizing the conditions for entry into specific professions. It applies to 'any

[65] Ibid.
[66] OJ 1989 L19/16. See also Dir 92/51 on a second general system for the recognition of professional education and training to supplement Dir 89/48, OJ 1992 L209/25.

national of a Member State wishing to pursue a regulated profession in a host Member State in a self-employed capacity or as an employed person', although it does not cover professions which are the subject of separate directives on the mutual recognition of qualifications.[67] In place of the traditional approach the directive introduces what has been described as a 'principle of mutual trust'.[68] That principle is reflected in Article 3 of the directive, which provides: 'Where, in a host Member State, the taking up or pursuit of a regulated profession is subject to possession of a diploma, the competent authority may not, on the grounds of inadequate qualifications, refuse to authorize a national of a Member State to take up or pursue that profession on the same conditions as apply to its own nationals . . .' if the applicant is qualified to exercise the profession concerned in another Member State. The national authorities are, however, permitted in certain circumstances to require nationals of other Member States to provide evidence of professional experience, to complete an adaptation period or to take an aptitude test.[69] The competent authorities of the host State are required by Article 8(2) to deal promptly with applications to pursue regulated professions and to communicate the outcome in a reasoned decision addressed to the person concerned within a specified time limit. That decision must be open to challenge in the national courts.

There is evidence here of a striking symbiosis between the Court of Justice on the one hand and the Commission and the Council on the other. The *Heylens* case was decided on 15 October 1987. Directive 89/48 was adopted on 21 December 1988 and had to be implemented by 4 January 1991.[70] The *Vlassopoulou* case was decided on 7 May 1991. Article 8(2) of the directive clearly reflects the *Heylens* decision. This is entirely sensible: decisions of national authorities would almost certainly have had to comply with the requirements laid down by the Court in that case in any event and Article 8(2) provides useful clarification of the point. However, the Court seems to have been influenced in *Vlassopoulou* by the content of the directive, which is mentioned in the judgment and in the Opinion of Advocate General van Gerven. Thus, the Court was aware that the Member States were required by the directive to establish mechanisms for dealing with applications to pursue regulated professions and for deciding whether applicants should be asked for evidence of professional experience, to complete an adaptation period or take an aptitude test. Such mechanisms should have been in place by the time the Court gave judgment. The impression given by the Court that the Member States were being required to put in place new procedures for assessing the qualifications and experience of those seeking to exercise a profession in a Member State other than their own is therefore apt to mislead.

In one sense, all the Court was doing in *Vlassopoulou* was to extend to V the benefits of a directive which was not applicable on the facts but which was now in

---

[67] Art 2. The term 'regulated profession' is defined in Art 1.

[68] See Pertek, 'Free movement of professionals and recognition of higher-education diplomas' (1992) 12 YEL 293, 312.

[69] Art 4.   [70] *Vlassopoulou, supra,* para 12.

force. However, there are a number of problems with this approach. Since it seems doubtful whether the same approach would have been taken had Directive 89/48 not been adopted, it follows that the content of the directive was allowed to influence the requirements of the Treaty. This seems wrong in principle and it led the Court to impose detailed requirements on national authorities which, while acceptable in a legislative act, look too precise to constitute an acceptable judicial gloss on the requirements of Article 43 (ex 52). In practical terms, the significance of *Vlassopoulou* is now confined to cases which fall outside the scope of Directive 89/48,[71] but this too is problematic: it effectively extends the approach embodied in that directive to cases it was not intended to cover.

Discrimination and the rule of reason

In order to ensure the removal of restrictions on the freedom of establishment and the right to provide services in accordance with the policy underlying the Treaty, the Court has on the whole adopted a broad view of the material and personal scope of Articles 43 (ex 52) and 49 (ex 59). However, the Court has not generally been neglectful of the limits to the judicial function or unsympathetic to the legitimate concerns of Member States. The balance it has sought to strike between these considerations and making the common market function properly notwithstanding the failure of the Council, at least initially, to discharge its responsibilities effectively is particularly evident in the approach the Court has taken to non-discriminatory national restrictions and the circumstances in which they may be justified. In that context there has been a marked convergence between the case law on establishment and particularly services and that on the free movement of goods.[72] That convergence undoubtedly has a certain intellectual appeal, but the applicable provisions remain distinct and the approach taken by the Court is not entirely uniform.

It was suggested at the beginning of this chapter that the Treaty provisions on establishment and services are perfectly capable of being interpreted as prohibiting not just discriminatory but also non-discriminatory national measures which restrict the exercise of the freedoms those provisions lay down. We are not here talking about measures which are merely non-discriminatory in a formal sense: it is well established that, where the Treaty prohibits discrimination, the prohibition applies to both direct and indirect discrimination. The issue for present purposes is whether the Treaty rules on establishment and services catch domestic restrictions which affect nationals of the State imposing them in the same way as nationals of other Member States. To put the point another way, if a rule applied by one Member State impedes the right of a national of another Member State to establish

---

[71] And Dir 92/51. Cf Case C–319/92 *Haim* [1994] ECR I–425; Case C–19/92 *Kraus v Land Baden-Württemberg* [1993] ECR I–1663. The *Kraus* case is discussed below.
[72] See Bernard, 'Discrimination and free movement in EC law' (1996) 45 ICLQ 82.

himself or provide services in the first State, can it be defended on the basis that the rights of the first State's nationals are restricted in the same way?[73]

In the case of Article 49 (ex 59), there are indications in the early decisions of the Court that the prohibition laid down in that article is not confined to discriminatory national rules. Thus, in *van Binsbergen* the Court stated:[74]

> The restrictions to be abolished pursuant to Articles 59 [now 49] and 60 [now 50] *include all requirements* imposed on the person providing the service by reason *in particular* of his nationality or of the fact that he does not habitually reside in the State where the service is provided, which do not apply to persons established within the national territory *or* which may prevent or otherwise obstruct the activities of the person providing the service.

A line of later cases, beginning with *Ministère Public and ASBL v van Wesemael*,[75] suggested that non-discriminatory national rules which restricted the freedom to provide services would be caught by Article 49 unless necessary to protect some public interest which was important enough to take precedence over that freedom. The Court summarized its previous case law on the matter in *Collectieve Antennevoorziening Gouda*,[76] which concerned the compatibility with Article 49 of Netherlands legislation restricting the transmission by cable of radio and television programmes broadcast from other Member States containing advertising aimed specifically at the Dutch public. Similar restrictions applied to programmes broadcast in the Netherlands.[77]

The Court declared that, in the absence of harmonization or a system of equivalence, restrictions on the freedom to provide services could arise from the application of national rules affecting anyone established in the State concerned to those providing services there from another Member State who already had to satisfy the legislation of the State where they were established. Although discriminatory national restrictions could only be justified under an express exemption, such as Article 46 (ex 56),[78] restrictions of the type at issue here would not come within the scope of Article 49 (ex 59) if their application to foreign providers of services was 'justified by overriding reasons relating to the public interest or if the requirements embodied in that legislation are already satisfied by the rules imposed on those persons in the Member State in which they are established'.[79] The Court went on to list 'the overriding reasons relating to the public interest' which it had already recognized. These included professional rules intended to protect recipients

---

[73] See generally Marenco, 'The notion of restriction on the freedom of establishment and provision of services in the case law of the Court' (1991) 11 YEL 111.

[74] Para 10, emphasis added.

[75] Joined Cases 110 and 111/78 [1979] ECR 35.   [76] Case C–288/89 [1991] ECR I–4007.

[77] See the referring court's first question. Cf Joined Cases C–34/95, C–35/95 and C–36/95 *KO v De Agostini and TV-Shop* [1997] ECR I–3843.

[78] Para 11 of the judgment. The Court sometimes examines both an express derogation and the rule of reason in order to avoid having to classify a national rule as discriminatory or non-discriminatory: see eg Case C–158/96 *Kohll v Union des Caisses de Maladie* [1998] ECR I–1931, discussed below, and in particular the Opinion of AG Tesauro at pp I–1861–3.

[79] Para 13.

of the service; the protection of intellectual property; the protection of workers; the protection of consumers and the conservation of the national historic and artistic heritage.[80]

The Court made it clear, however, that the application of national rules to providers of services established in other Member States had to be 'such as to guarantee the achievement of the intended aim and must not go beyond that which is necessary in order to achieve that objective'.[81] In other words, the requirements of the principle of proportionality had to be satisfied. The Netherlands Government argued that the disputed legislation was intended to safeguard the freedom of expression of the various elements of Dutch society by limiting the influence of advertisers over the content of programmes. The Court accepted that a cultural policy of that nature was capable of constituting an overriding requirement relating to the general interest of such a nature as to justify restricting the freedom to provide services. However, the restrictions of the type at issue in the main proceedings went further than was necessary to protect that interest and could not be justified.

The *Gouda* case exemplifies what may be called a rule of reason approach to the scope of Article 49 (ex 59): non-discriminatory national rules may sometimes have the effect of restricting the right to provide services and should not therefore be excluded a priori from the scope of the article. However, they are generally less objectionable than national rules which discriminate against providers of services established in other Member States and the range of circumstances in which they will be regarded as acceptable is therefore broader. The parallel with 'Cassis de Dijon' and the mandatory requirements which apply in the context of Article 28 (ex 30) is clear.[82] However, although the Court treated the disputed legislation in *Gouda* as non-discriminatory,[83] it also acknowledged that it imposed a heavier burden on broadcasters established in other Member States because they would normally also have to comply with the rules in force there.[84] To that extent, the legislation might have been considered discriminatory, although only indirectly. That this was not important in determining whether Article 49 was applicable is confirmed by another case decided on the same day as *Gouda*.

In *Säger*,[85] a German patent agent (S) tried to prevent an English company (D) from providing patent renewal services in Germany on the basis that its activities were incompatible with German law. D's business was carried on from its base in the United Kingdom on behalf of the holders of patents established in other

---

[80] See para 14 of the judgment, which contains references to the Court's earlier case law. In *Kohll*, *supra*, the Court accepted that preserving the financial balance of the social security system might also constitute an overriding reason in the general interest capable of justifying a barrier to freedom to provide services.

[81] Para 15.   [82] See ch 7.   [83] See para 16 of the judgment.

[84] The same was also true of the national rules at issue in 'Cassis de Dijon.' The position might be different where a broadcaster's output is not aimed at its State of establishment: see Case C–23/93 *TV10* [1994] ECR I–4795.

[85] Case C–76/90 [1991] ECR I–4221.

Member States. It monitored its clients' patents, advised them when renewal fees were due, and paid the fees on their behalf when asked to do so. D acted on the basis of information furnished by its clients and did not provide them with advice as to the consequences of non-payment. It charged its clients a commission which was generally lower than the fees charged by German patent agents who offered a similar service. Advocate General Jacobs explained that German law did not permit the activity in question to be carried on by a limited company like D but only by a patent agent or a lawyer in their personal capacities. D was therefore in exactly the same position as a company established in Germany. Indeed, the Bundesgerichtshof had held that a German company providing the same type of service as D should be prohibited from doing so. The Advocate General therefore took the view that the case 'should be approached on the basis that no discrimination, either overt or covert, has taken place'.[86] He went on to observe:[87]

I do not think that it can be right to state as a general rule that a measure lies wholly outside the scope of Article 59 [now 49] simply because it does not in any way discriminate between domestic undertakings and those established in other Member States. Nor is such a view supported by the terms of Article 59: its expressed scope is much broader . . . The principle should, I think, be that if an undertaking complies with the legislation of the Member State in which it is established it may provide services to clients in another Member State, even though the provision of such services would not normally be lawful under the laws of the second Member State. Restrictions imposed by those laws can only be applied against the foreign undertaking if they are justified by some requirement that is compatible with the aims of the Community.

That view was endorsed by the Court, which made it clear that:[88]

Article 59 [now 49] of the Treaty requires not only the elimination of all discrimination against a person providing services on the ground of his nationality but also the abolition of any restriction, even if it applies without distinction to national providers of services and to those of other Member States, when it is liable to prohibit or otherwise impede the activities of a provider of services established in another Member State where he lawfully provides similar services.

The Court went on to find that the activity in question was of a straightforward nature and did not call for specific professional skills. There was therefore no justification for reserving it to lawyers and patent agents.

We have seen that the extension of Article 28 (ex 30) to genuinely non-discriminatory restrictions on imports led the Court in *Keck and Mithouard*[89] to limit the application of that article in order to avoid having to decide whether national rules having only a remote impact on the free movement of goods were justified. In *Alpine Investments*, which concerned the compatibility with Article 49 (ex 59) of a national prohibition on cold calling imposed on businesses providing financial services, the Court was invited to treat the contested legislation as analog-

---

[86] See p I–4233.   [87] p I–4235.   [88] Para 12.
[89] Joined Cases C–267/91 and C–268/91 [1993] ECR I–6097, discussed in ch 7.

ous to non-discriminatory rules governing selling arrangements which, according to *Keck and Mithouard*, fell outside the scope of Article 28. That invitation was firmly rejected by both Advocate General Jacobs and the Court, which declared:[90]

A prohibition such as that at issue is imposed by the Member State in which the provider of services is established and affects not only offers made by him to addressees who are established in that State or move there in order to receive services but also offers made to potential recipients in another Member State. It therefore directly affects access to the market in services in the other Member States and is thus capable of hindering intra-Community trade in services.

The attempt to draw an analogy between the national rules at issue in *Alpine Investments* and those at issue in *Keck* was obviously misguided and the decision in the former case does not rule out the possibility that the latter case will be extended to Article 49 (ex 59) in the future. It is submitted that this would be a retrograde step for the reasons given in chapter 7. If the Court refuses to depart from or attenuate the *Keck* rule in the context of the free movement of goods, it should be regarded as a response to a particular problem encountered in defining the scope of Article 28 (ex 30). To apply a similar approach in the context of the other freedoms would have a detrimental effect on the functioning of the common market.[91]

The case law on Article 43 (ex 52) has been slower to develop. Although some decisions in which that article was found to have been breached could be analysed as involving non-discriminatory national rules, most could also be seen as involving rules which imposed a heavier burden on foreigners than on the nationals of the State which applied them.[92] In *Säger*, Advocate General Jacobs distinguished Article 43 from Article 49 (ex 59) and expressly reserved his position on the question whether the former did more than merely prohibit discrimination. In *Konstantinidis*, he said that he did not think 'that the case-law should be read as establishing that a measure can never be contrary to Article 52 [now 43] simply because it is non-discriminatory'.[93] However, the national provisions at issue in that case—concerning the transliteration of Greek names into Roman characters— were obviously discriminatory and they were treated as such by the Court.

A sign that the Court's view of the scope of Article 43 (ex 52) was beginning to shadow its approach to Article 49 (ex 59) came with *Kraus v Land Baden-Württemberg*,[94] which concerned the compatibility with Articles 39 (ex 48) and 43 (ex 52) of a German rule restricting the use, without prior authorization, of a post-graduate academic title awarded in another Member State. Although the applicant

---

[90] Case C–384/93 [1995] ECR I–1141, para 38. See also Case C–415/93 *URBSFA and Others v Bosman and Others* [1995] ECR I–4921, para 103, discussed in ch 8, where the Court rejected an attempt to rely on *Keck and Mithouard* in the context of Art 39 (ex 48).

[91] See further Weatherill, 'After *Keck*: some thoughts on how to clarify the clarification' (1996) 33 CMLRev 885; Daniele, 'Non-discriminatory restrictions to the free movement of persons' (1997) 22 ELRev 191.

[92] See eg *Klopp* and *Vlassopoulou, supra*; Marenco, op cit, pp 116–21.

[93] Case C–168/91 [1993] ECR I–1191, 1212.   [94] Case C–19/92 [1993] ECR I–1663.

was himself German, the contested rule was clearly discriminatory because it did not apply to academic titles awarded in Germany. It was therefore more likely to affect foreigners than German nationals. None the less, the Court made a broad statement about the scope of the relevant provisions of the Treaty:[95]

Articles 48 [now 39] and 52 [now 43] preclude any national measure governing the conditions under which an academic title obtained in another Member State may be used, where that measure, even though it is applicable without discrimination on grounds of nationality, is liable to hamper or to render less attractive the exercise by Community nationals, including those of the Member State which enacted the measure, of fundamental freedoms guaranteed by the Treaty. The situation would be different only if such a measure pursued a legitimate objective compatible with the Treaty and was justified by pressing reasons of public interest . . . It would however also be necessary in such a case for application of the national rules in question to be appropriate for ensuring attainment of the objective they pursue and not to go beyond what is necessary for that purpose . . .

The Court concluded that the need to protect the public against the abuse of foreign academic titles constituted a legitimate interest such as to justify restricting the fundamental freedoms guaranteed by the Treaty.[96]

The *Kraus* case was cited by the Court in *Gebhard v Consiglio dell'Ordine degli Avvocati e Procuratori di Milano*,[97] which it will be remembered arose out of an attempt by the Milan Bar Council to prevent G, a German national and a qualified German lawyer, from practising in Italy from his own chambers under the title *avvocato*. The Court pointed out that the pursuit of some self-employed activities was conditional on compliance with national rules 'justified by the general good, such as rules relating to organization, qualifications, professional ethics, supervision and liability'.[98] Such rules might restrict a particular activity to the holders of certain qualifications or the members of a professional body. They might also restrict the use of professional titles such as *avvocato*. The Court made it clear that, where a Member State made the pursuit of a given activity subject to conditions of this nature, 'a national of another Member State intending to pursue that activity must in principle comply with them'.[99] It went on to stipulate,[100] however, that:

— . . . national measures liable to hinder or make less attractive the exercise of fundamental freedoms guaranteed by the Treaty must fulfil four conditions: they must be applied in a non-discriminatory manner; they must be justified by imperative requirements in the general interest; they must be suitable for securing the attainment of the objective which they pursue; and they must not go beyond what is necessary in order to attain it;
—likewise, Member States must take account of the equivalence of diplomas and, if necessary, proceed to a comparison of the knowledge and qualifications required by their national rules and those of the person concerned.

---

[95] Para 32.
[96] The Court proceeded to lay down certain procedural requirements with which the procedure for granting authorization had to comply.
[97] Case C–55/94 [1995] ECR I–4165.   [98] Para 35.   [99] Para 36.

This is a passage of considerable significance. It makes it clear that a Member State cannot justify applying to the nationals of other Member States local rules on the pursuit of self-employed activities simply on the basis that they are non-discriminatory. Even non-discriminatory rules must be justified in the public interest and comply with the principle of proportionality if they are to be applied to the nationals of other Member States. Moreover, it will be noted that, in both *Kraus* and *Gebhard*, the Court spoke in general terms of 'fundamental freedoms guaranteed by the Treaty', a clear indication that there is no difference of principle in this regard between Articles 39 (ex 48),[101] 43 (ex 52), and 49 (ex 59). As far as Articles 43 and 49 are concerned, the distinction lies in the impact of the principle of proportionality. As Advocate General Jacobs explained in *Säger*,[102] while it may in principle be acceptable to expect a person who intends to participate on a stable and continuous basis in the economic life of a Member State to comply with all the relevant legal requirements of that State, it may be harder to justify the imposition of a burden of that magnitude on someone who is merely pursuing his activities there on a temporary basis. That distinction was endorsed by the Court in *Gebhard*, where the Court accepted that a person wishing to establish himself in a Member State other than his own in order to pursue an activity would in principle have to comply with the relevant local rules.[103]

The Court has shown great flexibility in reconciling the principle of freedom of movement for persons and services with the need to ensure that the legitimate interests of the Member States are protected. The rule of reason enables Member States to justify non-discriminatory and proportionate restrictions on the fundamental freedoms guaranteed by the Treaty while at the same time ensuring that disproportionate restrictions, even if non-discriminatory, are struck down. To interpret it as a device for extending the reach of the Treaty and the jurisdiction of the Court would be misguided: it in fact amounts to a recognition by the Court that there are some interests enshrined in national law which should be given precedence over the dictates of the common market. The circumstances in which that is so can ultimately only be determined by the Court itself, for otherwise the uniform application of Community law and the proper functioning of the common market would be at the mercy of the transient political pressures to which all national governments are subject.

[100] Para 39.
[101] Cf Case C–415/93 *URBSFA and Others v Bosman and Others* [1995] ECR I–4921, discussed in ch 8, where it was accepted that non-discriminatory obstacles to the free movement of workers might be caught by Art 39 (ex 48) unless justified by pressing reasons of public interest: see paras 96 and 104. The Court cited *Kraus* and *Gebhard*.
[102] At p I–4234. The relevant passage was quoted at the beginning of this chapter.
[103] Para 36.

Judicial restraint

Enough has been said to demonstrate that the Court has on the whole sought to tackle restrictions on freedom of establishment and the right to provide services in a bold and inventive way, bringing within the scope of the Treaty a range of such restrictions which are only indirectly related to the exercise of commercial activities. However, it would be wrong to give the impression that the Court always seizes any opportunity to extend the reach of Articles 43 (ex 52) and 49 (ex 59). The rule of reason discussed in the previous section represents one area where the Court has shown sensitivity to national concerns. The present section is concerned with other cases where the Court has taken a less expansive approach to the scope of the Treaty.

The *Grogan* case

A remarkable example of judicial restraint in the application of Article 49 is provided by *Grogan*,[104] where the Court was asked to consider the legality of national provisions restricting the publication of information about the availability of abortions in other Member States. The case was referred to the Court by the High Court of Ireland in the context of a dispute between the Society for the Protection of Unborn Children Ireland Ltd (SPUC), whose purpose was to prevent the decriminalization of abortion and promote human life from the moment of conception, and a number of officers of various student bodies, which had distributed in Ireland leaflets containing information about the identity and location of clinics in the United Kingdom where abortions were lawfully carried out. Abortion was prohibited in Ireland by statute and, since 1983, the right to life of the unborn had been acknowledged in Article 40.3.3 of the Irish Constitution. The Irish Supreme Court had held that it was incompatible with that provision to assist pregnant women in Ireland to travel abroad to obtain abortions. That decision had been taken without the benefit of a preliminary ruling from the Court of Justice and the High Court therefore decided to seek guidance from Luxembourg on the compatibility with Community law of a national rule prohibiting the distribution of information about clinics in another Member State where abortions were lawfully performed.

The referring court's first question asked whether performing an abortion was capable of constituting the provision of a service for the purposes of Article 50 (ex 60) EC. That question did not detain the Court for long. As Advocate General van Gerven pointed out, it was not disputed that medical termination of pregnancy was normally carried out for remuneration. Article 50 expressly included 'activities of

---

[104] Case C–159/90 *Society for the Protection of Unborn Children Ireland v Grogan and Others* [1991] ECR I–4685. Judgment was given on 4 October 1991. The significance of that date will become apparent in due course.

the professions' among the notion of services and Article 47(3) (ex 57(3))—applicable to services by virtue of Article 55 (ex 66)—expressly contemplated the abolition of restrictions on the 'medical and allied' professions. If that were not enough, the Court had regarded medical treatment as a service in *Luisi and Carbone*. SPUC maintained that the provision of abortion could not be considered a service because it was grossly immoral, but that argument was dismissed by the Court as irrelevant: 'It is not for the Court to substitute its assessment for that of the legislature in those Member States where the activities in question are practised legally.'[105]

That conclusion was criticized on the basis that 'the Court extended the scope of EC law by substituting the social legislation of the United Kingdom . . . for the direct choice of the people of another Member State to protect the right to life of the unborn'.[106] It is submitted that that criticism is misplaced. The Court's decision involved no extension of the scope of the Treaty. The referring court would have been justified in treating the question whether the medical termination of pregnancy constituted a service within the meaning of Article 50 (ex 60) as *acte clair*. That is why Advocate General van Gerven was effectively able to answer the High Court's first question in a single paragraph of a lengthy Opinion. The fact that the right to life of the unborn had been enshrined in a constitutional amendment made after a referendum could not in itself affect the scope of the Treaty. Otherwise Member States would be able to excuse themselves unilaterally from Treaty obligations they find unpalatable or inconvenient and the common market would quickly become a dead letter. Moreover, far from substituting United Kingdom social policy for the choice of the Irish people, the Court's decision quite properly ensured that professional activities which were lawful in the State where those carrying them out were established and the activities in question were performed were not deprived of the potential protection of the Treaty because the legislature of another State considered them immoral. The opposite result might have been interpreted as substituting Irish social policy for the choice of the United Kingdom legislature.

The values underlying the disputed provision of the Irish Constitution and the status they might enjoy in Community law were relevant, not to the definition of a service, but to the question whether any restriction on the freedom to provide services could be justified. Advocate General van Gerven considered that question at great length but it was not addressed by the Court, which took the view that the circumstances of the case did not involve a restriction for the purposes of Article 49 (ex 59). The link between the activities of the defendants and abortions carried out in clinics in other Member States was, it said, 'too tenuous for the prohibition on the distribution of information to be capable of being regarded as a restriction within the meaning of Article 59 [now 49] of the Treaty'.[107] The Court observed

---

[105] Para 20.

[106] Phelan, 'Right to life of the unborn v promotion of trade in services: the European Court of Justice and the normative shaping of the European Union' (1992) 55 MLR 670, 673.

[107] Para 24.

that the information circulated by the defendants was 'not distributed on behalf of an economic operator established in another Member State. On the contrary, the information constitutes a manifestation of freedom of expression and of the freedom to impart and receive information which is independent of the economic activity carried on by clinics established in another Member State.'[108]

That conclusion enabled the Court to escape, Houdini-like, from the dilemma posed by the referring court's questions. Had it examined the issue of justification, it would have been forced to confront difficult and highly delicate questions about the relative importance of the freedom to provide services, the right to receive and impart information protected under the European Convention on Human Rights, and the moral choice made by the Irish people. Those questions had all been tackled by Advocate General van Gerven, who had concluded essentially that the disputed restrictions were justified. However, his analysis of the case has not in all respects been found convincing[109] and the attraction for the Court of a solution which avoided those issues while producing the same result will readily be appreciated.

However, the reasoning of the Court lacks conviction. It is almost self-evident that restricting the information available about a service amounts to restricting the provision of the service itself. A person who is unaware that a service is available is unable to consider receiving it. The question whether the information is distributed by or on behalf of the provider or by an independent third party seems irrelevant. This was the view taken by Advocate General van Gerven, who referred to the decision in *GB-INNO-BM*,[110] where the Court acknowledged the adverse consequences for the free movement of goods of denying consumers access to advertising. He argued:[111]

I can see no reason why the position should be otherwise with regard to information provided about a service: individuals' freedom to go to another country in order to receive a service supplied there may also be compromised if they are denied access in their own country to information concerning, in particular, the identity and location of the provider of the services and/or the services which he provides.

In my view, the answer given holds good where the information comes from a person who is not himself the provider of the services and does not act on his behalf.

The view taken by the Court, while adequate to answer the questions put by the referring court, did not address what the position would have been had an attempt been made to prevent United Kingdom clinics where abortions were performed from advertising their services in Ireland. It seems clear that there would be a

---

[108] Para 26.

[109] See eg de Búrca, 'Fundamental human rights and the reach of EC law' (1993) 13 OJLS 283; O'Leary, 'The Court of Justice as a reluctant constitutional adjudicator: an examination of the abortion case' (1992) 16 ELRev 138.

[110] Case C–362/88 [1990] ECR I–667. The role of advertising was also considered by AG Jacobs in Case C–412/93 *Leclerc-Siplec v TF1 Publicité and M6 Publicité* [1995] ECR I–179, 186–7. See further ch 7.

[111] At p I–4713.

restriction within the meaning of Article 49 (ex 59) in those circumstances and that the question of justification would have to be confronted.

The restrictive nature of the Court's conclusion that there was no restriction within the meaning of Article 49 (ex 59) in the circumstances of *Grogan* is underlined by *Konstantinidis*,[112] an establishment case the facts of which were given in chapter 6. Briefly, the applicant was a Greek national residing in Germany, where he worked in a self-employed capacity. Following his marriage, he objected to the way in which German law required his name to be transcribed in the register of marriages in Roman characters, which he found offensive and liable to convey an inaccurate impression of the way his name was pronounced in Greek. Regarding the case as disclosing a potential breach of Article 43 (ex 52), the Court said that national rules on transcribing Greek names would be incompatible with that article if they had the effect of requiring a Greek national to spell his name in a way which was 'such as to modify its pronunciation and if the resulting distortion exposes him to the risk that potential clients may confuse him with other persons'.[113] The potential restriction constituted by the disputed German rules was marginal and indirect in the extreme. Although the position was not entirely clear, it appeared that it was only on official documents (such as birth, marriage, and death certificates) that the official spelling of his name would have to be used. For normal social and professional purposes, the applicant was free to spell his name in any way he pleased.[114] The Court seems to have considered the potential confusion that might be caused if the applicant used different spellings of his name for different purposes as sufficient to bring Article 43 into play.

The terse and unconvincing nature of the Court's reasoning in *Grogan* suggests a lack of agreement among the Judges on the best way of dealing with the questions raised by the case. A factor which is likely to have weighed heavily is the knowledge that proceedings were pending before the European Court of Human Rights in Strasbourg in which the compatibility with the European Convention on Human Rights of the Irish prohibition on the distribution of information about abortion facilities available abroad had been raised. As we saw in chapter 6, the fundamental rights enshrined in the Convention are regarded by the Court of Justice as a source of general principles of law which it is responsible for protecting, but there was at that time little guidance in the previous case law of the Strasbourg Court on the line it was likely to take.[115] The Court will therefore have been conscious of the danger that, if it had to consider the effect of the Convention, it might reach a conclusion which subsequently turned out to be at variance with that of the Strasbourg Court. By ruling that the circumstances of the case did not involve a restriction for the purposes of Article 49 (ex 59), it was able to avoid addressing the effect of the European Convention on jurisdictional grounds.

---

[112] Case C–168/91 [1993] ECR I–1191.   [113] Para 16.
[114] See AG Jacobs at pp I–1205–6.   [115] See AG van Gerven at pp I–4724–5.

In the event, the Court of Human Rights took a different view from Advocate General van Gerven and held[116] that an injunction granted by the Irish Supreme Court in circumstances similar to those of *Grogan* restraining the applicants from imparting or receiving information about abortion facilities available abroad amounted to a breach of the Convention guarantee of freedom of expression.[117] The question posed above about the right of foreign abortion clinics to advertise their services in Ireland should not therefore arise. If it does, the Court of Justice should have no hesitation in holding such a right to be vindicated by the EC Treaty.

It is sometimes suggested that the Luxembourg and Strasbourg Courts should be entitled to ask each other for preliminary rulings.[118] Such a facility would not have been helpful in the *Grogan* case. The Court of Justice was aware that a related case was already pending before the Court of Human Rights. One might be forgiven for wondering why the former did not simply wait until the latter had reached its decision before responding to the questions which had been referred to it. This would admittedly have entailed a further delay of over a year. However, since there was an injunction in force restraining the distribution of the contested information and the Court of Justice in any event decided that the restrictions applicable in Ireland were compatible with the Treaty, no adverse consequences would have followed from a decision to postpone judgment.

By way of footnote to this tale, a protocol agreed at Maastricht and annexed to the TEU and the Treaties establishing the European Communities provides that nothing in those Treaties 'shall affect the application in Ireland of Article 40.3.3 of the Constitution of Ireland'. Whatever political value it may have had, that protocol seems legally meaningless, for cases whose elements are confined to Ireland would in any event fall outside the scope of the Treaty as purely internal within the meaning of the Court's case law. Cases like *Grogan* which concern abortion but which possess factors linking Ireland with another Member State would not be confined to 'the application in Ireland of Article 40.3.3' and would not therefore be covered by the Protocol in any event. Indeed, the protocol does not seem to have been intended to apply in such circumstances for, according to a declaration subsequently made by all the then Member States (including Ireland), 'it was and is their intention that the Protocol shall not limit freedom either to travel between Member States or, in accordance with conditions which may be laid down, in conformity with Community law, by Irish legislation, to obtain or make available in Ireland information relating to services lawfully available in Member States'.[119]

---

[116] *Open Door and Dublin Well Woman v Ireland* (1993) 15 EHRR 244. Judgment was given on 29 October 1992.

[117] See Art 10.

[118] See the observations submitted to the Court of Justice in Opinion 2/94 [1996] ECR I–1759; ch 6, *supra*.

[119] Declaration adopted on 1 May 1992 in Guimarães (Portugal) by the High Contracting Parties to the TEU.

Other examples of restraint

The *Grogan* case may be regarded as exceptional, touching as it did on a matter of extreme moral delicacy regulated in a provision of a national constitution which enjoyed the democratic legitimacy of having been approved by referendum. However, although out of line with the prevailing trend of the case law, it is not the only case in which the Court has taken a restrictive line.

A limitation on the scope of Article 49 (ex 59) of potentially broad scope was suggested by Advocate General Slynn in *Gravier v City of Liège*,[120] which concerned the right of a French student to attend a course in Belgium without paying a fee which Belgian students were not required to pay. One of the arguments put forward by the applicant was that to require her to pay the fee would be inconsistent with her rights under Article 49 as a recipient of services. The Court dealt with the case on other grounds and did not deal with that argument, but it was considered by Advocate General Slynn, who drew a distinction between publicly funded education and private education:[121]

State education is not . . . provided as an economic activity with a view to recovering costs and making a profit, but as a matter of social policy, and the State bears the cost of all or a major part of the cost of tuition. Such education is not in my view provided 'for remuneration' within the meaning of Article 60 [now 50]. Accordingly, even if the nature of the services is similar, their economic classification is different. I would accordingly not regard education provided, or substantially provided, by the State as being a service for the purposes of the Treaty. The fact that the student pays something is not enough to convert it into a service. I take the view, however, that education provided by a private organization with a view to profit is a service.

The point was taken up by the Court in *Belgian State v Humbel*,[122] which concerned the legality of a fee demanded of a French boy in respect of his attendance at a school in Belgium but which Belgian pupils were not required to pay. The Court held that the circumstances of the case fell outside the scope of Article 49 (ex 59). The essential characteristic of the remuneration mentioned in Article 50 (ex 60) was 'that it constitutes consideration for the service in question, and is normally agreed upon between the provider and the recipient of the service'.[123] That characteristic was lacking in the case of courses provided under a national education system. The State was not seeking to make a profit and the system was funded essentially from the public purse, even if fees were sometimes charged.[124] This is a significant limitation on the scope of Article 49, particularly in the fields of education and medicine, where an important role is played by both the public and the private sector. It means that the effect of Article 49 may vary from State to State, and with the passage of time within the same State, according to the extent to which the private sector is involved in delivering services of general interest.

[120] Case 293/83 [1985] ECR 593. [121] At p 603.
[122] Case 263/86 [1988] ECR 5365. [123] Para 17. [124] See para 18.

A degree of judicial diffidence is perhaps also apparent in the case law of the Court on the extent to which national rules on social security are affected by the Treaty provisions on establishment and services.[125] *Sodemare and Others v Regione Lombardia*,[126] concerned a Luxembourg company, S, which had set up various companies in Italy to run old people's homes there. It applied to the Lombardy Region for authority to enter into contractual arrangements with local health and welfare centres for the provision of social welfare services. Such authority was necessary under the applicable regional legislation, but was only granted to bodies which were non-profit-making. S did not satisfy that condition and the necessary authority was refused. This meant it was not eligible to claim reimbursement from public funds of the cost of providing its services in Lombardy. Residents therefore had to bear a financial burden to which they would not have been subject had they been staying in a home which had concluded a contract with the local health and welfare centre. The level of occupancy of the homes run by the applicant companies in Lombardy was therefore relatively low, even though waiting lists existed for places in contracting homes. Before the national court, it was argued that the condition that only non-profit-making firms could enter into contracts with local centres was contrary to various provisions of Community law, including Articles 43 (ex 52) and 49 (ex 59).

As far as Article 43 was concerned, the Court ruled that the non-profit condition was a legitimate exercise of the powers which Member States retained to organize their social security systems as they saw fit.[127] The Court noted that commercial undertakings in other Member States were in no worse a position than commercial undertakings established in Italy, who were also unable to conclude contracts entitling them to reimbursement from public funds. That conclusion was reached against the advice of Advocate General Fennelly, who regarded the contested legislation as prima facie discriminatory:[128]

This legislation, in my view, necessarily favours domestic bodies. It is true that international charities exist, and some may operate in the sector of care for the elderly, but 'charity begins at home' and most charitable endeavour in this field takes place at national, regional or local level. This is certainly the case in Lombardy, as all of the private contracting homes are run by bodies based in the Region. Thus we are permitted to presume that non-Italian companies would be unwilling to assume a non-profit-making legal form in order to operate in Lombardy.

Citing the Court's case law to the effect that differences in treatment are not to be regarded as discrimination where they are objectively justified,[129] the Advocate General then considered whether there were any objective differences between

---

[125] Cf the Court's approach to the interpretation of Dir 79/7 on equal treatment for men and women in matters of social security, OJ 1979 L6/24, discussed in ch 13.

[126] [1997] ECR I–3395.

[127] See Case 238/82 *Duphar and Others v Netherlands* [1984] ECR 523; Joined Cases C–159/91 and C–160/91 *Poucet and Pistre v AGF and Cancava* [1993] ECR I–637.

[128] p I–3413.   [129] See generally ch 6.

non-profit-making and commercial companies in this context. He concluded that both were capable of performing the same function and that it had not been demonstrated that the decision to exclude commercially run homes from the system for reimbursing health-care costs was justified. The analysis of Advocate General Fennelly is on the face of it compelling. He examined a number of detailed points put forward by the Italian Government in an attempt to justify the difference in treatment and found them all wanting. By contrast, the Court merely asserted that the distinction constituted a legitimate exercise of the power retained by the Member State concerned to organize its social security system.

Equally unsatisfactory was the Court's approach to an argument based on Article 49 (ex 59). The applicant companies claimed that, having established themselves in Italy, they then provided services for beneficiaries many of whom were established in other Member States. The cross-frontier nature of those services entitled them, so they said, to rely on Article 49. *Alpine Investments*[130] showed that that article could be invoked by an undertaking against the State in which it was established if it provided services for recipients in other Member States. However, the Court regarded the circumstances of the present case as purely internal, because nationals from other Member States who travelled to Italy to stay in the applicants' homes there did so in order to enjoy the services provided in those homes on a permanent basis, or at least for an indefinite period. Article 49 did not apply where a national of a Member State went to the territory of another Member State and established his principal residence there in order to receive services in that State for an indefinite period.

That conclusion, this time consistent with the advice of Advocate General Fennelly, is perplexing. The Court cited its previous decision in *Steymann v Staatssecretaris van Justitie*,[131] but that case is distinguishable. It concerned the right of a national of a Member State, who had established his principal residence in another Member State in order to join a religious community, to claim a residence permit in the second State on the basis of the Treaty. The Court said that such a person did not fall within the scope of the rules on services, but might be covered by the rules on workers or the right of establishment. The rights of the religious community itself were not in issue. In *Sodemare*, it seems clear that the applicant companies' chances of attracting business from other Member States were limited by the contested legislation. It seems equally clear that the activities of S's Italian subsidiaries were not confined in all respects within a single Member State. The Court's unwillingness to tackle the substantive issues raised by the case perhaps reflects its sensitivity about interfering in the organization of national social security systems which are under increasing strain as a result of demographic factors and social changes.[132]

---

[130] See also Case C–18/93 *Corsica Ferries* [1994] ECR I–1783; Case C–379/92 *Peralta* [1994] ECR I–3453.

[131] Case 196/87 [1988] ECR 6159.

[132] Cf the amendments to Reg 1408/71 considered by the Court in Case C–20/96 *Snares v Adjudication Officer* [1997] ECR I–6057. The need to modernize Reg 1408/71 was considered by the High Level Panel on the Free Movement of Persons: see ch III of its report presented to the Commission on 18 March 1997.

The Court cited *Sodemare* in *Kohll v Union des Caisses de Maladie*,[133] where it accepted that the need to preserve the financial balance of a national social security system might in principle justify a restriction on the right to provide services. However, the Court made it clear that the powers of the Member States to organize their social security systems had to be exercised in a manner which was compatible with the Treaty. In *Kohll*, the Court found that condition not to have been satisfied, even though the threat to the freedom to receive and provide services was only indirect. The case arose out of a dispute between a Luxembourg national and the Union des Caisses de Maladie, with which he was insured, over a request that his daughter, a minor, should be authorized to receive dental treatment in Germany at the Union's expense. The Union rejected the request on the basis that the treatment was not urgent and could be provided in Luxembourg. The cost of the treatment was not in issue because the applicant was seeking reimbursement at the rate applicable in Luxembourg. The dispute was eventually referred to the Court of Justice by the Luxembourg Cour de Cassation, which asked whether Articles 49 (ex 59) and 50 (ex 60) precluded national rules which made reimbursement of the cost of dental treatment subject to authorization by the insured person's social security institution where the benefits were provided in another Member State.

It was argued by several Member States that the case was outside the scope of the rules on services and fell to be resolved instead on the basis of Regulation 1408/71, with which the disputed national provisions were said to be compatible. Notwithstanding the Court's sensitivity to the problems faced by Member States in the field of social security, it ruled that national rules on the matter were not automatically excluded from the scope of Articles 49 (ex 59) and 50 (ex 60). It added that the fact that a national measure was consistent with a provision of secondary legislation, such as those contained in Regulation 1408/71, could not have the effect of removing the measure from the scope of the Treaty. In any event, the Court said, Regulation 1408/71 did not directly govern the circumstances of the main action.

The Court then turned to the effect of the Treaty rules on services. There was no doubt that treatment provided for remuneration by an orthodontist established in another Member State constituted a service within the meaning of the Treaty. The Member States which had submitted observations argued, however, that the disputed national rules did not have the purpose or effect of restricting the right to provide services. The Court took a different view:[134]

While the national rules at issue in the main proceedings do not deprive insured persons of the possibility of approaching a provider of services established in another Member State, they do nevertheless make reimbursement of the costs incurred in that Member State sub-

---

[133] Case C–158/96 [1998] ECR I–1931. A parallel case concerning goods was decided on the same day: see Case C–120/95 *Decker v Caisse de Maladie des Employés Privés* [1998] ECR I–1831. Cf Case C–18/95 *Terhoeve v Inspecteur van de Belastingdienst Particulieren/Ondernemingen Buitenland*, judgment of 26 January 1999.

[134] Para 35.

ject to prior authorisation, and deny such reimbursement to insured persons who have not obtained that authorisation. Costs incurred in the State of insurance are not, however, subject to that authorisation.

Because such rules tended to deter patients from approaching providers of medical services established in other Member States, they constituted a barrier to the right to provide services. The Court rejected the argument that the contested rules were justified in order to preserve the financial balance of the social security system: 'it is clear that reimbursement of the costs of dental treatment provided in other Member States in accordance with the tariff of the State of insurance has no significant effect on the financing of the social security system'.[135] Attempts by the Luxembourg Government to justify the disputed rules by reference to the need to guarantee the quality of medical services provided in other Member States and to maintain a balanced medical and hospital service accessible to all were also dismissed by the Court.[136]

The conclusion reached by the Court in *Kohll* provided a vivid demonstration of the importance it continued to attach to the proper functioning of the internal market.[137] The way it handled the issue of justification showed that it is not always deterred from scrutinizing claims by Member States that the application of the Treaty would undermine their national social security systems. Those who are committed to consolidating the internal market will hope that the Court examines equally closely other attempts by Member States to rely on considerations such as those at issue in *Kohll*.

---

[135] Para 42.   [136] See further ch 10.
[137] Cf Case C–212/97 *Centros Ltd*, judgment of 9 March 1999, a right of establishment case.

10

Public policy, public service and official authority

The previous chapter emphasized the parallelism which has emerged through the case law between the Treaty rules on services and those applicable to quantitative restrictions on imports and measures having equivalent effect. It is unlikely that this development was foreseen when the Treaty was drafted, but it reflects the similarity between the issues with which the Court has been confronted in the two contexts. That similarity is in turn illustrative of the economic links which now exist between goods and services.[1] The case law on services has swept the rules on establishment and then workers along in its wake, with the result that it can be said that a body of principles, essentially crafted by the Court, on freedom of movement in general is beginning to emerge. An important distinction between the rules on persons and services and those on goods is that the Court has so far declined to apply an approach modelled on *Keck and Mithouard* in the context of the former. It is to be hoped that the Court will resist the temptation to do so, although it must be acknowledged that the theoretical and pragmatic reasons for taking that step are not inconsiderable.

The present chapter is concerned with two other areas in which the rules on persons and services have developed in parallel. Unlike the developments discussed in the preceding chapters, however, it must have been envisaged by the authors of the Treaty that this would occur. This is because, despite textual and contextual differences, the relevant provisions self-evidently address essentially the same questions and would inevitably give rise to similar difficulties of application. The approach of the Court to their interpretation has also on the whole been less dramatic: it has taken the only line compatible with the proper functioning of the common market, often leaving the national courts with a margin of discretion in applying its decisions to the facts of particular cases.[2]

---

[1] Cf the Agreement establishing the World Trade Organisation, which was considered by the Court of Justice in Opinion 1/94 [1994] ECR I–5267; Eeckhout, *The European Internal Market and International Trade: A Legal Analysis* (1994), ch 1.

[2] See generally Arnull and Jacobs, 'Applying the common rules on the free movement of persons: the role of the national judiciary in the light of the jurisprudence of the European Court of Justice', and Plender, 'The free movement of persons in Europe—the role of the national judiciary', in Schermers et al (eds), *Free Movement of Persons in Europe* (1993), pp 272 and 286 respectively.

The public policy proviso

According to Article 39(3) (ex 48(3)) EC, the right of workers to freedom of move-ment within the Community is 'subject to limitations justified on grounds of pub-lic policy, public security or public health'.[3] Article 46(1) (ex 56(1)) EC says that the chapter on the right of establishment does not affect national rules 'providing for special treatment for foreign nationals on grounds of public policy, public secur-ity or public health'. Article 46(1) also applies to the chapter on services by virtue of Article 56 (ex 66). More detailed rules on how these provisions, embodying what has come to be known as 'the public policy proviso', are to be applied were laid down by the Council in Directive 64/221.[4] According to Article 1, the direct-ive applies to 'any national of a Member State who resides in or travels to another Member State of the Community, either in order to pursue an activity as an employed or self-employed person, or as a recipient of services'. It also applies to the migrant's spouse and the members of his or her family. It is therefore clear that from the early days the Council saw the public policy proviso laid down in Article 39(3) as having the same substantive content as Article 46(1). That view has influ-enced the approach of the Court. In *Royer*,[5] the Court was asked various questions, some concerning the public policy proviso, which had arisen in the course of crim-inal proceedings against a French national for illegal entry into and residence in Belgium. At the time the reference was made, the national court had not deter-mined whether the defendant was to be regarded as an employed or self-employed person or as a member of a migrant worker's family. Referring *inter alia* to Article 1 of Directive 64/221, the Court said that this did not matter because the relevant provisions were 'based on the same principles both in so far as they concern the entry into and residence in the territory of Member States of persons covered by Community law and the prohibition of all discrimination between them on grounds of nationality'.[6] The Court proceeded to give a common interpretation to the public policy proviso in both Articles 39(3) and 46(1).

Article 2(1) of Directive 64/221 provides that the directive applies to 'all meas-ures concerning entry into their territory, issue or renewal of residence permits, or expulsion from their territory, *taken by Member States* on grounds of public policy, public security or public health'.[7] In the *Bosman* case,[8] it was argued that Article 39 (ex 48) could not extend to the actions of private bodies because, unlike the Member States, such bodies were unable to rely on the public policy proviso. The

---

[3] See also Arts 68 (ex 73p) EC and 35(5) (ex K.7(5)) TEU, discussed in ch 2.

[4] On the coordination of special measures concerning the movement and residence of foreign nationals which are justified on grounds of public policy, public security or public health, OJ Sp Ed, 1963–64, p 117.

[5] Case 48/75 [1976] ECR 497. See also Case 118/75 *Watson and Belmann* [1976] ECR 1185; Joined Cases 115 and 116/81 *Adoui and Cornuaille v Belgium* [1982] ECR 1665.

[6] Para 12.   [7] Emphasis added.

[8] Case C–415/93 [1995] ECR I–4921. See ch 8.

Court described that argument as 'based on a false premiss'. It explained: 'There is nothing to preclude individuals from relying on justifications on grounds of public policy, public security or public health. Neither the scope nor the content of those grounds of justification is in any way affected by the public or private nature of the rules in question.'[9] It therefore seems that, notwithstanding the wording of Article 2(1), Directive 64/221 extends by analogy to the actions of private bodies in the same way as those of the Member States. In practice, of course, it will usually be the Member States who seek to rely on it.

The potential of the public policy proviso, if construed too broadly, to undermine the Treaty rules on persons and services led the Council to take a robust approach to its use. Thus, by virtue of Article 2(2) of Directive 64/221, the proviso must not be used to achieve economic objectives. Article 3(1) provides that '[m]easures taken on grounds of public policy or of public security shall be based exclusively on the personal conduct of the individual concerned'. According to Article 3(2), '[p]revious criminal convictions shall not in themselves constitute grounds for the taking of such measures'. Only diseases or disabilities falling within one of the groups listed in an annex to the directive may be invoked to justify refusal of entry or a first residence permit.[10] Diseases or disabilities occurring after a first residence permit has been issued cannot be used to justify refusing to renew it or expulsion from the national territory.[11] The directive also lays down detailed requirements designed to ensure that, in the words of the preamble, 'in each Member State, nationals of other Member States . . . have adequate legal remedies available to them in respect of the decisions of the administration in such matters'.[12]

Taking its lead from the Council, the Court has sought to strike a balance between preventing abuse of the proviso by the Member States and recognizing that the national authorities may sometimes have legitimate reasons for wishing to restrict an individual's right to freedom of movement. One of the leading cases is *Regina v Bouchereau*,[13] where the Court gave some general guidance on the meaning of the term 'public policy' and the circumstances in which a previous criminal conviction might justify recourse to the proviso. The Court emphasized that, as a derogation from the fundamental principle of freedom of movement, the concept of public policy was to be interpreted strictly. This meant that the Member States were not at liberty to determine its scope unilaterally, free from scrutiny by the institutions of the Community. However, the Court did not seek to impose a uniform set of values on all the Member States. On the contrary, it reiterated that 'the particular circumstances justifying recourse to the concept of public policy may vary from one country to another and from one period to another and it is therefore necessary in this matter to allow the competent national authorities an area of

---

[9] Para 86.   [10] Art 4(1).   [11] Art 4(2).

[12] See Arts 8 and 9; Case 98/79 *Pecastaing v Belgium* [1980] ECR 691; Joined Cases C–297/88 and C–197/89 *Dzodzi* [1990] ECR I–3763; Martin and Guild, *Free Movement of Persons in the European Union* (1996), pp 114–22.

[13] Case 30/77 [1977] ECR 1999. See also Case C–348/96 *Calfa*, judgment of 19 January 1999.

discretion within the limits imposed by the Treaty and the provisions adopted for its implementation'.[14]

The Court summed up the position as follows:[15] '. . . recourse by a national authority to the concept of public policy presupposes . . . the existence, in addition to the perturbation of the social order which any infringement of the law involves, of a genuine and sufficiently serious threat to the requirements of public policy affecting one of the fundamental interests of society'. As for the relevance of a previous criminal conviction, the Court cited the terms of Article 3(2) of the directive and stated that such a conviction was only relevant 'in so far as the circumstances which gave rise to that conviction are evidence of personal conduct constituting a present threat to the requirements of public policy'.[16] Although it was possible that past conduct alone might constitute such a threat, the Court said that it would generally be necessary to show 'the existence in the individual concerned of a propensity to act in the same way in the future'.[17] The application of these criteria in particular cases was a matter for the authorities and courts of the Member States.

The same logic has inspired the Court's approach to the interpretation of Article 3(1) of the directive. It has held that the reference to 'the personal conduct of the individual concerned' in that provision means that measures taken by a Member State on grounds of public policy or public security must be based on the particular circumstances of that individual rather than merely general considerations.[18] The Court has, however, taken a relatively permissive approach to the interpretation of the term 'personal conduct', with the result that behaviour which is in itself innocuous may be treated by the national authorities as a threat to public policy or public security by reason of the context in which it takes place. This emerges from the decision in *van Duyn v Home Office*,[19] where a Dutch woman arrived in the United Kingdom to take up employment as a secretary with the Church of Scientology at its college in East Grinstead. She was refused leave to enter on the basis that 'the Secretary of State considers it undesirable to give anyone leave to enter the United Kingdom on the business of or in the employment of that organization'. Although the nature of the work which the applicant wished to undertake was not in itself objectionable, the Court accepted that the concept of 'personal conduct' was capable of embracing 'present association, which reflects participation in the activities of the body or of the organization as well as identification with its aims and designs'.[20]

The *van Duyn* case was decided in December 1974 against the background of the Labour Government's renegotiation of the United Kingdom's terms of entry into the Communities.[21] This factor may explain the sense of *realpolitik* which pervades the Court's response to another issue raised by the case. Although the British

---

[14] Para 34. The Court cited its decision in Case 41/74 *van Duyn v Home Office* [1974] ECR 1337. See also Case 36/75 *Rutili v Minister for the Interior* [1975] ECR 1219.

[15] Para 35. [16] Para 28. [17] Para 29.

[18] See Case 67/74 *Bonsignore v Stadt Köln* [1975] ECR 297; *Rutili, supra; Adoui and Cornuaille, supra.*

[19] Case 41/74 [1974] ECR 1337. [20] Para 17.

[21] See Irving, 'The United Kingdom referendum, June 1975' (1975) 1 ELRev 3.

Government had made it perfectly clear that it disapproved of the Church of Scientology, its activities were not prohibited and British nationals remained at liberty to join or to work for it. This did not in the Court's view prevent the United Kingdom from relying on Article 39(3) (ex 48(3)):

where the competent authorities of a Member State have clearly defined their standpoint as regards the activities of a particular organization and where, considering it to be socially harmful, they have taken administrative measures to counteract these activities, the Member State cannot be required, before it can rely on the concept of public policy, to make such activities unlawful, if recourse to such a measure is not thought appropriate in the circumstances.[22]

It was not relevant that the State concerned did not place the same restrictions on its own nationals as those it imposed on the nationals of other Member States. An element of discrimination was implicit in the application of the public policy proviso because, under international law, a State was not entitled to refuse the right of entry or residence to its own nationals.[23]

The judgment was less than wholly convincing, for it overlooked a vital question: if employment with the Church of Scientology was really considered a threat to public policy, why were British nationals permitted to accept such employment? In other words, could the discrimination against the nationals of other Member States which inevitably resulted from the contested policy be considered arbitrary? The point was clearly expressed by Leleux: '[I]f a given form of conduct by a national is *not* a threat to public order and public security, can the *same* conduct become such a threat when a foreigner is involved?'[24]

The negative answer invited by Leleux's question was in due course supplied by the Court itself. In *Adoui and Cornuaille v Belgium*,[25] the Court was asked whether the authorities of one Member State could rely on the concept of public policy to refuse a residence permit to a national of another Member State who was suspected of being involved in prostitution if such involvement was not actually an offence in the first State. The Court emphasized that Member States could not invoke the public policy proviso to justify measures 'which would have the effect of applying an arbitrary distinction to the detriment of nationals of other Member States'.[26] It went on:[27]

Although Community law does not impose upon the Member States a uniform scale of values as regards the assessment of conduct which may be considered as contrary to public policy, it should nevertheless be stated that conduct may not be considered as being of a sufficiently serious nature to justify restrictions on the admission to or residence within the

---

[22] Para 19.

[23] Cf Art 3(2), Protocol No 4 to the European Convention on Human Rights. The protocol was signed by the UK in 1963 but has not been ratified.

[24] See 'Recent decisions of the Court of Justice in the field of free movement of persons and free supply of services' in Jacobs (ed), *European Law and the Individual* (1976), p 79 at p 90, emphasis in the original.

[25] *Supra.*   [26] Para 7.   [27] Para 8.

territory of a Member State of a national of another Member State in a case where the former Member State does not adopt, with respect to the same conduct on the part of its own nationals repressive measures or other genuine and effective measures intended to combat such conduct.

It seems unlikely that the steps taken by the British Government to impede the activities of the Church of Scientology would have satisfied that test.[28]

There is one final point which is worth making about *van Duyn*. As we saw in chapter 4, that case was one of the early decisions in which the Court recognized that directives were capable of producing vertical direct effect. Critics of the Court's alleged activism sometimes single out the Court's conclusion on that issue to support their thesis.[29] However, the conclusion reached by the Court in that case on the scope of the public policy proviso was an extremely cautious one which allowed the Member States a considerable margin of discretion. Far from supporting the allegation that the Court has been unduly activist, *van Duyn* merely demonstrates the futility of seeking to categorize the Court's case law in such crude terms.

The right of a Member State to rely on the public policy proviso may in practice be limited by the existence of directives harmonizing the conditions which must be satisfied by a person wishing to carry on a particular profession. An illustration of this point is provided by the decision in *Kohll v Union des Caisses de Maladie*,[30] which also offers guidance on the scope of the public health derogation. The facts of the case were set out in the previous chapter. The Court held that Articles 49 (ex 59) and 50 (ex 60) of the Treaty precluded national rules which made reimbursement of the cost of dental treatment, provided by an orthodontist established in another Member State, subject to authorization by the insured person's social security institution. It was argued by the State concerned that the contested rules were necessary to guarantee the quality of medical services and to ensure the provision of a balanced medical and hospital service open to all insured persons. The Court recognized that those objectives fell within the scope of the public health derogation contained in Article 46 (ex 56). However, the Court refused to accept that the quality of medical services could not be guaranteed when they were provided in other Member States. The medical and dental professions had been the subject of several Council directives, the effect of which was to co-ordinate or to harmonize the conditions under which those professions could be pursued. The Treaty provisions on services therefore entitled doctors and dentists established in other Member States to the same guarantees as those accorded to doctors and dentists established on national territory. The Court acknowledged that the public health derogation permitted Member States 'to restrict the freedom

---

[28] This point is made by Slynn, *Introducing a European Legal Order* (1992), p 108. For a different view, see Craig and de Búrca, *EU Law* (2nd edn, 1998), p 792.

[29] See eg Sir Patrick Neill, 'The European Court of Justice: A Case Study in Judicial Activism', Minutes of Evidence taken before the House of Lords Sub-Committee on the 1996 IGC (Session 1994–95, 18th Report, p 218); European Policy Forum (August 1995).

[30] Case C–158/96 [1998] ECR I–1931.

to provide medical and hospital services in so far as the maintenance of a treatment facility or medical service on national territory is essential for the public health and even the survival of the population'.[31] However, it had not been established that the contested rules were necessary to provide a balanced medical and hospital service accessible to all. Such rules were accordingly found not to be justified.

Two points are worth emphasizing. First, the existence of the Council directives mentioned by the Court removed the risk that those seeking treatment in other Member States would not receive appropriate standards of care. In the absence of concrete evidence to the contrary, the State whose rules were in issue had to assume that treatment carried out in other Member States was as effective as treatment provided on its own territory. Secondly, the Court took a fairly broad view of the scope of the public health derogation. Even if reimbursing the cost of seeking treatment abroad had been found to threaten the provision of a comprehensive health service, the threat to public health would have been indirect and speculative. The Court balanced that broad view by applying strictly the principle of proportionality and treating with a certain scepticism the claim of the State concerned that the disputed rules were necessary to preserve a balanced medical and hospital service open to all. The case shows that, notwithstanding the Court's reluctance to interfere in the organization and financing of national social security systems, it will not allow the powers of the Member States in those areas to be exercised in a manner which disregards the fundamental principle of freeedom of movement.[32] The judgment strikes a judicious balance between the competing interests at stake.

Public service and official authority

Like the public policy proviso, the exceptions for employment in the public service and activities connected with the exercise of official authority contained in Article 39(4) (ex 48(4))[33] and the first paragraph of Article 45 (ex 55) respectively have the potential to undermine the fundamental principle of freedom of movement.[34] The practical importance of ensuring the correct application of Article 39(4) in particular was underlined by the High Level Panel on the Free Movement of Persons, which pointed out that 'the public sector employs about 22 million workers in the Union and . . . public sector workers (teachers and health professionals) are among the most mobile (public and private sectors taken together)'.[35] Unlike the public policy proviso, however, there is no legislation to elucidate the

---

[31] Para 51. The Court referred to Case 72/83 *Campus Oil v Minister for Industry and Energy* [1984] ECR 2727, discussed in ch 7.

[32] See paras 17–20 of the judgment.   [33] See also Art 8(1), Reg 1612/68.

[34] See generally Handoll, 'Article 48(4) EEC and non-national access to public employment' (1988) 13 ELRev 223; O'Keeffe, 'Judicial interpretation of the public service exception to the free movement of workers' in Curtin and O'Keeffe (eds), *Constitutional Adjudication in European Community Law and National Law* (1992), p 89.

[35] See the Panel's report presented to the Commission on 18 March 1997, p 35.

scope of Articles 39(4) and 45.[36] It has therefore fallen to the Court to balance the dictates of free movement against the recognition by the Treaty's authors that certain activities may legitimately be confined to a State's own nationals. Most of the Court's decisions in this field have concerned Article 39(4). The reason for this is probably that, as the United Kingdom argued in *Commission v Belgium*,[37] the self-employed are only exceptionally involved in the exercise of official authority whereas those employed in the public service are often called upon to exercise such authority. However, it is clear from the case law that the Court takes a similar approach to the interpretation of both provisions. Attempts to restrict the scope of Article 39(4) by comparing it with the slightly different—and allegedly narrower—language of the first paragraph of Article 45 have been unsuccessful.[38]

A number of points may now be regarded as well established. Many of them may seem self-evident and they are only worth dwelling on in the present context because some Member States have been disappointingly reluctant to accept them. In *Lawrie-Blum v Land Baden-Württemberg*,[39] the Court made it clear that:

as a derogation from the fundamental principle that workers in the Community should enjoy freedom of movement and not suffer discrimination, Article 48(4) [now 39(4)] must be construed in such a way as to limit its scope to what is strictly necessary for safeguarding the interests which that provision allows the Member States to protect . . . [A]ccess to certain posts may not be limited by reason of the fact that in a given Member State persons appointed to such posts have the status of civil servants. To make the application of Article 48(4) dependent on the legal nature of the relationship between the employee and the administration would enable the Member States to determine at will the posts covered by the exception laid down in that provision.

Moreover, Article 39(4) (ex 48(4)) can only be used to justify the imposition of restrictions at the point of admission to the public service. The Court has held that it 'cannot justify discriminatory measures with regard to remuneration or other conditions of employment against workers once they have been admitted to the public service'.[40] In *Commission v Belgium*,[41] it was argued that this approach was liable to create anomalies, since a person admitted to the public service might later be promoted or transferred to a post to which he could have been refused direct admission under Article 39(4). That argument was brushed aside by the Court, which stated that the Member States were permitted to reserve certain posts within the public service to their own nationals where the criteria for the application of Article 39(4) were met. In other words, a person cannot be excluded from appointment as

---

[36] Although in 1988 the Commission published a Communication on the application of Article 39(4): see OJ 1988 C72/2.

[37] Case 149/79 [1980] ECR 3881, 3893.

[38] See Case 149/79 *Commission v Belgium* [1980] ECR 3881, 3888; Case 307/84 *Commission v France* [1986] ECR 1725, para 7.

[39] Case 66/85 [1986] ECR 2121, para 26. See also Case 152/73 *Sotgiu v Deutsche Bundespost* [1974] ECR 153; Case 307/84 *Commission v France* [1986] ECR 1725.

[40] *Sotgiu, supra*, para 4.   [41] *Supra.*

a driver in the Civil Service because she might one day rise to the rank of Permanent Secretary.

In the *Belgium* case, the Court sought to clarify precisely what criteria had to be met before Article 39(4) (ex 48(4)) could be invoked. The Court stated:[42]

That provision removes from the ambit of Article 48(1) to (3) a series of posts which involve direct or indirect participation in the exercise of powers conferred by public law and duties designed to safeguard the general interests of the State or of other public authorities. Such posts in fact presume on the part of those occupying them the existence of a special relationship of allegiance to the State and reciprocity of rights and duties which form the foundation of the bond of nationality.

The Belgian Government attempted, with the support of three other Member States, to persuade the Court to abandon this approach, sometimes described as 'functional' because it focuses on the functions to be performed by the holders of the disputed posts, in favour of an 'institutional' or 'organic' test under which the scope of Article 39(4) (ex 48(4)) would depend on the way in which posts were classified under national law. Such a test, it was said, would be easier to apply and more in keeping with the intentions of the Treaty's authors and the constitutional traditions of certain Member States, according to which non-nationals were not in principle eligible for employment in the public service. The Court was adamant, pointing out that, if the institutional approach were upheld, its effect 'would be to remove a considerable number of posts from the ambit of the principles set out in the Treaty and to create inequalities between Member States according to the different ways in which the State and certain sectors of economic life are organized'.[43]

The full implications of the approach advocated by the Belgian Government emerge more clearly if one considers the factual background to the case. The Commission had sought a declaration that Belgium had infringed its Treaty obligations because recruitment to a series of posts with various public bodies in Belgium was reserved to Belgian nationals. In its judgment, the Court described the contested posts thus:[44] 'trainee locomotive drivers, loaders, plate-layers, shunters and signallers with the national railways and unskilled workers with the local railways . . . hospital nurses, children's nurses, night-watchmen, plumbers, carpenters, electricians, garden hands, architects, and supervisors with the City of Brussels and the Commune of Auderghem'. This provided a very unpromising context in which to seek to change the direction of the Court's developing case law. Had the Court accepted that posts of this nature were not open to the nationals of other Member States, the fundamental principle of freedom of movement would have been seriously jeopardized. However, conscious of the sensitive issues raise by the case, the Court concluded that it did not have enough information about the precise nature of the duties attaching to these posts to decide which of them, if any, fell within the scope of Article 39(4) (ex 48(4)). It therefore invited the parties to re-examine the position in the light of the guidance it had given and report back for a final deci-

[42] Para 10.   [43] Para 11.   [44] Para 3.

sion. The Commission subsequently conceded that some of the disputed posts were covered by Article 39(4), but in its second decision in the case the Court ruled that the remainder fell outside the scope of that provision.[45]

The Court has taken a similar approach to the interpretation of the first paragraph of Article 45 (ex 55). In *Reyners v Belgium*,[46] the Court was asked for guidance on the extent to which the profession of *avocat* could be connected with the exercise of official authority. In language almost identical to that used in *Sotgiu* less than five months earlier in relation to Article 39(4) (ex 48(4)), the Court stated that '[h]aving regard to the fundamental character of freedom of establishment and the rule on equal treatment with nationals in the system of the Treaty, the exceptions allowed by the first paragraph of Article 55 [now 45] cannot be given a scope which would exceed the objective for which this exemption clause was inserted'.[47] The Court therefore held that the provision applied only to 'those activities which, taken on their own, constitute a direct and specific connexion with the exercise of official authority'.[48] It could only embrace an entire profession 'where such activities were linked with that profession in such a way that freedom of establishment would result in imposing on the Member State concerned the obligation to allow the exercise, even occasionally, by non-nationals of functions appertaining to official authority'.[49] It was not permissible where 'the activities connected with the exercise of official authority are separable from the professional activity in question taken as a whole'.[50] The Court went on to emphasize the need to endow the exception laid down in the first paragraph of Article 45 with a 'Community character' in order 'to avoid the effectiveness of the Treaty being defeated by unilateral provisions of Member States'.[51] The Court concluded that some of the typical activities of *avocats*, such as consultation and legal assistance and the representation of parties in court, could not be considered connected with the exercise of official authority, even if they were compulsory or the subject of a legal monopoly.[52]

The response of the Member States

Some Member States have shown extreme reluctance to give effect to the principles laid down by the Court in this area. In *Commission v France*,[53] in which France was accused of failure to fulfil its Treaty obligations by restricting employment as a nurse in public hospitals to French nationals, the French Government invited the Court to depart from its previous decisions and to recognize that the correct test for determining whether Article 39(4) (ex 48(4)) applied was an

---

[45] [1982] ECR 1845. The posts concerned are listed at pp 1847–8 of the report.
[46] [1974] ECR 631. Cf Case C–114/97 *Commission v Spain*, judgment of 29 October 1998.
[47] Para 43. Cf para 4 of the judgment in *Sotgiu, supra*.   [48] Para 45.   [49] Para 46.
[50] Para 47.   [51] Para 50.
[52] The criteria laid down in *Reyners* were applied in Case C–306/89 *Commission v Greece* [1991] ECR I–5863 and Case C–42/92 *Thijssen v Controledienst voor de Verzekeringen* [1993] ECR I–4047. See also Case C–272/91 *Commission v Italy* [1994] ECR I–1409.
[53] Case 307/84 [1986] ECR 1725.

institutional rather than a functional one. The Court simply applied its existing case law and granted the declaration sought by the Commission. A series of cases decided over ten years later,[54] which had been brought by the Commission to reinforce the guidelines set out in its 1988 Communication,[55] revealed a whole range of posts in the public sector for which the nationality of the States concerned was required even though they were unconnected with tasks belonging to the public service properly so-called. The disputed posts included employment with the Luxembourg city bus service and employment as a musician with the Athens Opera and with municipal and local orchestras in Greece. The Court emphatically endorsed its previous case law and once again rejected the institutional approach. It made it clear that Member States were not entitled to make all posts in certain areas subject to a nationality condition: '[t]he fact that some posts in those areas may, in certain circumstances, be covered by Article 48(4) [now 39(4)] of the Treaty cannot justify such a general prohibition'.[56] The Court thus neatly turned on their head the objections of the defendant Governments to the so-called global approach taken by the Commission, which consisted of excluding whole areas of the public service from the scope of Article 48(4) without carrying out a detailed examination of the precise posts affected. The judgments make it clear that it is the Member States which are not entitled to adopt a global approach and that they may only exclude nationals of other Member States from particular posts which satsify the 'very strict conditions'[57] laid down in Article 39(4).

In the case involving Luxembourg, one of the areas challenged by the Commission from which nationals of other Member States were excluded was that of teaching. The defendant Government maintained that, in view of Luxembourg's size and demographic situation, the imposition of a nationality requirement in this area was necessary to preserve its national identity. The cultural importance of the teaching profession was acknowledged by the Court in *Groener*[58] and the Union is required to 'respect the national identities of its Member States' by Article 6(3) (ex F(1)) TEU. None the less, the argument of the Luxembourg Government was treated by both Advocate General Léger[59] and the Court with a certain amount of scepticism: 'the interest pleaded by the Grand Duchy can, even in such particularly sensitive areas as education, still be effectively safeguarded otherwise than by a general exclusion of nationals from other Member States. As the Advocate General points out . . . nationals of other Member States must, like Luxembourg nationals,

---

[54] Case C–473/93 *Commission v Luxembourg* [1996] ECR I–3207; Case C–173/94 *Commission v Belgium* [1996] ECR I–3265; Case C–290/94 *Commission v Greece* [1996] ECR I–3285. The Opinions of AG Léger in the *Luxembourg* and *Greece* cases contain lists of the posts which had to date been held to fall outside the scope of Art 39(4): see pp I–3215 and I–3294–5 respectively.

[55] See OJ 1988 C72/2.

[56] *Luxembourg*, para 47; *Belgium*, para 19; *Greece*, para 36.

[57] This description was first used by the Court in *Lawrie-Blum, supra,* at para 28. It was repeated in the *Luxembourg* case at para 33.

[58] Case C–379/87 [1989] ECR 3967. This case is discussed in ch 8.

[59] See pp I–3233–4.

still fulfil all the conditions required for recruitment, in particular those relating to training, experience and language knowledge.'[60] Nationals of other Member States are in practice likely to find the last requirement mentioned by the Court very hard to satisfy because Luxemburgish, the national language of Luxembourg, is not widely spoken outside that country.

It is submitted that the functional approach to the scope of Article 39(4) (ex 48(4)) adopted by the Court is self-evidently correct and that no objective observer could fail to recognize the force of the objections to the institutional approach which the Court has spelled out. Why then have certain Member States, willing to endorse the establishment of the concept of citizenship of the Union and the creation of 'an area of freedom, security and justice' in which internal border controls are removed, been so reluctant to accept the principles laid down in the case law? That question was addressed by Advocate General Mancini in the 'Nurses' case:[61] 'Such resistance is not surprising if it is borne in mind how deep-rooted is the conviction that the public service is an area in which the State should exercise full sovereignty and how widespread is the tendency, in times of high unemployment, to see the public service as a convenient reservoir of posts. Such resistance is nevertheless a matter for concern and should be tackled head-on before cases similar to the present one multiply . . .' An alternative approach, more in keeping with the spirit of the Treaty, was put forward by the High Level Panel on the Free Movement of Persons:[62] 'the inclusion of Community citizens in the public services of the Member States should not be perceived as a form of disruption. On the contrary, in a European Union where collaboration between national governments is increasingly close, the presence of civil servants from different Member States within the public service of a particular State may add value and increase efficiency to a considerable extent.' It is a matter for regret that the concepts of primacy and direct effect[63] and the use by the Commission of proceedings under Article 226 (ex 169) do not yet seem to have secured universal acceptance of that view. It seems unlikely that anything useful would emerge from the Council if legislation on the matter were to be proposed under Article 40 (ex 49) of the Treaty.[64] Perhaps the principle of State liability[65] and exposure to financial sanctions under Article 228(2) (ex 171(2)) EC[66] will increase the pressure on delinquent Member States to conform to the principles laid down by the Court.

---

[60] Para 35 of the judgment.

[61] Case 307/84 *Commission v France* [1986] ECR 1725, 1728. See also O'Keeffe, op cit, p 105.

[62] See p 37 of its report.   [63] See further the *Greece* case, *supra*, at paras 25 and 29.

[64] The absence of such legislation was criticized by the Belgian Government in Case 149/79 *Commission v Belgium*: see [1980] ECR 3881, 3889.

[65] See ch 5.   [66] See ch 2.

11

The free movement of persons and services: supplementing the basic principles

The chapters of the EC Treaty on workers, establishment and services, and the legislation which has been adopted under them, are far-reaching in their implications, conferring a wide range of rights on migrants. However, they are far from comprehensive in their coverage and it gradually became apparent that there were gaps in the Treaty framework which the logic of free movement required to be filled. One such gap was the absence of any reference in Article 39 (ex 48) to the rights of those going to a Member State other than their own in search of work. We have seen how the Court filled that gap by a broad and flexible interpretation of Article 39.[1] Other gaps have proved less amenable to that type of solution and different responses have been required. The task of finding such responses has been undertaken by the Court of Justice, the political institutions, and the Member States themselves.

The Treaty prohibition of discrimination on grounds of nationality

Perhaps the main device employed by the Court to fill perceived gaps in the main provisions of the Treaty concerned with the free movement of persons and services has been the first paragraph of Article 12 EC,[2] which provides: 'Within the scope of application of this Treaty, and without prejudice to any special provisions contained therein, any discrimination on the grounds of nationality shall be prohibited.' The second paragraph of Article 12 empowers the Council to 'adopt rules designed to prohibit such discrimination'. This might be taken to imply that the first paragraph is not capable of producing direct effect and that the principle it lays down only becomes enforceable once implemented by the Council. However, because the prohibition contained in the first paragraph is complete and legally perfect in itself, this is not an implication the Court has been willing to draw.

[1] See Case C–292/89 *Antonissen* [1991] ECR I–745, discussed in ch 8.
[2] Formerly Art 6 and, before the TEU, Art 7.

Article 12 is not of course the only provision of the Treaty which prohibits discrimination on the grounds of nationality. We have encountered similar prohibitions in Articles 39(2) (ex 48(2)), 43 (ex 52), and 49 (ex 59). The Court has consistently held that Article 12 'applies independently only to situations governed by Community law in regard to which the Treaty lays down no specific prohibition of discrimination'. Thus, in *Commission v Greece*,[3] from which that quotation is taken, the Commission alleged that Greece had failed to fulfil its obligation under Articles 12, 39, 43 and 49 of the Treaty. The Court found that the contested Greek rules were incompatible with Articles 39, 43, and 49 and that 'there is no need to consider whether there has been a specific infringement of Article 7 [now 12] of the Treaty in so far as the Commission has not referred to any situations other than those covered by the aforesaid Articles 48 [now 39], 52 [now 43] and 59 [now 49]'.[4] However, the Court does not always examine closely whether a particular instance of discrimination on the ground of nationality is caught by a more specific prohibition than Article 12 if that article seems the most convenient provision to apply. This might be so where, for example, the Court wishes to make it clear that discrimination is prohibited not merely in circumstances subject to the same rules as the case under consideration but also in comparable situations which are subject to different rules.[5]

It is in the field of education that the potential of Article 12 first became apparent and in which its impact has been most dramatic.[6] The story begins with *Forcheri v Belgium*,[7] where the Italian wife of a Commission official, also an Italian national, who worked in Brussels, was asked to pay a fee for foreign students when she enrolled on a social work course at a further education institute approved and subsidized by the Belgian Government. The fee was not imposed on students of Belgian or Luxembourg nationality or on students falling within certain other categories, none of which included Mrs F. The matter eventually came before a Juge de Paix in Brussels, who made a reference to the Court of Justice. The Court held that Community officials enjoyed 'all the benefits flowing from Community law for nationals of Member States in relation to freedom of movement, freedom of establishment and social security'.[8] There was, however, no specific provision of Community law requiring the spouse of a migrant worker to be admitted under the same conditions as nationals of the host State to courses of education such as the one Mrs F had followed: Regulation 1612/68 reserves that right to the worker himself[9] and to his children if they are resident in that State.[10] The obvious route

---

[3] Case 305/87 [1989] ECR 1461. See para 13 of the judgment. The case concerned the right of foreigners to own immovable property in border regions of Greece and is discussed in more detail in ch 9.

[4] Para 28. See also Case C–10/90 *Masgio* [1991] ECR I–1119, para 12; Case C–179/90 *Merci Convenzionali Porto di Genova* [1991] ECR I–5889, para 11; Case C–18/93 *Corsica Ferries* [1994] ECR I–1783, para 19.

[5] See Joined Cases C–92/92 and C–326/92 *Collins and Others* [1993] ECR I–5145, discussed below.

[6] See generally McMahon, *Education and Culture in European Comunity Law* (1995); Lonbay, 'Education and law: the Community context' (1989) 14 ELRev 363; Lenaerts, 'Education in European Community law after "Maastricht" ' (1994) 31 CMLRev 7.

[7] Case 152/82 [1983] ECR 2323.   [8] Para 9.   [9] Art 7(3).   [10] Art 12.

for the Court was to consider whether the prohibition on discrimination contained in Article 39(2) (ex 48(2)) had been infringed. However, although the Court referred to Article 39 and to Regulation 1612/68 in emphasizing the fundamental importance of the right to freedom of movement, it chose to address the national court's questions from the perspective of Article 12. It therefore asked 'whether access to educational courses, in particular those concerning vocational training, falls within the scope of application of the Treaty'.[11] The EEC Treaty did not at that time give the Comunity competence in the field of educational and vocational training as such, as the Court acknowledged.[12] However, Article 128 EEC did provide[13] that the Council was to 'lay down general principles for implementing a common vocational training policy capable of contributing to the harmonious development both of the national economies and of the common market'. The Court referred to a Council decision adopted in 1963 to give effect to that provision in which the importance of a common vocational training policy had been emphasized. The Court concluded:[14]

if a Member State organizes educational courses relating in particular to vocational training, to require of a national of another Member State lawfully established in the first Member State an enrolment fee which is not required of its own nationals in order to take part in such courses constitutes discrimination by reason of nationality, which is prohibited by Article 7 [now 12] of the Treaty.

That ruling, delivered by a five-Judge chamber against the (admittedly rather superficial) advice of Advocate General Rozès, was bold and inventive. The case itself, concerning the spouse of a Community official who was required by the Staff Regulations of the Community to live in Belgium, might have seemed relatively limited in scope. But the only aspect of Mrs F's status that the Court treated as important was the fact that she was 'lawfully established' in the host State. The ruling therefore established that Member States were not entitled to charge nationals of other Member States who were lawfully present within their territory fees for access to vocational training which they did not expect their own nationals to pay. A number of questions would subsequently require clarification. When was a person to be regarded as lawfully established in a Member State other than his own? When was training to be considered vocational for these purposes? Was Article 12 confined to fees or did it apply to other conditions of access? Upon the answers to these questions would depend the full impact of the *Forcheri* ruling on the organization and financing of education in the Member States.

It was not long before the Court was called upon to develop the principles laid down in *Forcheri*. In *Gravier v City of Liège*,[15] a reference was made to the Court in the course of proceedings in which G, a student of French nationality at a Belgian art college, was arguing that she should not be required to pay an enrolment fee which students of Belgian nationality were not required to pay. The Court again

---

[11] Para 13.   [12] Para 17.   [13] See now Arts 149 (ex 126) and 150 (ex 127) EC.
[14] Para 18.   [15] Case 293/83 [1985] ECR 593.

held that the imposition of a registration fee in circumstances such as these was prohibited by Article 12 of the Treaty. That access to vocational training fell within the scope of the Treaty was confirmed by Articles 7 and 12 of Regulation 1612/68 as well as by Article 128 of the Treaty (as it then stood). The common vocational training policy envisaged by the latter provision constituted, the Court said, 'an indispensable element of the activities of the Community, whose objectives include *inter alia* the free movement of persons, the mobility of labour and the improvement of the living standards of workers'. The Court continued:[16]

Access to vocational training is in particular likely to promote free movement of persons throughout the Community, by enabling them to obtain a qualification in the Member State where they intend to work and by enabling them to complete their training and develop their particular talents in the Member State whose vocational training programmes include the special subject desired.

The course which G wished to follow involved studying the art of strip cartoons. Referring to initiatives taken by the Council to give effect to Article 128 EEC, the Court accepted that such a course constituted vocational training where the institution providing it 'prepares students for a qualification for a particular profession, trade or employment or provides them with the skills necessary for such a profession, trade or employment'.[17] This was so regardless of the level of the course and even if it included an element of general education.

Further guidance on the meaning of the term 'vocational training' was given in *Blaizot v University of Liège and Others*,[18] where the Court considered the extent to which it covered university studies. Pointing out that whether a particular subject was studied in universities or elsewhere varied from State to State, the Court ruled that university studies were in general to be considered vocational training within the meaning of the Treaty. The only exception the Court was prepared to recognize was 'certain courses of study which, because of their particular nature, are intended for persons wishing to improve their general knowledge rather than prepare themselves for an occupation'.[19] The concept was therefore a broad one, not limited to courses which qualified students for a particular occupation or those with a practical rather than a theoretical emphasis.

In *Gravier* it was argued that G could not be regarded as 'lawfully established' in Belgium since she was not herself a worker, nor was she the child or the spouse of a worker. Her situation was therefore distinguishable from that of Mrs F. Advocate General Slynn said[20] that he did not read *Forcheri* 'as laying down that a necessary precondition of the right to undertake a particular vocational course depends on a pre-existing right of residence . . . The question to my mind remains open as to whether a national of one Member State can be charged a higher fee to undertake a course of study solely on the grounds that her nationality is not that of the Member State in which the course is held.' In one sense, G was lawfully resident

---

[16] Para 24.   [17] Para 31.   [18] Case 24/86 [1988] ECR 379.   [19] Para 20.
[20] At p 599.

in Belgium at the time when she was asked to pay the contested fees because she held a residence permit, presumably granted to enable her to pursue the course. The permit lapsed as a result of her refusal to pay the fees, but she was able to comply with the relevant Belgian residence formalities because the defendant in the main proceedings ensured that she was issued with a provisional registration certificate while her case was pending. The argument was that the host State was not *obliged* to allow her to remain on its territory.

The Court evidently agreed with the view of its Advocate General on this point, for it is not mentioned in the judgment.[21] Some time later, it became clear why G had indeed been lawfully established in Belgium. In *Raulin*,[22] the Court held:

> The right to equality of treatment regarding the conditions of access to vocational training applies not only to the requirements laid down by the educational establishment in question, such as enrolment fees, but also any measure that may prevent the exercise of that right. It is clear that a student admitted to a course of vocational training might be unable to attend the course if he did not have a right of residence in the Member State where the course takes place. It follows that the principle of non-discrimination with regard to conditions of access to vocational training deriving from Articles 7 and 128 of the EEC Treaty implies that a national of a Member State who has been admitted to a vocational training course in another Member State enjoys, in this respect, a right of residence for the duration of the course.

The Court added that the right of entry and residence which a student who was a national of a Member State derived from Community law did not depend on the grant of a residence permit by the host State. It had thus fashioned out of the prohibition against discrimination on the grounds of nationality a right of entry and residence for a category of people who fell outside the scope of the Treaty chapters on the free movement of persons and services.

The Court has not been insensitive to concerns expressed by Member States about these developments. In *Gravier*, two Governments argued that Article 12 of the Treaty should not be regarded as overriding the special responsibilities in the area of education which Member States were said to have towards their own nationals. In response the Court emphasized that the case was not concerned with the organization or financing of education, but with 'the establishment of a financial barrier to access to education for foreign students only'. The limits of the emerging right of non-discriminatory access to vocational training became clearer in *Lair v Universität Hannover*[23] and *Brown v Secretary of State for Scotland*,[24] where the Court considered whether the first paragraph of Article 12 covered grants for maintenance and the payment of tuition fees.[25] In his Opinion in the *Brown* case, Advocate General Slynn said that there was no difference between enrolment fees

---

[21] An argument that G enjoyed rights of free movement as a recipient of services was not addressed by the Court. See ch 9.

[22] Case C–357/89 [1992] ECR I–1027, para 34.

[23] Case 39/86 [1988] ECR 3161.   [24] Case 197/86 [1988] ECR 3205.

[25] In both cases the Court also considered the extent of the applicants' rights under Art 39 (ex 48) EC and Reg 1612/68. Its conclusions on that issue are discussed in ch 8.

and tuition fees: the rule laid down in *Gravier* applied to both. However, he thought the position with regard to maintenance grants was different:[26]

Though of course I realize that if a student cannot eat or have a bed he cannot study, it does not seem to me that the means of subsistence have a sufficiently direct link with access to the course itself to fall within the principle of non-discrimination spelled out in *Gravier*. Direct access to a vocational training course is within the scope of application of Article 7 [now 12] of the Treaty; the means of subsistence, in the absence of more specific Community provisions, are not.

That advice was followed by the Court, which ruled 'that the payment by a Member State to or on behalf of students of tuition fees charged by a university falls within the scope of the EEC Treaty for the purposes of Article 7 [now 12] thereof, but the payment of grants for students' maintenance does not'.[27] The Court explained that the latter 'is, on the one hand, a matter of educational policy, which is not as such included in the spheres entrusted to the Community institutions . . . and, on the other, a matter of social policy, which falls within the competence of the Member States in so far as it is not covered by specific provisions of the EEC Treaty . . .'.[28]

The Court's conclusion on this point may be seen as a pragmatic response to the concerns expressed by some Member States about the potential consequences of its case law for the way in which financial assistance was granted to students. The artificiality of the distinction drawn by the Court between assistance with the payment of fees and help with the costs of maintenance was underlined in *Raulin*, where the Court was asked to rule on the effect of Article 12 of the Treaty in the context of a system of study finance which made no distinction between the costs of access and the costs of maintenance. The Court held, logically but rather impractically, that only the part of the overall package which was intended to cover enrolment and tuition fees was covered by Article 12. The national court was left to work out the proportion affected.

Although it is in the field of education that the prohibition against discrimination on the grounds of nationality laid down in the first paragraph of Article 12 of the Treaty has produced its greatest impact, its effect has not been confined to that field. In *Cowan v Trésor Public*,[29] the Court held that it was incompatible with that prohibition for a Member State to refuse compensation for criminal injuries to a national of another Member State who came within the scope of Community law as a recipient of services. The Court observed: 'When Community law guarantees a natural person the freedom to go to another Member State the protection of that person from harm in the Member State in question, on the same basis as that of nationals and persons residing there, is a corollary of that freedom of movement.'[30]

[26] p 3230.   [27] Para 19 of the judgment in *Brown*. See also para 16 of the judgment in *Lair*.
[28] *Brown*, para 18; *Lair*, para 15.
[29] Case 186/87 [1989] ECR 195. This case is also discussed in ch 9.
[30] Para 17.

In *Collins and Others*,[31] the Court invoked Article 12 in relation to a national rule which restricted the remedies available to performing artists from abroad where certain rights in their performances were infringed. The rule in question was laid down in German law, which permitted performing artists who had German nationality to restrain the distribution of recordings of their performances which were made without their permission. Foreign performers enjoyed no such rights in respect of performances given outside Germany. This situation, the Court said, was incompatible with Article 12. Intellectual property rights were 'by their nature such as to affect trade in goods and services and also competitive relationships within the Community'.[32] They therefore fell within the scope of the Treaty and were subject to the principle of non-discrimination laid down in the first paragraph of Article 12 'without there even being any need to connect them with the specific provisions of Articles 30 [now 28], 36 [now 30], 59 [now 49] and 66 [now 55] of the Treaty'.[33] Referring to *Cowan*, the Court said that Article 12 required that 'persons in a situation governed by Community law be placed on a completely equal footing with nationals of the Member State concerned'.[34] It therefore precluded a Member State from denying to the nationals of other Member States the same protection in respect of their performances as that enjoyed by its own nationals. The Court went on to make clear what was already implicit in its case law,[35] that the first paragraph of Article 12 produced direct effect.

Both *Cowan* and *Collins* illustrate the Court's willingness, also evident in *Forcheri*, to apply Article 12 in preference to more specific prohibitions on discrimination in order to make it clear that the precise circumstances in which the problem has arisen are not important. In *Cowan*, the rules on services could not be applied without a certain amount of stretching because the discrimination suffered by C was unconnected with the services he had received as a tourist. His situation may be contrasted with that of the applicant in *Gravier*, who was the victim of discrimination in relation to the very activity—the provision of vocational training—in respect of which she claimed rights as a recipient of services. In the latter case, the Court did not deal with the Treaty rules on services because it wished to make it clear that discrimination in relation to access to vocational training was prohibited regardless of whether or not the circumstances involved a provision of services within the meaning of Article 50 (ex 60).[36] There is a similar explanation for the Court's reliance on Article 12 in *Collins*. Advocate General Jacobs, who regarded the facts of the case as falling within the scope of Article 49 (ex 59) of the Treaty, emphasized that 'there are many ways in which the proprietor of intellectual property rights may seek to exercise those rights in pursuit of the economic freedoms guaranteed by the Treaty'[37] and that Articles 28 (ex 30) and 43 (ex 52) might also

---

[31] *Supra.*   [32] Para 22.   [33] Para 27.   [34] Para 32.

[35] See in particular Case 309/85 *Barra v Belgium and Another* [1988] ECR 355; AG Jacobs in Case C–295/90 *Parliament v Council* [1992] ECR I–4193, I–4228. The latter case is discussed below.

[36] Cf the Opinion of AG Slynn in that case, subsequently followed by the Court in Case 263/86 *Belgian State v Humbel* [1988] ECR 5365. See ch 9.

[37] p I–5164.

sometimes be relevant. Recourse to Article 12 made it clear that, whether the case involved the free movement of goods, the right of establishment or the right to provide services, a Member State was required to accord the nationals of other Member States the same level of protection as its own nationals.

Citizenship of the Union

The importance of the prohibition against discrimination on grounds of nationality laid down in Article 12 of the Treaty has grown with the insertion into the EC Treaty at Maastricht of a new Part Two entitled 'Citizenship of the Union'. Article 17(2) (ex 8(2)) provides that '[c]itizens of the Union shall enjoy the rights conferred by this Treaty and shall be subject to the duties imposed thereby'. The substantive rights conferred by Part Two of the Treaty on such citizens in the absence of further action by the Council appear at first sight to be relatively limited.[38] However, it is becoming apparent that appearances may be misleading.

The significance of Part Two when combined with the principle of non-discrimination first became apparent with the Court's decision in *Martínez Sala v Freistaat Bayern*.[39] The applicant in the main proceedings was a Spanish woman living in Germany. She had had a series of jobs, but at the material time she was unemployed and receiving social assistance. Until 1984, the applicant had obtained from the competent authorities a series of residence permits. Subsequently, she obtained documents certifying that she had applied for an extension of her residence permit. In 1994 she was again issued with a residence permit. During the period when she did not have a permit, the applicant gave birth to a child and applied to the respondent for a child-raising allowance. Her application was rejected on the grounds that she did not have German nationality, a residence entitlement, or a residence permit. The applicant challenged that decision and the case was eventually referred to the Court of Justice.

There were various ways in which the applicant might have been able to establish an entitlement to the allowance. The Court accepted that such a benefit fell within the *material* scope of both Regulation 1408/71 and Regulation 1612/68. However, the Court said that it did not have enough information to establish whether the applicant fell within the *personal* scope of those regulations and left that question to the national court to determine. That court had asked whether a Member State was entitled to require production of a formal residence permit in a case such as this. The Court's answer illustrated the difference which the provisions on citizenship were capable of making. The Court noted that, in order to establish entitlement to the contested allowance, a claimant had to be permanently or

---

[38] See ch 8.
[39] Case C–85/96 [1998] ECR I–2691. See O'Leary, 'Putting flesh on the bones of European Union citizenship' (1999) 24 ELRev 68; Fries and Shaw, 'Citizenship of the Union: first steps in the European Court of Justice' (1998) 4 European Public Law 533.

ordinarily resident in Germany. A national of another Member State who, like the applicant, was authorized to reside in Germany and actually resided there satisfied that condition and was in the same position as a German national resident in Germany. However, a non-national had in addition to produce a certain type of residence permit to receive the allowance. A document certifying that an application for a permit had been made was not enough, even though it established that the person concerned was entitled to stay in the country. The Court said that this amounted to discrimination on the basis of nationality, because German nationals were not required to produce any equivalent document. Such discrimination was prohibited by Article 12 within the scope of application of the Treaty. The Court had already found that the allowance fell within the material scope of Community law. It went on to rule that, even if the applicant did not come within the personal scope of Regulations 1408/71 or 1612/68, she fell within the personal scope of the Treaty provisions on citizenship because she was lawfully resident in another Member State.[40] It followed, the Court said, 'that a citizen of the European Union, such as the appellant in the main proceedings, lawfully resident in the territory of the host Member State, can rely on Article 6 [now 12] of the Treaty in all situations which fall within the scope *ratione materiae* of Community law . . .'.[41] She could not therefore be required to produce a formal residence permit before being granted the disputed allowance.

The emphasis placed by the Court in *Martínez Sala* on the personal scope of Regulations 1408/71 and 1612/68 may be justified on the basis that each of those regulations constitutes a *lex specialis* in relation to the provisions on citizenship, which therefore fall to be considered only where the rules on social security and freedom of movement do not apply. That view is supported by the judgment in *Skanavi and Chryssanthakopoulos*,[42] where the Court said that, since the facts of the case fell within the scope of Article 43 (ex 52), it was not necessary to consider the interpretation of Article 18 (ex 8a). None the less, there is a certain unreality in devoting so much attention to questions which the Court was ultimately unable to resolve. It seems unlikely that the referring court would have spent any more time trying to establish whether the applicant fell within the personal scope of either regulation when the answer made no practical difference.

The Court's decision showed that, even in the absence of action by the Council, Part Two of the Treaty was capable of enlarging the substantive rights enjoyed by Community nationals in areas beyond those which it specifically mentioned. The wider significance of the judgment for the Treaty provisions on citizenship was obscured by the peculiar circumstances of the case, and in particular by the fact that the applicant had been permitted to remain in Germany. The Court was not therefore called upon to consider whether Community law conferred on her a right to

---

[40] The Court expressly declined to rule on whether the applicant could have relied on Art 18 (ex 8a) to claim a right to reside in Germany had she not been authorized to reside there in any event: see para 60.

[41] Para 63.   [42] Case C–193/94 [1996] ECR I–929.

reside there or whether the Treaty was only applicable because she found herself lawfully present in Germany.

The Treaty provisions on citizenship were subsequently invoked by the Court in the *Bickel and Franz* case,[43] where it was clear that the right of the individuals concerned to be in the host State derived from Community law. B, an Austrian national, was a lorry driver who was charged in the Trentino-Alto Adige Region of Italy with driving while under the influence of alcohol. F, a German national, visited the same Region as a tourist and was charged with being in possession of a prohibited knife. Neither B nor F spoke Italian and they each asked that the proceedings be conducted in German. The proceedings against them had been brought in the province of Bolzano in the Trentino-Alto Adige Region, where there was a large German-speaking minority. Residents of Bolzano therefore had the right to require the German language to be used in criminal proceedings. Did Community law require that right to be extended to nationals of other Member States?

The case bore some resemblance to *Ministère Public v Mutsch*,[44] discussed in chapter 8, where a Luxembourg national employed in a German-speaking part of Belgium was held to be entitled under Article 7(2) of Regulation 1612/68 to rely on a provision of Belgian law giving Belgian nationals resident in German-speaking areas of Belgium the right to use German in certain court proceedings. However, F was not a worker and the status of B appears to have been unclear. *Mutsch* did not therefore provide a direct answer to the questions raised in *Bickel and Franz*. None the less, the Court gave two reasons for regarding the situation of both B and F as within the scope of the Treaty. First, it said, they were covered by Article 49 (ex 59), which extended to 'all nationals of Member States who, independently of other freedoms guaranteed by the Treaty, visit another Member State where they intend to or are likely to receive services'.[45] Such persons were 'free to visit and to move around within the host State'.[46] Secondly, Article 18 (ex 8a) gave every citizen of the Union a right to move and reside freely in other Member States, a right which was enhanced if such citizens 'are able to use a given language to communicate with the administrative and judicial authorities of a State on the same footing as its nationals'.[47] It followed that, 'in so far as it may compromise the right of nationals of other Member States to equal treatment in the exercise of their right to move and reside freely in another Member State, national rules concerning the language to be used in criminal proceedings in the host State must comply with Article 6 [now 12] of the Treaty'.[48]

In establishing that Article 12 was applicable, the applicants had overcome the main obstacle to the success of their claim, for the contested rules were clearly discriminatory. The right to have proceedings conducted in German was available only to German-speaking residents of the Province of Bolzano. Although that right apparently extended to German-speaking nationals of other Member States who

---

[43] Case C–274/96, judgment of 24 November 1998.   [44] Case 137/84 [1985] ECR 2681.
[45] Para 15.   [46] Ibid.   [47] Para 16.   [48] Para 18.

were resident there and did not extend to Italian nationals resident elsewhere, the Court pointed out that Italian nationals were at an advantage by comparison with the nationals of other Member States: 'The majority of Italian nationals whose language is German are in a position to insist that German be used throughout the proceedings in the Province of Bolzano, because they meet the residence requirement laid down by the rules in issue; the majority of German-speaking nationals of other Member States, on the other hand, cannot avail themselves of that right because they do not satisfy that requirement.'[49] Rules such as those in dispute were therefore incompatible with the principle of non-discrimination laid down in Article 12.

The Italian Government had argued that the disputed rules were justified by the need to protect the German-speaking minority in Bolzano. This bizarre argument was not surprisingly rejected. The Court accepted that objective considerations independent of nationality might justify a residence requirement of the type in question where the principle of proportionality was satisfied. It also acknowledged that the protection of a linguistic minority might constitute a valid objective. What was not clear, however, was how that objective would be undermined if the contested rules were extended to German-speaking nationals of other Member States exercising their right to freedom of movement. As Advocate General Jacobs observed,[50] 'the exclusivity of the rule, that is to say, the denial of the advantage to visitors from other Member States, is neither a necessary nor an appropriate means of achieving that aim. In other words the rule is disproportionate.' There were of course no practical reasons for refusing to extend the benefit of the rule to B and F: the local criminal courts were apparently set up to conduct proceedings largely in German and, in the case against B and F, the judges and Public Prosecutor were German-speaking.[51]

One might be forgiven for finding it somewhat depressing that, more than thirty years after the signing of the Treaty of Rome, even one of the founding Member States was practising the sort of blatant and unjustified discrimination at issue in *Bickel and Franz*. However, the case gave the Court the opportunity to reiterate its conclusion in *Martínez Sala* that a national of a Member State who is lawfully present in the territory of another Member State comes within the scope of the Treaty by virtue of Article 18 (ex 8a) and may therefore rely on Article 12. The principle of non-discrimination embodied in Article 49 (ex 59) was not mentioned. In the context of the free movement of persons, Article 12 seems to have subsumed all other more precise expressions of that principle.

In neither *Martínez Sala* nor *Bickel and Franz* was the Court called upon to decide whether Article 18 (ex 8a) conferred on Union citizens a directly effective right to move and reside freely within the Member States independently of other provisions. The class of people who enjoy such a right is in any event wider now than

[49] Para 25. [50] Para 41 of the Opinion.
[51] See para 39 of the Opinion of AG Jacobs. The language of the proceedings before the Court of Justice was Italian.

it once was, but it still does not extend to all citizens of the Union unless it can be derived from Article 18. In particular, a national of a Member State who is not economically active has no right to reside in another Member State if he is not covered by sickness insurance or does not have sufficent resources to avoid becoming a burden on the social assistance system of the host State.[52] It might be thought inconsistent with the very notion of citizenship of the Union for any national of a Member State to be denied the right to enter and reside in another Member State, at least where matters of public policy, public security, and public health are not in issue. Moreover, if no such right is conferred on citizens of the Union by Article 18, the paradoxical result would be to encourage Member States to expel all nationals of other Member States who cannot claim an entitlement under Community law to be there. Otherwise the host State might find itself required by Article 12 to extend to such nationals certain advantages enjoyed by its own nationals.[53] On the other hand, Article 18 provides expressly that the right of Union citizens to move and reside in the Member States is 'subject to the limitations and conditions laid down in this Treaty and by the measures adopted to give it effect'. That language is hard to reconcile with the view that the article creates a freestanding right of free movement and residence. While the Member States remain responsible for the organization and financing of health care and social assistance within their territories, there would be dangers in endowing Article 18 with that effect. A general right of movement and residence would presuppose a high degree of shared values and interests among the citizens of the Member States. Whether such a state of affairs yet exists is a political question which national governments and the other institutions might be thought better placed to answer than the Court.

Another question which the Court was not required to address in *Bickel and Franz* is whether, even where a citizen of the Union has not exercised his right to freedom of movement, criminal proceedings brought against him in another Member State are none the less subject to the Treaty prohibition against discrimination on grounds of nationality. Advocate General Jacobs thought that the time had perhaps come 'for even that question to be answered affirmatively. The notion of citizenship of the Union implies a commonality of rights and obligations uniting Union citizens by a common bond transcending Member State nationality.'[54] If that further step were to be taken by the Court, it would become even harder to justify the continued application of the case law on purely internal situations. If a citizen of the Union who has not exercised his right to freedom of movement can rely on the principle of non-discrimination against another Member State, why should he not be able to do so against his own?

As we saw in chapter 6, the Treaty of Amsterdam introduced a new provision, Article 13 (ex 6a), concerned with discrimination on a range of grounds other than nationality. The structure of the new provision may be seen as a reaction to the way

---

[52] See Dir 90/364, Art 1(1); Dir 90/365, Art 1(1); Dir 93/96, Art 1. These directives are discussed below.

[53] The point is made by O'Leary, op cit, p 78.   [54] Para 23 of the Opinion.

in which the Court has developed the principle of non-discrimination laid down in the first paragraph of Article 12. Article 13 EC provides:

Without prejudice to the other provisions of this Treaty and within the limits of the powers conferred by it upon the Community, the Council, acting unanimously on a proposal from the Commission and after consulting the European Parliament, may take appropriate action to combat discrimination based on sex, racial or ethnic origin, religion or belief, disability, age or sexual orientation.

It will be noted that, unlike Article 12, Article 13 contains no prohibition against the forms of discrimination to which it refers. As a result, it is almost certainly incapable of producing direct effect. Moreover, it is evidently intended to be the Council and not the Court which decides on the circumstances in which such discrimination is to be prohibited. Article 13 is therefore unlikely to develop in the same way as Article 12.

Legislative initiatives

In 1979 the Commission submitted to the Council a proposal[55] for a directive which would have conferred a right of movement and residence on nationals of the Member States who were not economically active and who consequently fell outside the scope of existing provisions of Community law. The proposal did not find favour with the Council and it was withdrawn almost ten years later. Shortly thereafter, however, in the context of the single market programme, the Council adopted three directives designed to fill certain gaps in the Treaty regime governing freedom of movement for persons. The directives concerned granted the right to reside in another Member State to Community nationals who were not economically active,[56] who had retired,[57] or who wished to follow a vocational training course there.[58] Those claiming rights under any of these directives would have to show that they had resources sufficient to avoid their becoming 'an unreasonable burden on the public finances of the host Member State'.[59] The right to reside conferred by the directives extended to certain members of the beneficiary's family and was subject to administrative arrangements similar to those laid down by Directive 68/360.

Directive 90/366 on the right of residence for students is worth examining in a little more detail in the present context. That directive was intended to clarify the

[55] OJ 1979 C207/14.

[56] Dir 90/364 on the right of residence, OJ 1990 L180/26 (legal basis: Art 308 (ex 235)).

[57] Dir 90/365 on the right of residence for employees and self-employed persons who have ceased their occupational activity, OJ 1990 L180/28 (legal basis: Art 308 (ex 235)).

[58] Dir 90/366 on the right of residence for students, OJ 1990 L180/30 (legal basis: Art 308 (ex 235)).

[59] See the preambles to all three directives. The wording of the substantive provisions of the directives varies: Dir 90/365 refers to 'the social security system of the host Member State' (Art 1(1)), while Dirs 90/364 (Art 1(1)) and 93/96 (Art 1) refer to 'the social assistance system of the host Member State'. Dir 93/96 replaced Dir 90/366 after the latter was quashed by the Court: see below.

implications of the Court's case law, discussed above, on the effect of Article 12 of the Treaty in the field of vocational training. In order to facilitate access to vocational training, the directive required Member States to grant a right of residence to any student who was a national of another Member State and to his or her spouse and dependent children, provided (a) that the student had sufficient resources to avoid becoming a burden on the social assistance system of the host Member State, (b) that the student was enrolled on a vocational training course at a recognized educational establishment, and (c) that the student and his or her family were covered by comprehensive sickness insurance. The right of residence was restricted to the duration of the course in question and the directive did not give rise to a right to the payment of maintenance grants by the host State. Member States were permitted to derogate from the provisions of the directive only on grounds of public policy, public security, or public health.

There is a remarkable similarity between the rights accorded to students by Directive 90/366 and those which the Court held in *Raulin* flowed directly from the first paragraph of Article 12 of the Treaty. Indeed, the Court acknowledged in that case that 'the right of residence can be made subject to conditions deriving from the legitimate interests of the Member State, such as the covering of maintenance costs and health insurance, to which the principle of non-discriminatory access to vocational training does not apply'.[60] Directive 90/366 was adopted over eighteen months before judgment was given in *Raulin* and, although the deadline for its implementation did not expire until just over four months later, the Court may have regarded the directive as encouraging it to apply the principle of non-discrimination laid down in the Treaty in this way. Support for that view may be found in the Opinion of Advocate General van Gerven, whose advice was followed by the Court and who considered his view of the effect of Article 12 of the Treaty 'confirmed' by Directive 90/366.[61] In this sense, the *Raulin* decision resembles *Vlassopoulou*, discussed in chapter 9, where the Court deduced from the provisions of the Treaty obligations similar to those imposed on Member States by Directive 89/48.

It might seem strange that the Court should seem to allow the effect of the Treaty to be influenced by legislative initiatives of this nature. However, it should not be forgotten that the relevant legislation was in both cases intended to build on previous case law of the Court. There can be little doubt that substantially the same outcomes would have emerged from the Court even in the absence of the directives concerned, although there might of course have been minor differences on points of detail and it might have taken several cases for the Court to build up a comprehensive body of principles. But it would make little sense for the Court to disregard legislative initiatives which have already been taken. Where the Court is in principle content with the regime laid down by the legislature, it would prejudice legal certainty for it to develop an inconsistent regime of its own based directly

[60] Para 39 of the judgment in *Raulin, supra.*   [61] See p I–1051.

on the Treaty in order to achieve basically the same result. Moreover, the existence of a satisfactory legislative regime may remove any doubts the Court might otherwise entertain about the political acceptability of its preferred solution to a particular problem.

The judgment in *Raulin* provided support for the view that Directive 90/366 should have been based on the second paragraph of Article 12 of the Treaty, as originally proposed by the Commission, rather than on Article 308 (ex 235), the legal basis preferred by the Council. That view was confirmed in *Parliament v Council*,[62] where the directive was annulled on the ground of its defective legal basis. Although the directive went further in some respects than the Court had been asked to go in *Raulin*, the Court found that 'the various elements of the contested directive are linked with the actual exercise of a student's right of residence for the purposes of vocational training. It must be emphasised in particular that the right of residence conferred on the spouse and dependent children of a student appears essential to the effective exercise of the student's right of residence, as is indeed expressly indicated in the eighth recital in the preamble to the directive.'[63] The Court decided, for reasons of legal certainty, to maintain the effects of the contested directive until it had been replaced with a new directive adopted on the correct legal basis.[64]

Expanding the scope of the Treaty

Perhaps the most significant gap in the Treaty system before the signing of the Treaty of Amsterdam was the absence of any clear provision requiring the abolition of internal border controls.[65] Directives 68/360 and 73/148 expressly permit the Member States to require nationals of other Member States seeking to exercise the rights of free movement conferred on them by the Treaty to produce a valid identity card or passport.[66] Moreover, in *Commission v Belgium*,[67] the Court accepted that other checks carried out at the frontier might also be permissible. The introduction into the EC Treaty by the Single European Act of Article 14 (ex 7a) gave rise to doubts about whether this situation could be allowed to persist beyond the end of 1992. Article 14 required the Community to adopt the measures necessary to establish, by 31 December 1992, an internal market comprising 'an area without internal frontiers in which the free movement of . . . persons . . . is ensured in accordance with the provisions of this Treaty'. The Commission took the view[68]

---

[62] Case C–295/90 [1992] ECR I–4193.

[63] Para 19. See also para 18 of the judgment and the Opinion of AG Jacobs at pp I–4225–6.

[64] Dir 93/96 on the right of residence for students, OJ 1993 L317/59 (legal basis: Art 7 EEC (now Art 12 EC)).

[65] See Handoll, *Free Movement of Persons in the EU* (1995), pp 33–5.

[66] Art 3(1) of both directives.   [67] Case 321/87 [1989] ECR 997. See ch 8.

[68] See eg its Communication to the Council and the Parliament entitled 'Abolition of border controls' (SEC (92) 877 final, 8 May 1992).

that Article 14 required the Community to legislate for the abolition of controls at internal frontiers on the movement of all individuals, not only those covered by Articles 39 (ex 48) to 55 (ex 66) of the Treaty but also those who were not economically active and the nationals of non-member countries. That view was not universally shared and was inconsistent with a declaration adopted by all the Member States when the Single European Act was signed to the effect that '[n]othing in these provisions shall affect the right of Member States to take such measures as they consider necessary for the purpose of controlling immigration from third countries and to combat terrorism, crime, the traffic in drugs and illicit trading in works of art and antiques'. The lack of political consensus on the scope of Article 14 meant that little progress was made.[69]

The declaration referred to in the preceding paragraph reflected a widely held view that the abolition of internal border controls could only be contemplated once some degree of coordination had been achieved of the controls applied by Member States at their external borders and steps had been taken to prevent any consequent growth in international crime. An attempt was made to address a range of such so-called flanking issues in Title VI of the TEU, which was originally concerned with co-operation in the field of justice and home affairs. In order to achieve the objectives of the Union, 'in particular the free movement of persons', the Maastricht version of Article K.1 required the Member States to regard as matters of common interest the 'rules governing the crossing by persons of the external borders of the Member States and the exercise of controls thereon', as well as related matters including the rights of third country nationals within Member States and the prevention of international crime. The Council was empowered to promote various forms of co-operation on such matters.[70]

Title VI was essentially intergovernmental in nature: the Council in principle acted unanimously, the role of the Commission and particularly the European Parliament was limited and the jurisdiction of the Court of Justice almost completely excluded.[71] Dissatisfaction with the functioning of these arrangements[72] led to the introduction into the EC Treaty by the Treaty of Amsterdam of a new Title IV (ex IIIa) entitled 'Visas, asylum, immigration and other policies related to the free movement of persons'. The new title was designed to establish 'an area of freedom, security and justice' and gave the Council new powers to act in a range of areas, some of which previously fell within the scope of Title VI of the TEU. Thus, Title IV expressly envisaged the adoption of measures to ensure the absence of any controls on persons, of whatever nationality, when crossing internal borders and common rules on the crossing of the Member States' external borders.[73] The

---

[69] An attempt to challenge frontier controls and passport checks directly on the basis of Art 14 (ex 7a) was rejected by the English Court of Appeal in *R v Secretary of State, ex parte Flynn* [1997] 3 CMLR 888.

[70] See the Maastricht version of Art K.3(2).   [71] Cf Arts 100c and 100d EC (now repealed).

[72] See ch 2 of the 'General Outline for a Draft Revision of the Treaties' drawn up by the Irish Presidency during the IGC which opened in 1996 (CONF 2500/96, 5 December 1996).

[73] See Art 62 (ex 73j) EC.

Treaty of Amsterdam also made provision for the integration into the framework of the European Union of the so-called Schengen acquis, that is, the agreement signed outside the Community framework by some of the Member States in Schengen in 1985 on the gradual abolition of checks at their common borders and certain related instruments.[74] In a startling example of the type of differentiated integration which is a feature of the Union in the post Amsterdam era, the United Kingdom and Ireland were not to be affected by Title IV or the Schengen acquis (to which they were not parties) unless they 'opted in' in accordance with arrangements set out in protocols annexed to the TEU and the EC Treaty.[75] A separate protocol[76] is designed to prevent these arrangements from being undermined by Article 14 (ex 7a) EC. It preserved the so-called Common Travel Area between the United Kingdom and Ireland and permitted those States to maintain border controls on persons seeking to enter their territory, whether or not they were nationals of a Member State. As a corollary, the other Member States were given the right to exercise controls at the frontier on those seeking to enter their territory from the United Kingdom or Ireland.

In order to prevent Title IV (ex IIIa) from contaminating other areas of Community law which apply to all the Member States, Article 2 of the Protocol on the Position of the United Kingdom and Ireland[77] provided that, unless they decided to 'opt in':

none of the provisions of Title IV of the Treaty establishing the European Community, no measure adopted pursuant to that Title, no provision of any international agreement concluded by the Community pursuant to that Title, and no decision of the Court of Justice interpreting any such provision or measure shall be binding upon or applicable in the United Kingdom or Ireland; and no such provision, measure or decision shall in any way affect the competences, rights and obligations of those States; and no such provision, measure or decision shall in any way affect the acquis communautaire nor form part of Community law as they apply to the United Kingdom or Ireland.

The sweeping terms of that provision were a response to the creativeness of the Court in finding ways of applying in one area principles laid down in another. They reflected a wish to seal off the Member States concerned from developments under the new title unless they decided they wanted to take part. It is submitted that the Court should, and will, respect that wish, although it cannot be prevented

---

[74] They are listed in the annex to the Protocol integrating the Schengen acquis into the framework of the European Union. The protocol is itself annexed to the TEU and the EC Treaty. See generally O'Keeffe, 'The Schengen Convention: a suitable model for European integration?' (1991) 11 YEL 185; Schutte, 'Schengen: its meaning for the free movement of persons in Europe' (1991) 28 CMLRev 549; Hailbronner and Thiery, 'Schengen II and Dublin: responsibility for asylum applications in Europe' (1997) 34 CMLRev 957.

[75] See the Protocol integrating the Schengen acquis into the framework of the European Union, Art 4; the Protocol on the position of the United Kingdom and Ireland.

[76] Protocol on the application of certain aspects of Art 14 (ex 7a) of the Treaty establishing the European Community to the United Kingdom and to Ireland, annexed to the TEU and the EC Treaty.

[77] Art 2 of the Protocol on the Position of Denmark, for which special provision has also been made, is, *mutatis mutandis*, in similar terms.

from deciding that a principle first laid down in a case concerning Title IV has independent utility and validity in other areas.

The role of the Court of Justice in cases covered by Title IV is more limited than in cases arising under other provisions of the EC Treaty. In particular, by virtue of Article 68 (ex 73p), lower national courts have no power to ask the Court for preliminary rulings in cases covered by the new title. Moreover, by virtue of Article 68(2) (ex 73p(2)), the Court does not have jurisdiction to rule on measures connected with the removal of controls on the movement of persons across internal borders 'relating to the maintenance of law and order and the safeguarding of internal security'. Article 68 is considered in more detail in chapter 2.

The insertion into the EC Treaty of Title IV led to a recasting of Title VI of the TEU, now renamed 'Provisions on police and judicial cooperation in criminal matters'. Article 35(1) (ex K.7(1)) gives the Court of Justice a preliminary rulings jurisdiction in relation to a range of measures adopted under the post-Amsterdam Title VI. In addition, the Court has a role to play under the last two paragraphs of Article 35. That article is also discussed in chapter 2.

12

The law of competition

The origins and development of Community competition law

The authors of the EEC Treaty saw a system of undistorted competition as an essential element of the common market. There were two reasons for this. One was that a system of vigorous competition was regarded as having an important role to play in creating the 'powerful unit of production' contemplated by the Spaak Report, which formed the basis of the negotiations which led to the Treaty. However, in the system established by the Treaty, competition also has another role to play. It was recognized from the outset[1] that a way needed to be found to prevent private undertakings from erecting barriers to inter-State trade which the Member States themselves were to be required to abolish by the rules on the free movement of goods. As the Court of Justice explained in *Consten and Grundig v Commission*:[2]

. . . an agreement between producer and distributor which might tend to restore the national divisions in trade between Member States might be such as to frustrate the most fundamental object[ives] of the Community. The Treaty, whose preamble and content aim at abolishing the barriers between States, and which in several provisions gives evidence of a stern attitude with regard to their reappearance, could not allow undertakings to reconstruct such barriers.

Article 3(1)(g) EC[3] accordingly includes among the Community's activities 'a system ensuring that competition in the internal market is not distorted', a theme now picked up in provisions added to the Treaty at Maastricht. Thus, according to Article 98 (ex 102a), the Member States and the Community are to conduct their economic policies 'in accordance with the principle of an open market economy with free competition'. Article 105(1) imposes the same duty on the European System of Central Banks when carrying out its tasks. Under Article 154(2) (ex 129b(2)), the Community's contribution to the development of trans-European

---

[1] Competition policy was also an important aspect of the ECSC Treaty: see further Goyder, *EC Competition Law* (3rd edn, 1998) (hereafter 'Goyder'), pp 17–24; Gerber, *Law and Competition in Twentieth Century Europe* (1998) (hereafter 'Gerber'), pp 335–42.

[2] Joined Cases 56 and 58/64 [1966] ECR 299, 340.

[3] Formerly Art 3(f), which spoke of 'the institution of a system ensuring that competition in the common market is not distorted'.

networks is to take place '[w]ithin the framework of a system of open and competitive markets'. By virtue of Article 157(1) (ex 130(1)), the Community and the Member States are to ensure that the conditions necessary for the competitiveness of the Community's industry exist 'in accordance with a system of open and competitive markets'. These provisions serve to emphasize the continuing importance of competition in the functioning of the Treaty system.[4] Detailed rules on the matter are laid down in Chapter 1 of Title VI (ex V) of the Treaty. The following discussion is concerned with two provisions in particular of that chapter, Articles 81 (ex 85) and 82 (ex 86). Something will also be said about the provisions on aids granted by States, Articles 87–9 (ex 92–4).[5]

Article 81(1) prohibits 'all agreements between undertakings, decisions by associations of undertakings and concerted practices which may affect trade between Member States and which have as their object or effect the prevention, restriction or distortion of competition within the common market . . .'. It then gives some examples of agreements, decisions or practices which are liable to be caught by that prohibition. By virtue of Article 81(2), prohibited agreements or decisions are 'automatically void'. However, Article 81(3) makes provision for the prohibition laid down in Article 81(1) to be declared inapplicable to certain agreements, decisions or practices which are on balance beneficial, provided they are proportionate and do not afford those involved the opportunity to eliminate competition 'in respect of a substantial part of the products in question'. Article 82 provides that '[a]ny abuse by one or more undertakings of a dominant position within the common market or in a substantial part of it shall be prohibited as incompatible with the common market in so far as it may affect trade between Member States'. It then gives some examples of practices constituting such an abuse.[6]

Articles 81 (ex 85) and 82 (ex 86) have assumed great practical importance, but it is evident that they left a number of questions unanswered.[7] It has been noted that, when the Treaty was signed, there was little experience in Europe of the use of the law to protect competition.[8] The authors of the Treaty envisaged that effect

[4] In some sectors, however, the effect of the competition rules is expressly attenuated. Thus, they do not automatically apply to production of and trade in agricultural products: Art 36 (ex 42) EC; there is a special rule about the compatibility with the Treaty of aids granted by States in the transport sector: Art 73 (ex 77).

[5] This chapter does not deal with Art 86 (ex 90) on public undertakings, undertakings to which Member States grant special or exclusive rights and undertakings entrusted with the operation of services of general economic interest or having the character of a revenue-producing monopoly. See generally Goyder, pp 531–43; Whish, *Competition Law* (3rd edn, 1993) (hereafter 'Whish'), pp 330–46; Edward and Hoskins, 'Article 90: deregulation and EC law' (1995) 32 CMLRev 157.

[6] Although apparently confined to undertakings, the Court has held that Arts 81 and 82 also impose certain obligations on Member States: see eg Joined Cases C–140/94, C–141/94 and C–142/94 *DIP and Others v Comune di Bassano del Grappa and Comune di Chioggia* [1995] ECR I–3257; Case C–96/94 *Centro Servizi Spediporto v Spedizioni Marittima del Golfo* [1995] ECR I–2883; Case C–35/96 *Commission v Italy* [1998] ECR I–3851; Goyder, pp 522–31.

[7] See Goyder, pp 30–2.

[8] Gerber, 'The transformation of European Community competition law?' (1994) 35 Harv Int LJ 97, 101.

would be given to the principles laid down in Articles 81 and 82 by legislation of the Council adopted under Article 83 (ex 87). In the meantime, the authorities of the Member States and the Commission were to have jurisdiction to apply Articles 81 and 82 under powers conferred on them by Articles 84 (ex 88) and 85 (ex 89) respectively.

The Council's responsibility to adopt legislation giving effect to Articles 81 and 82 depended on the submission to it by the Commission of a proposal and, during the early years of the Commission's existence, the efforts of DG IV, the Directorate General for Competition, were directed mainly to the preparation of an appropriate proposal.[9] On 6 February 1962, the Commission's proposal came to fruition with the adoption by the Council of Regulation 17.[10] That regulation, which remains in force,[11] gave the Commission extensive powers to investigate, determine the existence of, and penalize, by fine or periodic penalty payment, infringements of Articles 81 and 82. As a result, the Commission assumed responsibility for the development of the Community's competition policy, that is to say, the extent to which those articles should be used to regulate particular practices. The central role conferred on the Commission and the consequent marginalization of the national authorities reflected a feeling that only the Commission could be trusted to apply the Treaty rules correctly.[12] The inability of the Commission to cope with the resulting workload was to lead some years later to attempts to 'decentralize' the application of the Treaty competition rules.

The role of the Court of Justice in the field of competition law has been essentially secondary to that of the Commission, but it has none the less had an important influence on the application of Articles 81 (ex 85) and 82 (ex 86).[13] That influence has been exercised mainly through the decisions it has given in dealing with challenges under Article 230 (ex 173) EC to decisions of the Commission applying the Treaty competition rules in particular circumstances. An important body of case law has also developed as a result of references from national courts called upon to apply those rules. Not surprisingly, the Court showed itself willing from the outset to acknowledge the importance of competition law in the scheme of the Treaty. It has generally been supportive of the Commission's efforts to make Articles 81 and 82 vigorous and effective tools for achieving the aims of the Treaty's authors. Indeed, in the early years of the Community's development, the Court appeared to use the Treaty competition rules as a way of overcoming the baleful

---

[9] Goyder, pp 35–6.   [10] OJ Sp Ed, 1959–62, p 87.

[11] For discussion of the extent to which it now needs updating, see the Commission's White Paper on Modernisation of the Rules Implementing Arts 85 and 86 of the EC Treaty (28 April 1999). Cf the House of Lords Select Committee on the European Communities, *Enforcement of Community Competition Rules* (Session 1993–94, 1st Report).

[12] Gerber, pp 348–51.

[13] See generally Slynn, 'EEC competition law from the perspective of the Court of Justice' in *Antitrust and Trade Policy in the United States and the European Community*, Fordham Corporate Law Institute (1985), ch 19.

effect which the Luxembourg Compromise[14] was having on the process of integration. Gerber observes:[15] 'The role the Court sculpted for itself in this competition law system centred on intellectual leadership. The Court frequently enunciated broad principles and values rather than limiting itself to ruling on the facts of individual cases. It looked to the future and aimed at guiding the Commission in its development of competition policy. This role had no precedents in European national competition law systems.' From around the mid-1970s,[16] the Court began to feel the need to dampen the Commission's enthusiasm. In particular, it perhaps started to give more weight than the Commission to what might be called rule of law considerations, requiring the Commission to provide more detailed economic evidence and to show more respect for the procedural rights of undertakings.

The establishment in 1988 of the CFI together with the increasing complexity and sophistication of the competition rules led to a reduction in the influence of the Court. Most competition cases now come before it only by way of references from national courts or appeals against decisions of the CFI, which has assumed the main responsibility for reviewing the actions of the Commission in this field. This reduction in the number of competition cases dealt with by the Court itself has perhaps made it less self-confident about dealing with those that do reach it.[17] However, the CFI has now developed special expertise in the field of competition law and may even have increased the intensity of the judicial scrutiny to which the Commission is subject, especially on questions of fact.[18]

Vertical agreements

The system established by Regulation 17 imposed an enormous administrative burden on the Commission. Article 2 of the regulation enabled undertakings to apply to it for negative clearance, that is certification that, on the basis of the facts in the Commission's possession, there were no grounds for action on its part under Articles 81(1) (ex 85(1)) or 82 (ex 86). Article 9(1) of the regulation gave the Commission exclusive jurisdiction to grant exemptions under Article 81(3). As a corollary, Article 4(1) of the regulation required agreements caught by Article 81(1) coming into existence after the entry into force of the regulation and in respect of which the parties sought such an exemption to be notified to the Commission. It was expressly provided that, subject to limited exceptions,[19] no decision in

---

[14] See Wyatt and Dashwood, *European Community Law* (3rd edn, 1993), p 46.   [15] At p 352.
[16] Gerber, pp 361–2.   [17] Gerber, p 375.
[18] For further discussion of the CFI, see ch 1.
[19] The requirement of prior notification before an exemption could be granted did not apply to agreements of the type mentioned in Art 4(2). These were thought unlikely to prevent, restrict or distort competition or to interfere with trade between Member States, but the requirements laid down by Art 4(2) were restrictive and the number of agreements which fell within it was limited. The Commission has now proposed that the scope of Art 4(2) should be broadened to bring within it a large

application of Article 81(3) could be taken until such agreements had been notified.[20]

It was recognized from the outset that these provisions would result in the notification of large numbers of vertical agreements, that is, agreements between
undertakings operating at different economic levels (manufacturer and wholesaler,
wholesaler and retailer, for example). In the event, approximately 35,000 agreements, many of them of a vertical nature, had been lodged with the Commission
by the beginning of February 1963.[21] This presented DG IV with a problem of volume from which it has never really recovered. The Commission, with the support
of the Court, has addressed this problem in a number of ways, some of them
unlikely to have been foreseen by the authors of the Treaty or of Regulation 17.
The sheer number of vertical agreements with which the Commission was confronted within a year of the adoption of Regulation 17 also led it to concentrate its
attention on such agreements, which it considered particularly liable to damage the
devlopment of the common market, at the expense of horizontal agreements,
which it did not begin to tackle until later.[22]

The emphasis placed by the Commission on the need to eliminate certain types
of vertical restraint[23] attracted the support of the Court in *Consten and Grundig v
Commission*,[24] the first case in which the annulment of a measure applying Article
81 (ex 85) in a specific case was sought. G, a German manufacturer of electrical
goods, had granted C, a French company, the exclusive right to sell its products in
France, the Saar and Corsica. C had agreed, *inter alia*, not to sell competing products or to deliver the contract products directly or indirectly to the markets of other
countries. G had imposed similar restrictions on German wholesalers and distributors in other countries. By a separate agreement, C registered in France under its
own name the GINT trade mark owned by G, which was affixed to all G's products at the point of manufacture. C agreed that the trade mark would be used only
for G's products and that it would either be cancelled or reassigned to G if C ceased
to be G's sole distributor in France. G notified these agreeements to the
Commission under the provisions of Regulation 17 with a view to obtaining an
exemption under Article 81(3).[25] However, the Commission found that both

category of vertical agreements: see the Communication from the Commission on the application of
the competition rules to vertical restraints (Follow-up to the Green Paper on Vertical Restraints) OJ
1998 C365/3, 17–18.

[20] By virtue of Art 6(1), decisions taken by the Commission under Art 81(3) pursuant to a notification under Art 4(1) had to specify the date from which they took effect. That date could not be earlier
than the date of notification. Art 5 of Reg 17 laid down a special rule for agreements caught by Art 81(1)
which were in existence at the date of entry into force of the regulation and in respect of which exemption under Art 81(3) was sought. Unless dispensed from the requirement of notification by Art 4(2),
such agreements had to be notified to the Commission by 1 November 1962 (if there were more than
two parties) or 1 February 1963 (if there were only two parties).

[21] See Goyder, p 50; the *Sixth General Report on the Activities of the Community* (1963), p 63.

[22] Goyder, p 578.   [23] See Goyder, pp 47–8; Gerber, pp 354–6.

[24] Joined Cases 56 and 58/64 [1966] ECR 299.

[25] The Commission had also received a complaint about the agreements from another French company, which C had sought to prevent from importing into France products manufactured by G.

agreements were incompatible with Article 81(1) and that the conditions for the grant of an exemption under Article 81(3) were not satisfied. C and G thereupon challenged the Commission's decision before the Court.

One of the main arguments put forward by the applicants was that Article 81(1) did not apply to vertical agreements but only to horizontal ones. Vertical agreements in general, and distribution agreements in particular, were economically beneficial, it was argued, and the parties were not in any event in competition with each other. In support of this view, it was pointed out that none of the examples of unlawful agreements given in Article 81(1) specifically referred to vertical agreements. The Commission would subsequently accept that vertical agreements posed less of a threat to competition than horizontal agreements. However, had the Court been persuaded that the former fell completely outside the scope of Article 81, the Commission's policy of giving priority to tackling vertical restraints would have been undermined. In the event, the Court refused to accept that Article 81(1) should be read in the limited way advocated by the applicants. 'Article 85 [now 81]', it said,[26] 'refers in a general way to all agreements which distort competition within the Common Market and does not lay down any distinction between those agreements based on whether they are made between competitors operating at the same level in the economic process or between non-competing persons operating at different levels.' The absence of competition between the parties to the contested agreement was irrelevant:

Competition may be distorted within the meaning of Article 85(1) not only by agreements which limit it as between the parties, but also by agreements which prevent or restrict the competition which might take place between one of them and third parties. For this purpose it is irrelevant whether the parties to the agreement are or are not on a footing of equality as regards their position and function in the economy. This applies all the more, since, by such an agreement, the parties might seek, by preventing or limiting the competition of third parties in respect of the products, to create or guarantee for their benefit an unjustified advantage at the expense of the consumer or user, contrary to the general aims of Article 85.[27]

The applicants also challenged the Commission's conclusion that trade between Member States had been affected within the meaning of Article 81(1) by the contested agreements. According to the applicants, the effect of the agreements had been to *increase* trade between them. In order to succeed, the Commission therefore needed to show that trade between Germany and France would have increased even more in the absence of the agreements. Advocate General Roemer was sympathetic to the applicants' argument,[28] but the Court rejected it. The purpose of the requirement of an effect on trade was to mark the boundary between Community law and national law: if an agreement had no such effect, it fell to be dealt with exclusively under the latter. The Court continued:[29]

---

[26] p 339.   [27] Ibid.   [28] See pp 360–1.   [29] pp 341–2.

In this connexion, what is particularly important is whether the agreement is capable of constituting a threat, either direct or indirect, actual or potential, to freedom of trade between Member States in a manner which might harm the attainment of the objectives of a single market between States. Thus the fact that an agreement encourages an increase, even a large one, in the volume of trade between States is not sufficient to exclude the possibility that the agreement may 'affect' such trade in the abovementioned manner. In the present case, the contract between Grundig and Consten, on the one hand by preventing undertakings other than Consten from importing Grundig products into France, and on the other hand by prohibiting Consten from re-exporting those products to other countries of the Common Market, indisputably affects trade between Member States.

The applicants also maintained that the Commission, by emphasizing the effects of the contested agreements on competition between suppliers of products of the same make (so-called intra-brand competition), had failed to take due account of their effect on competition between different makes (so-called inter-brand competition). The Court was again unreceptive: 'Although competition between producers is generally more noticeable than that between distributors of products of the same make, it does not thereby follow that an agreement tending to restrict the latter kind of competition should escape the prohibition of Article 85(1) [now 81(1)] merely because it might increase the former.'[30] Moreover, there was no need to examine the concrete effects of an agreement if its object was to prevent, restrict, or distort competition. Since the contested agreements were designed to isolate the French market for G's products and to maintain artificially separate national markets within the common market, they were such as to distort competition for the purposes of Article 81(1). As for the exercise by C of its rights as holder in France of the trade mark GINT, this could not be allowed to undermine the competition rules of the Treaty, which would be rendered ineffective if C could use the trade mark to achieve the same object as an agreement which was prohibited by Article 81(1).

The Court also upheld the Commission's refusal to grant an exemption to the contested agreements. That refusal was based principally on the requirement laid down in Article 81(3) that, in order to qualify for exemption, an agreement which contributes to improving the production or distribution of goods or to promoting technical and economic progress must not 'impose on the undertakings concerned restrictions which are not indispensable to the attainment of these objectives'. In its decision, the Commission had been willing to recognize that the distributorship agreement contributed to an improvement in production and distribution, but had not accepted that those advantages could not be produced without absolute territorial protection. That finding was endorsed by the Court, which said that any improvement in the production and distribution of goods had to 'show appreciable advantages of such a character as to compensate for the disadvantages which they cause in the field of competition'.[31] The Court was not persuaded that the Commission had been wrong to conclude that the advantages claimed for the

[30] p 342.   [31] p 348.

agreement—enabling the distributor to plan its requirements in advance and pro-viding guarantee and after-sales services—could all have been realized without absolute territorial protection.

Only on one issue did the application to the Court succeed. The Commission had found in its decision that the distributorship agreement taken as a whole was caught by Article 81(1) (ex 85(1)). The Court said that this was too sweeping a con-clusion. The invalidity which resulted from Article 81(2) attached in principle merely to the parts of an agreement which infringed Article 81(1). Only if those parts could not be severed from the rest of the agreement would the agreement as a whole be void. The Commission should therefore have confined its finding of invalidity to those parts of the agreement which were caught by Article 81(1) or explained in the preamble to its decision why the parts concerned could not be sev-ered from the remainder of the agreement.

Notwithstanding the Court's finding on the question of severability, the *Consten and Grundig* case was a major victory for the Commission.[32] It endorsed the use of Article 81 (ex 85) to control vertical agreements and the importance attached by the Commission to the removal of obstacles to freedom of movement. More generally, the broad view taken by the Court of the circumstances in which an agreement might be regarded as affecting trade between Member States brought within the scope of Article 81 and the jurisdiction of the Commission a very wide category of agreements. Had the Court been less alive to the importance of com-petition in the scheme of the Treaty, it might have attached greater weight to other considerations, such as freedom of contract and upholding intellectual property rights. Had it been less alive to the importance of freedom of movement in the scheme of the Treaty, it might have been more willing to regard the restrictions imposed by the contested agreements as justifiable. However, as we shall see, the Court would later become more receptive to arguments designed to show that agreements which had economic benefits should sometimes be permitted even if they had deleterious effects on inter-State trade.

The Commission's growing workload

While the Commission was assessing the agreements between C and G, it was becoming increasingly concerned at its inability to make substantial inroads into the backlog of agreements which had been notified to it. It therefore began work on a proposal which eventually resulted in the adoption by the Council of Regulation 19/65 on the application of Article 81(3) (ex 85(3)) to certain categories of agree-ments and concerted practices.[33] The preamble to that regulation pointed out that Article 81(3) provided for Article 81(1) to be declared inapplicable to *certain categories* of agreement, decision, and concerted practice. It noted that the large

---

[32] See Goyder, pp 51–4.   [33] OJ Sp Ed, 1965–66, p 35.

number of notifications made under Regulation 17 made it desirable for the Commission to be given a power to declare Article 81(1) inapplicable to categories or groups of agreements and concerted practices where it had acquired sufficient experience through individual decisions to identify such categories in relation to which the application of Article 81(3) could be considered satisfied. Article 1 of Regulation 19/65 accordingly gave the Commission a power to declare by regulation that certain categories of agreement and concerted practice to which only two undertakings were party were not caught by Article 81(1) by virtue of Article 81(3). The categories mentioned included exclusive distribution and exclusive purchasing agreements and agreements restricting the acquisition and use of intellectual property rights. Those categories reflected the largest groups of agreement which had been notified to the Commission.

Regulation 19/65 offered the Commission the opportunity to remove at a stroke the need to deal individually with large numbers of the agreements which had been notified to it. However, before it could take advantage of that opportunity it had to call upon the Court to reject a challenge to the validity of the regulation by Italy.[34] The Court gave judgment on the same day as *Consten and Grundig*: it reiterated that Article 81(1) (ex 85(1)) was capable of applying to both vertical and horizontal agreements. The fact that Article 1 of Regulation 19/65 treated certain categories of such agreement as falling under Article 81(1) could not therefore cast doubt on the regulation's validity. Nor was the validity of the regulation vitiated by the reference to agreements containing restrictions relating to intellectual property rights, since such agreements were also capable of falling within Article 81(1). More generally, the Court rejected the argument that the regulation implied that agreements which were not capable of exemption under the powers granted to the Commission were necessarily caught by Article 81(1).

Thus, the Court showed itself supportive of the Commission, not just at the substantive level but at the procedural level too.[35] Less than a year later, the Commission adopted Regulation 67/67 on the application of the Treaty to certain categories of exclusive dealing agreements,[36] automatically exempting a large number of the agreements which had been notified to it. This paved the way for the Commission to devote more attention to the problems of horizontal agreements. Here, too, it would receive the backing of the Court, although in due course the Court would intervene to curb its activites.

---

[34] Case 32/65 *Italy v Council and Commission* [1966] ECR 389.

[35] See also Case 45/69 *Boehringer Mannheim v Commission* [1970] ECR 769; Case 48/69 *ICI v Commission* [1972] ECR 619. The *ICI* case is discussed below.

[36] OJ Sp Ed, 1967, p 10. Reg 67/67 was replaced by Reg 1983/83 on exclusive distribution agreements, OJ 1983 L173/1, and Reg 1984/83 on exclusive purchasing agreements, OJ 1983 L173/5. The validity of those regulations was extended pending the outcome of the Commission's review of the treatment of vertical restraints: see OJ 1997 L214/27. A block exemption regulation for patent licensing agreements did not come into force until 1985: see Reg 2349/84, OJ 1984 L219/15. That regulation, and a parallel block exemption for know-how licensing agreements (Reg 556/89, OJ 1989 L61/1), was replaced by Reg 240/96 on the application of Art 85(3) to certain categories of technology transfer agreements, OJ 1996 L31/2. See Goyder, ch 13.

Horizontal agreements, concerted practices, and oligopolies

The adoption of Regulation 67/67 automatically exempting certain categories of exclusive distribution agreement from Article 81(1) (ex 85(1)) allowed the Commission to devote more attention to horizontal agreements and practices. Certain types of horizontal agreement, such as those involving price fixing or collective discrimination, had long been regarded as anti-competitive,[37] but eventually horizontal agreements generally came to be regarded as posing a more serious threat to competition than vertical agreements.[38] One type of horizontal behaviour which the Commission has encountered particular difficulty in regulating is the parallel conduct characteristic of oligopolies, that is, markets in which a preponderant share is held by a small number of participants. It is difficult for competition authorities to ensure effective competition in such markets because the participants may naturally tend to align their behaviour with that of their rivals.[39] They may seek to extend the effects of natural parallelism by concluding anti-competitive arrangements with each other. This will rarely be done overtly because a price-fixing or market sharing agreement between the members of an oligopoly would constitute too naked an infringement of competition law. Instead less direct methods will be employed. The problem for competition authorities is to distinguish the type of parallelism which may be regarded as acceptable because it is merely a response to market conditions from unlawful collusion designed to exaggerate those conditions. The Commission's main weapon against such collusion has been the prohibition in Article 81(1) against 'concerted practices', but the Court proved unwilling to allow the Commission to push that concept as far as it would have liked. The Commission therefore adopted an alternative tactic, paradoxically with the encouragement of the Court.[40]

The first occasion on which the Court was called upon to consider the notion of a concerted practice was the so-called 'Dyestuffs' case.[41] There the applicant sought the annulment of a Commission decision imposing fines on a number of producers of dyestuffs for having, as a result of unlawful concertation, introduced between 1964 and 1967 three general and uniform increases in the prices of dyestuffs in the Community. The applicant argued[42] that the mere fact that undertakings operating on an oligopolistic market had consciously adopted a parallel

[37] See the list in Art 85(1).
[38] See eg the Commission's Communication on the application of the Community competition rules to vertical restraints, OJ 1998 C365/3 at p 9.
[39] See the remarks of AG Mayras in the 'Dyestuffs' case, *infra*, at p 677.
[40] See the discussion of collective dominance under Art 82 (ex 86), below.
[41] Case 48/69 *ICI v Commission* [1972] ECR 619. See Mann, 'The Dyestuffs case in the Court of Justice of the European Communities' (1973) 22 ICLQ 35; Joliet, 'La notion de pratique concertée et l'arrêt ICI dans une perspective comparative' (1974) CDE 251.
[42] See p 638.

attitude was not enough to establish the existence of a concerted practice. It had to be shown that their conduct was the result of a common plan of action and of a mutual will to act in accordance with that plan. The Commission accepted[43] that parallel conduct did not in itself amount to concertation, but maintained that Article 81(1) (ex 85(1)) did not require the parties to have drawn up a common plan with a view to adopting a common course of behaviour. It was enough that they let each other know beforehand what attitude they intended to adopt so that each could regulate its conduct safe in the knowledge that its competitors would act in a similar way. According to the Commission, evidence that the contested price increases were the result of concerted action was to be found in the facts that the rates introduced for each increase by the different producers in the countries affected were the same, that the same dyestuffs were nearly always involved, and that the increases took effect within a very short period. Although the market was an oligopolistic one, this did not, according to the Commission, explain the increases. In the Commission's view, it was unrealistic to suppose that without previous concertation the main producers could have increased their prices in this way.

The Commission's view of the effect of Article 81(1) (ex 85(1)) in these circumstances was largely accepted by the Court, which stated that the object of the term 'concerted practices' was 'to bring within the prohibition of that article a form of coordination between undertakings which, without having reached the stage where an agreement properly so-called has been concluded, knowingly substitutes practical cooperation between them for the risks of competition'.[44] Although the Court accepted that parallel behaviour did not of itself amount to a concerted practice, it made it clear that such behaviour 'may however amount to strong evidence of such a practice if it leads to conditions of competition which do not correspond to the normal conditions of the market, having regard to the nature of the products, the size and number of the undertakings, and the volume of the said market'.[45]

The Court proceeded to carry out a detailed analysis of the market in dyestuffs. It noted that, with regard to two of the increases, the undertakings which took the initiative announced their intentions some time in advance. This allowed them 'to observe each other's reactions on the different markets, and to adapt themselves accordingly'.[46] The Court observed that these advance announcements allowed the undertakings concerned to eliminate all uncertainty as to their future conduct and thereby 'eliminated a large part of the risk usually inherent in any independent change of conduct . . .'.[47] The Court did not believe that this conduct could have been spontaneous:

Although a general, spontaneous increase on each of the national markets is just conceivable, these increases might be expected to differ according to the particular characteristics of the different national markets.

---

[43] See p 639.   [44] Para 64.   [45] Para 66.   [46] Para 100.   [47] Para 101.

Therefore, although parallel conduct in respect of prices may well have been an attractive and risk-free objective for the undertakings concerned, it is hardly conceivable that the same action could be taken spontaneously at the same time on the same national markets and for the same range of products.[48]

The Court accepted that producers were free to change their prices in the light of the conduct of their competitors, but said that it was contrary to the Treaty 'for a producer to cooperate with his competitors, in any way whatsoever, in order to determine a coordinated course of action relating to a price increase and to ensure its success by prior elimination of all uncertainty as to each other's conduct regarding the essential elements of that action, such as the amount, subject-matter, date and place of the increases'.[49] The Court concluded that the applicants' conduct had been designed to replace the risks of competition and the hazards of competitors' spontaneous reactions by co-operation constituting a concerted practice prohibited by Article 81(1) (ex 85(1)) of the Treaty.

The Court expanded on the definition of a concerted practice in the subsequent 'Sugar' cases,[50] a complex dispute involving an allegation by the Commission that a number of sugar manufacturers throughout the Community had tacitly agreed to restrict deliveries to each other's markets according to the principle of *chacun chez soi*.[51] Two of the producers involved argued that the concept of a concerted practice presupposed the existence of a plan and the aim of removing in advance any doubt as to the future conduct of competitors. The mere fact that competitors were aware of each other's commercial policies and had independently adapted their own policies accordingly could not amount to a concerted practice, for otherwise every attempt by an undertaking to react intelligently to the behaviour of its competitors would fall foul of Article 81 (ex 85). The Court rejected the suggestion that the Treaty required 'the working out of an actual plan' and emphasized that 'each economic operator must determine independently the policy which he intends to adopt on the common market including the choice of the persons and undertakings to which he makes offers or sells'.[52] Although this requirement of independence did not deprive undertakings of 'the right to adapt themselves intelligently to the existing and anticipated conduct of their competitors',[53] it did rule out any direct or indirect contact between undertakings which was liable to influence the conduct on the market of an actual or potential competitor or to disclose to a competitor the course of conduct which an undertaking intended to pursue. The evidence put forward by the Commission showed that the applicants had contacted each other and attempted to remove in advance any uncertainty about the future conduct of their competitors.[54]

[48] Paras 108–9. [49] Para 118.
[50] Joined Cases 40 to 48, 50, 54 to 56, 111, 113 and 114/73 *Suiker Unie v Commission* [1975] ECR 1663.
[51] See p 1680. [52] Para 173. [53] Para 174.
[54] For a straightforward example of a case where the Court found the evidence put forward by the Commission insufficient to establish the existence of a concerted practice, see Joined Cases 29 and 30/83 *CRAM and Rheinzink v Commission* [1984] ECR 1679.

The Court's decisions in 'Dyestuffs' and 'Sugar' were largely supportive of the Commission in its efforts to regulate disguised horizontal cartels through the use of the Treaty prohibition of concerted practices. The Court had not been receptive to claims by undertakings that their behaviour simply amounted to a sensible reaction to that of their competitors. However, the emphasis placed by the Court on the need for the Commission to show that competitors had co-operated with a view to eliminating uncertainty about each other's behaviour raised doubts about whether Article 81 (ex 85) would ever be an entirely adequate weapon for combating the threats to competition posed by oligopolies. One reason for this was that Article 81 did not appear to be applicable in cases of so-called conscious parallelism, where undertakings align their behaviour without any contact between them. Another is that the tendency for oligopolistic markets to be naturally transparent made it relatively easy for undertakings to conceal the type of contact which might bring them within the scope of Article 81(1).

An attempt by the Commission to broaden the scope of the Treaty prohibition on concerted practices to give it more powers to tackle oligopolies came before the Court in the long-running 'Wood Pulp' saga, which took nearly eight years to resolve. The case concerned bleached sulphate pulp used in the manufacture of paper. In 1984, the Commission addressed a decision to forty-three producers of pulp, most of them established in Canada, the United States, Sweden, or Finland. The Commission alleged essentially that the addressees of the decision had concerted on prices of wood pulp by announcing the prices they were going to charge some time before the beginning of each quarter. The announcements were made to the producers' customers but were quickly publicized in the trade press and through agents who acted for several producers. Prices were generally announced in US dollars regardless of the country in which the producer concerned was based.

In 1985, an application was made to the Court for the annulment of the Commission's decision.[55] Advocate General Darmon gave his Opinion in July 1992. He took the view[56] that, in order to establish a concerted practice, it was necessary to show that there had been reciprocal communication between two competitors. Article 81(1) (ex 85(1)) was not in his view aimed at unilateral conduct by undertakings. Moreover, the concertation had to give those involved an assurance as to the conduct they could expect from their rivals: each had to be able to foresee how the others would behave. In short, the concept of a concerted practice implied reciprocal communication between competitors intended to give each other assurances about their commercial behaviour. The Advocate General recognized the difficulty of distinguishing a legitimate public announcement of prices from an illicit public exchange of information, but he did not accept that the notion

---

[55] Joined Cases C–89/85, C–104/85, C–114/85, C–116/85, C–117/85 and C–125/85 to C–129/85 *Ahlström Osakeyhtiö and Others v Commission* [1993] ECR I–1307. An earlier judgment in the same proceedings dealing with the territorial scope of Art 81 is considered below.

[56] See pp I–1482 *et seq*, where extensive reference is made to the literature on the subject and to the American case law.

of a concerted practice applied to the identical behaviour of undertakings. Article 81 did not in his view condemn parallel behaviour but only certain ways of producing such behaviour. Parallel behaviour was merely evidence from which the existence of a concerted practice might be inferred.

The Court took a similar approach, reiterating that parallel conduct did not constitute proof of concertation unless there was no other plausible explanation for the disputed behaviour. As far as the system of price announcements was concerned, the Commission was unable to produce any evidence directly establishing concertation between the producers concerned, so it was necessary to consider whether the producers' behaviour constituted 'a firm, precise and consistent body of evidence of prior concertation'.[57] Relying on a report produced by two experts appointed by the Court to examine the characteristics of the market for bleached sulphate pulp during the period covered by the contested decision, the Court came to the conclusion that concertation was not the only plausible explanation for the conduct of the applicants, but that it was at least as likely to have resulted from the characteristics of the market. The Court therefore found that the Commission had failed to establish concertation regarding announced prices.[58]

The Court in 'Wood Pulp' was noticeably less encouraging than it had been in earlier cases about the potential of Article 81 (ex 85(1)) as a tool for regulating oligopolies.[59] In the absence of direct evidence of concertation, something undertakings have learned to take care to conceal, the Court is reluctant to accept that mere parallel conduct establishes concertation. Advocate General Darmon counselled caution when relying on indirect evidence, declaring:[60] 'it is necessary to establish a degree of certainty that goes beyond any reasonable doubt. In accordance with the principles governing the burden of proof, it is for the Commission to demonstrate that: the burden of proof cannot be shifted simply by a finding of parallel conduct.' Although the Court did not use the same language as its Advocate General, it took a similar approach. The Court evidently shares the same disquiet as courts in the United States[61] at the idea of using a provision designed to regulate collusive behaviour against behaviour which may well have been decided on independently as a normal response to market conditions. The problems posed by oligopolies are of a structural nature and the Court understandably seems reluctant to allow a provision concerned with behaviour to be used to deal with them. The area is one of several in which the Court has felt compelled to restrain the

---

[57] Para 70. The Court ruled inadmissible certain documents produced by the Commission to substantiate the evidence it had put forward based on the applicants' parallel behaviour: see paras 68–9.

[58] The Court upheld the Commission's decision in so far as certain other less significant infringements were concerned: see para 205. In particular, the Court accepted that producers belonging to an association known as the KEA which met periodically to fix sales prices and to announce those prices to their customers had engaged in a concerted practice on prices for wood pulp: see paras 130–2.

[59] Craig and de Búrca observe: 'It may have been no coincidence that the *juge rapporteur* in *Wood Pulp* was Joliet who had, a number of years earlier, expressed misgivings about the possible impact of the *Dyestuffs* case': *EU Law* (2nd edn, 1998), p 902, n 25. Joliet's article is cited above.

[60] At p I–1493.   [61] See the Opinion of AG Darmon at pp I–1491–2.

enthusiasm of the Commission and give greater weight to the legitimate concerns of business. The case law undermines the notion that the Court always takes an expansive view of the scope of the Treaty and of the powers of the Community institutions.

One consequence of the 'Wood Pulp' decision was that the Commission began to explore the potential of Article 82 (ex 86) as a weapon in its campaign against oligopolies. Here the Court (under the prompting of the CFI) has not been unreceptive, although the extent to which Article 82 can be used in this context remains unclear. This is an issue to which we return below.

The role of the national courts

Direct effect and provisional validity

In *BRT v SABAM*,[62] the Court confirmed what seemed implicit in several earlier cases, namely that 'Articles 85(1) [now 81(1)] and 86 [now 82] tend by their very nature to produce direct effects in relations between individuals'. In principle, that conclusion was probably inevitable in view of the unequivocal language of those provisions and their importance in the scheme of the Treaty. None the less, it was liable to cause difficulty if a national court reached a conclusion on the legality of a particular agreement or practice which was inconsistent with that of the Commission. The danger of inconsistent decisions was particularly acute in cases where there was a possibility that an agreement, although caught by Article 81(1), qualified for exemption under Article 81(3). This was because the Commission had exclusive jurisdiction, by virtue of Article 9(1) of Regulation 17, to grant such exemptions. The position was further complicated by the special provisions contained in Regulation 17 for so-called old agreements, that is, agreements concluded before that regulation took effect. Where the Commission grants an exemption pursuant to Article 81(3), the normal rule, laid down in Article 6(1) of Regulation 17, is that the exemption cannot take effect from a date earlier than that of notification. By virtue of Article 6(2), however, that rule did not apply to old agreements which were notified within certain time limits specified in Article 5(1). Moreover, where such agreements did not qualify for exemption, the Commission had a discretion[63] to determine the extent to which Article 81(1) applied to them if the parties ceased to give effect to them as to the future or modified them so as to take them outside the scope of Article 81(1) or within the scope of Article 81(3).

These provisions posed a potentially serious problem of legal certainty in cases where the validity of an old agreement was challenged before a national court. Such an agreement, valid until the entry into force of the Treaty, might then have become invalid as a result of the effect of Article 81(1). If the agreement was notified to the Commission on the entry into force of Regulation 17, an exemption

---

[62] Case 127/73 [1974] ECR 51, para 16.   [63] Art 7(1).

might then be granted with effect from the date on which Article 81(1) first applied to it. Thus, an initially valid agreement which subsequently became invalid might later be retrospectively revalidated by an act of the Commission. The problem was rendered more acute by the volume of agreements which had been notified to the Commission by the expiry of the deadlines laid down in Article 5(1) of Regulation 17, for it then became clear that there might be a considerable delay before the Commission was in a position to take a decision.

The Court sought to deal with this problem essentially by qualifying the direct effect of Article 81(1) (ex 85(1)).[64] In a line of cases beginning with *Bosch v Van Rijn*,[65] it developed the doctrine of so-called provisional validity.[66] As the Court explained in *De Bloos v Bouyer*,[67] until the Commission takes a decision on the applicability of Article 81(3), '[national] courts before which proceedings are brought relating to an old agreement duly notified or exempted from notification must give such an agreement the legal effects attributed thereto under the law applicable to the contract, and those effects cannot be called in question by any objection which may be raised concerning its compatibility with Article 85(1) [now 81(1)]'.[68] The benefit of provisional validity did not, however, extend to new agreements, that is, agreements concluded after the entry into force of Regulation 17. As the Court explained in *Brasserie de Haecht v Wilkin-Janssen*,[69] in the case of agreements falling into that category, Regulation 17 assumed 'that so long as the Commission has not taken a decision the agreement can only be implemented at the parties' own risk'. It followed that 'notifications in accordance with Article 4(1) of Regulation No 17 do not have suspensive effect'.[70]

The doctrine of provisional validity is of more than historical interest for at least two reasons. First, it is assumed to apply to so-called accession agreements, that is, agreements brought within the scope of Article 81 (ex 85) by virtue of the accession to the Union of new Member States and which are notified to the Commission within six months of accession.[71] Secondly, the Court has accepted that an agreement concluded after the entry into force of Regulation 17 which merely reproduces the terms of a provisionally valid old agreement, or which mitigates its restrictive effect, benefits from the provisional validity attaching to the

---

[64] See Wyatt and Dashwood, op cit, p 491. A further qualification results from Joined Cases 209 to 213/84 *Ministère Public v Asjes* [1986] ECR 1425, discussed below.

[65] Case 13/61 [1962] ECR 45. This case was the first to be referred to the Court under Art 234 (ex 177).

[66] See generally Kerse, *EC Antitrust Procedure* (4th edn, 1998) (hereafter 'Kerse'), pp 422–9.

[67] Case 59/77 [1977] ECR 2359, para 15. See also Case C–234/89 *Delimitis* [1991] ECR I–935, para 48.

[68] Provisional validity may also be terminated by a decision of the Commission under Art 15(6) of Reg 17 terminating the immunity from fines conferred by notification (see Case 10/69 *Portelange v Marchant* [1969] ECR 309, paras 18 and 19) and by an administrative letter (commonly known as a 'comfort letter') from the Commission informing the addressee that no action is to be taken with regard to an agreement and that the file on the matter is being closed (see Case 99/79 *Lancôme v Etos* [1980] ECR 2511, para 17).

[69] Case 48/72 [1973] ECR 77, para 10.   [70] Ibid.

[71] See Art 25 of Reg 17; Kerse, pp 424–5.

original agreement.[72] The development of the doctrine is hard to reconcile with the view that the policy of the Court is to expand the jurisdiction of the Community and its institutions at the expense of the Member States. As the Court pointed out in *Brasserie de Haecht*, from its entry into force the Treaty rendered agreements contrary to Article 81 automatically void and contained no transitional provisions to take account of agreements already in existence when either the Treaty itself or Regulation 17 entered into force. Those factors, together with the undoubted importance of Article 81 in the scheme of the Treaty, might have led the Court to conclude that all agreements which had not been exempted pursuant to Article 81(3) were to be treated as void. The Court's determination, in the interests of legal certainty, to avoid that conclusion in the case of duly notified or non-notifiable old agreements shows its willingness to recognize that the strict application of the Treaty might sometimes need to give way to other more pressing considerations.

The problems of legal certainty are less acute in the case of new agreements because, although any exemption granted by the Commission may not take effect from a date earlier than that of notification, it is open to the parties to notify such agreements to the Commission as soon as they have been concluded. Moreover, notification gives the parties immunity from fines in respect of acts falling within the scope of the notified agreement even if exemption is ultimately refused.[73] However, since the compatibility of a new agreement with Article 81(1) (ex 85(1)) may be challenged before the national courts from the moment it is concluded and the national courts have no jurisdiction (in the absence of a relevant block exemption) to apply Article 81(3) themselves, there remains a risk that conflicting decisions will be given. As the Court acknowledged in the *Delimitis* case,[74] '[s]uch conflicting decisions would be contrary to the general principle of legal certainty and must, therefore, be avoided when national courts give decisions on agreements or practices which may subsequently be the subject of a decision by the Commission'. The Court offered national courts the following guidance on how to deal with such cases.

Where it is clear that Article 81(1) does not apply and there is 'scarcely any risk of the Commission taking a different decision',[75] the national court may proceed to rule on the agreement. It may do likewise where the incompatibility of the agreement with Article 81(1) is beyond doubt and it can be stated with confidence that no exemption decision will be forthcoming from the Commission. Where there is a possibility that an exemption decision might be adopted, 'the national court may decide to stay the proceedings or to adopt interim measures pursuant to

---

[72] See Case C–39/96 *KVBBB v Free Record Shop* [1997] ECR I–2303.
[73] Art 15(5), Reg 17. Immunity may be withdrawn where the Commission forms the preliminary view that an exemption is unlikely to be granted: Art 15(6). Withdrawal of immunity may be challenged before the Community Courts: Joined Cases 8 to 11/66 *Cimenteries v Commission* [1967] ECR 75.
[74] *Supra*, para 47.   [75] Para 50.

its national rules of procedure'.[76] The Court pointed out that national courts are at liberty (at least as a matter of Community law) to ask the Commission for information on the state of any proceedings pending before it under Regulation 17 and the likelihood that a formal decision will be adopted on the contested agreement. The Commission could also be asked to supply economic and legal information of a more general nature. Finally the Court reminded national courts of their right to make a reference for a preliminary ruling under Article 234 (ex 177).

There is no doubt that the risk that the Commission and a national court might give conflicting decisions on the compatibility of an agreement with Article 81 (ex 85) represents a serious flaw in the machinery established by Regulation 17. One way of avoiding that risk would of course be to deprive national courts of the right to apply Article 81(1) at all.[77] That would, however, undermine the effectiveness of the article and would be liable to increase the burden on the Commission. Another possibility would be to give the national courts the power to grant exemptions under Article 81(3). Notwithstanding the difficulty of ensuring uniformity of approach in different Member States, that is now the Commission's preferred solution.[78]

The approach taken by the Court to the problem of conflicting decisions is an ingenious one which in many cases will avoid difficulty.[79] However, it assumes the existence of appropriate national rules of procedure and a degree of deference among national judges for the views of the Commission. Moreover, difficulties are liable to arise where the validity of an agreement is challenged before a national court after the Commission has issued a so-called comfort letter declaring that the agreement satisfies the requirements of Article 81(3) and that the file on the matter is being closed. Because of their informality and the speed with which they can be issued, the Commission often makes use of comfort letters.[80] However, since they do not amount to a formal decision of exemption and implicit in the Commission's finding on Article 81(3) is the conclusion that the agreement is caught by Article 81(1), a national court may feel it has no alternative but to declare the agreement void. It is hard to see what the Court could do about this conundrum, but it would be avoided if national courts were given the power to apply Article 81(3) themselves.[81]

---

[76] Para 52. The Court added that a stay of proceedings or the adoption of interim measures should also be envisaged where there is a risk of conflicting decisions in the context of the application of Arts 81(1) and 82.

[77] This is the position under the ECSC Treaty: see Case C–128/92 *Banks* [1994] ECR I–1209.

[78] See its White Paper on Modernisation of the Rules for Implementing Arts 85 and 86 of the EC Treaty (28 April 1999). Cf Kon, 'Article 85, para 3: a case for application by national courts' (1982) 19 CMLRev 541; Steindorff, 'Article 85, para 3: no case for application by national courts' (1983) 20 CMLRev 125.

[79] See Temple Lang, 'General Report', XVIII FIDE Congress, Stockholm (1998), p 278.

[80] Such letters may also state that an agreement is not regarded as falling within the scope of Art 81(1) or that it is covered by a block exemption. See generally Kerse, pp 275–6.

[81] Another possibility would be for the Council to stipulate that, where the validity of a duly notified or non-notifiable agreement was challenged in a national court and no decision of the Commission

The obligations of the Commission on receipt of a complaint

The role of the national courts in applying the Treaty competition rules was re-inforced by a decision delivered by the CFI just over eighteen months after the judgment in *Delimitis* concerning the rights of complainants. Article 3 of Regulation 17 allows Member States and 'natural and legal persons who claim a legitimate interest' to complain to the Commission that Articles 81 (ex 85) or 82 (ex 86) are being infringed.[82] In *Automec v Commission*,[83] the CFI was asked to con-sider the Commission's obligations when it received a complaint under Regulation 17. Citing the Court's decision in *GEMA v Commission*,[84] the CFI held that the Commission was not obliged to adopt a final decision on the existence or other-wise of the infringement alleged by the complainant.[85] Argument concentrated on the circumstances in which the Commission might legitimately decline to pursue a complaint.

The CFI accepted that the Commission was entitled to prioritize complaints in accordance with its view of the Community interest. This involved balancing 'the significance of the alleged infringement as regards the functioning of the common market, the probability of establishing the existence of the infringement and the scope of the investigation required in order to fulfil, under the best possible condi-tions, its task of ensuring that Articles 85 [now 81] and 86 [now 82] are complied with'.[86] The Commission was also entitled to take account of the extent to which the complainant's rights could be protected by the competent national courts. The Commission was required to set out the considerations which had led it to con-clude that there was insufficient Community interest to justify pursuing a com-plaint. The reasons given would be subject to review by the CFI, which would intervene if the complainant could establish that the contested decision was 'based on materially incorrect facts or is vitiated by an error of law, a manifest error of appraisal or misuse of powers'.[87]

The decision in *Automec II* is a striking example of the willingness of the CFI to develop the case law of the Court of Justice. In subsequent cases, the CFI took a

as to the applicability of Art 81(3) had been taken, a party should have the right to require a decision to be taken within, say, six months. If, after the expiry of that period, no decision had been taken, the agreement might be treated as exempt. Cf the so-called opposition procedure laid down in some block exemption regulations (eg Reg 240/96 on technology transfer agreements, Art 4(1), OJ 1996 L31/2); Forrester and Norall, 'The laicization of Community law: self-help and the rule of reason: how com-petition law is and could be applied' (1984) 21 CMLRev 11, 42–3.

[82] The Member States have not in practice made much use of their right to complain to the Commission under this provision: see Kerse, 'The complainant in competition cases: a progress report' (1997) 34 CMLRev 213, 217 (n 15).

[83] Case T–24/90 [1992] ECR II–2223 (*Automec II*).   [84] Case 125/78 [1979] ECR 3173.

[85] See para 75. The CFI made an exception for cases falling within the Commission's exclusive juris-diction, such as those involving the withdrawal of an exemption granted under Art 85(3). Here a com-plainant is entitled to a decision on the substance of his complaint: see eg Case T–23/90 *Peugeot v Commission* [1991] ECR II–653, para 47.

[86] Para 86.   [87] Para 80.

fairly strict line in reviewing the reasons given by the Commission for declining to pursue a complaint.[88] Be that as it may, taken together with the judgment in *Delimitis* the decision gave a boost to a campaign the Commission had been waging for some time[89] to promote the application of the Treaty competition rules by national courts. That campaign marked a significant change of direction from the period when Regulation 17 was being prepared, during which the central role of the Commission was emphasized.[90] In February 1993 the Commission seized the opportunity presented by these developments in the case law to issue a notice on co-operation between it and the national courts in applying Articles 81 (ex 85) and 82 (ex 86).[91]

In its notice the Commission explained that it intended 'to concentrate on notifications, complaints and own-initiative proceedings having particular political, economic or legal significance for the Community. Where these features are absent in a particular case, notifications will normally be dealt with by means of comfort letters and complaints should, as a rule, be handled by national courts or authorities.'[92] The Commission considered that 'there is not normally a sufficient Community interest in examining a case when the plaintiff is able to secure adequate protection of his rights before the national courts'.[93] Perhaps inevitably, however, the notice failed to deal satisfactorily with the difficult issues discussed above which arise from the inability of the national courts to grant individual exemptions under Article 81(3). Where a comfort letter has been issued stating that the Commission considers the conditions for applying Article 81(3) to have been met, the notice simply stated that 'the Commission considers that national courts may take account of these letters as factual elements'.[94] The case law which gave rise to the notice none the less constitutes a clear illustration of the sensitivity of the Community Courts to the problems faced by the Commission in applying Articles 81 and 82 and of their ability to influence the direction of its enforcement policy through their case law. The success of the initiative to date has, however, been limited: the notice seems to have had little effect on the willingness of undertakings to turn voluntarily to the national courts in place of the Commission.[95]

---

[88] See eg Case T–7/92 *Asia Motor v Commission* [1993] ECR II–669; Case T–37/92 *BEUC and NCC v Commission* [1994] ECR II–285; Case T–548/93 *Ladbroke Racing v Commission* [1995] ECR II–2565; Case T–387/94 *Asia Motor France and Others v Commission* [1996] ECR II–961; Maselis and Gilliams, 'Rights of complainants in Community law' (1997) 22 ELRev 103.

[89] See the *Thirteenth Report on Competition Policy* (1984), pp 135–6.   [90] Gerber, p 349.

[91] OJ 1993 C39/6.

[92] Para 14. A separate notice was subsequently issued on co-operation between national competition authorities and the Commission in handling cases covered by Arts 85 or 86: see OJ 1997 C313/3. See also the White Paper on the Modernisation of the Rules Implementing Arts 85 and 86 of the EC Treaty (28 April 1999).

[93] Para 15. Cf Case T–114/92 *BEMIM v Commission* [1995] ECR II–147; Case T–5/93 *Tremblay and Others v Commission* [1995] ECR II–185 (appeal to the Court dismissed: Case C–91/95 P [1996] ECR I–5547).

[94] Para 25.

[95] See Temple Lang, 'General Report', XVIII FIDE Congress, Stockholm (1998), p 288. The national reports deal with the effect of the notice in each Member State. For a detailed general account

The importance of implementing legislation

The importance for the direct effect of Article 81(1) (ex 85(1)) of implementing rules adopted by the Council under Article 83 (ex 87) of the Treaty became clear with the decision of the Court in *Ministère Public v Asjes* ('Nouvelles Frontières').[96] That case, a reference for a preliminary ruling from the Paris Tribunal de Police, a first instance criminal court, raised the question whether the referring court had jurisdiction to apply Article 81(1) in criminal proceedings against defendants who had been charged with infringing French legislation by selling air tickets at prices which had not been approved by the competent minister. It might have been thought that the direct effect of Article 81(1) meant that that question should be answered in the affirmative. However, the Court pointed out that no measures to give effect to the Treaty competition rules in the air transport sector[97] had yet been adopted by the Council.[98] In the absence of such measures, the transitional provisions of Articles 84 (ex 88) and 85 (ex 89) continued to apply. It will be recalled that those provisions confer on the national competition authorities and the Commission respectively powers to apply the Treaty competition rules pending the adoption of implementing rules under Article 83 (ex 87). Those powers had not been exercised in this case. The Court reiterated[99] that their mere existence did not suffice to establish that Article 81 (ex 85) had been fully effective since the Treaty entered into force since they were not such as 'to ensure a complete and consistent application of Article 85'. In those circumstances, the Court concluded that a national court such as the Tribunal de Police did not have jurisdiction to apply Article 81(1) itself. It added that, should action be taken against the contested conduct under Articles 84 (ex 88) or 85 (ex 89), all national courts would be required to draw the necessary conclusions.

By contrast, in the subsequent 'Air Tariffs' case[100] the Court held that the right of national courts to apply Article 82 (ex 86) was not affected by the absence of implementing rules adopted by the Council pursuant to Article 83 (ex 87). The Court's reasoning sheds light on its concerns in 'Nouvelles Frontières':

The sole justification for the continued application of the transitional rules set out in Articles 88 [now 84] and 89 [now 85] is that the agreements, decisions and concerted practices cov-

---

of the way in which the national courts apply Arts 81 and 82, see Braakman (ed), *The Application of Articles 85 and 86 of the EC Treaty by National Courts in the Member States*, published by the European Commission in 1997.

[96] Joined Cases 209 to 213/84 [1986] ECR 1425.

[97] Although the Treaty contains special provisions on transport (see Arts 70–80 (ex 74–84)), the Court ruled that that sector was also subject to the general rules of the Treaty, including the competition provisions. See also Case 167/73 *Commission v French Republic* [1974] ECR 359.

[98] Transport was excluded from the scope of Reg 17 by Reg 141/62, OJ, Sp Ed 1959–62, p 291. Implementing rules had subsequently been adopted in relation to other modes of transport but not transport by air, although the Commission had submitted a proposal on the matter.

[99] See Case 13/61 *Bosch v Van Rijn* [1962] ECR 45, 51, a case on provisional validity.

[100] Case 66/86 *Ahmed Saeed Flugreisen and Others v Zentrale zur Bekämpfung unlauteren Wettbewerbs* [1989] ECR 803.

ered by Article 85(1) [now 81(1)] may qualify for exemption under Article 85(3) and that it is through the decisions taken by the institutions which have been given jurisdiction, under the implementing rules adopted pursuant to Article 87 [now 83], to grant or refuse such exemption that competition policy develops. In contrast, no exemption may be granted, in any manner whatsoever, in respect of abuse of a dominant position; such abuse is simply prohibited by the Treaty . . .[101]

In other words, the mechanisms established pursuant to Article 83 for the grant of exemptions under Article 81(3) were essential to the healthy development of the Community's competition policy. Until those mechanisms were in place, there would be a risk that that policy would be undermined if national courts were to declare conduct incompatible with Article 81(1) in the absence of action under Articles 84 or 85.

Although the Commission had argued in 'Nouvelles Frontières' that the absence of implementing rules under Article 83 did not deprive Article 81(1) of direct effect, the outcome of the case to some extent strengthened its position.[102] Shortly after the judgment, the Commission began to flex the muscles the Court had reminded it that it had under Article 85 (ex 89). This underlined to previously sceptical Member States the desirability of measures under Article 83 to apply Articles 81 and 82 to air transport in a more structured way. Accordingly, in December 1987 the Council finally adopted a package of measures dealing with air transport, including two regulations based on Article 83.[103] The case shows that even an apparently conservative ruling from the Court can succeed in unblocking the legislative process if exploited intelligently by the Commission.

Parallel proceedings

A final question affecting the powers of national courts on which the Treaty is silent and which the Court has been called upon to address is the relationship between the competition rules of the Treaty and national competition law. The question arises where the same practice is the subject of proceedings under both the Treaty and the competition rules of a Member State. In *Wilhelm v Bundeskartellamt*,[104] the Court ruled that parallel proceedings were in principle acceptable: 'Community and national law on cartels consider cartels from different points of view. Whereas Article 85 [now 81] regards them in the light of the obstacles which may result for trade between Member States, each body of national legislation proceeds on the basis of the considerations peculiar to it and considers

---

[101] Para 32 of *Ahmed Saeed*. See also the reference to Art 81(3) in *Bosch v Van Rijn, supra*, at p 51.
[102] See Goyder, pp 82–5.
[103] Reg 3975/87 laying down the procedure for the application of the rules on competition to undertakings in the air transport sector and Reg 3976/87 on the application of Art 85(3) of the Treaty to certain categories of agreements and concerted practices in the air transport sector, OJ 1987 L374 1 and 9 respectively. See Whish, pp 363–7.
[104] Case 14/68 [1969] ECR 1.

cartels only in that context.'[105] However, the parallel application of the two sets of rules was not to be allowed to prejudice the uniform application of the provisions of the Treaty and the full effect of the measures adopted in implementation of them. The Court made it clear that 'conflicts between the rules of the Community and national rules in the matter of the law on cartels must be resolved by applying the principle that Community law takes precedence'.[106] Moreover, where a given practice was the subject of parallel proceedings, an allowance was to be made for any penalty which might previously have been imposed.[107]

What are the implications of the Court's ruling? A Member State is obviously not entitled to treat as lawful, conduct which is prohibited by the Treaty, whatever may be the position in national law.[108] Conversely, behaviour which falls outside the scope of the Treaty may be prohibited by national law, as the Court made clear in *Procureur de la République v Giry and Guerlain*.[109] Less clear is the situation where a practice is covered by a block exemption or has been the subject of an individual decision of exemption. That issue was sidestepped by the Court in *Giry and Guerlain* but it was examined in some detail by Advocate General Tesauro in two cases decided in 1995, *Bundeskartellamt v Volkswagen and VAG Leasing*[110] and *BMW v ALD*.[111] The Advocate General took the view that agreements which had been exempted under Article 81(3) (ex 85(3)) were outside the jurisdiction of the national authorities. Otherwise, he said, the agreement's status might vary from State to State and the full effectiveness of the decision of exemption would be undermined. Advocate General Tesauro thought that the position was the same where an agreement enjoyed the benefit of a block exemption regulation. The issue was not considered by the Court, but the views of the Advocate General are convincing: for a national authority to prohibit an agreement which has been exempted from Article 81(1) would undermine the choice of economic policy reflected in the exemption. This would be to prejudice the full effect of measures adopted in implementation of Article 81, which the Court said in *Wilhelm* was unacceptable.

The *Wilhelm* decision is now often seen as a product of its time. In the late 1960s, both the common market and Community competition law were only partially developed. The Commission's main concern was with removing obstacles to trade between Member States and it expected to be able to deal by decision with the practices brought to its attention. The context now is different. Partly as a result of the Court's encouragement, partly as a result of greater economic integration between the Member States, the Commission now gives more emphasis to the promotion of a healthy competitive process. On a more mundane level, its inability to

---

[105] Para 3.   [106] Para 6.
[107] Cf *Boehringer Mannheim v Commission, supra,* paras 60–1; Case T–141/89 *Tréfileurope Sales v Commission* [1995] ECR II–791, para 192; Kerse, pp 326–8.
[108] Cf Case C–7/97 *Bronner v Mediaprint* [1999] 4 CMLR 112.
[109] Joined Cases 253/78 and 1 to 3/79 [1980] ECR 2327.
[110] Case C–266/93 [1995] ECR I–3477, 3500–3.
[111] Case C–70/93 [1995] ECR I–3439, 3454–8.

deal with its workload has led it, again with the encouragement of the Community Courts, to promote decentralization in the enforcement of Community law. The latter trend has been seen as consistent with the development since the Maastricht Treaty of subsidiarity as an organizing principle of the constitutional order of the Union.[112] These developments have led to calls for the principle laid down in *Wilhelm* to be revised, either by giving national courts greater responsibility for applying the Treaty competition rules[113] or by confining Community law to cases which are of significance to the Community and leaving others to be dealt with by national authorities under the applicable national law.[114] Both proposals would make it difficult to ensure the application of a uniform standard throughout the Member States. Be that as it may, if any change in the present position is to be made, it would probably be preferable for this to be done in a comprehensive manner by Treaty amendment or Council regulation under Article 83(2)(e) of the Treaty rather than by the Court, which would have to wait for the vagaries of litigation to throw up a suitable case.[115]

The territorial scope of the Treaty competition rules

The Treaty competition rules apply only where the disputed practice affects trade between Member States. They are clearly infringed where the practice in question has been put into effect within the territory of the EU by undertakings established there. However, trade between Member States may also be affected by anti-competitive practices implemented in non-member States. Neither the Treaty nor Regulation 17 makes it clear whether Community competition law is intended to apply to practices taking place outside the EU but which affect the conditions of competition within it.[116] The right of States to regulate acts carried out abroad is a matter of public international law. However, the extent to which a State is entitled in public international law to regulate the behaviour abroad of foreign undertakings simply because it produces an effect within the territory of the State concerned is unclear. Moreover, the EU is not a State.

Courts in the United States have adopted a far-reaching 'effects doctrine' enabling them to assert jurisdiction over foreign undertakings which have done something which produces commercial effects there. The Commission has sought

---

[112] See further ch 16.

[113] See Walz, 'Rethinking *Walt Wilhelm*, or the supremacy of Community competition law over national law' (1996) 21 ELRev 449.

[114] Wesseling, 'Subsidiarity in Community antitrust law: setting the right agenda' (1997) 22 ELRev 35. Cf the Commission's notice on co-operation between national competition authorities and the Commission in handling cases falling within the scope of Arts 85 or 86 EC, *supra*.

[115] Cf Kerse, pp 440–1.

[116] This is sometimes called subject-matter or prescriptive jurisdiction and is to be distinguished from enforcement jurisdiction, that is jurisdiction to enforce compliance. The latter form of jurisdiction has posed fewer theoretical problems, at least in the Community context, than the former. For excellent short accounts of this area, see Whish, ch 11; Goyder, pp 545–53; Kerse, pp 337–47.

to apply a similar doctrine in the context of the EC Treaty. However, the approach of the US courts has encountered stiff opposition from other States, some of which have adopted so-called blocking statutes,[117] and the Court of Justice has conspicuously failed to endorse the line taken by the Commission. In its case law in this area, the Court has sought to strike a balance between the demands of international comity and the need to prevent the Community's competition policy from being undermined by the conduct of undertakings in third countries. It has to a large extent succeeded in doing this without acceding to the more extravagant claims of the Commission.

The issue of the extraterritorial application of the Treaty competition rules was first addressed by the Court in the 'Dyestuffs' case, discussed above.[118] The Commission adopted a decision finding that several undertakings had infringed Article 81(1) (ex 85(1)). The applicant was established in the United Kingdom, which at the time was not a Member State. It did, however, have subsidiary companies within the Community. The Commission asserted jurisdiction over the applicant's disputed practices on two bases. First, it maintained that the applicant's subsidiaries merely carried out its orders and were therefore to be regarded as forming a single undertaking with their parent for the purposes of the Treaty competition rules. If the Court was unwilling to go behind the separate legal personality of the applicant and its subsidiaries, the Commission maintained that the effect produced within the Community by the applicant's conduct outside it was enough to bring it within the scope of the Treaty.

The applicant sought to rebut both claims and produced an opinion by Professor R Y Jennings, then Professor of International Law at the University of Cambridge and later judge and President of the International Court of Justice. Professor Jennings argued[119] that the contemporary practice of States was strongly opposed to the extraterritorial application of competition laws. He observed that such application could not be applied in one direction only. If Article 81 (ex 85) were to be held to have extraterritorial effect, the Community and the Member States would not be able to resist similar claims by third countries against undertakings established within the Community. It would be absurd to suppose that the Member States had intended to confer such jurisdiction on the Community when they had rejected as contrary to principle the claims of the American authorities to exercise that jurisdiction. Professor Jennings also maintained that, since the applicant's subsidiaries had not acted as agents for their parent, the separate legal personality of the subsidiaries should be respected. Otherwise the way would be open for the economic policies of third countries to be imposed on the Community through the foreign subsidiaries of undertakings established in the Member States.

---

[117] eg the UK Protection of Trading Interests Act 1980.

[118] Case 48/69 *ICI v Commission* [1972] ECR 619. See Mann, 'The Dyestuffs case in the Court of Justice of the European Communities' (1973) 22 ICLQ 35. For the position under Art 82 (ex 86), see Case 6/72 *Europemballage and Continental Can v Commission* [1973] ECR 215. The Court took essentially the same approach as the one it adopted in 'Dyestuffs'.

[119] See pp 624–6.

Advocate General Mayras also took the view that the conduct of its subsidiaries could not be attributed to the applicant: '[t]aken to an extreme, this argument would amount to denying any substance to the legal personality of the subsidiaries'.[120] However, he was more receptive to the Commission's argument that an effects doctrine was applicable. Although the Community was not a State, it possessed the powers which were necessary to enable it to carry out its tasks: 'Where such powers have been granted to it—and this includes in the field of cartels—the Community possesses just as much power as a State, provided that cartels affecting competition in the Common Market are concerned.'[121] International law did not preclude the assertion of jurisdiction where an agreement or practice produced direct, foreseeable, and substantial effects on competition within the Community and it should be recognized that Article 81 could be applied in such circumstances. The Advocate General asked:[122]

Surely the Commission would be disarmed if, faced with a concerted practice the initiative for which was taken and the responsibility for which was assumed exclusively by undertakings outside the Common Market, it was deprived of the power to take any decision against them? This would also mean giving up a way of defending the Common Market and one necessary for bringing about the major objectives of the European Economic Community.

The approach of Advocate General Mayras might have been thought likely to commend itself to the Court. It was consistent with the wording of Article 81 (ex 85) and would have mirrored the approach taken by one of the Community's major trading partners. It would also have reinforced the effectiveness of the Treaty by protecting the proper functioning of the common market from being undermined by undertakings based abroad. The Court preferred to rely, however, on what is sometimes called the 'enterprise entity principle', that is, the fact that the contested practices had been implemented in the Community by subsidiaries of the applicant. The conduct of a subsidiary could be imputed to its parent, the Court said, '. . . in particular where the subsidiary, although having separate legal personality, does not decide independently upon its own conduct on the market, but carries out, in all material respects, the instructions given to it by the parent company'.[123] At the material time the applicant held the majority of the shares in its subsidiaries and was therefore in a position 'to exercise decisive influence over the policy of the subsidiaries as regards selling prices in the Common Market and in fact used this power upon the occasion of the three price increases in question'.[124] The Court therefore concluded that it was 'the applicant undertaking which brought the concerted practice into being within the Common Market'.[125]

The ruling in 'Dyestuffs' did not exclude the possibility that the Court might be prepared to uphold the effects doctrine where the 'enterprise entity' principle did not apply. Limited support for the view that the doctrine did apply to the Treaty competition rules was to be found in *Béguelin Import v G L Import Export*,[126] where

---

[120] p 693.   [121] p 693.   [122] p 696.   [123] Para 133.   [124] Para 137.
[125] Para 141.   [126] Case 22/71 [1971] ECR 949.

the Court said that Article 81 (ex 85) would apply to an agreement if it was 'operative on the territory of the common market'.[127] Apart from the fact that one of the parties to the agreement in question in that case was established in the Community, it was highly unlikely that the Court intended to resolve so controversial an issue in such an indirect way. Advocates of the effects doctrine were also encouraged by the Court's remark, in *Walrave v Union Cycliste Internationale*,[128] a case on the free movement of persons, that the Treaty prohibition against discrimination on grounds of nationality 'applies in judging all legal relationships in so far as these relationships, by reason either of the place where they are entered into or of the place where they take effect, can be located within the territory of the Community'.[129] It was far from clear whether that conclusion applied in the context of competition law, where different considerations had to be taken into account.

The Court did not consider the issue again until the famous 'Wood Pulp' case,[130] discussed above, where the Commission imposed fines on several producers of wood pulp established outside the Community for engaging, in breach of Article 81(1) (ex 85(1)), in concertation on the prices at which pulp was to be sold to customers in the Community. In its decision, the Commission stated that the fact that the parties to a restrictive practice were established outside the Community, or that the disputed practices also affected markets outside the Community, did not rule out the application of Article 81. The applicants took the view that only the effects doctrine could justify the assertion by the Community of jurisdiction over them, but they pointed out that that doctrine had never been accepted by the Court of Justice.

After a detailed examination of the relevant principles of international and United States law, Advocate General Darmon reiterated the conclusion of his predecessor in the 'Dyestuffs' case:

. . . there is no rule of international law which is capable of being relied upon against the criterion of the direct, substantial and foreseeable effect. Nor does the concept of international comity, in view of its uncertain scope, militate against that criterion either.

In the absence of any such prohibitive rule and in the light of widespread State practice, I would therefore propose that in view of its appropriateness to the field of competition, it be adopted as a criterion for the jurisdiction of the Community.[131]

Once again, however, the Court managed to avoid the issue of the extraterritorial effect of Article 81 (ex 85). It ruled that, where producers established in third countries sold directly to purchasers established in the Community and engaged in price

---

[127] Para 11. The French text reads '. . . dès lors que l'accord produit ses effets sur le territoire du marché commun'.

[128] Case 36/74 [1974] ECR 1405.   [129] Para 28.

[130] Joined Cases 89, 104, 114, 116, 117 and 125 to 129/85 *Åhlström v Commission* [1988] ECR 5193. See Lange and Sandage, 'The *Wood Pulp* decision and its implications for the scope of EC competition law' (1989) 26 CMLRev 137.

[131] p 5227.

competition in order to win orders from such customers, that constituted competition within the common market. It followed 'that where those producers concert on the prices to be charged to their customers in the Community and put that concertation into effect by selling at prices which are actually coordinated, they are taking part in concertation which has the object and effect of restricting competition within the common market within the meaning of Article 85 of the Treaty'.[132] The decisive factor, the Court said, was not the place where the agreement or practice was formed but the place where it was implemented. Otherwise it would be too easy for undertakings to evade the rules laid down in the Treaty. In this case, the wood pulp producers had implemented their pricing agreement within the common market. It was immaterial whether or not they had had recourse 'to subsidiaries, agents, sub-agents, or branches within the Community in order to make their contacts with purchasers within the Community'.[133]

Although the Court has shown extreme reluctance to embrace directly the effects doctrine, it may be thought that the broad approach it has taken to the territoriality principle amounts to much the same thing. The 'Wood Pulp' judgment suggests[134] that any practice which produces an effect on competition within the Community may be regarded as having been implemented there and as falling for that reason within the scope of the Treaty.[135] There is a danger that this approach will lead to conflicts of jurisdiction with third countries which take a similarly expansive approach to their own jurisdiction, notably the United States. In 1991 the Commission signed an agreement with the US Government in an attempt to increase coordination in the enforcement of the parties' respective competition rules.[136] However, in proceedings brought by France,[137] the Court held that, although the agreement was binding on the Community under international law, the Commission lacked competence to conclude it. In 1995, the Council authorized the Commission to conclude an agreement on the same subject with the US Government.[138] The Commission subsequently proposed the establishment of an

---

[132] Para 13.   [133] Para 17.

[134] Its precise effect is not free from controversy: see Goyder, pp 550–1; Kerse, pp 342–3. However, the CFI took a broad view of the judgment in Case T–102/96 *Gencor v Commission*, [1999] 4 CMLR 971, where it held that Reg 4064/89 on the control of concentrations between undertakings applied to a proposed concentration notified by undertakings whose registered offices and production activites were located outside the Community. Reg 4064/89 is discussed below.

[135] For an example of a situation which might not be covered by the Court's case law, see Whish, p 382, who refers to 'a non-EEC cartel refusing to supply customers within the EEC: could one argue in such circumstances that this agreement is "implemented" within the EEC by the refusal to supply there? Linguistically this seems hard to sustain; however there is no doubt in this situation that the *effects* of the agreement are felt within the EEC' (emphasis in the original).

[136] For the text of the agreement, see [1991] 4 CMLR 823.

[137] Case C–327/91 *France v Commission* [1994] ECR I–3641.

[138] See the decision of the Council and the Commission concerning the conclusion of the Agreement between the European Communities and the Government of the United States of America regarding the application of their competition laws, OJ 1995 L95/45. Cf the Agreement between the European Communities and the Government of the United States of America on the application of positive comity principles in the enforcement of their competition laws, OJ 1998 L173/28.

international framework for the enforcement of competition rules under the aegis of the WTO.[139]

This area exemplifies the restraining influence the Court has sometimes been called upon to exercise. The Court recognizes and endorses the importance of the competition rules in the scheme of the Treaty and the role attributed by the Treaty and Regulation 17 to the Commission in formulating the competition policy of the Community and in applying and enforcing Articles 81 and 82. However, the Court has perhaps shown greater sensitivity than the Commission to the concerns of Member States and the international context in which the Treaty rules are applied. It has also been concerned to ensure respect for the institutional balance established by the Treaties.

The *de minimis* doctrine and the rule of reason

We now turn to two devices the Court has employed to attenuate the effect of Article 81 (ex 85). This has had two advantages: first, it has reduced the workload of the Commission; secondly, it has reduced the extent to which the Treaty interferes with commercial freedom without significantly undermining the achievement of its authors' objectives.

The *de minimis* doctrine

The first device to be noted is the *de minimis* doctrine which the Court has read into Article 81(1). As it said in *Beguelin Import v G L Import Export*,[140] 'in order to come within the prohibition imposed by Article 85 [now 81], the agreement must affect trade between Member States and the free play of competition to an appreciable extent'. This doctrine has been enthusiastically embraced by the Commission, which has published a succession of notices on so-called agreements of minor importance with a view to giving guidance to undertakings and their advisers on when in the Commission's view the *de minimis* rule may be regarded as satisfied. In an explanatory note which accompanied a draft of the latest version of the notice,[141] the Commission said that one of its purposes was to avoid imposing unnecessary administrative burdens on undertakings and the Commission by discouraging the submission for its consideration of agreements which clearly did not have an appreciable effect on trade or competition. That statement reflected the growing importance attached by the Commission to reducing the administrative burden placed on it by its duty to police the application of the Treaty competition

---

[139] See the communication from the Commission to the Council entitled 'Towards an international framework of competition rules', COM(96) 284 final. Cf Torremans, 'Extraterritorial application of EC and US competition law' (1996) 21 ELRev 280; Whish, pp 387–9.

[140] Case 22/71 [1971] ECR 949, para 16. See also Case 5/69 *Volk v Vervaecke* [1969] ECR 295.

[141] See [1997] 4 CMLR 500. The notice itself is published at OJ 1997 C372/13.

rules. The notice has no formal status and the guidance it gives is of a non-binding nature. As an inducement to undertakings to rely on it, the Commission states that '[w]here undertakings have failed to notify an agreement falling within the scope of Article 85(1) [now 81(1)] because they assumed in good faith that the agreement was covered by this notice, the Commission will not consider imposing fines'.[142]

There was a danger that the *de minimis* rule would deprive the Commission of the power to act against agreements which might seem innocuous when taken in isolation but which were in widespread use in a given market, in which competition was as a result restricted to a more than insignificant extent. The case law of the Court therefore recognizes that, in order to assess the effect of an agreement on competition, it is necessary to take account of the economic and legal context and in particular the existence of other similar contracts. That case law is reflected in the Commission's notice on agreements of minor importance, which states[143] that the Commission reserves the right to intervene where competition in the relevant market is restricted by the cumulative effects of parallel networks of similar agreements. The leading case in this area is now *Delimitis*,[144] which was referred to the Court by the Oberlandesgericht Frankfurt am Main and concerned the validity of a contract entered into between a publican and a brewery in Germany. According to the test laid down by the Court in that case, the validity of the individual agreement in dispute would be affected by whether access to the market was restricted and 'the extent to which the agreements entered into by the brewery in question contribute to the cumulative effect produced in that respect by the totality of the similar contracts found on that market'.[145] In other words, the national court was being asked to analyse the market in which the parties were operating and to consider the effect on competition in that market, not only of the contract which had been entered into between the parties, but also of contracts between the brewery and other publicans and even of contracts entered into by their competitors. This is such a difficult task that many national courts might consider it impossible for them to undertake. In an attempt to meet that objection, the Commission stated in its notice on co-operation with national courts that 'national courts can obtain information from the Commission regarding factual data: statistics, market studies and economic analyses. The Commission will endeavour to communicate these data . . . or will indicate the source from which they can be obtained.'[146] The Commission pointed out, however, that 'the requisite data must actually be at its disposal'.[147]

---

[142] Para 5. Whether an agreement has an appreciable effect on competition is not simply a function of the size of the parties to it. Unlike previous versions of the notice, the latest version therefore makes no reference to the turnover of the parties. See the Commission's explanatory note, para 5.
[143] See paras 18 and 20.
[144] Case C–234/89 [1991] ECR I–935; see also Case 23/67 *Brasserie de Haecht v Wilkin* [1967] ECR 407; Case C–393/92 *Almelo* [1994] ECR I–1477; Case T–7/93 *Langnese-Iglo v Commission* [1995] ECR II–1533; Case T–9/93 *Schöller v Commission* [1995] ECR II–1611; Joined Cases C–319/93, C–40/94 and C–224/94 *Dijkstra and Others v Friesland (Frico Domo) Coöperatie and Others* [1995] ECR I–4471.
[145] Para 24.   [146] Para 40.   [147] Para 41.

The *de minimis* doctrine began life as a device for excluding unimportant agreements from the scope of Article 81, thereby reducing the burden on business and the Commission and relaxing the constraints on the freedom of action of national courts. However, the need to qualify the doctrine to take account of the problems posed by networks of similar agreements has resulted in the imposition on national courts of responsibilities they are liable to find very hard to discharge, even with the assistance of the Commission and the Court under Article 234 (ex 177). The danger is that the result will either be to damage the effectiveness of Article 81 or to require the Commission to intervene after all.

The rule of reason

Another device developed by the Court to temper the constraints imposed on business by Article 81 (ex 85) and to reduce the burden on the Commission is sometimes called the rule of reason. That term originated in the United States, where some anti-competitive agreements are regarded as illegal *per se*. In order to assess the legality of others, the courts adopt a rule of reason approach, which involves balancing an agreement's beneficial effects against any restrictions on competition which it contains. The terms 'rule of reason' and '*per se*' are not employed by the Court of Justice, but commentators seeking to encourage the Court to be more economically sophisticated in determining whether or not Article 81(1) applies to particular agreements have urged it to espouse a rule of reason approach. Other writers object to the use of the terms '*per se*' and 'rule of reason' in the Community context on the basis that they are liable to cause confusion by blurring the distinction between US and EC competition law and the contexts in which they apply.[148] However, it is clear from the case law that some restrictive agreements are treated by the Court as caught automatically by Article 81(1)[149] while the validity of others depends on an assessment of their economic effects. Although the Court itself is probably wise to eschew the term 'rule of reason', its use does not seem inapt to describe its approach as long as it is remembered that the term does not have precisely the same significance in EC law as it does in American law. The term is often used to describe the approach taken by the Court to assessing the lawfulness of non-discriminatory obstacles to freedom of movement, in particular whether such obstacles can be justifed by reference to mandatory requirements of public policy.[150] The use of the term in the context of Article 81 serves to underline the similarity in the approaches taken by the Court in these different contexts.

An early case in which the Court suggested that a rule of reason analysis might be appropriate under Article 81(1) (ex 85(1)) was *Société Technique Minière v Maschinenbau Ulm*,[151] in which the Court was asked for a preliminary ruling in the

---

[148] See Whish and Sufrin, 'Article 85 and the rule of reason' (1997) 7 YEL 1; Whish, p 209.
[149] See Rose (ed), *Bellamy and Child's Common Market Law of Competition* (4th edn, 1993), p 91.
[150] See chs 7–9.   [151] Case 56/65 [1966] ECR 235.

context of a dispute over the validity of an agreement under which a French company was given the exclusive right to sell in France machinery manufactured by a
German company. The parties agreed that the delivery of competing machinery
would only take place with the consent of the German company and that the
French company could not assign its rights under the agreement to a third party
without the German company's consent. It might have been thought that the
agreement clearly restricted the commercial freedom of the parties and affected
trade between Member States. However, the Court said that the concept of competition for the purposes of Article 81(1) 'must be understood within the actual
context in which it would occur in the absence of the agreement in dispute. In particular it may be doubted whether there is an interference with competition if the
said agreement seems really necessary for the penetration of a new area by an
undertaking.'[152] In order to establish whether the agreement should be regarded as
prohibited, it was necessary to take account of a range of factors including the
nature of the products concerned, the position of the parties, whether the agreement was an isolated one or one of a series, and the severity of its terms.

A perhaps more striking example of the adoption of a rule of reason approach by
the Court is its decision in *Metro v Commission*,[153] which concerned the compatibility with Article 81(1) (ex 85(1)) of selective distribution systems. These are used
by manufacturers to restrict the supply of their products to dealers whose premises
are appropriate and whose staff are suitably qualified. Approved dealers will be prevented from selling to non-approved dealers, who may not meet the standards set
by the supplier. As Goyder explains,[154] '[t]he essence of selectivity . . . is not simply that the supplier selects its main distributors or wholesalers . . . It is rather that
the supplier limits the distribution of goods only to those wholesalers and retailers
which satisfy appropriate criteria and as a result have been allowed to join the system.' The rationale for such systems is to ensure that the product is handled properly and that customers receive appropriate levels of advice and after-sales service.
However, their effect is to reduce competition between distributors of the same
brand of product[155] and they would therefore seem liable to fall foul of Article
81(1).

The *Metro* case arose out of attempts by M, an electrical wholesaler, to gain
admission to the selective distribution system operated by S, a manufacturer of electrical equipment. When S refused to admit M to the system, M complained to the
Commission. The Commission decided that certain aspects of S's distribution system fell outside Article 81(1) while others qualified for exemption under Article
81(3). Metro sought the annulment of the Commission's decision, but was unsuccessful. The Court said:[156]

---

[152] At p 250.   [153] Case 26/76 [1977] ECR 1875.   [154] At p 214.
[155] So-called intra-brand competition. Competition between different brands (inter-brand competition) may not be affected to the same extent because dealers may be entitled to sell several brands of
the same product: see para 22 of the judgment in *Metro*.
[156] Para 20.

... the Commission was justified in recognizing that selective distribution systems constituted, together with others, an aspect of competition which accords with Article 85(1) [now 81(1)], provided that resellers are chosen on the basis of objective criteria of a qualitative nature relating to the technical qualifications of the reseller and his staff and the suitability of his trading premises and that such conditions are laid down uniformly for all potential resellers and are not applied in a discriminatory fashion.

The Court noted the tendency of such systems to reduce price competition but maintained that this was not the only effective form of competition. Specialist wholesalers and retailers were entitled to maintain certain price levels where this was necessary to preserve a distribution network which was appropriate to the nature of the product and restrictions designed to achieve that objective would not necessarily fall within Article 81(1).[157]

There are several other cases in which the Court has accepted that restrictions on the behaviour of one or more of the parties to a contract do not fall within Article 81(1) if objectively justified. Particularly worthy of note is *Pronuptia*,[158] where the Court considered the compatibility with Article 81(1) of distribution franchises, under which the franchisee sells certain products in a shop bearing the franchisor's business name or symbol. The nature of such agreements, then relatively novel in Europe, was considered in some detail by Advocate General VerLoren van Themaat, who said that 'the significant distinguishing features of a franchise agreement for the sale of products are the independence of the undertakings involved, the existence of a licence for the use of a company name, trade name, emblem or other symbols, and for know-how in a broad sense, together with a uniform manner of presentation, the usual consideration being the payment of a royalty by the franchisee for the licences granted'.[159]

As the Court explained,[160] such agreements enable the franchisor to profit from its expertise without investing its own capital. The franchisee gains access to methods which it could not have learned without considerable effort and it benefits from the franchisor's reputation. The Court declared: 'Such a system, which allows the franchisor to profit from his success does not in itself interfere with competition.' The Court accepted that restrictions placed on the franchisee which were essential to make the system work did not constitute restrictions on competition for the purposes of Article 81(1). This was true of provisions designed to prevent the know-how and assistance provided by the franchisor from benefiting its competitors and of provisions establishing the control strictly necessary for maintaining the identity and reputation of the network identified by the franchisor's name or symbol. However, provisions which shared markets between the franchisor and the franchisee or between franchisees were caught by Article 81(1).

---

[157] On selective distribution, see further Goyder, pp 214–36; Whish, pp 584–97; Case T–19/92 *Leclerc v Commission* [1996] ECR II–1851.

[158] Case 161/84 [1986] ECR 353. See also Case 258/78 *Nungesser v Commission* [1982] ECR 2015; Case 262/81 *Coditel v Cine-Vog Films II* [1982] ECR 3381; Case 42/84 *Remia v Commission* [1985] ECR 2545; Case C–250/92 *Gottrup-Klim v Dansk Landbrugs Grovvareselskab AmbA* [1995] ECR I–5641.

[159] At p 362.   [160] See para 15.

The Court's decision had a strong influence on the development of the Commission's policy on franchise agreements, which at the start of the proceedings was not clearly defined,[161] and led to the adoption of a block exemption regulation on the matter.[162] The influence of the Court's judgment is particularly evident in recital 11, which states:

It is desirable to list in the Regulation a number of obligations that are commonly found in franchise agreements and are normally not restrictive of competition and to provide that if, because of the particular economic or legal circumstances, they fall under Article 85(1), they are also covered by the exemption. This list, which is not exhaustive, includes in particular clauses which are essential either to preserve the common identity and reputation of the network or to prevent the know-how made available and the assistance given by the franchisor from benefiting competitors.

The list referred to (the so-called white list) is set out in Article 3 of the regulation.

In the above discussion it has been convenient to use the term 'rule of reason'. Whether the use of that term is appropriate in the field of EC competition law is not of great importance in the present context. What is important is that the Court has, by means of a creative and flexible approach to the interpretation of Article 81 (ex 85), excluded from the scope of that provision a series of agreements which might on the face of things have seemed restrictive of competition. It was by no means self-evident that the Court would take this approach, which did not, at least initially, commend itself to the Commission. The factors which the Court has taken into account in applying the rule of reason approach might have been thought relevant, not to the scope of Article 81(1), but to whether an exemption was available under Article 81(3), a provision which has no counterpart in US law. It may be noted that much of the Court's judgment in the *Metro* case was concerned with whether aspects of S's distribution system were to be regarded as caught by the former or entitled to exemption under the latter. The Court found certain requirements which the Commission had exempted to fall outside the scope of Article 81(1).[163] However, as Forrester and Norall pointed out in a prescient article published in 1984,[164] '[t]he intensity of the debate over whether Europe has or should have a rule of reason is not principally about the meaning or the language of Article 85(1). It fundamentally concerns who shall interpret and apply the competition rules. By arguing against a rule of reason, the Commission is seeking to maximize the number of cases about which it receives detailed information through the notification process.' That is a view with which the Court might have been expected to have some sympathy.

---

[161] See AG VerLoren van Themaat at p 355.

[162] Reg 4087/88 on the application of Art 85(3) of the Treaty to categories of franchise agreements, OJ 1988 L359/46.

[163] See eg paras 23–7.

[164] 'The laicization of Community law: self-help and the rule of reason: how competition law is and could be applied' (1984) 21 CMLRev 11, 37. Some of the reasons underlying the Commission's attitude are summarized at p 13.

The enormous practical advantage of treating mitigating factors as relevant to the applicability of Article 81(1) is that Article 81(3) cannot yet be applied by the national courts.[165] To rely on the latter provision would therefore have increased the burden on the Commission caused by applications for individual decisions of exemption. Although the prevailing orthodoxy is now that the national courts should be encouraged to give effect to the Treaty competition rules, this is not without dangers for the effective and uniform application of the law. A less creative Court might well have taken the view that the resources available to the Commission were not its concern. The approach taken by the Court in an area universally acknowledged to be fundamental to the proper functioning of the common market shows how facile it is to argue that the Court always seeks to broaden the scope of the Treaty and to maximize its own powers and those of the other institutions.

Abuse of a dominant position

The prohibition against abuse of a dominant position laid down in Article 82 (ex 86) EC constitutes the second pillar of the competition rules applicable to undertakings laid down in the Treaty. The Commission did not initially seek to exploit the potential of Article 82, unwilling to interfere with the development of powerful European businesses capable of competing effectively in international markets.[166] However, the Commission's attitude began to change in the 1970s[167] and the Court was called upon to give a series of major rulings which helped to define the scope of the article. Although it has not given rise to such an abundant case law as Article 81 (ex 85), it has come to play an important part in achieving the objectives of the Community's competition policy.

In order to establish an infringement of Article 82, there are essentially four issues that need to be addressed. It should be emphasized that the language of Article 82 was initially considered somewhat vague and that it is largely as a result of the Court's case law, particularly in the 1970s, that it is now possible to identify these questions.[168] They are as follows. First, what is the relevant market? Secondly, is the undertaking concerned dominant on that market? Thirdly, if so, has the undertaking in question abused its dominant position? Fourthly, if so, is that abuse liable to affect trade between Member States? The fourth issue has not proved any more significant an obstacle to the application of Article 82 than it has to the application of Article 81. Although there was at one time a suggestion that the test applicable was stricter under Article 82,[169] the Court seems to have reverted in more recent

---

[165] Art 9(1), Reg 17.   [166] Gerber, pp 356–8.
[167] See Gerber (1994) 35 Harv Int LJ 97, 121–2, who suggests that the Commission saw Art 82 as a way of preventing dominant firms from adding to the inflationary pressures caused by the oil crisis.
[168] Gerber, p 356.
[169] See Case 22/78 *Hugin v Commission* [1979] ECR 1869.

decisions[170] to something closer to the broad test applied in its early case law.[171] As for the first three issues mentioned above, these require examination in a little more detail.

The relevant market

Since a dominant position cannot exist in a vacuum, the first question which arises is how the relevant market is to be defined. As the Court said in *United Brands v Commission*:[172]

The opportunities for competition under Article 86 [now 82] of the Treaty must be considered having regard to the particular features of the product in question and with reference to a clearly defined geographic area in which it is marketed and where the conditions of competition are sufficiently homogeneous for the effect of the economic power of the undertaking concerned to be able to be evaluated.

Sometimes temporal factors may be relevant in addition to the product and geographical area. The defendant undertaking will attempt to show that the relevant market is a broad one, since this will make it more likely that it faces competition from other undertakings. Conversely, the Commission will seek to define the relevant market as narrowly as possible because, if it succeeds, it will be easier to establish that the undertaking concerned is dominant. The Court has been sympathetic to attempts by the Commission to achieve this. A good example is *Hugin v Commission*,[173] where the Commission found that H had infringed Article 82 by refusing to supply spare parts for its cash registers to L, an independent undertaking which specialized in the maintenance and repair of cash registers, and by prohibiting its subsidiaries and distributors from selling such spare parts outside its distribution network. Although the market for cash registers was highly competitive, the Court upheld the Commission's finding that the relevant product market for the purposes of Article 82 was that constituted by spare parts for cash registers manufactured by H, because undertakings like L depended on supplies of such parts.

The geographic market was defined by the CFI in *Tetra Pak II*[174] as 'the territory in which all traders operate in the same conditions of competition in so far as concerns specifically the relevant products . . .'. According to the text of Article 82 (ex 86), the geographic market must constitute at least 'a substantial part of the common market', but the Court has accepted that relatively localized markets may

---

[170] See eg Case 322/81 *Michelin v Commission* [1983] ECR 3461, paras 103–4; Joined Cases C–241/91 P and C–242/91 P *RTE and ITP v Commission* [1995] ECR I–743, paras 69–70.

[171] See eg Joined Cases 6 and 7/73 *Commercial Solvents v Commission* [1974] ECR 223, para 33.

[172] Case 27/76 [1978] ECR 207, para 11.

[173] *Supra.* Cf Case 26/75 *General Motors v Commission* [1975] ECR 1367; Case 77/77 *BP v Commission* [1978] ECR 1513; Case 226/84 *British Leyland v Commission* [1986] ECR 3263; Case C–53/92 P *Hilti v Commission* [1994] ECR I–667.

[174] Para 91. See also the description of the relevant geographic market given in Form CO, which must be used to notify concentrations to the Commission under Reg 4064/89 on the control of concentrations between undertakings, discussed below.

satisfy this criterion. An example is *Merci Convenzionali Porto di Genova*,[175] where the Court was asked to consider whether an undertaking enjoying the exclusive right under Italian law to organize dock work in the port of Genoa occupied a dominant position for the purposes of Article 82. In answering that question in the affirmative, the Court said this about the relevant market:[176]

As regards the definition of the market in question . . . it is that of the organization on behalf of third persons of dock work relating to ordinary freight in the port of Genoa and the performance of such work. Regard being had in particular to the volume of traffic in that port and its importance in relation to maritime transport and export operations as a whole in the Member State concerned, that market may be regarded as constituting a substantial part of the common market.

Dominance

Having identified the relevant market, the Commission will then need to establish that the defendant undertaking holds a dominant position on that market. In *Hoffmann-La Roche v Commission*,[177] the Court said that the expression dominant position meant 'a position of economic strength enjoyed by an undertaking which enables it to prevent effective competition being maintained on the relevant market by affording it the power to behave to an appreciable extent independently of its competitors, its customers and ultimately of the consumers'. The Court has made it clear that establishing dominance is only an intermediate step on the road to showing that Article 82 (ex 86) has been infringed. However, it regards a dominant undertaking as having 'a special responsibility not to allow its conduct to impair genuine undistorted competition on the common market'.[178] Thus, conduct which might be acceptable from an undertaking facing strong competition may be regarded as unlawful if perpetrated by an undertaking in a dominant position. Businesses endowed with statutory monopolies[179] and even the holders of intellectual property rights[180] may find themselves burdened with the 'special responsibility' to preserve undistorted competition to which the Court has referred.

Of particular importance in determining whether an undertaking holds a dominant position for the purposes of Article 82 is the size of its market share and that of its rivals.[181] The Court has also taken account of a wide range of so-called barriers to entry. An example is the *United Brands* case,[182] which concerned an allegation by the Commission that the applicant had abused its dominant position on the

[175] Case C–179/90 [1991] ECR I–5889. Cf 'Sugar', paras 441–51; AG Warner in *BP* at p 1537.
[176] Para 15.   [177] Case 85/76 [1979] ECR 461, para 38.
[178] Case 322/81 *Michelin v Commission* [1983] ECR 3461, para 57.
[179] See eg Case C–41/90 *Höfner and Elser* [1991] ECR I–1979; Case C–260/89 *ERT* [1991] ECR I–2925; Case C–179/90 *Merci Convenzionali Porto di Genova* [1991] ECR I–5889; Case C–320/91 *Corbeau* [1993] ECR I–2533.
[180] See Joined Cases C–241/91 P and C–242/91 P *RTE and ITP v Commission* [1995] ECR I–743.
[181] See eg *Hoffmann-La Roche, supra*, paras 39 and 41; *Gottrup-Klim, supra*, para 48.   [182] *Supra*.

market for bananas in certain Member States. In assessing the strength of the applicant's position on the relevant market, the Court noted:[183]

The particular barriers to competitors entering the market are the exceptionally large capital
investments required for the creation and running of banana plantations, the need to increase
sources of supply in order to avoid the effects of fruit diseases and bad weather (hurricanes,
floods), the introduction of an essential system of logistics which the distribution of a very
perishable product makes necessary, economies of scale from which newcomers to the market cannot derive any immediate benefit and the actual cost of entry made up *inter alia* of all
the general expenses incurred in penetrating the market such as the setting up of an adequate
commercial network, the mounting of very large-scale advertising campaigns, all those
financial risks, the costs of which are irrecoverable if the attempt fails.

Although competitors could use the same methods of production and distribution
as the applicant, they would be faced with 'almost insuperable practical and financial obstacles'.[184] The Court said that this was one of the factors 'peculiar to a dominant position'.[185]

The Court therefore seems to regard as barriers to entry not only practices deliberately designed by an incumbent undertaking to exclude competitors but also anything that makes it more difficult for new participants to enter the market, even if
the same obstacles had to be overcome by incumbents. The effect of this approach
may be to bring within the scope of Article 82 a category of undertakings whose
dominance might be regarded as questionable. As Bork observes:[186] 'It is harder to
enter the steel industry than the business of retailing shoes or pizzas, and it is harder
to enter either of these fields than to become a suburban handyman. But these difficulties are natural; they inhere in the nature of the tasks to be performed. There
can be no objection to barriers of this sort.' Bork argues that competition law
should concern itself only with artificial entry barriers, that is, with exclusionary
practices by incumbents which are deliberately designed to block entry. On this
view, the danger of taking too wide an approach to what constitutes a barrier to
entry is that undertakings will be penalized for behaviour that, far from being
abusive, is in fact pro-competitive. This could actually discourage firms from competing.[187]

Two points might be made in response to Bork's penetrating analysis.[188] The
first is that it was written from the viewpoint of the United States, which constitutes (at least for the moment) a much more integrated market than the European
Union. Given the close link between the Treaty competition rules and the proper
functioning of the common market, it is perhaps legitimate for a broader view of
what constitutes a barrier to entry to be taken in the European context than is
appropriate in the United States. The second point is linked to the first. As Bork

---

[183] Para 122.   [184] Para 123.   [185] Para 124.
[186] *The Antitrust Paradox: A Policy at War with Itself* (1978), p 311.
[187] See Whish, p 268. Cf Craig and de Búrca, op cit, pp 953–4.
[188] See further Green, Hartley and Usher, *The Legal Foundations of the Single European Market* (1991),
chs 14 and 15, esp pp 203–5.

himself points out,[189] '[a]ntitrust is valuable because in some cases it can achieve results more rapidly than can market forces'. It may be argued that Article 82 (ex 86) has an important role to play in speeding up the process of removing barriers to trade within and between Member States. In any event, as pointed out above, an infringement of Article 82 is not established simply by showing that an undertaking is dominant: an abuse must also be proved. Here the Court and particularly the Commission, the guardian of the Community's competition policy, must be alert not to penalize efficiency.

The Court's willingness to take a broad view of the scope of Article 82 (ex 86) is clearly illustrated by its case law on so-called collective dominance, that is, the possibility that a number of independent undertakings might together hold a dominant position on a particular market.[190] The idea might at first sight seem fanciful: how can an undertaking be dominant if its position of market strength is dependent on its relationship with one or more other undertakings? Is it not the purpose of Article 81 (ex 85), which catches not only agreements but also concerted practices, to regulate anti-competitive behaviour by several undertakings acting together? These assumptions have been challenged by the Commission as part of its campaign against the threats to competition posed by oligopolies.

The view that Article 82 (ex 86) was confined to undertakings which alone held dominant positions appeared to secure the approval of the Court in *Hoffmann-La Roche v Commission*,[191] where the Court seemed to rule out the application of Article 82 in cases of collective dominance. The Court said[192] that it was necessary to distinguish a dominant position 'from parallel courses of conduct which are peculiar to oligopolies in that in an oligopoly the courses of conduct interact, while in the case of an undertaking occupying a dominant position the conduct of the undertaking which derives profits from that position is to a great extent determined unilaterally'. However, the Commission began to find Article 81 (ex 85) and the concept of the concerted practice increasingly inadequate as a device for controlling oligopolies. There were essentially two reasons for this. The first was the Court's insistence that parallel conduct could constitute proof of concertation only where there was no other plausible explanation for the conduct of the undertakings concerned.[193] The second was that undertakings became more adept at concealing direct evidence of unlawful concertation.

The Commission accordingly began to explore the potential of Article 82 in this context. That article speaks of abuse 'by one *or more* undertakings'[194] and the Commission maintained that the prohibition it laid down was therefore capable of applying in cases of collective dominance. The phrase could not be limited to

---

[189] Op cit, p 311.

[190] See Whish, pp 486–90; Whish and Sufrin, 'Oligopolistic markets and EC competition law' (1992) 12 YEL 59.

[191] Case 85/76 [1979] ECR 461.   [192] Para 39.

[193] See Joined Cases 89, 104, 114, 116, 117, 125 to 129/85 *Ahlström and Others v Commission* ('Wood Pulp') [1993] ECR I–1307, para 71. The 'Wood Pulp' case is discussed above.

[194] Emphasis added.

members of the same group, it argued, because the Court's case law on Article 81 established that a group of companies was to be considered a single undertaking.[195] In 'Italian Flat Glass',[196] that argument was favourably received by the CFI, which said that the term 'undertaking' was to be given the same meaning in Article 82 as in Article 81. The reference in Article 82 to an abuse by more than one undertaking must therefore have been intended to catch the behaviour of independent firms which, because of the economic links between them, held a collective dominant position on the relevant market.

That view of the scope of Article 82 was subsequently endorsed by the Court of Justice,[197] although it is clear that a finding of collective dominance is not one which the Community Courts will readily reach. In 'Italian Flat Glass', the CFI found that the Commission had failed to establish the existence of a collective dominant position on the facts; in the *DIP* case, the Court of Justice emphasized that, in order for such a position to exist for these purposes, 'the undertakings in question must be linked in such a way that they adopt the same conduct on the market . . .',[198] clearly a difficult test to satisfy and one that was not satisfied on the facts of that case.[199]

However difficult it may be to establish in practice, the notion of collective dominance clearly extends considerably the potential scope of Article 82 (ex 86). The result seems hard to reconcile with the Court's apparent reluctance to allow Article 81(1) (ex 85(1)) to be used to regulate parallel behaviour. Can it be justified? The line of reasoning endorsed by the CFI in 'Italian Flat Glass' has not subsequently been challenged by the Court, but it does not seem wholly convincing. Surely the real reason why an arrangement between a parent company and a subsidiary which it controls falls outside Article 81(1) is not that only one undertaking is involved, but that the notion of agreement implies the prior exercise by the parties of some degree of independent judgment. In any event, it was not self-evident when the Treaty entered into force how the term 'undertaking' would be defined. The wording of Article 82 might simply have been intended to make it clear that the article extended to abusive behaviour by the members of a group of companies.[200]

[195] See eg Case C–73/95 P *Viho v Commission* [1996] ECR I–5457.
[196] Joined Cases T–68/89, T–77/89 and T–78/89 *SIV v Commission* [1992] ECR II–1403. See in particular paras 357–8.
[197] See Case C–393/92 *Almelo* [1994] ECR I–1477; Joined Cases C–140/94, C–141/94 and C–142/94 *DIP and Others v Comune di Bassano del Grappa and Comune di Chioggia* [1995] ECR I–3257. See also AG Lenz in Case 66/86 *Ahmed Saeed Flugreisen and Others v Zentrale zur Bekämpfung unlauteren Wettbewerbs* [1989] ECR 803, 824.
[198] *Supra*, para 26.
[199] The notion of collective dominance is potentially important in the transport sector. Cf Joined Cases T–24/93, T–25/93, T–26/93 and T–28/93 *Compagnie Maritime Belge Transports and Others v Commission* [1996] ECR II–1201, where the CFI held that the members of a shipping conference had abused the collective dominant position they held as a result of the close relations between them. That judgment is at the time of writing the subject of an appeal to the Court: see Joined Cases C–395/96 P and C–396/96 P.
[200] This is how it appears to have been understood by the Court in *Continental Can*: see para 28.

From a policy point of view too the desirability of extending the limits of Article 82 in this way seems doubtful. The reasons for this are similar to those advanced by critics of the Court's approach to barriers to entry. Even if it is accepted that the perceived dangers of oligopolies are not adequately countered by the possibility that anti-competitive behaviour by incumbents will attract new entrants (or growth by smaller firms already in the market),[201] the extent of the links between under-takings which are necessary to establish a collective dominant position is always likely to cause controversy.[202] The result is that undertakings which do not hold individual dominant positions cannot be sure that they will escape unwelcome attention from the Commission merely by avoiding any infringement of Article 81. Such undertakings may therefore be induced to avoid practices which are in fact pro-competitive. Having accepted the Commission's invitation to travel down this road, the Community Courts will need to be alert to the need to set clearly defined limits to the application of the notion of collective dominance.

Abuse

The second paragraph of Article 82 (ex 86) sets out a non-exhaustive list of exam-ples[203] of practices constituting an abuse. The Court said in *Continental Can*[204] that it was apparent from the list that the article was 'not only aimed at practices which may cause damage to consumers directly, but also at those which are detrimental to them through their impact on an effective competition structure . . .'. The Court has supplemented the list by recognizing a range of behaviour as abusive for these purposes. Practices condemned by the Court include granting customers so-called loyalty or fidelity rebates, that is discounts conditional on the customer's obtaining all or most of its requirements from the dominant undertaking,[205] and refusing to supply other undertakings.[206] More controversially, the Court has also held that in exceptional circumstances the exercise of an intellectual property right conferred by national law might constitute an abuse.[207]

[201] For a sceptical view of the dangers posed by oligopolies, see Bork, op cit, ch 8, who observes at p 195: 'The absence of entry or the lack of growth by the smaller firms already in the industry suggests that one of two things is true. Either there is no restriction of output, and hence no greater-than-competitive profit, to induce entry or the growth of smaller firms; or the large firms are so far superior in efficiency that, even if there is a restriction of output, no new firm would find entry profitable and no small firm is able to grow. Of course, there may be both superior efficiency and absence of output restriction. These conclusions are awkward for the oligopolyphobe . . .' See also Whish, p 490.

[202] Cf the findings of the CFI on the issue in *Gencor v Commission, supra*, paras 273–84, a merger case.

[203] *Continental Can*, para 26: '[t]he list merely gives examples, not an exhaustive enumeration . . .'.

[204] At para 26.

[205] See eg Case 85/76 *Hoffmann-La Roche v Commission* [1979] ECR 461; Case 322/81 *Michelin v Commission* [1983] ECR 3461. Fidelity rebates are to be distinguished from quantity rebates, which are based on the volume purchased from a producer and are considered economically justifiable.

[206] See eg *United Brands*; Joined Cases 6 and 7/73 *Commercial Solvents v Commission* [1974] ECR 223. Cf Case 77/77 *BP v Commission* [1978] ECR 1513; Case 22/78 *Hugin v Commission* [1979] ECR 1869.

[207] See Case 238/87 *Volvo v Veng* [1988] ECR 6211; Joined Cases C–241/91 P and C–242/91 P *RTE and ITP v Commission* [1995] ECR I–743. The latter case was seen by some commentators as an

One of the abuses mentioned in Article 86 is 'imposing unfair purchase or selling prices'. In *United Brands* the Commission alleged that the defendant undertaking's prices were excessive because those it charged in some parts of the Community were considerably higher than those charged in other parts for the same product. The Court found that the allegation had not been proved, but it accepted that 'charging a price which is excessive because it has no reasonable relation to the economic value of the product supplied'[208] would constitute an abuse. One way of establishing this would be to ask whether the difference between the costs actually incurred by an undertaking and the price it charged was excessive and, if so, whether the price was unfair in itself or when compared to competing products.[209] An example of a case in which an allegation of excessive pricing was found to have been substantiated is *British Leyland v Commission*,[210] where a car manufacturer's practice of charging higher fees for issuing certificates of conformity for left-hand-drive than for right-hand-drive vehicles when the inspection was essentially the same was condemned as abusive. The Court thought that the level of the fee 'was fixed solely with a view to making the re-importation of left-hand-drive vehicles less attractive'.[211]

Prices may be unfairly low as well as unfairly high and the Court has accepted that charging excessively low prices (known as 'predatory pricing') may also be abusive if done to damage a competitor. This was established in *AKZO v Commission*,[212] where the Court upheld the Commission's finding that the low prices charged by the applicant on the flour additives market in order to prevent a competitor active in that market from expanding into the lucrative organic peroxides market, where the applicant was dominant, were abusive. The Court looked at the relationship between the prices charged by the applicant and its costs, of which it distinguished three categories: variable costs, which vary according to the quantity produced; fixed costs, which remain the same regardless of the quantity produced; and total costs, that is, fixed costs plus variable costs. The Court said that predation had to be assumed where prices were below average variable costs, because on every sale the dominant firm would be losing fixed costs and at least part of the variable costs relating to the unit produced. Where prices were above average variable costs but below average total costs, the undertaking would be guilty of predatory pricing if an intention to eliminate a competitor could be shown.[213]

endorsement of the essential facilities doctrine, under which an undertaking in a dominant position may sometimes be required to grant rivals access to a facility which it controls and which is essential to enable them to compete with it. That doctrine was treated by the Court with a certain amount of scepticism in Case C–7/97 *Bronner v Mediaprint* [1999] 4 CMLR 112. See generally Goyder, pp 346–50.

[208] Para 250.
[209] See para 252. This aspect of the decision is criticized by Bishop, 'Price discrimination under Article 86: political economy in the European Court' (1981) 44 MLR 282, 288–9.
[210] Case 226/84 [1986] ECR 3263.
[211] Para 29. Cf Case 26/75 *General Motors v Commission* [1975] ECR 1367.
[212] Case C–62/86 [1991] ECR I–3359.
[213] See paras 71–2; Whish, p 531; Goyder, p 342. For a brief general discussion of the issue of predatory pricing, with references to the considerable volume of literature on the subject, see Whish, pp 508–10.

The difficulty of calculating and classifying costs makes the apparent precision of the *AKZO* test misleading.[214] However, the Commission was again successful in establishing predatory pricing in *Tetra Pak v Commission (Tetra Pak II)*,[215] where the *AKZO* approach was followed. The Court made it clear that it was not necessary to show that the predator had a realistic chance of recouping its losses: 'It must be possible to penalise predatory pricing whenever there is a risk that competitors will be eliminated . . . The aim pursued, which is to maintain undistorted competition, rules out waiting until such a strategy leads to the actual elimination of competitors.'[216]

As with some of the Court's other case law on Article 82 (ex 86), the line of authority discussed above has been subject to criticism on the basis that it is liable to discourage behaviour (in this case, vigorous price competition) which is in fact liable to promote consumer welfare. Writing from a US perspective, Bork observes[217] 'that predatory price cutting is most unlikely to exist and that attempts to outlaw it are likely to harm consumers more than would abandoning the effort'. In addition, it has been persuasively argued that the 'mechanical application of the accounting formulae' laid down in *AKZO* is not appropriate where prices below average variable costs are economically justified, for example on the launch of a new product or to dispose of perishable or out-of-date products. The Court's reliance on intent has also been criticized on the basis that increasing market share and seeking to eliminate competitors is a normal and healthy part of the competitive process.[218]

There is another sense in which *AKZO* and *Tetra Pak II* illustrate the expansive attitude taken by the Court to the scope of Article 82 (ex 86). Both cases involved the behaviour of an undertaking in a market distinct from the one in which it held a dominant position, but in neither of them did this prevent Article 82 from applying. In *AKZO* the applicant's pricing policy in the flour additives market was held to amount to an abuse of the dominant position it held in a distinct market, that for organic peroxides. The applicant's behaviour in the former market was intended to reinforce its position in the latter. In *Tetra Pak II*, the situation was slightly different. The case concerned the markets in packaging for liquid and semi-liquid food. The contested conduct was carried out in the market for non-aseptic cartons and packaging machinery. The applicant did not hold a dominant position on that market but on the associated market for aseptic cartons and packaging machinery, which were used for foods requiring a higher degree of sterility. Thus, the applicant's dominant position in one market facilitated its behaviour in an associated market in which it wished to strengthen its position. The Court acknowledged that '[i]n the case of distinct, but associated, markets, as in the present case,

---

[214] Compare the approach of the Court in *AKZO* with that of AG Lenz, who concluded 'that it was impossible to determine what prices were economically justifiable or reasonable': see p I–3422.
[215] Case C–333/94 P [1996] ECR I–5951.   [216] Para 44.   [217] Op cit, p 155.
[218] See Art and Van Liederkerke, 'Developments in EC competition law in 1996: an overview' (1997) 34 CMLRev 895, 932–4.

application of Article 86 [now 82] to conduct found on the associated, non-dominated, market and having effects on that associated market can only be justified by special circumstances'.[219] The Court accepted that such special circumstances were present here: 'The fact that the various materials involved are used for packaging the same basic liquid products shows that Tetra Pak's customers in one sector are also potential customers in the other . . . the quasi-monopoly enjoyed by Tetra Pak on the aseptic markets and its leading position on the distinct, though closely associated, non-aseptic markets placed it in a situation comparable to that of holding a dominant position on the markets in question as a whole'.[220] This was a very far-reaching conclusion: the applicant was found to have infringed Article 82 even though it did not hold a dominant position on the market in which the abuse took place and even though the abuse had no effect on the dominated market.

The judgment in the *Continental Can* case

It is convenient to end this brief discussion of Article 82 (ex 86) by examining the judgment of the Court in *Europemballage and Continental Can v Commission*.[221] That case has the merit of drawing together several of the issues touched on in the preceding discussion and of illustrating in the context of Article 82 the general approach taken by the Court in resolving disputes over the correct interpretation of the Treaty.

Continental Can was a company registered in New York which manufactured various types of packaging. It owned 85.8 per cent of a German company called SLW, which was active in the market for metal containers. In 1970, Continental Can set up a subsidiary called Europemballage under the legislation of the State of Delaware. Europemballage opened offices in New York and Delaware and, later the same year, acquired an 80 per cent share in a Dutch packaging company called TDV. The Commission objected, arguing that Continental Can held, through SLW, a dominant position on the markets for (a) light packaging for preserved meat, fish, and crustacea, and (b) metal caps for glass jars. According to the Commission, the acquisition of TDV by Continental Can's subsidiary, Europemballage, constituted an abuse of that dominant position. The Commission claimed that the purchase of TDV had practically eliminated competition in the products concerned in a substantial part of the common market. It addressed a decision to Continental Can requiring it to put an end to the infringement. In proceedings for the annulment of the Commission's decision, the Court dismissed a number of procedural arguments raised by the applicants as well as a challenge to the jurisdiction of the Commission.[222] The crux of its judgment concerned two

---

[219] Para 27.   [220] Paras 29–31.   [221] Case 6/72 [1973] ECR 215.
[222] See paras 14–16. The Court held that the conduct of Europemballage could be attributed to its parent. Since the acquisition of TDV influenced market conditions in the Community, the fact that Continental Can did not have its registered office there did not remove it from the reach of Community

issues: did the facts of the case disclose an abuse within the meaning of Article 82 and had the Commission defined the relevant market correctly?

With regard to the first issue, the applicants maintained that the Commission was attempting unlawfully to use Article 82 as a means of controlling mergers. Article 82, they said, did not apply to structural measures taken by undertakings but only to behaviour which affected the market and damaged consumers or competitors. Furthermore, Article 82 was infringed only if the economic power enjoyed by an undertaking in a dominant position had been exploited.

The Court began the passage addressing these arguments with a statement reminiscent of *Van Gend en Loos*, saying it was necessary to 'go back to the spirit, general scheme and wording of Article 86 [now 82], as well as the system and objectives of the Treaty'.[223] The Court pointed out that Article 82 was one of several provisions designed to ensure, in accordance with Article 3(f) EEC,[224] that competition in the common market was not distorted. This *a fortiori* required that competition must not be eliminated, a requirement 'so essential that without it numerous provisions of the Treaty would be pointless'.[225] Article 82 was designed to achieve on a different level the same objective as Article 81 (ex 85), namely the maintenance of effective competition within the common market. The Court took the view that the proper functioning of the common market would be jeopardized if, 'in order to avoid the prohibitions in Article 85 [now 81], it sufficed to establish such close connections between the undertakings that they escaped the prohibition of Article 85 without coming within the scope of that of Article 86 [now 82] . . .'.[226] In the light of these considerations, the Court concluded that Article 82 was not confined to conduct which harmed consumers directly, but also extended to that which damaged their interests through its impact on the structure of a market. An abuse therefore took place 'if an undertaking in a dominant position strengthens such position in such a way that the degree of dominance reached substantially fetters competition, i.e. that only undertakings remain in the market whose behaviour depends on the dominant one'.[227] Strengthening the position of a dominant undertaking could fall within the scope of Article 82 regardless of the means by which it was achieved.

This section of the judgment in *Continental Can* provides a striking example of the teleological approach to interpretation for which the Court has become well known[228] and a clear illustration of its commitment to the competition policy enshrined in the Treaty. The Court peremptorily dismissed the suggestion that a comparison with the ECSC Treaty, which in Article 66 deals expressly with merger control, showed that the scope of Article 82 was more limited. The Court

law. The issue of the territorial jurisdiction of the Community under Arts 81 and 82 is discussed in more detail above.

[223] Para 22.   [224] See now Art 3(1)(g) EC.   [225] Para 24.   [226] Para 25.
[227] Para 26.

[228] Gerber (1994) 35 Harv Int LJ 97, 116, describes the *Continental Can* decision as 'the apotheosis of the teleological method'.

focused instead on the need to achieve the objective set out in Article 3(f) and to read Article 82 in a way which was consistent with Article 81. There are few clearer examples of the Court's techniques of resolving difficulties of interpretation by reference to the context in which a disputed provision is situated and the objectives of the Treaty.[229]

As for the definition of the relevant market, here the Commission was less successful. The Court found that it had failed to show how the markets on which SLW was said to be dominant differed from each other or from the wider market for light metal containers generally. In an important statement on the significance of so-called supply-side substitutability, the Court said:[230]

In order to be regarded as constituting a distinct market, the products in question must be individualized, not only by the mere fact that they are used for packing certain products, but by particular characteristics of production which make them specifically suitable for this purpose. Consequently, a dominant position on the market for light metal containers for meat and fish cannot be decisive, as long as it has not been proved that competitors from other sectors of the market for light metal containers are not in a position to enter this market, by a simple adaptation, with sufficient weight to create a serious counterweight.

The Commission had also failed to consider adequately the extent to which SLW faced potential competition from large consumers capable of manufacturing their own cans. The contested decision was therefore quashed.

The procedural framework for the application of the Treaty competition rules

Regulation 17 provided the Commission with a panoply of powers virtually unequalled[231] in any other field of Community law.[232] Just over a year after its adoption, it was supplemented by Regulation 99/63[233] laying down detailed rules on the conduct of the hearings which in certain circumstances Regulation 17 required to be held. The extent to which the powers enjoyed by the Commission under Regulation 17 have subsequently been subject to scrutiny by the

[229] See Craig and de Búrca, op cit, pp 957–8. The Court's approach to interpretation is discussed in more detail in ch 14.

[230] Para 33. Cf *Michelin, Hugin, supra.*

[231] Cf Arts 65 and 66 ECSC; Gerber, pp 335–42; Goyder, pp 22–4.

[232] See generally Kerse; Ortiz Blanco, *European Community Competition Procedure* (1996); Slot and McDonnell (eds), *Procedure and Enforcement in EC and US Competition Law* (1993); House of Lords Select Committee on the European Communities, *Enforcement of Community Competition Rules* (Session 1993–94, 1st Report).

[233] OJ Sp Ed, 1963–64, p 47. See now Reg 2842/98 on the hearing of parties in certain proceedings under Arts 85 and 86 of the EC Treaty, OJ 1998 L354/18, which replaced Reg 99/63 with effect from 1 February 1999. Note also Reg 27/62, OJ Sp Ed, 1959–62, p 132, now replaced by Reg 3385/94 on the form, content and other details of applications and notifications provided for in Council Reg No 17, OJ 1994 L377/27.

Community Courts is the result of three factors: the importance of Articles 81 (ex 85) and 82 (ex 86) in the scheme of the Treaty, the breadth of the powers conferred on the Commission under Regulation 17, and the resources of many of the undertakings who found themselves on the receiving end of those powers. The result has been a substantial judicial gloss on the text of the regulation. The case law provides evidence of the lengths to which the Court of Justice in particular has gone to balance the achievement of the policy goals underlying Articles 81 and 82 with rule of law considerations, which the Court has sometimes found more pressing than the Commission.

An early example of the Court's approach is the famous *Transocean Marine Paint Association* case,[234] where the applicant association challenged a condition attached by the Commission to the grant of an exemption under Article 81(3) (ex 85(3)) in respect of an agreement concluded between the applicant's members. The applicant's main objection was that it had not been aware of the Commission's intention to impose the disputed condition until it appeared in the text of the decision. The applicant had not therefore had an opportunity to express its views on it. The problem faced by the applicant was that, although Regulation 99/63 required the Commission in certain circumstances to give undertakings an opportunity to comment on objections raised against them, it did not expressly extend that requirement to cases where the Commission intended to subject the grant of an exemption to conditions. Advocate General Warner stated that '[t]here is a rule embedded in the law of some of our countries that an administrative authority, before wielding a statutory power to the detriment of a particular person, must in general hear what that person has to say about the matter, even if the statute does not expressly require it'.[235] He proceeded to review the laws of all the then Member States and concluded 'that the right to be heard forms part of those rights which "the law" referred to in Article 164 [now 220] of the Treaty upholds, and of which, accordingly, it is the duty of this Court to ensure the observance'.[236] Taking its lead from the Opinion of Advocate General Warner, the Court took the view that Regulation 99/63 simply applied 'the general rule that a person whose interests are perceptibly affected by a decision taken by a public authority must be given the opportunity to make his point of view known. This rule requires that an undertaking be clearly informed, in good time, of the essence of conditions to which the Commission intends to subject an exemption and it must have the opportunity to submit its observations to the Commission.'[237]

Advocate General Warner pointed out in the *Transocean Marine Paint* case[238] that the right to a hearing is sometimes classified in French law under the concept of

---

[234] Case 17/74 *Transocean Marine Paint v Commission* [1974] ECR 1063.

[235] p 1088. As the Advocate General showed, the rule is particularly firmly established in English law. For an up-to-date account of the rule, see Wade and Forsyth, *Administrative Law* (7th edn, 1994), ch 15; Craig, *Administrative Law* (3rd edn, 1994), ch 8. The *Transocean* case therefore provides an early example of Community law being influenced by English law.

[236] p 1089.   [237] Para 15.   [238] p 1088.

the rights of the defence. That concept has been employed by the Court in several subsequent cases to limit the investigatory powers enjoyed by the Commission under Articles 11 and 14 of Regulation 17. Article 11 empowers the Commission (subject to certain conditions) to compel undertakings to supply information to it on pain of financial penalties should they fail to comply. Article 14 empowers the Commission to enter premises and examine documents. Undertakings which fail to submit to duly authorized investigations under Article 14 may also have financial penalties imposed on them. These potentially far-reaching powers are essential weapons in the Commission's ongoing campaign against infringements of the Treaty competition rules but it is evident that the Court, and since 1989 the CFI, must be alert to ensure that they are not abused.

A striking example of the importance attached by the Court to the rights of the defence in this field is its decision in *AM & S v Commission*,[239] where the applicant challenged a claim by the Commission to be entitled under Article 14 of Regulation 17 to require the production of documents which were legally privileged. Regulation 17 contained no provision protecting such documents from disclosure to the Commission, but all the Member States recognized, albeit to varying degrees, the confidentiality of communications between lawyer and client. The Court observed that 'Community law, which derives from not only the economic but also the legal interpenetration of the Member States, must take into account the principles and concepts common to the laws of those States concerning the observance of confidentiality, in particular, as regards certain communications between lawyer and client.'[240] Regulation 17, the Court said, contained provisions[241] designed to 'ensure that the rights of the defence may be exercised to the full, and the protection of the confidentiality of written communications between lawyer and client is an essential corollary to those rights'.[242] The Court concluded that such protection attached to written communications concerning proceedings under Regulation 17 which were exchanged with a lawyer in private practice who was qualified to exercise his or her profession in a Member State. Where the status of a document was disputed, the Commission could order its production by decision under Article 14(3) of Regulation 17. Such a decision would be amenable to review by the Court (now the CFI) in annulment proceedings, in the course of which the undertaking's claim to confidentiality could be examined.[243] The Court's failure to extend the benefit of privilege to communications with in-house lawyers, even where subject to the same rules of professional conduct as those in private practice, caused some resentment, but the Court may have felt that it would not be right to distinguish such lawyers from those who were qualified in Member States where full-time employment was regarded as incompatible with the

---

[239] Case 155/79 [1982] ECR 1575. [240] Para 18.
[241] See in particular Art 19 on hearings, a provision which is elaborated on by Reg 99/63.
[242] Para 23.
[243] Cf Case 53/85 *AKZO Chemie v Commission* [1986] ECR 1965, where the Court ruled that a similar procedure should be applied in disputes over whether a document contained business secrets.

professional status of a lawyer.[244] The important point in the present context is that the Court was prepared to recognize that there were circumstances in which documents undoubtedly relevant to proceedings under Regulation 17 did not have to be disclosed to the Commission even though the circumstances in question were not mentioned in the text of the regulation.

The Court was again required to balance the need to ensure the effectiveness of Regulation 17 against the rights of the defence in the *Hoechst* case,[245] where the applicant again challenged a Commission decision based on Article 14 of Regulation 17. The Court noted that all the Member States provided protection, to varying degrees, against 'arbitrary or disproportionate intervention' and accepted that the need for such protection should be recognized as a general principle of Community law.[246] The difficulty was reconciling that principle with the need to ensure that the Commission had the investigative powers it needed. The problem was especially acute where an undertaking opposed an inspection by the Commission under Article 14. In trying to resolve this conundrum, the Court took as its starting point the first sentence of Article 14(6), which provides that '[w]here an undertaking opposes an investigation ordered pursuant to this Article, the Member State concerned shall afford the necessary assistance to the officials authorized by the Commission to enable them to make their investigation'. The Court ruled that, in determining the conditions under which the national authorities gave assistance to the Commission, the Member States were required to ensure both that the Commission's action was effective and that the general principles applicable were respected. Within those limits, the procedural rules and guarantees applicable were those laid down by national law, which the Commission had to respect. The national supervisory body, whether or not it was a court, was not entitled to substitute its own view for that of the Commission as to whether or not an investigation was needed, but it was entitled to 'consider whether the measures of constraint envisaged are arbitrary or excessive having regard to the subject-matter of the investigation and to ensure that the rules of national law are complied with in the application of those measures'.[247] The Court's ruling may be criticized on the basis that it offers insufficient guidance to national supervisory bodies on how to assess the proportionality of the measures envisaged. It may also be said that it is inconsistent to ask a national authority to examine that question but at the same time to prevent it from concluding that no inspection is justified in the circumstances. None the less, the ruling imposes a significant limit on the powers of the Commission under Article 14 of Regulation 17, powers which the Court accepted were essential to maintain the system of undistorted competition contemplated by the Treaty.

---

[244] AG Slynn had taken the view that privilege should be extended to such lawyers: see p 1655.

[245] Joined Cases 46/87 and 227/88 *Hoechst v Commission* [1989] ECR 2859. See also Case 85/87 *Dow Benelux v Commission* [1989] ECR 3137; Joined Cases 97 to 99/87 *Dow Chemical Ibérica v Commission* [1989] ECR 3165. See also ch 6.

[246] Para 19.   [247] Para 35.

Criticism has also been levelled at the Court's hostility in *Hoechst* to the applicant's attempt to rely on a right to the inviolability of the home.[248] Such a right is enshrined in Article 8 of the European Convention on Human Rights, paragraph 1 of which states: 'Everyone has the right to respect for his private and family life, his home and his correspondence.' In its judgment, the Court accepted that, as far as individuals were concerned, a right to the inviolability of the home was recognized by Community law as a principle common to the laws of the Member States. However, it refused to accept that any such right extended to businesses because there were considerable divergences between the laws of the Member States on the extent to which business premises enjoyed protection against intervention from public authorities. The Court considered such a limitation consistent with Article 8 of the European Convention, which was 'concerned with the development of man's personal freedom and may not therefore be extended to business premises. Furthermore, it should be noted that there is no case-law of the European Court of Human Rights on that subject.'[249]

The Court's conclusion that Article 8 of the European Convention did not extend to business premises was subsequently overtaken by the decision in *Niemietz v Germany*,[250] where the European Court of Human Rights found that a search of a lawyer's office came within the scope of Article 8 and declared:[251] 'to interpret the words "private life" and "home" as including certain professional or business activities or premises would be consonant with the essential object and purpose of Article 8, namely to protect the individual against arbitrary interference by the public authorities'. None the less, it is by no means clear that the outcome would have been much different even if the Court of Justice had accepted in *Hoechst* that Article 8(1) of the Convention was applicable. That provision is subject to a broadly-worded derogation in Article 8(2) and, as we have seen, it was accepted that national supervisory bodies were entitled to review the proportionality of the measures of constraint envisaged by the Commission.

The question raised in *Orkem v Commission*[252] was whether undertakings which are being investigated by the Commission may claim privilege against self-incrimination. The applicant was seeking the annulment of a Commission decision adopted under Article 11 of Regulation 17 requiring certain information to be supplied. The applicant argued that the Commission had used Article 11 to force it to incriminate itself by confessing to an infringement of the competition rules and to

---

[248] See Duffy, memorandum submitted to the House of Lords Select Committee on the European Communities, paras 9–10, in *Enforcement of Community Competition Rules* (Session 1993–94, 1st Report); Ryssdal, 'Human rights in the European Union' in *The Developing Role of the European Court of Justice* (European Policy Forum/Frankfurter Institut, 1995), pp 11–12. See generally Waelbroeck and Fosselard, 'Should the decision-making power in EC antitrust procedures be left to an independent judge? The impact of the European Convention on Human Rights on EC antitrust procedures' (1994) 14 YEL 111; Wils, 'La compatibilité des procédures communautaires en matière de concurrence avec la Convention européenne des droits de l'homme' (1996) 32 CDE 329.

[249] Para 18.   [250] (1993) 16 EHRR 97.   [251] Para 31.

[252] Case 374/87 [1989] ECR 3283. See also Case 27/88 *Solvay v Commission* [1989] ECR 3355 (summary publication). See also ch 6.

inform against other undertakings. This, the applicant argued, was contrary to the principle that no one may be compelled to give evidence against himself, a principle which formed part of Community law.

The Court began[253] by ruling that the Commission was entitled to compel an undertaking to provide all necessary information concerning the facts that were known to it and to disclose documents relating to those facts which were in its possession, even if they could be used to establish, against it or against another undertaking, the existence of conduct contrary to the Treaty competition rules. There is an apparent inconsistency[254] between that part of the Court's ruling and the later judgment of the European Court of Human Rights in *Funke v France*,[255] where it was held that the right to a fair trial enshrined in Article 6(1)[256] of the European Convention embodied a right to remain silent and not to contribute to incriminating oneself. However, that view perhaps fails to take due account of the importance attached by the Court of Justice in *Orkem* to the rights of the defence, which it described as 'a fundamental principle of the Community legal order'.[257] That principle led the Court to rule that the Commission could not compel an undertaking 'to provide it with answers which might involve an admission on its part of the existence of an infringement [of the Treaty competition rules] which it is incumbent upon the Commission to prove'.[258] There may admittedly be room for argument over whether the rights of the defence under EC law have precisely the same scope as the right not to incriminate oneself under Article 6 of the Convention, but any discrepancy is likely to be marginal. What is important to emphasize in the present context is that, notwithstanding the importance of enforcing the Treaty competition rules, the Court was willing, in *Orkem* as in *Hoechst*, to impose a limitation on the Commission's investigatory powers which was not expressly spelled out in Regulation 17.

These cases illustrate well the willingness of the Court to temper the effect of a Community act in the light of what might be called due process considerations, even though the importance of the act and of the policy it is designed to achieve is not in doubt. It would be misleading, however, to give the impression that the Court has only acted creatively in order to limit the Commission's powers under Regulation 17. In *Camera Care v Commission*,[259] the Court held that, although

---

[253] Para 34.

[254] See Duffy, op cit, para 7; Van Overbeek, 'The right to remain silent in competition investigations: the *Funke* decision of the Court of Human Rights makes revision of the ECJ's case law necessary' [1994] 15 ECLR 127.

[255] [1993] 1 CMLR 897. See also *Murray v United Kingdom* (1996) 22 EHRR 29; *Saunders v United Kingdom* (1997) 23 EHRR 313; Kerse, pp 151–3.

[256] 'In the determination of his civil rights and obligations or of any criminal charge against him, everyone is entitled to a fair and public hearing within a reasonable time by an independent and impartial tribunal established by law . . .'

[257] Para 32.

[258] Para 35. For the position in proceedings before the national courts between private parties in which a breach of Arts 81 or 82 is alleged, see Case C–60/92 *Otto v Postbank* [1993] ECR I–5683.

[259] Case 792/79 R [1980] ECR 119.

Regulation 17 was silent on the matter, the Commission had the power in urgent cases to adopt interim measures where necessary to ensure the effectiveness of any subsequent decision finding that the Treaty competition rules had been infringed.[260] The Commission has become reluctant to exercise this potentially significant power[261] because it is time-consuming and inconsistent with its present policy of encouraging undertakings to pursue their remedies in the national courts.[262] Be that as it may, the *Camera Care* case is a good example of the Court's willingness to interpret the powers of the Community institutions more expansively where this seems necessary to ensure that the policy underlying the Treaty is not frustrated.

It is appropriate to end this section with a brief discussion of the *BASF* case[263] which, although it did not actually concern Regulation 17, provides a good example of the range of responses liable to be provoked by a failure by the Commission to comply with procedural requirements in competition cases. In that case the applicants, who were based in several Member States, sought the annulment before the CFI of a Commission decision finding that they had infringed Article 81 (ex 85) of the Treaty and imposing fines on them. It was established during the course of the proceedings that a number of requirements applicable generally to the adoption of Commission acts had not been strictly followed. The CFI found, for example, that the decision adopted in one language version did not correspond with that adopted in other language versions or with that which was notified and published; the versions notified and published in some languages contained a paragraph which did not appear in the draft adopted by the College of Commissioners; some language versions had been adopted by the Commissioner responsible for competition when they should have been adopted by the College of Commissioners; although the Commissioner concerned had the power to sign copies of the decision adopted by the College for the purposes of notification, his signature had been affixed to the measures after his mandate had expired. The CFI concluded as a result of these defects that it could not determine with sufficient certainty the precise date on which the contested measure was capable of producing legal effects, the precise terms of the statement of reasons which it was required by the Treaty to contain, the extent of the obligations it imposed on its addressees, the identity of those addressees or that of the authority which issued the definitive version. The CFI ruled that, for these and other reasons, the contested measure was 'vitiated by particularly serious and manifest defects'[264] and that it was to be considered non-existent.

---

[260] For an indication of the limits to this power, see Joined Cases 228 and 229/82 *Ford v Commission* [1984] ECR 1129.

[261] See eg Case T–44/90 *La Cinq v Commission* [1992] ECR II–1.

[262] Discussed above. The Commission's notice on cooperation with national courts, *supra*, states that 'national courts can usually adopt interim measures and order the ending of infringements more quickly than the Commission is able to do' (point 16).

[263] Case C–137/92 P *Commission v BASF and Others* [1994] ECR I–2555.

[264] Joined Cases T–79/89, T–84/89, T–85/89, T–86/89, T–89/89, T–91/89, T–92/89, T–94/89, T–96/89, T–98/89, T–102/89 and T–104/89 *BASF and Others v Commission* [1992] ECR II–315, para 96.

This was a potentially devastating conclusion because measures which are legally non-existent can be challenged outside the normal time limits applicable to actions for annulment. If, as seemed possible, there were other decisions suffering from similar defects, the decision of the CFI might have rendered them vulnerable to challenge even if adopted many years previously. The Commission therefore brought an appeal before the Court of Justice. In a characteristically painstaking and closely argued Opinion, Advocate General van Gerven found that none of the defects from which the contested measure was alleged to suffer were enough even to render the decision void and he recommended that the Court should set aside the decision of the CFI. The Court itself found that 'the irregularities of competence and form found by the Court of First Instance, which related to the procedure for the adoption of the Commission's decision, do not appear of such obvious gravity that the decision must be treated as legally non-existent'.[265] Because of its gravity, such findings were reserved 'for quite extreme situations'.[266] However, since essential procedural requirements had been infringed, the decision would be declared void.

The significance of the case in the present context lies in what it reveals about the Court's attitude to the Commission in the field of competition law. Readers will have their own views about which of the three possible outcomes was preferable. The doctrine of non-existence is so ill-defined—indeed, the Court in *BASF* did not attempt to define it in anything other than the most subjective terms—that none can be regarded as untenable. The case therefore turned on the extent to which those sitting in judgment were willing to impose strict procedural requirements on the Commission and the practical consequences of breaching them. The solution preferred by the Court was typical of the balance the Court has sought to strike between the need to protect the rights of undertakings and at the same time not to make the Commission's task of applying the Treaty competition rules excessively onerous.

Merger control

Although the Court's decision in *Continental Can* confirmed that the acquisition of a competitor might in some circumstances constitute an abuse of a dominant position, Article 82 (ex 86) suffered from several drawbacks as a means of regulating mergers and takeovers ('concentrations' in Community parlance). First, Article 82 applies only where there is a pre-existing dominant position to be abused. The creation of a dominant position as a result of a merger between two undertakings which did not previously occupy one would therefore fall outside the scope of the article. Secondly, there is no mechanism under Article 82 for the prior authorization of a merger. The Commission's decision in *Continental Can* required the

[265] Para 52.   [266] Para 50.

addressee to submit proposals to it as to how the alleged infringement of Article 82 could be terminated, but mergers are hard to unravel once they have taken place. Thirdly, the Court in *Continental Can* seemed to envisage that a merger must have a particularly drastic effect on competition before it would qualify as an abuse.[267] The Commission therefore made relatively little use of Article 82 as a means of regulating mergers.[268]

Could Article 81 (ex 85) be used to overcome these drawbacks? When *Continental Can* was decided, it was widely believed that Article 81 did not apply to mergers. Some years previously, the Commission had come to the conclusion that 'it is not possible to apply Article 85 to agreements whose purpose is the acquisition of total or partial ownership of enterprises or the reorganisation of the ownership of enterprises (merger, acquisition of holdings, purchase of part of the assets)'.[269] The Commission gave a number of reasons for that conclusion. Concentrations sometimes brought about desirable changes in industrial structure, it claimed,[270] but the exemption criteria set out in Article 81(3) were inappropriate in this context. Furthermore, the sanction of nullity under Article 81(2) was less suitable than deconcentration.[271] Article 81 could not in any event apply to concentrations taking place other than by agreement, for example through Stock Exchange transactions.

The *Continental Can* case reflected a change in the Commission's perception of the potential dangers posed by mergers. Although doubtless pleased to have confirmation from the Court that Article 82 (ex 86) had a role to play in regulating them, the decision had served to clarify its limits. Shortly after the Court's decision, the Commission therefore submitted to the Council a proposal for a regulation specifically designed to deal with the problems posed by mergers.[272] For many years little progress was made. Then in 1987 a judgment of the Court undermined the view set out by the Commission in its 1966 memorandum that Article 81 (ex 85) did not apply to mergers. In *BAT and Reynolds v Commission*,[273] it was held that Article 81 was applicable to the acquisition by one company of an equity interest in a competitor where the acquisition served 'as an instrument for influencing the commercial conduct of the companies in question so as to restrict or distort

---

[267] See the last sentence of para 26 of the judgment, quoted above; Wyatt and Dashwood, *The Substantive Law of the EEC* (2nd edn, 1987), p 428 (the point is not made in the third edition).

[268] See further Downes and Ellison, *The Legal Control of Mergers in the European Communities* (1991), pp 12–13; Cook and Kerse, *EC Merger Control* (2nd edn, 1996), pp 2–3.

[269] Memorandum on the problem of concentration in the common market (Competition Series, Study No 3, Brussels, 1966).

[270] According to Jones and González-Díaz, '[i]n the late 1950s and early 1960s it was generally considered that one of the main European industrial policy objectives was to encourage industry to concentrate to enable it to attain the economies of scale necessary to compete effectively with the very large US corporations': *The EEC Merger Regulation* (1992), p 83. For a typically sceptical view of the extent to which competition law should seek to regulate mergers, see Bork, op cit, chs 9–12. He takes the view that 'the only mergers properly limited by law are very large horizontal mergers': p 199.

[271] Cf Art 66(5) ECSC, second para.   [272] OJ 1973 C92/1.

[273] Joined Cases 142 and 156/84 [1987] ECR 4487.

competition on the market on which they carry on business'.[274] The Court said that this would be the case in particular 'where, by the acquisition of a shareholding or through subsidiary clauses in the agreement, the investing company obtains legal or *de facto* control of the commercial conduct of the other company or where the agreement provides for commercial cooperation between the companies or creates a structure likely to be used for such cooperation'.[275] The criteria laid down by the Court were liable to prove problematic. The questions whether a company had acquired, through the purchase of shares, the ability to influence the conduct of a competitor or the possibility of being able to exercise such an influence in the future would inevitably give rise to controversy. Moreover, the Court emphasized the need to take account not only of the immediate effects of the agreement but also of its potential effects and to assess it in the light of the overall economic context.

If, by making it clear that Article 81 was capable of applying to some types of merger but creating doubt about precisely when this would be so, the Court intended to prompt the Council into action, it was successful. The resulting uncertainty was skilfully exploited by the Commission[276] which in 1989 succeeded in persuading the Council to adopt Regulation 4064/89 on the control of concentrations between undertakings.[277] Under that regulation, the Commission in principle has exclusive jurisdiction over concentrations with a Community dimension, that is, where certain thresholds defined in terms of the turnover of the undertakings concerned are met.[278] By virtue of Article 2(3) of the regulation, '[a] concentration which creates or strengthens a dominant position as a result of which effective competition would be significantly impeded in the common market shall be declared incompatible with the common market'. Proposed concentrations have to be notified to the Commission and must not be put into effect until cleared. Because time is usually of the essence, the regulation lays down a streamlined procedure which the Commission must follow in making its appraisal. It has a wide range of powers it can invoke to enforce the obligations which the regulation imposes on undertakings.

Although there is a rapidly developing body of Commission decisions on the scope of Regulation 4064/89, the influence of the Court on the way in which it is applied has so far been limited. An important reason for this is that the parties to a

---

[274] Para 37.   [275] Para 38.

[276] See Cook and Kerse, op cit, p 4; Venit, 'The "Merger" Control Regulation: Europe comes of age . . . or Caliban's dinner' (1990) 27 CMLRev 7, 13; Dehousse, *The European Court of Justice* (1998), pp 82–4. The absence of a proper Community framework for the regulation of cross-border mergers had become increasingly anachronistic in the light of the impending completion of the internal market. See Gerber, p 369, who comments on the 'rapid economic restructuring' caused by the single market programme.

[277] OJ 1989 L395/1, OJ 1990 L257/14 (corrigendum). Reg 4064/89 was subsequently amended by Reg 1310/97, OJ 1997 L180/1. A consolidated text of the regulation was published at [1997] 5 CMLR 387.

[278] Art 1. Concentrations which do not have a Community dimension fall in principle within the jurisdiction of the Member States.

merger are unlikely to challenge a Commission decision blocking it or imposing unacceptable conditions because the delay involved makes such a course of action commercially unrealistic. In evidence submitted to the House of Lords Select Committee on the European Communities, an experienced practitioner said that judicial review of Commission decisions in the field of merger control was 'in danger of becoming theoretical because, by the time when the CFI will have decided an application for the annulment of a Commission decision, the damage will to a material extent already have been done (if a merger has been permitted when it should not have been permitted) or it will not be possible to resurrect the deal (if a merger has been prohibited when it should have been permitted)'.[279] Rather than mount a challenge to a Commission decision, the parties to a proposed merger are more likely to abandon it or accept the least onerous conditions the Commission is prepared to countenance as the price to be paid for clearance. Third parties do not suffer from the same inhibitions, but may have difficulty in overcoming the standing requirements of Article 230 (ex 173).[280] This situation poses a potential threat to the rule of law, for it means that the activities of the Commission in the field of merger control are to a large extent immune from review. The problem is in practice mitigated by the small number of proposed mergers which the Commission has so far blocked, although clearance is sometimes only conditional. The workload of the Community Courts is now such that a solution to this problem is only likely to be found in the context of a general review of the Union's judicial architecture.[281]

Notwithstanding the preceding remarks, the Community Courts have on occasion been called upon to address important questions concerning the scope of Regulation 4064/89. One of the most significant judgments to date was *France and Others v Commission*,[282] where the Court of Justice accepted that the concept of collective dominance developed in the context of Article 82 (ex 86) was applicable in cases dealt with under the regulation. The Commission first applied the concept of collective dominance in the context of merger control in Nestlé/Perrier,[283] where it maintained that Article 2(3) of the regulation was not confined to cases where the dominant position created or strengthened by the concentration was held by a single firm, but that it was also applicable where such a position was held

---

[279] *The Court of First Instance: Single Judge* (Session 1997–98, 25th Report), Memorandum by K P E Lasok QC, para 11.

[280] See eg Case C–480/93 P *Zunis Holding and Others v Commission* [1996] ECR I–1; Case T–96/92 *CCE de la Société Générale des Grandes Sources and Others v Commission* [1995] ECR II–1213; Case T–12/93 *CCE de Vittel and Others v Commission* [1995] ECR II–1247. Cf Case T–3/93 *Air France v Commission* [1994] ECR II–121; Case T–2/93 *Air France v Commission* [1994] ECR II–323. See Brown, 'Judicial review of Commission decisions under the Merger Regulation: the first cases' [1994] ECLR 296; Arnull (1996) 33 CMLRev 319.

[281] See ch 1.

[282] Joined Cases C–68/94 and C–30/95 [1998] ECR I–1375. See Venit, 'Two steps forward and no steps back: economic analysis and oligopolistic dominance after *Kali & Salz*' (1998) 35 CMLRev 1101.

[283] OJ 1992 L356/1. See Winckler and Hansen, 'Collective dominance under the EC Merger Control Regulation' (1993) 30 CMLRev 787.

'by two or more undertakings holding the power to behave together to an appreciable extent independently on the market'.[284] In the *France* case, Advocate General Tesauro took the view that, in the absence of an express indication that Regulation 4064/89 was applicable in cases of collective dominance, to hold that it did so apply would create uncertainty. While accepting that the opposite solution would have certain benefits from an economic point of view, the Advocate General took the view that the proper way to proceed was by amending the regulation.

The Court was more adventurous. It noted that the wording of Article 2 'does not in itself exclude the possibility of applying the Regulation to cases where concentrations lead to the creation or strengthening of a collective dominant position, that is, a dominant position held by the parties to the concentration together with an entity not a party thereto'.[285] The *travaux préparatoires* concerning the regulation offered no clear guidance on the matter.[286] Since the textual and historical approaches were of no help, the Court resorted to its customary teleological method of interpreting the contested provision 'by reference to its purpose and general structure'.[287] The Court observed that, like Articles 81 (ex 85) and 82 (ex 86), the regulation was intended to contribute to the establishment of the system of undistorted competition envisaged by the Treaty. A concentration which created or strengthened a dominant position on the part of the parties concerned with an undertaking which was not involved in the concentration was, the Court said, liable to prove incompatible with that system. 'Consequently,' it went on, 'if it were accepted that only concentrations creating or strengthening a dominant position on the part of the parties to the concentration were covered by the Regulation, its purpose . . . would be partially frustrated.'[288] Although the regulation did not expressly grant any procedural rights to third parties alleged to hold a collective dominant position with the parties to a concentration, such third parties could rely on the well established general principle that those adversely affected by a decision had the right to be heard in the proceedings which led to its adoption. The Court concluded that collective dominant positions fell within the scope of the regulation. However, as in 'Italian Flat Glass',[289] the Court went on to hold (this time in accordance with the advice of Advocate General Tesauro) that the Commission had failed to establish a collective dominant position on the facts.

The Court's decision in *France and Others v Commission* renders subject to appraisal under the regulation a significantly wider category of mergers than a strict reading of its provisions would suggest.[290] It seems unlikely that this result was

---

[284] Para 114.   [285] Para 166.

[286] Para 167. The judgment suggests that, at least in relation to acts of the institutions, *travaux préparatoires* are relevant in attempting to discern the meaning of terms which are unclear. See ch 14.

[287] Para 168.   [288] Para 171.

[289] Discussed above in connection with Art 82.

[290] The Commission succeeded in establishing that a proposed concentration would have led to the creation of a collective dominant position in Case T–102/96 *Gencor v Commission*, [1999] 4 CMLR 971.

intended by the Council, for otherwise it would surely have conferred on third
parties an express right to intervene in the proceedings before the Commission.
The use of a general principle initially designed to protect the rights of those
affected by the exercise by Community institutions of their powers as a justification for extending those powers is unconvincing.[291] Moreover, although the Court
said that its conclusion was not incompatible with Article 2 of the regulation, that
provision, unlike Article 82 (ex 86) of the Treaty with its reference to an abuse by
more than one undertaking, does not contain any suggestion that it applies in cases
of collective dominance. More fundamentally, the Court's decision is subject to the
same objections as those levelled against the case law on collective dominance
under Article 82.[292] Be that as it may, the case provides an example, over twenty-
five years after the judgment in *Continental Can*, of the Court's continued willingness to interpret creatively the terms of substantive provisions and its determination
to uphold the system of undistorted competition on which the Treaty is based.

State aid

The Treaty rules on aids granted by States,[293] Articles 87 (ex 92) to 89 (ex 94), are
contained in the same chapter[294] as Articles 81 (ex 85) and 82 (ex 86). The basic
rule is set out in Article 87(1), which provides: 'Save as otherwise provided in this
Treaty, any aid granted by a Member State or through State resources in any form
whatsoever which distorts or threatens to distort competition by favouring certain
undertakings or the production of certain goods shall, in so far as it affects trade
between Member States, be incompatible with the common market.' The Court
has taken a fairly broad view of the concept of aid, regarding it as encompassing not
only subsidies but also other forms of State intervention which mitigate the charges
which firms would normally have to bear. The basic test is 'whether the recipient
undertaking receives an economic advantage which it would not have received
under normal market conditions'.[295] However, the prohibition set out in Article
87(1) of the Treaty is 'neither absolute nor unconditional'.[296] Article 87(2) sets out
three categories of aid which are to be regarded as compatible with the common
market, while Article 87(3) sets out five further categories which may be so
regarded.

The main responsibility for policing the application of these provisions belongs
to the Commission by virtue of Article 88 (ex 93), although the national courts of

---

[291] Cf the CFI's discussion of this question in *Gencor, supra*, paras 141–7.

[292] In *Gencor, supra*, para 276, the CFI held that 'the relationship of interdependence existing
between the parties to a tight oligopoly' was sufficient to support a finding that they held a collective
dominant position. It is not entirely clear whether the same is true of Art 82 or whether in that context
the existence of structural links has to be shown. See Whish, p 489.

[293] See generally Evans, *European Community Law of State Aid* (1997).

[294] Title VI (ex V), ch I.   [295] Case C–39/94 *SFEI and Others* [1996] ECR I–3547, para 60.

[296] *SFEI, supra*, para 36.

the Member States also have an important role to play.[297] The authors of the Treaty envisaged that the Council too would become involved in the application of Article 87 (ex 92). In particular, Article 89 (ex 94) provides that the Council may 'make any appropriate regulations for the application of Articles 87 and 88 and may in particular determine the conditions in which Article 88(3) shall apply and the categories of aid exempted from this procedure'.[298] Although the Commission proposed the adoption of implementing rules under Article 89 in the 1960s, no action was taken by the Council.[299] As a result, there was for many years no equivalent of Regulation 17 in the State aid context and the enforcement of Article 87 took place largely on the basis of the procedural rules set out in Article 88. This is more detailed than the transitional provisions in the Treaty on the application of Articles 81 and 82, but it does not provide for all eventualities and the Court was called upon to exercise a certain amount of ingenuity in developing an appropriate procedural framework. In 1998 the Commission put forward a new proposal for a Council regulation laying down detailed rules for the application of Article 88[300] and in March 1999 the Council finally adopted a regulation on the matter based on the practice of the Commission and the case law of the Court.[301] That case law remains of particular interest in the present context, however, because it illustrates vividly the extent to which the Court has been willing to compensate for the inactivity of the legislator. We shall see that it was by no means neglectful of the concerns of the Member States.

Article 88(1) (ex 93(1)) requires the Commission to 'keep under constant review all systems of aid' existing in the Member States. If it finds that such aid is not compatible with the common market, Article 88(2) provides that it must require the State concerned to abolish or alter the contested aid within a deadline set by the Commission. If the State concerned does not comply, the Commission or any other interested State may bring the matter directly[302] before the Court. Plans to grant new aid or to alter existing aid are subject to a two-stage procedure laid down in Article 88(3). During the first stage, Member States are required to inform the Commission of such plans in sufficient time to enable it to submit its comments. If the Commission considers that the plan is not compatible with the common market, it is required to move to the second stage by initiating the procedure laid down in Article 88(2). In other words, it must require the plan to be abandoned or modified. The final sentence of Article 88(3) reads: 'The Member State concerned shall

---

[297] In *SFEI*, the Court described the roles of the national courts and the Commission as 'complementary and separate': para 41. The Commission has issued a notice on co-operation between it and the national courts in the State aid field: see OJ 1995 C312/7.

[298] See also the third and fourth subparas of Art 88(2), which enable the Council in exceptional circumstances to declare aid compatible with the common market notwithstanding Art 87 or any regulations adopted under Art 89.

[299] See Evans, op cit, pp 406–7.   [300] See COM(1998)73 final; OJ 1998 C116/13.

[301] See Reg 659/1999, OJ 1999 L83/1.

[302] ie without going through the more lengthy procedure laid down in Arts 226 (ex 169) and 227 (ex 170).

not put its proposed measures into effect until this procedure has resulted in a final decision.' There are several issues which Article 88 leaves unresolved. Given the urgent nature of some State aid cases,[303] how quickly must the Commission decide whether to move to the second stage of the procedure under Article 88(3)? To what extent, if any, does it have to give the State concerned an opportunity to be heard? What if a Member State fails to notify the Commission of plans to grant or alter aid? If a State does notify, what consequences ensue from a failure on its part to respect the last sentence of Article 88(3)? What role, if any, do the national courts have to play?

The effects of delay on the part of the Commission in completing the first stage of the procedure laid down in Article 88(3) (ex 93(3)) were considered in the *Lorenz* case.[304] The Court said that the Commission had to 'define its attitude within a reasonable period'[305] which, by analogy with Article 230 (ex 173) and 232 (ex 175), it set at two months. If the Commission failed to initiate the second stage of the procedure by the end of that period, the Member State could implement the plan provided it gave prior notice to the Commission. However, it did not follow from the Commission's failure to proceed to the second stage within the deadline fixed by the Court that the aid was compatible with the common market and it was from then on to be treated as an existing aid, subject as such to Article 88(1) and (2).

The Court also held that the general principle of the right to be heard meant that a Member State had to be given the opportunity to make known its views on observations submitted by interested third parties under Article 88(2) on which the Commission proposed to base its decision.[306] Moreover, it was established that the Commission had the power to require Member States to recover from recipients aid which had been granted illegally. Although the Treaty does not expressly give the Commission such a power, the Court said that it was necessary to render 'of practical effect'[307] the obligation of Member States under Article 88(2) to 'abolish or alter' aid found incompatible with the common market.[308]

The Court was asked in *Lorenz* whether the national courts had jurisdiction to apply the last sentence of Article 88(3) (ex 93(3)). It had ruled in *Costa v ENEL*[309] that Article 88 did not create individual rights, but it had made an exception for the last sentence of the third paragraph. The Court accordingly reiterated in *Lorenz* that that sentence had direct effect and explained that the right of individuals to rely on

---

[303] See Case 120/73 *Lorenz v Germany* [1973] ECR 1471, para 4.   [304] *Supra.*
[305] p 1481.
[306] See eg Case 234/84 *Belgium v Commission* [1986] ECR 2263; Case 259/85 *France v Commission* [1987] ECR 4393. Breach of the State's right to be heard would only lead to the annulment of the Commission's decision if it was established that the outcome of the procedure might otherwise have been different.
[307] Case 70/72 *Commission v Germany* [1973] ECR 813, para 13. See also Case 310/85 *Deufil v Commission* [1987] ECR 901, para 24.
[308] See now Art 14 of Reg 659/1999.
[309] Case 6/64 [1964] ECR 585, 596. See also Case 78/76 *Steinlike und Weinlig v Germany* [1977] ECR 595, para 14.

it before the national courts covered any aid which had been implemented without being notified 'and, in the event of notification, operates during the preliminary period, and where the Commission sets in motion the contentious procedure, up to the final decision'.[310]

It will be observed that Article 88 (ex 93) is based on an assumption of good faith on the part of the Member States. It therefore makes no provision for aid which is introduced without being notified to the Commission beforehand. The Court held in *Italy v Commission*[311] that the procedure laid down in Article 88(2) applied in such circumstances. Referring to the spirit and general scheme of Article 88, however, the Court said that the Commission was entitled to require new aid which had not been notified to it and which it considered incompatible with the common market to be abolished or altered forthwith, that is, without fixing the deadline which Article 88(2) envisaged in the case of existing aid and new aid which had been duly notified. The contrary interpretation, the Court said, 'would have the effect of depriving the provisions of Article 93(3) [now 88(3)] of their binding force and even that of encouraging their non-observance'.[312]

These decisions all involved some departure from the text of Article 88. Some were designed to ensure the effectiveness of the Treaty regime, some to protect the interests of the Member States. Most of the issues the Court was called upon to address in these cases might have been foreseen and dealt with by Council regulation.[313] Later cases raised more complex issues and the Court became increasingly creative in finding solutions.

In the 'Boussac' case,[314] the Court was asked to consider what consequences the Commission was entitled to draw from a breach by a Member State of the last sentence of Article 88(3) (ex 93(3)). The case arose out of financial assistance granted by the French authorities to a company called Boussac Saint Frères. The Commission was not notified in advance of the French authorities' plans to grant the aid. It therefore adopted a decision stating that the aid was unlawful because it had been granted in breach of Article 88(3), but that it could not in any event be considered compatible with the common market under Article 88(2). The French Government was required to recover part of the aid which had been granted. France brought proceedings for the annulment of the Commission's decision.

The most controversial aspect of the case was the Commission's claim that a finding of illegality under Article 88(2) could be based on a breach of Article 88(3) without considering the compatibility of the disputed aid with the common market. Advocate General Jacobs acknowledged that the Treaty did not expressly give the Commission a power to declare aid unlawful on that ground, but he took the view that the principle of effectiveness, which the Court had often relied on in interpreting the Treaty provisions on aid, pointed to the existence of such a power:

---

[310] Para 8.   [311] Case 173/73 [1974] ECR 709.
[312] Para 8.   [313] See now Reg 659/1999, *supra*.
[314] Case C–301/87 *France v Commission* [1990] ECR I–307. See also Case C–142/87 *Belgium v Commission* ('Tubemeuse') [1990] ECR I–959.

At the hearing, the Commission's agent stressed the difficulties created by the repeated failure of certain Member States to comply with their obligations under Article 93(3) [now 88(3)] of the Treaty. It is self-evident that the Commission is hindered from exercising in such cases the powers which the Treaty confers upon it under Article 93(2) [now 88(2)]. From the very fact that Member States are required by the Treaty not to implement proposed aid until it has been cleared by the Commission, it can in my view properly be inferred that where a Member State acts illegally, the Commission must be regarded as vested with the broadest powers.[315]

Although in the circumstances of the case it did not appear necessary to decide the point, Advocate General Jacobs also took the view that the Commission had the power to order recovery of aid on the basis of a breach of Article 88(3) alone. As to the compatibility of such aid with the common market, the Advocate General considered that the Commission was entitled to go on to examine that question where it considered it appropriate, but that it was not required to do so.

The Court evidently felt uneasy about the solution proposed by its Advocate General. It observed that the position of both the parties to the case could give rise to 'major practical difficulties'[316]: the Commission's, because it would lead to aid which was as a matter of substance compatible with the common market being declared unlawful on procedural grounds; the French Government's, because it would deprive Article 88(3) of any effect. The system laid down by the Treaty was designed to ensure that aid could not be introduced until the Commission had had an opportunity to assess its compatibility with the common market. Thus, once it had established that aid had been granted or altered without notification, the Commission had the power, after hearing the Member State concerned, to issue an interim decision[317] requiring it to suspend forthwith the payment of the aid pending an examination of its compatibility with the common market by the Commission. The State could also be required to provide the Commission with the information it needed to carry out the examination. These powers extended to cases where aid had been notified but then put into effect before it had been cleared by the Commission, contrary to the last sentence of Article 88(3). Where a Member State complied with the Commission's order, the Commission was required to examine the compatibility of the aid with the common market. If the Member State failed to provide the information requested, the Commission was entitled to rule on the compatibility of the aid with the common market on the basis of the information available to it. In appropriate cases it could order the recovery of any aid which had already been paid. If the State concerned failed to suspend payment of the aid pending the outcome of the Commission's examination, the Commission was entitled, while proceeding with that examination, to apply directly to the Court for a declaration that the payment constituted an infringement of the Treaty.

---

[315] p I–340.   [316] Para 11.

[317] Cf Case 70/72 *Commission v Germany* [1973] ECR 813, para 20; in the context of Reg 17, *Camera Care, supra*.

The Court's judgment in the 'Boussac' case has been summarized in some detail because it offers a striking combination of judicial pusillanimity and activism. Advocate General Jacobs had put forward a convincing case for regarding aid introduced in breach of Article 88(3) (ex 93(3)) as *ipso facto* unlawful. The reason given by the Court for rejecting that view is unconvincing, for the Treaty does not *require* aid to be granted but merely *permits* it to be granted where certain conditions are met. It requires very little stretching of the language of Article 88 to regard the legality of aid as dependent on compliance with not only the substantive but also the procedural requirements laid down in the Treaty, particularly in view of the widespread failure by Member States to comply with the Treaty regime. In any event, the remedy for the 'practical difficulty' which the Court perceived in this solution would always lie with the State concerned, which would merely have to notify to the Commission plans to grant or alter aid.

The Court's very pusillanimity on this issue led it to devise an extraordinary piece of judicial legislation in order to prevent Article 88(3) (ex 93(3)) from becoming a dead letter. The extent of the Court's activism becomes clear if we ask what was the legal basis for the Commission's power to go to the Court where a Member State failed to comply with an order to suspend payment of a non-notified new aid.[318] The most obvious basis was Article 88(2), yet it is apparent that that provision can only be used where a State fails to comply with a Commission decision taken at the end of its examination finding that the aid in question is not compatible with the common market. Indeed, the Court's judgment in 'Boussac' suggested that the power which the Court said the Commission enjoyed was not based on Article 88(2). The Court declared that referral to it:

is justified in respect of urgency because there has been a decision embodying an order, taken after the Member State in question has been given an opportunity to submit its comments and thus at the conclusion of a preliminary procedure in which it has been enabled to put its case, *as in the case of the means of redress provided under the second subparagraph of Article 93(2) [now 88(2)] of the Treaty*. This means of redress is in fact no more than a variant of the action for a declaration of failure to fulfil Treaty obligations, specifically adapted to the special problems which State aid poses for competition within the common market.[319]

Thus, the Court seemed to create a special procedure which had not previously been known to exist under which the Commission could bring a Member State directly before the Court. There are other contexts in which the Court has devised remedies for which the Treaties made no express provision,[320] but those remedies were designed to avoid the consequences of a certain lack of foresight on the part of the Treaties' authors. Here the remedy was necessary to mitigate the consequences of the Court's failure to give full effect to Article 88(3). That such a

---

[318] See now Art 12 of Reg 659/1999.   [319] Para 23, emphasis added.
[320] See eg Case C–70/88 *Parliament v Council* ('Chernobyl') [1990] ECR I–2041; Case C–2/88 Imm *Zwartveld and Others* [1990] ECR I–3365; Arnull, 'Does the Court of Justice have inherent jurisdiction?' (1990) 27 CMLRev 683.

remedy had to be devised might have given the Court cause to reflect on whether it had reached the right conclusion as to the results of failing to comply with that provision.

Any fears that the 'Boussac' case heralded a general relaxation in the constraints imposed by the State aid rules on Member States' freedom of action were soon dispelled. In *FNCE*,[321] the French Government argued that the effect of 'Boussac' was to qualify the case law on the direct effect of Article 88(3) (ex 93(3)) and that national courts therefore had no jurisdiction to declare aid unlawful solely on the basis that that provision had been breached. The Court held that the 'Boussac' ruling had no effect on the obligations of national courts, whose role was to protect the rights of individuals pending a ruling by the Commission on the compatibility of an aid with the common market.[322] Even if, by the time the national court came to give judgment, the Commission had found the aid to be lawful, its decision would not have retroactive effect. It would not therefore validate, *ex post facto*, national measures which had been taken in breach of the last sentence of Article 88(3). The Court observed that '[a]ny other interpretation would have the effect of according a favourable outcome to the non-observance by the Member State concerned of the last sentence of Article 93(3) [now 88(3)] and would deprive that provision of its effectiveness'.[323]

The situation was in principle the same where the Commission was seised of the matter but had yet to decide whether the national measures constituted aid when a national court was asked to apply Article 88(3). This was made clear in *SFEI and Others*,[324] where the Court rejected the argument that in these circumstances the national court should decline jurisdiction because of the risk that its decision might conflict with that of the Commission.[325] The Court explained that, where the national court was unclear whether the contested national measures constituted aid, it could seek clarification from the Commission[326] or ask the Court for a preliminary ruling on the interpretation of Article 87 (ex 92). Where some time was likely to elapse before it gave final judgment, the Court reminded the national court that it might also like to consider whether to grant interim relief to safeguard the interests of the parties in the meantime. However, once it was established that aid had been granted in breach of the last sentence of Article 88(3), the national court had to grant an order requiring the aid to be repaid unless there were exceptional circumstances making repayment inappropriate.[327]

---

[321] Case C–354/90 [1991] ECR I–5505.

[322] On the distinction between the role of the national courts and that of the Commission, see AG Jacobs at pp I–5519–20.

[323] Para 16.   [324] Case C–39/94, *supra*.

[325] A similar danger arises under Arts 81 and 82, as we have seen.

[326] The Court referred (at para 50) to the notice on co-operation between national courts and the Commission in the State aid field, *supra*, in which the Commission encouraged national courts to get in touch with it if they encountered difficulty in applying Art 88(3) and explained the type of information it was able to supply. Cf the corresponding notice on the application of Arts 81 and 82, *supra*.

[327] On what constituted exceptional circumstances for these purposes, see AG Jacobs at pp I–3572–3.

The absence until 1999 of Council legislation under Article 89 (ex 94) to give effect to the rules laid down in Article 88 (ex 93) forced the Court to be highly creative in devising a workable framework for the application of Article 87 (ex 92). Looking at the case law in the round, the Court sought to respect the balance reflected in the very text of Article 87 between avoiding distortions of competition and respecting the concerns of the Member States. However, although the Court repeatedly emphasized the importance of the procedural rules laid down in Article 88, in 'Boussac', one of its most creative decisions, it resorted to a naked piece of judicial legislation in order to avoid what might have been regarded as a natural implication of that provision. That case is a striking example of judicial activism, but it is not generally cited by critics of the interventionist approach sometimes taken by the Court. The mischievous might suggest that the reason for this is that the effect of the decision was to undermine the effectiveness of the Treaty, limit the powers of the Commission, and protect the freedom of action of the Member States. That is an outcome of which some such critics would approve.

13

Equal treatment for men and women

The legal framework

The provisions of the EEC Treaty on social policy and the decision in *Defrenne II*

By comparison with the provisions on freedom of movement and competition, those dealing with social policy in the original text of the EEC Treaty[1] were on the whole fairly anodyne. One reason for this seems to have been a widely held view that better living standards and working conditions would flow automatically from the proper functioning of the common market and that no specific intervention by the Community institutions would be necessary.[2] Of the provisions contained in the title devoted to social policy, however, one stood out. Article 119[3] provided, in its first paragraph, that '[e]ach Member State shall during the first stage ensure and subsequently maintain the application of the principle that men and women should receive equal pay for equal work'. Although originally introduced as the result of a French initiative to prevent competition from being distorted by differing national standards on the matter,[4] the article has been used by the Court of Justice in a bold and creative way to develop a powerful right to equal pay for equal work.

The end of the transitional period on 31 December 1969 led to a reappraisal by the Member States of the need for Community intervention in the field of social policy. That reappraisal seems to have been prompted by two related factors.[5] On the one hand, the optimism of the Treaty's authors that social progress would flow inevitably from the completion of the common market had been somewhat dampened by experience. On the other, concern was mounting that the Community was perceived by ordinary people as unduly preoccupied with commerce and trade. On the eve of the first enlargement and in an attempt to give the Community a 'human face', the Heads of State or Government meeting in Paris in

---

[1] Part Three, Title III (Arts 117–28).

[2] See Nielsen and Szyszczak, *The Social Dimension of the European Union* (3rd edn 1997), p 19; Bercusson, *European Labour Law* (1996), p 48; Hervey, *European Social Law and Policy* (1998), p 14; Shanks, 'The social policy of the European Communities' (1977) 14 CMLRev 375.

[3] See now Art 141 EC.

[4] Nielsen and Szyszczak, op cit, p 23; Barnard, 'The economic objectives of Article 119' in Hervey and O'Keeffe (eds), *Sex Equality Law in the European Union* (1996), ch 20.

[5] Nielsen and Szyszczak, op cit, p 25.

1972 declared that they attached 'as much importance to vigorous action in the
social field as to the achievement of economic union'. That declaration led to the
adoption by the Council in 1974 of an ambitious Social Action Programme covering the period 1974–6 which had been put forward by the Commission. That
Programme lies at the origin of many of the initiatives subsequently taken by the
Community in the field of social policy.[6]

It was in this context that the Court was called upon to decide the seminal case
of *Defrenne v SABENA*.[7] This was the second case to reach the Court of Justice
brought by the redoubtable air hostess, Ms Defrenne. Her complaint on this occasion was that she was paid less than male cabin stewards doing the same work. The
Court was asked by the Cour du Travail in Brussels to clarify the extent to which
she could rely on Article 119 (now 141) of the Treaty. The Court began, as it had
in *Van Gend en Loos*,[8] by observing that the answer to the question whether Article
119 had direct effect depended on 'the nature of the principle of equal pay, the aim
of this provision and its place in the scheme of the Treaty'.[9] The Court acknowledged that one of the aims of the article was to ensure a level competitive playing
field, but it went on to emphasize another aim:[10]

Secondly, this provision forms part of the social objectives of the Community, which is not
merely an economic union, but is at the same time intended, by common action, to ensure
social progress and seek the constant improvement of the living and working conditions of
their peoples, as is emphasized by the Preamble to the Treaty.

The dual aim of Article 119, economic and social, showed according to the Court
that 'the principle of equal pay forms part of the foundations of the Community'
and explained why the principle was to be implemented by the end of the first stage
of the transitional period. Moreover, since the first provision in the chapter of the
Treaty devoted to social policy, Article 117,[11] spoke of improving working conditions and the standard of living of workers, the Court stated that the equal pay principle could only be satisfied by raising the lower salary, not by reducing the
higher.[12]

The Court recognized, however, that the complete implementation of the equal
pay principle would entail further legislation at both the Community and the
national level. In the absence of such legislation, national courts would not be in a
position to make comparisons across different branches of industry or to analyse the
situation in the economy as a whole. There would therefore be some forms of discrimination in relation to which Article 119 (now 141) would not produce direct
effect. However, in the case of forms of discrimination which could be 'identified
solely with the aid of the criteria based on equal work and equal pay referred to by

---

   [6] See Bercusson, op cit, ch 4; Hervey, op cit, pp 16–19.
   [7] Case 43/75 [1976] ECR 455.
   [8] Case 26/62 *Van Gend en Loos v Nederlandse Administratie der Belastingen* [1963] ECR 1.
   [9] Para 7.   [10] Para 10.   [11] See now Art 136 EC.
   [12] The Court was later to qualify that conclusion: see Case C–200/91 *Coloroll* [1994] ECR I–4389,
discussed below.

the article in question', Article 119 would produce direct effect.[13] Although the article was formally addressed to the Member States, that did not preclude the grant of rights to 'any individual who has an interest in the performance of the duties thus laid down'.[14] Moreover, the prohibition laid down in the article 'applies not only to the action of public authorities, but also extends to all agreements which are intended to regulate paid labour collectively, as well as to contracts between individuals'.[15] In other words, Article 119 was capable of producing both vertical and horizontal direct effect even though this would interfere with the terms of private contracts and collective labour agreements.

The referring court had asked from what date Article 119 (now 141) might produce direct effect. Its text[16] might have appeared to provide the answer to that question, but doubt had arisen because of differing views taken by the Member States and the Commission about the effect of the article. As the Court explained, by the expiry of the deadline laid down in Article 119 the equal pay principle had not been implemented in some Member States. A resolution was therefore adopted purporting to require the elimination of all discrimination by the end of 1964, some three years after the expiry of the deadline laid down in the Treaty. Several Member States failed to observe even that extended deadline and the Commission, after further delay, threatened to bring proceedings under Article 169 (now 226) EC against some Member States. No proceedings were in fact instituted. The Commission did propose that a directive on the application of the equal pay principle be adopted by the Council and that proposal bore fruit when, in February 1975, the Council adopted Directive 75/117.[17] That directive gave Member States one year to take the steps necessary to implement it. This sequence of events had created considerable confusion as to the precise effect of Article 119, but the Court underlined that neither the 1961 resolution nor the 1975 Directive could have the effect of modifying the deadline laid down in the Treaty. The Court therefore ruled that the original Member States should have ensured the full application of Article 119 as from 1 January 1962. As for the Member States which acceded to the Community on 1 January 1973, the absence of any relevant transitional provisions in the Treaty of Accession meant that Article 119 became fully applicable there as from 1 January 1973, when that Treaty entered into force.

---

[13] In the *Defrenne* case, the Court used the terms 'direct and overt discrimination' and 'indirect and disguised discrimination' to distinguish the two. As AG Warner pointed out in Case 69/80 *Worringham and Humphreys v Lloyds Bank* [1981] ECR 767 and Case 96/80 *Jenkins v Kingsgate* [1981] ECR 911, the use of those terms was unfortunate because the distinction between direct and indirect discrimination, though important, had no bearing on whether or not Art 119 (now 141) should be considered directly effective. Thus, in *Worringham* the Court (citing *Defrenne*) spoke instead of Art 119 applying directly 'to all forms of discrimination which may be identified solely with the aid of the criteria of equal work and equal pay referred to by the article in question, without national or Community measures being required to define them with greater precision in order to permit of their application' (para 23).

[14] Para 31.					[15] Para 39. See also *Coloroll, supra*, para 26.

[16] 'Each Member State shall during the first stage ensure and subsequently maintain . . .'

[17] On the approximation of the laws of the Member States relating to the application of the principle of equal pay for men and women, OJ 1975 L45/19.

But the Court had not finished. The Governments of Ireland and the United Kingdom argued that attributing direct effect to Article 119 (now 141) retrospectively would impose an intolerable burden on the economies of the Member States and cause many employers to go out of business because they would not be able to meet claims for arrears of pay. Advocate General Trabucchi doubted the relevance of that argument, 'however pressing on grounds of expediency',[18] and observed: 'the financial consequences should not reach too high a level, having regard to the effects of limitation in the various Member States'.[19] The Court was more receptive. The objectivity of the law and its future application were not in principle to be compromised by the practical consequences of a judicial decision. However, in this instance the conduct of several Member States and of the Commission had created a misleading impression as to the effect of Article 119. In these circumstances, the Court said, 'it is appropriate to determine that, as the general level at which pay would have been fixed cannot be known, important considerations of legal certainty affecting all the interests involved, both public and private, make it impossible in principle to reopen the question as regards the past'. The Court concluded that, except in the case of those who had already brought proceedings or made an equivalent claim, Article 119 could not be invoked in support of claims for pay in respect of periods which preceded the date of the Court's judgment.[20]

The importance of *Defrenne II*

Two aspects of the judgment in *Defrenne II* are particularly worthy of note. The first is the particularly strong view taken by the Court of the importance and effect of Article 119 (now 141). Although forming part of a title of the Treaty which appeared largely programmatic in nature,[21] Article 119 imposed a clear obligation on the Member States and the Court evidently regarded their failure to comply with it as wholly unacceptable. No doubt the Court also saw itself as acting in accordance with the declaration made by the Heads of State and Government in Paris in 1972, to which Advocate General Trabucchi began his Opinion by referring.[22]

The second noteworthy aspect of the judgment is the limitation imposed by the Court on its temporal effect. This was a device which the Court had never before employed and it soon attracted criticism from a distinguished quarter. In a paper presented at a conference held in Luxembourg less than six months after *Defrenne* was decided, Professor C J Hamson of the University of Cambridge argued that the Court had arrogated to itself 'a dispensing power which is I believe not known to

---

[18] p 492.   [19] p 493.   [20] 8 April 1976.
[21] Cf Case 149/77 *Defrenne v SABENA* (*Defrenne III*) [1978] ECR 1365; Case 126/86 *Giménez Zaera v Instituto Nacional de la Seguridad Social y Tesorería General de la Seguridad Social* [1987] ECR 3697; Joined Cases 281, 283 to 285 and 287/85 *Germany, France, Netherlands and United Kingdom v Commission* [1987] ECR 3203; Joined Cases C–72/91 and C–73/91 *Sloman Neptun v Bodo Ziesemer* [1993] ECR I–887.
[22] See [1976] ECR 455, 483.

any modern court of any of the Member States', namely the power to declare what the law is as to the future but to leave the past untouched. That power, he observed, 'is inherently the mark of the legislative function and there is an obstinate belief upon the continent of Europe that a court does not have a legislative function'. In Hamson's view, the Court had been driven to take this position as a result of its unduly enthusiastic development of the doctrine of direct effect, which might otherwise have produced 'chaos'.[23]

Hamson's case is powerfully argued but it is ultimately unconvincing because it seems to be based on a view that courts do not have a law-making function.[24] That view was abandoned long ago in the common law world and has always been hard to apply to the Court of Justice.[25] The doctrines of direct effect and primacy are implicit in the Treaty because without them the common market could not have functioned properly.[26] Indeed, although Hamson thought there were important differences between *Van Gend en Loos* and *Defrenne II*, he shrank from attacking the former as wrongly decided.[27] A useful precedent for limiting the retrospective effect of judicial decisions existed in the practice of the United States Supreme Court.[28] Hamson acknowledged this, but seemed to regard the practice as incompatible with European notions of the proper province of the courts. He was unwilling to concede the special nature of the Community and of the task the Court was called upon to perform.

A renewed attack on the limitation of the temporal effect of the ruling in *Defrenne II* came from Sir Patrick Neill in his paper on judicial activism. He argued that the effect of the judgment 'was to take away (confiscate is not too strong a word) the Article 119 [now 141] rights to which innumerable employees throughout the Community were and had for a long time been entitled'. The Irish and United Kingdom Governments were 'interested parties being themselves large employers of labour', yet no representations were heard on behalf of the employees whose rights would be prejudiced. Those who had been waiting for the Court to give judgment before bringing proceedings were denied the right to claim equal pay in respect of the past.

---

[23] Hamson, 'Methods of interpretation—a critical assessment of the results' in *Reports of a Judicial and Academic Conference* (Luxembourg, 1976), p II-15.

[24] See Keeling, 'In praise of judicial activism. But what does it mean? And has the European Court of Justice ever practised it?' in Curti Gialdino (ed), *Scritti in Onore di G Federico Mancini* (1998), p 505 at p 534: 'What matters is that the Court, like any law-maker, must perform that function responsibly and with due regard for the consequences of its actions on those who are likely to be affected by its rulings.'

[25] See the discussion of precedent in ch 15; Barav, 'Omnipotent courts' in Curtin and Heukels, *Institutional Dynamics of European Integration* (Vol II) (1994), p 265.

[26] See ch 3.   [27] See p II-25.

[28] See Dashwood, 'The principle of direct effect in European Community law' (1978) 16 JCMS 229, 237–8; Lord Lester, Minutes of Evidence taken before the Select Committee of the House of Lords on the European Communities in connection with its enquiry into the 1996 IGC (Session 1994–95, 18th Report). The practice of the US Supreme Court is discussed by Wyatt, 'Prospective effect of a holding of direct applicability' (1976) 1 ELRev 399. Cf van Gerven, 'Contribution de l'arrêt *Defrenne* au développement du droit communautaire' (1977) 13 CDE 131.

At this point it is helpful to emphasize a distinction. The questions whether the Court should in principle have the power to limit the temporal effect of its rulings and whether it should in any particular case exercise that power are separate and an affirmative answer to the first does not imply an affirmative answer to the second. Sir Patrick seemed to accept that there were cases when limitation of the temporal effect of a ruling would be appropriate, for he criticized the failure of the Court to follow the advice of Advocate General Mischo that it should do so in the *Francovich* case, where the principle of State liability was laid down.[29] If Sir Patrick was arguing that the device should not have been employed in *Defrenne II*, then the force of his argument must be conceded.[30] The Court does not seem to have examined very closely whether the fears of the Irish and United Kingdom Governments were justified. The potential exposure of employers in those States, where Article 119 (now 141) would in any event have been directly effective only from 1 January 1973, was much more limited than that of employers in the original six, but no objection on these grounds seems to have been taken by the Governments of States in the latter group. As Advocate General Trabucchi pointed out, all claims would in any event have been subject to national rules on limitation. As for the difficulty of establishing the general level at which pay would have been fixed had the requirements of Article 119 been respected, it is hard to see why this was regarded as relevant. The difficulty would have to be confronted in the case of Ms Defrenne and anyone else who had already brought proceedings. In any event, surely the claimant would merely be entitled (subject to the operation of national limitation periods) to the difference between what she was in fact paid and what she would have been paid had she been a man. Indeed, this was later conceded by the Court which ruled in a series of cases that, where Article 119 had not been respected, those who had been disadvantaged were entitled to the benefit of the regime applicable to their comparators since that regime constituted 'the only valid point of reference'.[31]

In more general terms, however, the device of limiting the temporal effect of a judgment might fairly be described as a stroke of genius, permitting the Court to consolidate the direct effect of sufficiently clear provisions of the Treaty while at the same time satisfying the requirements of legal certainty.[32] Other examples of the application of the device are to be found elsewhere in this book and later in this chapter. The Court has resorted to it only exceptionally and made it clear that it will only do so in the ruling which first establishes the point at issue and not in later

[29] See ch 5.

[30] See Arnull, *The General Principles of EEC Law and the Individual* (1990), p 227.

[31] Case C–33/89 *Kowalska* [1990] ECR I–2591, para 20. See also Case C–184/89 *Nimz* [1991] ECR I–297, para 21. This approach originated in cases concerned with the failure of Member States to implement on time Dir 79/7 on the progressive implementation of the principle of equal treatment for men and women in matters of social security, OJ 1979 L6/24: see eg Case 71/85 *Netherlands v Federatie Nederlandse Vakbeweging* [1986] ECR 3855, para 23; Case 286/85 *McDermott and Cotter v Minister for Social Welfare and Attorney-General* [1987] ECR 1453, para 19. Cf *Coloroll*, supra, discussed below.

[32] Cf the House of Lords Select Committee on the European Communities, *1996 Inter-Governmental Conference* (Session 1994–95, 21st Report), para 267.

cases where the same point is raised.[33] Indeed, there is a certain irony in the criticisms which the device has attracted. Its effect is of course to limit the scope of the rights conferred by the Treaty and therefore the extent to which national law is affected, yet many of those who have been most vociferous in attacking the device have at the same time tended to see the Court as too keen to extend the reach of Community law and interfere with the prerogatives of the Member States. Moreover, it will be observed that one of the States which was responsible in *Defrenne II* for the birth of the device was later to become associated with critics of the Court who cited the case as an example of excessive activism.

Equal pay for work of equal value

The Court's decision in *Defrenne II* was to render much of Directive 75/117 redundant. There was, however, one respect in which the directive appeared to go further than Article 119. According to Article 1, the principle of equal pay required, 'for the same work *or for work to which equal value is attributed*, the elimination of all discrimination on grounds of sex . . .'.[34] In its original form, Article 119 did not expressly refer to equal pay for work of equal value.[35] However, it soon became clear that the discrepancy was only apparent. In *Jenkins v Kingsgate*,[36] the Court observed that 'Article 1 of Council Directive 75/117/EEC which is principally designed to facilitate the practical application of the principle of equal pay outlined in Article 119 of the Treaty in no way alters the content or scope of that principle as defined in the Treaty.' In *Murphy v Bord Telecom Eireann*,[37] the Court was asked whether a worker could rely on Article 119 to claim equal pay with someone paid more but whose work was of *lower* value. The Court declared:[38]

It is true that Article 119 expressly requires the application of the principle of equal pay for men and women solely in the case of equal work or, according to a consistent line of decisions of the Court, in the case of work of equal value, and not in the case of work of unequal value. Nevertheless, if that principle forbids workers of one sex engaged in work of equal value to that of workers of the opposite sex to be paid a lower wage than the latter on grounds of sex, it *a fortiori* prohibits such a difference in pay where the lower-paid category of workers is engaged in work of higher value.

In the *Murphy* case, the value of the work performed by the claimant and that of the person with whom she was seeking to compare herself had been assessed by an Equality Officer, to whom the claim had been referred under the relevant national legislation. In the absence of intervention by such an agency, national courts might find that they were not in a position to assess equal value claims. In such

---

[33] See Case 61/79 *Amministrazione delle Finanze dello Stato v Denkavit Italiana* [1980] ECR 1205, paras 17–18. See generally Waelbroeck, 'May the Court of Justice limit the retrospective operation of its judgments?' (1981) 1 YEL 115.

[34] Emphasis added.

[35] But see now Art 141 EC.

[36] Case 96/80 [1981] ECR 911, para 22.

[37] Case 157/86 [1988] ECR 673.

[38] Para 9.

circumstances Article 119, although in principle applicable, would not produce direct effect because the conditions laid down in *Defrenne II* will not be satisfied. Here the Court used Directive 75/117 to reinforce Article 119. In *Commission v United Kingdom*,[39] it held that Member States were required to 'endow an authority with the requisite jurisdiction to decide whether work has the same value as other work, after obtaining such information as may be required'. That obligation flowed from Article 6 of the directive, which obliges Member States to take the measures necessary to ensure that the principle of equal pay is applied. Individuals who consider themselves the victims of a breach of that principle are therefore entitled by virtue of the directive to have the value of their work, and that of their comparator, assessed. It remains the case, however, that a claimant whose work is assessed as having marginally less value than that of a better-paid comparator falls outside the scope of the Community rules, even though the difference in pay is out of proportion to the difference in the value of their respective jobs. This weakness has been said to illustrate the limitations of the concept of equality, and its reliance on the so-called male norm, in redressing the chronically depressed level of women's pay.[40] This and related criticisms, and the extent to which they are applicable to the approach of the Court, are considered further below.

The equal treatment directives

The limits of Article 119 (now 141) were underlined in *Defrenne III*,[41] where the Court held that an air hostess could not rely on the article to challenge a provision in her contract of employment terminating it when she reached the age of 40, even though no such provision was inserted in the contracts of male cabin attendants doing the same work. Although, according to the Court, the elimination of sex discrimination formed part of the fundamental rights which it had a duty to protect, there was at the material time no Community rule requiring equal treatment in matters other than pay. By the time the Court gave judgment, however, Directive 76/207 on the implementation of the principle of equal treatment for men and women as regards access to employment, vocational training and promotion and working conditions[42] had been adopted. This measure, sometimes known as the Equal Treatment Directive, laid down a principle of equal treatment for men and women which extended far beyond the issue of pay to a range of other matters connected with employment and it has proved considerably more significant than Directive 75/117 in the development of the Community law of sex discrimination. None the less, the principle it lays down is not an absolute one. By virtue of Article 2(2), Member States are free to exclude from its scope 'those occupational activities and, where appropriate, the training leading thereto, for which, by reason of their nature or the context in which they are carried out, the sex of the worker

---

[39] Case 61/81 [1982] ECR 2601.
[40] See Fredman, 'European Community discrimination law: a critique' (1992) 21 ILJ 119, 124–5.
[41] Case 149/77 *Defrenne v SABENA* [1978] ECR 1365.   [42] OJ 1976 L39/40.

constitutes a determining factor'. According to Article 2(3), the directive is without prejudice to 'provisions concerning the protection of women, particularly as regards pregnancy and maternity'. Article 2(4) provides that the directive is 'without prejudice to measures to promote equal opportunity for men and women, in particular by removing existing inequalities which affect women's opportunities . . .'. As we shall see, the scope and effect of Directive 76/207 have been the subject of several remarkable decisions of the Court.

Article 1(2) of the Equal Treatment Directive envisaged the adoption of further legislation to give effect to the principle of equal treatment in matters of social security. The first such measure to be adopted was Directive 79/7.[43] That directive applied to the working population, retired or invalided workers and self-employed persons[44] and prohibited discrimination on the ground of sex[45] in social security schemes providing protection against a range of specified risks. The principle of equal treatment laid down in the directive was stated to be 'without prejudice to the provisions relating to the protection of women on the grounds of maternity'.[46] Moreover, by virtue of Article 7(1), Member States were entitled to exclude a range of matters from the scope of the directive. One which was to prove especially important was 'the determination of pensionable age for the purposes of granting old-age and retirement pensions and the possible consequences thereof for other benefits'.[47] That exclusion was reflected in Directive 86/378,[48] which extended the principle of equal treatment to occupational social security schemes, that is, to schemes not covered by Directive 79/7 whose purpose was to provide workers[49] with benefits intended to supplement or replace those available under statutory social security schemes. Article 9(1)(a) gave Member States the right to defer implementation of the principle of equal treatment with regard to:

determination of pensionable age for the purposes of granting old-age or retirement pensions, and the possible implications for other benefits:

— either until the date on which such equality is achieved in statutory schemes,
— or, at the latest, until such equality is required by a directive.

As we shall see, subsequent developments in the case law of the Court on the effect of the Treaty required substantial amendments to be made to Directive 86/378.[50]

---

[43] OJ 1979 L6/24.   [44] Art 2.   [45] See further Art 4(1).   [46] Art 4(2).
[47] Art 7(1)(a).
[48] OJ 1986 L225/40. For a brief comment, see Arnull, 'A new directive on equal treatment' (1987) 12 ELRev 63.
[49] Including both employees and the self-employed, persons whose work has been interrupted by certain causes, and retired and disabled workers: Art 3. More detailed rules on the application of the principle of equal treatment to the self-employed were laid down by Dir 86/613, OJ 1986 L359/56.
[50] See Dir 96/97, OJ 1997 L46/20.

Changes to the Treaty

The Single European Act saw the introduction of a new Article 118a (now 138), which provided a legal basis for the adoption of directives on the health and safety of workers.[51] Article 119 was left untouched. During the negotiations which led to the adoption of the TEU, an attempt was made to insert into the EC Treaty a revamped chapter on social policy containing a slightly amended version of Article 119. Opposition from the United Kingdom to the incorporation of the new chapter in the Treaty itself resulted in the annexing to the Treaty of a Protocol on Social Policy, by which the United Kingdom agreed with the other Member States that they could 'have recourse to the institutions, procedures and mechanisms of the Treaty for the purposes of taking among themselves and applying as far as they are concerned the acts and decisions required for giving effect'[52] to an Agreement on Social Policy, itself annexed to the Protocol. The United Kingdom would not take part in the process leading to the adoption of such measures, which would not be applicable in that Member State. Along with the arrangements for economic and monetary union agreed at Maastricht, the Protocol and Agreement on Social Policy were harbingers of the provisions on closer co-operation or flexibility which would later be included in the Treaty of Amsterdam.[53] The Agreement itself[54] contained a series of potentially far-reaching provisions on working conditions and the labour market, as well as a slightly modified version[55] of Article 119. It had evidently been intended that this should replace the original version of the article, but in the event that provision remained in force.

Although doubts were initially expressed about the legality of the Protocol and Agreement on Social Policy,[56] it seems probable that, whatever view one takes of their desirability, they formed a valid part of Community law.[57] However, the Agreement proved to be a less fertile source of new initiatives than might once have been hoped[58] and, following a change of government in the United Kingdom, new versions of Articles 117 to 120 (now 136 to 143) EC were inserted into the Treaty

[51] Art 118a (now 138) was interpreted broadly by the Court in Case C–84/94 *United Kingdom v Council* [1996] ECR I–5755.

[52] Protocol on Social Policy, Art 1.

[53] See Title VII (ex VIa) TEU and Art 40 (ex K.12) TEU; Art 11 (ex 5a) EC. Cf Art 1 of the Protocol integrating the Schengen acquis into the framework of the EU, annexed to the TEU and the EC Treaty.

[54] Which built on the Community Charter of Fundamental Social Rights of Workers (COM(92)562 final) signed in 1989 by all the then Member States with the exception of the UK.

[55] See Art 6 of the Agreement, which contained a new third paragraph.

[56] See Curtin, 'The constitutional structure of the Union: a Europe of bits and pieces' (1993) 30 CMLRev 17, 52–61; Szyszczak, 'Social policy: a happy ending or a reworking of the fairy tale?' in O'Keeffe and Twomey (eds), *Legal Issues of the Maastricht Treaty* (1994), ch 20. Cf Barnard, 'A social policy for Europe: politicians 1, lawyers 0' (1992) 8 IntJCompLLIR 15.

[57] See Art 311 (ex 239) EC, which provides: 'The protocols annexed to this Treaty by common accord of the Member States shall form an integral part thereof.' In Case T–135/96 *UEAPME v Council*, judgment of 17 June 1998, the CFI treated a directive adopted under the Agreement on Social Policy as susceptible in principle to review under Art 230 (ex 173) EC.

[58] Nielsen and Szyszczak, op cit, p 48.

at Amsterdam[59] and the Protocol and Agreement on Social Policy repealed. The first paragraph of the new version of Article 119 (now 141) endorsed the case law of the Court, referred to above, to the effect that the equal pay principle extends to work of equal value. The third paragraph conferred on the Council, acting in accordance with the co-decision procedure referred to in Article 189b (now 251) EC, a power to 'adopt measures to ensure the application of the principle of equal opportunities and equal treatment of men and women in matters of employment and occupation, including the principle of equal pay for equal work or work of equal value'.[60] The fourth paragraph authorized the Member States to take positive action to promote the interests of an under-represented sex. It went further than the corresponding provision in the Agreement on Social Policy and seems to have been introduced in response to a controversial decision of the Court, discussed below.

The role of the Court

It will be apparent from what has been said so far that the enthusiasm of the Member States for Community action in the field of social policy in general and equal treatment for men and women in particular has waxed and waned.[61] The contribution of the Court of Justice in this field has on the whole been more consistent. *Defrenne II* set the tone for the development of a remarkable body of case law in which the Court insisted on strict compliance with their obligations by the Member States and seemed to have little hesitation about using the Treaty or general principles to override compromises carefully constructed by the Community legislator. Some of the Court's case law is examined in more detail below.

While the Court's contribution to the promotion of equal treatment for men and women is widely acknowledged,[62] the persistence of some forms of disadvantage suffered by women has led to criticism from a feminist perspective of the Community rules on equal treatment and the approach of the Court to their interpretation and application. Fredman[63] gives a concise summary of the criticism of this kind to which British and United States anti-discrimination laws have been subjected and which is now being extended to Community law:

[59] The Treaty of Amsterdam also added to Art 2 EC a reference to promoting equality between men and women and to Art 3 EC a new paragraph requiring the Community to aim to eliminate inequalities and to promote equality between men and women. In addition, a new Title XI (ex VIII) on employment was inserted.

[60] The EC Treaty did not previously confer on the Community legislator an express power to act in the field of equal treatment for men and women, the directives referred to above having been adopted on the basis of Art 100 (now 94) (75/117, 96/97) or Art 235 (now 308) (76/207, 79/7) or a combination of the two (86/378, 86/613).

[61] See generally Nielsen and Szcszyzak, op cit, ch 1.

[62] Nielsen and Szyszczak, op cit, p 55, describe the Court as 'a key actor in the legislative process' and acknowledge the 'remarkable role' it has played. Fenwick and Hervey describe the Court's contribution as 'significant': 'Sex equality in the single market: new directions for the European Court of Justice' (1995) 32 CMLRev 443, 448.

[63] 'European Community discrimination law: a critique' (1992) 21 ILJ 119, 120.

There are five inter-related characteristics of many anti-discrimination laws which have been the major targets of criticism. The first, and possibly most important, is the extent to which such laws rely on the pivotal concept of equality. This concept, runs the argument, is crucially limited by its dependence on a norm of comparison, which is generally the existing male norm. A second, and closely connected, characteristic is that such laws are constructed on the basis of an assumed dichotomy between 'equality' and 'difference'. The 'difference' angle is reflected in derogations from the equality principle, such as those for bona fide occupational qualifications or protective legislation. This, according to the critique, is a false dichotomy, for difference is dependent on a male norm as much as is equality; and differential treatment is in danger of simply perpetuating stereotypes. A third characteristic is the assumption of neutrality, i.e. that discrimination is equally pernicious against men as against women. It is argued that this makes it impossible to remedy the real problem, gender-based disadvantage. Fourthly, criticism has focused on the subordination of anti-discrimination legislation to the market order; and, finally, on its individualism.

Some of these criticisms will be addressed in the context of the discussion of the Court's case law which now follows. The discussion is not comprehensive in its coverage. Instead four groups of cases have been selected for more detailed examination because they illustrate particularly clearly the role played by the Court. The groups concern: (a) the material scope of the Community rules; (b) indirect discrimination; (c) pregnancy; and (d) positive action. Finally, some brief comments will be made about the Court's approach to the interpretation of the Social Security Directive.

The material scope of the Community rules

What is pay?

Article 141 (ex 119) applies to discrimination concerning 'pay', defined by the article itself as 'the ordinary basic or minimum wage or salary and any other consideration, whether in cash or in kind, which the worker receives, directly or indirectly, in respect of his employment from his employer'. The breadth of this definition will immediately be apparent[64] and in *Garland v British Rail Engineering*[65] the Court held that it covered special travel facilities granted by an employer to male employees on their retirement in respect of themselves, their wives, and dependent children. Article 141 was therefore infringed if such an employer did not extend the same facilities to former female employees. It made no difference that the employer was not contractually bound to grant any such facilities or that the employment relationship had now come to an end.[66] The *Garland* case was

[64] For a detailed discussion see Ellis, *EC Sex Equality Law* (2nd edn, 1998), pp 64–101.
[65] Case 12/81 [1982] ECR 359.
[66] Cf Case C–342/93 *Gillespie and Others v Northern Health and Social Services Board and Others* [1996] ECR I–475, where maternity pay was held to fall within the scope of Art 141 (ex 119) and Dir 75/117. However, the Court went on to hold that those provisions did not entitle women to full pay during maternity leave, merely to an amount which was not so low as to undermine the purpose of such leave.

cited by the Court in *Barber*,[67] where it was held that Article 141 embraced a redundancy payment made by an employer even though it was paid, not by virtue of a contract of employment, but on a voluntary basis or pursuant to a statutory obligation. Notwithstanding the fact that it reflected considerations of social policy, the crucial factor was that the worker's right to receive it derived from the employment relationship.[68]

The *Barber* case raised a series of further questions about the material scope of Article 141 (ex 119) and Directive 75/117 which were to lead the Court into much deeper water. B was a member of a non-contributory pension scheme wholly financed by his former employer, the Guardian Royal Exchange Assurance Group. The scheme was contracted out[69] of the earnings-related part of the State scheme, for which it was a substitute. The normal pensionable age for employees like B under the scheme was 62 for men and 57 for women, a difference which corresponded to that which existed under the State scheme. In the event of redundancy, members were entitled to an immediate pension if they had reached the age of 55 for men and 50 for women. B, a man, was made redundant when he was 52 and would not have been entitled to a pension for another 10 years. A woman in the same position would have received an immediate pension. The question which the Court was asked to resolve was essentially whether this state of affairs was compatible with Community law.

The *Barber* case was not the first in which the Court had been asked to consider the effect of Article 141 (ex 119) on pensions. In *Defrenne I*,[70] the Court ruled that 'social security schemes or benefits, in particular pensions, directly governed by legislation without any element of agreement within the undertaking or the occupational branch concerned, which are obligatorily applicable to general categories of workers'[71] did not constitute pay within the meaning of the article, being determined 'less by the employment relationship between the employer and the worker than by considerations of social policy'.[72] In *Bilka v Weber von Hartz*,[73] however, the Court held that Article 141 was potentially infringed if an employer excluded a category of employees consisting mainly of women from an occupational pension scheme, based on an agreement between the employer and its employees, which

---

[67] Case C–262/88 [1990] ECR I–1889.

[68] Cf Case 19/81 *Burton v British Railways Board* [1982] ECR 555. In Case C–167/97 *The Queen v Secretary of State for Employment, ex parte Seymour-Smith and Perez*, judgment of 9 January 1999, compensation for unfair dismissal was held to constitute pay for the purposes of Art 141.

[69] As the Court explained in Case 192/85 *Newstead v Department of Transport* [1987] ECR 4753, para 3, '[p]ersons covered by a scheme of this kind . . . make reduced contributions to the national scheme, corresponding to the basic flat-rate pension payable under the national scheme to all workers regardless of their earnings. On the other hand, they are required to contribute to the occupational scheme, in accordance with the conditions which it lays down.' As AG van Gerven emphasized in *Barber* at p I–1919, B was not required to contribute to the scheme to which he belonged. The concept of 'contracting out' was also considered by AG Warner in *Worringham and Humphreys v Lloyds Bank, supra*, p 798.

[70] Case 80/70 [1971] ECR 445.   [71] Para 7.   [72] Para 8.

[73] Case 170/84 [1986] ECR 1607.

supplemented benefits paid under a generally applicable statutory scheme with additional benefits financed solely by the employer. However, in *Worringham and Humphreys v Lloyds Bank*,[74] Advocate General Warner expressed the view that a contracted-out scheme designed, not as a supplement to the State social security scheme, but as a substitute for it or for part of it was to be regarded as outside the scope of Article 141. He thought it would produce an 'unbalanced result' to treat the private scheme as subject to the article when the State scheme which it replaced was not.

Advocate General Warner's view on this point was less than confidently expressed and in *Barber* the Court took a different approach. It pointed out that contracted-out private occupational pension schemes 'are the result either of an agreement between workers and employers or of a unilateral decision taken by the employer. They are wholly financed by the employer or by both the employer and the workers without any contribution being made by the public authorities in any circumstances.' The Court added that such schemes were not of general application but derived from the employment relationship between members and a particular employer. Moreover, as long as they satisfied the statutory requirements for contracting out, they were governed by their own rules. The Court then addressed directly the point raised by Advocate General Warner in *Worringham*: 'occupational schemes such as that referred to in this case may grant to their members benefits greater than those which would be paid by the statutory scheme, with the result that their economic function is similar to that of the supplementary schemes which exist in certain Member States, where affiliation and contribution to the statutory scheme is compulsory and no derogation is allowed'. The Court observed that, in the *Bilka* case, benefits paid under a supplementary pension scheme had been held to constitute pay for the purposes of Article 141 (ex 119). That article therefore covered a pension paid under a contracted-out private occupational pension scheme. The Court went on to draw the natural conclusion, that it was incompatible with Article 141 to pay pensions under such schemes at ages which differed according to sex, even if the difference was based on that laid down by the national statutory scheme.

The temporal effect of the Barber case

The widespread use of different pensionable ages for men and women in contracted out schemes in the United Kingdom and other Member States meant that the practical implications of the conclusion reached by the Court were immense. The Commission and the United Kingdom raised the possibility that the Court might limit the temporal effect of its judgment. The Court acknowledged that interested parties might legitimately have taken the view, in the light of the provisions in Directive 79/7[75] and Directive 86/378[76] which appeared to sanction for the time being different pensionable ages for men and women, that the principle of equal

---

[74] *Supra*, p 806.   [75] Art 7(1).   [76] Art 9(a).

treatment did not apply in its full rigour to pensions paid under contracted-out schemes. To avoid upsetting the financial balance of such schemes, the Court therefore ruled that the direct effect of Article 141 (ex 119), which it had reaffirmed earlier in its judgment, 'may not be relied upon in order to claim entitlement to a pension with effect from a date prior to that of this judgment, except in the case of workers or those claiming under them who have before that date initiated legal proceedings or raised an equivalent claim under the applicable national law'.[77]

Although some limitation on the temporal effect of the ruling was clearly justified, the manner in which the Court set out the extent of the limitation constituted a serious blunder. The words 'entitlement to a pension' concealed an essential ambiguity which was to produce several further references to the Court and an unprecedented intervention by the Member States. The key question was whether equality was required in relation to payments made after the date of the judgment (17 May 1990) or only in relation to contributions paid in respect of periods of employment completed after that date.[78] In *Ten Oever*, one of the cases in which the Court was asked to clarify this issue, Advocate General van Gerven said[79] that 'the practical importance of the answer to this question is enormous' and observed that the second of the two alternatives set out above[80] 'would deprive the *Barber* judgment of almost all retroactive effect. In practical terms, it would mean that the full effect of the judgment would be felt only after a period of about 40 years.'

What is the explanation for the Court's failure to explain more clearly the extent of the temporal limitation it laid down? Critics may say that the failure demonstrates the dangers of appointing as Judges people without experience of senior judicial office. However, it is unusual for the Court to make a mistake of this nature which even its best friends would have trouble defending. Perhaps the case represents a rare lapse by a Court labouring under an increasingly heavy workload. This may have played a part, but the most likely explanation is simply that the issue was not explored in sufficient depth by those who submitted observations to the Court. The issue was of no interest to the referring court or the applicant in the main action and of interest to the respondent only in so far as it would affect other claims which might be brought against it in the future.[81] If this is the real explanation, the case provides a salutary example of the dangers of dealing with an important issue in the absence of proper argument.[82]

---

[77] Para 45.			[78] See Curtin, op cit, 50–1.

[79] Case C–109/91 [1993] ECR I–4879, 4901.

[80] As AG van Gerven pointed out (pp I–4901–2), there was a number of intermediate possibilities. See also Honeyball and Shaw, 'Sex, law and the retiring man' (1991) 16 ELRev 47, 56–7.

[81] Art 41 of the EC Statute enables a party to a case before the Court to apply for a judgment to be revised where a fact which might have proved decisive subsequently comes to light. This procedure is not available in the case of judgments given under the preliminary rulings procedure because there are technically no parties to such proceedings. It is for the referring court to make a further reference if new factors emerge after the Court has given its ruling. See Case 69/85 *Wünsche v Germany* [1986] ECR 947; Case C–116/96 REV *Reisebüro Binder* [1998] ECR I–1889.

[82] Cf the discussion of the preliminary rulings procedure in ch 2.

The ambiguity created by the *Barber* judgment prompted the Member States to take action at the intergovernmental conference on political union which opened towards the end of 1990. The TEU included a protocol to be annexed to the EC Treaty. The so-called '*Barber* protocol', which would become an integral part of the EC Treaty on the entry into force of the TEU,[83] attributed to the Court's ruling the most limited form of retroactive effect compatible with the terms of the judgment. It stated:

For the purposes of Article 119 [now 141] of this Treaty, benefits under occupational social security schemes shall not be considered as remuneration if and in so far as they are attributable to periods of employment prior to 17 May 1990, except in the case of workers or those claiming under them who have before that date initiated legal proceedings or introduced an equivalent claim under the applicable national law.

The facts which gave rise to the *Ten Oever* case took place before the TEU had entered into force. The Court was not therefore bound, when the case fell to be decided, by the terms of the *Barber* protocol. Had the Court taken a broader view of the *Barber* case than that embodied in the protocol, it might have been necessary to distinguish three periods rather than two: the period prior to 17 May 1990, the period between that date and the entry into force of the TEU, and the period after the entry into force of that Treaty. Moreover, difficult questions about the protocol's capacity to take away rights and indeed its very legality[84] might have had to be confronted. In the event, however, these questions did not arise, the Court ruling that, subject to the normal exception for those who had already brought a claim, 'equality of treatment in the matter of occupational pensions may be claimed only in relation to benefits payable in respect of periods of employment subsequent to 17 May 1990, the date of the *Barber* judgment . . .'.[85] There is no doubt that this resolved much of the confusion occasioned by the *Barber* judgment. Moreover, given the Court's acceptance in that case that the practical consequences of its finding on the question of principle were significant enough to justify a limitation on its temporal effect, it would have required a very precise economic analysis to identify the point at which a less severe limitation would have made those consequences manageable.[86]

The ruling in *Ten Oever* on the temporal effect of *Barber* was subsequently confirmed on several occasions.[87] It soon became apparent that, although unwilling to challenge directly the interpretation of the *Barber* ruling embodied in the protocol, the Court was not prepared to give the protocol a broad interpretation. An exam-

[83] See Art 311 (ex 239) EC.
[84] See Hervey, 'Legal issues concerning the *Barber* protocol' in O'Keeffe and Twomey (eds), *Legal Issues of the Maastricht Treaty* (1994), ch 21; Curtin, op cit, pp 50–1.
[85] Para 19.
[86] Cf Moore, ' "Justice doesn't mean a free lunch": the application of the principle of equal pay to occupational pension schemes' (1995) 20 ELRev 159, 164.
[87] See eg Case C–110/91 *Moroni* [1993] ECR I–6591; Case C–152/91 *Neath v Steeper* [1993] ECR I–6935; Case C–200/91 *Coloroll* [1994] ECR I–4389.

plc of the Court's approach to the effect of the protocol is the *Vroege* case,[88] decided after the TEU had entered into force. The pension scheme operated by the employers of Miss V was only open to men and unmarried women who worked at least 80 per cent of the full day. Since Miss V had never worked more than 80 per cent of the full day, she was not allowed to pay contributions into the scheme and acquired no pension rights under it. In 1991 new rules came into force providing that any employee who had reached 25 years of age and who worked at least 25 per cent of normal working hours could join the scheme. Provision was made for some women who were not previously members of the scheme to purchase additional years of membership, but the unfortunate Miss V was not eligible and only began to accrue pension rights from the beginning of 1991. She maintained that this was incompatible with Article 141 (ex 119) and she claimed to be entitled to membership with effect from the date of *Defrenne II*, 8 April 1976.

The Court reiterated the reasons which had led it to limit the temporal effect of its ruling in *Barber*, concluding that the limitation 'concerns only those kinds of discrimination which employers and pension schemes could reasonably have considered to be permissible owing to the transitional derogations for which Community law provided [in Directives 86/378 and 79/7] and which were capable of being applied to occupational pensions'.[89] However, it had been clear since the *Bilka* case in 1986 that Article 141 (ex 119) covered not only entitlement to benefits paid by an occupational pension scheme but also the right to be a member of such a scheme, because the pay of those excluded from membership would be lower than that of members. Interested parties had no justification for thinking otherwise. Since the *Bilka* ruling had not been limited in time, Article 141 could be invoked to claim equal treatment in relation to the right to join an occupational pension scheme as from the date on which the article first produced direct effect, namely the date of the judgment in *Defrenne II*.[90] The Court added that it was not now open to it to impose a temporal limit on the extent to which Article 141 applied to the right to join an occupational pension scheme because such limits could be imposed only in the first judgment in which the rule concerned was laid down.

The Court then turned to the effect, if any, of the *Barber* protocol in these circumstances. In a small rewriting of history, the Court observed that the protocol 'essentially adopted the same interpretation of the *Barber* judgment as did the *Ten Oever* judgment'.[91] Whilst acknowledging that the protocol was an integral part of the Treaty, the Court made it clear that it related only to benefits and not to the right to belong to an occupational social security scheme. It therefore had no effect on the right to join an occupational pension scheme, which continued to be governed by the *Bilka* ruling.

---

[88] Case C–57/93 [1994] ECR I–4541. See also Case C–7/93 *Beune* [1994] ECR I–4471.

[89] Para 27.

[90] See further Case C–246/96 *Magorrian and Cunningham v EHSSB and DHSS* [1997] ECR I–7153, discussed in ch 5.

[91] Para 41.

However, what the Court gave with one hand in *Vroege* it took away with the other in *Fisscher*,[92] decided on the same day. F, a married woman, had only recently been allowed to join her employer's pension scheme following a change in the scheme's rules. She claimed to be entitled to membership under Article 141 (ex 119) from the moment she entered the employer's service ten years previously. The Court repeated its findings in *Vroege* as to the scope of Article 141 and the *Barber* protocol. However, the Court added that the claimant was not entitled to more favourable treatment than that which she would have received had she been allowed to join the scheme from the outset: 'the fact that a worker can claim retroactively to join an occupational pension scheme does not allow the worker to avoid paying the contributions relating to the period of membership concerned'.[93] The Court did not take up the suggestion of the United Kingdom Government that someone in the position of the claimant should be entitled to a pension reduced by the value of the contributions which she did not make.[94] However, Whiteford observes that '[i]t appears to have been considered beyond doubt by the parties to the litigation that where an individual wishes to claim retroactive membership the employer will be bound to pay the back-dated employer contributions'.[95]

Levelling down

Several of the cases decided in the aftermath of *Barber* raised the question of the application in the pensions context of the statement made by the Court in *Defrenne II* apparently ruling out so-called levelling down as a way of meeting the requirements of Article 141 (ex 119). Applied strictly, the ruling in *Defrenne II* would mean that pension scheme members in the disadvantaged category would henceforward have to be treated in the same way as remaining scheme members. This would evidently exacerbate the potential threat to the financial equilibrium of pension schemes and in *Coloroll*[96] the Court qualified its earlier stance. It held that, as long as a scheme had not been changed to bring about equal treatment, the advantages enjoyed by those in the privileged class had to be extended to the disadvantaged class. However, once rules to eliminate discrimination on the grounds of sex had taken effect, Article 141 did not preclude a reduction in the advantages enjoyed by those favoured by the previous rules. All that the Treaty required was 'that men and women should receive the same pay for the same work without imposing any specific level of pay'.[97] The Court reiterated the qualification in two other cases decided on the same day as *Coloroll*. In one of them, *Avdel Systems*,[98] the employer had sought to achieve equality by raising the retirement age for women to that for

---

[92] Case C–128/93 [1994] ECR I–4583.   [93] Para 37.
[94] See AG van Gerven at [1994] ECR I–4541, 4562–3.
[95] 'Lost in the mists of time. The ECJ and occupational pensions' (1995) 32 CMLRev 801, 813.
[96] Case C–200/91 [1994] ECR I–4389.   [97] Para 33.
[98] Case C–408/92 [1994] ECR I–4435. The other was Case C–28/93 *van den Akker* [1994] ECR I–4527.

men but had made transitional arrangements in an attempt to minimize the consequences of the change for women whose benefits would otherwise be adversely affected. This the Court said was unlawful. Once discrimination contrary to Article 141 had been identified, employers were required to ensure immediate and full compliance with the article: 'achievement of equality cannot be made progressive on a basis that still maintains discrimination, even if only temporarily'.[99]

The relevance of actuarial considerations

A final point of controversy raised by the *Neath* and *Coloroll* cases concerned the question whether Article 141 (ex 119) permitted the payments made under a pension scheme to be calculated in accordance with actuarial factors which differed according to sex, in particular assumptions about the life expectancy of men and women. Advocate General van Gerven set out the issues involved:[100]

The pension fund and pension fund administrators as well as most of the intervening Member States . . . say that such actuarial calculation factors are based on reliable and objective statistical data which are related to life expectancy after pensionable age has been reached. Since those factors vary from sex to sex—on average women live longer and therefore on average receive their pension over a longer period of time than men—actuarial factors are, according to their arguments, essential for evaluating the liabilities assumed by a pension scheme and consequently for the financial structuring of the entire pension scheme.

The Commission took a different view on the basis that the equal pay principle had to be applied on an individual basis rather than on the basis of categories. Advocate General van Gerven summarized the Commission's argument as follows:

The fact that women generally live longer than men has no significance at all for the life expectancy of a specific individual and it is not acceptable for an individual to be penalized on account of assumptions which are not certain to be true in his specific case. Moreover, there are a number of risk factors which are not taken into account: risks associated with certain occupations, smoking, state of health and so on. Finally, there is no technical necessity for pension schemes to have a distinction based on life expectancies: some pension schemes, and all State pension schemes, use a system of risk compensation which covers differences in the probable lifespan of men and women.

The issue arose in *Neath v Steeper*[101] in the following way.[102] Mr N was employed by S. His employment was terminated by reason of redundancy when he was aged 54. N was a member of an occupational pension scheme which provided employees on retirement with a defined pension corresponding to one-sixtieth of their final salary for each year of service. The scheme was a contributory one funded by contributions by both employer and employee. When N was made redundant, he was not entitled to an immediate pension. He was therefore offered the choice of a deferred pension (payable at the age of 65) or a transfer payment to another

[99] Para 26 of *Avdel Systems*.
[100] See [1993] ECR I–4879, 4913. See also Whiteford, op cit, pp 828–32.   [101] *Supra.*
[102] See the Report for the Hearing, [1993] ECR I–6935, 6938–9.

scheme. If he opted for a transfer payment, a sum which was actuarially equivalent to the benefits which he had accrued as a result of his membership would be transferred to another scheme of his choice. The size of the sum transferred would vary according to the sex of the member. This was because, when the capital value of the member's accrued benefits were calculated, it was assumed that a woman would live longer than a man. The cost to the scheme of providing a retirement pension for a woman would therefore be greater than the cost of providing such a pension for a man. The transfer value of a woman's accrued rights was correspondingly higher than that of a man. If, on the other hand, N opted for a deferred pension, he would have to wait five years longer than a woman before receiving it. Moreover, if at that point he decided to exercise his right to exchange part of his pension for a tax-free lump sum, he would receive a smaller amount than a woman in the same position because the amount due to him would be worked out on the basis of actuarial tables which assumed that women lived longer than men.

The Court approached the problem by asking whether transfer benefits and lump-sum options constituted pay within the meaning of Article 141 (ex 119). It said that the basis of its previous case law on the matter, including *Barber*, was that the employer gave a unilateral commitment to pay his employees defined benefits or to grant them specific advantages which employees in turn expected the employer to pay. The concept of pay was confined to matters which were a consequence of that commitment and which fell within the corresponding expectations of employees. The Court continued:[103]

In the context of a defined benefit occupational pension scheme such as that in question in the main proceedings, the employer's commitment to his employees concerns the payment, at a given moment in time, of a periodic pension for which the determining criteria are already known at the time when the commitment is made and which constitutes pay within the meaning of Article 119. However, that commitment does not necessarily have to do with the funding arrangements chosen to secure the periodic payment of the pension, which thus remain outside the scope of application of Article 119.

Contributions made by employees had to be the same for all employees, male and female, because they were deducted directly from the salary of employees and therefore constituted part of their pay.[104] Contributions made by the employer were different. They ensured 'the adequacy of the funds necessary to cover the cost of the pensions promised, so securing their payment in the future, that being the substance of the employer's commitment'.[105] The Court therefore ruled that 'the use of actuarial factors differing according to sex in funded defined-benefit occupational pension schemes does not fall with the scope of Article 119 of the EEC Treaty'.[106]

---

[103] Para 30.

[104] See Case 69/80 *Worringham and Humphreys v Lloyds Bank* [1981] ECR 767.   [105] Para 31.

[106] Para 34. In *Coloroll*, where similar questions were raised, the Court followed the *Neath* approach, adding that 'inequalities in the amounts of capital benefits or substitute benefits whose value can be determined only on the basis of the arrangements chosen for funding the scheme are likewise not struck at by Article 119': para 85.

An assessment of the case law

How is one to assess the Court's case law on pay in general and pensions in particular? There is no doubt that in principle a broad interpretation of the concept of pay in Article 141 (ex 119) strengthens its capacity to promote substantive equality between men and women.[107] Moreover, in *Barber* the Court emphasized that the equal pay principle applied to each element of the remuneration received by men and women. If Article 141 only required a global assessment of the consideration paid to workers, the Court said, 'judicial review would be difficult and the effectiveness of Article 119 [now 141] would be diminished as a result'.[108] None the less, Fredman identifies a paradox in the case law on the application of Article 141 in the pensions context:[109] 'Whereas the large majority of successful cases are those brought by men claiming that they have been less favourably treated than similarly situated women, statistical evidence demonstrates clearly that women are at a distinct disadvantage compared to men in their ability to secure an adequate independent pension in their old age.' She observes that the attraction of women's lower pensionable age in the late 1980s and early 1990s was attributable to rising unemployment and compulsory early retirement, although it had been introduced (at least in the United Kingdom) for quite different reasons: 'The first was . . . to assist married women who were younger than their husbands to draw their dependent wives' pensions when their husbands reached 65 . . . The change was also intended to assist single women, who found it difficult to sustain their contributions record until 65, usually because of their responsibilities for caring for elderly parents.'[110] The *Barber* case is described as 'based unquestioningly on a working pattern that takes no account of child care or other family responsibilities', with the result that '[i]n reality, the "female comparator" was simply Barber himself with a lower retirement age'.[111]

These thought-provoking observations serve to underline the limitations of the principle of equal treatment in eliminating disadvantage suffered by women.[112] As such they seem directed more at the Community legislature and the Member States than the Court of Justice. The Court itself had been called upon to apply a principle of equal treatment expressed in gender-neutral language. The coherence of its case law meant that the approach it took in the pensions cases had to fit reasonably well with its other case law on the meaning of the concept of pay for the purposes of Article 141 (ex 119). Bearing these constraints in mind, could the Court reasonably have been expected to take account of considerations such as those identified by Fredman?

---

[107] See Fenwick and Hervey, op cit, pp 447–9.

[108] Para 34 of *Barber*. See also Case 109/88 *Handels- og Kontorfunktionærernes Forbund i Danmark v Dansk Arbejdsgiverforening, acting on behalf of Danfoss* [1989] ECR 3199, below. Cf *Hayward v Cammell Laird* [1988] 2 All ER 257 (HL).

[109] 'The poverty of equality: pensions and the ECJ' (1996) 25 ILJ 91.

[110] Op cit, p 93. See also by the same author *Women and the Law* (1997), pp 345–8.

[111] (1996) 25 ILJ 91, 102.   [112] See Ellis, op cit, pp 322–31.

One possibility might have been to require the applicant in *Barber* to find a real-life comparator. If it was the case that very few women would have had his employment and contribution record, he might have found this a difficult burden to discharge. Support for this type of approach might be found in *Macarthys v Smith*,[113] where the applicant argued that a woman was entitled to the salary she would be paid if she were a man, even if no man had ever performed similar work (the so-called hypothetical male worker). The Court rejected the suggestion that the direct effect of Article 141 (ex 119) could be invoked on the basis of such a comparison: 'in cases of actual discrimination falling within the scope of the direct application of Article 119, comparisons are confined to parallels which may be drawn on the basis of concrete appraisals of the work actually performed by employees of different sex in the same establishment or service'.[114] However, the principle laid down in *Macarthys* does not apply where the claimant can establish discrimination by other means. In *Dekker*,[115] the Court held that it was incompatible with the Equal Treatment Directive for an employer to refuse to take on a woman because of a reason directly linked to her sex (pregnancy) even if there were no male candidates for the post. Thus, in *Barber* the applicant merely needed to show that there were female members of the pension scheme to which he belonged and that the rules applicable to them were more favourable than those applicable to men.[116] The Court's decision in *Macarthys* is generally regarded[117] as undermining the capacity of Article 141 to remedy low pay levels in jobs traditionally confined to women. It would be paradoxical to extend its scope in order to make it more difficult for men to claim the same pension rights as women.

Might the Court none the less have done more to protect the rights of women adversely affected by changes to the pension schemes to which they belonged following the *Barber* case? It is submitted that the Court was right in *Avdel* to rule out transitional arrangements for the benefit of women required to work an extra five years in order to qualify for a full pension. Once a practice which is contrary to a fundamental provision of the Treaty is detected, it must clearly be terminated forthwith. To allow such a practice to continue, even in an attenuated form, once its illegality has been definitively established would undermine the integrity of the legal order and set a potentially damaging precedent. This question would not have arisen if the Court had ruled out levelling down in order to comply with *Barber*. The stance taken by the Court in the pensions context represented a departure from its ruling in *Defrenne II*. However, while it is the responsibility of the Court to apply the principle of equal treatment, it was understandably unwilling to fix a uniform pensionable age when the Member States had been unable to do so.

[113] Case 129/79 [1980] ECR 1275.
[114] Para 15. The Court did accept, however, that a woman could compare her pay with that of a man who previously did the same job.
[115] Case C–177/88 [1990] ECR I–3941. This case is discussed further below.
[116] In *Coloroll*, the Court held that Art 141 (ex 119) did not apply to pension schemes which had at all times had members of only one sex: para 104.
[117] See eg Ellis, op cit, pp 105–7.

Harder to defend is the Court's conclusion in *Neath* and *Coloroll* that Article 141 (ex 119) did not affect the arrangements used to fund a pension scheme and that the use of actuarial factors which differed according to sex was therefore acceptable. As Advocate General van Gerven pointed out, 'not all individual men and women exhibit the average characteristics of their sex: many women live for a shorter time than the average man and many men live longer than the average woman'.[118] He argued that Article 141 'reflects the aspiration to treat the worker as an *individual* with regard to the worker's right to equal pay for equal work, and not simply as a member of one particular sex group . . . The mere fact that, in general, women live on average longer than men cannot, therefore, be a sufficient reason to provide for different treatment in the matter of contributions and benefits under occupational pension schemes.'[119] The Advocate General was not convinced that there were any technical reasons necessitating the use of sex-based actuarial tables. His argument seems compelling,[120] but as we have seen the Court took a different view. It may be noted that the outcome in the cases concerned favoured female members of the schemes at issue.

It is submitted that, with the exception of its initial failure to explain clearly the extent of the temporal limitation of the *Barber* ruling and its (admittedly more debatable) rulings on the use of sex-based actuarial tables, the Court's case law on pensions strikes a skilful balance between the rights of individual members on the one hand and the rights of employers and pension scheme members considered collectively on the other.[121] Fredman claims that in this field the Court has 'attempted to develop equality as an end in itself, against a background of minimal disruption of existing power structures'.[122] If this is an accurate summary of its approach, it seems entirely appropriate for a Court required to ensure that, in the interpretation and application of the Treaty, the law is observed.[123]

It remains to be noted that, towards the end of 1996, the Council adopted Directive 96/97[124] amending the provisions of Directive 86/378 which had been overtaken by the case law of the Court.[125] More radical legislation to address the problem of women's poverty in old age has yet to materialize.

---

[118] [1993] ECR I–4879, 4918–19.

[119] [1993] ECR I–4879, 4919 (emphasis in the original). The Advocate General referred to Curtin, 'Scalping the Community legislator: occupational pensions and *Barber*' (1990) 27 CMLRev 475, 495, where a similar argument is advanced.

[120] But see Jones, 'Sex equality in pension schemes' in Kenner (ed), *Trends in European Social Policy* (1995), ch 2, pp 134–5.   [121] Cf Whiteford, op cit, p 834.

[122] (1996) 25 ILJ 91, 109.   [123] See Art 220 (ex 164) EC.

[124] OJ 1997 L46/20.

[125] For an analysis of Dir 86/378, as amended, see Ellis, op cit, pp 87–95. She observes, at p 88, that the main changes effected by Dir 96/97 'were to make it clear that the substantive right to equality in this field flows from Article 119, not the Directive, and to reduce the number of exceptions permitted'.

The material scope of Directive 76/207

The Court's approach to the material scope of the Equal Treatment Directive has, if anything, been even more expansive. Two cases illustrate the point. In *Marshall I*,[126] the question arose whether an employer was entitled under the directive to dismiss its employees at the age at which social security pensions became payable. M, a woman, worked for the respondent employer. She was dismissed when she reached the age of 62 even though she had expressed a wish to continue working until she reached the age of 65. Under the applicable national legislation, State pensions were paid to men at the age of 65 and to women at the age of 60. The sole reason for M's dismissal was that she was over 60, although the employer had agreed to waive its normal policy for the previous two years. It will be recalled that the Equal Treatment Directive[127] envisages further action on the part of the Council to give effect to the principle of equal treatment in the field of social security. Acting on the basis of that provision, the Council adopted Directive 79/7, which permits Member States to exclude from its scope 'the determination of pensionable age for the purposes of granting old-age and retirement pensions . . .'.[128] It would not have been unreasonable to infer that the protection against dismissal conferred on employees by the Equal Treatment Directive ceased once an employee became entitled to an old-age pension under the applicable national legislation.

The Court took a more progressive approach. The case did not concern the conditions under which pensions were paid but dismissal and therefore fell to be dealt with under the Equal Treatment Directive. Article 5(1) provided that the conditions governing dismissal were to be the same for both men and women. Moreover, the term 'dismissal' was to be construed broadly. It followed that 'an age limit for the compulsory dismissal of workers pursuant to an employer's general policy concerning retirement falls within the term "dismissal" construed in that manner, even if the dismissal involves the grant of a retirement pension.'[129] The Court emphasized that, 'in view of the fundamental importance of the principle of equality of treatment',[130] the exclusion of social security matters from the scope of the Equal Treatment Directive was to be interpreted strictly. Since this case was concerned with dismissal within the meaning of Article 5 of the Equal Treatment Directive, the exception in Directive 79/7 concerning the consequences which pensionable age had for social security benefits was not applicable.[131] The approach of the Court in *Marshall I* is striking. Rather than seek to render coherent the relevant Community legislation, the Court attempted to give effect to what it considered its fundamental purpose. This involved drawing up a hierarchy in which the place of the relevant provisions varied. By this means the Court was able to con-

---

[126] Case 152/84 *Marshall v Southampton and South-West Hampshire Area Health Authority* [1986] ECR 723.

[127] See Art 1(2).   [128] Art 7(1)(a).   [129] Para 34.   [130] Para 36.

[131] The Court went on to address the question of the horizontal direct effect of directives. See ch 4.

fine the scope of the derogations within limited fields and to apply the fundamental principle laid down in Directive 76/207, that of equal treatment.

Marshall I clearly involved discrimination between men and women. The only question was whether it was compatible with the terms of the relevant directives. In *P v S and Cornwall County Council*,[132] the Court was asked to consider whether the Equal Treatment Directive extended beyond discrimination between men and women to encompass discrimination against transsexuals. P, whose biological sex was originally male, was employed by the respondent Council. A year after starting work, P informed the Council that he intended to undergo gender reassignment. This process involved a period during which P would dress and behave as a woman and would, if all went well, be followed by surgery to give P some of the physical attributes of a woman. After P had undergone a series of minor surgical operations, the Council gave P three months' notice of dismissal. The final surgical operation took place during the notice period.

P brought proceedings against the Council in which she claimed that she had been the victim of sex discrimination contrary to the Equal Treatment Directive. This was a bold claim because the directive is intended to ensure equal treatment for men and women. P had not been dismissed because she belonged to one sex rather than the other, but because she had changed sex. According to the referring court, P would have been dismissed had she originally been female rather than male.

In an Opinion unusual for the passionate language in which it was couched, Advocate General Tesauro urged the Court to rule that the directive precluded the dismissal of a transsexual on account of a change of sex. He declared:[133]

> I am well aware that I am asking the Court to make a 'courageous' decision. I am asking it to do so, however, in the profound conviction that what is at stake is a universal fundamental value, indelibly etched in modern legal traditions and in the constitutions of the more advanced countries: *the irrelevance of a person's sex with regard to the rules regulating relations in society* . . . Any other solution would sound like a moral condemnation—a condemnation, moreover, out of step with the times—of transsexuality, precisely when scientific advances and social change in this area are opening a perspective on the problem which certainly transcends the moral one.

The Court followed the line proposed by its Advocate General, ruling that the Equal Treatment Directive precluded the dismissal of a transsexual for a reason related to a gender reassignment. The Court's reasoning could not be described as expansive, but it contained echoes of the outspoken Opinion of Advocate General Tesauro. The Court began by emphasizing that the principle of equal treatment laid down in the directive meant that there should be no discrimination whatsoever on grounds of sex.[134] The directive constituted a particular expression of the principle of equality, which was one of the fundamental principles of Community

---

[132] Case C–13/94 [1996] ECR I–2143.   [133] p I–2157, emphasis in the original.
[134] See Arts 2(1) and 3(1).

law. The Court reiterated that the right not to be discriminated against on the ground of one's sex was one of the fundamental human rights it had a duty to uphold. 'Accordingly', the Court declared,[135] 'the scope of the directive cannot be confined simply to discrimination based on the fact that a person is of one or other sex. In view of its purpose and the nature of the rights which it seeks to safeguard, the scope of the directive is also such as to apply to discrimination arising, as in this case, from the gender reassignment of the person concerned.' Such discrimination was based essentially on the sex of the person concerned. 'To tolerate such discrimination would be tantamount, as regards such a person, to a failure to respect the dignity and freedom to which he or she is entitled, and which the Court has a duty to safeguard.'[136]

This remarkable ruling showed a good deal more sensitivity to the predicament of transsexuals than has been demonstrated by the European Court of Human rights,[137] even though the European Convention contains provisions[138] which seem better adapted to deal with transsexualism than those of the Equal Treatment Directive. Barnard underlines the Court's 'broad approach to the principle of equality, reinforcing the idea of equality as a fundamental right' and its willingness 'to recognise both the moral and economic content of the principle of equality'.[139] However, her suggestion that the Court might be in the process of creating 'a genuinely fundamental right which assumes a superior position in the hierarchy of norms'[140] was destined to be swiftly contradicted.

In *Grant v South-West Trains*,[141] the Court was asked whether the Community rules on sex discrimination prohibited discrimination on the ground of sexual orientation. G, a woman, was employed by a railway company. She was entitled under her contract of employment to travel concessions for herself, her spouse and dependants. Regulations adopted by her employer provided that employees were also entitled to concessions 'for one common law opposite sex spouse . . . subject to a statutory declaration being made that a meaningful relationship has existed for a period of two years or more . . .'.[142] G was a lesbian. She applied for travel concessions for her female cohabitee, with whom she declared she had had a 'meaningful relationship' for two years or more. Her application was rejected on the ground that travel concessions were not granted for cohabitees of the same sex.

G brought proceedings in which she argued that she had been the victim of discrimination based on sex, contrary to Community law. She pointed out that her

---

[135] Para 20. [136] Para 22.

[137] See eg *Sheffield and Horsham v United Kingdom* (1999) 27 EHRR 163.

[138] eg Art 8 (right to respect for private and family life), Art 12 (right to marry), and Art 14 (prohibition of discrimination).

[139] '*P v S*: kite flying or a new constitutional approach?' in Dashwood and O'Leary (eds), *The Principle of Equal Treatment in EC Law* (1997), ch IV, p 63.

[140] Op cit, p 74.

[141] Case C–249/96 [1998] ECR I–621. See also Case T–264/97 *D v Council*, judgment of 28 January 1999.

[142] The term 'common law spouse' means an unmarried cohabitee. It has no legal significance. See the Opinion of AG Elmer at p I–630–1.

predecessor, a man, had been granted travel concessions for his female cohabitee. There was a widespread assumption in the light of *P v S* that discrimination on the ground of sexual orientation would be found incompatible with the Community rules on equal treatment[143] and indeed Advocate General Elmer concluded that discrimination of the sort to which G had been subject was contrary to Article 141 (ex 119) of the Treaty.[144]

The Court took a different view. Rejecting the argument that the rules applied by the employer constituted discrimination directly based on sex, the Court pointed out that 'travel concessions are refused to a male worker if he is living with a person of the same sex, just as they are to a female worker if she is living with a person of the same sex'.[145] Moreover, neither the organs of the European Convention nor the Member States could be said to have elevated same-sex cohabitees to the status of married partners. The Court therefore ruled:[146]

It follows that, in the present state of the law within the Community, stable relationships between two persons of the same sex are not regarded as equivalent to marriages or stable relationships outside marriage between persons of opposite sex. Consequently, an employer is not required by Community law to treat the situation of a person who has a stable relationship with a partner of the same sex as equivalent to that of a person who is married to or has a stable relationship outside marriage with a partner of the opposite sex.

The Court said that the reasoning which had led it to the conclusion that discrimination based on gender reassignment was prohibited did not apply to differences of treatment based on sexual orientation. The position was not affected by international human rights instruments which might cover such discrimination. Although respect for fundamental rights was 'a condition of the legality of Community acts, those rights cannot in themselves have the effect of extending the scope of the Treaty provisions beyond the competences of the Community . . .'.[147] The Court found support for this conclusion in the Treaty of Amsterdam, which confers upon the Council a power to legislate against various forms of discrimination, one of which is discrimination based on sexual orientation.[148] The Court saw the new Treaty, not as justifying an expansive approach to the interpretation of the

---

[143] See Ellis, op cit, pp 196–7.

[144] The referring court raised both Dir 75/117 and Dir 76/207 in addition to Art 141 (ex 119). As AG Elmer pointed out, however, the disputed travel concessions constituted pay for the purposes of Art 141. Dir 75/117 had no significance independent of that article and Dir 76/207 did not apply to pay. 'The questions referred to the Court must therefore be answered on the basis of Article 119 of the Treaty alone': [1998] ECR I–621, 625. See also paras 13 and 14 of the judgment.

[145] Para 27.   [146] Para 35.

[147] Para 45. The Court cited Opinion 2/94 [1996] ECR I–1759, discussed in ch 6, where it held that the Community lacked competence to accede to the European Convention. The statement in *Grant* implies that, under the pre-Amsterdam version of the Treaty (see below), the Community lacked competence to legislate against discrimination on the ground of sexual orientation. However, in para 36 the Court said it was 'for the legislature alone to adopt, if appropriate, measures which may affect' the existing position. Perhaps the Court was anticipating the entry into force of the Treaty of Amsterdam.

[148] See Art 13 (ex 6a) EC.

existing rules of Community law, but as indicating a wish on the part of the Member States to deal with certain matters at the level of the Council.

Grant was not an ideal test case because the discrimination of which G had been the victim (refusal of travel concessions for her partner) was trivial compared with that to which P had been subjected (dismissal). Be that as it may, the Court's decision in *Grant* is in some respects a disappointing one. From a policy point of view, there seems little point in protecting transsexuals from discrimination but not homosexuals. Responsibility for removing the inconsistency now rests with the Council, which may not see the coherence of the law as a compelling reason for extending protection to homosexuals under the power conferred on it by the Treaty of Amsterdam. However, *Grant* does not detract from the generally expansive approach taken by the Court to the scope of the Community rules on equal treatment. Indeed, as Barnard points out,[149] the approach advocated by the applicant in that case required 'a bigger leap of faith . . . by the Court than *P v S*, since discrimination against transsexuals is on the grounds of their sex or gender whereas discrimination against homosexuals is on the grounds of their sexuality'. That *Grant* occasioned disappointment in some quarters merely serves to emphasize the boldness of the decision in *P v S*.

Indirect discrimination

One of the most fundamental of the criticisms formulated by some feminists of much anti-discrimination law concerns the extent to which it relies on comparing the situation of women with a so-called male norm. As Fredman explains:[150]

The paradigm worker is the married man whose wife works unpaid in the home, at least for some of her time, looking after children or the elderly and doing domestic work. Equality based on a male norm may be useful for women who are in a position to conform to the male norm. However . . . the penalties for divergence from the norm fall disproportionately on women. Thus it is the male norm itself which functions as an obstacle to the progress of women.

Fredman acknowledges[151] that one way of enhancing the capacity of rules which rely on a male norm to achieve substantive equality is through the concept of indirect discrimination. This concept involves treating as discriminatory rules which, on their face, apply to everyone in the same way but which in practice prejudice the interests of one group more than another. Indirect discrimination is expressly prohibited within the scope of Directives 76/207, 79/7, 86/378, and 86/613 and has now been defined specifically in a separate directive.[152] That definition reflects the case law on indirect discrimination elaborated by the Court, mainly in the field of equal pay.

---

[149] Op cit, p 79, n 88.   [150] (1992) 21 ILJ 119, 121.
[151] Op cit, p 125. See also Fenwick and Hervey, op cit, p 448, n 23.
[152] See Art 2(2) of Dir 97/80 on the burden of proof in cases of discrimination based on sex, OJ 1998 L14/6 (as amended by Dir 98/52, OJ 1998 L205/66); Ellis, op cit, pp 123–4.

The general rule laid down by the Court

An early case in which the Court accepted that indirect discrimination might fall within the scope of the prohibition contained in Article 141 (ex 119) was *Jenkins v Kingsgate*.[153] There the Court was asked whether it was contrary to that article for an employer to pay part-time workers at a lower hourly rate than full-time workers where the part-time workers affected were all, or nearly all, women. The Court said that a pay policy of this nature was acceptable if based on 'factors which are objectively justified and are in no way related to any discrimination based on sex'.[154] It went on:[155]

By contrast, if it is established that a considerably smaller percentage of women than of men perform the minimum number of weekly working hours required in order to be able to claim the full-time hourly rate of pay, the inequality in pay will be contrary to Article 119 of the Treaty where, regard being had to the difficulties encountered by women in arranging to work that minimum number of hours per week, the pay policy of the undertaking in question cannot be explained by factors other than discrimination based on sex.

It was for the national court to decide how the pay policy of the employer in that case was to be characterized.

The Court developed the criteria laid down in *Jenkins* in the later case of *Bilka v Weber von Hartz*,[156] one of the leading decisions of the Court on the concept of indirect discrimination. The case arose out of a challenge to the legality of a policy pursued by a department store called Bilka of excluding part-time employees from membership of an occupational pension scheme on the basis that the exclusion affected many more women than men. Having found, for the reasons given above, that the case fell within the scope of Article 141 (ex 119), the Court turned to the reasons which had been advanced by the store to justify excluding part-timers from its pension scheme. The store claimed that its policy was based on its need to ensure staff cover throughout its opening hours. In its experience, part-timers generally refused to work in the late afternoon and on Saturdays and an attempt had therefore been made to make full-time work more attractive than part-time work by excluding part-timers from the pension scheme.

The Court declared:[157]

It is for the national court, which has sole jurisdiction to make findings of fact, to determine whether and to what extent the grounds put forward by an employer to explain the adoption of a pay practice which applies independently of a worker's sex but in fact affects more women than men may be regarded as objectively justified on economic grounds. If the national court finds that the measures chosen by Bilka correspond to a real need on the part of the undertaking, are appropriate with a view to achieving the objectives pursued and are

---

[153] Case 96/80 [1981] ECR 911.
[154] Para 11. As an example of such a factor, the Court mentioned encouraging full-time work on economic grounds: see para 12.
[155] Para 13.   [156] Case 170/84 [1986] ECR 1607.   [157] Para 36.

necessary to that end, the fact that the measures affect a far greater number of women than men is not sufficient to show that they constitute an infringement of Article 119.

The threshold erected by the Court in *Bilka* for employers seeking to show that indirect discrimination was objectively justified was quite a high one, requiring a strict proportionality test to be satisfied.[158] The employer needed to establish that the objective in view was legitimate and that there was no non–discriminatory or less discriminatory way of achieving it. The approach of the Court has none the less attracted criticism because of the underlying assumption that economic considerations are capable of taking precedence over the principle of equal treatment.[159] It is submitted, however, that in view of the importance attached by the Treaty and the Member States to the operation of the market,[160] the balance struck by the Court is not an unreasonable one, limited as it is to conduct which is not designed to disadvantage women and which produces that result only through circumstances which lie beyond the control of the employer. This does not mean that the principle of equal treatment is not a fundamental one, simply that its application may sometimes have to be weighed against other principles which the legal order of the Community also regards as fundamental.[161] It is none the less appropriate to enter one proviso, namely that the Court should insist on strict compliance with the principle of proportionality when the question of objective justification is considered. Has that proviso been met in the subsequent case law of the Court?

The application of the general rule

It must be acknowledged that the Court has sometimes treated somewhat pusillanimously grounds of justification put forward by employers in cases of indirect discrimination. In *Danfoss*,[162] the Court was asked to consider the compatibility with the Equal Pay Directive of a pay policy under which an employee's basic wage could be supplemented by extra payments based on factors like mobility, training, and seniority. The applicant claimed that, as a result of the policy, the average wage paid to men was higher than that paid to women. One of the issues dealt with by the Court in its judgment was whether a policy such as this could be objectively justified. In one respect, the Court took a fairly robust line. There was some doubt

---

[158] See Ellis, 'The concept of proportionality in European Community sex discrimination law' in Ellis (ed), *The Principle of Proportionality in the Laws of Europe* (1999), p 165. Cf *Reg v Employment Secretary, ex p EOC* [1995] 1 AC 1 (HL).

[159] See Fredman (1992) 21 ILJ 119, 125. Cf Fenwick and Hervey, op cit, p 443.

[160] See Fredman, *Women and the Law* (1997), pp 403–11.

[161] Cf Case 165/82 *Commission v United Kingdom* [1983] ECR 3431, para 13, where the Court referred to the need to reconcile the principle of equal treatment with the principle of respect for private life, which it said was also fundamental; Case 5/88 *Wachauf v Bundesamt für Ernährung und Forstwirtschaft* [1989] ECR 2609, para 18.

[162] Case 109/88 *Handels- og Kontorfunktionærernes Forbund i Danmark v Dansk Arbejdsgiverforening, acting on behalf of Danfoss* [1989] ECR 3199.

as to the precise meaning of the criterion of mobility. In so far as it was used to reward the quality of an employee's work, the Court said it could not be justified if it systematically worked to the disadvantage of women, because it was 'inconceivable that the quality of work done by women should generally be less good'.[163] However, it appeared that the criterion of mobility was also used to reward adaptability to variable hours and places of work. The Court acknowledged that, used in this way, it was capable of working to the disadvantage of female employees whose domestic responsibilities frequently prevented them from being as flexible as male employees. However, citing *Bilka*, the Court rather lamely said that an employer may 'justify the remuneration of such adaptability by showing it is of importance for the performance of specific tasks entrusted to the employee'.[164] The position was the same with regard to the criterion of training. As for length of service, the Court declared that this went 'hand in hand with experience and since experience generally enables the employee to perform his duties better, the employer is free to reward it without having to establish the importance it has in the performance of specific tasks entrusted to the employee'.[165] The Court's failure to remind the national court that it needed to satisfy itself that the disputed criteria reflected the real needs of the employer and that they could not be met in a non-discriminatory way lends support to the view that the Court is unduly attached to the male norm. The conclusion reached by the Court on the length of service criterion was particularly damaging to the objective of equal treatment, for it gave employers a free hand to pay long-serving male employees more than female employees doing the same job without even asking whether the greater experience of the former was reflected in the quality of their work. As we shall see, the Court subsequently retreated from this extreme position.[166]

In *Kowalska*,[167] the Court was asked to rule on the compatibility with Article 141 (ex 119) of a provision of a collective agreement according to which only full-time workers were entitled to severance grants when their contracts of employment were terminated. As usual, most part-timers were women, but the employer maintained that the discrimination was justified because part-time workers were not usually responsible for providing for their own needs or for those of their families. The Court might have been expected to comment on the inherently implausible nature of this sweeping generalization, but it merely reiterated that it was for the national court to decide whether a provision which discriminated indirectly against women was objectively justified.[168]

A more complex claim of objective justification came before the Court in *Enderby*.[169] E was employed within the United Kingdom National Health Service

---

[163] Para 20.   [164] Para 22.   [165] Para 24.   [166] See *Nimz*, below.

[167] Case C–33/89 [1990] ECR I–2591.

[168] It is possible that the Court was merely intending to repeat in a concise form its conclusion on the question of objective justification in *Rinner-Kühn, infra*: see AG Darmon at pp I–2602–3.

[169] Case C–127/92 [1993] ECR I–5535. Cf Case C–167/97 *The Queen v Secretary of State for Employment, ex parte Seymour-Smith and Perez*, judgment of 9 January 1999.

as a speech therapist, an overwhelmingly female profession. She claimed that she was the victim of sex discrimination because she was paid considerably less than members of a comparable profession who were predominantly male and whose jobs were of equal value to hers. One of the questions submitted to the Court by the Court of Appeal asked whether, on the assumption that the two jobs were indeed of equal value, the pay differential could be justified by a shortage of candidates for one job and the need to attract them by higher salaries.

In a case decided under the Equal Pay Act 1970, Lord Denning had been unreceptive to this argument: 'An employer cannot avoid his obligations under the 1970 Act by saying: "I paid him more because he asked for more", or "I paid her less because she was willing to come for less". If any such excuse were permitted, the Act would be a dead letter. Those are the very reasons why there was unequal pay before the statute. They were the very circumstances in which the statute was intended to operate.'[170] Lord Denning preferred an approach based on the 'personal equation of the woman as compared to that of the man, irrespective of any extrinsic forces which led to the variation in pay'.[171] One might have expected the Court of Justice to take a similar approach, but instead the Court said[172] that '[t]he state of the employment market, which may lead an employer to increase the pay of a particular job in order to attract candidates'[173] was capable of justifying indirect discrimination. If the national court was in a position to assess what proportion of the differential was attributable to market forces, then it had to accept that the pay differential was objectively justified 'to the extent of that proportion'.[174] In other cases, it was for the national court to assess, taking account of the principle of proportionality, 'whether the role of market forces in determining the rate of pay was sufficiently significant to provide objective justification for part or all of the difference'.[175]

It is submitted that the Court's ruling in *Enderby* pushes the concept of objective justification too far. The capacity of Article 141 (ex 119) to tackle occupational segregation would have been enhanced had the Court ruled that the only non-discriminatory way of accommodating the need to attract candidates to the higher paid job was by extending the same salary to other jobs which were of equal value. The case might have been distinguished from those concerned with part-time workers for the reason given by Lord Denning, that the justification advanced for the pay differential was unconnected with the work and performance of the individual claimant.[176]

However, to focus exclusively on this aspect of the judgment in *Enderby* is perhaps misleading. It should not be overlooked that the Court laid down a strong

[170] *Clay Cross (Quarry Services) Ltd v Fletcher* [1979] 1 All ER 474, 477.
[171] Ibid. See also *Shields v E Coomes (Holdings) Ltd* [1979] 1 All ER 456. Ellis, op cit, p 126, comments that '[t]he *Bilka-Kaufhaus* decision forced the UK courts to retrench somewhat and to accept the possibility of an economic defence'.
[172] Citing *inter alia Bilka* and *Nimz*.   [173] Para 26.   [174] Para 27.   [175] Para 28.
[176] The Court acknowledged at para 15 of the judgment that the circumstances of the case were not the same as those involving part-time workers.

proportionality test requiring strict scrutiny by the national court of the employer's claim that the difference of treatment, if established, could be justified by market forces.[177] Moreover, the burden of establishing objective justification in cases of indirect discrimination rests with the employer. This was made clear in the *Danfoss* case[178] which, it will be recalled, concerned the legality of a pay policy under which the basic pay of employees was supplemented by payments made on various grounds capable of disadvantaging women. The system of individual supplements made it impossible for a woman paid less than a man doing the same work to establish why this was the case. The Court ruled that 'where an undertaking applies a system of pay which is totally lacking in transparency, it is for the employer to prove that his practice in the matter of wages is not discriminatory, if a female worker establishes, in relation to a relatively large number of employees, that the average pay for women is less than that for men'.[179] This was so even if it meant departing from national rules on the burden of proof. The importance of the Court's ruling on this point, which to some extent pre-empted a proposal for a directive on the burden of proof in sex discrimination cases,[180] was underlined in *Enderby*.[181] There the Court accepted that a *prima facie* case of discrimination might be established by statistics showing that there was a significant difference in pay between two jobs of equal value, one carried out mainly by women, one mainly by men. Provided the national court thought the statistics were reliable, the onus of showing that the difference was based on objectively justified factors unrelated to discrimination based on sex would then shift to the employer.

A more robust approach was taken to the question of objective justification in *Rinner-Kühn v FWW Spezial-Gebäudereinigung*,[182] which concerned the compatibility with Article 141 (ex 119) of national legislation permitting employers to refuse sick pay to employees who worked less than a certain number of hours per week or per month. Considerably fewer women than men worked the requisite number of hours. In seeking to show that the contested legislation was objectively justified, the German Government argued that the workers adversely affected were not as integrated in or dependent on the undertaking employing them as other workers. The Court said that 'those considerations, in so far as they are only generalizations about certain categories of workers, do not enable criteria which are both objective and unrelated to any discrimination on grounds of sex to be identified'.[183]

The Court took a similar approach in *Nimz*,[184] which concerned the compatibility with Article 141 (ex 119) of a provision in a collective agreement which

---

[177] Cf Fredman, 'Equal pay and justification' (1994) 23 ILJ 37.
[178] Case 109/88 *Handels- og Kontorfunktionærernes Forbund i Danmark v Dansk Arbejdsgiverforening, acting on behalf of Danfoss* [1989] ECR 3199. Cf Case C–326/96 *Levez v T H Jennings (Harlow Pools) Ltd*, judgment of 1 December 1998, discussed in ch 5.
[179] Para 16.
[180] The proposal was mentioned by AG Lenz in *Danfoss* at p 3216. See now Dir 97/80, *supra*.
[181] See also Case C–262/88 *Barber* [1990] ECR I–1889, paras 33–5.
[182] Case 171/88 [1989] ECR 2743.   [183] Para 14.
[184] Case C–184/89 [1991] ECR I–297. See also *Seymour-Smith, supra*.

adversely affected the promotion chances of employees working less than three-quarters of normal working time. The class of such employees consisted predominantly of women. It was claimed during the course of the proceedings that employees who worked more than three-quarters of normal working time acquired the necessary skills more quickly and had greater experience than other employees. The Court reiterated that generalizations such as these were not enough to show that the disputed provision, prima facie discriminatory, was objectively justified:

Although experience goes hand in hand with length of service, and experience enables the worker in principle to improve performance of the tasks allotted to him, the objectivity of such a criterion depends on all the circumstances in a particular case, and in particular on the relationship between the nature of the work performed and the experience gained from the performance of that work upon completion of a certain number of working hours.[185]

The Court appeared unreceptive to an attempt to show objective justification in *Bötel*,[186] a reference from the Landesarbeitsgericht Berlin. The case arose out of a dispute between B, a part-time home help, and her employer over compensation for attending training courses. In accordance with the applicable national legislation, B was not compensated for attendance outside her working hours at a course required for working on a staff council. Had she worked full time, her employer would have been required to pay her compensation up to the limit of the full-time working week. The number of women working part-time was significantly higher than the number of men. It might have been thought that, since both part-time and full-time employees received compensation for attending training courses during working hours, there was no discrimination in these circumstances and the case seems to have been argued on this basis. However, the Court took a broader view, observing that 'staff council members who work on a part-time basis receive less compensation than their full-time colleagues when in fact both categories of workers receive without distinction the same number of hours of training in order to be able effectively to look after the interests of employees for the sake of good working relations and for the general good of the undertaking'.[187] The Court added that this situation was liable to deter part-timers from serving on staff councils. The Court acknowledged that it remained open to the Member State concerned to prove to the satisfaction of the national court that legislation such as that in issue was objectively justified, but it gave no indication of any particular grounds on which that might be done.

The Court's judgment in *Bötel* provoked a 'heated debate' in Germany[188] and gave rise to two further references. The first to be decided was *Kuratorium für*

---

[185] Para 14. The Court went on to hold that, should the national court find the disputed provision to be incompatible with Art 141 (ex 119), it must apply to the disadvantaged group the arrangements applied to other employees, since those arrangements were 'the only valid system of reference': para 21. See also on this point Case C–33/89 *Kowalska* [1990] ECR I–2591.

[186] Case C–360/90 [1992] ECR I–3589.   [187] Para 24.

[188] According to AG Darmon in Case C–278/93 *Freers and Speckmann v Deutsche Bundespost* [1996] ECR I–1165, 1167.

Dialyse und Nierentransplantation v Lewark,[189] where the referring court, the Bundesarbeitsgericht, suggested that *Bötel* might have been based on a misunderstanding of the position of staff council members under the relevant German legislation. It emphasized that staff council functions were performed on an honorary and unpaid basis and that the compensation for which German law provided was intended merely to ensure that council members did not lose wages as a result of attending training courses connected with their council functions. These arrangements, it explained, were designed to ensure the independence of staff council members. The idea was that they should not be influenced by the attraction of a special payment or the fear of loss of earnings.

Broadly following the advice of Advocate General Jacobs, the Court observed that the aim of social policy underlying the contested legislation 'appears in itself to be unrelated to any discrimination on grounds of sex. It cannot be disputed that the work of staff councils does indeed play a part in German social policy, in that the councils have the task of promoting harmonious labour relations within undertakings and in their interest. The concern to ensure the independence of the members of those councils thus likewise reflects a legitimate aim of social policy.'[190] The Court reiterated, however, that such legislation was liable to deter part-time workers from serving on staff councils. It emphasized the need for the national court, in satisfying itself that the contested legislation represented a 'suitable and necessary'[191] means of achieving the social policy aim in question, to take into account the possibility that that aim might be achieved by other means. The Court took a similar line the following month in *Freers*.[192]

In commenting on these cases, Shaw highlights 'the remarkable failure to mention anywhere caring obligations which may fall upon part-time workers, especially if they are women, and may in fact be the main reason why they work part-time rather than full-time. The cases talk of part-timers sacrificing their "leisure time" and "free time" in order to attend training courses without "compensation". [The Court] does not address the issue that such time may not be "free" at all, and that women attending training courses outside their normal hours of work may be forced to pay for child care, for example.'[193] The point is well taken, although the Court would doubtless have regarded it as the responsibility of the national court to take account of matters such as these. As Shaw acknowledges,[194] the tone of the Court's remarks suggested a degree of scepticism about whether the disputed legislation was objectively justified.

There is no denying that attributing to the national courts responsibility for establishing whether a given rule is to be regarded as objectively justified creates a danger of inconsistency, both between and within Member States.[195] The possibility of inconsistent application by the national courts of the law laid down by the

---

[189] Case C–457/93 [1996] ECR I–243.   [190] Para 35.   [191] Para 38.   [192] *Supra.*
[193] 'Works councils in German enterprises and Article 119 EC' (1997) 22 ELRev 256, 261. See also Ellis, op cit, pp 131–2.
[194] Op cit, p 260.   [195] See Ellis, op cit, p 130.

Court of Justice is not confined to the field of equal treatment.[196] Indeed, it is probably inherent in a system like that established by Article 234 (ex 177) EC under which cases only reach the Court of Justice through the filter of the national court, which alone has a direct knowledge of the facts. The involvement of the national courts may even be regarded as having certain advantages. It enlists their help in reviewing the legality of the measures which have been challenged, thereby distancing the Court of Justice from the outcome, and implicitly acknowledges that they are better placed to take due account of domestic traditions and concerns. These matters are not without importance for the overall legitimacy of the legal order established by the Treaty.[197]

Pregnancy

The treatment of pregnant employees poses a particular dilemma for the law of sex discrimination. One might say that it is not discriminatory to dismiss, or to refuse to employ, a woman on the basis that she is pregnant because pregnant women simply cannot be compared with men.[198] Alternatively, it might be argued that a woman has been discriminated against on grounds of sex in these circumstances unless it can be shown that a man suffering from a medical condition which had a similar effect on his ability to do the job would have been treated in the same way.[199] A third view, which enhances considerably the protection afforded to pregnant women in the workplace and does not depend on a male norm of comparison, is that to treat a woman adversely because she is pregnant necessarily constitutes discrimination on grounds of sex because men cannot be in the same position. The Court of Justice has tried, with only limited success, to steer a middle course between the second and the third view.

In *Dekker*,[200] a woman who was three months pregnant applied for a job with a body known as the VJV. The committee responsible for assessing applications for the post in question was aware that the applicant was pregnant but recommended to the management of the VJV that she be appointed, as it considered her the best qualified candidate. The management none the less decided not to employ her. The reason it gave was that, since the applicant was already pregnant when she applied for the job, the VJV's insurer would not reimburse the maternity pay which the VJV would be obliged to pay her while she was on maternity leave. This would

---

[196] The same issue arose in the context of Art 28 (ex 30) EC in the Sunday trading cases, discussed in ch 7.

[197] See further ch 16.

[198] This was the view taken by the majority of the Employment Appeal Tribunal in *Turley v Allders Stores Ltd* [1980] ICR 66. The consequence of this view would be that, if society deems pregnant women worthy of protection, special rules to deal with them would be needed.

[199] This was the view taken by the Court of Appeal in *Webb v EMO Air Cargo (UK) Ltd* [1992] IRLR 116. See Arnull, 'When is pregnancy like an arthritic hip?' (1992) 17 ELRev 265.

[200] Case C–177/88 [1990] ECR I–3941.

have made it financially impossible for the VJV to employ anyone to replace her during that period. The applicant instituted proceedings against the VJV and the Court of Justice was eventually asked to rule on the effect of the Equal Treatment Directive in these circumstances.[201]

The Court began by observing that the question whether a refusal to employ someone in circumstances such as these was capable of amounting to direct sex discrimination for the purposes of the directive depended on whether the real reason for the refusal was one which applied to workers of both sexes or one which applied only to the members of one sex. In a strikingly unequivocal statement, the Court made it clear that, since only women could be refused employment because they were pregnant, a refusal on that ground constituted direct discrimination on grounds of sex. The Court added that a refusal to employ a pregnant woman because of the financial consequences of her absence during the pregnancy had to be considered due essentially to the pregnancy. Such discrimination could not be justified, the Court said, by the financial loss the employer would suffer while the woman was on maternity leave. The Court declared[202] that the discrimination it had identified 'was in direct contravention of the principle of equal treatment embodied in Articles 2(1) and 3(1)' of the directive. It made it clear that it would not make any difference if there were in fact no male candidates for the post and that it was not necessary for the claimant to show fault on the part of the employer or the absence of any grounds of justification recognized in national law.

This was a remarkably strong judgment for several reasons. The most obvious was the Court's espousal of the view that to treat a woman adversely because she is pregnant necessarily amounts to *direct* discrimination on grounds of her sex, which appeared to rule out any possibility that it might be justified.[203] The Court was also prepared to treat as attributable to the pregnancy adverse treatment which was, at least in part and indirectly, caused by the policy adopted by the employer's insurer with regard to maternity pay. In addition, as already noted, the case showed that it was not necessary for a claimant to point to a physical comparator if discrimination on the grounds of sex could be established in other ways.[204]

In another case decided on the same day as *Dekker*, the Court's approach was less bold. In the *Hertz* case,[205] a female employee who had recently given birth to a child was dismissed on account of absence due to illness. Although the employee's maternity leave had expired, it was common ground that the illness from which she was suffering was attributable to her pregnancy and confinement. The Court was asked to clarify the effect of the Equal Treatment Directive in circumstances such

---

[201] Although the employer was not an emanation of the State, the referring court thought that the meaning of the directive might affect the interpretation of the domestic law implementing it: see [1990] ECR I–3941, 3946.

[202] Para 14.

[203] See AG Darmon at p I–3960. The question whether direct discrimination should be treated as capable of justification is considered below.

[204] Cf in the context of Art 141 (ex 119) Case 129/79 *Macarthys v Smith* [1980] ECR 1275.

[205] Case C–179/88 *Handels- og Kontorfunktionærernes Forbund* [1990] ECR I–3979.

as these. The Court might have been expected to say that the dismissal of an employee in circumstances such as these was incompatible with the directive, for the dismissal was attributable essentially to the employee's pregnancy. The Court accepted that the protection afforded to pregnant women by the directive extended to dismissal as well as refusal to engage. However, it said that illnesses attributable to pregnancy or confinement which manifested themselves after the woman's maternity had come to an end could not be distinguished from other illnesses. It went on: 'Male and female workers are equally exposed to illness. Although certain disorders are, it is true, specific to one or other sex, the only question is whether a woman is dismissed on account of absence due to illness in the same circumstances as a man; if that is the case, then there is no direct discrimination on grounds of sex.'[206]

Being decided on the same day and by an identical formation of the Court, *Hertz* was evidently intended to qualify *Dekker*. However, the reason given by the Court for distinguishing the two cases is unconvincing. Although it is of course true that both men and women can fall ill and that some illnesses are sex-specific, pregnancy is not an illness. On the contrary, it is a normal condition, but one which only affects women. The Court accepted in *Dekker* that to treat a woman adversely on the basis that she is pregnant constitutes direct discrimination on grounds of sex. It might have been thought that dismissal due to an illness attributable to pregnancy 'must be regarded as based, essentially, on the fact of pregnancy' in the same way as a refusal of employment on account of the financial consequences of absence due to pregnancy.[207]

Whatever the logical basis for distinguishing between *Dekker* and *Hertz*, the outcome seemed to be that the protection enjoyed by pregnant women under the Equal Treatment Directive lasted only until the expiry of the maternity leave accorded to them under national law. In *Habermann-Beltermann*,[208] a case referred by the Arbeitsgericht Regensburg, the Court suggested that the protection enjoyed by pregnant women before that moment was not quite as extensive as *Dekker* might have been taken to imply. The applicant was engaged as a night attendant in an old people's home. It then transpired that she was pregnant. German law prevented pregnant women from being asked to work at night. The applicant's employment contract was therefore terminated. Two features of the case were emphasized by the Court: first, that the employment contract had been concluded for an indefinite period, and, secondly, that both employer and employee were unaware of the pregnancy at the time the contract was concluded.

It will be recalled that Article 2(3) of the Equal Treatment Directive provides that it does not prejudice 'provisions concerning the protection of women, particularly as regards pregnancy and maternity'. The Court said that the national rule preventing pregnant women from working at night was 'unquestionably compatible with Article 2(3)' and noted that it would have prevented the claimant from

---

[206] Para 17.   [207] Cf *Dekker*, para 12.   [208] Case C–421/92 [1994] ECR I–1657.

working only for a limited period in relation to the total length of the contract. It declared: 'In the circumstances, to acknowledge that the contract may be held to be invalid or may be avoided because of the temporary inability of the pregnant employee to perform the night-time work for which she has been engaged would be contrary to the objective of protecting such persons pursued by Article 2(3) of the directive, and would deprive that provision of its effectiveness.' The directive therefore precluded the termination of an employment contract in a case such as this. The judgment strongly implied, however, that the outcome would have been different had the claimant's pregnancy prevented her from working during a significant part of the duration of the contract or had the claimant sought to conceal the fact she was pregnant when appointed.

In *Webb v EMO Air Cargo*,[209] the Court again emphasized the importance of the duration of the term for which the claimant had been employed. A woman employed to cover for a pregnant employee was dismissed when she found that she was herself pregnant and would be absent at roughly the same time as the person for whom she had been employed as cover. A man recruited for the same purpose would also have been dismissed if he had announced that, for medical or other reasons, he would be absent during the relevant period. In ruling that the Equal Treatment Directive precluded the dismissal of a female employee in circumstances such as these, the Court made a number of strong statements about the position of pregnant women. First, it explicitly dismissed the idea that the position of a pregnant woman could be compared with that of a man incapacitated for medical or other reasons: 'pregnancy is not in any way comparable with a pathological condition, and even less so with unavailability for work on non-medical grounds, both of which are situations that may justify the dismissal of a woman without discriminating on grounds of sex'.[210] Secondly, it roundly rejected the suggestion of the United Kingdom Government that dismissal of a woman in circumstances such as these might be justified because of her inability to fulfil a fundamental condition of her employment contract. The Court observed: 'The availability of an employee is necessarily, for the employer, a precondition for the proper performance of the employment contract. However, the protection afforded by Community law to a woman during pregnancy and after childbirth cannot be dependent on whether her presence at work during maternity is essential to the proper functioning of the undertaking in which she is employed. Any contrary interpretation would render ineffective the provisions of the directive.'[211] The Court concluded that, in a case like this, the 'termination of a contract for an indefinite period on grounds of the woman's pregnancy cannot be justified by the fact that she is prevented, on a purely temporary basis, from performing the work for which she has been engaged . . .'.[212] Once again, the judgment suggested that the outcome might have been different had the claimant not been employed for an unlimited term.

---

[209] Case C–32/93 [1994] ECR I–3567.   [210] Para 25.   [211] Para 26.   [212] Para 27.

The notion that the Equal Treatment Directive conferred special protection on female employees who fell ill as a result of pregnancy was challenged in *Brown v Rentokil*.[213] The *Hertz* ruling had not made it entirely clear whether the decisive factor was the fact that the employee there had been dismissed after the end of her maternity leave or the fact that her dismissal was due to illness. In *Larsson v Føtex Supermarked*,[214] a five-Judge chamber of the Court rather surprisingly took the latter view, ruling that, outside the period of maternity leave, the directive did not protect a woman from dismissal on grounds of absence due to illness attributable to pregnancy, since male and female workers were equally exposed to illness.[215] In *Brown* a full Court of eleven Judges[216] expressly overruled *Larsson*, declaring that 'dismissal of a female worker during pregnancy for absences due to incapacity for work resulting from her pregnancy is linked to the occurrence of risks inherent in pregnancy and must therefore be regarded as essentially based on the fact of pregnancy. Such a dismissal can affect only women and therefore constitutes direct discrimination on grounds of sex.'[217]

Although not applicable at the material time, the Court's decision in *Brown* was consistent with Article 10 of Directive 92/85 on the safety and health at work of pregnant workers and workers who have recently given birth or are breastfeeding.[218] Adopted under Article 138 (ex 118a) EC, Directive 92/85 was cited by the Court in *Webb*, *Larsson* and *Brown* as part of the general context. Article 10(1) precludes the dismissal of female employees 'during the period from the beginning of their pregnancy to the end of the maternity leave referred to in Article 8(1), save in exceptional cases not connected with their condition . . .'.[219] However, the Equal Treatment Directive remains the only instrument covering other forms of adverse treatment suffered by pregnant women in the workplace.

There are differing views on the desirability of the approach exemplified by Directive 92/85. Fenwick and Hervey maintain that conferring on women what they call special protection 'has great costs for women, since it permits unfavourable as well as favourable treatment of women where differences between women and men can be perceived'.[220] They prefer an approach which seeks to achieve substantive equality between men and women and which 'seeks to confine mandatory protective treatment for women arising from their child bearing function to as narrow a scope as possible'.[221] Ellis takes a different view. She argues that, to the extent that the directive creates a special regime for pregnant workers, it is to be wel-

---

[213] Case C–394/96 [1998] ECR I–4185. See also Case C–66/96 *Handels- og Kontorfunktionærernes Forbund i Danmark and Others v Fællesforeningen for Danmarks Brugsforeninger and Others*, judgment of 19 November 1998.

[214] Case C–400/95 [1997] ECR I–2757.

[215] For a defence of *Larsson*, see Ellis, op cit, pp 206–7.

[216] Including four of the Judges who decided *Larsson*.   [217] Para 24.

[218] OJ 1992 L348/1.

[219] Art 8(1) of the directive lays down minimum requirements as to maternity leave. See Case C–411/96 *Boyle and Others v EOC*, judgment of 27 October 1998.

[220] Op cit, p 455.   [221] Ibid.

comed: 'since pregnancy and childbirth are situations which are unique to women, it is inappropriate to use the anti-discrimination legislation as the chief legal vehicle to cater for them. It is certainly vital to the concepts of equality or identity of opportunity for special rules to exist to cater for maternity rights for workers, but such rules need to be additional to the normal equality principle.'[222] Fredman also points to the advantages of conferring specific rights on certain categories of women: 'The advantage of such a strategy is that it does not rely on the general anti-discrimination principle, with its problematic dependence on equality. Thus pregnancy attracts rights for its own sake, rather than on the basis of an artificial comparison.'[223]

It is submitted that, while comprehensive legislation setting out the rights of pregnant workers is desirable, the principle of equal treatment also has a useful role to play, particularly in cases arising before any such legislation has entered into force or which fall outside its scope. However, the Court has not been wholly consistent in applying the principle in the context of pregnancy and maternity. The general approach laid down in *Dekker* was bold and progressive, but the Court rather unconvincingly tried to sugar the pill for employers by holding in *Hertz* that the *Dekker* principle ceased to apply once the period of maternity leave had come to an end. Of wider significance is the suggestion in *Habermann-Beltermann* and *Webb v EMO Air Cargo* that to dismiss a woman employed on a fixed term contract on the basis that she is pregnant might be consistent with the Equal Treatment Directive. Since the Court has classified adverse treatment which is only indirectly attributable to pregnancy as direct discrimination on grounds of sex, it seems to be acknowledging in those cases that there are some circumstances in which direct discrimination may be justified.

Such a development would be of considerable importance for the whole of the law of equal treatment. Although it would be met with disapproval in some quarters,[224] Advocate General van Gerven has given two reasons why direct discrimination should in exceptional cases be regarded as capable of objective justification.[225] One is that the general principle of equality, of which the rules on equal treatment for men and women may be regarded as a specific application,[226] is not infringed where differentiation between similar situations is 'objectively justified'.[227] Another

---

[222] Op cit, p 261. Ellis goes on to criticize as 'inaccurate and patronizing' the extent to which the directive treats pregnant women and women who have recently given birth in the same way as sick workers.

[223] 'European Community discrimination law: a critique' (1992) 21 ILJ 119, 134.

[224] See eg Ellis, op cit, pp 134–6.

[225] See his Opinion in Case C–132/92 *Birds Eye Walls v Roberts* [1993] ECR I–5579, 5592–4. Cf the Court's case law on freedom of movement and the composition of national sports teams, discussed in ch 8.

[226] See *P v S and Cornwall County Council, supra*.

[227] See eg Joined Cases 117/76 and 16/77 *Ruckdeschel v Hauptzollamt Hamburg-St Annen* [1977] ECR 1753, para 7; ch 6, above. The European Court of Human Rights takes a similar approach: see eg the *Belgian Linguistic Case* [1979–80] 1 EHRR 252, para 10; *Abdulaziz, Cabales and Balkandali v United Kingdom* [1985] 7 EHRR 471, para 78.

is that the opposite view attaches too much significance to the question whether a particular form of discrimination should be classified as direct or indirect. Indeed, it might be said that it is liable to lead to some forms of discrimination being classified as indirect solely in order to permit them to be treated as objectively justified. As we have seen, the Community legislature has not hesitated to exclude certain forms of discrimination from the scope of the principle of equal treatment laid down in the various directives it has adopted on the matter, an approach endorsed by the Amsterdam version of Article 141 (ex 119) of the Treaty.[228] It is therefore submitted that the Court could legitimately conclude that cases of direct discrimination are capable of objective justification, although the fundamental nature of the principle of equal treatment would mean that such a possibility should be confined to wholly exceptional cases. A strict proportionality test would provide one way of keeping the possibility within bounds.

Positive action

Nowhere is the Court's growing uncertainty about the proper scope of the Community rules on equal treatment for men and women more apparent than in its case law on so-called positive action.[229] According to Fredman,[230] positive action 'denotes the deliberate use of race- or gender-conscious criteria for the specific purpose of benefiting a group which has previously been disadvantaged on grounds of race or gender'. As she points out, it is inherently controversial: 'How can it be legitimate for an anti-discrimination policy to include measures which actively discriminate on grounds of race or sex?'

The Equal Treatment Directive contains a provision which might seem to authorize positive action, at least to some extent. According to Article 2(4), '[t]his Directive shall be without prejudice to measures to promote equal opportunities for men and women, in particular by removing existing inequalities which affect women's opportunities' in areas falling within the scope of the directive. Article 2(4) is the third of three qualifications to the principle of equal treatment.[231] Article 2(2) says that Member States may exclude from the scope of the directive 'those occupational activities and, where appropriate, the training leading thereto, for which, by reason of their nature or the context in which they are carried out, the sex of the worker constitutes a determining factor'. Article 2(3) has already been mentioned. It provides that the directive does not prejudice 'provisions concerning the protection of women, particularly as regards pregnancy and maternity'. All

---

[228] Discussed below.

[229] Sometimes called reverse discrimination or affirmative action: see the Opinion of AG Tesauro in Case C–450/93 *Kalanke v Bremen* [1995] ECR I–3051, 3057–8; Fredman, 'Reversing discrimination' (1997) 113 LQR 575.

[230] Ibid.

[231] Defined by Art 2(1) as meaning that 'there shall be no discrimination whatsoever on grounds of sex either directly or indirectly by reference in particular to marital or family status.'

three paragraphs appear to authorize some form of action that would otherwise be contrary to the principle of equal treatment. It would seem to follow that each may be used to justify a degree of discrimination in favour of members of the privileged sex. In *Johnston v Chief Constable of the Royal Ulster Constabulary*,[232] the Court said that Article 2(2), 'being a derogation from an individual right laid down in the directive, must be interpreted strictly'[233] and that the same was true of Article 2(3). However, in *Hofmann v Barmer Ersatzkasse*,[234] Advocate General Darmon described Article 2(4) as 'in a category of its own . . . It merely appears to make an exception to the principle [of equal treatment]: in aiming to compensate for existing discrimination it seeks to re-establish equality and not to prejudice it. In other words, since it presupposes that there is an inequality which must be removed, the exception must be broadly construed.' The Advocate General appeared to envisage that Article 2(4) might therefore be used to justify some forms of positive action.

An indication that the Court did not share the view that Article 2(4) was to be construed broadly came in *Commission v France*,[235] where the Commission sought a declaration that France had breached its obligations under the Equal Treatment Directive by failing to prohibit the inclusion in collective agreements of certain provisions granting special rights to women. Such special rights included:[236]

the extension of maternity leave; the shortening of working hours, for example for women over 59 years of age; the advancement of the retirement age; the obtaining of leave when a child is ill; the granting of additional days of annual leave in respect of each child; the granting of one day's leave at the beginning of the school year; the granting of time off work on Mother's Day; daily breaks for women working on keyboard equipment or employed as typists or switchboard operators; the granting of extra points for pension rights in respect of the second [child] and subsequent children; and the payment of an allowance to mothers who have to meet the cost of nurseries or child-minders.

An attempt by the French Government to rely on Article 2(3) and (4) of the directive was unsuccessful. As far as the former was concerned, the Court pointed out that some of the contested special rights related 'to the protection of women in their capacity as older workers or parents—categories to which both men and women may equally belong'.[237] As for Article 2(4), that provision was 'specifically and exclusively designed to allow measures which, although discriminatory in appearance, are in fact intended to eliminate or reduce actual instances of inequality which may exist in the reality of social life. Nothing in the papers of the case, however, makes it possible to conclude that a generalized preservation of special rights for women in collective agreements may correspond to the situation envisaged in that provision.'[238] The Court's ruling left unclear the extent to which more specific provisions would have been justified if intended to eliminate actual instances of inequality.

---

[232] Case 222/84 [1986] ECR 1651.   [233] Para 36.
[234] Case 184/83 [1984] ECR 3047, 3082.   [235] Case 312/86 [1988] ECR 6315.
[236] Para 8 of the judgment.   [237] Para 14.   [238] Para 15.

It was against that background that the case of *Kalanke v Bremen*[239] was referred to the Court. The facts were fairly straightforward. The Bremen Law on Equal Treatment for Men and Women in the Public Service provided that female candidates for a job or for promotion were to be given priority over male candidates with the same qualifications in sectors where women were under-represented. This would be the case where women did not make up at least half of the staff in the individual salary brackets in the relevant personnel group within a department. The applicant, a man, was one of two candidates shortlisted for a post in the Bremen Parks Department. The other candidate was a woman who was considered equally qualified. She was given the job because women were under-represented in the Bremen Parks Department. The applicant brought proceedings against the City of Bremen and they were in due course referred to the Court of Justice by the Bundesarbeitsgericht, which sought guidance on the scope of the derogation from the principle of equal treatment set out in Article 2(4) of Directive 76/207.

Advocate General Tesauro did not think that Article 2(4) could be used to justify legislation such as that in issue before the referring court. He declared: 'To my mind, giving equal opportunities can only mean putting people in a position to attain equal results and hence restoring conditions of equality as between members of the two sexes as regards starting points.'[240] He concluded that '[p]ositive action must therefore be directed at removing the obstacles preventing women from having equal opportunites by tackling, for example, educational guidance and vocational training. In contrast, positive action may not be directed towards guaranteeing women equal results from occupying a job, that is to say, at points of arrival, by way of compensation for historical discrimination. In sum, positive action may not be regarded, even less employed, as a means of remedying, through discriminatory measures, a situation of impaired inequality in the past.'[241]

The Court agreed. Article 2(4), it said, permitted 'national measures relating to access to employment, including promotion, which give a specific advantage to women with a view to improving their ability to compete on the labour market and to pursue a career on an equal footing with men'.[242] However, as a derogation from an individual right laid down in the directive, Article 2(4) was to be interpreted strictly. National rules which guaranteed women 'absolute and unconditional priority for appointment or promotion'[243] went beyond the promotion of equal opportunities and fell outside the scope of Article 2(4). The Court added: 'in so far as it seeks to achieve equal representation of men and women in all grades and levels within a department, such a system substitutes for equality of opportunity as envisaged in Article 2(4) the result which is only to be arrived at by providing equality of opportunity'.[244]

The referring court had pointed out that the contested law did not involve a system of strict quotas because a woman was not accorded priority unless her qualifications were equivalent to those of a male candidate for the same post. A male

---

[239] *Supra.*   [240] [1995] ECR I–3051, 3060.   [241] [1995] ECR I–3051, 3063.
[242] Para 19.   [243] Para 22.   [244] Para 23.

candidate with better qualifications would not therefore be affected by it. This made the case an ideal test of the extent to which Article 2(4) permitted positive action. The Court's judgment caused consternation in several Member States, appeared to undermine a recommendation on positive action for women issued by the Council in 1984,[245] and cast doubt on the Commission's own employment practices.[246] Shortly after the judgment was delivered, the Commission issued a communication in which it suggested that it was limited to national rules which gave women an absolute and unconditional right to appointment or promotion: 'The Commission therefore takes the view that quota systems which fall short of the degree of rigidity and automaticity provided for by the Bremen law have not been touched by the Court's judgment and are, in consequence, to be regarded as lawful.'[247]

Whether that interpretation of the judgment was correct was put to the test in *Marschall v Land Nordrhein-Westfalen*,[248] another reference from Germany, this time by the Verwaltungsgericht Gelsenkirchen. The Law on Civil Servants of the Land of North Rhine-Westphalia contained a provision which stated: 'Where, in the sector of the authority responsible for promotion, there are fewer women than men in the particular higher grade post in the career bracket, women are to be given priority for promotion in the event of equal suitability, competence and professional performance, unless reasons specific to an individual [male] candidate tilt the balance in his favour.' The applicant applied for promotion but an equally qualified woman was appointed on the basis of that provision. The Court was asked whether such a rule was compatible with Article 2(4) of the directive.

The proviso contained in the contested provision appeared to distinguish it from the provision at issue in *Kalanke* and a number of those who submitted observations argued that, since the rule at issue in *Marschall* did not guarantee women absolute and unconditional priority, it was acceptable under Article 2(4). Advocate General Jacobs did not find that argument convincing.[249] As he pointed out, the Court had acknowledged in *Kalanke*[250] that the provision at issue there had to be interpreted in accordance with the German Basic Law, the Grundgesetz, which had the effect of requiring exceptions to be made in appropriate cases even where priority for promotion was in principle to be given to women. The effect of the Court's ruling in that case was, according to the Advocate General, 'that any rule which goes beyond the promotion of equal opportunities by seeking to impose instead the desired result of equal representation'[251] was outside the scope of Article

[245] Recommendation 84/635, OJ 1984 L331/34.
[246] See Ellis, op cit, pp 257–8. Keeling, op cit, pp 516–17, points out that the rule at issue in *Kalanke* 'was similar to a rule developed by the Court of Justice whereby the European institutions may take into account the nationality of a candidate, as a tie-breaker, when several candidates for employment are equally qualified and a particular nationality is underrepresented'.
[247] COM(96) 88 final, p 9.   [248] Case C–409/95 [1997] ECR I–6363.
[249] See [1997] ECR I–6363, 6372–5. The Opinion of AG Jacobs makes extensive reference to the barrage of academic comment which *Kalanke* attracted.
[250] See para 9 of the Court's judgment.   [251] p I–6374.

2(4) of the Equal Treatment Directive and unlawful. The Advocate General took the view that the rule at issue in *Marschall* could not be saved by the proviso, because its practical application might involve the use of traditional criteria which discriminated against women.[252] A rule which discriminated against the members of one sex could not be saved by a proviso which discriminated against the members of the other sex.[253] Advocate General Jacobs concluded that the contested national rule was unlawful having regard to the judgment of the Court in *Kalanke*. He urged the Court to resist any temptation to distinguish that case 'on narrow technical grounds'.[254]

The arguments marshalled by the Advocate General seem to have fallen on deaf ears. The Court pointed out that, 'unlike the provisions in question in *Kalanke*, the provision in question in this case contains a clause ("Öffnungsklausel", hereinafter "saving clause") to the effect that women are not to be given priority in promotions if reasons specific to an individual male candidate tilt the balance in his favour'.[255] There was evidence that, even where male and female candidates were equally qualified, male candidates tended to be preferred on account of prejudices and stereotypes about women in the workplace. The mere fact that a male candidate and a female candidate had the same qualifications did not mean that they had the same chances. A national rule which, subject to the application of a saving clause, gave female candidates priority over equally qualified male candidates in sectors where women were under-represented might therefore be covered by Article 2(4) 'if such a rule may counteract the prejudicial effects on female candidates of the attitudes and behaviour described above and thus reduce actual instances of inequality which may exist in the real world'.[256] A national rule which sought to give female candidates absolute and unconditional priority would fall outside the limits laid down in Article 2(4). However:

Unlike the rules at issue in *Kalanke*, a national rule which, as in the case in point in the main proceedings, contains a saving clause does not exceed those limits if, in each individual case, it provides for male candidates who are equally as qualified [*sic*] as the female candidates a guarantee that the candidatures will be the subject of an objective assessment which will take account of all criteria specific to the individual candidates and will override the priority accorded to female candidates where one or more of those criteria tilts the balance in favour of the male candidate. In this respect, however, it should be remembered that those criteria must not be such as to discriminate against female candidates.[257]

It was for the national court to examine whether the contested provision satisfied those conditions.

---

[252] eg preferring a man due to the fact that he is more experienced because he has had fewer career breaks or preferring a male with dependants to a male earner's wife: see the observations of the Land summarized at p I–6366 of the Opinion of AG Jacobs.

[253] See pp I–6375–6.   [254] p I–6376.   [255] Para 24.

[256] Para 31.   [257] Para 33.

It appears that provisions such as those at issue in *Kalanke* have had little effect on the development of women's careers[258] and one may ask how likely it is that the qualifications of two candidates for promotion will ever be genuinely equal. The answer is perhaps that such rules can only operate where the discretion of the committee considering the merits of the various candidates is strictly limited by rules which attribute precise values to certain attributes. However, one can envisage other more overtly discriminatory types of positive action and the Court's decisions in *Kalanke* and *Marschall* are important authorities on the extent to which such action falls within the scope of Article 2(4) of the Equal Treatment Directive. Unfortunately they left the law in a state of considerable confusion. The thirteen-Judge full Court which decided *Marschall* was evidently more sympathetic to measures of positive action than the eleven-Judge full Court which heard *Kalanke*. However, it is by no means clear that the former decision overrules the latter. Certainly it does not do so expressly and the language used by the Court in *Marschall* to describe the effect of *Kalanke* suggests that, notwithstanding the line taken by Advocate General Jacobs, it regarded that case as indeed confined to national measures giving absolute and unconditional priority to female candidates. That view seems to be supported by the way in which the *Kalanke* ruling was applied by the referring court, which took the view that the scope left by the contested rule for exceptions was too limited to meet the requirements of the directive.[259]

If the Court in *Marschall* intended to leave *Kalanke* in place, the result is that only the mildest form of positive action is compatible with Article 2(4) of the directive. Does the manner in which the Court dealt with this issue reveal anything about the nature of the principle of equal treatment? In *Marschall*, Advocate General Jacobs observed that 'the Court is not being asked—nor would it be appropriate for it to be asked—to rule on the desirability of positive discrimination or affirmative action generally: the national court's question concerns the conformity of the national rule at issue with two specific provisions of the Equal Treatment Directive. Similarly the Court in its recent decision in *Kalanke* relating to a similar national rule was focusing solely—notwithstanding the tenor of some of the academic reaction to the case—on the compatibility of that rule with those provisions.'[260] In formal terms, the Advocate General was clearly right: whether or not affirmative action is desirable is a matter for the Community legislature. However, the relevant provisions of the Equal Treatment Directive, and in particular Article 2(4), did not indicate with any degree of clarity the extent to which positive action was permitted. As a result, the Court had to have regard to the spirit and general scheme of the directive. The scheme of Article 2 might well have been thought to justify a more

---

[258] See Szyszczak, 'Positive action after *Kalanke*' (1996) 59 MLR 876, 879; AG Jacobs in *Marschall* at pp I–6378–9.

[259] See Senden, 'Positive action in the EU put to the test. A negative score?' (1996) 3 MJ 146, 157; Prechal (1996) 33 CMLRev 1245, 1249.

[260] [1997] ECR I–6363, 6367–8. See also pp I–6378–9.

relaxed approach to positive action than that taken by the Court. The article consists of four paragraphs. The first defines the principle of equal treatment and the second, third, and fourth qualify that principle in various ways. As was pointed out above, they seem to be intended to authorize acts which would otherwise be caught by the principle defined in paragraph 1. It would therefore have been consistent with the wording and scheme of the directive for Article 2(4) to have been interpreted as authorizing a measure of discrimination against the members of one sex.[261] Why did the Court resist that conclusion?

A technical reason given by the Court was that, as a derogation from the principle of equal treatment, Article 2(4) was to be interpreted strictly.[262] Given that the Court had previously taken the same approach to the interpretation of Article 2(2) and (3), this was not surprising. However, it may be observed that Article 2(4) is a somewhat peculiar type of derogation since, even if interpreted broadly, it could be seen not as jeopardizing but as contributing to the achievement of the directive's underlying aims.[263] A more fundamental reason for the conclusion reached by the Court is its attachment to the principle of equal treatment as an individual right enjoyed by men and women on the same terms.[264] That approach is not without its critics. Fredman, for example, argues that 'since discrimination on grounds of race or sex has consistently worked to the detriment of black people and women, discrimination in their favour should be viewed quite differently from invidious and detrimental discrimination. A law which genuinely aims to narrow the disparities and eventually achieve equality must tolerate unequal treatment where necessary to achieve more equal results.' She also advocates 'a movement beyond pure individualism: a recognition of the role of group membership in shaping an individual's choices; and of the social responsibility of citizens regardless of individual fault. Taking race or sex into account is crucial in this enterprise.'[265] Although this approach might perhaps have been accommodated within the framework of the Equal Treatment Directive, it is at odds with the line preferred by the Court.

The entry into force of the Treaty of Amsterdam rendered the debate over the precise scope of *Kalanke* and *Marschall* somewhat academic due to the insertion, mentioned above, in Article 141 (ex 119) of a new paragraph 4, providing:

With a view to ensuring full equality in practice between men and women in working life, the principle of equal treatment shall not prevent any Member State from maintaining or adopting measures providing for specific advantages in order to make it easier for the under-

---

[261] See Ellis, op cit, pp 255–7.

[262] See *Kalanke*, para 21. Cf *Johnston*, para 36 (concerning Art 2(2)) and para 44 (concerning Art 2(3)).

[263] The Court's insistence on interpreting Art 2(4) strictly is criticized by Prechal (1996) 33 CMLRev 1245, 1255, and Szyszczak (1996) 59 MLR 876, 883.

[264] Cf AG Tesauro in *Kalanke* at p I–3057; AG Jacobs in *Marschall* at pp I–6374–5.

[265] See 'Reversing discrimination' (1997) 113 LQR 575, 596. This article contains an excellent survey of the theoretical issues raised by affirmative action and of the legal responses in the UK, the EC and the USA. See also Fredman, 'European Community discrimination law: a critique' (1992) 21 ILJ 119, 128.

represented sex to pursue a vocational activity or to prevent or compensate for disadvantages in professional careers.

Nothwithstanding the gender-neutral language of the paragraph, it is intended to be of benefit primarily to women. This emerges from a declaration adopted by the IGC[266] according to which, when acting within the scope of Article 141(4), 'Member States should, in the first instance, aim at improving the situation of women in working life.' The new paragraph is based on Article 6(3) of the Agreement on Social Policy, but that provision was more limited in scope, being confined to the field of equal pay. Moreover, it contained no reference to the need to ensure full equality in practice between men and women in working life. It therefore seems likely that Article 141(4) will be interpreted as permitting a wider range of positive action than Article 2(4) of the Equal Treatment Directive, as interpreted by the Court in *Kalanke* and *Marschall*.[267]

The social security directive

The approach taken by the Court to the application of Directive 79/7 on equal treatment in social security has on occasion been less firm than that taken in the context of equal treatment in employment.[268] In particular, it has appeared unwilling in the social security field to subject to strict scrutiny claims advanced by Member States that indirectly discriminatory national rules are objectively justified. An example is *Nolte v Landesversicherungsanstalt Hannover*.[269] N did not qualify for an invalidity pension under German law because the employment in which she had been engaged was classified as minor and was not subject to compulsory insurance. Employment was regarded as minor where it occupied the person concerned for fewer than 15 hours per week and the monthly income it produced fell below a certain level. Considerably more women than men were affected by the relevant national provisions and the Court was asked whether they were compatible with Directive 79/7. The Court accepted that someone in N's position fell within the personal scope of the directive. However, it ruled that legislation such as this was not to be considered indirectly discriminatory 'since the national legislature was reasonably entitled to consider that the legislation in question was necessary in order to achieve a social policy aim unrelated to any discrimination on grounds of sex', in particular to meet demand for minor employment. The Court reached a similar conclusion in *Megner and Scheffel v Innungskrankenkasse Rheinhessen Pfalz*,[270] decided on the same day.

[266] No 28.
[267] The amendment to the Treaty rendered a Commission proposal to amend Art 2(4) of Dir 76/207 redundant. See the comments of AG Jacobs in *Marschall* at p I–6379–80 before the outcome of the IGC was known.
[268] See generally McCrudden (ed), *Equality of Treatment between Women and Men in Social Security* (1994); Ellis, op cit, ch 4.
[269] Case C–317/93 [1995] ECR I–4625.   [270] Case C–444/93 [1995] ECR I–4741.

Although the Court was in these cases dealing with the question whether indirect discrimination could be justified, the test which the Member State concerned was required to satisfy was remarkably lax. The Court seemed reluctant to subject the justification advanced to close scrutiny, merely observing that 'in the current state of Community law, social policy is a matter for the Member States . . . Consequently, it is for the Member States to choose the measures capable of achieving the aim of their social and employment policy. In exercising that competence, the Member States have a broad margin of discretion.'[271] The Court in these cases seemed effectively to abdicate responsibility for ensuring that the national court applied an appropriately strict proportionality test. Its approach was markedly less demanding than that taken in the context of the Equal Treatment Directive and equal pay. The Court's caution is perhaps attributable, at least in part, to the growing pressure on the social security systems of the Member States. None the less, the Social Security Directive, however vigorously applied, has only a limited capacity to improve the position of women under the social security schemes of the Member States. The main reason for this is that it is confined essentially to the 'working population'[272] and does not therefore protect women who have chosen to be economically inactive.[273] There are of course many more women in this position than men.[274] This is clearly not a matter which it is the responsibility of the Court to deal with.

It would, however, be misleading to suggest that the Court has never taken a firm approach to the interpretation of the directive. In *Secretary of State for Social Security v Thomas and Others*,[275] for example, the Court was asked to clarify the meaning of Article 7(1)(a). By virtue of that provision, it will be recalled, Member States may exclude from the scope of the directive 'the determination of pensionable age for the purposes of granting old-age and retirement pensions and the possible consequences thereof for other benefits'. The Court held that discrimination under benefit schemes other than old-age and retirement pension schemes could be justified under Article 7(1)(a) 'only if such discrimination is objectively necessary in order to avoid disrupting the complex financial equilibrium of the social security system or to ensure consistency between retirement pension schemes and other benefit schemes'.[276]

The Court's decision significantly curtailed the potential scope of Article 7(1)(a). The ruling was applied in *R v Secretary of State for Health, ex parte Richardson*,[277] which concerned the compatibility with the directive of national legislation under which women who had reached the age of 60 were exempt from prescription

---

[271] *Nolte*, para 33; *Megner and Scheffel*, para 29.

[272] See Art 2; Joined Cases 48, 106 and 107/88 *Achterberg-te Riele and Others v Sociale Verzerkeringsbank* [1989] ECR 1963.

[273] The directive does apply to workers whose activity is interrupted by illness, accident, or involuntary unemployment: Art 2.

[274] See further Sohrab, 'Women and social security: the limits of EEC equality law' [1994] JSWFL 5.

[275] Case C–328/91 [1993] ECR I–1247.   [276] Para 12.   [277] [1995] ECR I–3407.

charges, while men did not enjoy exemption until they reached the age of 65. Those ages corresponded to the ages at which old-age and retirement pensions became payable, but there was no evidence that treating men in the same way as women would jeopardize the financial equilibrium of the social security system or that the discrimination was objectively necessary to ensure consistency between the disputed system and the retirement pension scheme. The Court therefore concluded that overtly discriminatory legislation of this nature could not be saved by Article 7(1)(a). It declined to limit the temporal effect of its ruling notwithstanding its financial consequences for the State concerned.

Concluding remarks

The decision of the Court in *Defrenne II* set the tone for the vigorous development of its case law on equal treatment for men and women in the years which followed. If the Court was motivated initially by a desire to secure compliance by the Member States with their obligations under the Treaty, it showed sensitivity to the special problems faced by women in the workplace in its decisions on the concept of pay, indirect discrimination, and the treatment of pregnant women.

Some of the criticism which the Court's case law has attracted has been examined above. Particularly disappointing is the Court's apparent unwillingness to insist on strict compliance with the proportionality principle when employers or Member States seek to justify indirect discrimination. That unwillingness seems especially marked in the field of social security. Much of the remaining criticism which has in recent years been directed at the Court's case law in this field seems to be motivated by disappointment at the failure of equal treatment legislation to eradicate inequality between men and women and a belief that a more radical approach is necessary if that goal is to be achieved. Fredman, one of the Court's most incisive critics, observes: 'A fully fledged equal opportunities programme requires a radical reshaping of the world of paid and unpaid work to accommodate the combination of paid and family work for both men and women. It also requires a sea change in both the quantity and quality of both education and training available to ethnic minorities and women. Equalising the starting points therefore demands not only careful thought and planning but a high level of resource input reflecting a strong political commitment.'[278]

However desirable such a programme might be, it is not the responsibility of the Court to seek to create one in the absence of the appropriate initiatives by the Community institutions and the Member States. The Court's task is in principle to give effect to the policy choices made by the authors of the applicable Community rules. Critics sometimes overlook the limits on the role of the Court. A case which

---

[278] 'Reversing discrimination' (1997) 113 LQR 575, 600. See also Fredman, 'European Community discrimination law: a critique' (1992) 21 ILJ 119, 134; Fenwick and Hervey, op cit, pp 443–8.

has attracted comment is *Integrity*,[279] where the Court was asked for a ruling on the compatibility with the Social Security Directive of a national rule exempting married women, widows, and students from the requirement to pay social security contributions in respect of self-employed activities if their income therefrom did not exceed a certain level. The Court held that in principle such a national rule was incompatible with the directive because exemption from liability to pay contributions was not extended to married men and widowers. Advocate General Jacobs observed: 'Directive 79/7 makes no distinction between positive discrimination in favour of the members of a particular sex and negative discrimination. Within its field of application, it requires all discrimination on the grounds of sex to be abolished. Member States cannot therefore justify inequalities of treatment on the basis that the provisions at issue are favourable to women.'[280] That remark has acquired a certain unjustifed notoriety. Fredman, for example, comments: 'Such a view illustrates the central flaw of equality as neutrality. It assumes that equality is an end in itself, rather than a mechanism for correcting disadvantage, and in doing so, it makes it impossible for the anti-discrimination principle to make real inroads into the disadvantaged position of women.'[281] The Advocate General went on to show that the objectives of the contested national rule could be met in a non-discriminatory way, but in any event he was expressing no view about the desirability in principle of a neutral application of the principle of equal treatment. He was merely summarizing the effect of the directive, which it was the task of the Court to apply.

A similar point may be made about the Court's reluctance to interfere directly in the allocation of domestic tasks. In *Hofmann v Barmer Ersatzkasse*,[282] for example, the Court said that the Equal Treatment Directive was not designed 'to settle questions concerned with the organization of the family, or to alter the division of responsibility between parents'.[283] Thus, the father of a baby who had taken unpaid leave to care for it while the mother continued working was unable to rely on the directive to claim an allowance payable to mothers on maternity leave. In *Bilka v Weber von Hartz*,[284] the Court held that Article 141 (ex 119) did not require an employer to organize its occupational pension scheme so as to take account of the particular difficulties faced by female workers in satisfying the requirements for a pension. These decisions have been the subject of criticism,[285] but the Court was constrained by the terms of the provisions in issue: as we have seen, Article 2(3) of the Equal Treatment Directive permits Member States to introduce provisions for the protection of women who are pregnant or who have recently given birth; the concept of pay is too limited to require pension schemes to be organized in the way suggested by the applicant in *Bilka*. The Court was not, however, expressing a view about the desirability on policy grounds of the outcome sought by the applicants

---

[279] Case C–373/89 [1990] ECR I–4243.   [280] p I–4254.

[281] 'European Community discrimination law: a critique' (1992) 21 ILJ 119, 129; see also Fredman, 'Reversing discrimination' (1997) 113 LQR 575, 585; Sohrab, op cit, p 13.

[282] [1984] ECR 3047.   [283] Para 24.   [284] [1986] ECR 1607.

[285] See eg Fredman, 'European Community discrimination law: a critique' (1992) 21 ILJ 119, 126–7.

in those cases. Indeed, where a case falls within the scope of a Community provision, there is now evidence that the Court will endeavour to take account of an employee's family responsibilities. In *Hill and Stapleton v Revenue Commissioners and Department of Finance*,[286] a dispute concerning female job-sharers who had converted to full-time employment and which fell within the scope of Article 141 and the Equal Pay Directive, the Court declared: 'Community policy in this area is to encourage and, if possible, adapt working conditions to family responsibilities. Protection of women within family life and in the course of their professional activities is, in the same way as for men, a principle which is widely regarded in the legal systems of the Member States as being the natural corollary of the equality between men and women, and which is recognized by Community law.'[287]

It is perhaps a reflection of the vigour with which the Court developed its case law on equal treatment for men and women in the years immediately following *Defrenne II* that remarks like those in *Integrity*, *Hofmann*, and *Bilka* should cause disappointment in some quarters. However, the Court's social conservatism is not confined to the present context: as we have seen, striking examples may also be found in its case law on freedom of movement. In the view of the present writer, this is in principle an entirely appropriate stance for the Court to adopt. There is no reason to doubt that, if the Member States or the Council were to put in place a more radical equal opportunities programme, the Court would do its best to make it work.

[286] Case C–243/95 [1998] ECR I–3739.   [287] Para 42.

The Court's general approach

14

Methods of interpretation

This chapter is concerned with the way in which the Court of Justice determines the meaning and effect of the written provisions it is called upon to apply.[1] The Court has become famous for its preference for a purposive or teleological approach to questions of interpretation, construing ambiguity in the light of the objectives of the provision concerned. That approach is a controversial one, for it may lead the Court to interpret a provision in a way which might seem surprising to those who are accustomed to seeing judges accord greater weight to the terms in which the legislature has chosen to express itself. As we shall see, however, there are a number of reasons why the teleological approach—not in any event invariably applied by the Court—is especially well suited to the problems of interpretation to which Community law sometimes gives rise.

In the White Paper it issued on the eve of the 1996 IGC, the United Kingdom Government observed: 'There is concern that the ECJ's interpretation of laws sometimes seems to go beyond what the participating Governments intended in framing these laws.'[2] That observation echoed a comment of Sir Patrick Neill QC in his paper on judicial activism: 'The methods of interpretation adopted by the ECJ appear to have liberated the Court from the customarily accepted discipline of endeavouring by textual analysis to ascertain the meaning of the language of the relevant provision.' To what extent is the criticism implicit in those remarks justified?

In order to form an objective assessment of the Court's methods of interpretation, it is necessary to take account of 'the characteristic features of Community law and the particular difficulties to which its interpretation gives rise', as the Court itself put it in *CILFIT v Ministry of Health*.[3] The approach of the Court, like that of the national courts, is governed not so much by rigid rules as by maxims and aids. There are, however, certain principles of a relatively precise nature which may conveniently be mentioned at the outset. First, derogations from general provisions are normally interpreted strictly.[4] This principle has been applied not only to

---

[1] For a theoretical analysis of this and related issues, see Bengoetxea, *The Legal Reasoning of the European Court of Justice* (1993).

[2] 'A Partnership of Nations' (Cm 3181), para 37.

[3] Case 283/81 [1982] ECR 3415, paras 17–20.

[4] It is not always clear which provision lays down the general rule, which the derogation: see AG Léger's Opinion in Case C–84/94 *United Kingdom v Commission* [1996] ECR I–5755, 5766–74, where the relationship between Arts 118a (now 138) and 100a (now 95) EC is discussed. The point is dealt with by the Court at paras 11 and 12 of the judgment (Art 118a not to be interpreted strictly).

provisions of the Treaty, such as Articles 30 (ex 36)[5] and 39(3) (ex 48(3)),[6] but also to those contained in Community acts.[7] Its rationale is that a derogation should not be interpreted in such a way as to extend its effects beyond what is necessary to safeguard the interests it seeks to protect.[8] If the derogation were to be interpreted more broadly, it might undermine the general rule, thereby jeopardizing the attainment of the overall objective of the provisions concerned. In addition (and some of this may seem self-evident), the Court has said that:[9]

When the wording of secondary Community legislation is open to more than one interpretation, preference should be given as far as possible to the interpretation which renders the provision consistent with the Treaty. Likewise, an implementing regulation must, if possible, be given an interpretation consistent with the basic regulation . . . Similarly, the primacy of international agreements concluded by the Community over provisions of secondary Community legislation means that such provisions must, so far as is possible, be interpreted in a manner that is consistent with those agreements.

The scope of the principles referred to in the previous paragraph is limited. What approach does the Court take where they are not applicable? In the *CILFIT* case, the Court underlined three features which needed to be borne in mind when dealing with problems of interpretation in Community law. First, Community legislation is drafted in several languages. This means that the different language versions are all equally authentic and may have to be compared. Secondly, Community law uses terminology which is peculiar to it. Legal concepts do not necessarily have the same meaning in Community law as in the laws of the Member States. Thirdly, every provision of Community law must be placed in its context and interpreted in the light of the provisions of Community law as a whole. Regard must be had to the objectives of Community law and to its present state of development.

The special features of Community law to which the Court drew attention in the *CILFIT* case do not mean that no account is taken of the wording of the provision in question. Sometimes the Court will conclude that the ordinary meaning

[5] See eg Case 95/81 *Commission v Italy* [1982] ECR 2187, para 27. Cf the *Primecrown* case, *infra*. On the question whether the so-called mandatory requirements introduced in the 'Cassis de Dijon' case are to be considered derogations from Art 28 (ex 30), see ch 7.

[6] See eg Case 30/77 *Regina v Bouchereau* [1977] ECR 1999, paras 31–5. But even where the derogations contained in Art 39(3) are not relevant, the Court has accepted that restrictions on the free movement of persons are permissible where they pursue a legitimate aim compatible with the Treaty and are justified by pressing reasons of public interest: see eg Case C–19/92 *Kraus v Land Baden-Württemberg* [1993] ECR I–1663, para 32; Case C–415/93 *URBSFA and Others v Bosman and Others* [1995] ECR I–4921, para 104. These cases are discussed in ch 8.

[7] See eg Case 222/84 *Johnston v Chief Constable of the Royal Ulster Constabulary* [1986] ECR 1651, para 36; Case C–450/93 *Kalanke v Bremen* [1995] ECR I–3051, para 21; Case C–321/96 *Mecklenburg v Kreis Pinneberg—Der Landrat* [1998] ECR I–3809, para 25; Case C–149/97 *Institute of the Motor Industry v Commissioners of Customs and Excise* [1999] 1 CMLR 326, para 17.

[8] See *Mecklenburg v Kreis Pinneberg*, *supra*, para 25.

[9] Case C–61/94 *Commission v Germany* [1996] ECR I–3989, para 52. See also Case C–135/93 *Spain v Commission* [1995] ECR I–1651, para 37; Case C–284/95 *Safety Hi-Tech v S & T*, judgment of 14 July 1998, para 22.

of the words used can be applied. In *Marshall I*[10] and *Faccini Dori v Recreb*,[11] for example, the Court said that directives were not binding on individuals because Article 249 (ex 189) of the Treaty, which describes the characteristics of the legislative acts which the political institutions are empowered to adopt, only says that they are binding on Member States. In *Netherlands v Reed*,[12] the Court said that Article 10(1) of Regulation 1612/68, which confers on the 'spouse' of a migrant worker the right to install him or herself in the territory of the host State, did not extend to unmarried partners. However, there are two reasons why the wording cannot always be treated as decisive: one is the way in which many Community provisions are drafted; the other, mentioned by the Court in *CILFIT*, is the multilingual character of Community law. These factors have made a teleological and contextual approach by the Court to questions of interpretation not only especially well suited to the requirements of the Community legal order but also unavoidable. Each will now be examined in more detail.

The drafting of Community provisions

In the English case of *Customs and Excise v ApS Samex*,[13] Bingham J observed: 'The interpretation of Community instruments involves very often not the process familiar to common lawyers of laboriously extracting the meaning from words used but the more creative process of applying flesh to a spare and loosely constructed skeleton.' In the case of provisions contained in the Treaty, the teleological method is facilitated by its preamble and opening provisions, which set out the principles on which the system it establishes is based. The body of the Treaty is also peppered with articles explaining the purpose of more detailed provisions.[14] As for Community acts, these are required by Article 253 (ex 190) of the Treaty to 'state the reasons on which they are based'. It therefore comes as no surprise to find that the Court has made extensive use of the teleological and contextual approaches, not only to resolve divergences between different language versions but also to confirm interpretations suggested by the wording,[15] to clarify ambiguity and to fill in gaps in the legal framework. It would be quite wrong to suggest that the Court pursues some hidden agenda of its own in its approach to questions of interpretation. If there is an

[10] Case 152/84 *Marshall v Southampton and South-West Hampshire Area Health Authority* [1986] ECR 723.
[11] Case C–91/92 [1994] ECR I–3325. See also Case C–192/94 *El Corte Inglés v Blásquez Rivero* [1996] ECR I–1281.
[12] Case 59/85 [1986] ECR 1283.
[13] [1983] 1 All ER 1042, 1056. See also *Bulmer Ltd v Bollinger SA* [1974] Ch 401, 425, per Lord Denning.
[14] See eg Arts 33 (ex 39), 131 (ex 110) and 136 (ex 117) EC.
[15] See eg Case C–260/90 *Leplat* [1992] ECR I–643; Case C–84/95 *Bosphorus v Minister for Transport, Energy and Communications, Ireland and the Attorney General* [1996] ECR I–3953.

agenda pursued by the Court, it is one set by the authors of the Treaties and by the Community legislature.[16]

A good illustration of the methods employed by the Court is the famous *Van Gend en Loos* case.[17] There, it will be recalled,[18] the Court was asked whether Article 12 (now 25) of the Treaty, which concerns the elimination of customs duties between Member States, might have direct effect. In order to resolve that question, the Court said it was 'necessary to consider the spirit, the general scheme and the wording' of the Treaty.[19] As to its spirit, the Court inferred that the object-ive of the Treaty was to create 'a new legal order of international law for the ben-efit of which the states have limited their sovereign rights . . . and the subjects of which comprise not only Member States but also their nationals'. Turning to the general scheme of the Treaty, the Court observed that an essential element of the customs union on which the Community was based was the prohibition of cus-toms duties and charges having equivalent effect. That prohibition was laid down in a part of the Treaty entitled 'Foundations of the Community'.[20] As for the wording of Article 12, the Court pointed out that it contained 'a clear and uncon-ditional prohibition' which was not qualified by any reservation making its imple-mentation dependent on national legislation. The Court therefore concluded that 'Article 12 must be interpreted as producing direct effects and creating rights which national courts must protect.' The contrary view, that the effect of the Treaty in the national legal systems should have been left to depend on the constitutional law of the country concerned, would have fatally undermined the common market. Had the effect of the Treaty been determined by national law, it would have had direct effect in some States but not in others. It is plain that the common market could not have functioned properly on that basis.[21]

In *Van Gend en Loos*, the Treaty was silent on the question the Court had been called upon to resolve. A case in which the natural meaning of an express provi-sion of the Treaty was overridden on the basis of pressing contextual and teleolog-ical considerations is *Foto-Frost v Hauptzollamt Lübeck-Ost*.[22] As we saw in chapter 2, the Court held in that case that national courts have no jurisdiction to declare acts of the Community institutions invalid, even though the terms of Article 234 (ex 177) EC might have suggested the contrary. The Court's ruling was based on

---

[16] Cf Mancini and Keeling, who observe that the 'preference for Europe is determined by the genetic code transmitted to the Court by the founding fathers': 'Democracy and the European Court of Justice' (1994) 57 MLR 175, 186.

[17] Case 26/62 [1963] ECR 1.   [18] See ch 3.

[19] Cf Case 53/81 *Levin* [1982] ECR 1035, para 9, where the Court said that, in order to determine the meaning of two terms which had not been expressly defined, it was appropriate 'to have recourse to the generally recognized principles of interpretation, beginning with the ordinary meaning to be attributed to those terms in their context and in the light of the objectives of the Treaty'.

[20] The Treaty no longer contains a part with that title. Art 12 (now 25) is located in Title I of Part Three, which is entitled 'Community Policies'. This does not reflect any diminution in its importance.

[21] This was acknowledged in Case 6/64 *Costa v ENEL* [1964] ECR 585, 594.

[22] Case 314/85 [1987] ECR 4199, paras 16 and 17. See also Case 294/83 *Les Verts v Parliament* [1986] ECR 1339.

the objectives of the preliminary rulings procedure and the system of judicial protection established by the Treaty. The Court evidently took the view that the opposite result would have been so damaging to the Community system that it could be produced only by the clearest of language.

Both *Van Gend en Loos* and *Foto-Frost* also illustrate the Court's general aversion to *a contrario* reasoning to resolve questions of interpretation. In the former, the Court rejected the view that Articles 226 (ex 169) and 227 (ex 170) EC, by enabling proceedings to be brought against a Member State which failed to comply with its Treaty obligations, implied that individuals could not rely on those obligations before the national courts.[23] In the latter, the Court refused to accept that, because Article 234 (ex 177) permitted national courts to refer to the Court of Justice questions on the validity of Community acts, it had settled the question whether such courts (other than those of last resort) could themselves declare Community acts invalid. In some circumstances, however, the legal context might render an *a contrario* argument appropriate. In *Marshall I*,[24] for example, the Court held that, because Article 249 (ex 189) of the Treaty only expressly made directives binding on the Member States to which they were addressed, they could not in themselves impose obligations on individuals.

In principle the Court takes a similar approach where it is called upon to interpret an act of one of the Community's political institutions. In *France and Others v Commission*,[25] the Court was called upon to decide whether the Merger Regulation[26] was confined to concentrations which created or strengthened a dominant position in the hands of a single firm or whether it extended to the creation or strengthening of collective dominant positions, where a dominant position is held by two or more firms jointly. Article 2(3) of the regulation spoke of '[a] concentration which creates or strengthens a dominant position . . .', but the Court regarded that provision as inconclusive. Various *travaux préparatoires* had been brought to the Court's attention, but the Court said that they 'cannot be regarded as expressing clearly the intention of the authors of the Regulation as to the scope of the term "dominant position" '.[27] Since what the Court called 'the textual and historical interpretations of the Regulation' did not offer any useful guidance, the Court turned to the 'purpose and general structure' of the regulation.[28] It regarded the regulation as 'intended to apply to all concentrations with a Community dimension in so far as they are likely, because of their effect on the structure of competition within the Community, to prove incompatible with the system of

---

[23] See also Case 43/75 *Defrenne v SABENA* [1976] ECR 455, para 31.

[24] *Supra*, para 48. See the remarks of AG Jacobs in Case C–316/93 *Vaneetveld* [1994] ECR I–763, 771. *Marshall I* is discussed in more detail in ch 4.

[25] Joined Cases C–68/94 and C–30/95 [1998] ECR I–1375. See ch 12. For an example of the teleological approach in another context, see Case C–13/94 *P v S and Cornwall County Council* [1996] ECR I–2143, discussed in ch 13.

[26] Reg 4064/89 on the control of concentrations between undertakings, OJ 1990 L257/14.

[27] Para 167.					[28] Para 168.

undistorted competition envisaged by the Treaty'.[29] That consideration led the Court to the conclusion that collective dominant positions were within the scope of the regulation:

A concentration which creates or strengthens a dominant position on the part of the parties concerned with an entity not involved in the concentration is liable to prove incompatible with the system of undistorted competition which the Treaty seeks to secure. Consequently, if it were accepted that only concentrations creating or strengthening a dominant position on the part of the parties to the concentration were covered by the Regulation, its purpose . . . would be partially frustrated. The Regulation would thus be deprived of a not insignificant aspect of its effectiveness, without that being necessary from the perspective of the general structure of the Community system of control of concentrations.[30]

Where a Community act is silent or inconclusive on a question raised in a case, the Court sometimes supplements the teleological approach by undertaking a comparative analysis of the laws of the Member States on the question in the search for a solution. An example is *AM & S v Commission*.[31] There, having examined the position in the Member States, the Court accepted that a limited doctrine of legal professional privilege applied in EC competition cases, notwithstanding the silence of the relevant provisions on the matter.[32] It may be noted that the effect was to limit, on the basis of the approach taken by the Member States, the Commission's powers to enforce fundamental rules of the Treaty. The case provides a striking example of the Court's willingness to incorporate into Community law the legal values of the national systems, even where the result is to impose on the powers of the Community institutions limits which go beyond those laid down by the legislator.

   The Court may give less emphasis to the objective of a provision and to its legal context where there is a detailed legislative scheme,[33] such as those that have been laid down in the fields of social security and agriculture.[34] Indeed, where the legislature has made its intentions clear through the use of detailed provisions, the Court may feel bound to acknowledge the results which the provisions concerned

---

[29] Para 170. A concentration has a Community dimension where it meets the thresholds laid down in Art 1(2) and (3) of the Merger Reg. See further ch 12.

[30] Para 171.

[31] Case 155/79 [1982] ECR 1575, discussed in chs 6 and 12. See also Case 374/87 *Orkem v Commission* [1989] ECR 3283. For an unsuccessful attempt to persuade the Court to adopt a principle of Roman law in the interpretation of a directive, see Case C–296/95 *The Queen v Commissioners of Customs & Excise, ex parte EMU Tabac* [1998] ECR I–1605.

[32] Cf Case C–84/94 *United Kingdom v Council* [1996] 3 CMLR 671 concerning Directive 93/104 on the organization of working time (OJ 1993 L307/18), where AG Léger referred to Danish law in interpreting Art 118a (now 138) EC, which originated in a proposal made by the Danish Government at the IGC preceding the Single European Act: see para 42 of the Opinion.

[33] Although even relatively detailed legislation may leave crucial questions unresolved: see eg the attempts of AG Lenz and the Court to establish the requirements of a directive on television broadcasting in Case C–222/94 *Commission v United Kingdom* [1996] ECR I–4058 and Case C–11/95 *Commission v Belgium* [1996] ECR I–4115.

[34] By contrast, the Court has relied extensively on the teleological and contextual methods in interpreting the Community's detailed VAT legislation: see Farmer and Lyal, *EC Tax Law* (1994), pp 89–90.

were designed to produce. Thus, in a series of cases referred to in chapter 6,[35] the Court struck down successive Council regulations designed to curb milk production on the ground that they failed to respect the legitimate expectations of a particular class of producers. The Court's decisions exposed the Community to substantial claims for compensation[36] and severely hampered the Council's attempts to achieve an objective which was in itself entirely legitimate. However, as Advocate General Jacobs observed in the *Dowling* case:[37]

. . . the Court did not feel itself able to interpret those provisions in such a way as to bring them into conformity with Community law. It seems to me that the Court was unable to do so because the intention of the legislation, however defective, was abundantly clear, and there was accordingly no occasion to depart from the literal meaning of the provisions in which it was expressed. Since the intention of the legislator was inconsistent with a general principle of Community law, the Court had no choice but to declare invalid the provisions which gave effect to that intention.

Sometimes Member States or Community institutions make statements, which may be recorded in the Council minutes, when a measure is adopted about what they consider its scope to be.[38] Whether or not they are made public, such statements cannot affect the objective meaning of the measure. In *Antonissen*,[39] a case concerning the free movement of workers, the English High Court asked the Court of Justice 'what weight if any is to be attached by a court or tribunal of a Member State to the declaration contained in the minutes of the meeting of the Council when the Council adopted Directive 68/360?' The Court replied:[40] 'Such a declaration cannot be used for the purpose of interpreting a provision of secondary legislation where, as in this case, no reference is made to the content of the declaration in the wording of the provision in question. The declaration therefore has no legal significance.'[41] In *Denkavit Internationaal and Others v Bundesamt für Finanzen*,[42] several Member States argued that a provision contained in a directive

---

[35] Case 120/86 *Mulder* [1988] ECR 2321; Case 170/86 *von Deetzen* [1988] ECR 2355; Case C–189/89 *Spagl* [1990] ECR I–4539; Case C–217/89 *Pastätter* [1990] ECR I–4585.

[36] See Joined Cases C–104/89 and C–37/90 *Mulder and Others v Council and Commission* [1992] ECR I–3061.

[37] Case C–85/90 [1992] ECR I–5305, 5320–2.

[38] See eg the accompanying statements, some by the Commission, some by the Council, some by both institutions jointly, entered in the minutes of the Council when the Merger Reg was adopted, [1990] 4 CMLR 314. See AG Tesauro in *France and Others v Commission, supra*, p I–1420.

[39] Case C–292/89 [1991] ECR I–745. See also Case C–25/94 *Commission v Council* [1996] ECR I–1469, para 38; Hartley, 'Five forms of uncertainty in European Community law' [1996] CLJ 265, 274–8.

[40] Para 18. Declarations published when the Treaties were signed or on the occasion of later amendments may be of greater significance, especially when endorsed by all the Member States: see Schermers, 'The effect of the date 31 December 1992' (1991) 28 CMLRev 275; cf Toth, 'The legal status of the declarations annexed to the Single European Act' (1986) 23 CMLRev 803.

[41] Cf Case C–368/96 *The Queen v The Licensing Authority established by the Medicines Act 1968, ex parte Generics (UK) Ltd*, judgment of 3 December 1998, where the Court cited *Antonissen* but said that a declaration of that kind could be taken into consideration in so far as it served to clarify a general concept used in a directive.

[42] Joined Cases C–283/94, C–291/94 and C–292/94 [1996] ECR I–5063.

should not be interpreted restrictively because, 'when the Directive was being adopted by the Council, it was agreed that relatively vague terms should be used in order to allow for differing interpretations according to the requirements of the domestic legal systems'.[43] That argument was rejected by the Court, which stated: 'Expressions of intent on the part of Member States in the Council, such as those on which the Governments rely in their observations, have no legal status if they are not actually expressed in the legislation. Legislation is addressed to those affected by it. They must, in accordance with the principle of legal certainty, be able to rely on what it contains.'[44]

The multilingual nature of Community law

The multilingual nature of Community law poses problems of varying degrees of complexity which do not arise in the national systems.[45] Although some Member States have more than one official language, none has as many as the European Union. The Court's general approach is to seek to interpret provisions in a way which is consistent with all (or nearly all) of the language versions. If that does not prove possible, it turns for guidance to the purpose and context of the provision. An overriding consideration is the need to ensure the uniform interpretation of the provision concerned throughout the Member States.

In *The Queen v Commissioners of Customs & Excise, ex parte EMU Tabac*,[46] two language versions of a particular provision were clearer than the others. The provision in question was contained in a directive on excise duty. It concerned the circumstances in which private individuals resident in one Member State had to pay duty there on products acquired for their own use in another Member State. The question was whether individuals could avoid paying duty in their State of residence by employing an agent to purchase the goods for them, or whether the purchase had to be effected personally by the individual for whom the goods were intended. The Court pointed out that none of the language versions expressly provided for the involvement of an agent and that 'the Danish and Greek versions indicate particularly clearly that, for excise duty to be payable in the country of purchase, transportation must be effected personally by the purchaser of the products subject to duty'.[47] It was argued that those versions should be ignored on the basis that, at the time when the directive in question was adopted, Denmark and Greece represented only 5 per cent of the total population of the Member States and that their languages were not widely understood by the nationals of other Member States. That unattractive argument not surprisingly failed to commend itself to the

---

[43] Para 28.   [44] Para 29.

[45] See Van Calster, 'The EU's Tower of Babel—the interpretation by the European Court of Justice of equally authentic texts drafted in more than one official language' (1997) 17 YEL 363.

[46] *Supra.* See also *Mecklenburg v Kreis Pinneberg, supra.*

[47] Para 33.

Court, which pointed out that the Danish and Greek versions were not inconsistent with the other language versions. It continued:[48]

> Furthermore, to discount two language versions, as the applicants in the main proceedings suggest, would run counter to the Court's settled case-law to the effect that the need for a uniform interpretation of Community regulations makes it impossible for the text of a provision to be considered in isolation but requires, on the contrary, that it should be interpreted and applied in the light of the versions existing in the other official languages . . . Lastly, all the language versions must, in principle, be recognised as having the same weight and thus cannot vary according to the size of the population of the Member States using the language in question.

Where one language version is out of line with the others, the Court may be prepared to disregard it. An example is *Denkavit Internationaal and Others v Bundesamt für Finanzen*,[49] where the Court attached significance to the use of the present tense in all the language versions except the Danish of a provision contained in a directive. The interpretation preferred by the Court was not, it said, 'invalidated by the fact that the Danish version uses a past tense',[50] although the Court sought confirmation for its view in the purpose of the directive as explained in particular in its preamble.

Sometimes comparison of the different language versions reveals the text to be completely inconclusive. In *Regina v Bouchereau*, the United Kingdom Government sought to rely on the use of the same term in the English text of separate provisions of a Community directive. The Court observed:[51] 'A comparison of the different language versions of the provisions in question shows that with the exception of the Italian text all the other versions use different terms in each of the two articles, with the result that no legal consequences can be based on the terminology used.' A similar problem arose in *Merck and Others v Primecrown and Others* and *Beecham and Europharm*.[52] The plaintiffs in the main action were seeking to restrain imports into the United Kingdom from Spain and Portugal of drugs for which they held patents. The drugs concerned were not patentable in Spain or Portugal. The case turned on the interpretation of transitional provisions in the Act of Accession of Spain and Portugal giving the holder of a patent granted in a Member State the right in certain circumstances to oppose the importation of the patented product from Spain and Portugal. That right could be invoked until the end of the third year after Spain and Portugal had made pharmaceutical products patentable, which they were required to do within a certain period. The question which the Court had to decide was whether the transitional period expired exactly three years after the date on which pharmaceutical products became patentable there or at the end of the third calendar year after that date. The Court pointed out that that question

---

[48] Para 36.
[49] *Supra.* Cf Case C–64/95 *Lubella v Hauptzollamt Cottbus* [1996] ECR I–5105.   [50] Para 25.
[51] Case 30/77 [1977] ECR 1999, para 13. See also Case 29/69 *Stauder v Ulm* [1969] ECR 419; Case 9/79 *Koschniske v Raad van Arbeid* [1979] ECR 2717.
[52] Joined Cases C–267/95 and C–268/95 [1996] ECR I–6285.

could not be resolved solely on the basis of the wording of the relevant provisions of the Act of Accession: '[w]hile the wording of most of the language versions favours the first solution, that of the other versions favours the second'.[53]

In situations such as these, the Court treats—and has to treat—the objective of the provision and its legal context as decisive. In *Bouchereau*,[54] it declared: 'The different language versions of a Community text must be given a uniform interpretation and hence in the case of divergence between the versions the provision in question must be interpreted by reference to the purpose and general scheme of the rules of which it forms a part.' Similarly, in *Merck v Primecrown*, the Court said it was appropriate to take into account criteria other than the wording of the provisions at issue, 'in particular the general scheme and the purpose of the regulatory system of which the provisions in question form part'.[55] In that case, it went on to point out that the contested provisions of the Act of Accession 'introduced a derogation from the principle of free movement of goods and that it is settled case-law that such derogations are to be interpreted strictly . . .'.[56] It concluded that '[t]he provisions in question must therefore be interpreted in [such] a way that the transitional periods expire on the date which ensures the earliest application, in the field concerned, of the principle of free movement of goods in Spain and Portugal'. They therefore came to an end exactly three years after pharmaceutical products became patentable in those States.

Conversely, the Court may seek support in the different language versions for an interpretation it has arrived at through a teleological approach. In *Henke v Gemeinde Schierke and Verwaltungsgemeinschaft 'Brocken'*,[57] for example, the issue was whether a directive on the safeguarding of employees' rights in the event of transfers of undertakings, businesses or parts of businesses[58] applied to the transfer of administrative functions from a municipality to an administrative collectivity formed by neighbouring municipalities in order to strengthen their administration. The Court observed: 'As appears from the preamble to the Directive, in particular the first recital, the Directive sets out to protect workers against the potentially unfavourable consequences for them of changes in the structure of undertakings resulting from economic trends at national and Community level, through, *inter alia*, transfers of undertakings, businesses or parts of businesses to other employers as a result of transfers or mergers.'[59] It followed that reorganizing the structure of the public administration or transferring administrative functions between public

[53] Para 21.

[54] *Supra*, para 14. See also Case C–372/88 *Cricket St Thomas* [1990] ECR I–1345, paras 13–25; Case C–236/97 *Skatteministeriet v Aktieselskabet Forsikringsselskabet Codan*, judgment of 17 December 1998, paras 22–30.

[55] Para 22. See also Case C–72/95 *Kraaijeveld and Others v Gedeputeerde Staten van Zuid-Holland* [1996] ECR I–5403, paras 29–30.

[56] Para 23. Cf Case C–149/97 *Institute of the Motor Industry v Commissioners of Customs and Excise*, *supra*.

[57] Case C–298/94 [1996] ECR I–4989. Cf Case C–84/95 *Bosphorus v Minister for Transport, Energy and Communications, Ireland and the Attorney General* [1996] ECR I–3953.

[58] Dir 77/187, OJ 1977 L61/26.   [59] Para 13.

authorities did not constitute a 'transfer of an undertaking' within the meaning of the Directive. That interpretation, the Court said, 'is borne out by the terms used in most of the language versions of the Directive in order to designate the subject of the transfer . . . [the Court then quoted a number of them] . . . or the beneficiary of the transfer . . . [the Court again quoted several language versions] . . . and is not contradicted by any of the other language versions of the text'.[60]

An assessment of the Court's approach

It would be a mistake to think that the Court's approach to the interpretation of provisions of Community law is especially unorthodox. According to Article 31(1) of the Vienna Convention on the Law of Treaties, '[a] treaty shall be interpreted in good faith in accordance with the ordinary meaning to be given to the terms of the treaty in their context and in the light of its object and purpose'. That is not a bad summary of the Court's approach in the cases mentioned above. Article 31 of the Vienna Convention was mentioned by the Court in its first Opinion[61] on the compatibility with the Treaty of the draft agreement establishing a European Economic Area (EEA) extending certain provisions of Community law to the EFTA States and to Liechtenstein. It was the intention of the authors of the agreement that its substantive provisions should be interpreted and applied in the same way as the corresponding provisions of Community law. To that end, identical language had where possible been used. However, the Court pointed out that this was not in itself enough: 'The fact that the provisions of the agreement and the corresponding Community provisions are identically worded does not mean that they must necessarily be interpreted identically.'[62] Referring to the Vienna Convention, the Court noted that the objectives of the Community and the context in which they were pursued differed from those of the agreement, which merely created rights and obligations between the Contracting Parties and did not provide for the transfer of sovereign rights. It followed, the Court said, 'that homogeneity of the rules of law throughout the EEA is not secured by the fact that the provisions of Community law and . . . the corresponding provisions of the agreement are identical in their content or wording'.[63] There could be no clearer illustration[64] of the importance attached by the Court to the objectives and context of a provision in establishing what it means.

---

[60] Para 15.   [61] Opinion 1/91 [1991] ECR I–6079.   [62] Para 14.

[63] Para 22. Cf Case C–355/96 *Silhouette International v Hartlauer* [1998] 2 CMLR 953, where the Court adopted an interpretation of a directive which differed from that which had been taken by the EFTA Court. See AG Jacobs at pp 965–6; Alexander, 'Exhaustion of trade mark rights in the European Economic Area' (1999) 24 ELRev 56.

[64] But see also Case C–312/91 *Metalsa* [1993] ECR I–3751; Case 104/81 *Hauptzollamt Mainz v Kupferberg* [1982] ECR 3641; Case 270/80 *Polydor v Harlequin Record Shops* [1982] ECR 329. Cf Case C–163/90 *Administration des Douanes et Droits Indirects v Legros and Others* [1992] ECR I–4625.

As a supplementary means of interpretation, Article 32 of the Vienna Convention envisages recourse to the preparatory work (or *travaux préparatoires*) of a treaty in order to confirm the meaning resulting from the application of Article 31 or to remove ambiguity or absurdity. This is not a method which has in the past commended itself to the Court in cases concerning the interpretation of the Treaties themselves. As a former Judge has explained:[65]

The Court cannot rely on preparatory work which provides a history of how the Treaties came into being. In so far as any such preparatory work exists at all—essential questions were obviously only discussed and decided within working groups—it has in any case not been published. Documents which are not generally accessible must, however, be ruled out as aids to interpretation for constitutional reasons.

It is possible that this approach will in future be modified. The Court is willing to look at *travaux préparatoires* in cases concerning the interpretation of Community acts.[66] Increasing pressure for transparency[67] and the development of the Internet have now brought some *travaux préparatoires* concerning the Treaties into the public domain. This was particularly noticeable during the IGC which resulted in the Treaty of Amsterdam, when a series of drafts, some with explanatory comments indicating areas of disagreement, were widely circulated outside government circles. Indications given by *travaux préparatoires* would, however, have to be particularly compelling in order for them to be given precedence over the purpose and general scheme of the Treaty.

It is sometimes suggested that the interests of the Member States are accorded less weight in Community law than in public international law. In a memorandum on the Court submitted to the IGC by the United Kingdom in July 1996, it was even proposed that a protocol should be added to the EC Treaty providing that, 'when faced with more than one possible interpretation of provisions of Community law, the Court shall, unless there is a clear contrary intention, prefer the interpretation which least constrains the freedom of the Member States'. That proposal was not taken up by the conference. The philosophy underlying it is not rigidly adhered to in public international law and is incompatible with the very nature of the Community legal order, which the Court has said entails a limitation of the sovereign rights of the Member States and whose beneficiaries include individuals.[68] Moreover, it underestimates the extent to which the Court has sought in

---

[65] See Kutscher, 'Methods of interpretation as seen by a judge at the Court of Justice' in *Reports of a Judicial and Academic Conference* (Luxembourg, 1976), p I–21.

[66] See *France and Others v Commission*, *supra*, para 167; Case 15/60 *Simon v Court* [1961] ECR 115, 125. Cf *Mecklenburg v Kreis Pinneberg*, *supra*, para 28.

[67] See eg Arts 207(3) (ex 151) and 255 (ex 191a) EC; Case C–58/94 *Netherlands v Council* [1996] ECR I–2169. The pressure has grown since the accession of Sweden, where the law on access to documents is highly developed. See Österdahl, 'Openness v secrecy: public access to documents in Sweden and the European Union' (1998) 23 ELRev 336.

[68] See the *Van Gend en Loos* case and Opinion 1/91, *supra*.

appropriate cases to protect the interests of the Member States.[69] If there is any truth in the suggestion that it gives those interests less weight than other international tribunals,[70] its approach may be justified by the unprecedented degree of economic and political integration contemplated by the Treaties on which the European Union is based.

[69] See eg Opinion 1/94 'WTO' [1994] ECR I–5267; Opinion 2/92 'Third Revised Decision of the OECD on national treatment' [1995] ECR I–521; Opinion 2/94 'Accession of the Community to the European Convention on Human Rights' [1996] ECR I–1759. See further ch 16.

[70] For the approach of the European Court of Human Rights, see Matscher, 'Methods of interpretation of the Convention', and Golsong, 'Interpreting the European Convention on Human Rights beyond the confines of the Vienna Convention on the Law of Treaties?', in Macdonald, Matscher and Petzold (eds), *The European System for the Protection of Human Rights* (1993), chs 5 and 8 respectively; cf the Separate Opinion of Judge Fitzmaurice in *Golder v United Kingdom* (1979–80) 1 EHRR 524. On the interpretation of treaties generally, see Brownlie, *Principles of Public International Law* (5th edn, 1998), pp 631–8; Jennings and Watts (eds), *Oppenheim's International Law*, Vol I (9th edn, 1992), pp 1266–84.

15

Precedent

The capacity of courts to create law, although widely acknowledged in the common law world,[1] has not, at least until recently, been accepted in the civil law tradition. However, it should by now be apparent that many of the most important principles of Community law are to be found, not in the Treaties or the acts of the Community legislature, but in the case law of the Court. That case law is often now classified, even by continental observers, as a source of Community law.[2] Wider recognition of the normative character of the Court's decisions, together with their ever-increasing volume, has produced a significant evolution in the way in which the Court deals with its own decisions in the judgments it delivers. The establishment in 1988 of the CFI raised new questions about the status of judicial precedents in Community law. It will be convenient to examine the two Courts separately.[3]

The Court of Justice

In the common law world, the doctrine of precedent embodies more than the elementary principle that courts should try to be consistent. In certain circumstances, it may have the effect of requiring a judge to follow a decision given in a previous case even though, in the absence of precedent, he might have decided the case in

[1] See Dicey's *Lectures on the Relation between Law and Public Opinion in England during the Nineteenth Century* (1926), Lecture XI of which is entitled 'Judicial Legislation' and the Appendix to which contains an extensive note (at pp 483–94) on 'Judge-Made Law'. In that note, it is suggested (at p 483) that the existence of judge-made law is due in part to the doctrine of precedent. See also Sir Kenneth Diplock, 'The courts as legislators' in Harvey (ed), *The Lawyer and Justice* (1978), p 265. Lord Reid once described the suggestion that judges do not make law as a fairy tale: see 'The judge as law maker' (1972–73) XII JSPTL (NS) 22.

[2] See Shapiro, 'The European Court of Justice' in Craig and de Búrca (eds), *The Evolution of EU Law* (1999), ch 9, p 325; Dehousse, *The European Court of Justice* (1998) pp 71–2; Barav, 'Omnipotent courts' in *Institutional Dynamics of European Integration (Vol II)* (1994), p 265; Charrier, 'L'*obiter dictum* dans la jurisprudence de la Cour de justice des Communautés européennes' (1998) 34 CDE 79, 101; Simon, *Le Système Juridique Communautaire* (1997), p 234; Haguenau, *L'application effective du droit communautaire en droit interne* (1995), pp 549–50.

[3] The discussion which follows does not address the effect of decisions of the Community Courts in the national courts of the Member States. For a brief summary of the position, see Arnull, 'Interpretation and precedent in English and Community law: evidence of cross-fertilisation?' in Andenas (ed), *English Public Law and the Common Law of Europe* (1998), ch 6, pp 127–9. For a detailed analysis, see Toth, 'The authority of judgments of the European Court of Justice: binding force and legal effects' (1984) 4 YEL 1.

hand differently. Does the Court of Justice consider itself constrained in this way to follow its own decisions? The general position may be stated very simply: the Court of Justice is not bound by its previous decisions but in practice it does not often depart from them.[4] A doctrine of binding precedent on common law lines would have been entirely inappropriate in what was originally a court of first and last resort, many of whose decisions could only be changed by amending the Treaties, a lengthy process requiring the agreement of all the Member States and ratification by each of them in accordance with their respective constitutional requirements. It was therefore imperative that the Court should have the power to change the direction of its case law and to depart from its previous decisions, particularly in cases with important constitutional implications. The general position is exemplified by the extent of the freedom enjoyed by the national courts of the Member States to request preliminary rulings from the Court of Justice under Article 234 (ex 177) EC. Since the Court of Justice is not bound by its own previous decisions, the national courts are not precluded from taking that step merely because the point of Community law at issue has already been dealt with by the Court of Justice.[5]

A corollary of the absence of a doctrine of binding precedent in Community law is that the distinction between the *ratio decidendi* of a judgment of the Court and its *obiter dicta* loses much of its significance.[6] The distinction is important in the common law because it is only the *ratio* of a case which is capable of binding other courts in the future.[7] However, in principle everything that is said in a judgment of the Court of Justice expresses the Court's opinion and is therefore capable of having the same persuasive force.[8] This point may be illustrated by the decision in *Marshall I*,[9] where the Court held that directives were not in themselves capable of imposing obligations on individuals, that is, of producing horizontal direct effect. That decision was reached in proceedings in which the appellant was seeking to enforce a directive against a public authority. It was therefore not strictly necessary for the Court to decide whether directives could be enforced against individuals,[10] but this factor had no effect on the status of the

---

[4] See further Arnull, 'Owning up to fallibility: precedent and the Court of Justice' (1993) 30 CMLRev 247.

[5] See Joined Cases 28, 29 and 30/62 *Da Costa v Nederlandse Belastingadministratie* [1963] ECR 31; Case 66/80 *International Chemical Corporation v Amministrazione delle Finanze dello Stato* [1981] ECR 1191, para 14; Case 283/81 *CILFIT v Ministry of Health* [1982] ECR 3415, paras 14 and 15; Case C–91/92 *Faccini Dori v Recreb* [1994] ECR I–3325.

[6] See further Toth, op cit, pp 36–42; Cross and Harris, *Precedent in English Law* (4th edn, 1991), pp 17–18. Cf Koopmans, '*Stare decisis* in European law' in O'Keeffe and Schermers (eds), *Essays in European Law and Integration* (1982), p 11, at pp 22–4; Charrier, op cit, p 84.

[7] See further Cross and Harris, op cit, ch II.

[8] See AG Roemer in Case 9/61 *Netherlands v High Authority* [1962] ECR 213, 242. Cf AG Warner in Case 112/76 *Manzoni v FNROM* [1977] ECR 1647, 1661–3.

[9] Case 152/84 [1986] ECR 723.

[10] Cf Case C–316/93 *Vaneetveld* [1994] ECR I–763, 770, where AG Jacobs suggested that it would be 'disproportionate' for the Court to address issues of great importance for the Community legal order in a case where they did not need to be decided.

Court's judgment on that point and it has been followed in a number of subsequent cases, notably *Faccini Dori*.[11]

Occasionally, however, the Court seeks to distinguish a case on which a party has sought to rely. In order to perform this exercise, the Court has to establish what the previous case, properly construed, in fact decided. This process is analogous to that of identifying the *ratio* of a judgment given by a common law court.[12] Of course, like all courts the Court of Justice tries to be consistent in the decisions it reaches. Thus, in proceedings under Article 234 (ex 177) EC in which the Court is asked to rule on a point it has already dealt with, it will, in the absence of any suggestion that the previous case was wrongly decided, simply repeat its earlier ruling.[13]

English lawyers might be tempted to say that the Court's general approach is not dissimilar to that which, following the 1966 Practice Statement,[14] now prevails in the House of Lords. However, that would be to underestimate the influence on the Court's practice of its civil law origins. In the civilian tradition, the judge is merely the mouthpiece of the law[15] and does not feel compelled to analyse or reconcile earlier judgments in the manner of the common law judge.[16] Indeed, for many years the Court rarely referred in its judgments to its previous decisions, even when repeating a passage verbatim. Perhaps under the influence of the common law, the Court of Justice now deals more fully with previous cases in its judgments. But the analysis may appear superficial and selective by the standards of common law courts. Previous decisions are sometimes only cited by the Court where they support its argument. Authorities which point the other way are sometimes not mentioned at all, sometimes presented as if they support the line the Court has chosen to take.

An example is *Familiapress v Bauer Verlag*,[17] where the Court held that, where a Member State seeks to rely on an overriding (or mandatory) requirement to justify a measure which is liable to obstruct the free movement of goods, it must show that

---

[11] *Supra*. See also Case 80/86 *Kolpinghuis Nijmegan* [1987] ECR 3969, para 9; Case C–221/88 *Busseni* [1990] ECR I–495, para 23.

[12] See eg Case C–313/90 *CIRFS v Commission* [1993] ECR I-1125; Case C–188/92 *TWD Textilwerke Deggendorf* [1994] ECR I-833; Case C–194/94 *CIA Security v Signalson and Securitel* [1996] ECR I-2201.

[13] See eg Case C–350/89 *Sheptonhurst Ltd v Newham Borough Council* [1991] ECR I–2387, where the Court repeated its ruling in Case C–23/89 *Quietlynn Ltd v Southend Borough Council* [1990] ECR I–3059. Where a question referred to the Court for a preliminary ruling is 'manifestly identical to a question on which the Court has already ruled', the Court is empowered by Art 104(3) of its Rules of Procedure to give its decision by reasoned order in which reference is made to its previous judgment.

[14] [1966] 1 WLR 1234.

[15] See Montesquieu, *De l'esprit des lois*, Livre XI, Chapitre 6: 'Mais les juges de la nation ne sont . . . que la bouche qui prononce les paroles de la loi; des êtres inanimés qui n'en peuvent modérer ni la force ni la rigueur.' The English rendition is taken from the Opinion of AG Léger in Case C–84/94 *United Kingdom v Council* [1996] ECR I–5755, 5791.

[16] See Brown and Kennedy, *Brown and Jacobs' Court of Justice of the European Communities* (4th edn, 1994), p 344.

[17] Case C–368/95 [1997] ECR I–3689, discussed in more detail in ch 7. Cf Case C–358/89 *Extramet Industrie v Council* [1991] ECR I–2501; Case 302/87 *Parliament v Council* ('Comitology') [1988] ECR 5615; Case C–70/88 *Parliament v Council* ('Chernobyl') [1990] ECR I–2041.

the general principle of respect for fundamental rights has been observed. The Court did not refer to its previous ruling in *Cinéthèque v Fédération Nationale des Cinémas Français*,[18] where, rejecting the advice of Advocate General Slynn, it had held that national legislation which was justified under the mandatory requirements doctrine was not subject to the general principle of respect for fundamental rights. It seems that *Cinéthèque* is no longer good law on this point. The reason is perhaps that the mandatory requirements are now seen by the Court as derogations rather than as removing national legislation from the scope of the Treaty entirely and consequently from that of the general principles of law. It would, however, have been preferable had the Court explained the effect of *Familiapress* on its earlier decision.[19]

There have, however, been signs since the beginning of the 1990s of a growing willingness on the part of the Court to confront the implications of earlier case law. In *HAG II*,[20] the Court for the first time expressly overruled one of its own previous decisions. Following the advice of Advocate General Jacobs, the Court in that case abandoned the much-criticized doctrine of common origin laid down in *HAG I*,[21] which limited the circumstances in which the owner of a trade mark in one Member State could restrain imports of products legally bearing the mark in another Member State. Advocate General Jacobs stated that, if he were to be followed, 'the Court should in my view make it clear, in the interests of legal certainty, that it is abandoning the doctrine of common origin laid down in *HAG I*'. He went on: 'That the Court should in an appropriate case expressly overrule an earlier decision is I think an inescapable duty, even if the Court has never before expressly done so.' In the Advocate General's view, to depart from *HAG I* without abandoning the doctrine or to seek to rationalize such an outcome on some other ground 'would be a recipe for confusion'. The remarks of Advocate General Jacobs seem to have produced the desired result, for the Court said that it considered it 'necessary to reconsider the interpretation given in [*HAG I*]'.[22] The remainder of the judgment made it clear that the doctrine of common origin no longer formed any part of the Community rules on intellectual property, a result subsequently confirmed in the *Ideal Standard* case.[23]

In a subsequent case concerning the scope of Article 28 (ex 30) EC, *Keck and Mithouard*,[24] the Court also departed from previous case law, but it did so less candidly. The Court stated that it considered it 'necessary to re-examine and clarify its case-law on this matter' and concluded, 'contrary to what has previously been decided', that certain types of national legislation which might appear to hinder imports were none the less compatible with the Treaty. Unlike *HAG II*, however,

---

[18] Joined Cases 60 and 61/84 [1985] ECR 2605.
[19] Cf the line of cases leading to the demise of the rule laid down in Case C–208/90 *Emmott* [1991] ECR I–4269, discussed in ch 5. Without actually overruling that case, the Court made it clear that it was confined to wholly exceptional circumstances.
[20] Case C–10/89 *CNL-Sucal v HAG GF* [1990] ECR I–3711.
[21] Case 192/73 *Van Zuylen v HAG* [1974] ECR 731. See further ch 7.   [22] At para 10.
[23] Case C–9/93 *IHT Internationale Heiztechnik v Ideal Standard* [1994] ECR I–2789.
[24] Joined Cases C–267/91 and C–268/91 [1993] ECR I–6097. See further ch 7.

the Court did not make clear precisely what it was overruling. The effect of its judgment was therefore to leave the status of its previous decisions on the matter unclear. While a willingness to depart from previous decisions which are producing unsatisfactory effects is wholly desirable, it is imperative that, when the Court decides to take that course, it explains clearly which of its previous decisions are no longer to be treated as authoritative.

The criticism which this aspect in particular of the ruling in *Keck and Mithouard* attracted[25] seems to have produced an effect. In *Cabanis-Issarte*,[26] a social security case,[27] the Court made it clear that an earlier ruling[28] was to be regarded as confined to its facts and that a series of specified later cases based on it were no longer good law. The Court went on to limit the temporal effect of its judgment in order to 'preclude legal situations being called into question which have been definitively settled in accordance with the Court's previous case law, whose scope is limited by this judgment'.[29] In *Brown v Rentokil*,[30] a case on the protection conferred by the Equal Treatment Directive on female employees who fall ill as a result of pregnancy,[31] the Court expressly overruled its ruling in *Larsson v Føtex Supermarked*.[32] The latter case was decided by a five-Judge chamber little more than a year before *Brown*, a decision of the full Court. The full Court has always had a responsibility for correcting wrong turnings by chambers, but the express overruling in *Brown* of the earlier decision was a decisive step which left the legal position relatively clear.

By contrast, in *Merck and Others v Primecrown and Others* and *Beecham and Europharm*[33] the Court refused to depart from the rule laid down in a previous case, *Merck v Stephar and Exler*,[34] on the circumstances in which patent rights were to be considered exhausted. Although Advocate General Fennelly had recommended that the earlier case should no longer be applied, he also pointed out that it was 'obvious that the Court should, as a matter of practice, follow its previous case law except where there are strong reasons for not so doing'.[35] The Court undertook a detailed examination of the arguments for reconsidering the rule in *Merck v Stephar*, but concluded that it had struck the right balance in that case between the principle of the free movement of goods and the interests of patentees.

---

[25] See eg Gormley, 'Reasoning renounced? The remarkable judgment in *Keck and Mithouard*' (1994) EBLR 63, 66; Reich, 'The "November revolution" of the European Court of Justice: *Keck, Meng* and *Audi* revisited' (1994) 31 CMLRev 459, 471.

[26] Case C–308/93 [1996] ECR I–2097.

[27] The case concerned the right of a widow of a migrant worker to rely on the principle of equal treatment laid down in Art 3(1) of Regulation 1408/71 on the social security rights of migrants.

[28] Case 40/76 *Kermaschek v Bundesanstalt für Arbeit* [1976] ECR 1669.

[29] Para 47.

[30] Case C–394/96 [1998] ECR I–4185.   [31] See further ch 13.

[32] Case C–400/95 [1997] ECR I–2757.

[33] Joined Cases C–267/95 and C–268/95 [1996] ECR I–6285. See also Case C–85/96 *Martínez Sala v Freistaat Bayern* [1998] ECR I–2691, paras 22–4.

[34] Case 187/80 [1981] ECR 2063.

[35] [1996] ECR I–6285, 6344. It may be noted that AG Fennelly comes from Ireland, a common law country.

These cases reflect increasing sophistication on the part of the Court of Justice in handling its previous case law. The principle that the Court may depart from previous decisions is now firmly established. However, it also now seems to be recognized that such departures require an explanation of the cases affected in order to avoid an unacceptable degree of uncertainty about the new legal position. Where the Court declines to reverse a previous decision, it appears to accept that a detailed explanation of its reasoning may be equally necessary. It remains true that the Court does not often depart from its previous decisions. The difference is that it is now less common for the Court to ignore or misrepresent inconvenient earlier authorities.

The Court of First Instance

The establishment of the CFI raised two further questions about the status of judicial precedents in Community law: (a) is the CFI bound by its own previous decisions; and (b) is it bound by the decisions of the Court of Justice? The answer to the first question is that, like the Court of Justice itself, the CFI is not strictly bound by its own decisions but that it endeavours to be consistent. The second question needs to be explored at somewhat greater length in order to discover the answer.

A common lawyer might be tempted to say that, because the Court of Justice is hierarchically superior, its rulings ought to bind the CFI in the interests of legal certainty and the coherence of the law.[36] A more technical argument might be based on Article 51 of the EC Statute of the Court, according to which one of the grounds on which appeal lies to the Court against decisions of the CFI is 'infringement of Community law by the Court of First Instance'. It has been argued that '[t]he precedents set by the Court are, of course, part of Community law, so that where these are clear and consistent the lower court would regard itself as bound to follow them at risk of its decision being set aside on appeal. Only in the presence of unclear or conflicting decisions of the higher court would it feel free to decide the matter as it thought fit.'[37] On the other hand, it might be said that the decisions of the Court were not concieved of as a source of law in themselves, but merely as illustrations of the way in which the law has in the past been applied. In the absence of any written rule to the contrary, the case law of the Court should of course be treated as influential, but it would not be in keeping with the civilian tradition for the CFI to regard it as strictly binding. From a more pragmatic point of view, it might seem improbable that the Court of Justice would ever uphold an appeal on the sole ground that its own case law had not been followed. The Court would surely be more likely to ask whether the CFI had reached the right result, itself qualifying any of its own previous decisions which might seem to stand in the way.[38]

[36] Cf Slynn, *Introducing a European Legal Order* (1992), pp 165–6.
[37] Brown and Kennedy, op cit, p 351.   [38] See Arnull (1993) 30 CMLRev 247, 263.

In practice, the CFI makes extensive reference to the Court's case law in its judgments and clearly considers it highly persuasive. However, where the CFI believes it is liable to produce adverse results, it has not hesitated to look for ways of avoiding it. Indeed, since it heard its first case in 1989, the CFI's attitude to the case law of the Court has become increasingly robust. An early case in which the CFI demonstrated its readiness to distinguish inconvenient rulings of the Court of Justice was *BASF and Others v Commission*,[39] where the applicants sought the annulment of a Commission decision relating to proceedings under Article 81 (ex 85) of the Treaty. One of the grounds put forward by the applicants was that the Commission had infringed the first paragraph of Article 12 of its own Rules of Procedure,[40] which provided that '[a]cts adopted by the Commission, at a meeting or by written procedure, shall be authenticated in the language or languages in which they are binding by the signatures of the President and the Executive Secretary'. The Commission sought to rely on the judgment in *Nakajima v Council*,[41] where the Court of Justice said that 'the purpose of the rules of procedure of a Community institution is to organize the internal functioning of its services in the interests of good administration'. According to the Court of Justice, it followed 'that natural or legal persons may not rely on an alleged breach of those rules since they are not intended to ensure protection for individuals'. Notwithstanding the apparently general terms of that ruling, in *BASF* the CFI took the view that it was limited in scope:

The Court [of First Instance] considers that that judgment must be interpreted as meaning that it is necessary to distinguish between those provisions of an institution's Rules of Procedure whose infringement may not be relied upon by natural and legal persons because they are concerned solely with the internal working arrangements of the institution and cannot affect their legal situation and those whose infringement may be relied upon because, as is the case with Article 12 of the Commission's Rules of Procedure, they create rights and are a factor contributing to legal certainty for such persons.

The CFI went on to find that the contested measure was vitiated by such serious defects that it was to be considered non-existent. The Commission then appealed to the Court of Justice,[42] which set aside the conclusion of the CFI that the measure was non-existent. However, without referring to its decision in *Nakajima*,[43] it declared that '[a]uthentication of acts referred to in the first paragraph of Article 12 of the Commission's Rules of Procedure . . . constitutes an essential procedural requirement within the meaning of Article 173 of the EEC Treaty [now Article 230 EC] breach of which gives rise to an action for annulment'.[44] Since the

---

[39] Joined Cases T–79/89, T–84/89, T–85/89, T–86/89, T–89/89, T–91/89, T–92/89, T–94/89, T–96/89, T–98/89, T–102/89 and T–104/89 [1992] ECR II–315 para 78. Cf Case T–353/94 *Postbank v Commission* [1996] ECR II–921, para 70.

[40] OJ, English Sp Ed, Second Series VII—Institutional Questions, p 9, as amended by Commission Decision 75/461, OJ 1975 L199/43.

[41] Case C–69/89 [1991] ECR I–2069, paras 49 and 50.

[42] Case C–137/92 P *Commission v BASF and Others* [1994] ECR I–2555.

[43] But see the Opinion of AG van Gerven at pp 2598–605.   [44] Para 76.

Commission had failed to authenticate the contested decision in accordance with the requirements laid down in its Rules of Procedure, the Court concluded that the decision should be annulled.[45]

Perhaps emboldened by that episode, the CFI subsequently appeared to depart from the decision of the Court of Justice in 'Dutch Books'[46] that Community law did not require the Commission to divulge the contents of its files to the parties in competition cases. In *Solvay v Commission* and *ICI v Commission*, the CFI described access to the file as 'one of the procedural safeguards intended to protect the rights of the defence' and declared that '[r]espect for the rights of the defence in all proceedings in which sanctions may be imposed is a fundamental principle of Community law which must be respected in all circumstances . . .'.[47] Again, in *Kotzonis v ESC*,[48] the CFI expressly stated that the case law of the Court of Justice on the effect of a provision of the Staff Regulations 'ought to be reconsidered' and went on to depart from it. The CFI also displayed a marked reluctance to follow the lead apparently given by the Court in *Codorniu v Council*[49] on the standing conditions which natural and legal persons must satisfy in order to bring proceedings under Article 230 (ex 173) EC for the annulment of Community acts.[50]

A clear statement of the attitude of the CFI to the case law of the Court of Justice is to be found in *NMB France and Others v Commission*.[51] In that case (*NMB II*), the applicants sought the annulment of a series of Commission decisions concerning the refund of anti-dumping duties[52] collected on imports of ball-bearings from Singapore which had been fixed at too high a rate. According to the applicants, the method used by the Commission to calculate the amount of the refunds was unlawful. A curious feature of the case was that, before the CFI acquired jurisdiction in dumping cases, the applicants had already brought an unsuccessful action before the Court of Justice (*NMB I*)[53] for the annulment of Commission decisions on the refund of anti-dumping duties they had paid on the same product from the same origin. The decisions contested in *NMB II* related to different periods but the arguments advanced by the applicants were essentially the same as those previously rejected by the Court.

The Commission argued that the second action constituted an abuse of procedure, in that the applicants were in reality seeking to challenge the judgment of the Court in *NMB I*. The Commission was supported by a federation representing European bearing manufacturers, which maintained that the second action

---

[45] In a subsequent case, the Court cited its rulings in *Nakajima* and *BASF* as if they were consistent: see Case C–58/94 *Netherlands v Council* [1996] ECR I–2169, para 38.

[46] Joined Cases 43 and 63/82 *VBVB and VBBB v Commission* [1984] ECR 19, para 25.

[47] Case T–30/91 [1995] ECR II–1775, para 59, and Case T–36/91 [1995] ECR II–1847, para 69, respectively. In both cases, the contested decision was annulled. See Moore (1996) 33 CMLRev 355.

[48] Case T–586/93 [1995] ECR II–665, para 92.

[49] Case C–309/89 [1994] ECR I–1853.   [50] See further ch 2.

[51] Case T–162/94 [1996] ECR II–427 (Second Chamber, Extended Composition).

[52] Dumping takes place when a product is imported into the Community from a non-member country at a price which is lower than its normal value in that country and the result is to cause injury to a Community industry. Dumped products may be the subject of anti-dumping duties.

[53] Case C–188/88 *NMB and Others v Commission* [1992] ECR I–1689.

constituted a 'disguised appeal against the first judgment'.[54] However, the CFI held that the second action was admissible, declaring:[55]

It must be borne in mind at the outset that the Court of First Instance is only bound by the judgments of the Court of Justice, first, in the circumstances laid down in the second paragraph of Article 54 of the Statute of the Court of Justice of the European Community, and, secondly, pursuant to the principle of *res judicata*.

Article 54 of the Statute is concerned with the consequences where an appeal to the Court against a decision of the CFI is upheld. One of the options open to the Court is to refer the case back to the CFI for judgment. When that option is exercised, the second paragraph of Article 54 states that the CFI 'shall be bound by the decision of the Court of Justice on points of law'. In the interests of completeness, the CFI might also have mentioned Article 47 of the Statute. According to that provision, where the Court finds that an action which has been brought before it falls within the jurisdiction of the CFI, it must refer the action to the CFI, which 'may not decline jurisdiction'. In other words, the CFI is bound by the finding of the Court of Justice that the former Court has jurisdiction to hear the action. However, neither Article 47 nor Article 54 of the Statute was relevant in the circumstances of *NMB II*, so the CFI went on to consider whether the status as *res judicata*[56] of the judgment of the Court of Justice in *NMB I* rendered the second action inadmissible. The CFI observed: 'It is settled case-law that this can be the case only if the proceedings disposed of by the judgment in [*NMB I*] were between the same parties, had the same purpose and were based on the same submissions as the present case . . . those conditions necessarily being cumulative.'[57] The CFI pointed out that the second action concerned 'different, later decisions relating to other quantities [of ball-bearings] and import periods and reimbursements of different amounts'.[58] It followed that the status of the judgment in *NMB I* as *res judicata* could not affect the admissibility of the second action.

The CFI went on to note that, although the complaints put forward in the second action largely coincided with those advanced in *NMB I*, there were none the less significant differences: the international legal context had changed and the Community had adopted a new basic regulation on protection against dumping. The second action could not therefore be considered 'a mere replication'[59] of the first. Moreover, one of the applicants in *NMB II* had not been involved in *NMB I*. It followed, said the CFI, that 'this action is entirely admissible and that the Court of First Instance must therefore examine its merits. In so doing, it should take account simultaneously of the judgment in [*NMB I*] and of the new issues raised

[54] Para 31 of the judgment in Case T–162/94.
[55] Para 36. See also joined cases T–177/94 and T–377/94 *Altmann and Others v Commission* [1996] ECR II–2041.
[56] See further Toth, *The Oxford Encyclopaedia of European Community Law* (1990), Vol I, pp 464–7.
[57] Para 37 of the judgment in *NMB II*.
[58] Para 38.
[59] Para 39.

by these proceedings.'[60] After a detailed examination of the grounds put forward by the applicants, the CFI dismissed the action as unfounded.

The judgment in *NMB II* confirmed the indications given by earlier cases that the CFI does not consider itself bound by decisions of the Court of Justice except in certain exceptional and clearly defined circumstances. Those decisions are treated by the CFI merely as persuasive, although the more there are in support of a given proposition, the less likely the CFI will be to depart from them.

An assessment

The volume of previous case law with which the Court of Justice must now deal has both advantages and disadvantages. On the one hand, few cases now require the Court to invent the wheel: many can be decided simply be applying principles which have become fairly well established. On the other hand, the principles which emerge from the decided cases may not be entirely apt and the process of deciding whether and to what extent it is desirable to move in a new direction may require a considerable investment of intellectual stamina. In these circumstances, it is essential that the Court makes apparent to readers of its judgments precisely how they fit in with relevant previous case law. The technique once applied, of passing over in silence cases which might have appeared to point to a different result or of presenting them as if they were consistent with the Court's preferred solution in the instant case, would create intolerable confusion against the background of the present volume of case law. The Court seems to have recognized this and now deals with its own case law in a much more satisfactory manner, explaining when cases are no longer to be regarded as good law or alternatively when they remain good law notwithstanding an attempt to have them overruled. Although the Court's current approach may seem unremarkable to those brought up in the common law tradition, it is not in keeping with the practice traditionally followed by courts in many Member States. The Court deserves praise for departing from its previous approach in this way.

The CFI has faced a problem of precedent of a different order and has struck a nice balance between deference to the case law of the Court of Justice and a natural desire to do justice in the cases it is called upon to decide. The creative tension which results from the unwillingness of the CFI to follow without question the decisions of the Court is on the whole conducive to the healthy development of Community law. Although the present writer regrets the failure of the CFI to grasp the baton extended by the Court in *Codorniu*, the remedy lay with the Court itself in the exercise of its appellate jurisdiction. As we saw in chapter 2, far from reiterating the message apparently delivered by that case, the Court appeared to endorse the reservations of the CFI about making it easier for natural and legal persons to bring annulment proceedings. The attitude of the CFI may therefore be said to have had the benefit of concentrating the Court's mind on the consequences of taking that step.

---

[60] Para 41. The CFI referred to Joined Cases 311/81 and 30/82 *Klöckner-Werke v Commission* and Case 136/82 *Klöckner-Werke v Commission* [1983] ECR 1549 and 1599 respectively, para 5.

16

Judging Europe's Judges

Some of the preceding chapters have sought to trace the way the Court's approach to the questions it has been called upon to decide has changed with the passage of time in particular contexts. Others have mentioned apparent links between specific decisions of the Court and developments at the political level. The aim of this final chapter is to examine more generally the extent to which the approach of the Court to its task has evolved over time and to speculate about the causes of any such variation.[1] For the purposes of the discussion, three broad phases in the Court's case law are identified. The first runs from the entry into force of the EEC Treaty until the breakdown of the Luxembourg Compromise in the early 1980s. During this phase, the Council was handicapped by the need to reach a consensus before acting and the Court took a number of bold decisions which had the effect of 'constitutionalizing'[2] the Community and achieving some at least of the Treaty's policy objectives notwithstanding the absence of much of the legislation it envisaged. The second phase runs from the transition in the early 1980s to qualified majority voting in the Council until the signature on 7 February 1992 of the TEU. This heralded the start of the third phase. The nature of the TEU and the unprecedented public debate which accompanied its ratification by the Member States produced a fundamental change in the political climate which affected all the institutions of the Community, including the Court of Justice. The chapter concludes with some brief remarks about the relationship between the Court of Justice and the national courts of the Member States and the question of the Court's legitimacy.

---

[1] For a path-breaking analysis of some of these issues, see Weiler, *The Constitution of Europe* (1999) (hereafter 'Weiler'), chs 2 and 5. Those chapters are based respectively on well-known papers first published elsewhere, namely 'The transformation of Europe' (1991) 100 Yale LJ 2403 and 'Journey to an unknown destination: a retrospective and prospective of the European Court of Justice in the arena of political integration' (1993) 31 JCMS 418. See also Lenaerts, 'Some thoughts about the interaction between judges and politicians in the European Community' (1992) 12 YEL 1; Dehousse, *The European Court of Justice* (1998), ch 6; Shapiro, 'The European Court of Justice' in Craig and de Búrca (eds), *The Evolution of EU Law* (1999), ch 9.

[2] See Weiler, ch 6; 'The European Courts of Justice: beyond "beyond doctrine" or the legitimacy crisis of European Constitutionalism' in Slaughter, Stone and Weiler (eds), *The European Court and National Courts—Doctrine and Jurisprudence* (1998), 365.

The first phase: from consensus to qualified majority

Making the system work

During the first phase of the Community's existence, the Court was called upon to address a variety of issues which were self-evidently fundamental to the functioning of the Treaty system. The Court's overriding concern seems to have been to ensure that the Treaty system worked and that the Member States complied with the obligations imposed on them. Although the Treaty itself contained, in Article 169 (now 226), a procedure for achieving that objective which was in itself quite radical, the Court appreciated that the Treaty's capacity to bind the Member States would be greatly enhanced if it were to confer on individuals rights which the national courts had to uphold. Thus, in a series of cases beginning with *Van Gend en Loos*, the Court held that Treaty provisions which were sufficiently clear and precise were capable of producing that effect, not just against the State and its emanations but also, in appropriate cases, against private parties.[3] Moreover, such provisions would take precedence over inconsistent provisions of domestic law. Although not expressly spelled out in the Treaty, these principles of direct effect and primacy were wholly consistent with its spirit and general scheme for without them the uniform application of Community law throughout the Member States, essential to the proper functioning of the common market, could not have been achieved. It was not therefore surprising when the Court made it clear that Community law took precedence regardless of the constitutional status of conflicting provisions of national law or the date on which they were adopted. The contrary conclusion would have enabled the Member States to absolve themselves at will from the requirements of the Treaty.

The transition to qualified majority voting which should have taken place at the beginning of 1966 might have led the Court to pass the baton to the Member States. However, the Luxembourg Compromise agreed in January of that year led to the development in the Council of a practice under which measures were not adopted until a consensus had emerged in their support. That practice hampered the Council's ability to fulfil the responsibilities cast upon it by the Treaty in two ways. First, the process of finding a consensus was immensely time-consuming; secondly, it tended to result in a dilution of the proposals put forward by the Commission which were usually required to set the process in motion. Against that background, the Court followed the path on which it had set out into the field of substantive law, with crucial decisions on the scope of the Treaty rules on freedom of movement[4]

---

[3] See Case 127/73 *BRT v SABAM* [1974] ECR 51; Case 43/75 *Defrenne v SABENA* (*Defrenne II*) [1976] ECR 455.

[4] eg Case 2/74 *Reyners v Belgium* [1974] ECR 631; Case 8/74 *Procureur du Roi v Dassonville* [1974] ECR 837; Case 33/74 *van Binsbergen v Bedrijfsvereniging Metaalnijverheid* [1974] ECR 1299; Case 120/78 *Rewe v Bundesmonopolverwaltung für Branntwein* ('Cassis de Dijon') [1979] ECR 649. See chs 7 and 9.

and competition.[5] In addition, the growing importance attached by the Member States to action in the social field provided the context for the Court's decision in *Defrenne II*,[6] which triggered the development of a remarkable body of case law on equal treatment for men and women.[7]

It was during the period in which the practice of consensus became firmly established that the Court gave a decision which emphasized once more the profound consequences which the entry into force of the Treaty had produced for the sovereignty of the Member States. This was its judgment in the 'ERTA' case,[8] where the Court addressed a long-running controversy about the extent of the Community's power to enter into international agreements. The EEC Treaty gave the Community legal personality[9] and express powers to conclude agreements with third States and international organizations in particular fields.[10] Such agreements are negotiated by the Commission in accordance with instructions issued by the Council, which concludes the agreement on the Community's behalf if the negotiations are successful.[11] In 'ERTA' the Court recognized that, even in the absence of express Treaty authority, the Community might have implied power to conclude such agreements. It declared:[12]

To determine in a particular case the Community's authority to enter into international agreements, regard must be had to the whole scheme of the Treaty no less than to its substantive provisions.

Such authority arises not only from an express conferment by the Treaty . . . but may equally flow from other provisions of the Treaty and from measures adopted, within the framework of those provisions, by the Community institutions.

In particular, each time the Community, with a view to implementing a common policy envisaged by the Treaty, adopts provisions laying down common rules . . . the Member States no longer have the right, acting individually or even collectively, to undertake obligations with third countries which affect those rules.

As and when such common rules come into being, the Community alone is in a position to assume and carry out contractual obligations towards third countries affecting the whole sphere of application of the Community legal system.

With regard to the implementation of the provisions of the Treaty the system of internal Community measures may not therefore be separated from that of external relations.

---

[5] eg Joined Cases 56 and 58/64 *Consten and Grundig v Commission* [1966] ECR 299; Case 48/69 *ICI v Commission* [1972] ECR 619; Case 6/72 *Europemballage and Continental Can v Commission* [1973] ECR 215; Case 27/76 *United Brands v Commission* [1978] ECR 207. See ch 12.

[6] *Supra.*   [7] See ch 13.

[8] Case 22/70 *Commission v Council* [1971] ECR 263.   [9] See Art 210 (now 281).

[10] See in particular Art 113 (now 133) on the common commercial policy and Art 238 (now 310) on association agreements.

[11] See now Art 300 (ex 228) EC. The present text of that article is based on provisions introduced at Maastricht, which laid down procedures modelled on practice under the EEC Treaty. For detailed discussion, see Macleod, Hendry and Hyett, *The External Relations of the European Communities* (1996), pp 80–105; Dashwood, 'External relations provisions of the Amsterdam Treaty' (1998) 35 CMLRev 1019, 1023–8. A shorter account may be found in Hartley, *The Foundations of European Community Law* (4th edn, 1998), p 157. For a description of the procedure followed before the entry into force of the TEU, see the 2nd edn of that work at pp 148–50.

[12] Paras 15–19.

Subsequent case law[13] built on the foundations laid in 'ERTA' so that by the end of the 1970s it was clear that the Community's implied power to enter into international agreements was not confined to areas in which common rules had been laid down. Wherever the Community institutions had the power to act in order to achieve a particular policy objective in the internal sphere, the Community had the power to enter into international commitments with a view to achieving the same objective notwithstanding the absence of an express provision authorizing it to do so. Moreover, that power would become exclusive[14] once the Community exercised its powers, whether internally or externally.[15]

This line of case law was of enormous significance in equipping the Community with the powers it needed to achieve the objectives laid down in the Treaty. It provided a striking example of the extent to which, to borrow the language of the Court in *Van Gend en Loos*, the Member States had limited their sovereign rights for the benefit of the Community. It is also worth noting that, to enable it to police the jurisdictional boundary between the Community and the Member States in the field of external relations, the Court took a characteristically broad approach to its own powers. The Treaty contained a provision, Article 228(1),[16] enabling the Council, the Commission, or a Member State to ask the Court for its opinion on whether an international agreement which the Community was proposing to conclude was compatible with the Treaty. If the Court's opinion was adverse, the agreement (unless modified) could only enter into force if the Treaty were amended. The notion of compatibility might have been interpreted as limited to whether or not the substantive provisions of the agreement envisaged were consistent with the Treaty, but the Court took a broader view. In an opinion delivered in late 1975 at the request of the Commission,[17] the Court ruled:

. . . the fact that the Commission raised the problem of the compatibility of this agreement with the provisions of the Treaty for the purpose of obtaining the opinion of the Court of Justice on the extent of the Community's powers to conclude the agreement envisaged cannot be sufficient of itself to render the request inadmissible . . .

The compatibility of an agreement with the provisions of the Treaty must be assessed in the light of all the rules of the Treaty, that is to say, both those rules which determine the extent of the powers of the institutions of the Community and the substantive rules.

---

[13] See in particular Joined Cases 3, 4 and 6/76 *Kramer* [1976] ECR 1279; Opinion 1/76 'Draft Agreement Establishing a European Laying-Up Fund for Inland Waterway Vessels' [1977] ECR 741.

[14] That is, action by the Member States in the field in question would be precluded or 'pre-empted'. See further Weatherill, *Law and Integration in the European Union* (1995), ch 5.

[15] Until that point, the Member States would have concurrent powers to enter into international commitments in the field in question.

[16] The procedure was moved to Art 228(6) (now 300(6)) EC by the TEU.

[17] Opinion 1/75 'Understanding on a Local Cost Standard' [1975] ECR 1355, 1360. See also Opinion 1/78 'International Agreement on Natural Rubber' [1979] ECR 2871, para 30; Opinion 3/94 'Framework Agreement on Bananas' [1995] ECR I–4577, paras 16–17; Opinion 2/94 'Accession by the Communities to the Convention for the Protection of Human Rights and Fundamental Freedoms' [1996] ECR I–1759, paras 3–5.

The Court pointed out that, if it were to rule, after the conclusion of an international agreement binding on the Community, that it was incompatible with the Treaty by reason either of its content or the procedure adopted for its conclusion, serious difficulties might arise for all interested parties. It was the purpose of the procedure laid down in Article 228 of the Treaty to avoid such difficulties.

Had the Court adopted a more limited view of its jurisdiction under Article 228 (now 300), it is hard to see how disputes between the Commission and the Member States on the matter could have been settled. Be that as it may, the outcome was to give the Court a pivotal role in defining the extent of the Community's power to enter into international agreements and to underline the extent to which the sovereignty of the Member States had been curtailed in the field of external relations. Not only were there some fields in which they had lost the power to enter into international agreements with third countries, but those fields would in cases of dispute be determined by a supranational Court which evidently attached greater importance to achieving the Treaty's objectives than to preserving the traditional prerogatives of the Member States.

Protecting the rights of individuals

During the initial phase, protecting the rights of individuals seemed to be another of the Court's major preoccupations. Indeed, in *Van Gend en Loos* the Court emphasized that the Treaty was intended to confer upon individuals 'rights which become part of their legal heritage'.[18] Much of the Court's case law during this phase had the effect of strengthening the capacity of individuals to benefit from Community law, whether it took the form of rules laid down in the Treaty or in directives, the capacity of which to produce direct effect in the vertical sense started to emerge at the beginning of the 1970s with the decision in *Grad v Finanzamt Traunstein*.[19]

However, in most of the cases in which the rights of individuals were upheld by the Court, the Member States were as a corollary required to comply with their own obligations. In cases where individuals sought to claim rights against the institutions of the Community, the Court was less sympathetic. Thus, in *Producteurs de Fruits v Council*,[20] decided towards the end of 1962, the Court was called upon to consider the circumstances in which a natural or legal person could challenge the validity of a Community act which had been called a regulation by the institution which adopted it. The Treaty entitled such an applicant to contest a decision 'in the form of a regulation' and the Court accepted that it was indeed the substance rather than the form of the contested act which was important. However, it went on to define the characteristics of a regulation in a way which was to make it extremely difficult for natural or legal persons to show that a measure which car-

---

[18] [1963] ECR 1, 12.   [19] Case 9/70 [1970] ECR 825.
[20] Joined Cases 16 and 17/62 [1962] ECR 471.

ried that label in fact constituted a decision.[21] In the same vein was *Plaumann v Commission*,[22] decided in July 1963. The applicant sought the annulment under Article 173 (now 230) of a Commission decision addressed to the Federal Republic of Germany. The Treaty allowed a natural or legal person to challenge a decision addressed to another person which was of direct and individual concern to the applicant. The Commission argued that a Member State could not constitute 'another person' within the meaning of Article 173. That argument was unconvincing: it was tolerably clear from the text of the Treaty that a natural or legal person was intended to have the capacity to challenge any decision which, while not addressed to him, was of direct and individual concern to him. That was the conclusion reached by the Court, which declared: 'The words and natural meaning of this provision justify the broadest interpretation. Moreover provisions of the Treaty regarding the right of interested parties to bring an action must not be interpreted restrictively.'[23] However, on the more difficult question of individual concern, that is precisely what the Court did, ruling that the applicant was not individually concerned because it was only affected by the contested decision 'by reason of a commercial activity which may at any time be practised by any person . . .'. The *Producteurs de Fruits* and *Plaumann* decisions became classic authorities on the right of individuals to bring annulment proceedings under the EC Treaty and for many years had the effect of making it extremely difficult for such an applicant to challenge any Community act other than a decision addressed to him. Their impact is still being felt today.

The Court's reluctance to allow individuals to challenge the activities of the institutions was also evident in *Zuckerfabrik Schöppenstedt v Council*,[24] decided in late 1971, where the Court addressed the circumstances in which damage resulting from a legislative act of the Community might fix it with liability under the second paragraph of Article 215 (now 288). The Court declared:[25] 'Where legislative action involving measures of economic policy is concerned, the Community does not incur noncontractual liability for damage suffered by individuals as a consequence of that action . . . unless a sufficiently flagrant violation of a superior rule of law for the protection of the individual has occurred.' The restrictive nature of the *Schöppenstedt* formula made it very difficult for individuals to recover damages for loss caused by legislative acts.[26]

The Court's early case law on the action for annulment and the action for damages appears at first sight to be inconsistent with the emphasis placed by the Court on protecting the rights of individuals in *Van Gend en Loos*. How can this

---

[21] See eg Joined Cases 789 and 790/79 *Calpak v Commission* [1980] ECR 1949.
[22] Case 25/62 [1963] ECR 95.   [23] pp 106–7.
[24] Case 5/71 [1971] ECR 975.   [25] Para 11.
[26] See further Arnull, 'Liability for legislative acts under Article 215(2) EC' in Heukels and McDonnell (eds), *The Action for Damages in Community Law* (1977), ch 7. The Court in due course took a slightly more receptive approach to claims arising out of loss caused by administrative acts: see van der Woude, 'Liability for administrative acts under Article 215(2) EC' in Heukels and McDonnell, op cit, ch 6.

discrepancy be explained? It seems likely that the Court was influenced by a variety of factors. In the case of the action for annulment, some of these are mentioned in chapter 2. In the case of the action for damages, it was no doubt mindful of the difficulty of recovering compensation for loss caused by legislative action in the national laws of the Member States.[27] However, the boldness of the Court's case law on direct effect and primacy makes explanations such as these inadequate. It seems probable that the Court was also motivated by a desire to shield the Community's as yet immature institutions from legal challenge. Allowing Community acts to be challenged or damages to be sought by potentially large numbers of private applicants might have caused serious disruption to a decision-making process which, either *de iure* (before 1966) or *de facto* (after 1966), required the Council to act unanimously. By the time qualified majority voting had become the norm in the early 1980s, a substantial body of case law on both the action for annulment and the action for damages had built up which considerations of legal certainty made it hard to abandon.

The second phase: from QMV to EU

A reduced role for the Court?

The practice of consensus which developed as a result of the Luxembourg Compromise began to break down in the early 1980s and voting in accordance with the Treaty became the normal practice.[28] This trend was reinforced by the Single European Act, signed in February 1986, which inserted into the EEC Treaty a new provision[29] requiring the Community to 'adopt measures with the aim of progressively establishing the internal market over a period expiring on 31 December 1992'. All the Member States understood that that objective would be impossible to achieve if the Council did not take advantage of the new legal bases introduced by the Single European Act which provided for qualified majority voting, particularly Article 100a (now 95). Against that background it might have been thought that the Court would begin to play a less prominent role in the Community's development.[30] An activist approach by the Court could no longer be justified on the basis that the Community legislature was not functioning prop-

---

[27] Especially as the second para of Art 215 (now 288) referred expressly to 'the general principles common to the laws of the Member States'. See AG Darmon in Case C–282/90 *Vreugdenhil v Commission* [1992] ECR I–1937, 1958.

[28] See Dashwood, 'Majority voting in the Council' in Schwarze (ed), *Legislation for Europe 1992* (1989), p 79. The Treaty of Amsterdam introduced three provisions which are reminiscent of the Luxembourg Compromise: see Arts 23(2) (ex J. 13(2)) and 40(2) (ex K. 12(2)) TEU and Art 11(2) (ex 5a(2)) EC. It remains to be seen what effect, if any, these provisions will have on recourse to the Compromise where they do not apply.

[29] Art 8a (now 14).

[30] Cf Koopmans, 'The role of law in the next stage of European integration' (1986) 35 ICLQ 925; Mancini, 'The making of a constitution for Europe' (1989) 26 CMLRev 595.

erly. Even changes to the Treaty itself now seemed a practical possibility in suitably pressing cases.

To some extent the Court may be said to have responded to the new climate. In *Marshall I*,[31] decided between the two dates on which the Single European Act was signed, the Court finally decided that directives did not have horizontal direct effect. It doubtless took account of the hostile reception of some national courts to its case law on the vertical direct effect of directives. However, it may also have been influenced by the importance which directives were to play in the establishment of the internal market and the consideration that to endow them with horizontal direct effect would be to upset the bargain struck by the Member States in the Single European Act. *Marshall I* is a leading example of the Court's capacity for restraint, but it came to be overshadowed by the Court's attempts to attenuate the damaging effects the decision had for the uniform application of the law and the rights of individuals, particularly the principle of consistent interpretation first articulated in *Von Colson*[32] and later developed in *Marleasing*.[33]

In the field of substantive law too the Court began to show greater deference to national sensitivities. In *Reed*,[34] decided in April 1986, the Court refused to assimilate unmarried partners to spouses for the purposes of the rules on the free movement of workers. In *Groener*,[35] decided in late 1989, the Court held that a Member State could require a worker from another Member State to demonstrate competence in a language having constitutional status, even if knowledge of that language was not necessary to enable the worker to do the job she was seeking. In *Grogan*,[36] the Court took a restrictive approach to the rules on services in order to avoid addressing the compatibility with the Treaty of national rules prohibiting abortion. In the field of competition law the Court seemed more reluctant than previously to articulate 'major new conceptual developments or ideals'.[37]

The momentum of the case law

The Single European Act did not, however, contain any indication that the Member States were dissatisfied with the role which had hitherto been played by the Court. On the contrary, the Member States accepted a proposal from the Court itself[38] that the Council should be empowered to reinforce judicial protection in

---

[31] Case 152/84 *Marshall v Southampton and South-West Hampshire Area Health Authority* [1986] ECR 723. See ch 4.

[32] Case 14/83 *Von Colson and Kamann v Land Nordrhein-Westfalen* [1984] ECR 1891.

[33] Case C–106/89 [1990] ECR I–4135.   [34] Case 59/85 *Netherlands v Reed* [1986] ECR 1283.

[35] Case C–379/87 *Groener v Minister for Education and the City of Dublin Vocational Education Committee* [1989] ECR 3967.

[36] Case C–159/90 *Society for the Protection of Unborn Children Ireland v Grogan and Others* [1991] ECR I–4685.

[37] Gerber, *Law and Competition in Twentieth Century Europe* (1998), p 372.

[38] See Millett, *The Court of First Instance of the European Communities* (1990), p 6; Kennedy, 'The essential minimum: the establishment of the Court of First Instance' (1989) 14 ELRev 7, 13–15.

the Community by establishing a court of first instance. Moreover, the case law of the Court had by the 1980s developed a certain momentum of its own which did not entirely correspond with developments at the political level. This phenomenon is clearly illustrated by the fields of equal treatment for men and women and remedies.

Following its decision in *Defrenne II*, in 1981 the Court made it clear in *Jenkins v Kingsgate*[39] that Article 119 (now 141) of the Treaty was not confined to cases of direct discrimination. In *Garland*,[40] the following year, the Court underlined the breadth of the notion of pay for the purposes of that article. By the late 1980s the Court had started to show some reluctance to subject to close scrutiny claims that indirect discrimination was objectively justified,[41] a reluctance which was to extend to the social security directive. None the less the Court continued to adopt a robust approach to the material scope of Article 119,[42] an approach it extended to Directive 76/207.[43]

Making up for lost time

The case law on remedies is less nuanced. Mounting frustration with the lack of Council legislation on the procedural conditions under which Community rights were to be protected in the Member States led the Court in the early 1980s to reduce the deference it had previously shown for the procedural autonomy of the Member States.[44] The increased vigour with which the Court started to intervene in the circumstances in which Community rights were protected in the national courts culminated in *Factortame I*,[45] *Francovich*,[46] and *Emmott*.[47] The case law on remedies and that on equal treatment for men and women merged in *Marshall II*,[48] where the Court held that the Member States were not permitted to set an upper limit to the amount of compensation payable to the victims of discrimination contrary to Directive 76/207.

Moreover, the improvements in the functioning of the decision-making process of the Community and the single market programme, which first saw the light of day in the form of the Commission's White Paper entitled 'Completing the Internal Market' presented to the European Council at the end of June 1985, served to emphasize the lack of progress that had been made hitherto and in particular the failure of the Community and its Member States to establish the

---

[39] Case 96/80 [1981] ECR 911.
[40] Case 12/81 *Garland v British Rail Engineering* [1982] ECR 359.
[41] See eg Case 109/88 *Handels- og Kontorfunktionærernes Forbund i Danmark v Dansk Arbejdsgiverforening, acting on behalf of Danfoss* [1989] ECR 3199. See ch 13.
[42] eg Case C–262/88 *Barber* [1990] ECR I–1889.
[43] eg Case C–177/88 *Dekker* [1990] ECR I–3941. See ch 13.   [44] See ch 5.
[45] Case C–213/89 [1990] ECR I–2433.
[46] Joined Cases C–6/90 and C–9/90 *Francovich and Others* [1991] ECR I–5357.
[47] Case C–208/90 [1991] ECR I–4269.
[48] Case C–271/91 *Marshall v Southampton and South-West Hampshire AHA* [1993] ECR I–4367.

common market by the deadline laid down in the original version of the EEC Treaty.[49] A collective realization of the need to make up for lost time seems to have galvanized the Member States and the institutions into action and the Court was conscious of the opportunity this presented for it to continue its own efforts to make the Community work.

It was around the mid-1980s that the Court started to make serious use of Article 5 EEC (now 10 EC), requiring the Member States to 'facilitate the achievement of the Community's tasks' and to 'abstain from any measure which could jeopardize the attainment of the objectives of this Treaty'.[50] Article 5 played an important part in the Court's reasoning in *Von Colson*,[51] where it was held that the obligations it laid down extended to the national courts and required them to interpret their national law in the light of the wording and the purpose of relevant directives. In the field of competition law too Article 5 was used to reinforce the effectiveness of the Treaty rules. In *Leclerc v Au Blé Vert*,[52] for example, the Court declared: 'Whilst it is true that the rules on competition are concerned with the conduct of under-takings and not with national legislation, Member States are none the less obliged under the second paragraph of Article 5 of the Treaty not to detract, by means of national legislation, from the full and uniform application of Community law or from the effectiveness of its implementing measures; nor may they introduce or maintain in force measures, even of a legislative nature, which may render ineffect-ive the competition rules applicable to undertakings.' Even more dramatically, the Court held in *Francovich*[53] that Article 5 provided one reason (among others) why Member States were required to make good loss caused by breaches of Community law for which they were responsible. In *Zwartveld and Others*,[54] the Court even held that the 'principle of sincere cooperation' enshrined in Article 5 extended to the Community institutions in their relations with the authorities of the Member States, especially national courts who were seeking to ensure respect for Community law in the national legal systems. The Court proceeded to order the Commission to co-operate with an investigation being carried out by a Dutch judge into an alleged fraud relating to the Community legislation on fisheries. The background to the case was certainly unusual, but in *Delimitis*[55] the Court used the same reasoning in emphasizing the duty of the Commission to co-operate with national courts called upon to apply the Treaty competition rules.

---

[49] That is, 31 December 1969 (the end of the transitional period): see Art 8(7) EEC; Gormley (ed), *Kapteyn and VerLoren van Themaat's Introduction to the Law of the European Communities* (3rd edn 1998), pp 132–3.

[50] See Temple Lang, 'Community constitutional law: Article 5 EEC Treaty' (1990) 27 CMLRev 645.

[51] *Supra.*

[52] Case 229/83 [1985] ECR 1, para 14. See also Case 231/83 *Cullet v Leclerc* [1985] ECR 305, para 16.

[53] *Supra*, para 36.   [54] Case C–2/88 Imm [1990] ECR I–3365.

[55] Case C–234/89 [1991] ECR I–935.

Protecting the institutional balance

The transition to qualified majority voting and the single market programme also focused the Court's attention on an issue which had previously been somewhat neglected, that of the institutional balance. The importance which this issue assumed during this phase of the case law seems to be attributable to a variety of factors. One of these is the importance of the legal basis chosen for Community acts. While the Council followed the practice of consensus, the legal basis chosen did not have much practical effect on the way in which the Council reached its decisions. The demise of the practice of consensus meant that the legal basis assumed greater importance because it determined the voting procedure which the Council had to follow. The introduction by the Single European Act of the so-called co-operation procedure,[56] giving the European Parliament greater influence over the content of Community acts where that procedure applied, increased the significance of the legal basis still further, for it became crucial to know not only how the Council was to vote but also the extent to which the Parliament was entitled to take part in the process. These developments were themselves attributable, at least in part, to the first set of direct elections to the Parliament, which took place in 1979.

The co-operation procedure reflected the increased status of the Parliament and reduced the discrepancy between its role in the Community's general decision-making process and the important powers it had enjoyed in the budgetary field since the mid-1970s.[57] It seems self-evident that a mechanism would have to be found of subjecting to judicial scrutiny the way in which a more confident Parliament exercised its powers and ensuring respect for the prerogatives it now enjoyed in the institutional architecture of the Community. However, the Member States failed to address the issue in the Single European Act and it fell to the Court to deal with it. In *Les Verts*[58] the Court held that acts of the Parliament which affected the legal rights of third parties were open to challenge under Article 173 (now 230), notwithstanding the absence of any reference to the Parliament in the version of that article which was then in force. The acts contested in *Les Verts*, concerning the reimbursement of election expenses, were perhaps of limited importance but an early beneficiary of the ruling was the Council which, with the support of three Member States, successfully challenged the Parliament's exercise of its budgetary powers.[59] In the subsequent 'Chernobyl' case,[60] the Court accepted, after some hesitation,[61] that the Parliament could itself bring annulment

---

[56] See Art 149(2) EEC. The procedure is now set out in Art 252 (ex 189c) EC but, since the entry into force of the Treaty of Amsterdam, its importance has diminished.

[57] See further Gormley, op cit, pp 374–89.

[58] Case 294/83 *Les Verts v European Parliament* [1986] ECR 1339.

[59] Case 34/86 *Council v Parliament* [1986] ECR 2155.

[60] Case C–70/88 *Parliament v Council* [1990] ECR I–2041.

[61] See Case 302/87 *Parliament v Council* ('Comitology') [1988] ECR 5615.

proceedings where necessary to ensure respect for its prerogatives. The 'Chernobyl' case involved a claim by the Parliament that its right to take part in the legislative process leading to the adoption of a regulation had been unlawfully curtailed through the use by the Council of the wrong legal basis. Had the Court rejected the Parliament's claim, the institution with the most immediate interest in the issue would have been deprived of any direct means of enforcing compliance with the legislative process envisaged by the Treaty, a result which would have been inconsistent with the enhanced status in the process which the Parliament had been given by the Member States.[62]

The controversy to which these decisions gave rise is discussed in chapter 2 and it is not proposed to rehearse the arguments again here. For present purposes it need merely be noted that the Court was not deterred from addressing the increasingly anomalous position of the European Parliament by the thought that the Member States could be trusted to deal with the matter themselves now that they had shown a willingness to amend the Treaty in appropriate cases. Indeed, the very amendments they had made in the Single European Act might be seen as justifying the bold approach taken by the Court.

The importance attached by the Court to respect for the institutional balance and the completion of the internal market produced a potent combination in the 'Titanium Dioxide' case decided in mid-1991.[63] In that case, the Commission asked the Court to quash a Council directive on the reduction of pollution caused by waste from the titanium dioxide industry. The directive was unanimously adopted by the Council on the basis of a provision introduced by the Single European Act, Article 130s EEC, which entitled the Council, acting unanimously and 'after consulting the European Parliament and the Economic and Social Committee', to take action to protect the environment.[64] The Commission saw the directive as a harmonizing measure connected with the functioning of the internal market. It had therefore proposed as its legal basis Article 100a EEC, which would then have required the co-operation procedure to be followed.[65] The Commission, supported by the European Parliament, asked the Court to quash the directive on the ground that it should have been based, not on Article 130s, but on Article 100a.

The Court observed that 'the choice of the legal basis for a measure may not depend simply on an institution's conviction as to the objective pursued but must be based on objective factors which are amenable to judicial review'.[66] Those factors included the aim and the content of the measure. The directive in question had two aims which were inextricably linked: the protection of the environment and the elimination of disparities in the conditions of competition. Thus, the directive constituted both a measure relating to the environment for the purposes of Article

---

[62] Cf the Court's rejection of the UK's argument on admissibility in Case C–295/90 *Parliament v Council* [1992] ECR I–4193, paras 8–10.

[63] Case C–300/89 *Commission v Council* [1991] ECR I–2867.   [64] See now Art 175 EC.

[65] See now Art 95 EC.   [66] Para 10.

130s and a harmonizing measure within the meaning of Article 100a. The Court noted that, under Article 130r(2), the objective of environmental protection was to be a component of the Community's other policies and that Article 100a(3) made it clear that that objective could be pursued by means of harmonizing measures adopted under Article 100a. It followed that the contested directive should have been based on that provision rather than on Article 130s and it was therefore quashed.

Article 130s EEC suffered from two disadvantages which seem in retrospect to have proved fatal to the Council's case: one was that it marginalized the European Parliament, the other that it required the Council to act unanimously. Although introduced by the Single European Act, the article was in those respects out of keeping with the overall climate which that Act created. The outcome seemed to render Article 130s almost a dead letter, since most measures laying down requirements relating to the protection of the environment at a Community level may be regarded as affecting the functioning of the internal market, even if only indirectly. After the TEU had altered the climate, however, it became clear that Article 130s still had a role to play.

The third phase: Maastricht and beyond

Conferred powers, subsidiarity, and public opinion

The TEU, which entered into force in November 1993, at one stage threatened to change nearly everything. The most striking feature of the new Treaty was probably the arrangements it made for the establishment of an economic and monetary union. Less dramatic but more significant for present purposes was the greater precision with which the powers of the Community were enumerated. This had the effect of emphasizing the limits to its competence and curtailing the Council's right to invoke the default power in Article 235 (now 308), which had in the past been applied rather loosely.[67] The new ethos was reflected in the first paragraph of Article 3b (now 5) EC, which stated: 'The Community shall act within the limits of the powers conferred upon it by this Treaty and of the objectives assigned to it therein.' Strictly speaking that paragraph merely repeated a principle on which the Community had always been based.[68] Taken together with the enlarged catalogue of specific powers which the Community was given to act, however, the first paragraph of Article 3b seemed to reflect a wish on the part of the Member States to set clearer limits to the Community's capacity to encroach on their prerogatives.

---

[67] See Dashwood, 'The limits of European Community powers' (1996) 21 ELRev 113. The use of Art 308 (ex 235) is discussed by Weiler, pp 52–6.

[68] Thus, Art 4(1) (now 7) EC provides: 'Each institution shall act within the limits of the powers conferred on it by this Treaty.'

The second paragraph of Article 3b (now 5) went further, laying down a principle of subsidiarity intended to make the Community legislature consider more closely whether it needed to exercise the powers it possessed. It provided:

In areas which do not fall within its exclusive competence, the Community shall take action, in accordance with the principle of subsidiarity, only if and in so far as the objectives of the proposed action cannot be sufficiently achieved by the Member States and can therefore, by reason of the scale or effects of the proposed action, be better achieved by the Community.

The third paragraph of Article 3b added that '[a]ny action by the Community shall not go beyond what is necessary to achieve the objectives of this Treaty'. This, of course, was the well-known principle of proportionality. In this context it had the effect of limiting the intrusiveness of what the Community was entitled to do even where it had been decided that, although the Community shared competence to act with the Member States, action by the Community would be more effective. As Advocate General Léger explained in *United Kingdom v Council*,[69] the principles of subsidiarity and proportionality operate 'at two different levels of Community action: "The first determines whether Community action is to be set in motion, whereas the second defines its scope. Hence the quesion of competence is dissociated from that of its exercise".'

Doubts were expressed about the justiciability of the principle of subsidiarity[70] and the Court showed a certain lack of enthusiasm for examining whether it had in substance been respected.[71] The Court is clearly competent to decide whether the principle is applicable, that is to say, whether or not an area falls within the exclusive competence of the Community. The Court has also shown that it is prepared to examine whether the preamble to a Community act contains an adequate explanation of why the adopting institution considered action by the Community to be necessary.[72] As for the substance of the principle, it is submitted that the Court is likely to allow the Community legislature a wide discretion in areas which involve policy choices. Where the exercise of that discretion is challenged, the Court may well confine itself to examining whether the contested act 'has been vitiated by manifest error or misuse of powers, or whether the institution concerned has manifestly exceeded the limits of its discretion'.[73] However, as

---

[69] Case C–84/94 [1996] ECR I–5755, 5783, referring to Lenaerts and van Ypersele, 'Le principe de subsidiarité et son contexte: étude de l'article 3B du traité CE' (1994) CDE 3.

[70] See generally Toth, 'Is subsidiarity justiciable?' (1994) 19 ELRev 268.

[71] See eg Case C–233/94 *Germany v Parliament and Council* [1997] ECR I–2405, paras 22–8; *United Kingdom v Council*, *supra*, paras 46–7 and 54–5. Cf Case C–415/93 *URBSFA and Others v Bosman and Others* [1995] ECR I–4921, para 81. The philosophy underlying the principle may have influenced the Court indirectly: see eg AG Jacobs in Joined Cases C–430/93 and C–431/93 *van Schijndel and van Veen v SPF* [1995] ECR I–4705, 4715 (see ch 5) and the case law supporting the Commission's attempts to encourage national courts to apply the Treaty competition rules (see ch 12).

[72] See *United Kingdom v Council*, *supra*, paras 80–1; *Germany v Parliament and Council*, *supra*, paras 26–8. In the latter case, the Court held that an express reference to the principle of subsidiarity in the preamble to an act was not required. Cf the views of AG Léger at p I–2428.

[73] See para 58 of the judgment in *United Kingdom v Council*, *supra*, in connection with the principle of proportionality.

important as the extent to which the Court is prepared to intervene is the effect produced by the principle of subsidiarity on the approach of the Community legislature. The European Council meeting in Edinburgh in December 1992 agreed on detailed guidelines for the application of the principle[74] which later formed the basis of a protocol annexed to the EC Treaty[75] at Amsterdam. That protocol underlines the political importance attached by the Member States to compliance with the principle of subsidiarity.

Significant though the technical changes wrought by the TEU were, the effect of the Treaty on public opinion was perhaps of greater importance. The Treaty underwent an exceptionally difficult process of ratification, being rejected by the people of Denmark in a referendum in June 1992 less than six months after it was signed[76] and securing only a narrow majority in a referendum held in France the following September. In Germany[77] and the United Kingdom,[78] challenges to the legality of ratification, albeit ultimately unsuccessful, were brought in the courts. As a result, the Treaty did not enter into force until nearly twenty-one months after it was signed. The public debate unleashed by the Treaty in the Member States revealed widespread misgivings about the nature of the proposed Union and an unwillingness to entrust the continued governance of Europe to the élites by which it had previously been dominated. This mood of public scepticism created a climate among some specialists in European law in which the legitimacy, not only of some new developments but also of certain well-established doctrines, began to be questioned. The body of specialists now comprised, as well as those who had been attracted to the study of Community law for its own sake, those whose main interests lay in some field of substantive law which they now found increasingly affected by Community legislation. Specialists in the latter group were perhaps particularly unlikely to accept at face value doctrines which had started to be taken for granted by some members of the former group.[79]

The Court's reaction

As for the Court, the TEU betrayed a certain ambivalence on the part of the Member States about the role it was henceforward to play. Some of the provisions of the new Treaty might have been interpreted as a rebuke to the Court. The most prominent was perhaps Article L (now 46), which excluded from the Court's juris-

[74] See Bull EC 12–1992, I.15–22.

[75] Protocol on the Application of the Principles of Subsidiarity and Proportionality. See also the Interinstitutional Agreement between the European Parliament, the Council and the Commission on procedures for implementing the principle of subsidiarity, OJ 1993 C329/132.

[76] The result was reversed in a second referendum held in May 1993. See Curtin and van Ooik, 'Denmark and the Edinburgh Summit: Maastricht without tears' in O'Keeffe and Twomey (eds), *Legal Issues of the Maastricht Treaty* (1994), ch 23.

[77] See *Brunner v European Union Treaty* [1994] 1 CMLR 57, discussed in ch 3.

[78] See *R v Secretary of State for Foreign and Commonwealth Affairs, ex parte Lord Rees-Mogg* [1993] 3 CMLR 101.

[79] See Weiler, pp 216–17. Dehousse, op cit, p 173, observes: 'From the standpoint of a national lawyer, European law is often a source of disruption. It injects into the national legal system rules which are alien to its traditions and which may affect its deeper structure, thereby threatening its coherence.'

diction all the new provisions on foreign and security policy and practically all those on justice and home affairs. Protocols were annexed to the EC Treaty with the apparent objective of limiting the potential effect of two controversial decisions of the Court, one on pensions,[80] the other on abortion.[81] At the same time, however, the Treaty endorsed the Court's case law on fundamental rights[82] and the status of the European Parliament in annulment proceedings[83] and granted the Court important new powers. These included the power to impose sanctions on Member States which failed to comply with rulings against them under Article 169 (now 226),[84] the power to review the legality of acts adopted by the European Central Bank,[85] and the power to hear actions brought by the Council of the European Central Bank against national central banks alleged not to have complied with the Treaty.[86]

Notwithstanding the equivocal nature of the message transmitted to the Court by the TEU, it was undoubtedly influenced by the profound change in the climate of opinion which the Treaty had caused. The limits on its jurisdiction imposed by Article L were accepted without question in *Grau Gomis*.[87] The Court showed no inclination to dissent from the solution agreed by the Member States in the *Barber* protocol to the problem of the extent to which men could claim equality with women in pensions.[88] Indeed, in the field of sex discrimination the Court at times seemed bereft of any sense of direction.[89] Against that background it is perhaps not surprising that in 1994 the Court declined to depart from its earlier case law denying that directives could produce horizontal direct effect.[90] It may also be noted that it was during this period that the gradual demise of the *Emmott* rule began.[91] It is true that the rationale for that rule was widely regarded as flawed and its days may have been numbered in any event. In so far as its decline reflected a renaissance in the principle of national procedural autonomy, however, the changed atmosphere after Maastricht may not have been devoid of significance.

---

[80] *Barber, supra.* See ch 13.

[81] *Grogan, supra.* See chs 6 and 9. See also the Protocol on the acquisition of property in Denmark, discussed in ch 9.

[82] See Art F(2) TEU. [83] See the post-Maastricht text of Art 173 EC.

[84] See Art 171(2) (now 228(2)) EC. [85] See the post-Maastricht text of Art 173 EC.

[86] See Art 180(d) (now 237(d)) EC.

[87] Case C–167/94 [1995] ECR I–1023. That case undermines the view that a remark in Opinion 1/91 'Agreement creating the European Economic Area' [1991] ECR I–6079, para 72, implied that the Court would treat certain amendments to the Treaties as invalid: see Arnull, 'The Community judicature and the 1996 IGC' (1995) 20 ELRev 599, 610–11.

[88] See ch 13. The Court was unwilling, however, to interpret the protocol broadly: see eg Case C–57/93 *Vroege* [1994] ECR I–4541.

[89] Compare Case C–45/93 *Kalanke v Bremen* [1995] ECR I–3051 with Case C–409/95 *Marschall v Land Nordrhein-Westfalen* [1997] ECR I–6363 and Case C–13/94 *P v S and Cornwall County Council* [1996] ECR I–2143 with Case C–249/96 *Grant v South-West Trains Ltd* [1998] ECR I–621. These cases are discussed in ch 13.

[90] See Case C–91/92 *Faccini Dori v Recreb* [1994] ECR I–3325, discussed in ch 4.

[91] See Case C–208/90 [1991] ECR I–4269. The process began in Case C–338/91 *Steenhorst-Neerings* [1993] ECR I–5475 and culminated in Case C–188/95 *Fantask and Others v Industriministeriet* [1997] ECR I–6783. See ch 5.

In addition, two opinions given by the Court on the external competence of the Community seemed to reflect the new emphasis on the need to define more precisely the scope of the Community's powers and to protect the prerogatives of the Member States.[92] In Opinion 1/94,[93] the Court was asked whether the Community had exclusive competence to conclude certain agreements annexed to the Agreement establishing the World Trade Organization (WTO) signed in 1994. Two of those agreements were of special importance: the General Agreement on Trade in Services (GATS) and the Agreement on Trade-Related Aspects of Intellectual Property Rights (TRIPS). The Commission argued that the Community had exclusive jurisdiction to conclude those agreements by virtue of Article 113 (now 133) EC, which gives the Community such jurisdiction in the context of the common commercial policy, regulating trade with third countries. The Court accepted that trade in services could not in principle be excluded from the scope of Article 113 and that there was a connection between intellectual property rights and trade in goods. However, neither factor was enough in itself to bring GATS and TRIPS within the exclusive competence of the Community, since the ambit of those agreements was too broad to be regarded as covered by Article 113. The Court also rejected the Commission's alternative argument that the Community had an implied exclusive competence to conclude GATS and TRIPS. It therefore ruled that the Community and the Member States were jointly competent to conclude those agreements.

The restrictive nature of the Court's approach to the scope of Article 113 was all the more striking given that, in late 1979, it had observed that Article 113 could not be interpreted so as to 'restrict the common commercial policy to the use of instruments intended to have an effect only on the traditional aspects of external trade to the exclusion of more highly developed mechanisms . . .', adding that a commercial policy understood in that limited sense 'would be destined to become nugatory in the course of time'.[94] Opinion 1/94 attracted criticism,[95] but it reflected increased sensitivity on the part of the Court to the desire of Member States to ensure that their national interests were adequately protected in international trade negotiations. The cautious approach of the Court was vindicated at the IGC which resulted in the Treaty of Amsterdam, where a proposal to extend the scope of the common commercial policy to trade in services and trade related aspects of intellectual property failed to secure the unanimous support of the Member States.[96]

[92] On the position of the Member States, see further Dashwood, 'States in the European Union' (1998) 23 ELRev 201.

[93] [1994] ECR I–5267. See generally Tridimas and Eeckhout, 'The external competence of the Community and the case law of the Court of Justice: principle versus pragmatism' (1994) 14 YEL 143.

[94] Opinion 1/78, 'International Agreement on Natural Rubber' [1979] ECR 2871, para 44.

[95] See eg Bourgeois, 'The EC in the WTO and Advisory Opinion 1/94: an Echternach procession' (1995) 32 CMLRev 763.

[96] Instead it was agreed that the Council should be empowered, acting unanimously, to extend the application of Art 133 to international negotiations and agreements on services and intellectual property in so far as they were not already covered by it: see para 5.

A similarly restrained view of the Community's competence was evident in Opinion 2/94,[97] where the Court was asked whether accession by the Community to the European Convention on Human Rights would be compatible with the EC Treaty. Referring to Article 3b (now 5), the Court emphasized that the Community only had the powers which had been conferred on it. That principle of conferred powers, it said, had to be respected by the Community in both the internal and the external spheres.[98] No Treaty provision gave the Community institutions any general powers to lay down rules on human rights or to conclude international conventions on the matter. The Commission had suggested that accession might be based on Article 235 (now 308), but that view was rejected by the Court, which said that that article could not be used as the basis for a step which would have fundamental constitutional implications for the Community and for the Member States. The Court concluded that the Community lacked competence to accede to the Convention. Opinion 2/94 may be said to illustrate the Court's reluctance, in the post-Maastricht era, to take upon itself responsibility for bringing about major constitutional change. Once again, the Court's Opinion attracted criticism. Once again, a proposal to give the Community competence to accede to the European Convention was put to the IGC which led to the Treaty of Amsterdam. Once again, the proposal failed to secure the unanimous support of the Member States. Once again, the outcome may be seen as a vindication of the restraint shown by the Court.

It was during this phase that coping with its workload, a matter of concern to the Court for many years, became one of its principal preoccupations. Important sources of extra work included the large body of legislation adopted to give effect to the single market programme and the national courts in the newer Member States, which were becoming increasingly familiar with the preliminary rulings procedure.[99] The growing pressure under which the Court found itself is reflected in the case law requiring national courts to set out clearly the legal and factual context of a case when making a reference for a preliminary ruling[100] and the Court's refusal, after the false dawn of *Codorniu*,[101] to relax significantly the standing requirements which have to be satisfied by private applicants in annulment proceedings.

Even in cases touching the functioning of the internal market, the Court at times seemed less resolute than previously. In *Commission v Council*,[102] another directive

---

[97] [1996] ECR I–1759. See further ch 6.

[98] Cf Case C–106/96 *United Kingdom v Commission* [1998] ECR I–2729, where the Court found that the Commission had failed to respect the principle of conferred powers in the internal sphere.

[99] Of particular concern to the CFI was the volume of litigation expected to be generated by Reg 40/94 on the Community trade mark, OJ 1994 L11/1. See ch 1.

[100] See eg Joined Cases C–320 to C–322/90 *Telemarsicabruzzo v Circostel* [1993] ECR I–393. See ch 2.

[101] See Case C–309/89 *Codorniu v Council* [1994] ECR I–1853, discussed in ch 2.

[102] Case C–155/91 [1993] ECR I–939. The notorious 'Belgian Waste' case (Case C–2/90 *Commission v Belgium* [1992] ECR I–4431, discussed in ch 7) was decided less than six months after the TEU was signed.

on waste was challenged. As in 'Titanium Dioxide', the Council had based the directive in question on Article 130s.[103] The Commission, with the support of the European Parliament, maintained that it should instead have been based on Article 100a.[104] The Court acknowledged that certain provisions of the directive had an effect on the operation of the internal market. This might have seemed enough, in the light of 'Titanium Dioxide', to establish that the directive should indeed have been based on Article 100a. None the less, the Court ruled that the mere fact that the establishment or functioning of the internal market was affected was not sufficient for Article 100a to apply. The Court said that there was no justification for having recourse to that article 'where the measure to be adopted has only the incidental effect of harmonizing market conditions within the Community'.[105] In the Court's view, that was so in this case. The main object of the harmonization provided for by the directive was to ensure the effective management of waste in the Community in the interests of environmental protection. Unlike the directive at issue in the 'Titanium Dioxide' case, the one at issue here had only an incidental effect on competition and trade. It had therefore been validly adopted under Article 130s. The Court's judgment prompted Dashwood to observe, in response to Sir Patrick Neill's claim that the Court had a federalizing mission, that 'a missionary Court would certainly have grasped the opportunity . . . of establishing that any measure affecting the internal market, however remotely, falls to be adopted under Article 100a'.[106]

There is a temptation to mention *Keck and Mithouard*[107] in this context. There the Court held, overruling unspecified earlier case law, that Article 30 (now 28) EC did not apply to national provisions regulating the circumstances in which a product could be sold as long as they affected domestic and imported products in the same way. That conclusion, which weakened one of the very cornerstones of the internal market, was reached even though the Court seemed to accept that at least some national rules on 'selling arrangements' could have the effect of reducing sales of products imported from other Member States. However, *Keck and Mithouard* seems to have been a response, not so much to the change in climate brought about by the TEU, as to the particular problem, posed in acute form by the Sunday trading cases, of defining the scope of Article 30 (now 28). Indeed, the TEU was not intended to mark a fresh start but to 'maintain in full the "acquis communautaire" and build on it'.[108] While the Treaty therefore led to some reappraisal of the Court's priorities, it was not intended to produce a complete change of direction and nor did it have that effect.

---

[103] See now Art 175.   [104] See now Art 95.
[105] Para 19. On distinguishing the predominant components of a Community act (its so-called 'centre of gravity') from those which are merely incidental, see further Case C–42/97 *Parliament v Council*, judgment of 23 February 1999; Joined Cases C–164/97 and C–165/97 *Parliament v Council*, judgment of 25 February 1999.
[106] See 'The limits of European Community powers' (1996) 21 ELRev 113, 128.
[107] Joined Cases C–267/91 and C–268/91 [1993] ECR I–6097.
[108] Art B (now 2) TEU.

That the *Keck and Mithouard* ruling was confined essentially to Article 30 (now 28) and did not reflect any general reduction in the Court's commitment to the importance of freedom of movement was confirmed in *Bosman*[109] and *Alpine Investments*,[110] where the Court rejected attempts to extend the reasoning in *Keck and Mithouard* to workers and services respectively.[111] Even in the context of the free movement of goods, the Court remained capable of applying Article 30 in an extensive manner. Thus, in *Decker v Caisse de Maladie des Employés Privés*,[112] the Court held that it prevented a national social security institution from refusing to contribute to the cost of spectacles purchased from an optician established in another Member State on the ground that prior authorization was needed for the purchase of medical products abroad. Overcoming its initial reluctance, the Court also began to explore the potential of the provisions on citizenship of the Union introduced at Maastricht.[113] In the field of competition law, the Court gave a decision[114] on the scope of the Merger Regulation based on its 'purpose and general structure'[115] which demonstrated clearly the continued importance attached by the Court to avoiding distortions of competition in the internal market. The Court's commitment to preserving the uniform application of the law was evident in its refusal to depart from the case law establishing the right of national courts to request preliminary rulings in cases where Community law was applicable only because its scope had been enlarged by national law.[116] It may also be noted that, notwithstanding the Court's greater respect for the rights of the Member States, in the 'Airport Transit Visas' case it firmly asserted its jurisdiction to ensure that acts which the Council claimed fell within the scope of the third pillar did not encroach on the powers conferred on the Community by the EC Treaty.[117]

As in the pre-Maastricht era, the momentum of the case law also led it to develop principles which might have seemed out of keeping with the prevailing mood. This is clearly illustrated by the Court's decisions on the scope of the principle of State liability, which was laid down in the *Francovich* case shortly before the TEU was signed. The Court's insistence on drawing a parallel between the liability of

[109] *Supra*, para 103. See ch 8.

[110] Case C–384/93 [1995] ECR I–1141, paras 33–9. See ch 9.

[111] Other cases notable for their contribution to the functioning of the internal market decided during this period are Case C–118/96 *Safir v Skattemyndigheten i Dalarnas Län* [1998] ECR I–1897 (freedom to provide services); Case C–212/97 *Centros Ltd*, judgment of 9 March 1999 (right of establishment).

[112] Case C–120/95 [1998] ECR I–1831. A parallel case on the freedom to provide services, Case C–158/96 *Kohll v Union des Caisses de Maladie* [1998] ECR I–1931, is discussed in ch 9.

[113] See Case C–85/96 *Martínez Sala v Freistaat Bayern* [1998] ECR I–2691; Case C–274/96 *Bickel and Franz*, judgment of 24 November 1998. See ch 11.

[114] Joined Cases C–68/94 and C–30/95 *France and Others v Commission* [1998] ECR I–1375. See chs 12 and 14.

[115] Para 168.

[116] See Case C–28/95 *Leur-Bloem v Inspecteur der Belastingdienst/Ondernemingen Amsterdam 2* [1997] ECR I–4161; Case C–130/95 *Giloy v Hauptzollamt Frankfurt am Main-Ost* [1997] ECR I–4291, discussed in ch 2.

[117] See Case C–170/96 *Commission v Council* [1998] ECR I–2763. See ch 2.

Member States in damages and that of the Community itself under the second paragraph of Article 215 (now 288) may have limited the scope of the principle to a greater extent than might once have been anticipated. None the less, it remains the case that the principle is capable of fixing Member States with liability in circumstances where no such liability would arise under national law. Moreover, the Court did not shrink from indicating in appropriate cases whether it considered the conditions to which liability under Community law was subject had been met.[118]

The Treaty of Amsterdam

The Treaty of Amsterdam may well encourage the Court to exercise its powers with renewed confidence.[119] It is true that the Treaty contains a provision[120] designed to reverse a decision of the Court,[121] but the provision in question had been overtaken by developments in the case law by the time it entered into force.[122] Moreover, while the result of the decision it was aimed at was undoubtedly controversial, the reasoning was somewhat conservative. Of greater general significance are Articles 68 (ex 73p) EC and 35 (ex K.7) TEU, which give the Court jurisdiction over a range of matters which previously either fell outside the scope of the Treaties entirely or were covered by the Maastricht version of the third pillar, over which the Court had virtually no control. Moreover, there are several areas of potential political controversy in which the Court seems to be intended to intervene in cases of dispute. One such area is that of closer co-operation, under which a majority of the Member States may use the institutions, procedures and mechanisms laid down in the TEU and the EC Treaty to take action furthering the objectives of the Union but in which a minority of the Member States do not wish to participate.[123] Recourse to the mechanism of closer co-operation is subject to a number of procedural and substantive conditions, some of them highly political in character, which it will ultimately be for the Court of Justice to enforce.[124] A second area in which the Court may find itself called upon to intervene is that of the suspension of the rights of Member States which are found to be in serious and persistent breach of the founding principles of the Union set out in Article 6(1)

---

[118] See eg Joined Cases C–46/93 and C–48/93 *Brasserie du Pêcheur and Factortame* [1996] ECR I–1029; Case C–5/94 *The Queen v MAFF, ex parte Hedley Lomas* [1996] ECR I–2553. See ch 5.

[119] See Arnull, 'Taming the beast? The Treaty of Amsterdam and the Court of Justice' in Twomey and O'Keeffe (eds), *Legal Issues of the Amsterdam Treaty* (1999); Kapteyn, 'The Court of Justice after Amsterdam: taking stock' in Heukels, Blokker and Brus (eds), *The European Union after Amsterdam* (1998), ch 7; Albors-Llorens, 'Changes in the jurisdiction of the European Court of Justice after the Treaty of Amsterdam' (1998) 35 CMLRev 1273.

[120] Art 141(4) (ex 119(4)) EC.

[121] Case C–450/93 *Kalanke v Bremen* [1995] ECR I–3051. The *Kalanke* decision is discussed in ch 13. Cf Hartley, *Constitutional Problems of the European Union* (1999), pp 53–4.

[122] See Case C–409/95 *Marschall v Land Nordrhein-Westfalen* [1997] ECR I–6363.

[123] See Art 11 (ex 5a) EC and Arts 40 (ex K.12) and 43–5 (ex K.15-K.17) TEU.

[124] See Arts 40(4) and 46(c) TEU; Edwards and Philippart, 'Flexibility and the Treaty of Amsterdam: Europe's new Byzantium', CELS Occasional Paper No 3 (1997), pp 14–15.

TEU.[125] A third is that of the application of the principle of subsidiarity. The guidelines set out in the protocol on the matter agreed at Amsterdam already had considerable political force due to their origins in the conclusions of the Edinburgh European Council of December 1992. The protocol therefore seems designed, at least in part, to encourage the Court to apply the principle. As striking as these new provisions is the absence in the Treaty of Amsterdam of any attempt to address concerns about the Court's general approach such as those expressed by the British Conservative Government in the White Paper it issued on the eve of the 1996 IGC.[126]

The relationship between the Court of Justice and the national courts of the Member States

Fundamental to the ability of the Court to influence the development of Community law throughout the three periods identified above has been its relationship with the national courts of the Member States.[127] It was they who, through the preliminary rulings procedure, brought before it the cases which enabled it to see the problems to which the application of Community law in the Member States gave rise. It was they who asked the questions which enabled the Court to develop many of the doctrines which became fundamental to the way in which the new legal order created by the EEC Treaty functions. Crucially, it was the national courts who applied the answers given by the Court to the questions which had been referred to it.

Had the national courts been less willing to play their part in giving effect in concrete cases to the principles laid down in Luxembourg, the development of the Community would have followed an entirely different path. There was admittedly the occasional hiccup. Some national courts had misgivings about the protection of fundamental rights in the new legal order, some about the capacity of directives to produce vertical direct effect. The Court responded to the first concern, not by judging Community acts against national standards, which would have subverted the legal order, but by recognizing a Community principle of respect for fundamental rights. That principle, born in the first phase, reached adolescence in the second phase and early adulthood in the third phase when it was enshrined in Article 6(2) (ex F(2)) TEU. It can be expected to develop further post-Amsterdam now that the Court has expressly been given jurisdiction to apply Article 6(2) to the activities of the institutions by Article 46 (ex L) TEU.[128] The second concern

---

[125] See Arts 7 TEU and 309 EC, discussed in ch 6.

[126] *A Partnership of Nations* (Cm 3181), para 37. See also the 'Memorandum by the United Kingdom on the European Court of Justice' tabled at the IGC by the British Government in July 1996. For a brief comment on that memorandum, see the editorial at (1996) 21 ELRev 349.

[127] See generally Slaughter, Stone and Weiler, op cit.

[128] It seems unlikely that the Court will permit the Member States to apply a lower standard when they act within the scope of the Treaties: cf Case 5/88 *Wachauf v Bundesamt für Ernährung und*

was met by denying directives the capacity to produce horizontal direct effect. The response of the Court in both instances in due course persuaded recalcitrant national courts to accept its case law. The Court has also begun to address a further concern, articulated by the Bundesverfassungsgericht in its Maastricht decision of 12 October 1993,[129] that the Community institutions do not respect sufficiently strictly the principle of conferred powers. The Court's concern to ensure compliance with that principle was manifest in Opinion 2/94 on the Community's competence to accede to the European Convention on Human Rights. That Opinion helped to convince the Danish Supreme Court that ratification by Denmark of the TEU was compatible with the Danish Constitution.[130] Although the attitude of the national courts has in these situations posed a potential threat to the cohesion of the Community legal order, the outcome has been largely beneficial. It should be apparent to national courts that the Court of Justice is prepared to take account of their concerns in so far as this is compatible with the functioning of the Community. The Court's response in the field of fundamental rights in particular strengthened the Community system by drawing on the constitutional traditions of the Member States and raising the political profile of the need to ensure adequate protection for such rights.

One of the reasons why we are struck by these instances of resistance to some of the incidents of Community membership among the national courts is their relative rarity. On the whole, the national courts have complied conscientiously with their duty to decide cases in accordance with the principles laid down by the Court of Justice. This should not cause surprise. Why should the national courts have resisted the case law of a court established by the Member States to secure observance of the rule of law in the pursuit of policy objectives on which they were all agreed? Indeed, if those objectives were taken for granted—and it was not for the national courts or the Court of Justice to question them—then the logic underlying the case law emanating from Luxembourg was compelling.[131]

The coherence of the Court's case law helps to explain the broadly favourable reaction to the Court's case law among academic lawyers in the early years of the Community's development.[132] Many of those who were drawn to the study of Community law in that period were essentially sympathetic to the underlying objectives of the Treaty. For scholars who came from a background in public inter-

---

Forstwirtschaft [1989] ECR 2609; Case C–260/89 *ERT* [1991] ECR I–2925; Case C–368/95 *Familiapress v Bauer Verlag* [1997] ECR I–3689.

[129] [1994] 1 CMLR 57. See ch 3.

[130] Judgment of 6 April 1998, *Carlsen and Others v Prime Minister*. The Danish Supreme Court made it clear, however, that a Community act would in theory be inapplicable in Denmark if it went beyond the extent to which sovereignty was surrendered to the Community by the Danish Act of Accession. See Høegh, 'The Danish Maastricht judgment' (1999) 24 ELRev 80; Hartley, *Constitutional Problems of the European Union* (1999), pp 157–9.

[131] See further Weiler, pp 32–4 and 192–7; Alter, 'Explaining national court acceptance of European Court jurisprudence: a critical evaluation of theories of legal integration' in Slaughter, Stone and Weiler, op cit, ch 8; Dehousse, op cit, pp 135–41; Hunnings, *The European Courts* (1996), pp 145–51.

[132] See Weiler, pp 203–6.

national law, Community law showed what treaties could achieve. As Weiler explains:[133] 'In some ways, Community law and the European Court were everything an international lawyer could dream about: the Court was creating a new order of international law in which norms were norms, sanctions were sanctions, courts were central and frequently used, and lawyers were important. Community law as transformed by the European Court was an antidote to the international legal malaise.' Comparatists saw Community law as a fascinating experiment in the comparative method and the success of the Court as a vindication of the practical benefits of comparative law. The importance traditionally accorded to 'la doctrine' in civil law countries means that the reaction of the academic community is likely to have had an effect on the response of national judges and practitioners.

To a large extent, the Court of Justice continues to enjoy the confidence of the Member States, the national courts, and many academic lawyers. That confidence is reflected in the important new responsibilities given to the Court by the Treaty of Amsterdam and the substantial portion of the Court's current workload represented by requests for preliminary rulings. There is no doubt, however, that the Court now attracts more criticism than before the signature of the TEU. One reason for this may be that some traditional supporters of the Community were alienated by its transformation into the Union with all that that implied about its ambitions and the substantive scope of the Treaties. Another is that those who were unsympathetic to the very idea of European integration started to identify the Court as the origin of much of which they disapproved. Paradoxically, the Court's responsiveness to the change of public mood consequent on the ratification of the TEU attracted criticism from friends concerned that it was retreating with undue haste. A consequence of this upsurge in criticism has been increased questioning of the Court's very legitimacy.[134] The Court is not of course unique in this respect. Public bodies in general and the legal system in particular are now subject to an unprecedented degree of critical scrutiny. Institutions which can withstand it emerge with their reputations and authority enhanced. What then is the basis of the Court's claim to the confidence of those it serves?

The legitimacy of the Court

Weiler[135] underlines the importance of the distinction between formal legitimacy and the wider notion of social legitimacy. The former implies that all relevant legal

---

[133] Weiler, pp 205–6.

[134] An early critic of the Court's legitimacy was Rasmussen, *On Law and Policy in the European Court of Justice* (1986). See generally Weiler, 'The European Courts of Justice: beyond "beyond doctrine" or the legitimacy crisis of European Constitutionalism' in Slaughter, Stone and Weiler, op cit, p 365; Chalmers, *European Union Law (Volume I): Law and EU Government* (1998), pp 326–34; Ward, *A Critical Introduction to European law* (1996), pp 52–77. A reviewer of a recently published book on European public law observed critically that the book 'hardly questions the right of the ECJ to lay down the law on the sensitive issue of state liability (or, for that matter, any other issue)': see Harlow (1998) 18 LS 558, 562.

[135] Weiler, pp 77–86, in particular pp 80–1.

requirements were met when the institution or polity in question was established, the latter broad societal acceptance of the system. Formal legitimacy will generally be necessary but not sufficient for an institution such as the Court to enjoy assent and acceptance among those who are subject to it.[136] The formal legitimacy of the Court of Justice is clearly not open to challenge. It was constituted in its present form by the Convention on Certain Institutions Common to the European Communities signed by the Member States on 25 March 1957 alongside the EEC and EAEC Treaties. That Convention was ratified, like those Treaties, by the Member States in accordance with their own constitutional requirements. The Court's powers were subsequently amended by further treaties which entered into force only after ratification by the Member States, again in accordance with their respective constitutional requirements. The social legitimacy of the Court, a more nebulous concept, is harder to assess. To an extent, it depends on the social legitimacy of the European Union in general and the degree to which it meets public expectations of accountability, openness and probity. There are limits to the influence which the Court can exert on matters such as these. However, the Court's own legitimacy also depends on the way it discharges the particular responsibilities conferred on it.

It is sometimes suggested that the social legitimacy of the Court and Community law generally is strengthened by the conferral on individuals of rights which take precedence over inconsistent provisions emerging from the domestic political process.[137] As the Court recognized in *Van Gend en Loos*, that characteristic of the Community system certainly gives individuals a role in policing the application of Community law and a voice in its development. However, it is as likely to undermine as to reinforce the social legitimacy of the Court for the simple reason that many of those who rely on Community law are seeking to challenge the laws of another Member State which confer some advantage on its own nationals. They are unlikely to have much sympathy with either the applicant or the system which enables him to bring his claim. The public of his own State may be more supportive, but is likely to see the situation as one in which the applicant is simply claiming his legitimate entitlement and may not be prepared to give much credit to the Court, whose rulings have made the claim possible. This was clearly illustrated in the *Factortame* cases, discussed in chapter 5, where Spanish fishing interests successfully invoked Community law against United Kingdom legislation designed to stop them fishing against the quota allocated to the United Kingdom under the Community's common fisheries policy. The main effect of the litigation in the United Kingdom, where it received considerable publicity, was to underline the extent to which national sovereignty had been curtailed by accession to the Communities.[138] Even where the applicant is a national of the State in which pro-

---

[136] See Birks, 'The academic and the practitioner' (1998) 18 LS 397, 401.

[137] See the discussion in Poiares Maduro, *We the Court: the European Court of Justice and the European Economic Constitution* (1998), pp 27–30.

[138] Cf the remarks of Lord Bridge in *R v Secretary of State for Transport, ex parte Factortame* [1990] 3 CMLR 375, 379–80.

ceedings are brought, there may be little public sympathy for the claim and oppro-
brium may consequently attach to the institutions which are perceived as enabling
it to be brought.[139] The effect on the Court's social legitimacy of the role played
by individuals in enforcing Community law therefore seems at most to be neutral.

Habermas observes that the law's claim to legitimacy 'requires decisions that are
not only consistent with the treatment of similar cases in the past and in accord with
the existing legal system. They are also supposed to be rationally grounded in the
matter at issue so that all participants can accept them as rational decisions.'[140] It is
submitted that, judged against that yardstick, the Court has a very strong claim to
social legitimacy. That is not to say that none of its decisions is open to criticism:
it would be foolhardy to defend the entire corpus of any court's case law and the
Court of Justice is no exception. But it cannot seriously be denied that the Court
strives to be consistent and that most objective observers are able to identify and
accept the rational basis for the vast majority of its decisions.[141]

In this respect lawyers have a crucial role to play. Just as the lay person must turn
to scientists for advice on the causes and risks of global warming or the threat to
human health caused by 'mad cow disease',[142] so it is lawyers that the general public must rely on for an assessment of the rational acceptability of the Court's judgments and overall approach. A court which is taken seriously by lawyers deserves
to be taken seriously by the public in the absence of clear evidence that something
is amiss. Thus, it is only partly true that 'no matter how much a court follows the
rules of due process and is seen to reach decisions in an impartial manner, it will
not enjoy support if it consistently reaches decisions which are unacceptable to
society at large'.[143] Whether decisions are acceptable to society at large will
depend, at least to some extent, on whether they are acceptable to lawyers, whose
views are liable to be affected by whether the rules of due process have been followed.[144] Evidence of widespread endorsement among lawyers and informed
commentators of the role played by the Court may be found in the evidence
submitted to the House of Lords Select Committee on the European Communities
in the course of its enquiry into the IGC which opened in 1996 and in the

---

[139] See eg the public response to the claims based on Community law brought against the UK
Government by servicewomen dismissed when they became pregnant. The claims are discussed by
Arnull, 'EC law and the dismissal of pregnant servicewomen' (1995) 24 ILJ 215. It may be noted that
they were dealt with before the scope of the *Emmott* rule had been clarified. See further ch 5.

[140] *Between Facts and Norms* (1996), p 198.

[141] To the criteria identified by Habermas might be added a third, that judgment should be given
within a reasonable period of time. If that criterion is not always met by the Court of Justice, ultimate
responsibility lies with the Member States, who are responsible for refurbishing and extending as appropriate the judicial architecture of the Union. See ch 1.

[142] Otherwise known as bovine spongiform encephalopathy or BSE. See Case C–157/96 *R v MAFF
and Others, ex parte National Farmers' Union and Others* [1998] ECR I–2211; Case C–180/96 *United
Kingdom v Commission* [1998] ECR I–2265.

[143] Chalmers, op cit, p 329.

[144] Chalmers seems to acknowledge this: see 'Judicial preferences and the Community legal order'
(1997) 60 MLR 164, 171.

conclusion, quoted in chapter 1, at which the Select Committee arrived.[145] This is not to deny the misgivings, even hostility, which undoubtedly exist among some sections of the public about certain aspects of the Union's activities. But the existence of the Union and the functions it performs are the responsibility not of the Court but of the Member States, the 'Masters of the Treaties' as the Bundesverfassungsgericht reminded us in the Maastricht decision.[146] The legitimacy of the Court is not undermined but enhanced when it seeks to comply with its duty to ensure that the law is observed in the application of the Treaties, for a Union which was not based on the rule of law would be a much more threatening animal.

We have seen that the Court's overall approach has varied with the passage of time and, albeit perhaps to a lesser extent, according to the nature of the substantive issues it has been called upon to decide. Is it none the less possible to give a simple description of its approach? The term 'activist' will not do because there are many examples of restraint by the Court. Indeed, if we are to play the game of activism-spotting, some cases might be presented as examples of both activism and restraint.[147] However, it would clearly be misleading to describe the Court in general terms as restrained in the way it has developed the law. At considerable risk of oversimplification, it is submitted that one phrase which helps encapsulate the Court's approach is radical conservatism.[148] The Court's inventiveness has been most apparent in devising mechanisms, such as direct effect, primacy, and the principle of State liability, which go with the grain of the EC Treaty by enhancing its capacity to achieve its objectives. The Court has also displayed great ingenuity in seeking to protect basic values implicit in the Treaty and the laws of the Member States, such as the institutional balance and fundamental rights. On matters of economic and social policy, however, the Court has been more willing to defer to the choices made by the Member States, at least where they have acted in a proportionate and non-discriminatory manner. Although it has on the whole taken an expansive view of the scope of substantive rules, it shrunk from telling the United Kingdom that it would have to proscribe the Church of Scientology before it could prevent nationals of other Member States from working for it, or that its restrictions on Sunday trading were incompatible with the rules on the free movement of goods. It declined to assimilate unmarried partners to spouses, or homosexual couples to heterosexual couples,[149] or to interfere with the organization of the family or the division of responsibility between parents. It resisted claims that Irish rules on the use of the Irish language and the protection of the unborn were incompat-

---

[145] See *1996 Inter-Governmental Conference* (Session 1994–95, 21st Report), para 256.

[146] [1994] 1 CMLR 57, 91.

[147] Classic examples are Case 41/74 *van Duyn v Home Office* [1974] ECR 1337, discussed in ch 10, and Case C–301/87 *France v Commission* ('Boussac') [1990] ECR I–307, discussed in ch 12.

[148] The phrase was used by Stephen Sedley to describe Lord Denning in an obituary published in the *Guardian* on 6 March 1999.

[149] See *Grant v South-West Trains Ltd*, *supra*. The decision in *P v S and Cornwall County Council*, *supra*, affording protection under Dir 76/207 to transsexuals therefore seems all the more surprising, perhaps even an aberration.

ible with, respectively, the rules on the free movement of workers and the right to provide services.

It is true that the Court's systemic radicalism added to the broad view it has taken of many of the rules contained in the EC Treaty and in legislation made under it has produced a potent combination, capable of upsetting regulatory choices made by Member States. This is perhaps most apparent in the field of the free movement of goods,[150] though a similar phenomenon is evident in the fields of the right to provide services and competition.[151] None the less, it was always inevitable that some national policy choices would have to give way to the dictates of the common market. Moreover, to the extent that the Court's case law reflects a preference for a liberal over a regulated economy, that preference can be detected in the EC Treaty itself and, before that, in the Spaak Report. But the Treaty is not concerned exclusively with the promotion of free competition and deregulation[152] and the Court has also taken an expansive approach to the interpretation of provisions on social policy, such as Articles 138 (ex 118a) and 141 (ex 119).[153]

Of course, judges are not computers and deciding cases invariably involves the exercise of a greater or lesser degree of discretion. However, the main influence on the choices made by the Court from the range of possible outcomes in a given case is always the need to give effect to the fundamental policy preferences of the Member States (represented by the government for the time being in office) and the Community legislature. A radically conservative approach of this type seems especially well suited to the Court. It is, however, one which is virtually guaranteed to attract criticism, either from those who would prefer the Court to be socially radical or from those who would rather see a greater degree of systemic conservatism. The Court is therefore likely to remain the subject of sometimes fierce controversy.

---

[150] See eg Case C–189/95 *Franzén* [1997] ECR I–5909, where the Court held that domestic provisions allowing only traders holding certain types of licence to import alcoholic beverages were disproportionate to the public health aim pursued; Poiares Maduro, op cit; Weatherill, 'Recent case law concerning the free movement of goods: mapping the frontiers of market deregulation' (1999) 36 CMLRev 51.

[151] The effect of some internal market case law on national labour laws is analysed by Davies, 'Market integration and social policy in the Court of Justice' (1995) 24 ILJ 49. See also Barnard, 'EC "social" policy' in Craig and de Búrca (eds), *The Evolution of EU Law* (1999), ch 13, pp 494–5.

[152] Shapiro, op cit, p 341, observes: 'Like the rest of the industrialized world, Europe is now caught up in the politics of simultaneous de-regulation and re-regulation.'

[153] See ch 13; Davies, 'The European Court of Justice, national courts, and the Member States' in Davies et al (eds), *European Community Labour Law: Principles and Perspectives* (1996), ch 5.

Select bibliography

Albors-Llorens, *Private Parties in European Community Law* (1996)
—— 'Changes in the jurisdiction of the European Court of Justice after the Treaty of Amsterdam' (1998) 35 CMLRev 1273
Alston and Weiler, *The European Union and Human Rights: Final Project Report on an Agenda for the Year 2000* (European University Institute, 1998)
Andenas (ed), *Article 177 References to the European Court: Policy and Practice* (1994)
Anderson, 'The admissibility of preliminary references' (1994) 14 YEL 179
—— *References to the European Court* (1995)
Arnull, 'The use and abuse of Article 177 EEC' (1989) 52 MLR 622
—— 'Does the Court of Justice have inherent jurisdiction?' (1990) 27 CMLRev 683
—— *The General Principles of EEC Law and the Individual* (1990)
—— 'What shall we do on Sunday?' (1991) 16 ELRev 112
—— 'Owning up to fallibility: precedent and the Court of Justice' (1993) 30 CMLRev 247
—— 'Refurbishing the judicial architecture of the European Community' (1994) 43 ICLQ 296
—— 'EC law and the dismissal of pregnant servicewomen' (1995) 24 ILJ 215
—— 'Private applicants and the action for annulment under Article 173 of the EC Treaty' (1995) 32 CMLRev 7
—— 'The Community judicature and the 1996 IGC' (1995) 20 ELRev 599
—— 'Challenging Community acts—an introduction' in Micklitz and Reich (eds), *Public Interest Litigation before European Courts* (1996), p 39
—— 'The European Court and judicial objectivity: a reply to Professor Hartley' (1996) 112 LQR 411
—— 'Interpretation and precedent in English and Community law: evidence of cross-fertilisation?' in Andenas (ed), *English Public Law and the Common Law of Europe* (1998), ch 6
—— 'Taming the beast? The Treaty of Amsterdam and the Court of Justice' in Twomey and O'Keeffe (eds), *Legal Issues of the Amsterdam Treaty* (1999)
Audretsch, *Supervision in European Community Law* (2nd edn, 1986)
Barav, 'Preliminary censorship? The judgment of the European Court in *Foglia v Novello*' (1980) 5 ELRev 443
—— 'La répétition de l'indu dans la jurisprudence de la Cour de Justice des Communautés Européennes' (1981) CDE 507
—— 'Damages in the domestic courts for breach of Community law by national public authorities' in Schermers, Heukels and Mead (eds), *Non-Contractual Liability of the European Communities* (1988), p 149
—— 'Enforcement of Community rights in the national courts: the case for jurisdiction to grant an interim relief' (1989) 26 CMLRev 369
Barnard, 'A social policy for Europe: politicians 1, lawyers 0' (1992) 8 IntJCompLLIR 15
—— 'The economic objectives of Article 119' in Hervey and O'Keeffe (eds), *Sex Equality Law in the European Union* (1996), ch 20

Barnard and Sharpston, 'The changing face of Article 177 references' (1997) 34 CMLRev 1113

Beatson and Tridimas (eds), *New Directions in European Public Law* (1998)

Bebr, 'Directly applicable provisions of Community law: the development of a Community concept' (1970) 19 ICLQ 257

—— 'The existence of a genuine dispute: an indispensable precondition for the jurisdiction of the Court under Art 177 EEC Treaty?' (1980) 17 CMLRev 525

—— 'The possible implications of *Foglia v Novello* II' (1982) 19 CMLRev 421

Bengoetxea, *The Legal Reasoning of the European Court of Justice* (1993)

Bercusson, *European Labour Law* (1996)

Bernard, 'Discrimination and free movement in EC law' (1996) 45 ICLQ 82

Birks, 'The academic and the practitioner' (1998) 18 LS 397

Bishop, 'Price discrimination under Article 86: political economy in the European Court' (1981) 44 MLR 282

Bonnie, 'Commission discretion under Article 171(2) EC' (1998) 23 ELRev 537

Borgsmidt, 'The Advocate General at the European Court of Justice: a comparative study' (1988) 13 ELRev 106

Bork, *The Antitrust Paradox: A Policy at War with Itself* (1978)

Bourgeois, 'The EC in the WTO and Advisory Opinion 1/94: an Echternach procession' (1995) 32 CMLRev 763

Bradley, A., 'Administrative justice: a developing human right?' (1995) 1 European Public Law 347

Bradley, K., 'The variable evolution of the standing of the European Parliament in proceedings before the Court of Justice' (1988) 8 YEL 27

Brealey and Hoskins, *Remedies in EC Law* (2nd edn, 1998)

Bridge, 'Procedural aspects of the enforcement of European Community law through the legal systems of the Member States' (1984) 9 ELRev 28

British Institute of International and Comparative Law, *The Role and Future of the European Court of Justice* (1996)

Brown, A., 'Judicial review of Commission decisions under the Merger Regulation: the first cases' [1994] ECLR 296

Brown, L. N., 'The first five years of the Court of First Instance and appeals to the Court of Justice: assessment and statistics' (1995) 32 CMLRev 743

Brown, L. N., and Kennedy, *Brown and Jacobs' The Court of Justice of the European Communities* (4th edn, 1994)

Brownlie, *Principles of Public International Law* (5th edn, 1998)

Campbell and Voyatzi (eds), *Legal Reasoning and Judicial Interpretation of European Law* (1996)

Capotorti, Hilf, Jacobs and Jacqué, *The European Union Treaty* (1986)

Cappelletti, 'Is the European Court of Justice "running wild"?' (1987) 12 ELRev 3

—— *The Judicial Process in Comparative Perspective* (1989)

Caranta, 'Judicial protection against Member States: a new *jus commune* takes shape' (1995) 32 CMLRev 703

Cardwell, *Milk Quotas* (1996)

Catchpole and Barav, 'The public morality exception and the free movement of goods: justification of a dual standard in national legislation?' (1980/1) LIEI 1

Chalmers, 'Judicial preferences and the Community legal order' (1997) 60 MLR 164

—— *European Union Law (Volume I): Law and EU Government* (1998)

Charrier, 'L'*obiter dictum* dans la jurisprudence de la Cour de justice des Communautés européennes' (1998) CDE 79

Christiansen, 'The EFTA Court' (1997) 22 ELRev 539

Clapham, 'A human rights policy for the European Community' (1990) YEL 309

Closa, 'The concept of citizenship in the Treaty on European Union' (1992) 29 CMLRev 1137

Convery, 'State liability in the United Kingdom after *Brasserie du Pêcheur*' (1997) 34 CMLRev 603

Cook and Kerse, *EC Merger Control* (2nd edn, 1996)

Coppel and O'Neill, 'The European Court of Justice: taking rights seriously?' (1992) 29 CMLRev 669

Craig, 'Sovereignty of the United Kingdom Parliament after *Factortame*' (1991) 11 YEL 221

—— '*Francovich*, remedies and the scope of damages liability' (1993) 109 LQR 595

—— *Administrative Law* (3rd edn, 1994)

—— 'Directives: direct effect, indirect effect and the construction of national legislation' (1997) 22 ELRev 519

—— 'Once more unto the breach: the Community, the state and damages liability' (1997) 105 LQR 67

Craig and de Búrca, *EU Law* (2nd edn, 1998)

—— (eds), *The Evolution of EU Law* (1999)

Cross and Harris, *Precedent in English Law* (4th edn, 1991)

Cruz Vilaça, 'The Court of First Instance of the European Communities: a significant step towards the consolidation of the European Community as a Community governed by the rule of law' (1990) 10 YEL 1

Currall, 'Some aspects of the relation between Articles 30–36 and Article 100 of the EEC Treaty, with a closer look at optional harmonisation' (1984) 4 YEL 169

Curtin, 'Directives: the effectiveness of judicial protection of individual rights' (1990) 27 CMLRev 709

—— 'Scalping the Community legislator: occupational pensions and *Barber*' (1990) 27 CMLRev 475

—— 'The province of government: delimiting the direct effect of directives in the common law context' (1990) 15 ELRev 195

—— 'State liability under Community law: a new remedy for private parties' (1992) 21 ILJ 74

—— 'The constitutional structure of the Union: a Europe of bits and pieces' (1993) 30 CMLRev 17

Curtin and Heukels (eds), *Institutional Dynamics of European Integration* (Vol II) (1994)

Curtin and O'Keeffe (eds), *Constitutional Adjudication in European Community Law and National Law* (1992)

Daniele, 'Non-discriminatory restrictions to the free movement of persons' (1997) 22 ELRev 191

Dashwood, 'The principle of direct effect in European Community law' (1978) 16 JCMS 229

—— 'The Advocate General in the Court of Justice of the European Communities' (1982) 2 LS 202

—— 'The Cassis de Dijon line of authority' in Bates et al (eds) *In Memoriam J D B Mitchell* (1983), p 157

Dashwood, 'Majority voting in the Council' in Schwarze (ed), *Legislation for Europe 1992* (1989), p 79
—— (ed), *Reviewing Maastricht: Issues for the 1996 IGC* (1996)
—— 'The limits of European Community powers' (1996) 21 ELRev 113
—— 'External relations provisions of the Amsterdam Treaty' (1998) 35 CMLRev 1019
—— 'States in the European Union' (1998) 23 ELRev 201
Dashwood and O'Leary (eds), *The Principle of Equal Treatment in EC Law* (1997)
Dashwood and White, R., 'Enforcement actions under Articles 169 and 170 EEC' (1989) 14 ELRev 388
Dauses, 'The protection of fundamental rights in the Community legal order' (1985) 10 ELRev 398
Davies, 'Market integration and social policy in the Court of Justice' (1995) 24 ILJ 49
—— 'The European Court of Justice, national courts, and the Member States' in Davies et al (eds), *European Community Labour Law: Principles and Perspectives* (1996), ch 5
de Búrca, 'Giving effect to European Community directives' (1992) 55 MLR 215
—— 'Fundamental human rights and the reach of EC law' (1993) 13 OJLS 283
—— 'The principle of proportionality and its application in EC law' (1993) 13 YEL 105
Dehousse, *The European Court of Justice* (1998)
Dicey, *Lectures on the Relation between Law and Public Opinion in England during the Nineteenth Century* (1926)
Diplock, 'The courts as legislators' in Harvey (ed), *The Lawyer and Justice* (1978), p 265
Downes and Ellison, *The Legal Control of Mergers in the European Communities* (1991)
Due, 'The Court of First Instance' (1988) 8 YEL 1
Easson, 'The "direct effect" of EEC directives' (1979) 28 ICLQ 319
—— 'EEC directives for the harmonisation of laws: some problems of validity, implementation and legal effects' (1981) 1 YEL 1
Edward, 'Establishment and services: an analysis of the insurance cases' (1987) 12 ELRev 231
—— 'How the Court of Justice works' (1995) 20 ELRev 539
Edward and Hoskins, 'Article 90: deregulation and EC law' (1995) 32 CMLRev 157
Edwards and Philippart, 'Flexibility and the Treaty of Amsterdam: Europe's new Byzantium', CELS Occasional Paper No 3 (1997)
Eeckhout, *The European Internal Market and International Trade: A Legal Analysis* (1994)
Ellis, *EC Sex Equality Law* (2nd edn, 1998)
—— (ed), *The Principle of Proportionality in the Laws of Europe* (1999)
Emiliou, *The Principle of Proportionality in European Law* (1996)
Emmert and Pereira de Azevedo, 'L'effet horizontal des directives. La jurisprudence de la CJCE: un bateau ivre?' (1993) 29 RTDE 503
Evans, 'The enforcement procedure of Article 169 EEC: Commission discretion' (1979) 4 ELRev 442
—— *European Community Law of State Aid* (1997)
Everling, 'The Maastricht judgment of the German Federal Constitutional Court and its significance for the development of the European Union' (1994) 14 YEL 1
—— 'Will Europe slip on bananas? The bananas judgment of the Court of Justice and national courts' (1996) 33 CMLRev 401
Farmer and Lyal, *EC Tax Law* (1994)
Feldman, 'Public interest litigation and constitutional theory in comparative perspective' (1992) 55 MLR 44

Fennelly, 'Reflections of an Irish Advocate General' (1996) Irish Journal of European Law 5

Fenwick and Hervey, 'Sex equality in the single market: new directions for the European Court of Justice' (1995) 32 CMLRev 443

Forrester and Norall, 'The laicization of Community law: self-help and the rule of reason: how competition law is and could be applied' (1984) 21 CMLRev 11

Foster, 'The German constitution and EC membership' [1994] PL 392

Fredman, 'European Community discrimination law: a critique' (1992) 21 ILJ 119

—— 'Equal pay and justification' (1994) 23 ILJ 37

—— 'The poverty of equality: pensions and the ECJ' (1996) 25 ILJ 91

—— 'Reversing discrimination' (1997) 113 LQR 575

—— Women and the Law (1997)

Gerber, 'The transformation of European Community competition law?' (1994) 35 Harv Int LJ 97

—— Law and Competition in Twentieth Century Europe (1998)

Gormley, Prohibiting Restrictions on Trade within the EEC (1985)

—— 'Recent case law on the free movement of goods: some hot potatoes' (1990) 27 CMLRev 825

—— 'Reasoning renounced? The remarkable judgment in Keck & Mithouard' (1994) EBLR 63

—— (ed), Kapteyn and VerLoren van Themaat's Introduction to the Law of the European Communities (3rd edn, 1998)

Goyder, EC Competition Law (3rd edn, 1998)

Green, 'Directives, equity and the protection of individual rights' (1984) 9 ELRev 295

Green and Barav, 'Damages in the national courts for breach of Community law' (1986) 6 YEL 55

Green, Hartley and Usher, The Legal Foundations of the Single European Market (1991)

Habermas, Between Facts and Norms (1996)

Haguenau, L'application effective du droit communautaire en droit interne (1995)

Hamson, 'Methods of Interpretation—A Critical Assessment of the Results' in Reports of a Judicial and Academic Conference held in Luxembourg on 27–28 September 1976, p II-3

Handoll, 'Article 48(4) EEC and non-national access to public employment' (1988) 13 ELRev 223

—— Free Movement of Persons in the EU (1995)

Harding, 'The private interest in challenging Community action' (1980) 5 ELRev 354

Harlow, 'Towards a theory of access for the European Court of Justice' (1992) 12 YEL 213

—— 'Francovich and the problem of the disobedient State' (1996) 2 ELJ 199

Hartley, 'Five forms of uncertainty in European Community law' [1996] CLJ 265

—— 'The European Court, judicial objectivity and the constitution of the European Union' (1996) 112 LQR 95

—— The Foundations of European Community Law (4th edn, 1998)

—— Constitutional Problems of the European Union (1999)

Herdegen, 'Maastricht and the German Constitutional Court: constitutional restraints for an "ever closer union" ' (1994) 31 CMLRev 235

Hervey, European Social Law and Policy (1998)

Heukels and McDonnell (eds), The Action for Damages in Community Law (1997)

Hilson and Downes, 'Making sense of rights: Community rights in EC law' (1999) 24 ELRev 121

Himsworth, 'Things fall apart: the harmonisation of judicial procedural protection revisited' (1997) 22 ELRev 291

Hoskins, 'Tilting the balance: supremacy and national procedural rules' (1996) 21 ELRev 365

Howe, 'Euro-justice: yes or no?' (1996) 21 ELRev 187

Hubeau, 'La répétition de l'indu en droit communautaire' (1981) RTDE 442

Hunnings, *The European Courts* (1996)

Jacobs (ed), *European Law and the Individual* (1976)

Jacobs and Roberts (eds), *The Effect of Treaties in Domestic Law* (1987)

Jacobs and White, R., *The European Convention on Human Rights* (2nd edn, 1996)

Jacqué and Weiler, 'On the road to European Union—a new judicial architecture: an agenda for the intergovernmental conference' (1990) 27 CMLRev 185

Jarvis, *The Application of EC Law by National Courts* (1998)

Jennings and Watts (eds), *Oppenheim's International Law*, Vol I (9th edn, 1992)

Joliet, 'La notion de pratique concertée et l'arrêt ICI dans une perspective comparative' (1974) CDE 251

—— 'The reimbursement of election expenses: a forgotten dispute' (1994) 19 ELRev 243

Jones, B., 'Sex equality in pension schemes' in Kenner (ed), *Trends in European Social Policy* (1995), ch 2

Jones, C., and González-Díaz, *The EEC Merger Regulation* (1992)

Kapteyn, 'The Court of Justice after Amsterdam: taking stock' in Heukels, Blokker and Brus (eds), *The European Union after Amsterdam* (1998), ch 7

Keeling, 'The free movement of goods in EEC law: basic principles and recent developments in the case law of the Court of Justice of the European Communities' (1992) 26 The International Lawyer 467

—— 'In praise of judicial activism. But what does it mean? And has the European Court of Justice ever practised it?' in Curti Gialdino (ed), *Scritti in Onore di G Federico Mancini* (1998), p 505

Kennedy, 'The essential minimum: the establishment of the Court of First Instance' (1989) 14 ELRev 7 and (1990) 15 ELRev 54

Kerse, 'The complainant in competition cases: a progress report' (1997) 34 CMLRev 213

—— *EC Antitrust Procedure* (4th edn, 1998)

Kon, 'Article 85, para 3: a case for application by national courts' (1982) 19 CMLRev 541

Koopmans, 'The role of law in the next stage of European integration' (1986) 35 ICLQ 925

—— 'The technique of the preliminary question—a view from the Court of Justice' in Schermers et al (eds), *Article 177 EEC: Experiences and Problems* (1987), p 327

—— 'The future of the Court of Justice of the European Communities' (1991) 11 YEL 15

Kutscher, 'Methods of interpretation as seen by a Judge at the Court of Justice' in *Reports of a Judicial and Academic Conference held in Luxembourg on 27–28 September 1976*, p I-29

Lackhoff and Nyssens, 'Direct effect of directives in triangular situations' (1998) 23 ELRev 397

Lange and Sandage, 'The *Wood Pulp* decision and its implications for the scope of EC competition law' (1989) 26 CMLRev 137

Langrish, 'The Treaty of Amsterdam: selected highlights' (1998) 23 ELRev 3

Lasok, *The European Court of Justice: Practice and Procedure* (2nd edn, 1994)

Lauwaars, *Lawfulness and Legal Force of Community Decisions* (1973)

Laws, 'Law and democracy' [1995] PL 72

Lecourt, *L'Europe des Juges* (1976)

Lenaerts, 'The development of the judicial process in the European Community after the establishment of the Court of First Instance' in Clapham (ed), *Collected Courses of the Academy of European Law* (1990), Vol I, Book 1, p 53

—— 'Fundamental rights to be included in a Community catalogue' (1991) 16 ELRev 367

—— 'Some thoughts about the interaction between judges and politicians in the European Community' (1992) 12 YEL 1

—— 'Education in European Community law after "Maastricht" ' (1994) 31 CMLRev 7

Lenaerts and van Ypersele, 'Le principe de subsidiarité et son contexte: étude de l'article 3B du traité CE' (1994) CDE 3

Lewis, *Remedies and the Enforcement of European Community Law* (1996)

Lewis and Moore, 'Duties, directives and damages in European Community law' [1993] PL 151

Lonbay, 'Education and law: the Community context' (1989) 14 ELRev 363

Lonbay and Biondi (eds), *Remedies for Breach of EC Law* (1997)

MacCormick, 'The Maastricht-Urteil: sovereignty now' (1995) 1 ELJ 259

Macdonald, Matscher and Petzold (eds), *The European System for the Protection of Human Rights* (1993)

Macleod, Hendry and Hyett, *The External Relations of the European Communities* (1996)

Maltby, '*Marleasing*: what is all the fuss about?' (1993) 109 LQR 301

Mancini, 'The making of a constitution for Europe' (1989) 26 CMLRev 595

Mancini and Keeling, 'From *CILFIT* to *ERT*: the constitutional challenge facing the European Court' (1991) 11 YEL 1

—— 'Democracy and the European Court of Justice' (1994) 57 MLR 175

Manin, 'L'invocabilité des directives: quelques interrogations' (1990) 26 RTDE 670

Mann, 'The Dyestuffs case in the Court of Justice of the European Communities' (1973) 22 ICLQ 35

Marenco, 'Pour une interprétation traditionnelle de la notion de mesure d'effet équivalant à une restriction quantitative' (1984) CDE 291

—— 'The notion of restriction on the freedom of establishment and provision of services in the case law of the Court' (1991) 11 YEL 111

Martin and Guild, *Free Movement of Persons in the European Union* (1996)

Maselis and Gilliams, 'Rights of complainants in Community law' (1997) 22 ELRev 103

McCrudden (ed), *Equality of Treatment between Women and Men in Social Security* (1994)

McMahon, *Education and Culture in European Community Law* (1995)

Millett, 'The new European Court of First Instance' (1989) 38 ICLQ 811

—— *The Court of First Instance of the European Communities* (1990)

Moore, ' "Justice doesn't mean a free lunch": the application of the principle of equal pay to occupational pension schemes' (1995) 20 ELRev 159

Mortelmans, 'Article 30 of the EEC Treaty and legislation relating to market circumstances: time to consider a new definition?' (1991) 28 CMLRev 115

Neill, 'The European Court of Justice: a Case Study in Judicial Activism', Minutes of Evidence taken before the House of Lords Sub-Committee on the 1996 IGC (Session 1994–95, 18th Report, p 218); European Policy Forum (August 1995)

Neuwahl, 'Article 173, paragraph 4 EC: past, present and possible future' (1996) 21 ELRev 17

Neuwahl and Rosas (eds), *The European Union and Human Rights* (1995)

Nielsen and Szyszczak, *The Social Dimension of the European Union* (3rd edn, 1997)

Nihoul, 'La recevabilité des recours en annulation introduits par un particulier à l'encontre d'un acte communautaire de portée générale' (1994) 30 RTDE 171

O'Keeffe, 'The Schengen Convention: a suitable model for European integration?' (1991) 11 YEL 185

—— 'Is the spirit of Article 177 under attack? Preliminary references and admissibility' (1998) 23 ELRev 509

O'Keeffe and Schermers (eds), *Essays in European Law and Integration* (1982)

O'Keeffe and Twomey (eds), *Legal Issues of the Maastricht Treaty* (1994)

O'Leary, 'Nationality law and Community citizenship: a tale of two uneasy bedfellows' (1992) 12 YEL 353

—— *The Evolving Concept of Community Citizenship* (1996)

Oliver, 'Non-Community nationals and the Treaty of Rome' (1985) 5 YEL 57

—— 'Enforcing Community rights in the English courts' (1987) 50 MLR 881

—— *Free Movement of Goods in the European Community* (3rd edn, 1996)

Ortiz Blanco, *European Community Competition Procedure* (1996)

Österdahl, 'Openness v secrecy: public access to documents in Sweden and the European Union' (1998) 23 ELRev 336

Pertek, 'Free movement of professionals and recognition of higher-education diplomas' (1992) 12 YEL 293

Pescatore, 'The doctrine of "direct effect": an infant disease of Community law' (1993) 8 ELRev 155

Phelan, 'Right to life of the unborn v promotion of trade in services: the European Court of Justice and the normative shaping of the European Union' (1992) 55 MLR 670

Picod, 'La nouvelle approche de la Cour de justice en matière d'entraves aux échanges' (1998) 34 RTDE 169

Plaza Martin, 'Furthering the effectiveness of EC directives and the judicial protection of individual rights thereunder' (1994) 43 ICLQ 26

Plender (ed), *European Courts Practice and Precedents* (1997)

—— 'Procedure in the European Courts: comparisons and proposals' (1997) 267 Recueil des Cours 13

Poiares Maduro, *We the Court: the European Court of Justice and the European Economic Constitution* (1998)

Prechal, 'Remedies after *Marshall*' (1990) 27 CMLRev 451

—— *Directives in European Community Law* (1995)

—— 'Community law in national courts: the lessons from *van Schijndel*' (1998) 35 CMLRev 681

Rasmussen, 'Why is Article 173 interpreted against private plaintiffs?' (1980) 5 ELRev 112

—— 'The European Court's *acte clair* strategy in *CILFIT*' (1984) 9 ELRev 242

—— *On Law and Policy in the European Court of Justice* (1986)

—— 'Between self-restraint and activism: a judicial policy for the European Court' (1988) 13 ELRev 28

Reich, 'The "November revolution" of the European Court of Justice: *Keck, Meng* and *Audi* revisited' (1994) 31 CMLRev 459

—— 'Judge-made "Europe à la carte": some remarks on recent conflicts between European and German constitutional law provoked by the banana litigation' (1996) 7 EJIL 103

Reid, 'The judge as law maker' (1972–3) XII JSPTL (NS) 22

Rose (ed), *Bellamy and Child's Common Market Law of Competition* (4th edn, 1993)

Ross, 'Beyond *Francovich*' (1993) 56 MLR 55

Schermers, 'The European Court of First Instance' (1988) 25 CMLRev 541

—— 'The effect of the date 31 December 1992' (1991) 28 CMLRev 275

—— 'Election of judges to the European Court of Human Rights' (1998) 23 ELRev 568

Schermers and Waelbroeck, D., *Judicial Protection in the European Communities* (5th edn, 1992)

Schermers et al (eds), *Free Movement of Persons in Europe* (1993)

Schockweiler, 'Le régime de la responsabilité extra-contractuelle du fait d'actes juridiques dans la Communauté européenne' (1990) 26 RTDE 27

—— 'La responsabilité de l'autorité nationale en cas de violation du droit communautaire' (1992) 28 RTDE 27

Scorey, 'A new model for the Communities' judicial architecture in the new Union' (1996) 21 ELRev 224

Senden, 'Positive action in the EU put to the test. A negative score?' (1996) 3 MJ 146

Shanks, 'The social policy of the European Communities' (1977) 14 CMLRev 375

Shaw, 'The many pasts and futures of citizenship in the European Union' (1997) 22 ELRev 554

Simon, *Le système juridique communautaire* (1997)

Slaughter, Stone and Weiler (eds), *The European Courts and National Courts: Doctrine and Jurisprudence* (1998)

Slot and McDonnell (eds), *Procedure and Enforcement in EC and US Competition Law* (1993)

Slynn, 'EEC competition law from the perspective of the Court of Justice' in *Antitrust and Trade Policy in the United States and the European Community*, Fordham Corporate Law Institute (1985), ch 19

—— *Introducing a European Legal Order* (1992)

Smith, 'A European concept of *condictio indebiti*' (1982) 19 CMLRev 269

Sohrab, 'Women and social security: the limits of EEC equality law' [1994] JSWFL 5

Sonelli, 'Appeal on points of law in the Community system' (1998) 35 CMLRev 871

Stein and Vining, 'Citizen access to judicial review of administrative action in a transnational and federal context' (1976) 70 AJIL 219

Steindorff, 'Article 85, para 3: no case for application by national courts' (1983) 20 CMLRev 125

Steiner, 'Direct applicability in EEC law—a chameleon concept' (1982) 98 LQR 229

—— 'Drawing the line: uses and abuses of Article 30 EEC' (1992) 29 CMLRev 749

—— 'From direct effects to *Francovich*: shifting means of enforcement of Community law' (1993) 18 ELRev 3

—— *Enforcing EC Law* (1995)

Szyszczak, 'European Community law: new remedies, new directions?' (1992) 55 MLR 690

—— 'Positive action after *Kalanke*' (1996) 59 MLR 876

Tatham, 'Restitution of charges and duties levied by the public administration in breach of European Community law: a comparative analysis' (1994) 19 ELRev 146

Temple Lang, 'Community constitutional law: Article 5 EEC Treaty' (1990) 27 CMLRev 645

—— 'General Report', XVIII FIDE Congress, Stockholm (1998)

Tesauro, 'The effectiveness of judicial protection and co-operation between the Court of Justice and the national courts' (1993) 13 YEL 1

Torremans, 'Extraterritorial application of EC and US competition law' (1996) 21 ELRev 280

Toth, 'The authority of judgments of the European Court of Justice: binding force and legal effects' (1984) 4 YEL 1

—— 'The legal status of the declarations annexed to the Single European Act' (1986) 23 CMLRev 803

—— 'The Court of First Instance of the European Communities' in White, R., and Smythe (eds), *Current Issues in European and International Law* (1990), p 19

—— *The Oxford Encyclopaedia of European Community Law* (1990), Vol I

—— 'Is subsidiarity justiciable?' (1994) 19 ELRev 268

—— 'The European Union and human rights: the way forward' (1997) 34 CMLRev 491

Tridimas, 'The Court of Justice and judicial activism' (1996) 21 ELRev 199

—— 'The role of the Advocate General in the development of Community law: some reflections' (1997) 34 CMLRev 1349

—— *The General Principles of EC Law* (1999).

Tridimas and Eeckhout, 'The external competence of the Community and the case law of the Court of Justice: principle versus pragmatism' (1994) 14 YEL 143

Usher, *General Principles of EC Law* (1998)

Van Calster, 'The EU's Tower of Babel—the interpretation by the European Court of Justice of equally authentic texts drafted in more than one official language' (1997) 17 YEL 363

Van den Bergh and Schäfer, 'State liability for infringement of the EC Treaty: economic arguments in support of a rule of "obvious negligence" ' (1998) 23 ELRev 552

Vandersanden, 'Pour un élargissement du droit des particuliers d'agir en annulation contre des actes autres que les décisions qui leur sont adressées' (1995) CDE 535

van Gerven, 'Contribution de l'arrêt *Defrenne* au développement du droit communautaire' (1977) 13 CDE 131

—— 'Non-contractual liability of Member States, Community institutions and individuals for breaches of Community law with a view to a common law for Europe' (1994) 1 MJ 6

—— 'Bridging the gap between Community and national laws: towards a principle of homogeneity in the field of legal remedies?' (1995) 32 CMLRev 679

—— 'Bridging the unbridgeable: Community and national tort laws after *Francovich* and *Brasserie*' (1996) 45 ICLQ 507

—— 'The role and structure of the European judiciary now and in the future' (1996) 21 ELRev 211

Van Overbeek, 'The right to remain silent in competition investigations: the *Funke* decision of the Court of Human Rights makes revision of the ECJ's case law necessary' (1994) 15 ECLR 127

Venit, 'The "Merger" Control Regulation: Europe comes of age . . . or Caliban's dinner' (1990) 27 CMLRev 7

—— 'Two steps forward and no steps back: economic analysis and oligopolistic dominance after *Kali & Salz*' (1998) 35 CMLRev 1101

Vesterdorf, 'The Court of First Instance of the European Communities after two full years in operation' (1992) 29 CMLRev 897

Wade, 'Sovereignty—revolution or evolution?' (1996) 112 LQR 568

Wade and Forsyth, *Administrative Law* (7th edn, 1994)

Waelbroeck, D., and Fosselard, 'Should the decision-making power in EC antitrust procedures be left to an independent judge? The impact of the European Convention on Human Rights on EC antitrust procedures' (1994) 14 YEL 111

Waelbroeck, D., and Verheyden, 'Les conditions de recevabilité des recours en annulation des particuliers contre les actes normatifs communautaires' (1995) CDE 399

Waelbroeck, M., 'May the Court of Justice limit the retrospective operation of its judgments?' (1981) 1 YEL 115

Walz, 'Rethinking *Walt Wilhelm*, or the supremacy of Community competition law over national law' (1996) 21 ELRev 449

Ward, *A Critical Introduction to European Law* (1996)

Weatherill, *Law and Integration in the European Union* (1995)

—— 'After *Keck*: some thoughts on how to clarify the clarification' (1996) 33 CMLRev 885

—— 'Recent case law concerning the free movement of goods: mapping the frontiers of market deregulation' (1999) 36 CMLRev 51

Weatherill and Beaumont, *EC Law* (2nd edn, 1995)

Weiler, 'The Court of Justice on trial' (1987) 24 CMLRev 555

—— *The Constitution of Europe* (1999)

Weiler and Lockhart, ' "Taking rights seriously" seriously: the European Court and its fundamental rights jurisprudence—Part I' (1995) 32 CMLRev 51; Part II (1995) 32 CMLRev 579

Wesseling, 'Subsidiarity in Community antitrust law: setting the right agenda' (1997) 22 ELRev 35

Whish, *Competition Law* (3rd edn, 1993)

Whish and Sufrin, 'Oligopolistic markets and EC competition law' (1992) 12 YEL 59

—— 'Article 85 and the rule of reason' (1997) 7 YEL 1

White, E., 'In search of the limits to Article 30 of the EEC Treaty' (1989) 26 CMLRev 235

Whiteford, 'Lost in the mists of time. The ECJ and occupational pensions' (1995) 32 CMLRev 801

Wils, 'La compatibilité des procédures communautaires en matière de concurrence avec la Convention européenne des droits de l'homme' (1996) 32 CDE 329

Winckler and Hansen, 'Collective dominance under the EC Merger Control Regulation' (1993) 30 CMLRev 787

Winter, 'Direct applicability and direct effect—two distinct and different concepts in Community law' (1972) 9 CMLRev 425

Woolf, 'Droit public—English style' [1995] PL 57

Wyatt, 'The direct effect of Community social law—not forgetting directives' (1983) 8 ELRev 241

Wyatt and Dashwood, *European Community Law* (3rd edn, 1993)

Zuleeg, 'The European constitution under constitutional constraints: the German scenario' (1997) 22 ELRev 19

Index